Disaster Recovery Planning

Preparing for the Unthinkable

Third Edition

Jon William Toigo

with illustrations by
Margaret Romao Toigo

Prentice Hall PTR
Upper Saddle River, New Jersey 07458
www.phptr.com

ISBN 0-13-046282-9

9 790130 462823

90000

Library of Congress Cataloging-in-Publication Data

Toigo, Jon William 1959-
  Disaster recovery planning: preparing for the unthinkable / Jon William Toigo; with illustrations by Margaret Romao Toigo.—3rd ed.
    p. cm.
  Previous ed. has different other title information.
  ISBN 0–13–046282–9
  1. Data recovery (Computer science)—Planning. 2. Data protection. 3. Emergency management. I. Title.
  QA76.9.D348 T653 2003
  658.4978—dc21   2002011553

Acquisitions editor: *Tim Moore*
Cover designer: *Talar Agasyan-Boorujy*
Editorial assistant: *Allyson Kloss*
Cover design director: *Jerry Votta*
Buyer: *Maura Zaldivar*
Marketing manager: *Bryan Gambrel*
Project coordinator: *Anne Garcia*
Compositor/Production services: *Pine Tree Composition, Inc.*

© 2003, 2000, 1989 Pearson Education, Inc.
Published as Prentice Hall, PTR
Upper Saddle River, New Jersey 07458

Prentice Hall books are widely used by corporations and government agencies for training, marketing, and resale.

For more information regarding corporate and government bulk discounts please contact:

> Corporate and Government
> Phone: 800–382–3419
> or
> E-mail: corpsales@pearsontechgroup.com

Printed in the United States of America
10   9   8   7   6   5   Fifth Printing

ISBN: 0–13–046282–9

Pearson Education Ltd., *London*
Pearson Education Australia Pty, Limited, *Sydney*
Pearson Education Singapore, Pte. Ltd.
Pearson Education North Asia Ltd. *Hong Kong*
Pearson Education Canada, Ltd., *Toronto*
Pearson Educación de Mexico, S.A. de C.V.
Pearson Education—Japan, *Tokyo*
Pearson Education Malaysia, Pte. Ltd.
Pearson Education, *Upper Saddle River, New Jersey*

Robert Cantor once noted that the Chinese expression for the word *disaster* consists of two symbols. One is the symbol for danger, the other for opportunity. *Disaster Recovery Planning* is an effort to minimize the former, while maximizing the latter.

Meeting the unthinkable with courage, principles, audacity, and wit makes all the difference in life as in business. This I learned from Esther and Bill Toigo, and it is to you, my parents, that this third edition is dedicated.

Contents

CHAPTER 3   Facility Protection   **63**

CHAPTER 4   Data Recovery Planning   **120**

Foreword

Michael Shannon
Accounting Supervisor
Port Authority of New York and New Jersey
And President
Institute of Management Accountants—New York City Chapter

On September 11, 2001, I had just arrived at my office on the 69th floor of Tower One of the World Trade Center prepared for another day of summarizing the revenues and expenses for the various transportation facilities of the Port Authority of New York and New Jersey. I turned on my Dell PC, waited for the local disk drive to boot-up and virus-checking software to complete its scan, and then signed on to the office Novell network. Then, suddenly, it happened.

There was a very loud explosion, followed by a buzzing or whirring noise. The entire building rumbled and swayed—what felt like 4 feet in one direction, a slight hesitation then continued another 4 feet in the same direction. At that time, I truly believed the building was going to topple over and wondered if anyone would be able to survive such a disaster. (I later learned that the building had swayed as much as 8 to 10 feet because of the impact of the aircraft—well beyond its normal sway of 1 foot.)

From my window facing the east side of the building, I saw an unbelievable shower of glass and debris falling through the air and the edges of a fireball that had ignited several floors above ours. It was then that I realized that there was a serious explosion somewhere on the floors above and we needed to move as quickly as possible to evacuate the building.

There was minor hysteria and concern, a co-worker grabbed me and held on for the 60 seconds or so that it took for the building to settle back into place. As soon as the building settled, everyone made for the hallway and immediately went for the stairs in an orderly way. In all probability, some of the elevators were working, but numerous fire drills had taught us not to go there.

I had been working at the WTC on February 26, 1993, but I wasn't in the building when the terrorist bomb detonated in the basement. On that day, I had left for a lunch meeting minutes before the explosion occurred at 12:18 P.M. Some people who had been in the building during the 1993 bombing seemed to know exactly what had happened this time around and later confirmed that the tremors felt in 1993 could not compare to the impact of September 11th.

As we headed for the stairs, we learned that a plane had struck the building. A co-worker whose office sits on the north side of the tower had seen the plane approaching. He later said that he knew this was a major airline carrier and had been able to identify the American Airlines plane seconds before impact.

Once in the stairwell, we were able to go down a couple of flights before the stairwell quickly filled with people from the floors below us. This was like sitting in bumper-to-bumper traffic. You would step down three or four steps, then wait; travel three or four more steps, then wait. There was a thin cloud of smoke with the obvious smell of aircraft fuel filling the stairwell.

With everyone covering their face with shirts, ties or napkins, there was concern as to why we were even experiencing fumes when the plane had hit above us. Back in 1993 the smoke was rising from the basement, which made the evacuation more difficult. Also, unlike 1993, the stairwells remained lit throughout our descent, which was the result of increased safety measures implemented since the 1993 bombing.

The trip down the stairs was somewhat surreal. We were making nervous jokes to help ease our concerns, and everyone was staying relatively calm. By the time we reached the 39th floor, we had to press ourselves into a single-file line against the wall to make room for the firemen who were climbing the stairs, humping their gear in the opposite direction.

I could only imagine what was going through the minds of these firefighters. They knew how severe the situation was and were still heading in as we were trying to exit. It was then that we learned about the second plane, from a firefighter who had paused a moment from his ascent, huffing and puffing. We did not talk very much about the incident because we didn't want to create additional hysteria, but in my own head, I realized that one plane might have been an accident, two planes however, within a few minutes of each other, had to be a deliberate attack of terrorism.

As the conditions worsened in the stairwell, the people from the lower levels would tell us about the hazards that lie ahead and we would do the same for the people who were behind us. As we reached the floors in the lower thirties, the stairs became slippery from the moisture and sweat of a crowded stairwell. By the time we reached the 25th floor, we were stepping through about two inches of running water—perhaps from broken pipes, sprinkler systems, or even firefighting efforts on the floors above, I could only speculate. The pace of our descent picked up slightly, though we were still slowed from people who were too weary to continue and had to be carried the last remaining floors.

We finally reached the second floor, the mezzanine/plaza level at about 9:40A.M. Now out of the stairwell and into the open space, the urgency and chaos had come in full force. Our slow descent down the stairs had changed to running to get a safe distance away from the buildings. Firefighters and police escorted us down through the Mall level, where water pouring over our heads like a heavy rain, then back up an escalator and out around the plaza. There in the center plaza grotto, where I had attended so many lunch hour concerts during the summer in Manhattan, there was now piles of debris: charred rubble, burning office furniture. . . and parts of what looked unmistakably like human beings.

We were moved quickly across the street, having to take cover once because of falling debris. We turned to catch our first glimpse of both towers, which were in flames and billowing smoke.

It was chaos on the streets and we moved en masse about four or five blocks away. I turned around, wanting to look again and dispel my disbelief, but the person I was with could not stand to look at this disaster and wanted to keep moving uptown.

We were able to board an uptown subway, when the train suddenly stopped. We sat unmoving for an hour, then finally proceeded to the next stop and were told to exit the train to Canal Street.

Once back on the street, I tried to look for the World Trade Center which would have been easily viewable from were I was standing but was unable to find them. When I asked a passerby, his response was, "They are gone, they both fell awhile ago." I could not believe what I was hearing and never could have imagined that the buildings would have collapsed.

By now I was frantically trying to reach my family to let them know I was safe. I was unable to contact them by phone until 1:00 P.M. and did not make it home until 7:30 that evening. That was the hardest part about the day, the anxiousness to get home and see my family. They were very frightened and unsure of my safety. My eight-year-old son, who had stayed home from school that day, had watched the events take place on television. Friends and relatives had come down to my home in New Jersey to be with the family while they waited for word. Once I managed to get home, it took two days for everyone, including me, to calm down.

Others, I later learned, did not have the luxury of time. Senior staff at the Port Authority gathered at the Emergency Command Center, which was in the World Trade Center Marriott Hotel. As they gathered to assess the situation, Tower Two collapsed on top of them. Those that climbed out of the rubble made their way to our New Jersey offices to reassemble what resources they could. That evening, staff was already at work trying to assess the damage and loss of life.

During this time, other Port Authority operations had to be tended to. The New York regions' three major airports, tunnels and bridges, bus facilities and PATH trains are the Port Authority's responsibility. For the next couple of days most of these facilities remained closed for security reasons, but plans were already in the works for additional security and reopening.

All the while that planning was underway, Port Authority emergency managers were calling around to identify our missing. We lost 75 employees that day, 37 police officers and 38 civilian employees. I had known many of them by name. Others were familiar faces I would pass in the hallways of the Trade Center. I had even worked with some of them over varying points of my Port Authority service.

Of key importance was the restoration of critical functions and operations. The recovery team for the accounting department worked to locate files, records, and gain access to critical systems that would enable the processing of payroll and accounts payable. Over 8,000 employees would depend on our department to ensure that they were able to cover their costs to feed and shelter their families during this difficult time as well as payment to the many vendors needed to replace destroyed equipment and keep operations going at our other facilities.

I was not part of the immediate recovery operation, but I was certainly among its beneficiaries. The incident took place on Tuesday and I received my paycheck on that Friday. My division was out of work for about a week and a half. The planning team slowly brought us back in, finding us new quarters in the Journal Square Transportation Center in Jersey City, New Jersey. Other departments were brought back to work at decentralized office space that included airport offices and port facilities.

We managed to set up some of our applications by getting access to the network. Fortunately, the Port Authority has decentralized offices that have access to a network maintained outside of the World Trade Center. We were able to log in to applications through this network by rerouting our computers and restoring our data from back-up tapes kept off-site.

Among the difficulties we confronted was the problem of simply finding workstations and telephones to use. Laptop computers became extremely popular because we were shuffling between workstations sometimes two-to-three times a day.

The first two weeks were spent assessing what files we still had, and what files were lost. Most of the files on local PC disk drives in the World Trade Center were lost forever. Our email system proved to be a useful resource to find lost computer files. As we move closer to a paperless society, the chances of finding a file improve if it has been emailed to a co-worker and a copy still exists in your in-box, deleted or sent folders.

One thing that was not in short supply was crisis management counseling. The counselors were available at all times and were tremendously helpful to many in my office. They were just as critical as the technicians providing telephone and LAN hook-ups to getting our group back to some sort of normalcy.

In addition to the on-going recovery activities at the Port Authority, I had the responsibility to regroup the more than 800 members of the Institute of Management Accountants, a professional accounting organization for which I had been appointed New York City Chapter President. The day of the attack was supposed to be our kick-off dinner meeting, which was cancelled for obvious reasons. I contacted the national office to advise them that we had lost most of our chapters' financial records in the World Trade Center. I arranged for ground mail and email for the chapter to be directed to my home and received emails of support from other chapter presidents across the nation.

As I write this, about two months have elapsed since the attack. Today, I look around the office and realize that people are actually coming in and settling into their chairs to work. This is a sign of healing, I think, and a contrast to the many weeks when we would need to interrupt our day every few minutes or so to converse and compare notes with each other about that tragic day.

Though we are still doubled-up in offices and a permanent office and corporate headquarters appears to be months in the future, not many people are complaining. The resolve of my Port Authority co-workers remained unbeaten and the proactive steps taken to start the rebuilding process is one that will be remembered forever. We all knew many of the co-workers whose lives were ended, but miraculously no one in our office on the 69th floor of One World Trade Center died on that tragic day of September 11th.

Foreword
Gregory Ferris
Executive Director
Global Business Continuity Planning (Institutional Securities)
Morgan Stanley

"When we think back on 2001, we are filled with deep sorrow and outrage over the events of September 11. Who among us will ever forget the shock and horror of that day? For the Morgan Stanley family, the attacks hit us right at home—3,700 of our people worked in the World Trade Center. Sadly, seven of them and six contract service professionals did not make it out that day.

"But we also take pride in the way our company responded in the immediate aftermath of the attacks and the weeks that followed. Through resolve, discipline and some individual acts of heroism, nearly all our employees evacuated the South Tower immediately after the North Tower was hit, executing planned and frequently practiced safety procedures. Many of our people immediately went to backup sites to begin to take care of customers and to protect the firm. We believe it was a defining moment for us — a summation of what we stand for and how we respond when tested by extreme circumstances."

— From the Letter to the Shareholders,
Annual Report of Morgan Stanley 2001.

It was a very special feeling to flip my calendar to January 1, 2002. It is human nature to want to get on with our lives and put 2001 behind us—way behind us. We continually hear how the tragic events of 9/11 changed our way of life forever. As difficult as it is to do, I think it is important that we occasionally stop and reflect on the enormity of what happened on that fateful day.

Many of us lost family, friends, and colleagues long before we were ready to say goodbye. We struggled, and we watched so many around us struggle, to accept such a senseless and barbaric act. Terrorists took our ingenuity and our liberties and turned them against us.

For the first time in our lives, we no longer had to imagine how our parents and grandparents felt on December 7th, 1941. Many of us went home and looked into the puzzled faces of our children and tried to help them rationalize something that we could not rationalize for ourselves. For the first time in recent memory, the White House was evacuated in fear of an attack. Not since the crash of 1929, have the U.S. equity markets been closed for three consecutive days. New York City was placed in complete lock-down, and for those of us who were unable to make it out of the city on September 11th, the sight of completely empty Manhattan streets, with the exception of busloads of National Guard and armored vehicles, is an image we will not soon forget. National air travel was halted for almost a week, also a first.

Major League Baseball and the National Football League suspended their schedules pushing the World Series into November and the Superbowl into February for the first time in history. Many television and radio broadcasters suspended their normal schedules and advertising for days after the attack. Hollywood awards shows were canceled and, for the first time in history, the National Anthem was played during the changing of the guard at Buckingham Palace.

Patrick Witty is the photographer who had the foresight to turn his camera in the opposite direction as Tower 2 started to implode. While all of his contemporaries were photographing similar images of the tower's demise, he captured the horror-stricken reaction of hundreds in the street in what is sure to become one of the defining portraits of September 11th. I'd like to tear a page from Mr. Witty's playbook and turn my camera in the other direction—from the negative to the positive.

Yes, dare I say it, there are many positives that have come and will continue to come from the events of September 11th. Many of us reprioritized our lives and found renewed solace in our families, our friends, and our faith. The petty events, to which we were so fixated, were purged from the front pages and lead broadcasts like yesterday's fads. For at least a brief moment in time, there were no political issues, race, or religion dividing us. There were just Americans, united in our effort to pick each other up and move forward. We have proven to ourselves, and the world, that America is still a great nation, capable of coming together during trying times despite what may divide us. We demonstrated that we can still make difficult decisions and rally behind them.

The President and his administration worked steadfastly to ascertain international consensus on the response to global terrorism. New York City's former mayor, his cabinet, and the New York Police and Fire Departments were finally recognized for the invaluable contributions they make every day on the job. To be sure, America turned a corner on September 11th, 2001, and we all had ringside seats.

We were amazed by the many acts of selfless bravery and heroism. We were touched by the outpouring of emotion from around the world. We feel reassured by the decisively swift success of our military campaign. The people involved are heroes one and all.

But, to me, there was an even more amazing feat. The American economy, while teetering on a high wire, took a direct hit right through its heart. Although it wobbled precariously, it never fell. There are many unsung heroes who should be recognized.

They are the people who wake up every morning and get the kids ready for school, and kiss their loved ones goodbye, and bring their intellect and imagination to the American workplace. They are the people who had no formal training in dealing with a crisis, yet did so brilliantly. They are the people whose hearts beat a little faster when they start their commute every morning, or board a plane, in the face of new uncertainty. They are the architects and custodians of the strongest, economic machine in the history of the world. They, my good people, are each and every one of you reading this book and the millions like you. The perseverance of American commerce, our ability to dust ourselves off and get right back in the game, was the most amazing story of all.

The consequences of not learning everything there is to learn from this experience, and modifying our behavior accordingly, are too staggering to fathom. Yes, our way of life and conducting business has changed forever. Our ability to recover critical functions can no longer be viewed as a reactive process and must be considered a primary operational risk. Our ability to recover mission-critical data is the most critical element. Without it, other strategies such as physical diversification and work area recovery are not possible.

An ancient Chinese proverb which says that every crisis brings opportunity. The opportunities before us are bountiful. Together, we can build a new and reinvigorated America, full of hope, strength and peace. Let's rise to the occasion.

I would like to dedicate this foreword to the memory of my brother-in-law, Stephen P. Dimino, a former partner of Cantor-Fitzgerald, who perished on September 11, 2001 in the attack on the World Trade Center.

Author's Preface
to the
Third Edition

On reading the forewords to this edition, which consist of first hand accounts of the events that occurred during and after the September 11, 2001 terrorist attacks on the World Trade Center, one cannot help but be moved—and somewhat awestruck.

In addition to the sadness and tragic loss associated with 9/11, we are also magnetized by the remarkable tenacity and heroism manifested by those who worked to save lives and to recover organizations in the hours, days, and weeks following the disaster. This edition is dedicated to spirit of the survivors and to the memory of the victims.

When my editor approached me to write a third edition of this book in the aftermath of the September incidents, my first reaction was one of hesitance. Was a new edition really justified, or was it simply a marketing ploy designed to capitalize on the current surge of interest in disaster recovery and risk management in the wake of 9/11? To keep things honest, I performed a quick inventory:

Question: Had September 11 changed what we know about disaster recovery?

Answer: Of course not. The methodologies and procedures and best practices that comprise disaster recovery planning did not change in the wake of this latest disaster any more than they had changed following Hurricane Andrew or the Kobe earthquake. If anything, 9/11 had confirmed the efficacy of planning and, once again, demonstrated the difficulties of undertaking recovery successfully in the absence of proactive DR planning.

Question: Is terrorism a new threat to organizations that requires new measures of preparedness?

Answer: Again, no. The terrorist threat potential has been an unfortunate fixture in the disaster scenarios of private and public institutions for many years—both in the United States and abroad. Moreover, disaster recovery planning is less concerned about the root cause of disasters (unless such knowledge can help disasters to be averted in the first place), than in coping with their consequences. From a disaster recovery standpoint, it mattered very little whether 9/11 was caused by Al Qaeda operatives, bin Laden fanatics, or insane hijackers of any political or religious stripe. The disaster might just as well have been the result of an electrical spark or other igniter.

What was important to disaster recovery planners was how the most critical assets of the organizations located in the WTC and the Pentagon—specifically, the trained personnel and the data—would be protected and returned to work quickly and efficiently in the wake of the disaster. Simply put, whatever the toll of the disaster, failing to respond to the events in a rational way would have made the costs much greater.

Question: Did the events of 9/11 change the milieu in which disaster recovery plans must execute?

Answer: Maybe. This event was not a manifestation of natural forces, nor a consequence of random circumstances. It was a deliberate act by hostile force that has touched off a response increasingly characterized as a war. As a consequence, it has placed certain societal and governmental institutions on a war footing. That does create a meaningful change in the milieu in which disaster recovery plans will need to be executed.

Without a doubt, new legal mandates will follow the events of 9/11. Some involve the "hardening" and protection of public infrastructure. Security has already been stepped up within the energy and transportation sectors. Information and communications are also coming under greater scrutiny as investigations turn to discovering how the terrorists obtained detailed intelligence on structural vulnerabilities and how they were able to establish false identities with such apparent ease.

When milieu changes occur, disaster recovery plans need to be re-tested. So too with books on disaster recovery: assumptions need to be re-visited and reconfirmed.

Question: Aside from 9/11, have any other technical changes occurred that merit revision of the content of this book?

Answer: Yes. Ten years elapsed between the first edition (1989) and the second edition (1999) of *Disaster Recovery Planning*, during which information technology moved from the data center and into the distributed environment of departments and workgroups within many organizations. The second edition endeavored to update the content of the original to reflect the new challenges and opportunities created by this shift.

In the comparatively brief period of time between 1999 and 2002, one could argue that an equally important technology shift has occurred. Several indicators testify to the truth of this assertion.

Data Growth: According to a study conducted by the University of California at Berkeley, the amount of data amassed by organizations and stored electronically in all of human history through 1999 totaled twelve exabytes (12,000,000,000,000,000,000 bytes). Researchers observed, however, that this number would double by mid-2002—a function of greater amount of information generated by a greater number of individuals.

The bulk of burgeoning data is being created by individuals and the lion's share, some 55 percent, is being stored on personal computers that are often not included in disaster recovery planning efforts. This is potentially an Achille's heel of disaster recovery—a point underscored by many 9/11 recovery efforts.

New Storage Technologies: Managing the data explosion referenced above—providing for its secure yet accessible storage—has become the central challenge confronting IT in the 21st century. Today, we are seeing the advent of nascent, "networked," storage technologies that portend to sever the connection between storage arrays and servers. Such technologies are expected to improve data accessibility and to provide nondisruptive scalability. Vendors claim that their wares also have potential for improving the resiliency of data storage and for reducing the timeframe for critical business process restoration, which is increasingly described by the metric "time-to-data." The truth of these assertions has yet to be demonstrated and interoperability problems continue to plague solutions, causing many more disasters than they prevent.

New Application Paradigms to Support Business Process Deconstruction: Currently, the industry is seeing the rise of new technologies such as XML-enabled "Web Services" that promise to enable an entirely new level of interoperation and integration between disparate systems in different companies. At the same time, new outsourcing paradigms, such as application service provisioning or ASP, are being introduced to reduce business costs and enhance business capabilities.

Such technologies are required to support the larger trend toward "business process deconstruction"—a means by which companies improve the efficiency of business processes by outsourcing more logistical responsibility to supply chain and value chain partners. The question is whether the still-evolving technologies will cause more disasters than they avoid. Will the use of ASPs increase the vulnerability of business processes to disaster or reduce it? Will application Web-enablement deliver less-costly and more secure B2B operations or simply succeed in making multi-tier client/server platforms even less stable than ever before?

The above list could go on, but by the conclusion of this brief inventory, I determined that a new edition of this book was indeed merited. A new edition was mandated not by the events of 9/11 directly, but by changes in the information technology infrastructure that supports key business processes and by changes in the organizational and external milieu in which disaster recovery plans must execute. It can be argued (and will be) that these changes require that the traditional approach to disaster recovery planning must also change.

Rather than being reactive, "playing the hand of cards they are dealt," DR planners will need to become more proactive in their efforts. They will need to begin to interact with application architects on an ongoing basis and to begin addressing the recoverability of applications, storage, and IT *infrastructure while they are still in their initial design phases.* DR planning can no longer be conceived as a "bolt on" or an afterthought: it must become an integral part of systems development.

Of course, to move into this role, planners themselves will need to become more technically astute. The days of "secretary friendly" plans are increasingly behind us. To interface with technical personnel—IT designers and architects, in particular—planners will need to become more proficient in the concepts and terminology of advanced technology domains. The modern planner will need to be conversant in object-oriented programming, middleware, extensible markup language, storage area networking, and many other rarified facets of information technology. To walk the walk of the IT architect, planners will need to talk the talk.

Planners will also need to become more business savvy. While it is a given that 9/11 has increased business awareness of the need for DR, history teaches us that business interest in DR has a tendency to wane over time. It is only natural: just as current events eventually become footnotes in history books, the more time that elapses following a disaster event, the less urgency business managers tend to place on disaster preparedness. Practicality dictates that companies spend money on projects that advance the goal of profitability.

Thus, business savvy planners will contextualize their efforts using a more robust business value proposition than mere "risk reduction." Dual use—the philosophy of delivering DR solutions that both reduce risk and enable business in normal day-to-day operations—must be paramount in DR strategy development going forward.

Ultimately, disaster recovery planning will need to become an integral part of the business and IT decision-making process. The development of a new business process and selection of every element and component of the technology infrastructure to support that business process should have recoverability as a key criterion.

When this happens, the discussion of disaster recovery planning as a separate discipline will be oxymoronical. *Disaster Recovery Planning* will no longer be a role for a select individual or dedicated cadre of planners. It will be the job of everyone in the organization—from the most senior manager to the most junior staff member, from the business professional to the IT professional.

And, of course, the need for new editions of this book will fade away. (I, for one, would welcome this outcome.)

But, until such a day arrives, new editions of *Disaster Recovery Planning* will be forthcoming to address the challenges of change in business, technology, and the backdrop of institutions and cultures in which we must all operate.

Preface to the Second Edition

This book is scheduled for publication on the eve of a new Millennium, as described in Western calendars. Indeed, for the past five years, "Year 2000 issues" have dominated discussions at every level of business and government—at least in the world's developed countries. Building to a crescendo of nearly deafening proportions by the end of 1999, the mainstream press has allocated millions of column inches to Y2K, creating a kind of mystique around a rather arbitrary date.

January 1, 2000 has been positioned as a watershed event in human history. Somehow, it is more than just another wintery pause in the seasonal cycles that determine agricultural prosperity, more than just another New Year's Day spent recovering from the Bacchanalian excesses of the previous evening's celebration, certainly more than just another Saturday spent working in the yard or watching TV or attending religious services.

For many, the date is loaded with symbolic significance. Year 2000 conjures to mind the conclusion of ten centuries of fast-paced technological innovation that has changed forever the society and culture in which we live. In just the past 100 years, we have witnessed the harnessing of the electron, the atom, the microwave, and the photon to meet the needs of everyday existence. The Industrial Revolution has come to flower, given way to a Computer Age, and now, courtesy of the global Internet, World Wide Web, and the ubiquitous Web browser, morphed analog reality into digital reality of the Information Age.

Doubtless, there are good reasons to select a day on which to pause and reflect on the past, to consider the present, and to prepare for the future. Some psychologists argue that the human mind requires bookmarks, milestones, and "closure events" to remain centered and healthy. One supposes that, to this end, January 1, 2000 is as good a date as any other.

However, Y2K has acquired a second symbolic meaning that is much less grounded in the psychological revolution that gave us Vatican II, no-fault divorce, and the self-help books of the 1980s. To many, the millennium is a mystical event, touching on a deeply rooted superstitious stratum seemingly present in the human psyche since the dawn of man. For a variety of reasons, Y2K is viewed as a harbinger of doom, a signal that some cataclysmic event is in the offing.

Hollywood understands the phenomenon and has provided a steady fare of disaster movies as the decade of the 1990s draws to a close. Recent wildly popular films have enabled audiences to "experience, " courtesy of Industrial Light and Magic and other computer graphic effects studios, the havoc and devastation caused by natural, man-made and even extraterrestrial disasters. With apologies to Bruce Willis and others, the acting and plot of these films do not explain their success. The real draw of the films appears to be the disasters themselves: tornadoes, volcanoes, earth-asteroid collisions, viral outbreaks, nuclear terrorism, and infrastructure collapse based on computer hacking. They satisfy a need in the viewers to confront their own mortality, if only vicariously.

Some of the movies are rooted in real-life disaster events, which seem to some observers to be coalescing as the end of the century approaches.

- The World Trade Center and Oklahoma City federal building bombings underscored the reality of terrorism for a heretofore-insulated North American audience.
- The eruption in 1980 of Mount Saint Helens, following a 128-year dormancy, and powerful earthquakes in California, including Loma Prieta/San Francisco earthquake of October 1989 and the Northridge/San Fernando Valley earthquake of January 1994, have stimulated concerns about geological disasters and their frequency. The National Earthquake Information Center of the U.S. Geological Survey is quick to point out that "while it may seem that we are having more earthquakes, earthquakes of magnitude 7.0 or greater have remained fairly constant throughout this century and, according to our records, have actually seemed to decrease in recent years."
- The 1990s also gave the North America the costliest hurricanes in its history. While 1969 Hurricane Camille was the most powerful storm to date, Hurricane Andrew in 1992 racked up $26 billion in damage—the highest costs associated with any natural disaster on record to that point. As this book goes to press, experts are still calculating the costs accrued to 1999's Hurricane Floyd, which may well top Andrew's record. Between these devastating storms have been a steady wave of less powerful but very destructive cyclone events.
- Some may say that life imitates art. Following the success of the movie, *Twister,* Bridge Creek, Oklahoma experienced a real-life encounter in May 1999 with an F5 tornado, a so-called a "Finger of God."[1] This and many other severe storms, made the 1999 tornado season the most active since 1992. In part because of the movie, these storms commanded the full at-

tention of the media, which subtly attributed the tornadoes, hurricanes, floods, and ice storms of the last decade to humanity's destruction of the environment and nature's reprisal. In some reports, the tornadoes were incorrectly correlated with the El Nino/Southern Oscillation effect.[2] According to government tornado watchers, the number of tornadoes have increased as the century draws to a close, but this phenomenon does not correlate to El Nino/El Nina weather patterns in any statistically meaningful way.

- The possibility of near-earth-orbit (NEO) asteroids and comets colliding with the earth has been part of science fiction lore since the Golden Age of the genre in the 1950s. As the millennium approaches, concerns about this threat have been fueled by several events. One was the 1994 collision of Comet Shoemaker-Levy 9 with Jupiter, which was photographed in brilliant color using NASA's Hubble Space Telescope and published in magazines and newspapers worldwide. The other was the hyperbole surrounding 1997 XF_{11}, an asteroid originally thought to be on a collision course with Earth, but later determined to be no threat when it passes the planet at a comfortable distance in 2028. The mistaken estimate sent many millennium watchers to their underground shelters and found NASA asking for authority to censor such predictions until they could be properly verified.

- One man-made disaster potential that has seen a marked increase as the millennium approaches is the computer virus. Bearing such innocuous names as Melissa, Chernobyl, and ExplorZIP, 1999's crop of viruses have already resulted in greater dollar losses than has malicious programs introduced in any previous year. Experts expect this trend to continue for three basic reasons. First, the widespread use of the Internet for email and file transfers provides a perfect mechanism for spreading viruses. Second, the increased sophistication of programming tools is enabling even novices to create powerful virus programs. Third, the increased complexity of common desktop applications, such as word processors, spreadsheets, and browsers, are providing a "target-rich environment" for exploitation by hackers and other malicious code writers.[3]

- According to the FBI and the Computer Security Institute, virus-related costs are only a subset of a growing trend in crime directed at companies and enabled by computers and networks. Directed against critical infrastructure systems, such as the power grid, telecommunications, air traffic control systems, and so on, malicious programs and computer terrorism could potentially be as devastating as nuclear weapons.

Given the perception in many minds that disasters are coalescing as the millennium approaches, it is easy to understand how Y2K has become so closely associated with Armageddon. However, upon more sober analysis, few indicators point to a cataclysmic end to human existence on the first Saturday in January. It is a safe bet that the day will come and go without the seas boiling, dogs and cats living together, or any other apocalyptic nightmares being realized. If we are wrong in this conclusion, then this book will have a rather short shelf life.

What we may have to look forward to on January 1, 2000 (and possibly for several months after) is a set of irritating, and in some cases hazardous, interruptions in services that are supported by information systems and networks. These interruptions will have nothing to do with Nature's wrath or Judgment Day. They will be linked to simple, software-based, date calculation errors.

The Y2K bug exists in many older software programs, those written at a time when programmers did not consider how programs would behave when the calendar turned over from 99 to 00. Some of the software is compiled to execute on computer systems. In other cases, the software is embedded in microchips that are installed on computing and networking devices themselves.

Obviously, government and industry have known about the Y2K problem for some time. Significant investments in Y2K code remediation efforts began in the mid-1990s in most developed countries. In 1998, however, validation and verification of these efforts by independent third parties revealed that substantial numbers of errors still existed in remediated code. The persistence of errors is attributed to the shortcomings of early Y2K code remediation tools and the failure of organizations to test adequately the code fixes that had been implemented. In a surge of effort and spending, many companies have addressed the problem in three ways:

- Continued remediation of persistent date calculation errors.
- Increased attention to contingency and disaster recovery planning to mitigate the operational impact of unresolved errors.
- Lobbying for liability caps in Y2K-related lawsuits that are expected to appear in droves as interruptions begin to occur.

As situations presently stand, the GartnerGroup, in testimony to the U.S. Senate,4 predicts that 25% of Y2K code problems will manifest themselves in the months preceding January 1, 2000, 55% during the first year of the new millennium, and 15% in the year 2001. Unremediated errors in chip-embedded software will likely manifest themselves immediately with the date change at 12:59 P.M. on December 31, 1999.

According to the analyst, only 10% of Y2K bug-related failures will occur within the first two weeks of 2000. Of the failures that occur, only 10% will result in service downtime for a period of three days or more. Finally, one out of 100,000 chips will fail due to Y2K bugs.

GartnerGroup's findings are echoed by other industry analysts, with a few criticizing the findings as too conservative or "feel good." Whether the numbers are exact is beside the point. The analysts agree that, despite the advanced knowledge of the problem, most companies did not build momentum to address date calculation issues until 1998. At that point, they were already behind the curve. As a consequence, the situation has taken disaster recovery planning from the backwaters of IT system stewardship—an audit checklist item—and elevated it to a managerial concern of the highest priority in many companies.

In a sense, Y2K has done what no other common-sense disaster recovery argument could do. It has crystallized for management the dependency of their businesses upon information systems and networks. Moreover, it has increased management's perception of the threat of unmitigated disasters—not only to business operations, but to corporate profits as well.

While government has acted to limit corporate liability and the deep-pocket lawsuits that Y2K outages were sure to generate, it did so after much debate. One issue that received much attention was the importance of due diligence as a modifier of corporate responsibility.

Due diligence mandates that a business, knowing that a potentially damaging situation exists, must take steps to rectify the situation or mitigate its consequences. With other disaster potentials, such as floods, fires, hurricanes, and earthquakes, the comparative rarity of the disaster potential manifesting itself into an actual disaster has limited the liability of most companies to lawsuits. The exception is in cases where legislative mandates required disaster recovery planning and testing of plans (in the financial sector, for example). In fact, shareholders and consumers can be pretty forgiving if a hurricane impacts a business and interrupts normal operations for a period of time.

In the case of the Y2K bug, the compassion of shareholders and consumers was likely to be much less forthcoming. U.S. lawmakers decided that shareholders and consumers would more likely to look for someone to blame and to sue. They would ask why, if business managers knew that a disaster was in the offing, did they do nothing to prevent the disaster from happening? And if the Y2K bug could not be excised from code in time, why didn't the company have a contingency plan that would minimize the impact of the disaster potential they could not prevent? Those questions go to the heart of due diligence and were central to the government's debate over Y2K liability limits.

Shortly after this book is published, Y2K—both the bug and the calendar change—will be ancient history. Interruptions resulting from the Y2K bug will become what many disaster recovery planners regarded them as all along: just another series of interruptions of business processes owed to software-related causes.

However, for some disaster recovery planners, Y2K—for all of its danger—will have also provided an opportunity. The sum of all of the practical and superstitious concerns about the millennium and the Y2K bug has, for a time, focused attention on the dependency of business on its information systems and their vulnerability to unplanned interruption. For now, DR planners are enjoying a bit of "face time" with corporate management. Used wisely, this increased level of awareness could be cultivated into an ongoing component of the corporate culture.

In this time of concern, disaster recovery planners would be well served to conduct themselves professionally and to vest all of their skills, knowledge, and experience to assisting their senior management in coping with the Y2K bug (as well as any millennium superstitions they may harbor). A well-developed plan will provide protection against a much more varied set of disaster recovery scenarios, of course. However, by emphasizing Y2K issues as a planning objective, DR planners will identify themselves to management as intelligent and competent resources who can be depended upon to support business objectives. This political capital can serve the DR planner well as he or she works to address the broader spectrum of business process protection.

Welcome to the world of disaster recovery planning.

ENDNOTES

1. F5 refers to the Fujita Scale for tornado classification. A class five, or F5, tornado, sometimes called "the Finger of God," is extremely rare.

2. Despite the tendency of movies and the popular media to assign a correlation between tornadoes and El Nino, this does not stand up to scrutiny. See "The Relationship Between El Nino, La Nina, And United States Tornado Activity," Joseph T. Schaefer, Storm Prediction Center, Norman, OK, and Frank B. Tatom, Engineering Analysis Inc., Huntsville, AL, Preprints, 19th Conf. Severe Local Storms, Minneapolis, MN, October 1999.

3. Daniel Sforza, "New Terror Lurks in Computer Mailboxes," *The Record,* June 12, 1999 and Robert Gebeloff, "On-Line Perils, Pitfalls Growing for the Unwary, " The Record, June 12, 1999.

4. Lou Marcoccio, "Year 2000 International State of Readiness: Expert Testimony of Lou Marcoccio, March 5, 1999 to the U.S. Senate Special Committee on the Year 2000 Technology Problem, Washington, D.C.," GartnerGroup, 1999.

Acknowledgments

It has been three years since the second edition of this book, and thirteen since the first edition, were published. Originally, *Disaster Recovery Planning: Managing Risk and Catastrophe in Information Systems* was written out of practical necessity.

The MIS Director for a large financial company (and my boss at the time), Mary Kern, first placed me in the role of disaster recovery coordinator. The job was made extremely difficult both by Mary's desire to be an "early adopter" of distributed systems technology, and by the general lack of information available in print on the subject of disaster recovery for mainframes, let alone distributed information systems. The technical challenges were surpassed only by the political ones.

Fortunately, I discovered a band of "fellow travelers"—other MIS and IT personnel tasked with DR planning, as well as a few vendors of DR-related services. Together, we shared ideas and developed approaches and techniques that strengthened the plans we developed for our respective companies.

In time, this core group formed a organization for businesses located on Florida's Gulf Coast called the Disaster Avoidance and Recovery Information Group (DARING) that, together with one or two others throughout the United States, set the trend for the large national and international contingency planning associations that exist today.

The members of the DARING core group have since moved on to new adventures, but the fellowship and advice from Judith Brugner, John Flint, Joan Kobernick, Tom Little, Ross Markley, Pat O'Connell, Judy Ryan, Steve Glantz, Kevin Hephner, and Mark Sher contributed much to both the original edition of this book. The author wishes you well, wherever you are.

Staying current with the industry requires practice. DR books can't be written based on vicarious experience. The author wishes to extend special thanks to Frank McIntire, Craig Jensen, Charlie Fox, Jim Nowah, Milt Maughan, and many other friends at the ACP-Utah Chapter, as well as past and present editors Ceil Perry, Tony Strattner, Charlie Simpson, Linda Briggs, Michelle Hope, Steve LeSeuer, Bill Laberis, Bruce Hoard, Bonnie Anderson, and Julie Strasberg for providing me with opportunities to keep in touch with disaster recovery planning. Thanks to them, I have had ongoing assignments in the field—consulting on plans for a broad range of businesses, speaking at DR planning conferences, reporting firsthand on actual post-disaster business recovery efforts, and documenting my findings in the trade press. There are no experts in disaster recovery planning, but experience is a great teacher. You, my friends, have provided the means for me to continue to learn and grow.

Edward Yourdon is also owed a debt of gratitude for contributing a structured approach to the first edition, which continues in this version. Special thanks to Philip Jan Rothstein, as well, for serving as a reviewer of the second edition and contributing many insights that helped to improve the scope and content of the work.

The author was also fortunate to have a champion in the person of Tim Moore. He and his staff merit special recognition for bearing with my delays and seeing this book through another Prentice Hall edition. Thanks also to Patty Donovan and company at Pine Tree Composition. It is always a pleasure to work with you folks, and the results are marvelous.

Margaret, Alexandra, Maximilian, Mercedes, Vincent, Carrie and the entire Toigo and Romao clans kept the author alert, healthy, and positive about the effort. Tony Romao and his Nerd Herd filled my email inbox with jokes each day, while Lori provided babysitting services at critical times, freeing up the author to write the words and Margaret to do the graphics.

Last but not least, the author wishes to thank the many vendors, analysts, and DR planners who contributed information and interviews to this project. A special thanks also goes to the many readers who sent me their comments on the first and second editions, and also to the college professors, who continued to use the first edition, photocopied with my permission, for nearly a decade as a text in their classrooms.

As we complete a Third Edition, in the wake of 9/11, it is increasingly clear that disaster recovery planning is nothing less than a survival strategy for helping companies cope with the unthinkable. The author wants to thank you, the reader, for continuing to accompany me on my journey to define and document the most effective DR strategies and practices. I hope that this book will help you to weather whatever storms are ahead.

CHAPTER

1

Introduction

It is perhaps inevitable that for an entire generation of Americans, the word *disaster* will be inexorably linked to the horrific events that shattered a pleasant morning in New York City and Washington, D.C., on September 11, 2001. No other single incident, save perhaps the attack on Pearl Harbor, struck so profoundly or so deeply into the consciousness of the nation.

For most, the experience was a vicarious one—but one made more tangible by the video footage of commercial aircraft smashing into the twin towers of the World Trade Center (WTC) and the subsequent reduction of those buildings—and a wing of the Pentagon—into twisted masses of debris that CNN and other news agencies repeated over and over in the days and weeks that followed. For those who were actually at ground zero, who were working in the buildings when the terrorists struck or sifting through the rubble of the WTC or the Pentagon in the aftermath of the attacks, the reality of the disaster was overwhelming.

There had been other disasters before 9/11, and some had taken an even greater toll in terms of human life. However, none had generated such resonance in the minds of those who were not directly affected by the calamity.

It could be argued, of course, that this disaster was different from any other event, both in terms of its emotional impact on a nation and also in a number of other eminently practical ways. The fact that the attacks had been deliberate and intentional acts undertaken in accordance with a carefully thought-out plan, rather than a natural and random event, touched off an emotional whirlwind that for a time impacted the energy and attention spans of everyman. Moreover, as the government braced itself for the possibility of more attacks, air transportation and stock markets were shut down for several days. These actions changed the

milieu in which business recovery plans must execute and increased the scope
and duration of the disaster.

Aside from the social and political consequences of 9/11, perhaps the most
extraordinary thing about the disaster was that so many of the impacted organizations appeared to lack any sort of disaster recovery plan. Of the 440-odd businesses occupying the WTC, the thousands of businesses in Lower Manhattan
affected by the interruptions in power, telecommunications and access to facilities, and the numerous governmental entities in the Pentagon, only a small subset—perhaps as few as 200—evidenced preplanned continuity strategies.

This estimate is based on press accounts of the number of firms that formally declared a disaster and activated their contracts with any of the several
leading "hot-site" vendors. (A hot-site contract provides for a facility, computer
equipment and networks that can be put rapidly into service to replace a subscriber's "production" IT infrastructure when and if normal operations are interrupted by a disaster event.)

To be generous, a few organizations may not have needed the services of a
hot-site vendor in the wake of the disaster. In some cases, only "branch office operations," rather than a primary headquarters or important data center, were
hosted within or around the WTC, or inside the Pentagon. In a few more cases,
organizations may have activated "homegrown" recovery strategies that didn't
require the participation of a commercial service provider.

Even with these exceptions factored in, however, the number of companies that were not prepared for the possibility of a disaster like 9/11 were likely
the majority. The sad truth is that, as in the case of the 143 companies that simply disappeared in the months and years following the 1993 bombing of the
WTC, many of the companies that endured the 9/11 tragedy without a continuity plan will likely not see the end of the decade. These companies will learn
their lessons about the importance of disaster recovery planning the hard way,
adding further pain and anguish to the already sad memory of that awful
event.

Once the immediate sense of threat had ended and the period of mourning
had subsided, stories began to emerge about the efforts of organizations to recover from the disasters—to restore business critical operations to some sem-
blance of normalcy. Specific lessons were learned that will be referenced where
appropriate in the discussion that follows.

Perhaps the most important lesson to be learned from 9/11, from a disaster
recovery perspective, is one of business dependency on information technology
and, by extension, its vulnerability to the unplanned interruption of access to information technology (IT) of infrastructure.

Driven by the incentives of cost-efficiency and competition, business has
placed more and more of its critical information assets into automated systems
and networks. This, in turn, has made business dependent upon the uninterrupted function of the machine, a dependency rarely perceived by those within
the corporation who have no direct contact with the IT infrastructure itself. The

consequences of a loss of access to the IT infrastructure to the business may never be considered—until a disaster occurs. By then, it is often too late.

Recent business experience—both before and after 9/11—is replete with examples of companies that failed to recover from a disaster. Some were consumed by a flood or fire that demolished offices and data centers, leaving skeletons of twisted metal and smoking rubble. Others died gradually over several years, after being crippled by a catastrophe from which they could never fully recover.

However, in the same historical experience, there are also examples of companies that suffered disasters of the same magnitude and survived. They emerged from the crisis, with critical operations intact, to regain their position in the marketplace and to continue their commercial pursuits.

One must ask the reason for the different outcomes. Why do some companies survive when others fail? Is it simply fate or chance that determines success or failure in disaster recovery?

The word *disaster* connotes chance or risk. It is derived from the Latin word for "evil star"—a metaphor for a comet, once thought to be a harbinger of some impending doom. While the word embodies a fatalistic view of the unavoidable and inexplicable nature of disaster, it also communicates a positive corollary: Forewarned is forearmed. Knowing in advance that a disaster might happen provides the ability to prepare and to mitigate its consequences.

The insights of the ancient Romans continue to hold truth for modern organizations. Mounting evidence supports the contention that companies can take measures that will improve the likelihood of full recovery following a disaster. Companies that plan for the possibility of a disaster—that implement preventive measures to avoid predictable events and formulate strategies for recovering critical business processes in the wake of events that cannot be prevented—generally do survive disasters.

WHAT IS DISASTER RECOVERY PLANNING?

This book is about disaster recovery planning. As defined here, disaster recovery planning consists of a set of activities aimed at reducing the likelihood and limiting the impact of disaster events on critical business processes.

This preliminary definition may raise a few eyebrows. In the past few years, there has been an effort in some quarters to distinguish the concept of disaster recovery from a related concept, business continuity planning.

To some commentators, disaster recovery pertains to a specific domain of disaster events: recovery from natural disasters such as floods, hurricanes, and earthquakes. Business continuation planning, some argue, covers a broader domain of events, many of which may be less cataclysmic and life threatening in nature. Software viruses, hard disk failures, malicious attacks on systems and networks by hackers or disgruntled employees, and many other factors can and do cause interruptions in normal business processes without necessarily result-

ing in the widespread regional damage that might be left in the wake of a hurricane.

At the level of semantics, a measure of clarity is contained in the term "business continuity planning" that may not be present in the term "disaster recovery
planning." Business continuity more concisely describes the objective of this type of
activity, which is to sustain mission-critical business processes during an unplanned interruption event. By contrast, some would argue, the term "disaster recovery" is semantically flawed. By its nature, a disaster is a nonrecoverable event. If
recovery is possible, because of the implementation of some planned strategy, then
an unplanned interruption event does not, strictly speaking, constitute a disaster.

This book does not seek to contribute to the semantic debate. Suffice it to
say that the use of the term disaster recovery planning in this book encompasses
the objectives attributed to all of the other forms. Namely, it is a set of activities
intended to prevent avoidable instances of unplanned interruption, regardless of
cause, and to minimize the impact of interruption events that cannot be avoided.

PURPOSE OF THIS BOOK

This book is designed to equip company planners with the background knowledge and skills they need to develop an effective disaster avoidance and recovery
capability for their companies. It is also intended to serve as a primer for information technology managers and business executives in the critical and sometimes
mysterious discipline of disaster recovery planning. It may be useful as a guide
for managing the activities of the planning project, whether such a project is undertaken by internal personnel or outside consultants. Finally, it is a pragmatic
reference describing the products, practices, and politics of the disaster recovery
industry that has emerged over the past three decades.

After reading this book, the reader will understand the principles of disaster
recovery planning and will be equipped with a generic model for a DR planning
project that he or she may emulate to develop a workable disaster recovery plan.
Along the way, the reader will be exposed to some of the current debates and
emerging technologies of disaster recovery as well as firsthand experiences of numerous business planners in both the preparation and implementation of disaster
recovery plans. All that will remain is for the reader to select and apply what has
been learned to develop a workable plan for his or her own company.

A WORKING DEFINITION OF DISASTER

The term disaster, as used in this book, means the unplanned interruption of normal business processes resulting from the interruption of the IT infrastructure
components used to support them. This definition includes information systems
and networks and their hardware and software components—as well as data
itself.

Of IT infrastructure-related business process interruptions, those resulting from a loss of data itself are arguably the most devastating. Whether a loss of data results from accidental or intentional erasure and/or the destruction of the media on which data is recorded or from any of a number of manmade or natural phenomena, data is the most difficult of all infrastructure components to replace. As a result, interruptions of business processes resulting from data loss may be the most difficult to surmount.

In addition to data loss, business process interruptions can also result from a loss of IT infrastructure components used to transport, process, and/or present data for use. A broad range of factors can lead to infrastructure component loss. These may include events that cause the destruction of key system, network or storage hardware or software, such as fires or floods. Component "loss" may also be the by-product of disruptions in regional infrastructure supports such as power or telecommunications outages.

These infrastructure interruptions have the potential to wreak as much havoc within a company as the loss of the data itself. However, their effects can generally be minimized through the application of recovery or continuity strategies that are the result of advanced planning and preparation.

The above description of disaster may suggest that only a major calamity—a terrorist bombing, an earthquake, or even a war—would qualify as a disaster. The term disaster conjures to mind a smoking data center at Goliath, Inc., rather than an accidental hard disk erasure at the small business office down the block. In either case, if the result is an unplanned interruption of normal business processes, the event may be classified as a disaster. Disasters are relative and contextual.

THE TIME FACTOR IN DISASTER RECOVERY

However, despite contextual diversity, there are some constants about disasters. One is time.

Because of businesss' growing dependency on customized information systems and networks, alternatives to system-provided functions and information cannot be implemented readily. Yet, for a business to survive a disaster, the time factor for restoration of system functions is critical.

In the past, interruptions in normal processing could be withstood by most companies for a protracted period of time. A 1978 study by the University of Minnesota depicted the resilience of business to system interruptions, suggesting that most companies could survive interruptions of 2 to 6 days in length.[1]

Given the increased dependency of business today on information technology, it is hard to imagine a company withstanding an outage of more than 48 hours without incurring serious difficulties for its market position. Indeed, for companies ranging from brokerages and banks to e-commerce vendors and just-in-time manufacturers, the costs associated with even minimal system or network interruptions may be extremely high.

This is underscored by data from the Meta Group, describing the cost of downtime by industry segment. The Meta Group study looked at downtime costs from the perspective of employee idle time and suggested that the average cost to an organization an hour of downtime exceeded $1 million. (See Table 1–1.)

While industry- and application-specific averages for downtime cost are poor indicators of specific business vulnerabilities, they do point out the growing dependence of business processes on IT infrastructure. In view of business' dependence upon its information technology infrastructure and its vulnerability to an unplanned interruption of normal information processing activity, it makes sense for a company to plan and prepare for this possibility.

Recent events attest to the fact that those who plan for unplanned interruptions fare better than those who do not. A brief listing of some disaster recovery successes illustrates this point. In the last decade, publicized business process interruptions (excluding 9/11 attacks) included:

Table 1–1   The Cost of Downtime from the Perspective of Lost Revenues and Employee Idle Time

Industry Sector	Revenue/Hour	Revenue/Employee Hour
Energy	$2,817,846	$569.20
Telecommunications	2,066,245	186.98
Manufacturing	1,610,654	134.24
Financial Institutions	1,495,134	1,079.89
Information Technology	1,344,461	184.03
Insurance	1,202,444	370.92
Retail	1,107,274	244.37
Pharmaceuticals	1,082,252	167.53
Banking	996,802	130.52
Food/Beverage Processing	804,192	153.10
Consumer Products	785,719	127.98
Chemicals	704,101	194.53
Transportation	668,586	107.78
Utilities	643,250	142.58
Healthcare	636,030	142.58
Metals/Natural Resources	580,588	153.11
Professional Services	532,510	99.59
Electronics	477,366	74.48
Construction/Engineering	389,601	216.18
Media	340,432	119.74
Hospitality/Travel	330,654	38.62
AVERAGE	**$1,010,536**	**$205.55**

- An anthrax scare in November 2001 temporarily closes Empire Blue Cross/Blue Shield's data center.
- Tropical Storm Allison floods the Texas Medical Center Campus in June 2001, closing 54 medical institutions.
- Rolling power outages in California leave hundreds of companies in the dark during the summer of 2001.
- An earthquake measuring 6.9 on the Richter scale in the Seattle area hits numerous companies including Boeing Corporation in March 2001.
- A computer glitch causes Delta Airlines subsidiary, Atlantic Southeast Airlines, to cancel or delay over 400 flights in February 2001.
- In 1999, pipe break floods Charles Schwab and Company offices in San Francisco, California.
- In 1998, roof collapses and floods at Landstar Systems in Jacksonville, Florida.
- A tornado hits on Bank of America Corporation's Nashville, Tennessee, operations center in 1998.
- Hurricane Georges causes the evacuation of Degussa Corporation in Theodore, Alabama, in 1998.
- A 1996 data center fire occurs at Humana Inc. headquarters in Louisville, Kentucky.

The above examples, and many others, provide empirical evidence of the efficacy of disaster recovery planning. In virtually every case, companies that experienced potentially devastating disasters implemented tested contingency plans and survived to continue operating in the marketplace.

By contrast, as mentioned above, nearly 150 companies without disaster recovery plans were dealt a death blow in February 1993, when a bomb wracked the World Trade Center in New York.[2] These firms learned too late that when a company does not have a tested set of procedures for reacting to and recovering from a catastrophe, it places all of its other plans and objectives in jeopardy.

Business Continuity Planning Consultant Philip Jan Rothstein correctly observes that documented information about the outcomes of system or network interruption events, both in the presence and absence of recovery plans, remains very limited. He bristles at the use of gross estimates of downtime cost as a substitute for factual industry statistics.[3] The point is well-taken, especially as it pertains to business failures following disaster. In many cases, the relationship between a disaster event and business failure is not discussed publicly at all. Moreover, failures of businesses that are rooted in a disaster event may not occur until several years after the event, making the relationship difficult to document.

Based on available evidence, the time required to recover critical business processes following an interruption is a universal determinant of successful recovery. Unplanned interruption can cost a business dearly in revenues, reputation, customers, and investors. The objective of DR planning is to recover mission-critical processes as quickly as possible following the interruption event to mitigate its duration and costs.

However, evidence also suggests that interruption costs do not remain constant following a disaster event. They may rise exponentially, then decline over time. Assuming that a company can sustain itself through the initial high-cost interruption period, even those without tested DR plans may be able to recover their operations and live to fight another day.

While this may seem to contradict the recovery time factor argument cited above, in fact it confirms it. Companies can elect to expend time, effort, and resources in advance of a disaster to reduce the risk of business failure, or they can do nothing, accept the risk, and hope that their IT infrastructure can be repaired "on the fly" following an unplanned interruption.

Even in the absence of a statistical DR planning nirvana—the availability of exacting data on outage costs and business failure rates that would provide an airtight case for planning—numerous case studies can and do make a persuasive argument. Proactive planning can avoid certain risks and mitigate the impact of others.

THE NEED FOR DISASTER RECOVERY PLANNING

The need for disaster recovery planning is usually self-evident to an IT professional. Who, after all, has a more personal stake in the survival of a company's information systems than the manager whose position, prestige, and salary directly depend upon system performance?

In addition to self-interest, information managers often manifest a protective, almost parental attitude toward "their" systems. This is especially true when systems have been developed in-house. Effective IT managers and chief information officers (CIOs), like good parents, take a personal interest in the safety and health of their charges.

Beyond self-interest and psychological factors, the IT professional has an ethical mandate to protect data integrity and ensure system and network survivability. Service level agreements between the IT department and company's end user departments are one manifestation of this commitment to quality and excellence in IT services. Contingency plans must exist if service level agreements are to be made in good faith.

Given all the compelling arguments for undertaking disaster recovery planning, it may seem redundant for auditors and federal law to require it. Unfortunately, a 1998 survey of 4,255 IT and information security managers conducted by Ernst & Young and Computerworld revealed that over half had no disaster recovery plan in place for their companies.[4] The study further showed a decline in attention to disaster recovery planning generally, despite increasing downtime-related costs:

> While over 59% of this year's respondents said they experienced financial loss due to system downtime or failure within the past 12 months, only 41% of the organizations surveyed have a [disaster recovery] plan, compared to 55% last year; of that number, 34% have never tested the plan. In approximately 45% overall, there was no

budget for [DR planning] activities. . . . In 45% of the organizations surveyed, there were no full-time employees dedicated to [DR planning], while 26% had none last year. The number of part-time employees allocated has also decreased: in 1997, 20% had no part-time [DR planning] employees; this year it is 53%."[5]

One year before the Ernst & Young survey, the Meta Group interviewed 100 of its Fortune 1000 company clients and discovered that fewer than 5% had "back-to-front" disaster recovery plans in place. Missing were provisions for the recovery of client/server systems, even in those companies that were in the process of migrating mission critical legacy applications onto distributed platforms.[6]

In the absence of effective planning, it has fallen to auditors, and in some cases legislators, to apprise corporate information managers of disaster recovery planning requirements and to enforce them as a matter of law.

THE AUDITOR'S VIEW

Auditors tend to view disaster recovery planning as a facet of an organization's efforts to guarantee the security and integrity of its data processing capability. While in the past auditors may have been content with a regular schedule for off-site storage of backup tapes and a paper plan gathering dust on the IT manager's bookshelf, their level of sophistication has grown. Documented and tested disaster recovery plans are increasingly regarded by IT auditors as a necessary component of business operation integrity.

Internal auditors are also taking a more active role in helping develop business recovery plans, often to ensure that corporate management (for whom they serve as the "eyes and ears") is not exposed to lawsuits or regulatory censure in the event of a disaster. Another reason for their interest is a well-founded concern that the integrity and security of corporate information assets will be maintained as contingency plans are rolled out and critical business applications and data are transitioned to backup platforms. The importance of this aspect of contingency plan auditing was underscored in the late 1990s as auditors and IT managers alike troubled over the possibility of hacker attacks during the recovery of Y2K-related application failures.[7]

External auditors, especially the "Big Five" consulting/accounting firms such as Deloitte Touche Tohmatsu, Arthur Andersen, PricewaterhouseCoopers, KPMG International, and Ernst & Young, offer disaster recovery planning services to clients. The auditor-as-contingency-planner opens some controversial issues that will be explored later in this chapter.

IT audit handbooks now contain chapters devoted entirely to auditing the IT department's disaster recovery plan. Auditors are paying increasing attention to the following areas as they examine a company's disaster recovery plan.

- Plan revisions. While IT auditors may have no way to determine a plan's solvency or workability (unless they are invited to participate in an actual test), they may look to see when the plan was last revised. They are also interested in procedures providing for the regular review and revision of the document and for the regular reporting of system changes that must be accommodated within the plan. A list of revision dates should appear in the back matter of the plan document to answer these questions.

- Plan test schedule and results assessments. An untested disaster recovery plan cannot be assumed to provide an adequate measure of recoverability to corporate data assets. Tests provide the means for assessing the workability of strategies for evacuation and recovery that appear to work well on paper but may not perform well in real life. A schedule of regular testing and documentation of methods and results are important indicators to the auditor of management's attentiveness to the disaster recovery requirement. This is also typically added to the back matter of the plan.

- Training and awareness. It is often said at IT Security and Disaster Recovery Planning seminars that DR plans are "living documents." A disaster recovery plan addresses two time frames: the future time frame, when the plan will be implemented to cope with some manmade or natural catastrophe, and the present time frame, when the plan is maintained and tested, plan participants are trained, and every corporate employee is made aware of the principles of disaster preparedness and prevention. This dual focus of disaster recovery planning presumes an ongoing training effort. Thus, auditors may ask to see a schedule indicating the dates, topics, and attendance by key recovery personnel at training sessions covering the many aspects of the plan. They may also wish to see evidence of provisions made to increase safety awareness within the company as a whole. Awareness posters in dining areas and elevators, handouts for new employees, and even designated "disaster awareness days" may be some of the ways that this audit requirement can be satisfied.

In addition to these general items, there are many specific requirements of a disaster recovery plan that may be checked or verified by the auditor. These may include:

- A fully articulated planning rationale, providing an overview of threats and exposures and prioritization of risks based on potential business impact and other factors (e.g., likelihood of occurrence), plus a discussion of mitigation strategies considered and selection criteria applied.

- Effective disaster prevention and mitigation measures for all critical business process infrastructure components, including strategies for system, network, and end user work area recovery and evidence that these measures can be implemented in whole or part in response to various interruption scenarios.

- Documentation of relationships with other companies for backup of system platforms in the event of a facility disaster, including contracts with vendors of system backup facilities and services (hot sites, shell sites, mobile recovery facilities, etc.).

- Contracts and schedules for regular off-site storage for paper files and magnetic media backups, schemes for electronic tape vaulting, and/or remote data mirroring with off-site entities.
- Provisions for network recovery including contracts with network vendors for on-demand rerouting or automatic switching of voice and data communications services to a designated alternative work site.
- Specifications for fire protection systems, power continuation systems, water detection systems, and automated detection and alarm systems for other contingencies (disaster prevention capabilities).

AN IMPERFECT LEGAL MANDATE

In many industries, the dictates of common sense and audit requirements are supplemented by legal mandates for disaster recovery planning. The U.S. government has enacted legislation or issued regulations that require a broad range of contingency planning and related activities to be undertaken by businesses. A partial list of these provisions is provided in Table 1–2. In addition, many states are currently deliberating legislation pertaining to contingency planning, and some, including Florida and Maryland, have already passed laws requiring demonstrated disaster recovery capabilities for certain industry segments. Readers are urged to consult a lawyer specializing in computer and business law to determine the requirements that pertain in their respective states.

Federal mandates for disaster recovery planning affect various industry segments unevenly. Financial institutions, particularly those participating in the various components of the federal banking system, must comply with a well-rooted regimen of regulations on DR.

National banks, for example, must comply with Comptroller of the Currency Banking Circulars and Federal Financial Information Examination Council (FFIEC) guidelines that require them to develop means to reduce the impact and/or risk of losing IT support for business-critical applications.

In many cases, bank management is made directly responsible for determining critical functions at the bank, assessing the risk and potential impact of a loss of IT support for those functions, and developing plans to reduce the risk and/or impact of such a loss. Moreover, boards of directors are obligated to review the plans of bank management annually, approve them, record their approval in the board minutes, and provide the minutes for review by the bank examiners. The intent is to make both the board and bank management legally liable for a bank failure arising from inadequate preparation for an IT outage.

Other banking regulations extend management accountability for disaster recovery planning to include the performance of service bureaus. Banks using service bureaus to process information are required to investigate the financial

Table 1–2   Partial Business Recovery Regulatory Profile

Regulation	Industry	Description
Comptroller of Currency BC-177 (1983, 1987)	Banking	Amended since original in 1983; requires banking institutions to develop and maintain Business Recovery Plans
Federal Home Loan Bank Bulletin R-67	Banking	Follows intent of BC-177
Inter-Agency Policy from Federal Financial Institutions Examination Council (FFIEC—1989, 1996)	Banking and any related service bureaus	Requires business-wide data and IT protection planning for banking institutions and extends regulation to require contingency plans from any service bureaus or outsourcing companies which service such banks.
Financial Institution Letter from Federal Financial Institutions Examination Council (FFIEC—1997)	FDIC Supervised Banks	Emphasizes to the board of directors and senior management the importance of corporate data protection functions, also addresses issues that management should consider when developing a viable IT security plan
Fair Credit Reporting Act	Reporting Agencies	Ensures credit information is accurate and up-to-date
Foreign Corrupt Practices Act (1977)	Cross-Industry	Management accountability through record keeping
IRS Procedure 86-19	Cross-Industry	Legal requirements for protecting computer records containing tax information
IRS Procedure 97-22, Cumulative Bulletin 1997-1	Cross-Industry	Compliance requirements for electronic storage systems used to maintain record-keeping information
IRS Procedure 98-25, Internal Revenue Bulletin 1998-11	Cross-Industry	Requirements for documentation of machine-readable recordkeeping system processes
Federal Response Planning Guidance (1994) FRPG 01-94	Federal departments and agencies	Outlines responsibilities and objectives of data protection planning
GAO/IMTEC-91-56 Financial Markets: Computer Security Controls	Financial	Security guidelines for stock markets
Gramm-Leach-Bliley Act of 1999	Financial	Requirements for guaranteeing information privacy and security
Health Insurance Portability and Accountability Act of 1996 (HIPAA)	Healthcare	Requires adequate provisioning for health information privacy and security
Accreditation Manual for Hospitals (1994)	Healthcare	Guidelines for information management including security
Clinical Laboratory Information Act (1988)	Healthcare	Specifies requirements protection of critical laboratory data

Source: U.S. Government sources and William P. Dimartini, "What Drives Business Recovery Planning—The Carrot or the Stick?," *Contingency Planning & Management Magazine,* March/April 1996, © 1996 Witter Publishing Corp.

condition of their servicers annually and to develop alternate processing strategies if the servicer's financial condition is deteriorating or unsound. They are also required to prepare their own contingency plans for mitigating exposure to a failure of the service bureau's processing capability.

The focus of federal regulators on the disaster preparedness of financial institutions in particular originated in the wake of an actual disaster. Following a computer failure at the Bank of New York in 1985, senior officials of the bank were summoned to appear before a Congressional investigating committee that, at one point in its hearings, considered the possibility of removing senior managers from their positions for not adequately preparing for a disaster.[8]

Bank of New York, reputedly the state's largest broker for government securities, experienced an IT outage that lasted approximately 27 hours. To continue operations, the bank was forced to borrow $22 billion from the discount window of the Federal Reserve Bank. It did so at an interest rate well below prime. The huge loan briefly destabilized the weighted rate of federal funds and cost the bank (or its insurer) $4 to $5 million in interest.[9] While Congress did not remove management in this case, the Federal Reserve did issue a circular that set the rate for borrowing in the face of an IT failure at prime plus two.

Not all federal regulations are reactive, however. In the late 1990s, the Year 2000 (Y2K) problem focused the attention of some regulators on corporate contingency planning as a proactive measure—a hedge against widespread economic calamity.

The Securities and Exchange Commission (SEC), for example, required all publicly held companies to disclose the details of their Y2K remediation projects, including contingency plans, as part of their SEC filings. Presumably, this requirement was intended to pressure companies to deal with their Y2K vulnerabilities by making the status of their preparedness a matter of public record.

The regulation cajoles companies to perform Y2K remediation by providing prospective investors with an additional criterion for making investment decisions. It may also provide a basis for shareholder lawsuits in the wake of Y2K outages if false claims are made by companies about their preparedness.

The regulation further incites companies to remediate their application code or risk being dropped as suppliers by business customers who depend upon their products within their own supply chains. As the 1990s drew to a close, many companies were actively reviewing their supply chain providers and selecting new, Y2K-ready providers for critical supply sources.

The close attention paid to the disaster preparedness of the financial industry (and to Y2K remediation across all industries) by federal lawmakers and regulators is not indicative of a comprehensive DR planning mandate, however. In many cases, disaster recovery planning requirements must be interpreted from legal language pertaining to recordkeeping requirements.

The Foreign Corrupt Practices Act of 1977, for example, requires only indirectly that companies undertake contingency planning. The post-Watergate-era legislation was conceived as a mechanism for prosecuting companies that routinely used bribes to obtain business advantage in foreign markets. However, the recordkeeping provisions of the law are sweeping and have been adopted by the SEC and applied to all publicly held companies.

The recordkeeping provisions of the Act require companies to keep and safeguard records that clearly indicate how their assets are used. The original intent was to eliminate vaguely labeled accounting entries, such as "slush funds," which investigators found were often used to disguise bribery payments. According to the legislation, any accounting system that fails to indicate clearly how money is disposed of violates the Act. The SEC has since used the Act in several cases to prosecute wrongdoers who have not engaged in bribery of foreign officials, but whose actions technically violate the Act's accounting requirements (much like the federal government has used tax laws to prosecute organized crime figures whose "real" crimes cannot be proven).[10]

The Foreign Corrupt Practices Act pertains to any company using manual or computerized ledger, accounts receivable/accounts payable, or other accounting systems. Under the law, a business must take measures to guarantee the security and integrity of its recordkeeping system—a provision that has been widely interpreted as a requirement to undertake contingency planning. The Act further provides the means to prosecute individual managers and corporate executives who fail to comply with the Act. By legal extension, management can be prosecuted for failing to plan adequately for recordkeeping system recovery following a disaster.

Individual fines of up to $10,000, 5 years in prison, and corporate penalties of more than $1 million have been established. To date, however, no penalties have been exacted under the provisions of this law against companies or their executives simply for failing to develop disaster recovery plans.

Another government regulation, from the Office of Management and Budget, requires government agencies to take adequate measures to safeguard the operations of their IT processing facilities. This rule has been interpreted to extend to government contractors and subcontractors and is being rigidly enforced as a matter of national defense. Proponents of the regulation argue that because the design and production of military equipment and other contracted goods are being conducted or controlled using computer systems, the inadequate safeguarding of these systems represents an economic and military threat to the security of the United States. Plans must be made by federal contractors and subcontractors to ensure the availability and integrity of these systems.

The assignment of the ultimate responsibility—in legal terms—for the protection and preservation of corporate assets to corporate management has precedents. The Internal Revenue Service (IRS), for example, has articulated a number of strict rules pertaining to secure storage of business records. Management is often liable if IRS rules have not been observed and the records are lost.

For example, IRS Procedure 64-12 requires that recorded and reconstructable data be maintained in accordance with the Internal Revenue Code of

1954 and that program and source documentation be securely stored so that an audit trail from source documents to final accounting balances and totals may be demonstrated in the event of an IRS audit.[11] IRS Ruling 71–20 goes further to describe the requirements for retaining and safeguarding machine-readable records (including punched cards, disks, and other machine-sensible data media) that may become material in the administration of any IRS law.[12] Corporate officers are subject to penalties if these rulings and regulations are not observed.

Besides making provisions for disaster recovery and secure storage of data, the U.S. government further requires all businesses to safeguard the health and safety of employees and to refrain from activities that could harm the community in which facilities are located. The Occupational Safety and Health Administration (OSHA) and the Environmental Protection Agency (EPA) have issued enforceable codes and regulations aimed at "disaster avoidance" that make company management prosecutable if avoidable disasters occur.[13] At the state level, numerous agencies and departments have followed the federal government's lead with fire, building, and emergency management codes that impact on disaster avoidance and recovery planning.[14]

BUILDING MANAGEMENT CONSENSUS FOR DISASTER RECOVERY PLANNING

This brief survey demonstrates that the disaster recovery planning project is propelled by a number of considerations, ranging from a common-sense business impetus to safeguard corporate assets from loss or damage to a natural desire to reduce legal exposure and personal loss. This is not to say, however, that corporate management is aware of all of the legal penalties, or even the risks, associated with not having an effective disaster recovery capability. In some cases, management consensus must be cultivated by an information manager or auditor.

The above observation may seem out of step with the current elevated level of attention being paid to disaster preparedness in the wake of 9/11. However, history has demonstrated over and over again that there is a tendency for interest in DR to spike in the aftermath of a disaster, then to diminish rather quickly as the memory of the disaster fades.

Even after a consensus is built to support the planning for business interruption and recovery, sustaining the consensus when it comes time to implement the paper plan—to install the recovery capability—can be difficult. The reasons for the breakdown of the consensus are numerous. In some cases, management exhibits reluctance to spend money acquiring the services and products that are intrinsic to the plan. This often occurs when management does not fully understand the risks and exposures a company faces without a recovery capability.

To address this dilemma, DR consultants recommend that a formal risk analysis process be undertaken early in the disaster recovery planning project.

An assessment should be made of the impact of unplanned interruption events on the business as a whole—including a detailed assessment of tangible and intangible costs accrued to the unplanned interruption of each automated application that supports a mission-critical business process.

As an adjunct to this analysis, any legal requirements that compel management to undertake planning should be cited and clearly communicated. Where the law does not directly mandate disaster recovery planning, other strategies have to be found to convince reluctant senior managers of plan benefits. Effective strategies are often difficult to find.

Convincing corporate management to shoulder the costs of a disaster recovery capability can often be a greater challenge than surmounting the technical problems involved in backing up critical systems and networks. In the final analysis, however, management will play the most critical role in the planning effort—the role of underwriter.

Following are some typical problems reported by the information managers who had to sell their plans to senior management, and the successful strategies they developed to overcome them.

- "You haven't cost-justified the plan."

  This criticism usually reflects the disaster recovery planner's failure to document adequately the exposures and risks of not having a plan. Often, planners first encounter this objection when they seek management approval to conduct an analysis of risks and exposures. That is, management may ask the planner to cost-justify the plan before they have authorized an investigation of whether such a disaster recovery capability is necessary!

  How does one cost-justify a capability that, in the best circumstances, will measure its success in nonevents? This dilemma was perhaps best expressed in a humorous anecdote that followed January 1, 2000 in which a chief executive officer railed at his IT manager, "You mean we spent all that money on Y2K preparations and nothing happened?!" A good disaster recovery plan, after all, sets the stage for disaster avoidance by providing the means to detect and react to potential problems, in many cases, before they become disasters. Strategies for successfully addressing this problem generally fall into two categories.

  One strategy for responding to this criticism is to assign a dollar value to an hour of downtime. Calculate the average hourly earnings of employees who use an application that provides a business process for which a recovery capability will be planned. This provides an estimate of the cost of an hour of lost productivity were an application outage to occur. Assuming that the data could be entered at a later time without other adverse consequences, repeat the above calculation for 1 hour of average overtime salary (i.e., the amount of time all system users would need to work to make up for lost time). Then, add the two dollar costs as the total average labor cost for one hour of downtime.

For applications used by greater numbers of end users, this number by it-self could be sufficient to demonstrate the benefit of a disaster recovery ca-pability that would avoid outages or minimize the duration of unavoidable outages. By multiplying the number to reflect 10 hours, 24 hours, 48 hours, and so on, the statistic could be quite compelling.

This approach, while simplistic, can be augmented by citing any docu-mented costs associated with outages that have previously been experi-enced by the company. However, the planner must keep in mind what was said earlier about the tendency of outage costs to decline over time.

In some cases, the better case can be made by referencing intangible costs. The loss of customer satisfaction, the abrogation of service level commit-ments, potential legal liability, lost sales opportunities, negative press, and a host of other non-dollar-based factors may hold significant meaning for management. Arguments based on these non-quantifiable factors may actu-ally be more compelling than cost-justification and other quantitative meth-ods. The latter are inherently flawed, in any case, by the lack of reliable data on the likelihood of occurrence for any given disaster potential.

Another way to justify the plan is to demonstrate the collateral benefits of such a plan. An effective disaster recovery capability can actually reduce business insurance costs in some situations. Premiums for facility or busi-ness interruption insurance may be substantially reduced in many cases where disaster recovery planning identifies the specific coverages required and blanket insurance policies are replaced with targeted and less-expensive plans.[15]

Some disaster recovery capabilities, such as uninterruptible power sup-plies (UPS), actually do double-duty. They can sustain critical business sys-tems or network devices for a time so that organized shutdowns can be accomplished or independent generators started up in the event of a disas-trous power outage. In addition to its use in a disaster, the UPS also sup-ports equipment during the occasional surges, dips, and flickers of a typical business day. In so doing, the UPS can actually prolong the useful life of connected equipment.

Another dual-use scenario may apply to an end-user or workgroup oper-ations center—a facility designed to house users if the main business facility becomes uninhabitable for a period of time. Such a facility may also be used during non-disaster periods as a training or conference facility.

A practical example of dual-use may be found in the case of a certain Midwestern state government's IT department. In the wake of 9/11, the politicians in the state made compelling speeches about the need for disas-ter recovery but allocated no money for building such a capability. The IT manager for the government did, however, manage to receive funding for an "application development and testing center." Determined to build a re-dundant facility for disaster recovery, the savvy IT manager replicated vir-tually all critical production systems and networks at the alternate site and

created an internal hot site while also providing a location for developing
and testing new systems before they were deployed into production for the
state. Sometimes, as this case suggests, planners may need to become down-
right sneaky to overcome obstacles to effective planning.

Dual-use benefits can usually be discerned for most disaster recovery
plan components, given sufficient time and creative energy. When a particularly compelling benefit cannot be found to outweigh a cost, the impact of
the cost may be softened if it is examined from the perspective of tax deduc-
tions, health and safety of personnel, or good corporate citizenship.

- "Our insurance will cover an outage, so why do we need the plan?"

Even if a consensus exists for developing a plan on paper, management
may resist spending money for implementation, especially if the disaster recovery capability is viewed as just so much more insurance. According to
spokespersons for two data processing insurers, the right insurance policy
will cover operating costs that are above the normal costs of business operations, provided that the appropriate "extra" costs are spelled out in the policy. This business interruption insurance, however, should not be viewed as
business resumption insurance.[16] An information manager may need to educate management in the following facts.

Insurers can readily cover the costs of facility damage (and, in some
cases, replacement), and they can provide coverage for hardware and
media. However, while insurers are willing to underwrite the reconstruction of data lost to a natural or manmade disaster, it would be cost prohibitive to the client to underwrite the value of the data.

Without a disaster recovery plan, the client would be hard pressed to estimate the cost of reconstructing data or to buy adequate insurance for doing
so. In all likelihood, without a disaster recovery capability, there would be
nothing with which to reconstruct the data: no extant records, no systems,
no location for personnel to work. Purchasing extra coverages under these
circumstances would be pointless.

In a disaster situation, a company protected only by business interruption
insurance is placed in the unenviable position of relying on the progress of
the claims adjustment cycle to drive the recovery. While top insurers generally provide excellent turnaround on disaster claims and may even provide
support services to facilitate the insured's recovery activities, this is generally less desirable than controlling recovery within the business itself and
capitalizing on the determination and commitment of trained recovery
teams who are employees of the company.

If management does not understand the problems inherent in depending
on insurance to recover from disaster, planners should provide information
about the experience of companies that have experienced disasters firsthand. The aftermath of Hurricane Andrew—the subsequent flight (and, in
some cases, bankruptcies) of property and casualty insurers from the state
of Florida—attests to the impact of a regional disaster on insurance compa-

nies as well as the potential problems companies confront in obtaining the timely handling of insurance claims.

The bottom line is that business interruption insurance is properly regarded only as a supplement to a tested disaster recovery capability. It is never a substitute for planning.

- "The purpose of the plan is to satisfy the auditors."

While it may seem blasphemous, managers often express this sentiment in spoken or unspoken terms. One manager of a national financial concern remarked, off the record, that the best disaster recovery plan he could get his company to fund was an up-to-date resume. Sadly, in the absence of rigidly enforced laws, auditors' comments are often the only incentive for management to undertake disaster recovery planning. Auditors seldom have the power to compel management to do anything it is not inclined to do.

One strategy for surmounting management indifference is to barrage corporate officers with news clippings about business disasters, although this may ultimately cost the sender some prestige or power. The object of this strategy is not to aggravate or frighten, but to create awareness in senior management that disasters do happen and that those who prepare for them generally recover normal operations far more readily than those who do not.

Another method for reducing senior management indifference is to demonstrate that the planner understands and participates in management's priorities and objectives. This may be reflected in the methods used to create and articulate the plan. For example, every effort should be made to maximize the plan's protection while minimizing its cost. Despite his or her personal investment in systems and networks, the planner should strive to assess IT resources dispassionately for their criticality to the corporation. Certain applications are more vital than others, a fact that is underscored by carefully analyzing the impact of an unplanned interruption on business applications. It needs to be clearly communicated to senior management that the plan will target the largest share of budget expenditures for the most important applications.

Furthermore, plans must ultimately encompass not only the recovery of IT and network resources but also the user departments. It makes little sense to restore applications if no provision is made to restore the user community. By involving the managers of user departments in the planning project, the planner may be able to cultivate a corporate climate of support for disaster recovery planning. This, in turn, may reinforce senior management's perception of the value of the disaster recovery planning effort and result in a more comprehensive and effective recovery capability.

Only a few years ago, the Y2K Bug, and the legal exposure it created for a company, captured the attention of senior management. In some companies, it provided an opportunity for DR planners to demonstrate to senior management that what they do is motivated by concern for the business and for management. While Y2K was merely another software-related disaster potential from the DR perspective, some savvy DR planners were able to leverage management concern to gain political capital that could be used later to expand the scope of DR planning into other areas. The same opportunities exist in the wake of 9/11 and should not be overlooked.

These are only a few of the common problems and strategies used by DR planners to obtain senior management approval for disaster recovery planning costs. Other problems may develop that reflect the particular circumstances of a business, the distribution of information systems, or even the individual personalities of senior managers themselves. Whenever possible, disaster recovery planning should be depoliticized and depersonalized. Since the initial focus of the planning effort is on information systems, the information manager will play an important role in setting the stage for the entire corporate disaster recovery plan.

WHO SHOULD WRITE THE PLAN?

Once the decision has been made to undertake disaster recovery planning, the information manager must first determine the method to be used to develop the plan. One option is to hire a consultant to perform this task. Another is to develop the plan in-house. Valid arguments exist to support each option.

At first glance, hiring a consultant with X years of experience in developing this type of project may seem the best choice. Indeed, this approach has several distinct advantages.

First, the disaster recovery planning project is just as complicated as a major system development project and, in fact, parallels the systems development life cycle (SDLC). (Figure 1–1 depicts the similarity.)

Like a system development project, a disaster recovery planning project begins with analysis. A risk analysis process is undertaken to identify potential threats and vulnerabilities, while business impact analyses and application impact analyses are undertaken to identify critical business processes and their IT infrastructure supports and to discern recovery priorities, objectives, and requirements.

Recovery strategies are then outlined and tasks are prioritized much in the same way that an analyst would set forth a general system design. This general design is subjected to user review and, if it is approved, a detailed system description is articulated. At this point, development costs are specified and a project time-and-money budget is developed.

In systems development, the project would be approved by management, and coding would begin. Similarly, the disaster recovery planning budget is presented to senior management and, if approved, vendors are contacted, products and services purchased, and recovery procedures developed and documented.

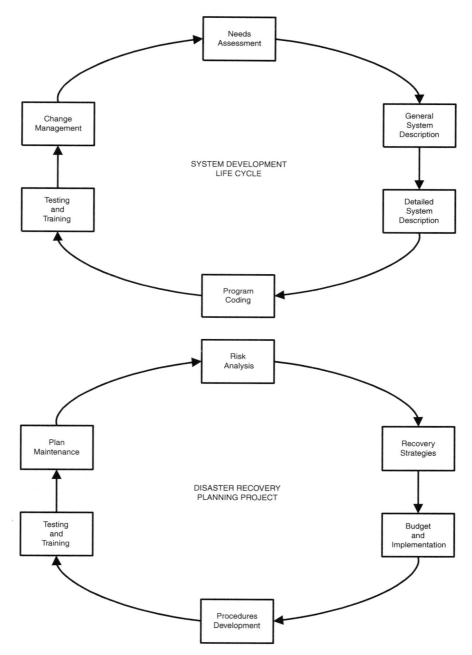

Figure 1-1 Comparison of systems development life cycle (SDLC) to disaster recovery planning project.

Plan testing and user training follow, just as comparable activities would follow the conclusion of coding. Finally, when the system is released or the plan is placed into effect, it is integrated into a change management system to provide for periodic review, revision, and maintenance.

An IT manager, realizing the scope and complexity of the planning project, may decide that a consultant is needed to manage it. The IT manager either cannot reassign an employee to manage the project or feels that no employees are equal to the assignment. There may also be other factors that favor the consultant option:[17]

- Consultants bring specialized knowledge to the planning project that may facilitate the speedy development of an effective plan. An experienced consultant knows how a disaster recovery plan is constructed, knows the right questions to ask, and typically knows who's who in the disaster recovery products and services industry. Consultants who work within a specific industry may combine an understanding of the industry with a methodology for disaster recovery planning. This reduced learning curve, in turn, can help to speed plan development.

- Consultants can bring a fresh eye to the project, noticing recovery requirements that may be overlooked by someone who is too close to the data center he or she is seeking to protect. One consultant relayed a story about a client who had hired her to perform a risk analysis of a data center. In conferences, the client confidentially reassured her that all vital processing equipment had been identified. Then, during a preliminary visit to the data center, the consultant nearly tripped over an ancient time card reader. She asked what it was and learned that no payroll checks could be generated without its use. A vital piece of equipment, yet it had not been mentioned anywhere in the lists that otherwise documented completely the state-of-the-art hardware installed in the shop.

- Consultants are expensive. While this may be viewed as a drawback of the consultant option (and will be discussed later in this chapter), it may actually favor plan development in certain cases. Disaster recovery planning requires the interaction of users and information systems and network technical personnel. Within a large information systems shop, where rivalries frequently exist among applications support personnel, systems administrators, and operations, disaster recovery planning will also require the interaction of these groups. Often the only way to get all of the relevant parties to sit down as a group and discuss critical issues is to make it clear that a great deal of money is being spent for the consultant's time. Similarly, senior management, having invested a considerable sum of money for a consultant-developed plan, may be less inclined to withdraw support for the implementation of the plan.

Consultant-driven plans are similar to computer hardware acquisitions: They are usually available with a maintenance agreement. For a fee, the consultant will return on a semiannual basis to aid in the testing and updating of the original plan. Furthermore, since the plan usually reflects the "favored" (read "proprietary") methodology of the consultant, many consulting firms offer a training service to educate personnel in the client company who will maintain or use the plan.

Good consultants usually produce good plans and provide competent maintenance and training services. Unfortunately, not all consultants are good consultants. As of this writing, the disaster recovery planning consultancy is an unpoliced field. In the late 1960s, there were only handfuls of disaster recovery consulting firms. Since that time, the number has increased exponentially. It is not uncommon for consulting firms to open and close their doors within the same year. This bodes ill for the industry as a whole.

Consultants may attempt to demonstrate their competence by referencing a certification from a DR planning certification body. Several certification organizations have evolved over the past decade with the stated objective of training novice planners and, for a fee, "certifying" the skills of those who have learned their trade "on the job." Contrary to the view of many who have obtained certifications, the kindest thing that this author has to say about certification programs is that, at present, they provide little assurance about the capabilities of those who hold them.

This assertion is likely to draw fire from several quarters, so it merits further discussion. In the early 1990s, the originator of one of the first certification programs for DR planning contacted this author to solicit his participation in promoting a "marketing concept": disaster recovery certification. The proposal consisted of selling certifications for a fee to anyone who could pass a multiple-choice test consisting of easy-to-answer questions such as the meanings of familiar acronyms and the definitions of DR-specific concepts such as "dial backup" and "hot site." Not to be exclusionary, DR practitioners would also be invited to participate. They would be "grandfathered in"—that is, provided the certification without testing in exchange for dues payment. The fellow was clearly delighted with the concept, which he viewed as a "sure money-maker" on three grounds:

1. Many individuals responsible for disaster recovery planning for their organizations suffered from a lack of confidence. They feared that they were not as professional as consultants who developed DR plans for many companies. The certification program would not make them better planners, but it would give them the appearance of professionalism when they interacted with other professionals and with management. Basically, the certification program was a confidence game.
2. The certification program would become a discriminator between consultants in a highly competitive and totally unregulated disaster recovery consulting industry. The revenue potential for the program based on "grandfathering" fees alone was enormous, even if the certification program was meaningless.

3. The certification program would be a great way to amass the world's best database of DR planner names and addresses, which could subsequently be resold to vendors of DR products and services, producing another revenue stream.

Demonstrating a lack of business acumen, the author declined to participate. Nevertheless, the program was launched and became one of the most successful certification programs today.

Recently, an acquaintance of many years, who had retired as the chief disaster recovery planner for a major financial institution, complained that he was required to obtain a certification before he could join the consulting group of a major systems integrator. The fellow was told that in spite of his extensive experience in DR planning, his intimate familiarity with planning methods and tools, his thorough knowledge of vendors and their offerings, his former senior role within a major disaster recovery planning user group, and his numerous references, he was unmarketable without the letters of a certification program following his name on his business card. The situation has achieved the status of a mind-boggling absurdity.

While numerous organizations, including the well-respected National Fire Protection Association, are working to develop objective DR planning standards, effective DR planning remains at this writing a mixture of art and science. Effective planners require a broad base of knowledge across a variety of technologies and business practices. For this reason, disaster recovery planning is not a skill set that is easily tested or certified.

Thus, this book contends that, despite the fact that a consultant's business card contains an acronym for a disaster recovery certification body, this alone is insufficient evidence that the consultant is competent to do an acceptable job for the business client. Some of the best consultants in the field do not have letters following their names on a business card or brochure.

Speaking of credentials, over the past decade, many "Big Five" accounting firms entered the contingency planning business. In other words, the same firm that performs the company's annual audit probably offers a disaster recovery planning service as well.

Despite claims by these organizations that their audit and planning organizations are entirely separate, it is not uncommon, following an audit that discovers a missing or inadequate disaster recovery plan, for a representative of the planning services arm of the firm to pay an impromptu courtesy call on the IT manager, CIO, or other business manager. The accounting firms argue that there is nothing incestuous about this practice, but concerned observers have asked how an auditor can objectively assess a DR plan bearing the label of his or her own firm.

Undoubtedly, there are good and bad consultants in "Big Five" accounting firms just as there are in the "pure" disaster recovery consultancies. The business or IT manager should use the same criteria when evaluating either type of consulting service. The following guidelines may be useful when considering the hiring of consultants to develop the disaster recovery plan.

1. **Check the qualifications of the consultant.** It is important to know the name and background of the consultant who will be providing services. Find out how many and which companies the consultant has served and check directly with the clients for recommendations and criticisms. Be wary of using an inexperienced consultant, even if he or she reputedly has access to more experienced hands. Ideally, the consultant will be able to demonstrate a knowledge of the IT and network technology used at the prospective client's company, will understand the specific requirements within a prospective client's industry, and will have developed satisfactory disaster recovery plans for at least two other businesses within the same industry.

2. **Ask for a project roadmap.** Ask for a proposal that shows the phases and tasks of the planning project. The consultant should not view this as an illegitimate request. Over the past few years, with the increasing availability of excellent DR planning project models and improved information on the techniques and methods of recovery planning, consultants have been hard pressed to portray what they do as secret, mysterious, or otherwise beyond the reach of nonconsultants. Most consultants have planning methodologies that they adapt to accommodate specific client requirements. All the manager needs is enough information about techniques and methods to evaluate the validity of the methodology. (For this reason, even if a manager elects to use a consultant, this book will help the manager to evaluate the consultant's planning methodology.)

3. **Check and validate proposed time and cost estimates.** Read consultant proposals carefully and note, first, whether time and dollar cost estimates have been assigned to parts of the project. Unless consulting services are packaged as fixed-price contracts, there is no way that a consultant can develop meaningful time and cost estimates. The manager should be especially wary if the consultant quotes exact prices or times before knowing anything about the particular requirements of the company.

   Estimates provided by the consultant can be of value to the information manager in other ways. For example, valid time and cost estimates can provide a useful benchmark for comparing various consultant proposals, especially if each consultant states that he or she is basing estimates on similar projects performed for similar businesses. This is about the only way "comparison shopping" can be performed for this type of service.

   To ensure that the data being collected from each candidate is not skewed by anything other than unknown factors, ask whether all predictable costs, including the consultant's travel and lodging, are reflected in the estimated cost.

   IT managers should be aware that some consultants tend to push their premium service initially, and offer less-expensive shared responsibility approaches only if they sense that they may be pricing themselves out of a contract. Faced with the prospect of losing a potential client, some consultants can become very creative in finding cost-saving measures. One manager reported that he cut the cost of consultant-aided plan development in half by offering to provide "administrative assistance" (someone to do word processing, etc.) to the consultant, and by allocating one of his employees to work with the consultant on a full-time basis, replacing the assistant to be provided by the consulting firm. Other managers have discovered that they could purchase the consultant's PC-based disaster recovery planning tool and utilize the consultant's personal services only in the up-front analysis and data collection phases of the project. Substantial cost reductions resulted in each case.

Another manager reported that the business ethics of the consultant could be discerned from the way in which he reacted to the manager's reluctance about costs. In one instance, a consultant offered to reduce costs by dropping the final two phases of the proposed project. These phases consisted of training personnel who would play key roles in the plan and maintenance of the plan document itself. Implied in this offer was the consultant's willingness to develop a paper plan that would sit on a shelf and satisfy a casual audit but provide no meaningful recovery capability!

Cases such as the one described above are certainly the exception rather than the rule. No stereotyping of disaster recovery consultants is intended—some of the author's best friends are disaster recovery planners.

4. Ask about the consultant's relationships with vendors of disaster recovery products and services. Managers who are considering the use of consultants also need to be aware that many consulting firms have formal or informal relationships with vendors of disaster recovery products and services. These relationships can profit the consultant's client in some cases. Using a particular consultant, for example, may qualify the client for discount rates on fire protection systems, off-site storage, or hot sites (subscription-based system backup facilities).

There is, however, a potential for misuse of these relationships. An unethical consultant may be willing to sacrifice the objective analysis of client requirements in favor of recommending a product or service from which the consultant receives a kickback. It is valuable to know whether and with whom the consultant has marketing agreements, and how these agreements may result in price advantages for the client. Most vendors will openly admit to any special arrangements, particularly when they may profit the client and improve the marketability of their service. Some consultants argue that it is partly their extensive knowledge of the disaster recovery industry that qualifies them for the rates they command.

Should the manager decide to use a consultant, whether or not the consultant admits having special marketing arrangements with vendors, he or she should pay particular attention to soliciting competitive bids for any product or service that the consultant recommends.

For many managers, the cost of a consultant-driven disaster recovery plan is the major drawback. Plans can range from $20,000 to upwards of $120,000. This is generally perceived as a cost over and above the cost for in-house plan development. Consultants respond that their price is reasonable from many perspectives.

A company electing to use in-house personnel to develop a plan must patiently wait for the novice disaster recovery coordinator to acquire knowledge that the consultant already possesses and finance the coordinator's education and pay his or her salary while doing so. Plan development is a slower process when performed by a novice in the field. In the meantime, the company's vital information asset remains exposed. Consultants also point to the fact that most plans begun by in-house personnel are never completed.

Despite these arguments, many companies elect to use in-house personnel. Even consultant plans ultimately require that in-house skills and knowledge be developed. Someone must coordinate plan revisions and maintain the plan between visits by the consultant. In addition, much of the consultant's work must be overseen by in-house personnel since the consultant is essentially an outsider who does not participate in day-to-day business operations. Also, in-house personnel must perform all evaluations of products and services to be used in the plan, partly to ensure the honesty of the consultant.

Finally, in-house personnel now have access to information about disaster recovery planning techniques and methods through special training courses, published articles and books, the Internet and World Wide Web, and by participating in "sharing" groups. So, the learning curve for the in-house planner is drastically reduced.

Generic PC-based planning tools are also now available, and several consulting firms market their own software package containing their proprietary planning tool. These tools provide a structured approach to planning for common equipment configurations. They need to be modified by the purchaser to account for specific applications, networks, decentralized processors, and other characteristics peculiar to the customer site.

Although the PC-based planning tool does not provide comprehensive answers for the novice planner, it can offer valuable models that the planner can imitate when customizing the plan to meet his or her requirements.

Another change that is supporting the development of disaster recovery plans by in-house personnel is the improvement of project management skills across all industries and business activities. The development of a disaster recovery capability is essentially a project with discrete tasks, milestones, resources, and budget. Once the principles peculiar to disaster recovery planning are understood, any person skilled in the techniques of project management can develop a competent disaster recovery plan. Many, including this author, have found that the only tools they require are old-fashioned research and communication skills; email and web browser; a word processor; and a generic, off-the-shelf, spreadsheet, database, or PC-based project management software package.

A final word on the consultant versus in-house development strategy is suggested by consultant Philip Jan Rothstein, who notes that there are other roles for consultants than performing or managing the plan development process.

Consultants can be used in connection with in-house planning efforts "to perform or support certain planning phases" (such as analysis or testing) with specialized methods or techniques, "or to serve as a true consultant—meaning, a knowledge base or coach."[18]

Given the right consultant, such an approach has the potential to deliver the best of both the in-house and the consultant-driven planning project models.

A STRAIGHTFORWARD, PROJECT-ORIENTED APPROACH

This book presents a straightforward project-oriented approach to DR planning. Each chapter provides cogent, practical information about the major tasks involved in developing a disaster recovery capability. Each chapter clearly defines the objectives of a development task, describes typical methods used to realize objectives, defines what resources are typically required, identifies sources for specific products and services, and discusses methods for evaluating task fulfillment.

In some cases, the IT manager or his or her designee serves as the disaster recovery coordinator for the company. In other cases, planning is undertaken by a group of users representing both information systems and the user community. If planning is undertaken by a group, however, it will need a person who will serve sometimes as researcher, sometimes as data collector, sometimes as honest broker, and ultimately as the person responsible for maintaining the plan in the face of almost daily shifts in recovery requirements. All these responsibilities are implied in the title DR coordinator.

In many cases, the IT or business manager will either hire a new employee to serve as disaster recovery coordinator or transfer an employee to fill the position full-time. The critical phrase is full-time. In very small companies, the IT manager is likely to serve as disaster recovery coordinator. In medium to large companies, developing and maintaining the disaster recovery plan is a full-time job.

Who is the ideal disaster recovery coordinator? There is no pat answer to this question. The coordinator does not require the highly technical skills set of a programmer, network analyst, hardware specialist, or systems administrator, but it is important that the candidate be able to communicate with technical staff and correctly interpret what they say in order to communicate it effectively to non-technical users in reports, procedures, and other documentation.

It is important that the coordinator be organized, detail-oriented, and a competent writer. The candidate should be able to work methodically through complex problems and issues and be experienced in managing vendors and evaluating product offerings. He or she should also be fluent in project management principles and techniques. In addition to these skills, the coordinator will need highly developed qualities of patience, perseverance, and diplomacy.

A common theme emerges in meetings of organizations for disaster recovery coordinators. Regardless of the initial level of enthusiasm and team spirit participants bring to the disaster recovery planning project, a substantial effort will be required to keep participation levels high. Planners need to cultivate enthusiasm and constantly reinforce the buy-in of plan participants. Unless participants see the plan as their creation, nearly everyone will develop a resentment of the planning process.

DR planning is demanding work. IT operations personnel can easily come to view the coordinator's insistence on routine backups as an unwarranted interruption of their already overcrowded processing schedules. They need to be applauded for the work they are doing to safeguard the corporation's most important asset, information.

Similarly, application developers may be put off by the DR requirement that they pause periodically to document changes made to programs and systems so that work can be reconstructed in the event of disaster. Reinforcing the importance and value of their work—known in the vernacular as stroking their egos—may ensure their continued enthusiastic cooperation.

User departments may develop an intense dislike of the coordinator's constant testing and probing for possible gaps in their preventive and protective measures. The coordinator needs to work with users and ensure that they regard the procedures involved as their own effort, rather than a task that is being imposed on them from outside.

Senior management may even come to disdain spending money on a project that delivers little tangible return on investment. Coordinators can diffuse this trap before it occurs by exploring every possible dual-use or dual-value opportunity for disaster avoidance and recovery components.

The relationship with management works both ways. To supplement the skills that the coordinator brings to the job, the IT or business manager will have to provide the coordinator with authority to make decisions and to quell dissent, visible (and budgetary) support and enthusiasm for the planning effort, and personal support for the coordinator's ego.

No statistics are available to demonstrate the stress level associated with the position of disaster recovery coordinator, but considering the nature of the job—the need to confront the dark side of business survival daily and make the safety and security of fellow employees one's personal concern—the coordinator's stress level must rate somewhere between that of a dentist and a Middle East peace negotiator. The manager needs to recognize this and compensate for it, not only in salary, but by freeing the coordinator from other tasks and giving personal recognition and reinforcement for the valuable work that the coordinator is performing.

The above may convey the impression that fulfilling the role of DR coordinator is a thankless task. Before readers rush to put this book back on the shelf, it should be observed that there are few business roles that are more compelling and challenging than disaster recovery planning. Creating an effective team, working across the exclusive territories established by business units, developing innovative strategies to fit requirements, and playing the ombudsman for corporate safety and continuity comprise a dynamic set of tasks that appeal to one's creativity and provide an enormous sense of accomplishment.

A NOTE ON METHODOLOGY

A cursory examination of the literature will confirm that there are as many methodologies for developing disaster recovery plans as there are plan authors. This book seeks to find common ground by returning to the fundamental methodology of project management.

Fortunately, disaster recovery planning is too young an endeavor to have spawned argumentative schools of adherents to this or that guru's methodology. There are no gurus except, perhaps, those who have experienced and recovered from an actual disaster. Having talked with many of them in research for this book, they are wiser and somewhat modest about their accomplishment. Hardly the guru type.

This is not to say that there are not pretenders. In certain facets of disaster recovery plan development, one is almost certain to run up against a vendor representative, a plan author, or a risk manager who is convinced he or she has all the answers. It would seem that, in the wake of 9/11, everybody from the value added reseller to the local cellular telephone salesman has decided to hang out a DR consulting shingle. The best policy is to listen. They may, after all, have a few worthwhile observations.

In the meantime, there are far more important and basic skills to master. One of the most important is one's ability to think systematically about the planning task. This is no simple feat: One must, after all, superimpose rationality on an event that is inherently chaotic—disaster.

It cannot be overstressed that disaster recovery planning is not something that one can do perfectly the first time. Only by putting the plan on paper and testing it can its errors be realized and corrected. The only effective method for DR planning is trial and error.

There are a few other points to make about the approach of this book to its subject. As previously observed, developing a disaster recovery plan is a project entailing the performance of many discrete tasks and the allocation of fixed resources. The end product of the effort is less a plan document than a recovery capability. The plan is only a roadmap for yet another project: recovery from an actual disaster.

To help the reader understand the objectives and alternative strategies that must be considered in the formulation of the plan, it is sometimes necessary to describe in detail how the plan will be implemented in a disaster recovery project. To aid the reader, a simple diagrammatic distinction has been made between the planning project and the recovery project. When this book describes the plan development project, the accompanying illustrations use the techniques of data flow diagramming. When the recovery project is described, flow charts are used.

Data flow diagrams, or DFDs, seem appropriate to the description of the plan development project since the project generally consists of acquiring, processing, and presenting information.[19] Figure 1–2 provides the context for the disaster recovery planning project. It shows the plethora of organizations—

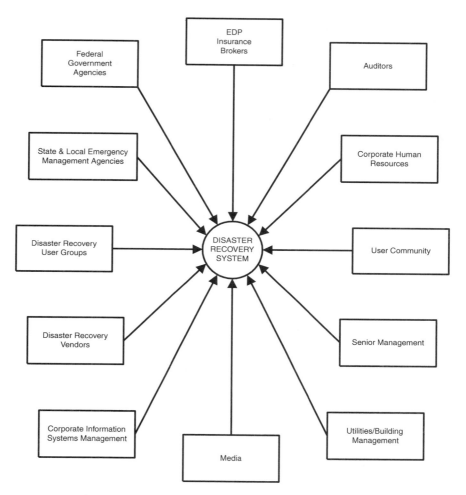

Figure 1–2   The context of disaster recovery planning.

including corporate departments, professional groups, and regulatory agencies—
that shape the environment of the planning endeavor and form the reality against
which plan adequacy is judged.

From this simple diagram, however, little can be discerned about the components of disaster recovery planning. Thus, in the coming chapters, the reader
will find other DFDs that illustrate the major activities involved in the planning
project.

For example, Figure 1–3 is a DFD depicting data flows and activities described in Chapter 1. Information resources, such as industry standards, published

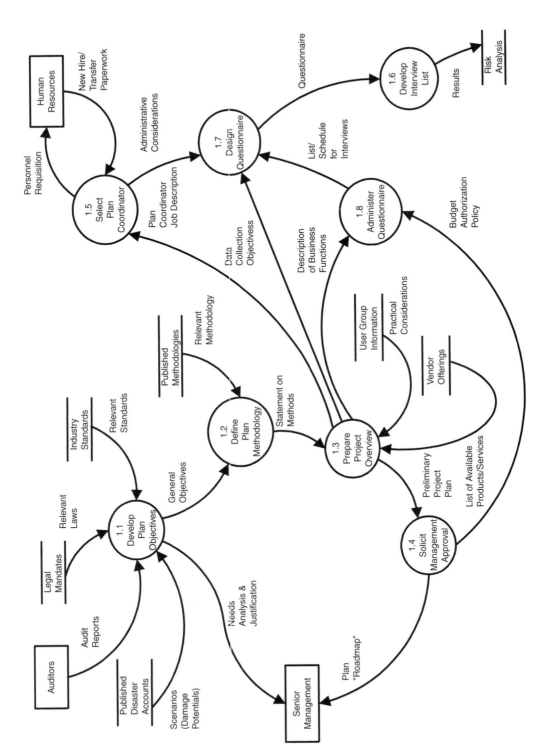

Figure 1-3 Initialization phase data flow diagram.

disaster accounts, and legal mandates, are used to develop a rationale for the plan development project for presentation to senior management. Data from these sources is used to define methods (consultant or in-house development) and to create project outlines. Other inputs and outputs are also presented to account for the numerous tasks involved in the initial start-up phase of disaster recovery planning.

DFDs do not necessarily show precedence or chronological order of tasks. They are flexible, spatial constructs that the reader, it is hoped, will find easy to apply to his or her planning requirements. As such, DFDs are preferable to the linear and rigid structure of a flowchart depicting tasks and milestones in the plan development project.

Elsewhere in this book, the reader will encounter flowcharts that provide examples of master plans for various aspects of the recovery project. These flowcharts attempt to superimpose order and sequence on recovery events. Flowcharts are not intended as models to be rigorously followed, but as guides for creating and organizing one's own implementation plan. A concatenated flowchart is provided at www.drplanning.org, a web site that has been established to serve as a "living appendix" to this book.

It is hoped that this distinction in illustrations will help to clarify any confusion that may arise between the planning project and the implementation project that is its product.

ENDNOTES

1. D. O. Aasgaard et al., "An Evaluation of Data Processing 'Machine Room' Loss and Selected Recovery Strategies," MISRC Working Papers (Minneapolis, MN: University of Minnesota, 1978).
2. Thomas Hoffman, "Denial Stalls Disaster Recovery Plans," *Computerworld,* 2/23/98.
3. Philip Jan Rothstein, Rothstein Associates, Brookfield, CT, comments to the author, 07/99.
4. Gary H. Anthes, "Lotsa Talk, Little Walk," *Computerworld,* 9/21/98.
5. "6th Annual Information Security Survey," conducted in conjunction with *Computerworld,* Ernst & Young LLP, 1998.
6. Jaikumar Vijayan, "Client/Server Disaster Plans Fall Short," *Computerworld,* 11/03/97.
7. Bruce Caldwell, "Homestretch," *Information Week,* 7/19/99.
8. Eddy Goldberg, "DP Nightmare Hits N.Y. Bank," *Computerworld,* 12/02/85.
9. Ibid.
10. Dale Stackhouse and Kenneth T. Ungar, "The Foreign Corrupt Practices Act: Bribery, Corruption, Recordkeeping and More," *The Indiana Lawyer,* 4/21/93.
11. William Perry, "The Auditor, EDP, and the Federal Government," in *Data Processing Management* (New York: Auerbach Publishers, 1979).
12. Ibid.
13. Ibid.
14. Interview with Inspector Roy Williams, St. Petersburg, FL Fire Department, 9 January 1987.

15. Interviews with Maar Haack, EDP Underwriter, The St. Paul Insurance Companies, and Tom Cornwell, CHUBB Insurance Company, December 5–6, 1987.

16. Ibid.

17. Jon Toigo, "Alternatives for Disaster Recovery Plan Development," *Data Security Management* (New York: Auerbach Publishers, 1988).

18. Rothstein, op. cit.

19. Data flow diagram (DFD) standards taken from Tom DeMarco, Structured Analysis and System Specification (New York: Yourdon, 1979).

CHAPTER

2

Analyzing the Risk

Just as a systems development project responds to user needs, a disaster recovery planning project responds to an organization's needs for survival and business resumption in the wake of a disaster. In disaster recovery planning, defining corporate needs is synonymous with identifying risks and exposures. This is accomplished through a series of analytical procedures.

- The business processes of a company need to be identified, together with the components of the IT infrastructure used to support each process. IT infrastructure components may include application software; servers and operating systems; data and data storage systems; local and wide area networks; and client systems including PCs, thin client devices, and terminals. Key peripheral devices, such as printers, must also be identified.
- With business processes and their IT resources identified, disaster recovery planners need to turn their attention to measuring the impact of unplanned interruption on each business process. This is done for two reasons: first, it provides insights which are used to justify measures that must be taken to safeguard or provide continuity for the process. Second, the analysis assists in gauging the relative criticality of business processes to overall business continuity so that recovery efforts can be prioritized.
- Most analyses also include the development of a list of threats and the ranking of threats according to some rational strategy (i.e., likelihood of occurrence, depth or breadth of impact on company business processes, anticipated cost to company, etc.). One benefit of a threat assessment is that it can help guide the development of a plan so that the plan can be imple-

mented flexibly—in whole or in part—in response to a broad range of disaster scenarios.

This description covers considerable territory. It embraces concepts and activities that some DR methodologists prefer to break down into discrete practices such as business impact analysis, application impact analysis, threat and exposure analysis, and risk impact analysis. To avoid becoming identified with any of the rarefied or proprietary methodologies that exist in the field, this discussion subsumes all of the preceding activities under a single rubric: risk analysis. In the broadest sense, risk analysis assesses what is vulnerable, the causes of vulnerability, and what needs to be given priority for recovery.

Figure 2–1 is a DFD showing typical inputs and outputs of a risk analysis. As one can readily see, risk analysis is key to the development of objectives for many of the disaster recovery tasks that will follow. Its many activities involve interviewing company IT personnel and users, collating responses into a comprehensive view of the corporate information asset—segregated by business processes and their associated resource requirements—and formulating criteria and objectives for the plans that will be created to safeguard this asset.

THE PURPOSES OF RISK ANALYSIS

Risk analysis is perhaps the single most misunderstood aspect of disaster recovery planning. To many, the term is vague and mysterious, connoting rarefied techniques and unintelligible calculations known to only a very few privileged practitioners. To others, risk analysis is perceived as an irritating process of formalizing what is self-evident or obvious to anyone with a modicum of horse sense.

As one information manager put it, "There is a generally accepted statistic that places the likelihood of a major disaster for any business at right around 1% per year. This is the risk. And when you have a disaster, you either have one or you don't. That's the exposure. That's all the risk analysis that you need. You just prepare for the worst."

This is an oversimplification, of course, but the meaning is clear. Risk analysis is a big term for what is essentially a straightforward application of good research and common sense. This is indicated by the three basic objectives of risk analysis:

1. Identify business processes and their associated IT infrastructure resource requirements (that is, the data, applications, systems, and networks that are used in delivering the business process). Prioritize business processes according to time sensitivity and criticality.
2. Identify existing threats to business processes and infrastructure resources.
3. Define objectives for strategies to eliminate avoidable risks and to minimize the impact of risks that cannot be eliminated.

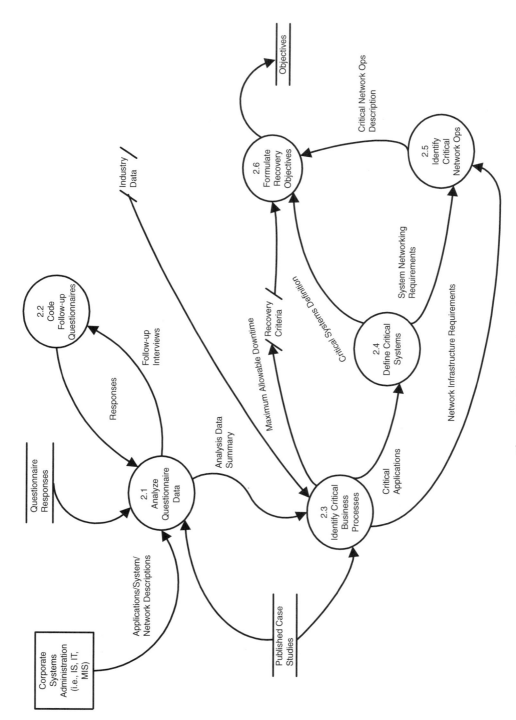

Figure 2–1 The analysis phase.

IDENTIFYING AND PRIORITIZING ASSETS AND FUNCTIONS

Risk analysis consists of two basic operations: data collection and data analysis. The data collected in risk analysis should include a comprehensive list of business processes and their infrastructure supports, including computer and network hardware and applications, databases, and system software. From these data, business process flow diagrams are created and annotated to show resource requirements. Additionally, planners need to collect information about the amount of activity, traffic, or use of infrastructure resources to deliver each business process during a normal business hour, day, week, or month.

Typically, the data listed above is collected from end-users and IT personnel, often through the use of a paper questionnaire. Other collection methods may include in-person interviews, on-line or diskette-based surveys, and so on.

Users are in an excellent position to identify work procedures and overall business process criticality (see below). Technical personnel can usually address more specific questions such as operational hardware configurations, locations of data stores, and network connections. They also have access to data on numbers of transactions, traffic volumes, and other measures of business process activity.

The ultimate purpose of the questionnaire is to collect information on each business process and its infrastructure supports so that the criticality and recovery requirements can be assessed. Secondarily, the planner uses the data to develop a deeper understanding of dependencies that may exist between business processes.

With this data collected and analyzed, risk analysis can commence. Risk analysis seeks to identify which business processes and related infrastructure resources are critical to the business, what threats or exposures exist to unplanned interruption of business processes, and what costs accrue to an interruption based on duration.

The ability of a company to cope with the interruption of a business process determines the tolerance of the business process. In practical terms, tolerance may be expressed as a dollar value—the cost to the company if the business process is interrupted for a period of time.

It is worth noting that not all assessments of tolerance and cost are necessarily expressed as dollar values. Some organizations may be concerned about outages of applications for reasons other than lost dollars. A just-in-time manufacturer, for example, may be extremely concerned about the possibility that a temporary software outage might see the company cast in an unfavorable light on the industry media. The direct dollar costs of such an outage may be a smaller issue than the loss of customers resulting from a perceived lack of reliable service.

In general, business processes that maintain customer service levels, support reputation in the market, or provide some other intangible value to the company may be deemed just as critical as business processes whose interruption results in dollar costs. Planners need to be sensitive to this fact and avoid classifying all business processes based only on a dispassionate assessment of their dollar value. For this discussion, cost is used as a straightforward indicator of business process value.

If there is a very low tolerance within the company to the interruption of a business process (typically the result of an infrastructure resource outage), this low tolerance is typically expressed as a high dollar value or cost. If, on the other hand, the company can tolerate to a significant extent the interruption of a business process, this high tolerance is typically expressed as a low dollar value or cost.

This concept cannot be overemphasized. The dollar value to the company of a given business process may have little to do with the dollar cost of the hardware or software used in the system. A PC, using an off-the-shelf spreadsheet package and a few hundred bytes of corporate financial data, may actually support a low-tolerance/high-cost business process. The corporation might more keenly feel its loss than the loss of any application running on an expensive network or mainframe platform.

Applications or equipment whose loss or outage would impact low-tolerance business processes and entail great costs for the company are termed critical. Conversely, infrastructure resource supports for high-tolerance/low-cost business processes may be regarded as noncritical.

For example, the loss of a telemarketing company's telecommunications switch would represent a low-tolerance or high-dollar loss. For each minute that the switch is down, the company is unable to perform mission-critical business processes, resulting in serious dollar losses. The telecommunications private branch exchange (PBX) switch, therefore, would be regarded as a critical system.

If, on the other hand, the same telemarketing firm were to lose the function of a computer application that is used to generate random telephone numbers, a noncritical business process, the financial impact of the outage would be very different. Since the company could readily change over to a manual system of random number generation, this application would not cost the company nearly as much as a telecommunications outage of the same duration. Thus, the application could be considered noncritical.

Of course, most companies have numerous business processes that depend upon a variety of systems, networks, and applications whose loss or interruption can be tolerated to varying degrees. Thus, a spectrum of tolerances exists between those systems or applications that are critical and those that are noncritical. For this reason, business process criticality is often expressed in a ranking or scale. This may be reflected in the end-user questionnaire, which might ask the respondent to rate the criticality of a business process and explain the reasons for the ranking.

With many business processes, tolerance to an outage or interruption is contingent upon the length of the outage or interruption. In an electrical power company, for example, customer billing processes may be sustainable for a brief period of time by reverting to manual methods. However, because a large part of the customer base for a power company is transient (i.e., the customers associated with a given meter may change several times over the course of a month), the efficiency of manual billing processes may be degraded over time. It may become difficult to keep pace with the changes, driving up the costs of the interrupted business process. Hence, over time, the utility's tolerance for the interruption of the normal business process may decrease, and the criticality of the process may increase.

Variances in tolerance may also be linked to the time of the day or month an interruption occurs. For many companies, a loss of their payroll process for a two-week period at month's end may be devastating. However, if the same interruption occurred at mid-month, tolerance might be far greater. Risk analysis, in general, assumes that an outage will always occur at the worst possible time.

COLLECTING INPUT FROM END USERS

It is not uncommon for users to identify mitigating factors, such as the timing of a disaster, when they assess the criticality of their applications. Applications are increasingly engineered to provide discrete business processes. Where this is the case, application may be used as a synonym for a business process.

To end-users, time is a dynamic determinant of tolerance, for both economic and psychological reasons. Confronted with the news that an application is unavailable for use, the question that many users first ask is not why, but for how long. An outage of any length represents, in most cases, a need to make up time later—under stress or in costly overtime.

It is also quite common for users to begin a criticality assessment by stating that all of their applications (i.e., business processes) are critical—precisely because they are their applications. This categorization may seem like flagrant egotism, but it may reflect something quite different. Perhaps obtaining approval for application development was an uphill battle, or the development project itself took a deep personal toll. Whatever the rationale, few users (or systems administrators) like to believe that the work they do, or the applications they use, are anything less than critical to the company.

Planners are well advised to avoid provocative questions or insinuations when collecting end-user data. The criteria used to classify the criticality of applications must be clearly explained. The questionnaire should ask not how critical an application is but what steps a user would take to perform the same business function if the application were unavailable. Placed in this context, the determination of application criticality usually becomes less problematic for the questionnaire respondent.

More than one disaster recovery coordinator who has used the questionnaire method to gather information has discovered that users will provide a surprisingly fair assessment of their applications' criticality. One planner reported that three factors contributed to the success of a user poll at his company: First, each participant realized that other users were making similar concessions and complying with the classification scheme. Second, in group meetings held as a follow-up to the questionnaires, individuals who had displayed creativity or re-sourcefulness in developing coping strategies to deal with a hypothetical outage were given special praise or recognition by the coordinator. Third, everyone quickly realized that the classification of "his or her" business process or applica-tion as less-than-critical applied only in the event of a disaster. The coordinator stressed that, under normal conditions, every system or application played a nec-essary, vital role in the achievement of company goals.[1]

Critical applications are often defined as such because, regardless of duration of the outage or the time of month in which an outage occurs, there are no substi-tute methods for providing the functions of the application. Electronic commerce applications used by on-line brokers, for example, are clearly mission critical.

In April 1999, an outage of less than 2 hours at on-line broker, E-Trade™, and its subsequent reportage on the front page of the *Wall Street Journal,* resulted in a 50% drop in the company's stock price and a 330% increase in complaint calls to the Securities and Exchange Commission concerning on-line investing.[2] Ac-cording to George Ferguson, Hewlett Packard Company's Business Recovery Services Marketing Manager, this phenomenon has generated a "push in the mis-sion-critical industry."

> The first generation of e-commerce/e-services companies don't have service level objectives in place. Their customers are early adopters and are more tolerant of out-ages. But, this is changing quickly. The customer drives the requirement to bring up the service level. The next generation companies are entering a much more competi-tive market. Consumers are demanding more. They have a much lower tolerance to outages and interruptions and it is less costly for them to simply switch to another vendor if the one they normally use has an outage.[3]

This example illustrates clearly how the criticality of an application/busi-ness process may be directly linked to market forces. And e-commerce is not the only application area where this connection holds, according to industry insiders. Enterprise Resource Planning (ERP) software suites, ported to distributed sys-tems during Y2K preparedness programs, are also seen as critical in many firms.

ERP is used to manage the total supply chain for the company and is driv-ing new recovery technologies designed to eradicate downtime completely, ac-cording to one observer. These technologies include wide area disk storage mirroring as a replacement for tape backup. Mirroring, in theory, can provide au-tomatic, near instantaneous recovery of multiterabyte ERP databases at an alter-nate location in the event that access to data at the normal production facility is compromised. The expense of such a technology can only be cost-justified based on the absolute criticality of ERP business processes.[4] The benefits and potential drawbacks of mirroring are discussed in greater detail in Chapter 4.

The criticality of a business process extends to its infrastructure supports, such as a database in the example of an ERP system. In most cases, it is safe to categorize certain infrastructure components, including electrical power systems, air conditioning systems, communications network "local loops" (connections between the company premises and the telecommunications provider's local point of presence or central office), and other fundamental resources required by all business processes, as critical. Without backups or manual means of control, a loss of any of these systems at any time may represent a total cessation of normal business operations.

In engineering terminology, these resources are sometimes described as single points of failure. Within any complex system, there are usually components or processes that, if not replicated or otherwise backed up by redundant capabilities, represent points of failure for the entire system. A large part of disaster avoidance planning comes down to identifying single points of failure wherever they exist and eliminating them. This may include complex arrangements to secure alternate utility providers for the corporate data center to simple plans to eliminate notebook computer "docking stations" that can impair recovery efforts. (Docking stations provide desktop attachment points for some types of portable computers, providing such functions as auxiliary hard disk drives, LAN connectivity, and AC power when the computer user is in the office. Typically, docking stations are unusable when a power outage occurs and may prevent access to vital auxiliary disk-based data and LANs while the portable computer operates in battery power mode.)

In addition to fundamental infrastructure supports, other infrastructure components, including hardware, software, and networks, derive their criticality from the support they provide to a specific critical business process. Often criticality can be determined by asking end users a pointed question: How would you deal with an application interruption that was 1 hour in duration, or 24 hours, or 48 hours, or 72 hours? If no coping strategies can be identified by the respondent, and if tolerance to interruption is low, the application and its infrastructure resources are likely to be critical.

A CRITICALITY SPECTRUM

In the context of conventional information processing, applications may be defined on the following spectrum of tolerance:

- **Critical.** These functions cannot be performed unless identical capabilities are found to replace the company's damaged capabilities. Critical applications cannot be replaced by manual methods under any circumstances. Tolerance to interruption is very low, and the cost of interruption is very high. Thus, for critical systems and applications, the company would need to arrange to have access to hardware comparable to its own, and in an emergency, plan to transfer the application to the backup hardware in order to resume processing.

- **Vital.** These functions cannot be performed by manual means or can be performed manually for only a very brief period of time. There is somewhat higher tolerance to interruption and somewhat lower costs, provided that functions are restored within a certain time-frame (usually 4 or 5 days). In applications classified as vital, a brief suspension of processing can be tolerated, but a considerable amount of "catching up" will be needed to restore data to a current or usable form.
- **Sensitive.** These business processes can be performed, with difficulty but at tolerable cost, by manual means for an extended period of time. Sensitive applications, however, require considerable "catching up" once restored.
- **Noncritical.** These applications may be interrupted for an extended period of time, at little or no cost to the company, and require little or no "catching up" when restored.

Figure 2–2 illustrates this spectrum of tolerances. It should be noted that this classification scheme may be extended from business processes to their infrastructure resources, including hardware, software, networks, and even to data itself. Classification schemes employed by planners will vary from company to company. As previously noted, the basis for categorizing a specific business process as critical may have more to do with corporate culture than with prospec-

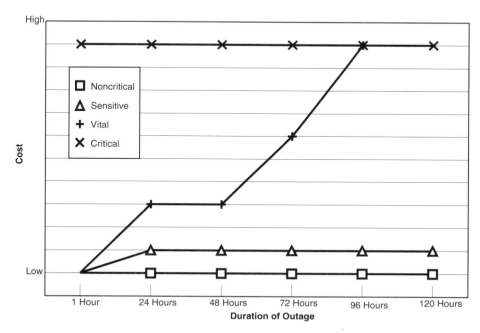

Figure 2–2   Relative tolerances to business process interruptions.

tive dollar losses accrued to an unplanned interruption. The important thing is to document the rationale used to assess criticality so that auditors and others can understand them.

Disaster recovery service providers, such as Hewlett Packard Business Recovery Services and IBM BCRS, are working on similar business process criticality assumptions to define appropriate services for their customers. In the case of Hewlett Packard, this takes the form of a "portfolio of services," which the company unveiled in 1999. According to Ferguson, "Certain business processes are worth every dime spent to recover them, while others are not so critical."

> At the very high end, we will offer data replication and other technologies designed to keep business processes available through all circumstances. Companies may be looking at $750,000 per year to achieve high availability uptime solutions. For other business processes, there are three lower availability solutions that extend recovery intervals to between eight hours and three days. The pricing reflects that. From $750,000, there is a huge price drop to below $100,000 per year for a lower availability solution.[5]

HP's example, which is likely to take hold industry-wide, underscores the importance of risk analysis. Choosing the appropriate services from a disaster recovery vendor will become increasingly tied to a customer estimate of business process criticality. One goal of risk analysis is to apply a classification scheme to each company process or asset that the disaster recovery plan will seek to protect.

COLLECTING DATA ON OUTAGE COSTS

In cases where business process interruptions may be measured in terms of dollar cost, the questionnaire analysis method can be harnessed to compile some compelling cost justifications for disaster recovery planning. In addition to asking users to classify their application's criticality and identify strategies for coping with outages, another question should be asked during initial data collection: What would outages of the specified duration cost the company?

User departments are often able to compile accurate estimates about the cost of downtime. They may have documented the impact of past interruption events or they may have compiled data describing normal operations costs for use in demonstrating departmental performance. Many times this data can be adapted to show the value of the work that would be lost if an interruption occurred.

For example, a marketing manager might keep data on the department's average daily sales of product in order to set sales goals for the next sales period. Using this statistic, the loss of on-line ordering systems for 2 days could be evaluated as a dollar loss.

The permutations, as those who regularly perform risk analyses have observed, can be quite ingenious. They can also be useful in addressing budgetary concerns that often arise when it comes time to fund disaster avoidance and recovery capabilities.

IDENTIFYING THREATS TO ASSETS AND FUNCTIONS

Once the criticality of business processes has been assessed, another objective of risk analysis is to identify what threats exist to normal business operations.

There are a variety of schemes for classifying threats, with most endeavoring to create a taxonomy for use in analysis. One scheme classifies threats by causal origin, either man-made or natural. Another classification scheme uses locational scope, with distinctions drawn between facility and regional disasters.

These taxonomies have little merit in planning, and the distinctions they introduce tend to obfuscate more than they clarify. The dividing line, for example, between man-made and natural disaster potentials is often unclear until long after the disaster event has passed. Whether a fire was started by a negligent employee or by a bolt of lightning is, practically speaking, irrelevant to disaster recovery.

Similarly, the regional-versus-facility distinction provides a poor analytical tool. Practically speaking, a regional disaster, such as a hurricane, may have a no less debilitating effect on business operations than would a facility disaster (and, in fact, a regional disaster will in many cases also damage the facility).

The best method for identifying threats is to look at the phenomena, regardless of root cause, that typically interrupt normal business processes. These may include:

- Water damage (whether from leaky pipes or floods)
- Fire (heat) damage (whether from arson, equipment overheating, environmental contamination, lightning strikes, etc.)
- Power failure (originating at the customer premises or across the power grid)
- Network failure (LAN or WAN, whether component or line based)
- Mechanical hardware failure or software failure (whether caused by human error, short circuits, normal parts wear and tear, or building collapse following an earthquake)
- Accidental or deliberate destruction or corruption of hardware, software, or data (by hackers, disgruntled employees, industrial saboteurs, terrorists, or misbehaving software)
- Other causes (including forced evacuation for environmental hazards, aircraft crashes, etc.)

Many novice planners become mired down in an effort to define every conceivable risk scenario. A preferred strategy is to plan for a worst-case scenario, one that portends an interruption of all business processes, and to develop a plan with such a scenario in mind. Organizing recovery procedures rationally—by business process, for example—provides for flexible implementation and enables the plan to be activated, in whole or in part, in response to a number of disaster events.

THE PROBLEM WITH PROBABILITY

If there is one debate in the disaster recovery planning field that equates to the "How many angels can dance on the head of a pin?" argument, it centers on which type of disaster occurs most frequently. Many planners wish that there was an actuarial table or set of probability statistics that could be used to assess the precise risk posed by each disaster potential. There isn't, and this fact has created more pointless discussions in DR circles than virtually any other issue.

Information security professionals point to the computer virus as the culprit behind the greatest number of business interruptions. Natural disaster statisticians point to the much greater dollar cost per incident of major hurricanes, earthquakes, floods, and tornadoes.

The Federal Emergency Management Agency (FEMA) points to fires as the number-one disaster potential, but quickly adds that floods are in second place. Floods account for nine out of ten presidential disaster declarations and cause property damage in excess of $1 billion per year.[6]

Hard-disk drive manufacturers, who equate disaster with data loss, blame user and software errors for the preponderance of drive failures. By contrast, data recovery vendors, such as Ontrack Data International, place the blame squarely at the feet of the hard-disk manufacturers, claiming that 44% of the data recovery jobs they receive are the result of hardware malfunctions (see Figure 2–3).[7]

Reliable business disaster data, organized by type of disaster, are difficult to obtain for a variety of reasons. For the purposes of this book, it will suffice to say that each of the disaster potentials addressed in the above list is a cause of significant interruptions each year in mission-critical operations. Having said this, some statistical information may be useful, not to evaluate threat probability, but to aid in building management awareness or to sensitize company employees about threats.

A FEW COMPELLING STATISTICS

It was the position of major EDP insurers about a decade ago that, because of improvements in fire detection and suppression systems and increased industry awareness to the threat of fire, flooding (water) was the number-one threat to corporate data processing.[8]

Water damage frequently results from fire-fighting techniques, but fires themselves claimed an annual average of 1,239 data centers and telephone switch rooms annually from 1980 to 1996, according to the National Fire Protection Association (NFPA). The direct property damage to facilities averaged $24.98 million in the same period.[9]

NFPA provides additional information on structure fires that were started by electronic equipment but did not originate in equipment rooms themselves (e.g., fires in user work areas, rather than data centers). These fires averaged 990

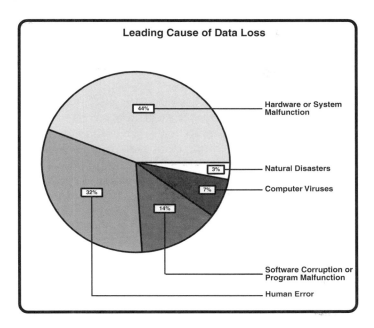

Figure 2–3   Leading causes of data loss. (*Source:* Ontrack Data International, Inc., Eden Prairie, MN. Reprinted with permission.)

in number, causing damage estimated at an average $20.47 million per year from 1992 through 1996, though the preponderance of events (320 in the period covered) originated in one- or two-family dwellings.[10]

The study goes on to point out that only 28% of the fires originating with electronic equipment were in facilities with automatic suppression equipment (such as sprinkler systems or other extinguishing agents).[11] This continues a "tradition" of unprotected user work areas that contributed to a fire at the U.S. Postal Service headquarters in October 1984. In that instance, fire claimed more than 500 PCs in user work areas and cost the USPS approximately $20 million. Disaster recovery planning and disaster prevention did not extend to user work areas where PCs were in great use.[12]

In addition to fires, floods, and other disaster potentials, power failures, mechanical breakdowns, software malfunctions, network outages, and computer sabotage, hacking and viruses account for the balance of the IT disasters that business suffers in any given year.

According to a survey conducted of 500 small businesses by Los Angeles, CA-based Impulse Research, 90% of those interviewed reported experiencing at least one power outage in 1998. Of this group, 26% reported two outages in the period, while 12% indicated that they had experienced five or more outages. The preponderance of interviewees attributed power outages to storms and lightning, but more than 50% blamed at least one of their power outages on problems at their power company. Of the outages blamed on the power company, further investigation revealed that accidents or construction accounted for 18% of blackouts; floods for 8%; with electrical fires, earthquakes, and strikes taking the blame for the balance.[13]

A June 1999 survey of more than 800 commercial and industrial companies by energy industry analyst E SOURCE gleaned an outage record bordering on insanity. Said respondents, their companies had sustained an average of nearly 15 outages during a 12-month period, at a total cost of more than $7 billion per year. Bill LeBlanc, Vice President of E SOURCE remarked, "This is a huge level of loss for US and Canadian businesses to sustain. If you look beyond the seven sectors surveyed in our study, national outage costs could be five to ten times as high." He also noted a growing market for uninterruptible power supplies (UPS), battery backups for commercial power that provide a hedge against momentary power outages.[14]

In July 2001, yet another report sponsored by the Electric Power Research Institute's (EPRI) Consortium to Support a Digital Society, found that the absence of "digital quality" electricity—meaning always perfect and always on—cost the US economy more than $119 billion annually.[15] The study of 985 companies in three sectors of the US economy representing 40 percent of the gross national product, found that $45.7 billion was lost annually to power outages, and another $6.7 billion to power quality disturbances such as voltage sags and other occurrences that do not allow equipment to function properly, causing temporary work stoppages, loss of data and other problems.

The EPRI study pointed out that a current-model unprotected microprocessor can malfunction if power is interrupted for even one-quarter of a single alternating current (AC) cycle—that is, 1/240th of a second. The study pointed out that the costs to properly equip a new facility with adequate, digital-quality electricity are high, citing one facility in which $300 of the $565 per square foot building costs went to power conditioning equipment. The alternative of doing nothing and absorbing downtime costs, study authors argue, is much more costly. "In the final analysis, most [technology-based firms] need power that is several magnitudes more reliable and distortion-free than what we typically get from a wall socket," said one spokesperson.

Like power outages, public telephone service outages also take a toll on business process availability annually. The Federal Communications Commission (FCC), concerned about a series of lengthy and extensive outages in 1991, created the Network Reliability Council in 1992 and issued a requirement for carriers to report outages lasting 30 minutes or longer and impacting 30,000 or more customers. Together with the Alliance for Telecommunications Industry Solutions (ATIS), the NRC began collecting data from carriers and generated a report in 1996, classifying telecom outages by cause.

Between 1992 and 1995, the leading causes of outages were line dig-ups, other line-related problems, and hardware failures. Procedural problems and software design errors filled out the causal list. The average number of reported failures between 1993 and 1994 was 180. This climbed to 280 in 1995, owing mainly to increases in dig-ups and hardware failures at telco facilities.

Dig-ups, especially of fiber-optic cable trunks (cable conduits carrying tens of thousands of fiber-optic cable strands), required on average 6 hours to repair in the 1992 to 1995 period. Switch related problems climbed steadily from an outage duration of 1.2 hours in 1992 to 2.5 hours of downtime per event in 1995.[16]

Analysts speculated in 1997 that increased demand for Internet access would increase trunking requirements (the number of communications lines—copper or fiber optic—that the telco needs to deploy and maintain) and place even greater loads on switches. This, in turn, could lead to a dramatic increase in the number of outages attributable to carrier overloads.[17] The many outages that have affected the Internet and World Wide Web through the end of the decade appeared to bear out these predictions, as do the major findings in the latest Annual Report from the Network Reliability Steering Committee (the NRC was rechartered as the NRSC in 2000) and ATIS, which disclosed the following major findings:[18]

- Outage frequency is increasing at a rate of 2.2% per year, still less than the annual growth of the network in lines or calls.
- The frequency of central office (CO) power outages was greater in 2000 than in any prior year and is increasing at the rate of 14% per year. The annual aggregated outage index of CO power outages has been higher on average since 1997.
- The frequency of tandem switch outages was greater in 2000 than in any prior year and significantly higher than its baseline level. The annual aggregated outage index of tandem switch outages has been higher on average since 1997.
- The frequency of common channel signalling (CCS) outages was significantly higher in 2000 than its baseline level and is increasing at the rate of 11% per year. The annual aggregated outage index for CCS outages was greater than in any prior year.
- Since 1994, digital cross-connect systems (DCS) outage frequency is increasing at a rate of 21% per year. The annual aggregated outage index of DCS outages has been higher on average since 1997.
- The number of outages with a procedural error as root cause was significantly higher than its baseline level and matched its highest annual total to date. The frequency of outages with a procedural error as a root cause are increasing at a rate of 8% per year.
- The annual aggregated outage index for facility outages was lower than in any prior year and significantly lower than its baseline level. The facility category had its lowest annual share of outages (34%) and of aggregated outage index (29%) to date.
- Outages had the lowest annual median duration to date, indicating more relatively short duration outages in 2000 than in the past.

The occasional stoppages of the public network and Internet may have an upside, however, as they offer a temporary respite from the seemingly endless barrage of e-mail viruses that became an almost weekly occurrence since 1999. Even as the reasonably benign "Happy99.exe" and "Melissa" Microsoft Word macro virus were becoming a memory, industry analysts were speculating in mid-April that mutant strains of Melissa, carrying destructive payloads, might be in the offing.

First "Chernobyl," then "Pretty Park," and in June, the extremely destructive "Explore.Zip" worm appeared. In response to the Explore.Zip worm infections, PricewaterhouseCoopers, Boeing, and Microsoft Corporation, and many other companies, were forced to take their Internet e-mail systems off-line for nearly 6 hours.[19]

By 2001, anti-virus software vendors, such as Panda Software, were actually publishing a "top-ten list" of most frequently encountered viruses in a given month. January 2002's list from Panda, taken from its website, provides an example:[20]

- Badtrans.B stole the march on all the rest in January and was responsible for over 22% of cases. The mass-mailing worm's capacity to exploit a vulnerability in Internet Explorer and run automatically when the message carrying it is viewed in the preview pane has no doubt contributed to its virulence.
- Sircam was a long way off in second place this month. However, its use of "social engineering" techniques still meant it was responsible for more than 10% of detected infections.
- Nimda, another virus that exploits software vulnerabilities, rose to third position accounting for nearly 7% of January's infections.
- The dangerous polymorphic virus Magistr.B also took up residence in users' computers, accounting for 6.48% of infections. A similar infection rate was registered by Klez.F, with 6.12%.
- Behind this group are two other persistent viruses, which have appeared in the ranking for the last few months, Help (known as Haptime) and Disemboweler, causing 4.57% and 4.40% of infections.
- The virus, Myparty which despite initial expectations also figures into the list, has not caused a widespread epidemic. In fact, it was only detected in 3.28% of cases, taking eighth place in the ranking.

By 2002, the situation bordered on the ridiculous as pundits reported that it had become a sign of popularity to have a virus named for one. The trend, which began with a virus named for professional tennis player Anna Kournikova, continued with an e-mail virus detected in February and named for pop singing star, Britney Spears. In both cases, victims received an e-mail instructing them to view an attached image of the "star." Doing so infected the e-mail application, causing the virus-laden message to be sent to every address in the infected party's e-mail directory.

The humor is missed, however, on those who must cope with the costs. According to a 2000 Computer Virus Prevalence Survey from the International Computer Security Association (ICSA), the rate of virus attacks has been growing steadily since 1996. Encounters with viruses grew from approximately one infection per 1000 PCs annually in 1994 to 31 per 1000 PCs annually in 1998 to nearly 91 per 1000 in 2000 (see Figure 2–4).[21]

The most common source of virus infections was tainted e-mail (87%), while the earlier predominant vector, infected diskettes brought to the workplace from home by employees, had dropped significantly in importance—accounting for only 7% of cases (see Figure 2–5).[22] The most important finding of the study, however, was the cost to organizations that were infected. In 2000, ICSA says that the median cost per incident was approximately $10,000 (up from $2400 in 1998) and complete recovery required a mean of 7 days per infection.[23]

Again, the purpose of citing industry statistics on disaster potentials is not to suggest that they are predictors of actual disasters. In risk analysis, it is valuable to know what the threats are in order to develop scenarios that will serve as the basis for planning prevention and recovery strategies. For example, it is valu-

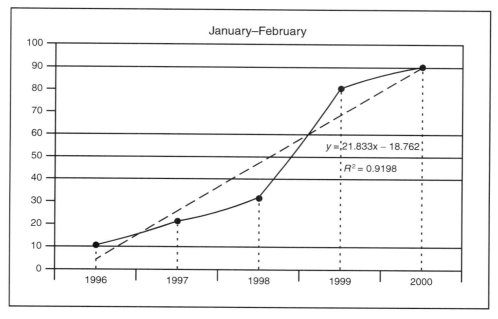

Figure 2–4   Virus infections per 1,000 computers per month, 1996–2000. (*Source:* ICSA Labs 6th Annual Computer Virus Prevalence Survey 2000, International Computer Security Association, ICSA.net, Reston, VA.)

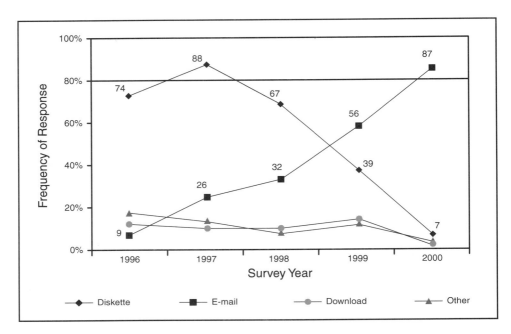

Figure 2–5   Sources of virus infection, 1996–2000. (*Source:* ICSA Labs 6ᵗʰ Annual Comptuer Virus Prevalence Survey 2000, International Computer Security Association, ICSA.net, Reston, VA.)

able to know at what temperatures various media burn (see Table 2–1) in order to assess the protection afforded by fireproof cabinets of various ratings.

On the other hand, there is a hardcore group of risk managers and analysts who take this investigation to the extreme by quantifying the likelihood of each threat and expressing this percentage as a corporate financial exposure. However, the admonition of the information manager quoted earlier should be observed: "Either you have a disaster or you don't." Hence, the practical value of threat identification is twofold: (1) It serves to point out where disaster avoidance measures (such as fire suppression systems, security access systems, and power

Table 2–1   Temperatures at which Damage Begins to Occur

Computer Equipment	175°F
Magnetic Tape/Diskettes	100–120°F
Magnetic Disk	150°F
Paper/Punch Cards	350°F
Microfilm/Microfiche	225°F (with steam)
	300°F (without steam)

protection systems) may be needed; and (2) it identifies specific vulnerabilities that plans and procedures must specifically address.

Another benefit of the threat identification process is less methodological than psychological. Focusing a group's attention on the threat potential can increase members' awareness and sensitivity. It can also facilitate group cohesion and unity in the disaster recovery planning effort because it helps the group recognize the importance of the work it will perform. This is extremely important, since there is much in the risk analysis process, including the classification of system criticality, to divide the group.

Threat identification may also serve to make participants more aware of the interdependencies that exist among them and build team unity by clarifying shared vulnerabilities. In this way, threat identification can set the stage for cost sharing in expensive threat avoidance systems and cooperation in other essential areas.

DEVELOPING PLAN OBJECTIVES

Having classified business process/application critically, assigned costs to outages of various duration, and identified threats to systems and data, it remains to analyze this data to formulate a set of specific objectives to guide the development of the recovery capability. The goal is to eliminate exposures that can be eliminated and to minimize the effects of those that cannot be eliminated.

This analysis does not lend itself readily to "group think," although follow-up interviews with users and system administrators may help the disaster recovery coordinator better understand requirements and set objectives. In fact, certain exposures may not fall under the aegis of the disaster recovery coordinator and, thus, require coordination with the security manager, auditor, or other authorized persons.

Threats related to the intentional abuse by persons who are not corporate employees are typically viewed as security threats. Obviously, if a hacker demolishes a network or erases critical data, these activities may have an impact equivalent to a disaster. Security planning is a companion discipline to disaster recovery planning, and the two functions must work together to accomplish their respective goals.

To address effectively the other threats to normal operations, such as fire and flooding, the disaster recovery coordinator will need to work with individuals at practically every level within the company. This is because of the nature of the planning project.

As Figure 2–6 illustrates, the objectives of disaster recovery planning are to develop both a plan and a permanent, ongoing disaster prevention and recovery capability. Installation of a fire prevention system will require the cooperation of the data center manager or department manager in whose area the system is being installed. Similarly, the coordination of a regular schedule of off-site stor-

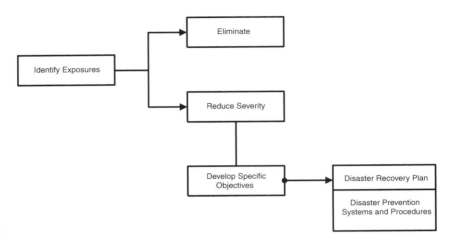

Figure 2–6   Objectives development in risk control.

age for important records, storage media, and microfiche will require the full participation of those who create and use these items.

A set of clearly stated objectives, identifying the conditions, tasks, and standards for each protection or recovery strategy, is often a prerequisite for justifying the strategy to those who will have to absorb the cost and/or modify their existing procedures. Representatives of the affected department and senior management will want to know what the coordinator is specifically seeking to do and will want to see how all of the objectives fit together in a comprehensive recovery strategy.

The following is a generic, but by no means comprehensive, set of objectives that may result from a risk analysis. Each objective assumes that sufficient information has been collected to justify the need for the tasks. Objectives are organized under section titles that define the function or area that the objectives are designed to address. (If the objectives seem a little bit like a job description for the disaster recovery coordinator, this is only because they reflect the assumption made at the outset: Disaster recovery planning is a full-time task.)

Company Policy

1. The disaster recovery coordinator will develop and seek senior management approval for a company policy for the protection of people, property, and assets (within a specified timeframe) that meets current company standards and format for documentation.

This objective addresses itself to the need to undertake disaster recovery planning, to obtain management approval and support, and to generate a paper plan within a set timeframe. It also assigns responsibility for the task to the disaster recovery coordinator.

Plan Maintenance

2. The disaster recovery coordinator will develop a schedule for periodic review and maintenance of the plan and advise all personnel of their roles and the deadline for receiving revisions and comments.

3. The disaster recovery coordinator will collate reviewer revisions and comments and update the plan within 30 days of the review date.

4. The disaster recovery coordinator will arrange and coordinate scheduled and unscheduled tests of the disaster recovery plan to evaluate its adequacy.

5. The disaster recovery coordinator will participate in scheduled plan tests that will be performed x times per year on (specific dates). For all scheduled and unscheduled tests, the coordinator will write evaluations of test results and integrate test results into the disaster recovery plan within 30 days.

6. The disaster recovery coordinator will develop a schedule for training recovery personnel in emergency and recovery procedures as set forth in the disaster recovery plan. Training dates should be scheduled within 30 days of each plan revision and scheduled plan test.

7. The disaster recovery coordinator will maintain records of plan maintenance activities (testing, training, and reviews) and submit these for examination by internal and external auditors.

This section sets forth the objectives for maintaining the plan and empowers the disaster recovery coordinator to initiate and supervise plan maintenance activities. Part of the IT manager's job is to ensure that the disaster recovery coordinator is provided with the authority to fulfill these responsibilities.

Physical Environment

8. The disaster recovery coordinator will collect information regarding company facilities and assess existing structures and facilities for their susceptibility to earthquake-, fire-, and water-related damage, as well as criminal intrusion, and will report the findings in memoranda to senior management, IT management, and departmental management.

This objective specifically seeks to assess facility-related risk factors so that they may be addressed in the disaster recovery plan or through the development of loss prevention capabilities. (Facility-related risk factors are explored in greater detail in Chapter 3.) Obviously, the results of the departmental risk analyses are provided to those persons who will need to underwrite the costs of acquiring a specific avoidance or recovery capability. Risk factors and potential costs are typically communicated as a part of a cost-justification for the capabilities that are being proposed.

Organizational Control

9. The disaster recovery coordinator will work with departmental managers or system/network administrators to develop informational programs to advise all employees within the department of the assets and functions they are expected to safeguard, the events they are to note and/or report, and the immediate actions they are to take in response to disaster events.

10. The disaster recovery coordinator will work with departmental management to develop a formal "ownership" program in order to assign responsibility for each and every resource to individual employees within the department.

This section provides the means for employees and managers to aid the disaster recovery coordinator in the early detection and correction of potentially hazardous or debilitating conditions or practices. The disaster recovery coordinator may be called upon to draft these disaster avoidance procedures, or the task may be assigned to the department manager once the specific procedures and guidelines have been identified.

The second objective, to establish an "ownership" program, may be familiar to security planners, with whom the concept originated. However, system or application ownership has relevance in the context of disaster recovery planning as well.[24] The practice of assigning ownership of equipment or functions to employees is tantamount to giving the employee "owner" the right to say who may use the resource. At first glance, this may seem to invite friction and disputes among employees. However, the experience of many organizations that use ownership programs demonstrates that the opposite effect typically results.

Ownership programs often help employees become more attentive to the secure and qualified use of "their" resources. Abuse of systems or misuse caused by inadequate training may be spotted sooner so that the detection and correction of errors can be undertaken before the problem creates an outage.

Human Resources

11. The disaster recovery coordinator will work with the human resources department to develop procedures for notifying IT managers of pending employee terminations or separations.

12. The disaster recovery coordinator will work with the human resources department to develop procedures for maintaining a telephone directory to be used in contacting recovery team members in the event of a disaster.

13. The disaster recovery coordinator will work with the human resources department to develop a program designed to foster safety awareness among employees of the company.

The human resources connection is a vital one for a variety of security and disaster recovery-related reasons. In some companies, human resources will be responsible for making employees aware of where to go to continue work in the event of a disaster.

Human resources may also be called upon to set a policy providing for the immediate dismissal of employees who abuse systems and to set into motion a procedure that will see a terminated employee's access passwords and file permissions revoked and company property reclaimed.

Human resources may also be asked to assess the psychological strengths of employees who will be called upon to provide key recovery functions. Knowing how an employee is likely to behave under stress and having access to the employee's personal data (marital status, home address, home and emergency contact telephone numbers) can be critical for evaluating his or her suitability to participate directly in recovery or salvage activities.

14. The disaster recovery coordinator will work together with systems administrators and network management personnel to coordinate data backup programs.
15. The disaster recovery coordinator will identify all documentation and forms required for continuation of normal operations following a disaster and ensure that adequate supplies are inventoried in a secure, access-controlled location.
16. The disaster recovery coordinator will document network and system integrity control measures.
17. The disaster recovery coordinator will ensure that master and/or firmware passwords and/or encryption/decryption standards are recorded and stored in a secure, access-controlled location.

Operational and access control measures are typical features of data processing or network operations; they are the backbone of security in normal, day-to-day operations. However, they can present a nightmare for disaster recovery. If systems administrators or network operations personnel cannot be located at the time of a disaster, it is possible that the recovery of impacted business processes will be delayed because master passwords or data encryption keys, known only to the administrator, are unavailable. A related concern: the lack of procedural or software documentation or preprinted forms used in normal operations can also delay recovery.

Applications Development

18. The disaster recovery coordinator will develop and implement a schedule of routine backup and documentation for applications under development.

Applications development projects, which represent a substantial investment of company time and resources, should be backed up to prevent disastrous loss. If industry-accepted documentation standards are observed and enforced, this objective may have already been met. However, the disaster recovery coordinator should verify this.

Systems and Networks

19. The disaster recovery coordinator will quantify, to the extent possible, the dollar loss potential to the company of business process/application outages of fixed duration for every business process/application in the company, identifying infrastructure components including mainframe, mini-, and microcomputer-based systems, telecommunications systems, and data networks.
20. The disaster recovery coordinator will develop a disaster recovery capability that provides for recovery of critical applications within x hours.
21. The disaster recovery coordinator will document responsibilities of key recovery personnel in the event of a disaster.
22. The disaster recovery coordinator will develop minimum acceptable configurations for systems and networks that will provide emergency service levels for x hours, or until normal operations are restored.
23. The disaster recovery coordinator will develop strategies for the replacement of business process infrastructure resources by manual or automated means for a period of x hours in the event of a disaster.
24. The disaster recovery coordinator will develop sufficient alternative vendors or sources of supply for each resource required for business process recovery in a minimum acceptable configuration in order to provide an acceptable level of risk mitigation.

These objectives begin to approach tasks that are generally recognized as the exclusive domain of disaster recovery planning. They set a timetable for recovery of interrupted business processes in emergency mode. This number is expressed as a goal: Critical applications will be up and running at emergency service levels within x hours.

Furthermore, the tentative recovery timeframe is set forth: Recovered applications will need to be operated at emergency levels for x hours/days, which is the estimated time required to relocate to the original or to a new permanent operating site.

The term "minimum acceptable system configuration" in the above objectives is also significant. It refers to the fact that recovery systems and networks need not be mirror images of pre-disaster systems and networks. If only critical application service levels are being provided, for example, end-user client workstation requirements might be drastically reduced. Also, storage capacity requirements may not be as great if the amount of data required by partially restored systems is reduced.

For voice and data communications, a smaller telecommunications switch might suffice to replace a full-sized private branch exchange (PBX). An analysis of capacity requirements might reveal that critical communications activity can be adequately sustained with fewer incoming trunks and fewer wide area service lines.

Whatever strategies are developed for system or network recovery, they must be cost-justified by demonstrating how much it would cost the company if it did not have the capabilities in the event of a disaster. The backup strategies and configurations that are formulated must be documented in advance, the documentation must be made available to those who will rebuild systems in an emergency, and provisions must be made for two or more sources to supply hardware and supplies that will be needed for reconstruction.

Backup/Off-Site Storage

25. The disaster recovery coordinator will assess and contract with a qualified vendor of off-site storage services according to the guidelines set forth by PRISM International (formerly, the Association of Commercial Records Centers), or some comparable body.
26. Having documented the criticality of data, applications, systems, and networks, the disaster recovery coordinator will identify the following resources for backup and/or removal to off-site storage:
    a. Hard copies of system documentation, user manuals, operating procedures, vital paper records, disaster recovery plans, and other documentation that might be useful or essential to recovery.
    b. Critical, vital, and sensitive data stored on magnetic or photographic media.
    c. Stocks of forms and supplies that are necessary for recovery and subject to delays in resupply.
27. The disaster recovery coordinator or designate will inventory materials stored off-site at 60-day intervals and periodically audit materials for completeness and integrity in accordance with the latest update of the plan.
28. The disaster recovery coordinator will assess options and recommend strategies for system and network backup that meet business process recovery requirements in the most cost-effective way.
29. The disaster recovery coordinator will make all advance arrangements that are necessary to facilitate the logistics of the transition from normal system operation to emergency system operation, including the transportation of resources, the acquisition and delivery of emergency supplies and materials, and the rerouting or activation of telecommunications networks.

These objectives go to the heart of the disaster recovery capability. When realized, they provide the means for recovery and the methods for implementing the recovery strategy.

Emergency Action

30. The disaster recovery coordinator will document all procedures and policies of civil or government organizations that might impact on the company's recovery strategy.
31. The disaster recovery coordinator will develop procedures that provide for the monitoring of all alarm sources, including fire alarms and weather and emergency radio.
32. The disaster recovery coordinator will develop clear decision trees (decision-making flowcharts) that assign specific personnel responsibility for invoking the disaster recovery plan. These procedures will fully identify the criteria for decision making.
33. The disaster recovery coordinator will document the notification procedure that will be observed when the plan is invoked.
34. The disaster recovery coordinator will develop sound evacuation and immediate action procedures and train all personnel in their use. Periodic drills in evacuation will be conducted with the consent of department managers.
35. The disaster recovery coordinator will develop a strategy/facility for management command, communication, and control of recovery efforts in the wake of a disaster.

The orderly evacuation of facilities is prerequisite in disaster recovery planning, which seeks first and foremost to safeguard human life. In addition to the need (and legal requirement) to assign evacuation routes and drill employees in their use, it is also necessary to identify how (and by whom) the disaster recovery plan will be invoked to initiate recovery strategies.

Some disasters occur suddenly and without warning. Others, such as hurricanes, may develop over a period of time, allowing for a last-minute backup and an orderly shutdown of systems. These differences would be reflected in the logic of a decision tree included in the plan.

Furthermore, the procedures for warning and evacuating populations used by civil government authorities can have a direct impact on the implementation of the disaster recovery plan. In hurricane-prone areas, for example, it is not unusual for businesses in vulnerable areas to be evacuated while a storm is still quite distant and has a very small chance of striking anywhere in the vicinity of the business. Evacuation orders employ the logic of mass population movements, not of business resumption. Thus, the timetable with which government emergency managers work may be very different from the timetable of the disaster recovery plan.[25]

Finally, this section introduces the idea of an Emergency Operations Center (EOC), a facility (physical or virtual) from which senior management will be able to monitor and manage the recovery effort.

Articulating Objectives

These 35 objectives are very general and generic. Those developed for a particular company will reflect the company's specialized needs in the area of disaster recovery. Once developed, plan objectives should be articulated to those who will provide spending authorization and those who will actually develop strategies and procedures based on the objectives.

Procedures development can be a lengthy process involving hours of research, consulting, writing, reviewing, and rewriting. During this process, the coordinator should take some immediate steps to provide basic protections for the data centers and user departments. These protective measures are the subject of Chapter 3.

ENDNOTES

1. Kenneth N. Myers, "Avoiding a Crisis," *Datamation,* 1/2/86.
2. Stacy Collett, "E-brokers' Snafus Provide Lessons," *Computerworld,* 4/12/99.
3. Interview with George Ferguson, Marketing Manager, Hewlett Packard Company Business Recovery Services, Palo Alto, CA, June 1999.
4. Interview with Tony Martinez, General Manager, IBM Business Continuity and Recovery Services, Sterling Forest, NY, June 1999.
5. Ferguson interview.
6. Federal Emergency Management Agency, "Backgrounder: Floods and Flash Floods," *FEMA Publication,* Washington, DC, January 1998.
7. Interview with Stuart Hanley, Vice President of World Wide Operations, Ontrack Data International, Eden Prarie, MN, June 1999.
8. Interview with Maar Haack, EDP underwriter for St. Paul Fire and Marine, St. Paul, MN, January 1987.
9. John R. Hall, Jr., Special Analysis Package: Computer Equipment and Computer Areas, National Fire Protection Association, Quincy, MA, February 1999.
10. Ibid.
11. Ibid.
12. Interview with Steve Skolochencko, data security branch, US Postal Service, Washington, DC, August and October 1987.
13. "Power Outages Cost Small Business Big Bucks," *Power Online,* 3/24/99.
14. "Electricity Outages Cost Corporations Billions And It Also May Make Them Run From Their Current Utility," E SOURCE Press Release, E SOURCE, Inc., Boulder, CO, 6/10/99.
15. "Electricity System Improvements Needed To Prevent Economic Losses," EPRI Journal Online, 7/01, EPRI, 3412 Hillview Avenue, Palo Alto, CA.
16. Alliance for Telecommunications Industry Solutions, Network Reliability Steering Committee, "Fixing Facility Outages: Building Tools to Make It Happen," ATIS Facilities Solution Team Report, November 1997.
17. William Taren, "How Reliable Is the Public Network?," *Internet Telephony,* 2/10/97.

18. "Annual Report 2000 of the Network Reliability Steering Committee," Network Reliability and Interoperability Council, http://www.nric.org/pubs/nric5/2B1appendixi.doc

19. Dick Satran, "Users Feel Bite In Year Of Computer Bug," Reuters, 6/15/99.

20. Panda Software Website, www.pandasoftware.com.

21. "ICSA Labs 6th Annual Computer Virus Prevalence Survey 2000," International Computer Security Association (ICSA.net), Reston, VA, September 2000.

22. Ibid.

23. Ibid.

24. Security Assessment Questionnaire, IBM Data Security Support Programs, May 1985.

25. Jon Toigo, "Storm Alarms Sound," *Databus*, 8/86.

CHAPTER 3

Facility Protection

Formulating the strategies and documenting the procedures for disaster recovery may be challenging and time-consuming processes. However, there are usually a number of action items, identified during risk analysis, which may be undertaken while procedures are being developed. These include the purchase and installation of systems to safeguard against certain avoidable disaster potentials, such as fire and flooding.

Figure 3–1 is a data flow diagram (DFD) showing many of the generic activities that aim at securing disaster avoidance capabilities for a company's user departments and information-processing facilities. As the chart suggests, the evaluation, selection, cost-justification and installation of these capabilities may be undertaken concurrently with the development of the paper plan.

As depicted in the data flow diagram, planning for disaster prevention capabilities requires, first, an evaluation of existing vulnerabilities and a survey of any existing prevention measures. Tests and inspections as well as consultations with civil emergency planners, fire protection officials, security professionals, police, and other experts facilitate threat assessments. Based on these assessments, objectives can be articulated that will be useful when identifying suitable preventive systems and when evaluating the proposals of vendors.

This chapter focuses on a specific set of preventive measures. These include:

- Systems for water detection that can provide early warning of leaks and other water-related hazards.
- Systems for the detection of pre-ignition gases, smoke and other indicators of impending fire to enable proactive response that will ensure the health and safety of personnel and prevent the loss of data and equipment to fire.

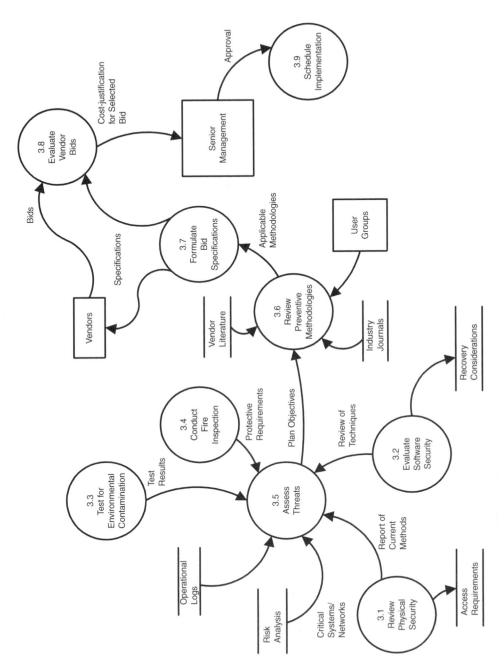

Figure 3–1 Disaster prevention system selection and implementation.

- Systems for the detection of airborne contamination levels that are associated with employee illness, data loss, equipment malfunction, and fires.
- Systems for the suppression of fires.
- Systems for the continuation of electrical power in the presence of a utility power outage.
- Systems for the physical security of corporate computing and telecommunications facilities.

A conscious decision has been made to exclude two additional disaster prevention systems from this discussion. The first is computer/network security systems. A complete discussion of this topic would require a book of its own, and there are more than a few good ones in print today. Moreover, many organizations have planners who are already tasked with computer and network security functions. DR coordinators should make every effort to develop working relationships with their peers in the security area and to include corporate computer and network security representatives on their disaster recovery planning teams. The second prevention system that is not included in the above list is a corporate data backup/restore system. This topic is covered in Chapter 4.

The purpose of disaster avoidance systems is to provide an automated mechanism for detecting certain disaster potentials (and to respond to them, where possible) before they develop into unplanned interruptions of normal business processes. The acquisition of disaster avoidance systems is rarely a simple matter of cutting a purchase order. Vendors must be identified, products evaluated, bids solicited, costs justified, and expenditures approved.

Furthermore, depending on the type of system, there may be an additional set of tasks to coordinate system installation (with the data center or user department), schedule work, prepare the installation site, or provide for the interruption of normal operations for training or installation work. Preparatory steps differ depending on a number of factors, ranging from the type of disaster avoidance system being installed to the work schedule of the affected department.

Under ideal circumstances, systems are installed during the preparation of new company quarters. However, more often than not, disaster avoidance capabilities are add-ons to existing facilities and must, to the extent possible, be implemented around normal business activities.

The following sections discuss several common disaster prevention and protection strategies that can be implemented to provide a disaster avoidance capability.

WATER DETECTION

As noted previously, flooding poses a significant threat to data processing and records management facilities. Annual costs to companies resulting from water damage are in the millions of dollars.

Some encounters with flooding are sudden and catastrophic. Landstar Systems, a transportation broker in Jacksonville, FL, learned about water damage firsthand in 1998, when 6 inches of rain, weighing an estimated 150 tons, collapsed the roof of its data center. Noting a trickle of water in the data center, the night operator managed to place one call to the vice president of IT before the flood moved from the second floor into the data center directly.[1]

Leaks can also develop slowly and, if detected and rectified in time, can be prevented from resulting in a facility outage. For example, a water pipe sharing the same channel as the building main electrical bus at Charles Schwab's Montgomery Street office building in San Francisco, CA, may have been leaking for some time before it finally broke in February 1999. The leak was not detected, however, until the pipe burst on Friday morning, spilling a torrent into the bus cabling, shorting out the building electrical system, and forcing the evacuation of 550 employees. Repairs to the pipe and the bus required 2 weeks while Schwab personnel operated from other company-owned space in the Bay Area.[2]

Water can intrude into sensitive information processing and storage facilities, as well as user work areas, in a variety of ways and from a variety of sources. Some common sources of flooding are:

- Facility plumbing leaks. Although well-designed data processing or storage facilities should be located away from building plumbing, they often are not. Water and sewer pipe leakage, particularly in multistory buildings, can travel along pipes and duct work and drain into data centers, records storage centers, communications equipment closets, or electrical panels.
- Air conditioning. In data centers, spot coolers and subfloor air conditioning plants can produce water, either through leakage or condensation. Roof-mounted air conditioners and improperly sealed building rooftops are also a potentially dangerous combination.
- Water cooling systems. Some larger mainframes are cooled, not by air, but by water. Leaks in the cooling system can show up as underfloor puddles in raised floor environments.
- Sprinkler systems. Sprinkler heads or piping can be damaged by workers carrying ladders or performing construction or repair work in crawl spaces or on facility ceilings and walls. Leaks may not be obvious for a protracted period of time.

Some hardware vendors suggest that their equipment is impervious to water damage, and it is not uncommon to hear a sales representative state assuredly that water poses no threat to de-energized equipment. If the computer is de-energized and becomes wet, says the rep (or service technician or field service agent), just disassemble it, dry it out, put it back together, and it will work properly.

This presumes that the information manager or computer operator will have the prescience to know when water will enter the facility, contacting energized equipment. With the exception of the times when facilities are intentionally evacuated in response to natural threats, such as hurricanes, storm surges, or rising water, there is rarely a clear indication of imminent water intrusion. Thus, it is likely that water will contact energized equipment, causing short circuits and damage.

Even if it were true that electronic components are waterproof if de-energized (and according to a US Air Force study, this is certainly not the case[3]), there are several problems with vendor optimism. For one, even if equipment is not energized, the presence of water may represent a shock risk to personnel. The health hazard represented by the combination of water and electronics should be paramount in any discussion of the subject.

Second, even if equipment is recently powered down prior to contact with water, components will still be warm and subject to warping caused by uneven cooling. Restarting a system with warped circuit cards will likely result in untrustworthy performance.

Third, the contaminants present in sprinkler systems and other sources of water intrusion, more so than the water itself, represent a continuing threat to the operation of electronic equipment. Even if water-laden components are dried perfectly, the evaporated water will likely leave behind a noxious mixture of organic and metallic particulate that, in turn, will leave components vulnerable to failure.

Fourth, insurance, warranties, and service agreements may be invalidated if equipment has gotten wet, is restarted, and fails.

Finally, even in the best-case scenario, when wet equipment is salvageable, the period required to dry and test components before re-energizing them is likely to be protracted. Thus, the claims of many vendors about the tolerance of their hardware to water intrusion may be a moot point. Disasters are disasters in part because they interrupt critical business processes for an unacceptable period of time.

To anticipate water intrusion before it contacts energized equipment, and in some cases, before a leak can become a disaster, planners may wish to consider any of a number of water detection and annunciation systems presently available on the market. Detection systems—ranging from simple battery-operated alarms to sophisticated sensing cables and ceiling or floor detection grids—are available to identify the presence of water wherever it is found and either signal an audible alarm or relay hazard alert messages to a system or network management console.

Figure 3–2 provides a schematic drawing of one water sensor product that can be deployed either as a standalone unit or as part of a cabled sensor network. Placed in strategic locations, the simple, battery-operated device deploys two metal contacts against the mounting surface. If a film of water touches both contacts, a circuit is completed and a buzzer sounds.

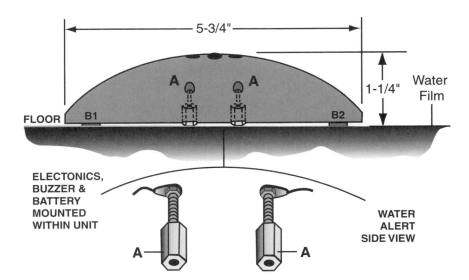

Figure 3–2   Water Alert® sensor schematic view. (*Source:* Dorlen Products, Milwaukee, WI.)

Another product, appropriate for applications ranging from structural risers to raised-floor environments, features a sensing cable consisting of a braid of wires and a fluoropolymer conductor, available in 3- to 50-foot lengths (see Figure 3–3). One or more cables can be connected together and deployed in a snake-like pattern to enable the coverage of a broad area of subfloor, wall, or other surface. Multiple cable branches can be deployed to provide coverage for different areas.

The branches return to an alarm and locating module, which provides both annunciation of the detected leak and a display of its exact location. When the system is deployed around subfloor air ducts, pipes, and fixtures in a raised-floor environment such as a data center, it can provide ongoing monitoring of moisture conditions and localize detected leaks to their source. In addition to signaling leakage with an alarm, systems can also provide the means for automatically de-energizing equipment when water intrusion is detected. Figure 3–4 depicts a common installation.

Figure 3–3   A Tracetek® cable asembly. (*Source:* Raychem HTS, Tyco International, Ltd., Menlo Park, CA.)

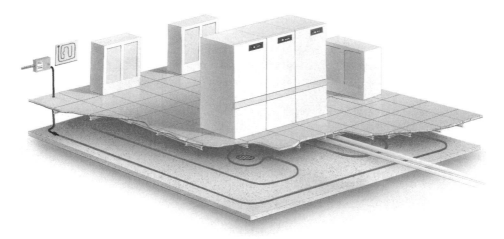

Figure 3-4   A Tracetek® data center deployment. (*Source:* Raychem
HTS, Tyco International Ltd., Menlo Park, CA.)

FIRE SUPPRESSION

Fire is typically the disaster scenario of choice for DR planning. Fires present very
directly the prospect of life safety issues and total property destruction that necessitate a total disaster recovery capability.

According to the National Fire Protection Association, most fires can be prevented before they cause smoke-and-rubble disasters through a combination of
prevention, detection, and suppression. Fire prevention begins with facility design and construction. Fire-resistant construction materials, firewall placement,
and facility compartmentalization can play major roles in limiting the scope, duration, and destructiveness of a fire. Also, when fire codes are observed in facility
construction, many building-related fire hazards can be minimized or eliminated.

However, despite the existence of some very thorough building and fire
codes (Disney World's EPCOT code being one of the more advanced), state laws
differ in terms of which codes they adopt and how rigorously code compliance is
enforced. Some states have adopted National Fire Protection Association standards in toto, while others have adopted only parts of the NFPA code. Even in
states that have adopted NFPA codes, nearly all lack sufficient enforcement personnel to inspect all new and existing construction for code adherence. Code violations often become evident only after a fire occurs.

A good starting point for the disaster recovery coordinator interested in installing fire prevention is to contact the local fire department. Fire inspectors are
generally willing to visit a site and provide practical (and legal) insights into the
adequacy or inadequacy of existing detection and suppression capabilities.

The inspector may find code violations in the building structure that will need to be rectified, regardless of the type of fire suppression system being considered for installation. However, few inspectors will penalize facility owners or tenants for less-than-life-threatening code violations discovered in an investigation prompted by an invitation, provided that the violations are remedied within a reasonable period of time.

The inspector can make recommendations regarding detection and suppression capabilities that can be used to support the case for spending money on an effective system. The inspector's comments should be requested in writing.

Another way in which fire departments (or fire protection engineers, consultants specially trained and certified in fire prevention methods and technologies) may assist during disaster recovery planning is by identifying the techniques that will likely be used if a fire occurs. More than one company has learned, to its chagrin, that the expensive, "clean-agent"-based fire suppression system it purchased proved useless in the case of a major fire originating in another part or on another floor of the building.

Clean agents are replacements for Halon™, a 30-year-old fire suppression workhorse that was determined to be hazardous to the Earth's ozone layer and banned by international treaty in 1993. The Environmental Protection Agency (EPA) enforces the ban on new production of Halon in the United States and is monitoring the phasing out of existing Halon systems. Companies with Halon systems already deployed may retain them but may not perform live tests of the systems, nor recharge them once used.[4]

The Halon ban prompted a quest for effective, environment-friendly alternatives, especially for data centers and certain industrial applications. To date, the EPA under its Significant New Alternatives Program (SNAP) has approved four alternatives (see Table 3–1).[5]

As with Halon in the past, the new crop of "clean" fire suppression agents must reach a certain concentration within the atmosphere of the protected environment (i.e., a data center, telecommunications equipment room, etc.) in order to be effective. Thus, the environment must be sealed. Fire-fighting techniques, however, may require that the integrity of the protected environment be violated by breaking windows or opening sealed doors.

Table 3–1   Clean Agent Replacements for Halon

Trade Name	Chemical Name	Manufacturer
Inergen™	IG-541	Ansul Fire Protection
FE 13™	HFC-23	DuPont Company
FM-200™	HFC-227ea	Great Lakes Chemical
CEA-410™	FC-3–1-10	3M Specialty Chemicals

Fire inspectors can often advise, based on facility design and probable fire-fighting techniques, whether a clean-agent system is appropriate for a given facility. In the case of one facility, an inspector observed that the data processing department's system would be useless: "We'd just open the doors at one end of the building and hose everything through the doors at the other end, and on into the parking lot. Computers, cubicles, chairs, the works."

This is not meant to imply that clean-agent systems are inappropriate in all cases. Brian Pung, President of Protective Systems, Inc., observes that the objective of a clean-agent system (as with Halon previously) is to stop electrical fires originating with electronic equipment from spreading.

> The intent is to limit fire to a specific component. The systems are designed to hold a sufficient concentration of the agent in a room so that people can shut down intelligently and exit safely, rather than doing these things reactively. We deploy systems so they will provide at least 10 minutes [of protection]. The national average for fire protection response is 6 minutes. These systems are not for building protection. Sprinkler systems are used for that. They are for fire protection in data centers and similar types of environments.[6]

In addition to providing advice on the selection of fire suppression systems and assisting with the determination of facility fire code compliance, fire inspectors can often identify fire hazards within company offices and recommend corrective measures. The coordinator should accompany the inspector through the facility and note any comments he or she may make. Some common observations and concerns may include:

- *The presence of combustibles located near potential ignition sources.* In a computer environment, for example, this may include cartons of paper located in close proximity to heat-generating hardware.
- *Exceeding the UL rating of extension cords and utilizing electrical devices that lack UL approval.* The Underwriting Laboratory rates a wide range of products for, among other things, their fire hazard potential. Many products do not bear the UL label and this may be a factor in determining fire risks.
- *Company smoking policy.* Lighted tobacco is an obvious hazard. However, in addition to the immediate danger of a fire, cigarette smoke can also invade and damage sensitive storage media and drives. Workplace smoking is obviously on the decline in most companies, either as a function of company policy or of local indoor antismoking ordinances.
- *Fire-related health hazards posed by certain types of fabrics and materials.* Some fabrics and materials, when burned, can release poisonous particles and gases into the atmosphere. Phosgene, hydrogen chloride, and hydrogen cyanide may be released by the burning of common plastics, while PCBs may be released from fires involving transformers and older electronic equipment that some companies may still have in service. These toxic

by-products can not only result in the loss of human life, but they can also delay reentry into the facility following a fire.

Besides hazards within the facility, a fire inspector is often in a position to warn the disaster recovery coordinator about neighbors with high potential for disaster. In multistory buildings, it may be valuable to know the lines of business of other occupants. If a neighbor engages in an activity that poses a substantial fire risk, this might affect the selection of fire avoidance systems. Such information may also be a springboard for opening discussions with fellow tenants in a shared office building setting regarding joint fire risk mitigation. With cooperation, tenants can watch out for each other in the area of fire detection and physical security.

Also, if a facility is located near a firm engaged in toxic chemical or other volatile product manufacturing or storage, the fire inspector usually knows this and can notify the disaster recovery coordinator.

Knowledge is power. However, knowing the risks does not necessarily mean that all threats can be eliminated. Just as the disaster recovery coordinator may have no control over the initial construction of the facility, he or she may have no control over where the facility is located in relation to high potential risks. The best one can do is to eliminate potential risks that can be eliminated and minimize exposure to those that cannot.

This strategy involves both preventive and prophylactic measures. Protecting against fires means identifying possible causes and controlling or eliminating them.

CONTAMINATION REDUCTION

An important and often overlooked root cause of fire in facilities where electronic equipment is used is environmental contamination. The entry of airborne contaminant particles into electronic equipment can cause short circuits and even flash fires in electronic equipment. Moreover, contamination has been the indirect cause of more IT downtime than all the fires, floods, hurricanes, earthquakes, and disgruntled employees combined.

Contaminants are microscopic particulate bearing such grandiose names as crystallines, carbonaceous particles, organic and synthetic fibrous particulate, and metallics (such as zinc). Without a degree in chemistry, a DR planner can be unimpressed by the reports and analyses conducted by research labs that explain how contaminants effect sensitive disk media, circuitry, and microswitches. Also, because of the minute size of many contaminants, industry specialists report that they are often hard pressed to convince a business manager that a contamination problem exists.

Concern with the destructive potential of contamination has long been an issue for agencies of the U.S. government. In the late 1960s, the General Services

Administration issued federal air standards for clean rooms and workstations in federal agencies. These were revised in 1973 and issued by the GSA under the unassuming title, Federal Standard 209B.

209B set forth three scientific classifications of environmental contamination and mandated that certain federal agencies and contractors comply with them. Class 100 facilities included certified clean rooms, such as those employed by NASA and the Department of Defense for the development of sensitive electronic devices. Class 10,000 facilities included government hospital operating theatres. Class 100,000 facilities included all federal data processing centers.

The classification nomenclature—100, 10,000, and 100,000—referred to particulate concentrations. It was determined that environments having less than 100,000 particulate (no larger than 0.5 microns in size) per cubic foot of air were optimal for data processing hardware.

209B was revised several times in the 1980s and in 1992 became Federal Standard 209E. The revised standard included classes of air cleanliness by metric measurements as well as newly defined criteria for ultrafine particles.[7]

While the 209 standards have not been enforced stringently in the private sector (except in the case of certain defense contractors and within certain facilities regulated directly by the federal government), the inclusion of an air standard for data centers does suggest the correlation the government has drawn between environment and system integrity. 209E specifies techniques for sampling air in the facility and for determining the concentration of contaminant particles it contains. Effective measurement requires multiple tests conducted at different locations in the room. Some of the more popular testing methods include:

- *"White-glove" method.* As the name suggests, this method assesses the level of contamination by wiping the exposed surface of a piece of equipment with a white glove. The particulate on the glove is analyzed to determine the type of contaminant in the center environment.
- *Petri-dish method.* With this method of checking contamination, a petri dish is used to collect particulate that fall out of the air.[8] After a period of time, the contents of the dish are analyzed to determine the amount and type of fallout.
- *Aspirating pump.* This method involves the installation of a pump in an area where air quality is to be measured. Air samples are collected through an air intake, and the contents are analyzed following several hours of operation.
- *Electronic particulate counter.* The electronic counter is one of the most advanced methods of airborne contaminant data collection. Most units are about the size of cellular phones, except that the "antenna" is actually a sensing tip that counts the number of particles that it contacts over a period of time (see Figure 3–5). To analyze the contaminants themselves, counter probes are wiped with a swab and the swab is then microscopically examined.

Figure 3–5   Electronic airborne particulate counters. (*Source:* Biotest Diagnostics Corporation, Denville, NJ.)

None of the above methods alone provides a means to both count and analyze the contents of airborne contamination. Hybrid systems are appearing in the market that count particulate moving with room air flow, while at the same time sampling the contaminants with special filters, so that it can be analyzed. The analysis can often reveal the sources of contamination so they can be corrected, if necessary.

Once the presence of contamination in the data center has been demonstrated and the threat it poses to personnel and equipment is understood, next it is necessary to develop strategies for eliminating or reducing contamination levels. A good way to begin is to answer the question: How are contaminants introduced into the clean environment of the data processing facility?

While certain contaminants are carried in by operators (including clothing fibers, hair and skin particles, and even cigarette smoke and ash), most particulates are airborne and, in data centers or other raised-floor environments, are transported into sensitive equipment through the data center sub-floor air supply. Examples of the more common contaminants follow.

- Cement dust, sand, plaster, and brick dust may be produced by the gradual erosion of the subfloor surface beneath a data center's raised floor. Even if the subfloor has been properly sealed with polyacrylic sealants, the dust that was generated during raised-floor installation may settle on the subfloor. This cement dust, propelled by air conditioning, can enter bottom-cooled equipment at high velocity and damage board components.

- Urban pollution, including carbon/coal dust, can enter the subfloor air supply by way of the air conditioning system. The wearing of drive belts or printer components and the release of laser printer toner can also introduce these contaminants to the DP area. These particulates are a special problem since they can conduct electricity and cause short circuits and cross-tracking.
- Electrically conductive metallic particulate can often be traced to equipment wear, wear of the air-conditioning plant, floor and ceiling suspension systems, and even to old-fashioned rust (iron oxide). Metallic contaminants are even more dangerous than carbon residue because they tend to "plate out" on components where they will cause the most damage.

Nearly any contaminant can conduct electricity—even paper dust. If the contaminant can absorb moisture, it can wreak the same sort of damage as the "bug" of computer legend that, when it straddled two poles of an open switch with its legs, made a circuit and short-circuited the first computer. As in the case of the first bug, it is almost impossible to determine the cause of the short circuit since fiber or paper particles disintegrate in the heat generated by the short.

Fortunately, the IT manager can take several steps to eliminate certain types of contamination and to minimize the impact of contaminants that cannot be completely eliminated. The good news is that most of these steps do not require that the equivalent of a NASA clean room be established in the data center or telecommunications switchroom.

1. Forbid cigarette smoking inside the data center or switch room. If smoking is now permitted, smoke particles and tar are already harming the health of computer equipment.
2. Remove wastepaper baskets and bulk paper containers from the computer room. These are prime sources of fiber and paper dust, which is a highly water-absorbent, therefore conductive, particulate.
3. Invest in a handheld vacuum that is fitted with brushless rotors and microstatic filters for use in general cleanup of paper handlers and printers in the center. Most portable vacuum cleaners add more contamination than they remove. Especially dangerous are the metallic particles from the motor brushes that are expelled in the vacuum exhaust and collected by sensitive equipment in the center.

Most modern data-center-grade vacuum cleaners feature "H.E.P.A." exhaust filtration. H.E.P.A. stands for high efficiency particulate air (or arresting) and a H.E.P.A. rating indicates that the filter media used on the vacuum is certified by the US government to comply with a specific filtration efficiency. The efficiency of a H.E.P.A. filter is evaluated in two ways. One measure is the proportion of particulate that the filter will trap: government-certified H.E.P.A. filters operate at 99.97% efficiency. The second measure of filtration efficiency is expressed as the smallest particle size that will be filtered: Particulate of 0.3 microns or greater are filtered by a certified H.E.P.A. filter.

Only those filters with the "S-CLASS H.E.P.A." printed on the filter are the genuine article. The periods between the letters in the acronym are important. Vendors who offer vacuum units emblazoned with the terms "true HEPA" or "HEPA-type" are not certified. Of course, H.E.P.A. filters are not the only media on the market that are effective for removing computer-killing contaminants. Independent laboratories have certified the 3M FILTRETE™ hospital filter, for example, with a filtration efficiency of 99.95% dust free at 0.1 microns. However, the media loses effectiveness as it is used.

Both H.E.P.A. and other high-efficiency filtration vacuums are expensive because of the frequency with which the filters must be changed. Replacement filtration media itself is costly. An alternative is to invest in a central vacuum system that empties its exhaust outside of the equipment room.

4. If space permits, move printers—especially laser printers—out of the vicinity of CPUs, tape drives, telecommunications switches, and disk drives. Ideally, computer and telecommunications equipment should be compartmentalized and printers should be in a separate room with separate air handling.
5. Observe proper computer floor tile maintenance practices, as recommended by the manufacturer. For example, perform all tile alterations outside the raised-floor environment. Cutting a tile inside the center will flood the environment with fiber and aluminum contaminants. In addition, always replace a tile in the same direction as it was removed. Replacing tiles incorrectly can cause them to wobble and wear, depositing contaminants into the plenary air supply below the raised floor.
6. Ensure that all equipment is fitted with the best filters that the equipment vendor can provide. This will not eliminate contamination altogether, but it will keep some of the larger particulate out of older drives and switches.

Most drive manufacturers insist that their disk products are safe from the airborne contamination that surrounds them because they are sealed. With the latest disk drives, this is likely the case. To achieve extremely high-storage capacities (a function of the areal capacity of a disk drive), vendors are using magnetoresistive heads that are very sensitive to particulate contamination and corrode easily. Moreover, in order to read more densely packed data from the disk platter, most vendors are reducing the head-fly height in their disk drives. Read/write heads fly approximately 2 to 3 microns above the media.

With such close tolerances, drives need to be sealed away from external contamination. Otherwise, catastrophe can result. Think of a 747 airplane flying at 400 miles per hour 3 feet off the ground and encountering a boulder 4 feet tall. This is actually a fair metaphor for current drive read/write heads (the airplane), disk platters (the runway 3 microns below) and a small particulate of 4 microns. The result can be a head crash.

With some older disk drives that may still be in service, however, contamination remains a threat to drive media. Previous generation drives featured so-called "absolute" filters or "breather" filters designed to vent heat or provide pressure equalization inside and outside the drive assembly during shipping. In some cases, particles that were small enough to pass through absolute filters were still large enough to cause disk crashing (see Figure 3–6).

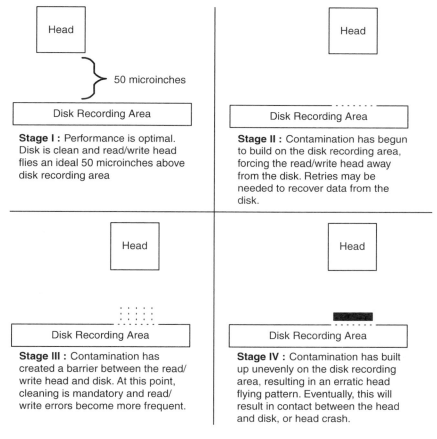

Figure 3–6   Chronology of a head crash. (*Source:* Jon William Toigo, "Environmental Contamination: Averting a Microscopic Threat to Data Center Operations," Data Center Operations Management [Auerback Publishers: New York, 1987].)

Furthermore, even when contaminants did not pass through the filter, but instead built up on its outer surface, they caused temperatures to build up in the drive to a point at which disk media was affected. Platter warble (or warping) occurs when heat inside the drive exceeds the upper limits for the disk media. When this happens, the media undergoes a molecular change that warps its surface. As with contamination buildup, an irregular surface caused by warping can lead to head crashes.

Frequent disk crashes were often cited as harbingers of environmental contamination. With newer drives, hermetic sealing largely eliminates the possibility of contaminants affecting disk media directly. Indirectly is another matter however.

Dust and contamination can still create heat problems for systems, switches and disk drives, causing shutdowns and failures. According to Eric Williamson, President of Worldwide Environmental Services, contamination is still a threat to hard disks and other electronic systems.

> Generally speaking, although it is true that the hardware is more reliable today than previous technologies, the environment, including contamination, is still a major issue, partly because availability requirements are so much higher today. [Vendors may have sealed their] hard disk assemblies against the introduction of external particulate. Unfortunately, there are still many components within the drives that CAN be affected by contamination. The mechanism for problems is sometimes quite complicated, but two ways that contamination can affect hardware are:
>
> a) Depending on its makeup, airborne contamination flowing through the drives may eventually coat hardware components, applying an insulative coating, and reducing the unit's ability to adequately shed its heat load, increasing the temperature, and leading to reduced mean time to failure (MTBF).
> b) Conductive particles can cause shorts or voltage aberrations on sensitive electronic components. Power supplies are particularly vulnerable to this phenomenon, and much has been written in recent years about this issue. [Disk drive vendors] are fully aware of this problem.[9]

The buildup of contaminants and dust on the filters covering power supply cooling fans remains a major source of disk problems today, according to Stuart Hanley, vice president of world wide operations at OnTrack Data International.

> There is plenty of evidence that heat is a disk drive's worst enemy [see Figure 3–7]. The first generation of 10,000 RPM drives had a major heat problem, though the newer ones run cooler. From a data recovery standpoint, we still see system cooling failures, usually poor or blocked ventilation of the system cabinet, that lead to hard disk crashes. Some box manufacturers have started adding temperature strips to their system cabinets [to check whether hard disk failures are the result of heat].[10]

Hanley further observes that root cause analysis is rarely performed on damaged drives. Therefore, the cause of a failure is usually listed as "mechanical problems," when blame should probably be placed on contamination-related heat in some cases.

Drive Reliability Typical Temperature Sensitivity

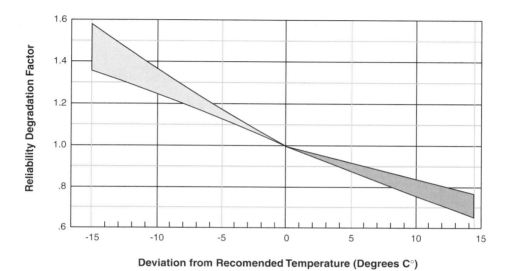

Reliability Degradation Factor

Deviation from Recomended Temperature (Degrees C°)

Figure 3–7 Heat and hard disk drive reliability. (*Source:* IBM.) "All escalating fires have four stages: Incipient (pre-combustion), Visible Smoke, Flaming Fire, and Intense Heat. The incipient stage of smoldering fires provides the widest window of opportunity to detect and control the spread of fire, before it develops into devastating stages. VESDA LaserPLUS can be configured to generate multiple alarms within this window."—Vision Systems VESDA LaserPlus marketing literature.

7. For data centers and equipment rooms, consult an engineer to determine how (and at what cost) a positive pressure air system can be established. In a positive pressure air system, air blows outward when the integrity of the room is violated (e.g., when a door is opened). If air blows outward, airborne contaminants are less likely to find ready access to the facility.

8. Remove all ion-generating air purifiers from the center environment. Also, deinstall any humidifiers or "toaster-element" space heaters and set up a schedule for thorough maintenance and inspection of air conditioners. All of these are major contributors to the contamination of environments where they are present. Ion-generating purifiers, nicronic wire heating elements (like those in a kitchen toaster), and the electrostatic precipitators found in

some older model air conditioning units produce electrostatic particulate that seek out electronic components like guided missiles.

9. Perhaps the most important step to take to control contamination is to contract with a reputable computer room maintenance company to perform routine cleaning.

Unfortunately, a number of firms claim to be competent in the field of computer room cleaning, and selecting one requires some savvy about the causes of environmental contamination and proper cleaning techniques. For example, many janitorial companies are more than willing to clean a company's computer facility using the same techniques that they use to keep other office areas neat and clean. The fact is that contracting with one of these services could well add to the problem of contamination.

Stories abound of janitorial services that wax and buff tile floors, creating a wax barrier that impairs the static grounding ability that was part of the floor's design. Another company found piles of sawdust under the computer room floor, deposited there by janitors to absorb water. More than one firm has experienced costly damage because janitors took up 20 or 30 raised-floor tiles at the same time to clean the subfloor beneath them "more efficiently."

According to industry specialists, most janitorial services do not know enough about the raised-floor environments to provide a service that will effectively reduce contamination. They use improper techniques and equipment that do more harm than good and possibly cause even more contamination-related downtime.

What should an IT manager or DR coordinator look for in a cleaning vendor? First, the best cleaning companies use only shielded, brushless-rotor equipment to avoid releasing ferromagnetic pollutants into the atmosphere and to prevent electromagnetic interference from affecting data processing equipment.

Furthermore, the cleaning company should clean tiles using OSHA-approved, nonionic solutions and lint-free towels, and should clean equipment exteriors with silicon-treated cloths that leave a silicon film that repels dust.

As with most service providers, companies are well served by asking for and checking provider references. The vendor should have a reputation for quality work and a pedigree of experience.

PRECOMBUSTION DETECTION

In the final analysis, the solution to the problem of contamination-related equipment failure and downtime will never be a comprehensive one. At best, an informed DR planner or IT manager, aided by a competent high-technology environmental maintenance service, will be able to reduce the amount of costly downtime and greatly offset the possibility of fire from this cause.

In addition to fire prevention through facility design and maintenance, it is necessary to take other measures to detect and suppress non-preventable fires. Detection systems are required by most states to counter the threat to human life posed by fire. Legal requirements for installing suppression capabilities vary widely, however.

The telltale signs of fire are, of course, heat and smoke. These by-products of fire can substantially damage an area, such as a computer facility or records storage area, that is never touched by flame itself. Heat can destroy CPUs and storage media. Furthermore, heat in the presence of water generates steam that can destroy microfilm and fiche at a substantially lower temperature than heat in the absence of steam. Finally, smoke can render equipment unusable, and corrosive gases can make the facility uninhabitable.

Protective Systems recommends that detectors be placed every 125 square feet in computer and switch rooms, and at least every 900 square feet in user work areas. Heat and smoke detectors are available in a variety of types, shapes, and sizes to alert personnel to hazardous conditions. Some types are:

- Photoelectric detectors, which detect the smoke produced by smoldering fires and fires that involve PVC insulation.
- Ionization detectors, which detect fires involving more flame than smoke.
- Temperature detectors, which detect heat in excess of a preset value.
- Rate of rise heat detectors, which monitor rates of heat increase and do not actuate alarms unless heat increases at a rate exceeding a preset threshold (useful in environments subject to significant ambient temperature changes such as nuclear power generation facilities or heavy manufacturing environments).
- Air sampling detectors, which detect the invisible by-products of materials as they degrade during the pre-combustion stages of fire. According to Vision Systems, detectors that capitalize upon this fact can shorten response times to fire events and even prevent them before combustion occurs (see Figure 3–8). The VESDA air sampling detection system continuously draws samples of room air into a "monitored environment"—a sampling pipe network—with the aid of a high-efficiency aspirator pump. There, the dust particles are filtered out and the sample is exposed to a high-intensity and broad-spectrum light source, such as a laser. The incident light scattered from smoke particles in the air sample passes through a series of optical components to a solid state light receiver, where it is analyzed for signs of pre-combustion. Depending upon smoke levels and the preprogrammed alarm levels, the appropriate output signals are generated and sent to a monitoring station or annunciator (see Figure 3–9).

It is advisable to select, purchase, and position detection devices on the advice of a fire protection official or a knowledgeable fire protection contractor—preferably a certified fire protection engineer with experience in computer room environments. This recommendation cannot be emphasized enough given the

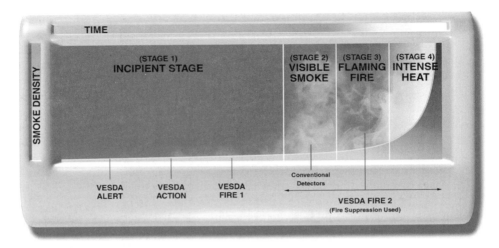

Figure 3–8   The window of opportunity in fire detection. (*Source: Vision Systems—VESDA, Hingham, MA.*)

special environmental characteristics of data centers and switch rooms (air conditioning, air streams, etc.), which can actually impede the effective detection of hazardous conditions.

Once a hazardous condition is detected, the purpose of the detector is to alert on- and/or off-site personnel to the situation. Audible alarms are typically connected to signaling systems. Says Pung, modern detection/suppression systems also typically provide automated functions that may include:

> annunciating the alarm to the building fire alarm system, automatically shutting power down to equipment, activating dampers to block air conditioning airflows so that a clean agent release will reach its optimal concentration. In many cases, the alarm will also turn off security systems so that card keys or digital codes do not need to be entered in order to access the room.[11]

Pung points out that the many functions associated with fire suppression systems require that the DR planner select a qualified contractor to deploy an effective solution.

> The protective systems contractor serves as a general contractor. He should have 5 years minimum in the business, use nationally recognized products, and have a qualified distributor. Beyond that, he needs to be able to manage a mechanical contractor who will install air conditioning dampers, an electrical contractor to power the dampers so that they provide a fail-safe close in the event of a fire, and a security systems contractor who will connect the fire suppression system to the security system.[12]

In addition to the above, the fire suppression system contractor will also need to specify a system that will effectively suppress fire. Knowledge of the new

Figure 3-9   How VESDA® works. (*Source:* Vision Systems—VESDA, Hingham, MA.)

"clean agent" technologies is particularly important (see Figure 3–10 for a simplified system layout diagram). These products are still new in the market and substantial misunderstanding surrounds them, according to Pung and others.

For example, the EPA warns users of FM-200™ that frostbite may occur if a hand or other body part comes into contact with the discharge of the chemical. Similarly, it warns of reduced visibility following a discharge. In general, the use of most clean agents seems fraught with peril, based on EPA caveats and warnings.

In the case of FM-200, says Pung, "no frostbite will occur unless you stick your hand into the discharge, which lasts for about 10 seconds. The reduced visibility results from humidity in the air contacting the chemical and dissipates very quickly as the agent mixes with the air." He adds that FM-200 is at least as "people safe" as Halon and notes that it has been used for years as the propellant in asthma inhalers.[13]

An equipment room fire that breaks out in the presence of a properly installed and tested suppression system, according to NFPA statistics, results in damage costs 53% lower than fires in unprotected areas.[14] This is true whether the system uses clean agents or water.

Obviously, with the distribution of electronic equipment throughout user work areas of a company, including LAN servers, desktop PCs, departmental

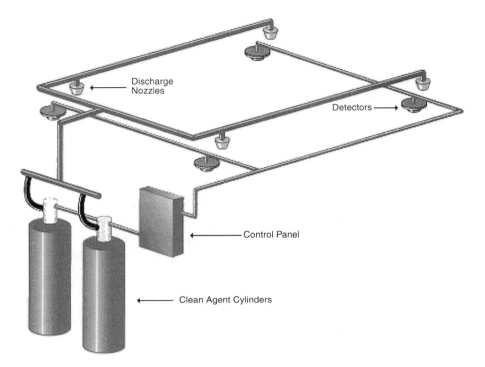

Figure 3-10   A simplified FM-200™ fire suppression system layout.

routers, switches and hubs, and even telecommunications systems, not every device can be adequately protected by clean agents. Sprinkler systems and hand-held extinguishers remain the primary fire suppression mechanism for distributed systems.

Sprinkling does have drawbacks, including the potential damage they cause to electronic gear and the delay to facility reentry associated with their use. This may be perceived as one more argument for re-centralizing servers and communications equipment into the glass house and deploying "thin client" devices on corporate desktops, with no local data storage. Centralization may make sense from a disaster avoidance standpoint (though it is offset to some degree by the advantages accrued to "target dispersal," as discussed in Chapter 6).

POWER PROTECTION

With all of the attention paid by information technology vendors and the trade press to the latest innovations in hardware or software, it may be easy to over-look the fact that virtually all networks and systems are dependent upon a continuous availability of clean electrical power in order to deliver their value. Truth be told, nearly every network, server, or peripheral component is delivered to an end user with at least two cables: one (or more) for integrating the component with the existing information technology infrastructure, and the other for connecting the component to the power infrastructure of the facility.

As a rule, organizations invest significant effort and resources to define and implement a server and networking infrastructure that provides scalability, accessibility, and availability features required to support mission-critical applications. Often, however, the need for intelligent power planning is overlooked.

Except in cases of components with special power conditioning requirements, most IT professionals tend to treat electrical power as a "given"—a utility service whose convenience is defined by the proximity of a power receptacle or multi-outlet power strip on a facility wall, equipment rack, cubicle, or closet to the component that is being installed. This view has its roots in tradition.

In most organizations, the power infrastructure was originally the domain of the facilities manager rather than the technology professional. However, as organizations have become increasingly dependent on their information systems and networks to perform useful work, and increasingly vulnerable to any potential interruption in normal system and network operations, the power infrastructure has become more and more a target of disaster recovery planning.

Perhaps the clearest example of the relationship between the reliability of utility power and system and network availability was provided in California at the beginning of this Millennium. The problem began with a state law passed in 1996, which eliminated price controls on wholesale power (the cost to utility companies to purchase supplies from power producers), while setting caps on what utilities could charge their customers.

The legislation was intended to encourage competition among power utilities, promote the use of alternative energy sources, and reduce the electricity bills paid by California consumers. Legislators did not anticipate, however, the increased demand for electricity that accompanied the Internet Revolution, or the reduction in supplies of power resulting both from the decommissioning of nuclear power plants and the drought that effected hydroelectric supplies from producers in the Pacific Northwest in late 1999 and early 2000.

In spring 2000, the problems began to show. Utility companies found themselves unable to purchase—profitably—sufficient power from producers to meet the needs of power consumers, whose requirements had grown three times faster than projected by legislators in 1996. A blackout warning for the San Francisco Bay Area was issued in summer 2000 when wholesale prices for electricity climbed to $522.55 per megawatt hour, a more than ten-fold increase over 1999 rates of $49.56 per megawatt hour.

The blackout warning was the first in a string of emergencies that reached a crescendo in spring 2001. As the situation worsened, organizations located in California became familiar with the procedures observed by utility companies to address discrepancies in supply and demand. The California Independent System

Operator (Cal-ISO), responsible for managing electrical power supplies for most of the state, issues warnings in response to a range of conditions including

- *Emergency Stage 1:* Occurs when power reserves in the day-ahead market are forecasted at less than 7%. Consumers are urged to reduce usage of power voluntarily to avoid a widespread emergency.
- *Emergency Stage 2:* Occurs when reserves are less than 5%. Customers who have agreed to go off-line in a crisis are required to do so.
- *Emergency Stage 3:* When reserves reach the 1.5% threshold, rotating outage plans are activated until the emergency is passed. These rolling blackouts, usually about an hour in duration, affect closely defined groups of customers sharing specific utility company circuits. Efforts are made by utilities to ensure that outages are shared evenly so that one group does not carry the entire load. Exemptions are available where public health, safety, or security concerns exist.

The direct impact of rolling blackouts was felt by more than two-thirds of the 192 members of the Silicon Valley Manufacturing Group[15], who collectively provide more than 250,000 jobs. Responding to a survey, member companies reported that the average blackout

- Lasted approximately 90 minutes
- Idled more than 100,000 workers
- Created immediate financial losses in the tens of millions of dollars

The organization also contested the representation of high technology companies as resource hogs responsible for the power shortfall. While Internet-facing data centers built in the area did add to the local demand, the increase was proportionately much lower than the increased consumer demand in a market that saw explosive population growth in the late 1990s.

Beyond California: Capacity and Transmission Issues Loom

While a considerable debate rages over the likelihood of a recurrence of the California experience elsewhere in the United States, especially given the unique set of circumstances that contributed to the energy problems in that state, industry watchers are projecting a potential crisis in terms of capacity and demand to appear by the middle of this decade.

As shown in Figure 3–11, US electrical energy demand is expected to grow from just above 700 MWh in 2001 to as high as 920 MWh in 2009, according to the North American Electric Reliability Council (NERC)[16], if trends persist. Capacities will become insufficient to meet demand as early as Summer 2006, NERC projects, if aggressive federal and commercial capacity supplements are not brought on line.

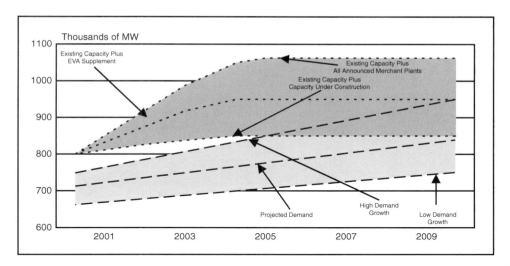

Figure 3–11 US capacity vs. demand—summer. (*Source:* North American Electric Reliability Council (NERC), Princeton, NJ, http://www. nerc.com.)

In addition to potential capacity shortfalls, the US also confronts a mounting problem with power transmission—that is, the means by which generated power is supplied to end-users. Most people believe that the power they use originates at a local utility generation facility. In point of fact, power may originate almost anywhere, in any region of the country. There is an active program in the United States for sharing energy production capacity that envisions production and transmission as a set of three loosely interlocking grids, as depicted in Figure 3–12.

The US power grid has been called the largest machine ever built by man. In actuality however, it comprises, not one, but three systems: one in Texas, and two others whose lines of demarcation follow roughly the Continental Divide. Some interconnection occurs between the three systems, but the grid itself is far from orderly.

Each system comprises a tangle of transmission lines operated by a set of owners ranging from federal power authorities to regulated utilities to utility industry conglomerates. Regulation of each grid involves a hodgepodge of state agencies and departments, and they decide how much power can enter and leave the grids and how much power can flow over each set of lines within the systems themselves.

The grid is designed for simple operation, owing to its origins in the days of electrical monopolies. It was developed by large regional power producers to meet the requirements of their primary customers—and no one else. However,

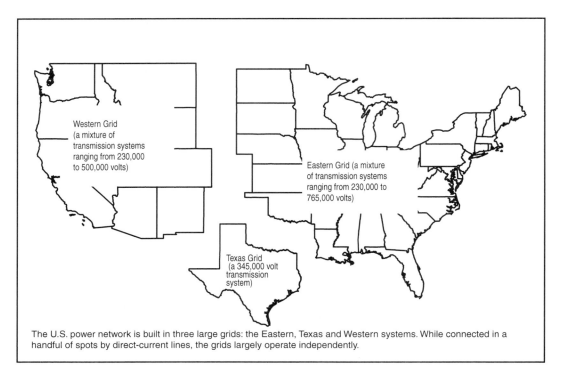

The U.S. power network is built in three large grids: the Eastern, Texas and Western systems. While connected in a handful of spots by direct-current lines, the grids largely operate independently.

Figure 3–12   Three primary power grids.

deregulation in the 1990s opened the door to newcomers with different objectives and differing construction roadmaps.

Buildouts no longer follow a "grand scheme" and power generation capabilities are no longer located where they can be readily served by transmission lines for efficient sharing. One analyst has described the situation succinctly, "The United States is a superpower, but it has the grid of a Third World country."

Since 1996, public- and private-sector organizations have announced far-reaching plans to increase the amount of available electricity by building new generation facilities. However, utilities are investing next to nothing to build additional transmission lines to deliver the energy to where it's needed. The major reason is that deregulation has caused most power companies to decouple their transmission business from their lucrative power plant operations. That little money is made from the maintenance and buildout of the transmission network, especially given concerns about the electromagnetic radiation potential of high-voltage power lines, explains why the Department of Energy anticipates only a modest increase (4.2%) in high-voltage transmission facilities over the next decade, but a 20% increase in power generation capacity in the same period. In the minds of many observers, it is the recipe for many disasters to come.

The situation is under study currently within the US Department of Energy and Congress, and numerous suggestions are being put forth to ease the transition to a "shared cost transmission system." However, until a solution is found, the potential for a utility service interruption is high through the end of this decade. What's more, the locations that experience blackouts may not be to blame for the overtaxing of supply: given the nature of the grid, demand generated in on geographic area can overtax supplies in another area.

In addition to its systemic problems, utility power can also be affected by problems in the local generation and transmission system. Figure 3–13 provides a simplified depiction of how power moves from the generation facility to business offices. The design of specific systems can be quite complex, but fundamentally all utility power systems are identical.

The earliest utility power systems were based on direct current (DC), but alternating current (AC) systems eventually predominated because AC systems permitted voltages to be stepped up and down using simple transformers. Step-up transformers at utility power plants increase the voltage for transmission over long distances. Then, nearer the delivery points, utility substations use step-down transformers to bring voltages down for distribution to business and residential communities. Finally, transformers on utility poles step the power down again before it enters most customer facilities.

This process minimizes energy loss in power distribution, which is caused by the resistance of "conductors"—the cables used to conduct power from point A to point B. Without transformers, utilities would need to force large currents (measured in amperes, or amps) through the resistance created by conductors, producing high power losses. Since increasing voltage in AC power decreases amperage, by stepping up the voltage in long distance transmission lines, utilities are able to minimize the current, and thereby minimize transmission losses.

This complex system of interconnected power generation, transmission, and transformation systems has its own risks and vulnerabilities, of course. A brief survey of recent event underscores this point.

- December 8, 1998: A major power outage, resulting from a voltage problem at a power substation in PG&E Corporation's San Mateo County facility, halted trading at the Pacific Stock Exchange, dimmed lights on the Golden Gate Bridge, cut power to 360,000 customers, and caused traffic chaos during a Tuesday morning rush hour. San Francisco International Airport stopped operations temporarily because computers were down. The city's bus system (electrical) was stopped. And, an untold number of persons were trapped in elevators in at least 50 high-rise buildings.
- October 8, 2000: A fire at an electrical substation in Chicago, IL sparked a power outage that affected a 2-mile by 3-mile section of downtown, according to Commonwealth Edison for 10 hours. Approximately 10,000 cus-

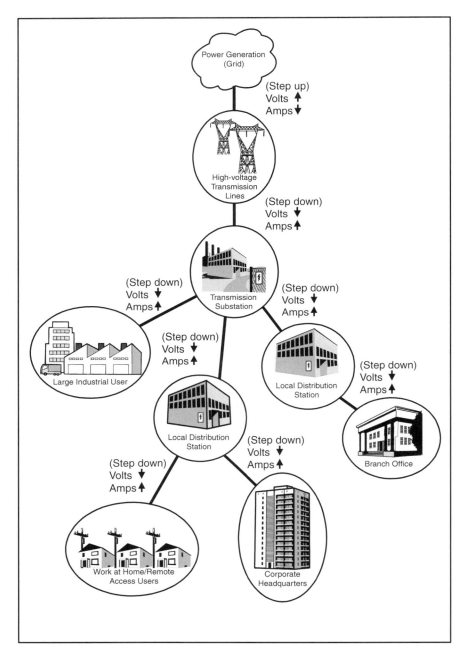

Figure 3-13   Power generation and transmission systems.

tomers, including a shopping mall and two television stations, were impacted. The temperature, a brisk 45° Fahrenheit, forced some evacuations of residences. According to a Department of Energy Power Outage Study Team report, the event was the result of several causes, including the inflexibility of the transmission network and the inadequacy component maintenance procedures, which increased the severity of the incident.

- May 8, 2001: As rising temperatures and increased power consumption threatened a Stage 3 Warning in California, no one expected an underground explosion that cut a PG&E power line, cutting power to web hosting company, Exodus Communications, Inc. Adding to problems was the fact that the backup generators installed by the company to continue operations in the event of an outage failed to kick in. Of the many companies hosted at the Exodus data center, one in particular—Yahoo!—was taken off-line by the incident from 4:45 PM until late in the evening. In addition to several millions of dollars in lost advertising revenues, the incident also exposed Yahoo! Instant Messenger service to increased criticism by foes AOL and Microsoft on the basis of reliability.

- September 11, 2001: Two Con Edison substations at 7 World Trade Center were consumed by fire following the terrorist attack on the World Trade Center and the subsequent collapse of the twin towers. A third substation was cut off from the power transmission system. As a result, all of lower Manhattan—some 12,000 customers, including most firms located in the financial district—was without power for the next 6 days. Through September 17, 1,900 Con Edison workers labored around the clock to run more than 26 miles of high-voltage cables and to isolate the damaged cables buried beneath debris-clogged streets. Partial power was restored to 1,800 customers on September 18, with the request that customers limit their use of power to avoid overtaxing the makeshift transmission system. Customers were also cautioned about the use of temporary generators that were providing power to some buildings. "In some cases," according to a Con Ed news release, "the generator cannot handle the entire building load, so building personnel have disconnected electrical service to some of their tenants." The electric company advised customers not to attempt to hook up generators themselves, but to call a licensed electrician. Also damaged were telephone lines to Con Ed itself. The company was forced to arrange for additional lines and to ask customers to use the lines for emergencies only, and not for billing or customer-service inquiries.

This sampling suggests that power-related outage events can result from a variety of sources that are outside the boundaries of the DR planner's own operational facility. In fact, a substantial number of temporary power outage and power quality events impact organizations annually as a result of natural events such as thunderstorms, which can create sudden and damaging changes in the voltage patterns of electricity conducted through the internal electrical distribution system (as well as other cabling infrastructures such as phone lines, cable television, and data communications networks). Additional external power problems are linked to

- Provider equipment failure.
- Vehicular accidents that impact transmission facilities.
- Environmental factors (wind, ice, flooding, etc.) that impact transmission facilities.
- Line cuts and other accidents (the dreaded back-hoe).
- Actions of utility companies (maintenance and alert-related outages).
- Collateral impact of incidents that occur at neighboring businesses.

Figure 3–14, drawn from National Weather Service data, illustrates the number of days per year, on average, that various parts of North America are impacted by thunderstorms. As the illustration shows, those seeking to eliminate all of the potential natural causes of power interruption events need to understand that there is, literally, nowhere to hide.

The good news is that, with intelligent power planning, and the selection and deployment of appropriate power conditioning and continuity technologies, DR coordinators can insulate their organizations from most power-related interruptions. Industry experts argue that developing, deploying, and managing a comprehensive conditioned power infrastructure can avoid up to 95% of power-related downtime. All it takes is some common sense, a bit of power savvy, and the selection of best-of-breed components to create a digital friendly power infrastructure for your environment.

Developing a Protected Power Architecture

To develop a power-related disaster avoidance capability, DR planners need to develop an understanding of power itself: How it is generated and transmitted to organizational facilities, and what happens to it once it enters the facility itself. The next step is to look for likely causes of power interruptions so that steps can be taken to prevent them altogether or to minimize their consequences if they can't be prevented.

Within the electrical utility industry, power providers often make the claim that 80% of power interruptions and power quality problems result from causes located inside the customer's own facility; only 20% of problems are the result of causes located in the utility service itself. While these statistics may strike some California-based energy consumers as rather self-serving—especially given the energy crisis confronting that state and the frequency of utility-initiated blackouts—the truth is that, for most other areas of the United States, the proportions are fairly accurate.

Most types of power quality problems and many types of interruptions (see Table 3–2) are caused by the internal electrical distribution system of a facility.

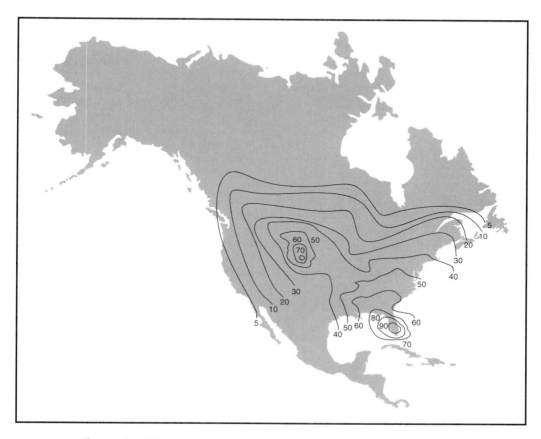

Figure 3–14   Thunderstorm frequency: average number of days per
year. (*Source:* National Oceanic and Atmospheric Administration Data.)

Many problems have to do with the number and types of devices that share internal facility electrical wiring, and how they interact with each other. For example,

- Starting and stopping equipment (i.e., motors, heating and cooling equipment, refrigerators, and elevators) can cause voltage surges or transients
  that destroy sensitive electronic circuit boards, degrade electrical insulation,
  cause unplanned server shutdowns or lock-ups, and damage computer or
  network equipment.
- Improper wiring or grounding can create voltage sags and swells that can
  result in data errors, memory loss, equipment shutdown, and power supply
  failures over time.

Table 3–2 Power Problems and their Causes

Power Problem (with wave form)	Description	Cause	Damage Potential
1 **Power** **Failure**	A total loss of utility power	Can be caused by a number of events: lightning strikes, downed power lines, grid over demands, accidents and natural disasters	Loss of data protracted denial of IT services to organization.
2 **Power** **Sag**	Short term low voltage	Triggered by the startup of large loads, utility switching, utility equipment failure, lighting and power service that's too small for the demand.	In addition to crashes, sags can damage hardware.
3 **Power** **Surge**	Short term high voltage	With voltages above 110% of nominal, surges can be triggered by a rapid reproduction in power loads, heavy equipment being turned off, or by utility switching	Can potentially damage hardware.
4 **Brownout**	Reduced line voltage for extended periods of a few minutes to a few days	Can be caused by an intentional utility voltage reduction to conserve power during peak demand periods or other heavy loads that exceed supply capacity.	See power sag.
5 **Electrical** **Line Noise**	High frequency waveform that piggybacks on the line waveform	Can be caused by either RFI or EMI interference generated by transmitters, welding devices, SCR driven printers, lightning etc.	Can cause data loss, interference with data communications and networks, processing errors, equipment lock-ups, and audio/video interference.
6 **High** **Voltage** **Spike**	Instant and dramatic increase in line voltage	Can be caused by lightning strike and can send line voltages to levels in excess of 6,000 volts.	A spike almost always results in data loss or hardware damage.

Table 3–2 Power Problems and their Causes

Power Problem (with wave form)	Description	Cause	Damage Potential
7 Frequency Variation	A change in frequency stability	Resulting from generator or small co-generation sites being loaded and unloaded.	Frequency variation can cause erratic operation, data loss, system crashes, and equipment damage.
8 Switching Transients	Instantaneous high voltage increase	Normal duration is shorter than a spike and generally fails in the range of nanoseconds.	Can cause processing errors, computer lockup, burned circuit boards, degradation of electrical insulation, or equipment damage.
9 Harmonic Distortion	Distortion of the normal waveform generally transmitted by nonlinear loads	Switched mode power supplies, variable speed motors and drives, copiers and fax machines are examples of nonlinear loads.	Can cause communication errors, overheating, and hardware damage.

Source: Various, IEEE E-050R adn FIPS PUB 94.

- Overloaded circuits can lead to power interruptions and, in some cases, fires.
- Improper grounding and the operation of certain types of equipment can also generate harmonics or line noise—that is, the distortion of normal voltage patterns—that can play havoc with data storage, data communications, and voice telephony.

Table 3–2 describes nine types of common power problems and provides the electrical "wave form" that might be associated with each problem type. A wave form is a graphical representation of AC power, which normally produces a "perfect" sine wave (or sideways "S" form) on an oscilloscope screen or other monitoring instrument if no trouble is present. Seeing wave forms requires the use of such monitoring instruments, which may be used as part of a power quality assessment procedure.

Power quality assessments are performed to aid in identifying power problems before they can create downtime. The steps involved are straightforward:

- First, define the characteristics of the "load" (the devices that use electricity are collectively referred to as the load), then assess the current power distribution system (the mechanisms used to distribute power in order to support the load) and identify risks/vulnerabilities.
- Next, review and optimize the design of the internal power distribution system to deliver improved availability and quality.
- Finally, implement the improved design using best-of-breed power conditioning and power availability components. Test and validate the optimized design, and manage change over time.

Often, as DR planners collect information on their existing utility service and internal electrical distribution systems, they will notice obvious risk potentials as well as telltale signs of other burgeoning problems. Specifically, be on the lookout for

- "Daisy chains" of electrical cords and power strips that indicate circuit overloading.
- Outlet covers with obvious charring that may signal a past short circuit or overload.
- Computer monitors with noticeable movement in the display tube and/or hums or other distortions in audio devices such as desktop speakers or phone handsets.
- Lights dimming on and off.
- Logs of data communications errors.
- Records of abnormal (or frequent) component failure and replacement cycles.
- User reports of any abnormal equipment operations.

To aid in localizing possible power-related problems, the planner may want to engage a qualified electrical contractor to provide power quality assessment services. Some utility companies provide this service for a nominal fee, but the comprehensiveness of tests varies. A skilled electrical contractor specialized in power quality assessment may provide a clearer view of the health of the electrical distribution system of the facility.

If an electrical contractor is engaged to perform a power quality assessment, the DR coordinator should expect several basic services. For one, the contractor should document the characteristics of the "load" (devices that consume power) that is being placed on the circuits comprising the internal power distribution system. Ensure that a copy of this inventory-by-circuit is obtained for future reference before the contractor leaves the facility.

Load characteristics determine, in part, the adequacy of the existing power system. In most environments, the load is distributed over several transmission circuits to prevent an overload on any single circuit.

To calculate the load on a given circuit, a technician needs to identify all devices connected to that circuit and add together the wattage requirement for each powered component. An exception to this rule is a device that uses an electrical motor. (See Table 3–3) Some electrical motors require up to three times their running wattage to start up, which explains why the startup of an air conditioner or other motorized device may cause a sudden dimming of lights or other devices on the same circuit. Ideally, motorized devices are placed on their own circuits, separate from non-motorized devices.

One point that should be made here is that many office equipment, computing and networking devices often do not express their operating power requirements in terms of watts on their nameplates. Often vendors use amps and volts to describe power consumption characteristics. To calculate watts, just multiply amps by volts. In the case of electrical engines, you need to multiply the resulting number by three to obtain a startup wattage requirement.

It should be further noted that these load calculations, while they are adequate for determining the size of the load on existing circuits and for projecting future load handling requirements of the infrastructure, are not sufficient for specifying the capacities of power protection components such as uninterruptible power supplies (UPS) or backup generators. Sizing requirements for these devices will be discussed in greater detail later.

Once the load on each facility transmission circuit has been calculated, the electrician should compare the load totals to the load capacity ratings of each circuit. This will help to identify overloaded circuits and to provide insights about changes that may be required to the existing electrical transmission system.

Table 3–3   Electrical Motor Load Estimation

	Electrical Motors: Approximate Starting Watts*				
Motor HP Rating	**Approximate Running Watts**	**Universal Motors (small appliance)**	**Repulsion Induction Motors**	**Capacitor Motors**	**Split-Phase Motors**
1/8	275	400	600	850	1200
1/4	400	500	850	1050	1700
1/3	450	600	975	1350	1950
1/2	600	750	1300	1800	2600
3/4	850	1000	1900	2600	x
1	1000	1250	2300	3000	x
1–1/2	1600	1750	3200	4200	x
2	2000	2350	3900	5100	x
3	3000	x	5200	6800	x

* Always use starting watts, not running watts, when figuring correct electrical load.

x Motors of higher horsepower are not generally used.

With load characteristics defined, a circuit testing procedure is often undertaken in which the technician validates wiring integrity and measures voltages in wires and at switches and outlets to detect any short circuits or over-voltage conditions that may exist. The next step is to deploy disturbance analyzers, which are connected to receptacles in the facility in order to monitor electrical wave forms over a period of time. Some types of disturbance analyzers are also capable of monitoring current so that low-level harmonic characteristics of power can be discerned and charted.

Once data has been captured, it needs to be analyzed carefully to discern trends, patterns and correlations that 1) identify any specific and recurring problems, and 2) suggest possible causes for the problems so they can be rectified. Improved software analysis tools can be leveraged to generate actionable information from the data, but even these tools require some experience on the part of the user for proper interpretation.

The truth is that quality assessment is not an exact science, and data often points to a number of potential causes rather than one specific cause to explain any event. That is because problems within the organization's electrical transmission system may originate virtually anywhere in the grander power generation and transmission network. A more experienced hand can often winnow out the less likely explanations.

On the other hand, a quality assessment may turn up no significant issues whatsoever, and will instead provide confidence that the organization has a well-structured electrical transmission system on which to build power safeguards. To determine what safeguards are appropriate, the load supported by the power system needs to be evaluated.

With the current electrical transmission system and current load documented, some immediate opportunities for optimization may present themselves. Adding circuits to address overloads, shifting certain devices to alternate circuits to minimize noise, and similar strategies may help to accomplish the first objective of power protection: prevent avoidable power-related interruptions. Experts claim that comparatively simple adjustments and modifications to the existing power transmission infrastructure can help to eliminate up to 95% of power-related downtime exposures.

Redundancy vs. Replacement

In addition to preventive measures, however, a variety of other options are available to mitigate the consequences of power-related problems that cannot be eliminated and to all but eliminate power outages. Most of these options fall into one of two categories: redundancy and replacement.

Redundancy options are those that duplicate key electrical transmission system operational features in order to provide a backup capability should the primary capability fail. Some organizations, for example, obtain power from two separate power substations. Each substation delivers power to the facility via a separate transmission cable terminating at a separate service entry point in the building. This configuration, as illustrated in Figure 3–15 adds several redundancies to mitigate the possibility of a utility power failure.

- Separate substations (or separate transformers at the same substation that are located on separate local "grids") provide power, so a fire or equipment failure at one substation (or a utility company-imposed "rolling blackout") will not deny utility power to the organization.
- Power traverses different transmission cables, thereby avoiding the possibility of an accidental cable cut that renders the facility without power.

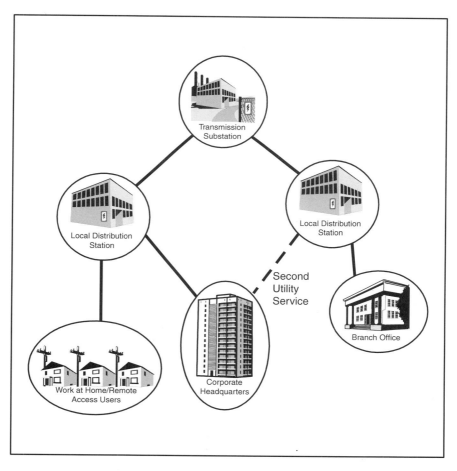

Figure 3–15   Redundant utility services.

- Separate service entry points provide the capability to access power from one entry point even if facility damage (from a fire or flood, for example) renders the other service entry point unusable.

Replacement options are used to shore up exposures that cannot be addressed through redundancy. For some organizations, for example, the option of developing a failover capability using two (or more) utility services may be too costly or simply unavailable. For organizations that cannot afford to be without power for any length of time, the only option is self-generation.

Self-generation, the provisioning of local generators, their fuel, and necessary switching equipment to handle the organization's equipment load if utility power is discontinued, is quite possibly the most expensive replacement strategy in power protection. However, in some locations, including energy-poor areas of California, government subsidies and incentives are being provided to help organizations live "off-grid"—particularly, if they invest in "clean" power generation, such as microturbines, small gas turbines, wind turbines, photovoltaics, fuel cells, and certain varieties of internal combustion engines, which are installed on the customer's side of the utility meter to provide electricity for a part or all of customer's electric load.

In the United States, the Department of Energy's Distributed Power Program is tasked with facilitating self-generation programs by conducting strategic research on advanced hardware and software for integrating distributed generation, storage technologies and load controls within the existing electric system and for interfacing distributed resources with power systems. The DOE program is also responsible for addressing safety, reliability, power quality, interconnection and environmental issues related to the integration of distribution generation and storage into a power system and for working with industry and state and local government organizations to eliminate unnecessary barriers to distributed power created by current policies, regulations and business practices.

The Distributed Power Program web site[17] notes several success stories, including the following:

- A bank in Omaha installed a fuel cell generation system to avoid power disturbances that were shutting down its computer systems—the bank was able to purchase an on-site generation system for about the cost of a 1-hour outage.
- A large grocery store chain operating in the Northeast estimates that an on-site generation system at a Portland, ME, store saves $50,000 to $80,000 every day during a power outage when the store can remain open and the competition closes.
- A fast-food restaurant in Chicago, Illinois gets most of its electricity from a natural gas-fired microturbine, cutting $1,500 off its monthly power bill while improving power reliability.

- A police station in New York's Central Park recently bought a fuel cell to run its electronic crime-fighting equipment, saving $200,000 over the cost of a line upgrade.

However, the organization is also quick to point out the hurdles that confront self-generation initiatives.

- Interconnection with the grid: Current technical interconnection requirements for distributed generation may differ from utility to utility and state to state. Customers attempting to install these technologies may also be required to pay for pre-interconnection engineering studies, which can add significant cost to the system. The typical lack of a single utility point of contact or defined process for distributed generation interconnection matters, and the absence of simple standardized applications and agreements serves to delay and discourage customer-owned projects.
- Utility pricing practices and tariff structures: Current utility use tariffs and rate design as a rule do not price distribution services to account for system benefits that could be provided by distributed generation. More appropriately designed tariffs can provide for standby and backup power services without incurring prohibitive charges. Standby services include power to supplement or replace a customer's on-site generation. Backup services include power supplied to a customer during an unscheduled or emergency outage of his on-site generation.
- Siting, permitting and environmental regulation: Zoning, air permitting, water use permits, comprehensive environmental plan approval, and other regulatory processes can both delay and increase the costs of distributed power projects. These issues typically relate to site-specific concerns. In general, distributed power technologies are not covered in national building, electrical, and safety codes. Local code and zoning officials are typically not familiar with these technologies. Environmental regulations are not currently administered in a way that gives credit for the overall pollution reduction effects of high efficiency distributed power technologies such as combined heat and power systems.
- Current business models and practices: Existing business practice and business models often reflect the old regulated electricity industry dominated by vertically integrated utilities and central station power plants. New business models are needed to capture the values of non-utility owned distributed power in delaying or avoiding transmission and distribution system upgrades, the use of distributed power for ancillary services and for improving system reliability, power quality and reducing line losses. New competitive business models need to be developed that will allow the realization of full economic value of distributed power in competitive markets.

As suggested by this list of barriers, planners may need to dedicate a significant amount of time and resources to identify a suitable self-generation option and to develop a plan for its implementation. Depending on several factors, including the size of the power plant, requirements for its fueling, and health, environmental and safety issues, DR planners may require the participation of government, technical and commercial entities in their planning efforts.

Of course, replacement of utility power through self-generation is the most extreme solution to the problem of protracted utility power outages. Other solutions, including redundant supplies from two or more substations, and more conventional battery-with-diesel-fueled standby generators may be easier to deploy and potentially less costly. All approaches, however, have their limitations.

Using the redundant substation option, for example, avoids only some downtime risks. If power is supplied through redundant transmission lines, the possibility of both being unearthed and cut by a backhoe (or two poles on opposite sides of the facility being hit by an automobile) is dramatically reduced. On the other hand, if both substations are in the same section of a region's local electrical grid, and rolling blackouts are ordered, chances are that both supplies will be cut off.

Moreover, natural disasters such as hurricanes, earthquakes or floods that are regional in scope may also cause the interruption of supplies from both sources of supply, and planners should be aware that most utilities, on the guidance of local government, restore power in a particular order: grids that support government and emergency services are restored first, then grids supporting healthcare, then financial institutions, then everyone else. Unless the planner's facility happens to be collocated to a facility containing a high-priority power restoral target, chances are that power will be restored whenever the proverbial number is called.

The self-generation option also carries with it certain vulnerabilities. While batteries (technically, uninterruptible power supplies, or UPS) and diesel generators have been the solutions of choice in the power protection field since the 1930s and came into great vogue with the advent of corporate computing in the 1960s, drawbacks of this strategy continue to be linked to the need to provide a facility to house the components, and to periodically test and maintain their operation to ensure proper function in an emergency. Concerns have also been raised about the ability to scale battery and generator capabilities to maintain their adequacy in handling critical load requirements. Moreover, the destructive potential of certain types of disasters, such as earthquakes, floods or hurricanes, introduce potential inefficacies into the use of this strategy. For instance, if roads are impassable, obtaining supplies of generator fuel may be difficult. Additionally, if facilities housing battery systems and generators become structurally compromised, they may not be able to be operated safely.

Ideally, planners should seek a solution for power protection that considers all objections, as well as practical constraints such as budget, to provide the organization with protection against the loss of utility power.

Beyond Utility Power Replacement: Power Quality Assurance

In addition to planning to prevent wholesale interruptions in the supply of utility power to the organization's facilities, planners also need to concern themselves with short duration power outages that may result from both external and internal causes, and also with the problem of power quality and its impact on equipment operation. The more that planners can do to prevent these power events from disrupting normal operations, the greater their contribution will be toward the goal of optimizing uptime.

There are as many different electrical distribution systems as there are facilities. Past efforts to create a generic model of an electrical infrastructure that would cover all installations have been largely unsuccessful. Yet, such a model would be very useful for analyzing vulnerabilities and creating high-level best practices for the planner to follow when developing a power protection strategy.

One model that described many organizations was originally advanced by Ken Brill, the author of several books on "uptime management science" in the 1980s.[18] According to Brill, nearly every organization with a data center has eleven power-related subsystems. These include lightning protection, building switch gear and utility service entry, critical power buses, air conditioning, frequency conversion equipment, UPS, UPS batteries, emergency generators, offline testing, computer room power distribution, and grounding. Brill used this model to test the capabilities of his clients to withstand power-related disasters, noting that the entire eleven-subsystem chain was only as resilient as its weakest link.

In the 1990s, with the advent of distributed client-server computing and enterprise networking, Brill's model was largely dismissed as increasingly irrelevant. Computing was no longer limited to the glass house of the data center, but had moved out into the department and workgroup environment. Power protection needed to be distributed as well.

The argument has merit, but several things prevent the simple dismissal of Brill's model. For one, in many organizations, computing is being returned to a centralized IT environment through a process called re-centralization. Even data storage is being recentralized by many organizations as a response to unprecedented data growth and the desire to make storage less costly by making it more manageable. As a result of these trends, many of the old concepts of data center management are coming back into vogue.

However, even with recentralization, many organizations continue to place important IT assets—in the form of PCs and workstations—on the distributed desktops of end users. Even those organizations that have adopted a "thin desktop model"—which entails the centralized hosting of applications with end user access provided via web browser-equipped terminal devices—distribute application services via mission-critical networks. The key components of these networks—switches, routers, and hubs—are themselves sensitive microprocessor- based devices and may be distributed throughout an organization's infrastructure.

Thus, in many organizations, the distributed nature of the equipment load that must be supplied with dependable and clean power argues against a strategy that focuses solely on a centralized UPS and power conditioning equipment set up to serve only a data center. Power protection is required throughout the organization.

An effective design for a power protection capability must address two objectives. First, it must provide a centralized architecture: one that enables the centralized management of both centralized and distributed power protection and power quality management components. Second, it must be flexible: enabling power protection and power quality assurance components to be installed where they can deliver the best value—whether that is at the desktop, in the network wiring closet, or in the data center.

Achieving the first goal requires some sort of network-based management capability. Traditionally, most power quality and power protection components were "stand-alone" devices. They could only be configured and monitored for status using faceplate controls or test switches on the equipment itself. This resulted in a fairly high total cost of ownership for the devices. That is, in addition to the cost to acquire the products and to deploy them, organizations also had to underwrite the often hidden costs for personnel to manage and maintain the devices wherever they were installed. For a large organization, technical support personnel might spend a considerable amount of time traveling from device to device to rectify error conditions or to check device status.

Recently, vendors of best-of-breed power protection and power conditioning components have begun enabling the devices to communicate either directly with the servers or PCs that they protect, or to a central management system via a network interface. Direct connect solutions often leverage a serial cable interface, or interfaces and cables based on the increasingly popular IEEE-1934 "Firewire" or Universal Serial Bus (USB) standards.

Network-based power protection management and monitoring is the ultimate expression of a centralized architecture. Using a protocol such as the Simple Network Management Protocol (SNMP), which has been adopted by the Internet Engineering Task Force (IETF) as a protocol standard for device management across a TCP/IP network, it is increasingly possible to receive alerts from distributed power protection devices regarding either their own operation or functions triggered by power problems.

SNMP-enabled power protection devices communicate their status and configuration via management information bases (MIBs). MIBs are small databases updated on a regular basis by the devices themselves. An SNMP management program periodically "polls" the MIBs (that is, reads their contents) and reports events to a centralized management console. In this way, literally hundreds of devices can be monitored from a single console (or from a web page).

For devices that don't support SNMP, a proxy agent may be used to translate data between the device and the network. This capability is valuable when power protection devices themselves lack any memory or microprocessing features.

In a growing number of cases, a power protection device offers a way for the remote administrator to interact directly with the device via the network. That is to say, the administrator can use the configuration software or toolset provided with the device remotely by issuing control commands from his or her console. This capability dramatically reduces cost of ownership for the power protection devices because it alleviates considerable administration and support costs.

Centralized architecture enables more devices to be managed by fewer administrative hands, plus it enables power protection devices to be deployed flexibly, in whatever manner makes sense for an organization's computing and networking infrastructure. Many best-of-breed vendors have begun to develop different categories of products to meet different needs.

APC Corporation, for example, offers its "Silicon" family of UPS products to support a large project or data center environment, plus it offers "Symmetra Power Arrays" to support zone-based power protection strategies and "Smart-UPS" products to support, depending on the model, everything from individual components and PCs up to a single rack of equipment.

Similarly, Powerware offers a line of products, described according to number of common power problems addressed by each product. Series 3 provides protection that makes it best suited to support an individual component or PC, according to the vendor. Series 5 units are appropriate for small to large networks, depending on the model. And, Series 9 units are recommended for mission-critical applications like server farms and hospital systems.

In the final analysis, the power protection capability designed by the DR coordinator should be driven, first and foremost, by a careful consideration of the unique characteristics of the facility electrical distribution system, the utility service, and the equipment load. The design should also factor in the budget available for power protection and the cost of ownership advantages of distributed protection with centralized management.

Building Blocks of Power Protection

Once the requirements for power protection and power quality are understood, and a strategy has been settled upon for power redundancy or replacement, planners need to turn their attention to acquiring the right components with which to build the power protection capability. As indicated above, one component that is often selected is a UPS.

As its name implies, an uninterruptible power supply (UPS) affords protection against both momentary and prolonged power outages. As previously mentioned, a UPS is a dual-value technology. It provides a hedge against disastrous data loss by supplying backup power for a sufficient amount of time to perform an organized shutdown of systems and other equipment. Additionally, a power conditioning UPS (a line interactive or on-line unit, see below) reduces the daily, power-related wear and tear on connected hardware and prolongs the useful life of hardware. Given this value proposition, planners often report that their recommendation to acquire UPS protection for key systems results in quick approval from senior management.

What is a UPS? Basically, it is an interface between critical electronic devices in a company and the local power company. Rich Feldhaus, a product specialist with Chicago, IL–based UPS maker, TrippLite, explains that there are three types of UPS systems. As shown in Figure 3–16, the first type is an off-line system.

Feldhaus explains that vendors prefer to use the term stand-by, mainly because of the negative connotations of the term "off-line." (Why would anyone want to buy something that is off-line—that is, not used?) Semantics and political correctness aside, this type of UPS is among the most popular for use with desktop and server systems—mainly because of its power protection capabilities and low price.

Stand-by UPS systems are characterized as such because they remain outside of the path between the utility and the load in normal operation. A trickle charger draws some current from the utility source in order to maintain batteries at full power. That way, if utility power is interrupted, the load can be switched automatically to UPS battery power.

A few years ago, Feldhaus says, the time required to switch the load—called the UPS transfer time—was a concern. If a stand-by UPS did not switch quickly enough to meet the needs of the connected load, a failure would occur in the connected device(s). Says Feldhaus, "The current state of the switching power supply has made transfer time a non-issue."[19]

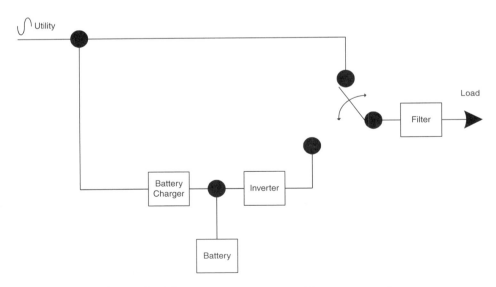

Figure 3–16   Stand-by uninterruptible power supply.

Today's switching power supplies make servers and desktop systems much more resilient. They can wait 30 to 200 milliseconds for load transfer to occur before failing. Most UPS systems today can switch loads in a much shorter amount of time: 2 to 4 milliseconds on average for a 2 kVA UPS, 4 to 6 milliseconds for a 5 kVA system.

The shortened transfer time is also a characteristic of the second type of UPS system: the line-interactive UPS. According to Feldhaus, line interactive UPS systems are a "hybrid line conditioner and stand-by UPS." As shown in Figure 3–17, the difference is that the UPS system unit filters the power supplied by the utility, even while the UPS itself is in stand-by mode.

Filtering circuitry conditions the power supplied to the load to remove electrical noise and to smooth surges and spikes. Additionally, this design provides low-grade voltage regulation by supplementing utility power with battery power if brownouts occur. Some experts claim that the price paid for this type of protection is shorter battery life in the line-interactive UPS than in either the stand-by or on-line UPS shown in Figure 3–18.[20]

With an on-line UPS, the UPS inverter and batteries are continuously used to deliver conditioned power to the load, effectively isolating the connected equipment completely from the vicissitudes of utility power. In operation, a rectifier circuit converts utility AC power into DC power, both to charge the UPS storage batteries and to supply the UPS inverter. The inverter converts DC power

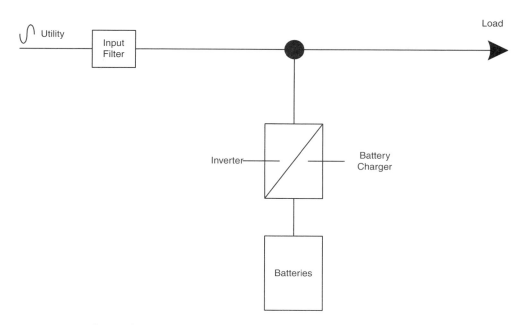

Figure 3–17   The line-interactive uninterruptible power supply.

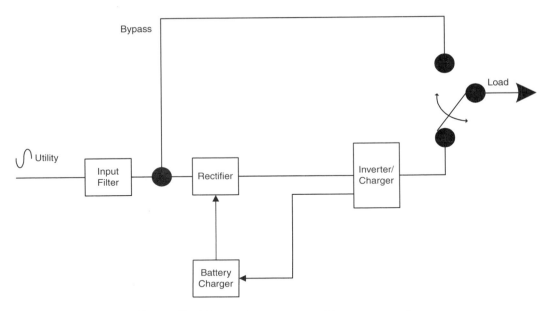

Figure 3–18   On-line uniterruptible power supply.

from the rectifier or storage batteries into a clean, continuous AC power supply for use in driving connected equipment.

On-line systems are commonly used with large systems whose load power requirements exceed 6 kVA, though some on-line units are available for much smaller loads. The on-line UPS also features a by-pass switch that serves as both a protective device, should the UPS itself fail, and as a mechanism for changing the load over to an alternative AC source such as a backup generator.

An on-line UPS remains in the line between the critical load and the power company at all times, while other types supply battery power only when switched. This configuration protects the load from transients that may be generated by the power switching process itself.

All UPS configurations share one thing in common: They provide a battery backup to commercial power. Typically, units will be selected based on the combined kVA or Wattage requirements of the load, the length of time that emergency power will need to be provided, physical characteristics of the unit itself (i.e., footprint, environmental conditions, etc.), and cost.

Units are available in a variety of kVA ratings and some feature rackmount configurations (see Figure 3–19) or modular battery designs (see Figure 3–20) enabling backup power durations to be extended. For smaller systems, vendors have increasingly taken to offering "configurators" on their Web sites. Configurators are useful in identifying which vendor UPS products are sized for certain

Figure 3-19 A rackmount UPS. (*Source:* American Power Conversion, West Kingston, RI. For more information: www.apcc.com.)

"name-brand" computer, peripheral or network components and help you to save time and effort in identifying wattage requirements from the name plates on the back or underside of your equipment. However, configurators are also limited in several ways. These include:

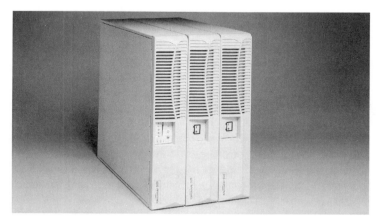

Figure 3-20 The Powerware 9125 two-in-one form factor (rack or tower installation) with extended battery modules. (*Source:* Powerware Corporation, An Invensys Company, Raleigh, NC, www.powerware.com.)

- Custom configurations of equipment: the configurator can tell you what the base line model of a PC, server, switch or array may require in terms of backup capacity, but it can't tell you specifically the requirements for a server or PC that is configured with many optional cards and capabilities.
- Special application requirements: the configurator cannot usually identify the type of UPS you should select based on factors such as application sensitivity to harmonic distortion.
- Compatibility with generators or other self-generation technologies: most configurators do not ask you about the generator you may be using to replace utility power in the event of a protracted utility outage. If self-generation or utility replacement is a strategy that you are pursuing, you will need to examine closely the compatibility of the UPS with the self-generation equipment. The important questions to be answered include how the UPS will handle the change-over from utility to generated power. An improper interface can create a sudden surge of frequency and voltage that can harm downstream equipment or the UPS itself. Also, the compatibility of the UPS with the characteristics of the power generated by the self-generation plant must also be considered carefully.
- Air conditioning requirements: a configurator may not address other requirements that will be mandated by products selection that will adversely effect the price of the solution. This is particularly the case with on-line UPS selection. Coordinators need to read the fine print to see whether an upgrade in the facility air conditioning plant will be required to support the UPS device that is under consideration.
- Battery life: a configurator may not provide information on the hidden cost of UPS—the operational life of its batteries. Be sure to find out the frequency with which batteries must be replaced and the costs. Also, find out whether the vendor offers any way to gauge the remaining life of batteries once they are installed.

It should also be mentioned that UPS products tend to be undersized for their loads. In other words, vendors recommend less battery backup than the consumer may think is needed, based on the simple calculation of wattage requirements of all the devices comprising the load for the unit. This should not be viewed as an error on the vendor's part, however.

In point of fact, equipment nameplate ratings are never lower, but often higher, than the actual power drawn by electronic equipment. Nameplate ratings are required by regulatory agencies and are required to represent a power or current rating which the equipment will never exceed. As a result, manufacturers often are extremely conservative and place high nameplate ratings on equipment. It is fairly common for the nameplate rating of computer equipment to be over two times the actual power draw of the equipment. Many UPS vendors maintain their own power ratings for equipment that more accurately reflect the load. This database of actual power measurements for systems and configuration options is often touted as a benefit of the vendor's configurator.

A final note: Before buying a UPS, DR coordinators need to ensure that it is manageable under the strategy that you have selected for your power protection design. If the planner intends to manage the UPS via a network management system console, for example, then it is necessary to ensure that the vendor has instrumented its product to support SNMP or some other network management method.

Beyond UPS

UPS systems are used primarily to address power outages. In addition to outages, planners should also consider other power quality issues including power spikes and sags, brownouts, noise, and harmonics. While not as dramatic as blackouts, these power quality issues probably do more damage and generate more downtime annually than all blackouts combined.

Not only can poor power quality reduce the operating life of sensitive electronics, leading to the crashing of servers or switches, it can also cause imperceptible errors in data that can corrupt databases, render data storage unreadable, or create havoc with print jobs, email and network communications. Intermittent power quality problems can be difficult and expensive to trace to their origin, consuming an inordinate amount of a tech support team's time in troubleshooting. *Bottom line:* bad power can spoil your whole day!

The tools for fighting power quality problems come in several forms:

Surge Suppressors

Surge suppressors are deployed on power lines as well as network cables, telephone lines, cable TV cables, and any other conductor that might possibly provide an inroad to equipment for a power surge or spike, whether caused by power company switch transients or by internal culprits (air conditioning compressors, motorized equipment, etc.). Suppressors keep the overvoltage from reaching protected equipment by "turning on" when a preset voltage is reached and then absorbing part of the energy of the surge and eventually diverting all surge energy to ground. Once the surge has been dissipated, the suppressor "resets" and waits for the next surge.

Crucial in the design of a suppressor is its ability to turn on rapidly and absorb or divert all the energy present in the surge and clamping or holding the "let through" overvoltage down to a level safe for exposed circuitry. Poorly designed and "low end" surge suppressors may protect equipment from minor overvoltages, however, severe spikes can stress the suppressor, causing failure in load equipment. Industry insiders describe this situation in terms of "let-through" voltage that occurs during a surge of larger amplitude. The overvoltage is caused by the inability of the suppressor to absorb or divert all of the surge energy present on the line.

There are a variety of quality, cost-effective products offered by vendors to meet all surge suppression requirements for applications ranging from the main power entry into the building to the various zones of a building, to the connected electronic equipment, as well as surge control devices which mount onto the internal circuit board of the equipment. Industrial products are also available that protect load devices such as process controls, machine controls, and data transmission instrumentation.

Some vendors offer configurators to guide the selection of surge protectors, but planners should do some fact checking before making any purchases. Here are a few pointers:

- *Energy Absorption:* Surge suppressors are normally rated by the amount of energy they can absorb, which is measured in joules. The higher the surge rating of the suppressor, the better the unit. Generally, 200 joules is basic protection, 400 is good protection, and 600 or higher is superior protection.
- *UL Standards for Voltage Let-Through:* Underwriters Laboratories has established standard UL 1449 for surge suppressors. This standard is used to rate suppressors by the amount of voltage they allow to pass through to protected equipment. In UL testing, the suppressors are subjected to a 500 A, 6000 V surge. The output measured to see what voltage level is let through to the equipment. Protection is rated in three levels – 330 V, 400 V and 500 V – and the lower the rating, the better the suppression. Even the 330 V number is triple the nominal voltage of a North American PC power supply and may still do damage to equipment, so you may want to find out from the vendor what additional capabilities they bring to their product design to keep the spikes out.
- *Protection Indicator:* Metal-oxide varistors (MOVs) used to redirect spikes to ground, have a useful life that decreases exponentially as the surge suppressor operates to clamp overvoltages over time. If the MOV is blown (e.g., ceases to operate), the surge suppressor is no longer protecting your equipment from voltage problems. On better units, an LED indicator or some other signal is provided to let you know that the MOV has failed.
- *Line Conditioning:* Better surge suppressors normally contain some line conditioning capabilities as well. (See below for more information on line conditioners and prefer a surge protector with this capability over one without it.)
- *Power Switch:* Some suppressors have a manual on/off switch, while others do not. Others offer some protected outlets and some unprotected outlets. Read the manual to find out the capabilities of your unit and to ensure that you aren't circumventing the protection that it offers through misuse.

- *Circuit Breaker or Fuse:* Most suppressors will have either a fuse or a resettable circuit breaker, which will blow or trip if there is a short circuit or severe surge that causes excessive current to flow. Breakers are preferred because fuses need to be replaced.
- *Protection Guarantee:* Many vendors provide an equipment protection guarantee that promises something to the effect that if connected equipment is damaged by a surge or spike, the vendor will pay for its replacement. Be sure to read the fine print to determine what terms and conditions apply. Keep in mind that guarantees typically cover only hardware losses, not data.

Line Conditioners

Surge suppressors are sometimes called the poor man's line conditioner, but a line conditioner has a significantly different purpose. Most line conditioners provide electronic circuits that filter and smooth the power stream to eliminate dips, fluctuations, and interference that can cause power to be "noisy." Noise reduction capability is measured in decibels over a given frequency range. The higher the decibel value, the better the conditioner—and the greater the cost.

Hybrid devices featuring both electromagnetic interference/radio frequency interference (EMI/RFI) filtering (also known as line conditioning) and surge protection have recently appeared in the market. Additionally, many better UPS products offer line conditioning as a part of their functionality.

Voltage Regulators

A surge suppressor may also be called a poor man's voltage regulator, since it performs one of the functions expected from most regulators—the amelioration of voltage irregularities. Of course, a voltage regulator also protects equipment against undervoltages that can accrue to power sags. Voltage regulators come in three forms: Tap-Switching, Ferroresonant, and Electronic. The characteristics of each type of voltage regulator determine its suitability to different applications.

Tap-switching systems have the advantage of a rather small footprint for a lot of capability. However, it is an expensive solution for low KVA applications and does not address harmonic distortion in current.

Ferroresonant voltage regulators operate very simply as in-line transformers that normalize current across their primary and secondary coils. They are unmatched in power conditioning and filtering of line noise and transients and have no moving parts. While they have a larger footprint than Tap-Switching devices, they are increasing in popularity in medical applications and in some data centers because of their robustness and low ground leakage.

Electronic Voltage Regulators use transformers and digital circuitry to reshape line voltages within a very narrow range of tolerances. Some disadvantages include the fact that units tend to be physically larger and heavier than

Tap-Switchers. Plus, units don't provide the same degree of power conditioning as the Ferroresonant or the speed of a Tap-Switching unit. Electronic Voltage Regulators tend to be used almost exclusively in industrial settings where motors and other high inrush devices are commonly deployed. Some UPS manufacturers have begun to use the technology in larger capacity products as a bypass filter.

This brief survey of power protection and power conditioning devices should underscore that equipment acquisition is not as simple as vendor-provided "configurators" might suggest. Considerable technical expertise is generally required, especially in the selection of voltage regulators and large UPS systems. The acquisition and installation of a centralized UPS is significantly more complex than the acquisition and deployment of multiple, smaller units. Facility preparation tasks may be extensive.

Figures 3–21 and 3–22 provide views of a distributed computing environment before and after they are equipped with power protection capabilities. In some environments, power protection measures will be distributed, but centrally monitored and managed. With others, power protection may be provided via more centralized power quality components.

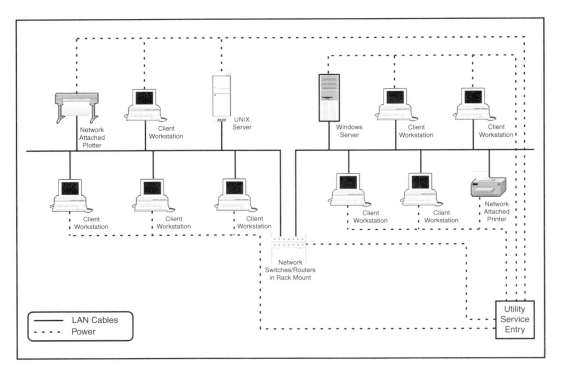

Figure 3–21   A distributed environment with minimal power protection.

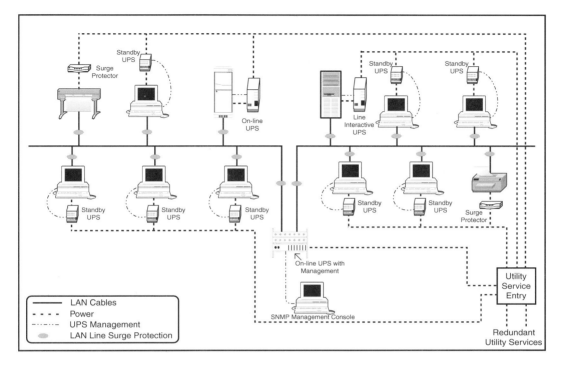

Figure 3–22   A distributed environment with a managed power protection capability.

Most vendors are extremely forthcoming with advice and information, and some even provide installation planning teams. Coordinators need to ensure that warranties and maintenance agreements are clearly understood and that thorough documentation and training are provided to those who will manage the power protection strategy that is implemented.

With the implementation of management software, the process for establishing a power protection capability for the organization is nearly complete. All that remains is to test and validate connections and controls, and to establish a routine for the periodic inspection, testing, and maintenance of the components that have been fielded.

One other matter requiring the attention of the DR coordinator is change management. A power protection strategy isn't something that is developed once, then forgotten. To maintain a power protection capability that is consistent with the requirements of the organization, it needs to be adapted on an ongoing basis to changes within the organizational facility. Both the electrical transmission system and the equipment load in most organizations are "moving targets" for power protection.

- Individual personnel, workgroups, and even whole departments change their physical locations on a more or less frequent basis in some settings, as is evidenced by the amount of time that most telephony and network administrators spend processing adds, moves, and changes in their shops. When personnel move, the power protection capability may need to be adjusted.
- New applications, and new networks and servers to support them, are being fielded on an on-going basis. When this happens, DR coordinators need to assess the power protection requirements for the new infrastructure.
- Improving remote management capabilities in power protection components may present new opportunities going forward to manage power in geographically-disbursed offices, equipment rooms and data centers—all from a centralized, web-accessible, management console. Taking advantage of these options can help improve the power protection afforded to the organization as a whole.
- The technology for power protection itself is changing constantly. New, more capable, high-end UPS systems—providing features such as network attachment for ease of management and new product designs for ease of expansion—may prompt planners to reconsider product choices at some point in the future and to deploy newer technology to achieve an even better level of protection and return on investment.

These are only a few of the many potential drivers for change in a power protection strategy. It is up to DR coordinators to put into place a change management process that will enable them to seize on opportunities when they arise and to leverage the organization's investment in power protection to the fullest possible extent.

PHYSICAL ACCESS CONTROL

Although commonly regarded as a security concern, facility access is another area with which the disaster recovery coordinator may need to become involved. An increasing number of disasters are the result of intentional or accidental damage to equipment and facilities by employees and others who have access to the corporate business offices and data centers. Disgruntled employees, corporate saboteurs, negligent users or vendors, and a host of others may cause fires, damage media, disrupt processes, or otherwise impair normal operations.

This has led to the installation of physical access control systems in many companies ranging from locked doors, security guards, and closed-circuit cameras to electronic card key systems and biometric access control systems. It is essential for the disaster recovery coordinator to fully understand systems that are already in place and to champion the physical security issue if inadequate access control methods are discovered.

The reasons for involving the disaster recovery coordinator in physical security matters are twofold. For one, effective access security can greatly reduce the risk of certain disaster potentials. The coordinator needs to document the capabilities that exist in the plan.

The second reason for the DR coordinator's concern with physical security is for post-disaster recovery. It is important to know how to circumvent security measures in the event of a disaster in order to evacuate personnel, to perform emergency equipment shutdowns, and to access and remove secure information that is at risk of loss or damage.

In a financial environment, for example, checks and other executable financial documents, printed on a daily basis, are often stored on-site in locked cabinets. Also, registers and logs, which are used to track the use of checks, may be stored in the cabinets where they can be accessed to record check processing runs. Assuming that a supply of checks is readily available from off-site storage or from vendors in the case of a disaster, the disaster recovery coordinator may see no reason to change the current security arrangement.

However, if the registers are important and irreplaceable, the coordinator may need to make provisions for accessing registers in order to remove them to a safe location in the event of an emergency.

The concept that disaster recovery planning may require security work-arounds is sometimes difficult for security administrators to accept. Implicit is the threat that security-breaking methods will become common knowledge, and that expensive and time-consuming systems will be rendered impotent. Considerable diplomacy and common sense may be required to cultivate the cooperation of security managers in those areas where access control and disaster recovery priorities conflict.

A comprehensive discussion of physical access controls and security management is beyond the scope of this book. However, there are some very basic tasks for the DR coordinator to undertake in order to facilitate the integration of security with disaster recovery.

- *Become familiar with current security industry practices.* The World Wide Web is a good place to begin. Numerous security trade associations and practitioner societies host extensive sites on the Web filled with technical papers, case studies of security system designs, and detailed guides. Attending security-oriented tradeshows and seminars and reading up on the latest techniques and methods are also excellent ways to become conversant with the field and its jargon.
- *Consult with experts.* If the corporate office facility or data center is currently without an access control capability, consult with one of the many vendors of security products and services to provide a preliminary analysis of facility security requirements. If knowledgeable security professionals are not part of the corporate organization, DR coordinators may want to consult with a security professional prior to inviting vendors into any discussion.

The American Society for Industrial Security (ASIS) is a good source for qualified security consultants.

- *Develop an understanding of security systems that are already in place.* If security consists of a locked door, cabinet, or drawer, find out who has the keys. Similarly, if a master card key, or special code number, or other device (sometimes called a token) exists that will open all doors, find out who possesses the token. The security administrator or a designee from the security organization should be a member of the recovery team. Not only will the individual be helpful in identifying current capabilities and security workarounds that may be needed for emergency response, a security professional can also contribute useful input about how security will be provided for business processes that are being operated in a disaster recovery mode.

- *Learn what is being safeguarded by security measures and determine if it is needed in day-to-day work at the facility or if it would be better stored in a secure, off-site location.* In some cases, companies have invested significant resources to secure sensitive documents and other private corporate materials from disclosure or theft, but have not considered their loss to fire, water damage, or other disaster potentials. Working with the security administrator, the DR coordinator may be able to find those materials a home in secure off-site storage, solving both their security and disaster recovery requirements.

- *Make provisions for the restoration of physical security at the recovery site.* It is important to ensure that security controls are reestablished at the same time as systems and networks are restored. Controls should also be established to safeguard data during evacuation and transport to the backup site.

The point is that physical security remains just as important in an emergency as it is during normal operations. Only by providing the means for replacing standard security procedures with emergency security procedures will the objectives of both security planning and disaster recovery planning be met.

In addition to physical security considerations, a host of application and network security measures may also need to be accounted for in the disaster recovery plan. These will be discussed in greater detail later in this book.

ENDNOTES

1. Hewlett Packard Case Study, 5/24/99, and Jeffrey Camp, "Flood Prods NT Move," *Computerworld,* 6/1/99.
2. Alan Radding, "Lights Out," *Computerworld,* 6/1/99.
3. "Report of Test Results: Halon 1301 vs. Water Sprinkler Fire Protection for Essential Electronic Equipment," Document ESL-TR-B2–28, Air Force Engineering and Services Laboratory (Tyndall AFB, FL: AFESL, 1982), pp. 75–76. Conclusions about water damage to computer equipment included: "water...produced many deleterious side ef-

fects, primarily through corrosion and staining of sensitive electronic components" and that "considerable downtime [was required] to dry out the electronic equipment and repair water damaged components."

4. "Facts about Clean Agent Suppression Systems," The Fire Suppression Systems Association (FSSA), Baltimore, MD, 1994.

5. Significant New Alternatives Program Preliminary Findings, Environmental Protection Agency, Washington, DC, 3/18/94.

6. Interview with Brian Pung, President, Protective Services, Inc., Hollywood, FL and Tampa, FL, 6/99.

7. Richard A. Matthews, "Cleanroom Velocity Not Subject to Outdated Standards," CleanRooms, 3/99.

8. According to studies published by the American Society of Heating, Refrigeration and Air Conditioning Engineers (ASHRAE), Handbook of Fundamentals (Atlanta, GA, 1986), particles have a calculable settling velocity. A particle one micron in size that is suspended in the air of a room eight feet tall, under ideal conditions of still air, will take nearly 19 hours to settle out. A .1 micron particle, under the same conditions, would take 72 days. In a typical data center—with doors opening and closing frequently, air conditioners blowing, and machines moving and generating electrostatic, thermal, and frictional influences—the settling rate would be very much prolonged. For this reason, contamination detection methods that rely on settled particulate are inherently flawed in their findings.

9. Interview with Eric Williamson, President, Worldwide Environmental Services USA Inc., Blue Bell, PA, 6/99.

10. Interview with Stuart Hanley, Vice President of World Wide Operations, OnTrack Data International, Eden Prarie, MN, 6/99.

11. Pung interview.

12. Ibid.

13. Ibid.

14. John R. Hall, Jr., "Special Analysis Package: Computer Equipment and Computer Areas," National Fire Protection Association, Quincy, MA, February 1999.

15. Silicon Valley Manufacturing Group press release (http://www.svmg.org).

16. "Reliability Assessment 2001–2010: The Reliability of Bulk Electric Systems in North America," Figure 6, North American Electric Reliability Council (NERC), October 2001, (http://www.nerc.com).

17. See the DOE Distributed Power Program web site at www.eren.doe.gov/distributedpower/.

18. Kenneth G. Brill, "Keeping Up Your UPS," Datamation, 7/15/87.

19. Interview with Rich Feldhaus, Product Specialist, TrippLite, Chicago, IL, 6/99.

20. "Uninterruptible Power Systems (UPS) Technology: Which UPS Is Right for My Systems?" Technical Paper, Powerware Corporation (formerly Exide Electronics), Raleigh, NC, 1999.

CHAPTER 4

Data Recovery Planning

Many experts believe that successful business recovery comes down to a simple axiom: shorten the time to data. For the company experiencing an unplanned interruption in time-sensitive, mission-critical business processes, the primary objective is to reestablish access to application data quickly and by whatever means possible.

Time to data is a determinant of post-disaster business survival. Companies that go too long without key business process restoration quickly amass lost revenues, lost customers, lost market position, and eventually lose everything. How long this takes for a particular company is a matter of conjecture because it depends so much on the unique characteristics and sensitivities of the company.

For most firms, failure to recover mission-critical business processes within a week virtually guarantees business failure within five years. For companies that are extremely dependent upon technology to support business processes—especially those engaged in electronic commerce or dependent upon extended supply chain management or Enterprise Resource Planning (ERP) applications—the timeframe may be much shorter.

From an IT perspective, creating strategies to shorten time to data is the primary mission of disaster recovery planning. Once provisions have been made to minimize the likelihood of avoidable disasters, attention turns to developing strategies to restore infrastructure supports for critical business processes in the wake of disasters that cannot be effectively avoided.

THE PRIMACY OF DATA

Recently, significant industry attention has turned to electronic data and its storage infrastructure (rather than processors or networks) as the focal point for effective information systems design and integration. Data storage is increasingly recognized as the center of the IT universe. Extending this metaphor, networks of servers and client devices provide a system of satellites that orbit the storage infrastructure.

The above is more than a metaphor. Companies are increasingly deploying large-scale, multi-server-attachable storage disk arrays, network-attached storage (NAS) appliances, or storage area networks (SANs) to serve as a centralized repository for corporate data. These platforms provide the means to share data among multiple, heterogeneous processor platforms, usually via high-speed interconnects such as SCSI, Fibre Channel, or even Gigabit Ethernet.

Many factors are driving this shift in the perspective of corporate IT architects and have been discussed in detail elsewhere.[1] For the disaster recovery coordinator, the relevance of the phenomenon is that data—its effective storage, management, and accessibility—is already a major concern for most businesses and their IT organizations. So, too, protecting data and assuring its availability for access following a disaster must be the central concern of disaster recovery. Without data, there can be no recovery at all.

Some vendors of disaster recovery planning products have already come to this conclusion. They argue that, following a disaster, alternate system processors might be able to be found "on the fly," that network backup strategies might be "pieced together" ad hoc, and that temporary user quarters might be set up just about anywhere. Without the recovery of data, however, all the other logistics and strategies of disaster recovery plans are meaningless.

While one cannot discount the value of advance planning for the recovery of servers and networks, the importance of safeguarding data assets required for business process recovery cannot be overstated. To understand why, one needs only recall some of the issues discussed earlier in this text.

As discussed previously, business interruption insurance can provide only for the restoration—not the replacement—of data. Restoration frequently requires that copies of electronic datasets and the most current updates to them (whether in the form of electronic update files or paper-based input documents) be available to the recovery effort.

To guarantee that data copies and other update sources are not consumed in the same disaster that renders the production environment untenable, these items should be stored at a safe location, preferably off-site and at a facility other than the one that houses the production systems.

PLANNING FOR DATA RECOVERY

Maintaining secure, off-site, copies of data is not enough to assure recovery, however. The time to data requirement means that companies must be able to restore electronic datasets to an accessible form efficiently so they may be processed by the systems, networks, and end users who make them purposeful. How quickly datasets must be restored to a usable form is determined by the sensitivity of the company to the duration of an unplanned interruption. To address different degrees of sensitivity, several techniques of data restoral have evolved over time. These include:

- Routine data backup to magnetic tape using backup/restore software and the removal of backups to off-site storage. Restoral requires the retrieval of stored backup tapes, transport to system recovery facility, and restoration of data to a new storage platform via software.
- Routine data backup to an electronic "tape vault" via a wide area network (WAN) interconnect or the Internet. Restoral may require the physical retrieval of tapes and their transport to a systems recovery site, or restoral may be possible using a WAN link between the recovery system and the electronic tape vault.
- Remote mirroring of data to a second (or third) storage platform via a wide area network (WAN) interconnect. Restoral is unnecessary. The recovery system is connected via WAN links to the remote mirror array, or the remote mirror may be located at the system recovery site.

A modern data recovery strategy may include one or more variations of the above techniques. The major differences between them are the data availability timeframes they provide and, of course, their cost (see Table 4–1). Choosing the appropriate set of techniques is usually a matter of balancing the time to data requirement of the business process and the willingness of senior management to invest in the data protection strategy.

Clearly, before a disaster recovery coordinator can approach senior management with a proposal for an expensive remote mirroring strategy, a careful analysis of data assets needs should be made. Despite improvements in data backup/restore technology, the underlying methods for determining what data assets need to be protected and how best to protect them have not changed significantly in the last decade or more. The data flow diagram in Figure 4–1 provides an overview of the complex network of activities involved in creating and maintaining an effective data recovery plan.

As suggested by the DFD, data recovery planning involves several activities. These include:

- The analysis and classification of data based on importance to recovery (and to the company)

Table 4–1   Data Backup and Restoral Alternatives

Strategy	Description	Pros	Cons	Cost
Traditional Backup to Tape	Manual process of copying data from hard disk to tape and transporting to secure facility.	Simple-to-implement technology, multiple price-point devices/software available.	Manual transportation and storage prone to risk and error. Potentially long lead time to restoral. Not always practical given available "windows" of processing time.	Low to Medium
Backup to Electronic Tape Vault	Copying data from disk to a remote tape system via a wide area network link.	Data is accessible in shorter timeframe, services becoming standardized, WAN link prices falling, exposure to risk/errors in manual methods reduced.	WAN links can introduce latency into backup process; depending on e-vaulting provider, storage may be difficult to restore; data restoral times potentially lengthy.	Medium to High
Disk Mirroring	Copying data written to one disk or array of disks to a second disk or array of disks via a wide area network link.	Instantaneous restoral of access to data possible (depending on WAN link availability and synchronicity of primary and mirrored arrays).	WAN links can introduce latency into production system operations; some mirroring systems reduce production system performance; logic errors may be repli= cated from original- to mirrored data sets.	High

- The review of existing backup procedures
- The evaluation and selection of a backup strategy
- The formalization of that strategy in the form of automatic and manual procedures for moving data to a secure, off-site location

Given its close relationship to system, network, and end-user recovery, data recovery planning is often undertaken concurrently with the development of other backup strategies and procedures in the disaster recovery planning project.

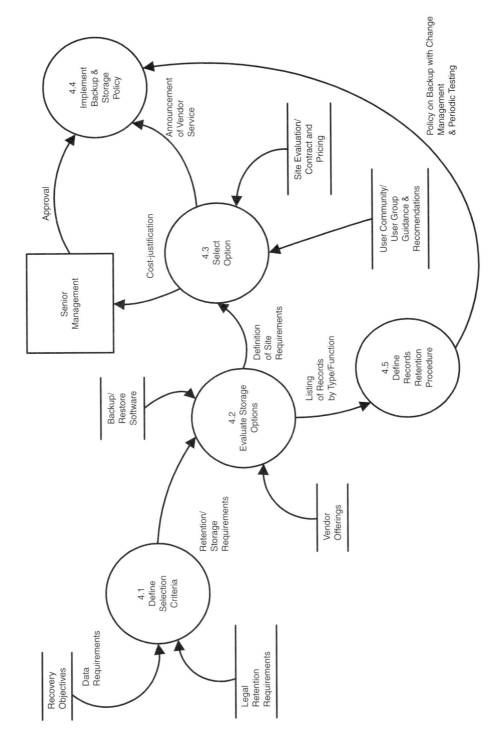

Figure 4–1 Data recovery planning.

IDENTIFYING THE INFORMATION ASSET

For a data recovery plan to be meaningful, it must ensure the "right" data—data that is required by critical business processes and necessary for recovery—is identified, safeguarded against loss, and made available in an acceptable recovery timeframe. This is a deceptively simple premise. Consider these facts:

- Depending on the analyst one reads, data is growing at a rate of between 70 to 100% per year in most corporations. Replicated data, "enhanced" data (e.g., document files with graphics, sound clips and other data objects embedded), and large program files account for some of this growth—perhaps as much as 50%, according to some analysts. However, the balance is new data, including e-mail and transaction entries in databases, that is constantly being created and stored by end-users and automated systems.

- A significant percentage (some argue as much as 80%) of the data stored on hard disk drives is never referenced again. This applies to databases as well as files, fostering significant discussion of the possibility of shortening data recovery timeframes by "prestaging" static or nonchanging data at the recovery center.

- Databases measured in terabytes are becoming commonplace within Fortune 1000 firms. Even in medium-sized firms, it is not uncommon to find databases sized in the 400 to 700 GB range.

- In most companies, policies and standards do not exist for the classification of data by its importance to the organization. According to the 1998 Information Week/PricewaterhouseCoopers Global Information Security Survey, 43% of the 1600 companies surveyed worldwide indicated that they never classify data and 14% classify their records only on an annual basis.[2] Says George Symons, Vice President of Product Management and Development with Legato Systems, Inc., "Today CIOs are being forced to determine the relative importance of different applications. They cannot afford to invest in tools and people to protect all applications at the 24 x 7 level. Decisions need to be made as to which applications must be available 24 x 7, which are 19 x 5 and which are 12 x 5."[3]

Against this backdrop, clearly the DR coordinator may confront a major challenge at the outset of data recovery planning: learning where the data is stored in the organization. This task, according to vendors, can be facilitated through the use of software products that automatically "discover" volumes, databases, and files recorded on data storage devices throughout the IT infrastructure. Storage management software is being pressed into service to aid in ferreting out data, determining its usage characteristics, and using this information to plan capacity requirements for recovery in the wake of a disaster.

Discovering the locations and usage characteristics of electronic files stored on PCs, server-captive storage arrays, stand-alone arrays, network attached storage (NAS) devices, and storage area networks (SANs) does not, however, define the criticality of the data or its suitability to a backup strategy. According to Legato's Symons, companies are not going to cull through data sets to assess their importance and set policies for backup, policies will be set based on the application producing the data, and the priority given to that application.

> To perform backups of distributed data effectively requires policy-driven management. Policy-driven backup and recovery [using an enterprise-wide data backup product like Legato NetWorker®,], helps reduce the staff requirements necessary to manager these complex environments. Policy- based systems automate key functions in order to provide consistent management of repetitive tasks.[4]

In addition to electronic or machine-readable data, data recovery planning must also concern itself with identifying business critical information stored on paper and with the interdependencies that may exist among paper or other documentation, electronic data, source documents, and worker knowledge that make all data usable. This, too, can be a laborious and time-consuming task. To the list of information storage repositories that must be examined by the DR coordinator an assortment of safes, file cabinets, microfiche and microfilm storage racks, and old-fashioned desk drawers must be added.

Paper and microform continues to proliferate in most companies, to the dismay of naturalists and efficiency experts alike. One vendor of electronic document management systems summarizes the problems associated with these popular information storage media:

> Upwards of 90% of all corporate knowledge is stored on paper—but paper itself is never a profit center. Filing, storing, and retrieving paper documents is an enormous drain on a company's resources....[Moreover,] paper documents and the data contained on them must be analyzed on a document by document basis. Sorting or searching for data is, practically speaking, impossible...3% of a company's documentation is misfiled—and 3% is lost...32% of a company's documentation is in use by a single user at any time—and is unavailable to any other users. The cost of locating a missing document is $6 to $120.[5]

These drawbacks of static storage media and the advantages of maintaining machine-readable copies is behind explosive growth in the knowledge management industry, which includes electronic document management systems, workflow management systems and related technologies. According to a joint survey of 500 IT managers by Information Week Research and Cap Ventures, total document management solutions spending jumped 38% in 1998 to $3.5 billion, up from $2.5 billion in 1997.[6]

If an organization has embraced electronic document management, the DR coordinator can leverage this effort to identify key documents for removal to off-site storage, of course. If not, disaster recovery may provide yet another justification to senior management for such an endeavor.

In the absence of an electronic document management capability, the DR coordinator may still be able to enlist the services of a corporate records manager, or clerical personnel at a departmental level to identify paper and microform-based information for inclusion in the data recovery strategy.

It is worth noting that, according to numerous studies, records managers are the forgotten asset in disaster recovery and security planning. These knowledgeable persons were members of recovery plans in fewer than 20% of plans reviewed in one 1997 survey. In another survey conducted in the same year, it was determined 70% of company executives excluded records managers from the process of assessing and mitigating risk to records—this despite the fact that 90% of businesses that lose their vital records are out of business within 1 year.[7]

CLASSIFYING CRITICALITY: INPUTS AND OUTPUTS

No data, whether paper-based or digital, is critical in and of itself. It is only critical insofar as it supports critical business processes or satisfies other legal or financial requirements of the business. Critical data includes all information files, regardless of storage media, that provide inputs to and, in some cases, the outputs from critical applications. Thus, in formulating a data recovery plan, the coordinator needs to:

- Identify input (and output) data sources for those critical business processes that were identified as part of risk analysis.

  Inputs may comprise source documents that are coded or otherwise rendered machine-readable by system users. These source documents (or copies of them) should be identified for removal to off-site storage.

  Output documents, such as reports or summaries, may also be critical if they are auditable records, used in important historical analyses, or used by others in their performance of vital work (e.g., account histories used by customer service, shipping records for recent deliveries to customers, etc.). These documents and/or the media on which they are recorded should be listed for regular removal off-site.

  Of course, licensed programs and systems software, and as well as source code and compiled source for custom-developed applications software, should also be earmarked for off-site storage. Be sure to include any software license information and registration keys that may be required to make software function or to obtain vendor support. More than one disaster recovery effort has been held up when it was discovered that software keys were omitted from recovery requirements lists and applications could not be restarted without them.

- Identify ancillary documentation required for restoring business processes.

  In addition to application programs and input source data and documents, a number of other items must be stored off-site to facilitate recovery. These may include insurance policy information, asset inventories, and other documentation required for efficient processing of insurance claims;

key operations and user manuals; preprinted forms such as blank check stock; and, of course, copies of the disaster recovery plan.
- Identify data that must be preserved to satisfy legal requirements and to reduce business loss.

  Auditors and records managers can assist in identifying data and documents that must be preserved to satisfy legal requirements. In addition, there may be a number of records—such as sales and marketing client contact lists and email directories, drafts of contracts, and intellectual properties such as designs for prototype systems—that would not be needed to restore vital business operations or to satisfy legal mandates, but which do represent substantial investments of company resources. These may be difficult, costly, or impossible to replace and would be a substantial business loss if destroyed. These files, too, are excellent candidates for secure off-site storage.

SETTING A POLICY ON DATA ASSET IDENTIFICATION, CLASSIFICATION, AND BACKUP

The identification of key business data is not a one-time undertaking. As information proliferates, an ongoing identification, classification, and protection strategy is required to keep the data protection plan in synchronization with the business. A formal policy or set of policies may need to be developed and enforced to facilitate data recovery requirements in the future. Elements of such a policy may include the following:

- Establish departmental "owners" of information. Make someone in each business unit, department, or workgroup responsible for providing the "brainwork" of data asset identification and classification on an ongoing basis.
- With the assistance of auditors, establish criteria for identifying the relative importance of records. The simplified method for classifying data criticality summarized in Table 4–2 may be adapted to the needs of virtually any company. As may be apparent, the same categories that are applied to applications in risk analysis may also be applied to classify the data required to restore the applications.

  With the help of auditors and in-house experts, it may be possible to correlate certain types of documents (e.g., forms with specific form numbers, specific "named" reports, etc.) with the generic categories identified in Table 4–2. These and other classification aids can assist data owners in keeping their off-site storage inventories current.

  Of course, classifying data may entail some of the same problems encountered when classifying application criticality during risk analysis. No one likes to believe that the data he or she "owns" is anything less than critical. However,

Table 4–2   Simplified Data Classification Scheme

Classification	Definition
Critical	Data or documentation that must be retained for legal reasons, for use in key business processes, or for restoration minimum acceptable work levels in the event of a disaster.
Vital	Data or documentation that must be retained for use in normal business processes and that represents a substantial investment of company resources that may be difficult or impossible to recoup, but may not be required in a disaster recovery situation. Information that requires special secrecy or discretion may also fall under this category.
Sensitive	Data or documentation that is needed in normal operations, but for which alternative supplies are available in the event of loss. Data that can be reconstructed fairly readily but at some cost could also be classified as sensitive.
Noncritical	Data or documentation that can be reconstructed readily at minimal cost, or duplicates of critical, vital, or sensitive data that have no prerequisite security requirements.

most owners will concede that third-generation copies of original documents are less critical than the originals, and many will comply with a definition of criticality that does not suggest that their work does not contribute to business success in day-to-day operations.

POLICY-BASED MANAGEMENT OF ELECTRONIC DATA VIA SOFTWARE

Considerable work is currently underway to establish a common mechanism for tagging electronic data as it is created with special "metadata" identifiers. When such a scheme becomes more universally adopted, it will deliver several benefits, including the means to assure data integrity and a method to facilitate the cost-effective deployment of data, based on usage characteristics, across media of different price points. Such a scheme would also be of enormous benefit to disaster recovery planning by providing a highly granular method for tagging which data is required to fulfill recovery objectives.

Until such time that an effective data classification scheme is ready for use, we must all depend on somewhat less refined data classification and management methods. Most of these require the use of storage management software.

Management of ongoing data identification, classification, and backup tasks for electronic data can be facilitated through the use of storage management software. A number of worthwhile enterprise-, workgroup-, and server-class tools are available today, as might be expected of a software market segment that is experiencing a period of significant growth, and most organizations are using an assortment of products to help cope with burgeoning data growth. DR coordinators need to develop an understanding of what products are currently being used and to determine whether they can be harnessed to assist in data disaster avoidance and storage recovery.

If storage management software is not already in use, the DR coordinator should work with IT or system administrators to identify appropriate candidates. But, be prepared for a significant amount of work just sifting through the products that are available.

As shown in Figure 4–2, there are several layers of software in the storage management space, from point products that perform a single task (such as mirroring or backup and restore) or work only with a single vendor's storage platform, to storage resource managers that aggregate multiple point products into an "integrated" suite, to framework managers that instrument all storage platforms—whether direct attached to servers (DAS), connected to IP networks (NAS), or configured in a Fibre Channel "fabric", often mistakenly called a storage area network or SAN. Additionally, vendors have just begun to appear in the market that offer a new "layer" of storage management functionality intended to enable the delivery of storage as a service. Bottom line: it can be quite confusing to sift through the literature of the many vendors that comprise this $20+ billion market to determine the best solution—usually a combination of products from several categories—to meet a specific company's requirements.

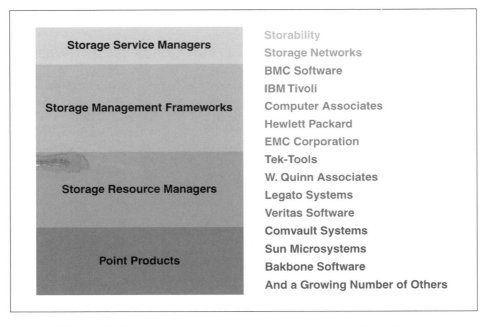

Figure 4–2   Types of storage management software: blurred lines.

However daunting the task, deploying an effective storage management capability is a critical requirement for data protection and recovery. The old adage that you can't manage what you can't see also applies in disaster recovery: You can't prevent avoidable disasters or recover from unavoidable disasters without the proper management tools.

Leading vendors in the storage management space include BMC Software, IBM, Tek-Tools, Hewlett Packard Company, Computer Associates, Legato Systems, Sun Microsystems, Veritas Software, Storability, Fujitsu Softek, W. Quinn Associates, Bakbone Software, Comvault Systems, and the redoubtable EMC Corporation. In addition, most storage equipment vendors either offer their own point management products or bundle products from third-party providers.

In the past, the only software product of interest to disaster recovery planners was backup and restore: software for copying data so that the copy can be removed from harm's way and restored if necessary. According to one vendor product manager, a comprehensive backup software solution is one that "provides logical views into data storage [and] that allows you to classify data and establish views of data on some logical basis (e.g., by the application that the data supports)."

> The package should also allow you to set policies on data backups and provide an event-correlating policy engine that enables the software to take certain actions when policy thresholds have been reached, such as forwarding alarms or backing up changed data automatically.[8]

Another industry insider notes that the performance of the product, in terms of both its speed of operation and its CPU resource utilization, are also important considerations.

> When [our company acquired a storage management product to sell as part of our product line], we went to existing customers and asked why they selected it. One of the largest telcoms was a user and their IT manager told us they bought the product because it could do everything that other packages could do, but on a smaller server—basically a desktop system. The others required high-powered servers. But, with [our product], they could run it on a large server and still have some resource left over to perform other tasks important to the business. The difference is in the product's use of memory. Many products rely on remote procedure calls (RPCs), involving many memory-to-memory data copies. [Our software] is unique in that it uses an asynchronous memory scheme. It makes for extremely efficient data movements with low CPU overhead. That is something others don't tell you when they announce the results of terabyte backup "speed trials"—what their resource utilization was like.[9]

Ken Barth, CEO of Tek-Tools, offers that backup and restore is no longer enough to ensure the recoverability of data. Rather, organizations need to supplement their backup software with storage management software that aids in identifying potential data disasters before they occur. It is critically important, according to Barth, that such solutions support heterogeneous computing platforms (platforms from different vendors) and heterogeneous deployment topologies—and that they enable management from any location. He notes that most enterprises still have distributed storage infrastructures comprised on many vendors' hardware.

> The key to effective storage management today is the ability of the management product to support multiple platforms and topologies for storage. Just because companies are deploying newer technologies like SAN or NAS doesn't mean that they are uninstalling their existing server-attached storage, so the storage infrastructure is becoming more complex. Management software is increasingly defined by its ability to manage the broadest possible number of storage devices, however they are configured. What's more, the management software must be flexible to address the different ways that organizations have deployed their storage—whether it is centralized in a data center or distributed throughout the enterprise. The management console should be portable—Web-based (see Figure 4–3)—so that those responsible for monitoring and management can use it to manage all storage wherever it resides.[10]

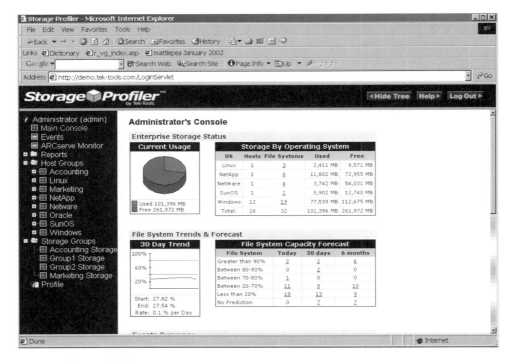

Figure 4–3   Tek-Tools Storage Profiler web-based management console. (*Source:* Tek-Tools, Inc., Dallas, TX. www.tek-tools. com.)

Legato's Symons agrees with this assessment, noting that his company's products provide both the heterogeneous support, and also the scalability to go from a department to a full enterprise solution.[11] He adds that, given the large volume of data and multiplicity of systems that need to be included in a distributed system backup strategy, an open tape format that stores data together with "self-describing metadata" is key for efficient recovery. Moreover, he adds, a comprehensive solution needs to support a broad range of backup devices and strategies.

> Recovery is the key for our customers to provide optimum business continuity. Many of them are looking at ways to recover data faster. Technology such as snapshots, and using lower cost disk as the backup target are becoming more popular. This does not eliminate the need for tape, but augments it with higher speed devices for a more expedient recovery.[12]

While these criteria are certainly helpful in guiding the selection of storage management software, there are several caveats that must be kept clearly in mind. For one, storage management remains more art than science. The problem is less with the software than with the hardware being managed.

Storage hardware vendors continue to resist the development of a common management standard that would threaten to commoditize their offerings. It is analogous to the response of Hannibal Lecter, the fictional serial killer in the novel and movie *Silence of the Lambs,* when he is presented with a questionnaire designed to obtain information for an FBI behavioral science database. He asks FBI Agent Clarice Starling whether she believes she can dissect him with "such a blunt instrument." Storage hardware vendors, like the Lecter character, insist that their products have special features that cannot be captured by a generic or standards-based management approach such as a Simple Network Management Protocol (SNMP) management information base (MIB), or a Common Information Model (CIM) object model currently in development at the Storage Networking Industry Association (SNIA). As a result, storage management software developers find themselves in a quandary. To sell products, they must be able to monitor or manage popular storage hardware. In the absence of a common, standards-based management approach, however, this requires that the bulk of their developer resources be allocated to developing custom interfaces to the products themselves.

More than one management software vendor has offered that this situation prevents storage management software from doing what it should do: automating routine management functions (like backups) and immediate actions taken in response to error conditions. Customers want more automation—so-called policy-based management—but software vendors lack the resources to develop it since they are continuously writing and re-writing hardware interfaces as hardware vendors release new platforms each year.

While work proceeds in the Internet Engineering Task Force (IETF), which oversees SNMP, and within SNIA, which oversees CIM, to garner support for standards-based storage management schemes, some vendors, like EMC, are offering their own proprietary management software technologies as de facto industry standards. Additionally, a few innovative software developers, like Tek-Tools, are working to develop intelligent agents that can obtain management status information from devices without using the proprietary interfaces of storage hardware vendors. This is one more area of technology development that DR coordinators and storage administrators need to monitor to reach a good storage management software acquisition decision.

Another point that DR planners should keep in mind about storage management software is that new technologies are entering the market that could actually compromise data recovery strategies. A prime example is storage virtualization and its potential impact on tape-based data restore.

A number of vendors, including StoreAge Networking Technologies, Data-Core Software, FalconStor Software, StorageTek, Veritas Software, and others, are introducing virtualization technologies to market with the goal of creating scalable "virtual volumes" from aggregations of physical disk drives and storage array logical partitions (a partition on an array is, itself, a virtualization of multiple physical disks into a logical entity). The objective is to enable a volume to scale non-disruptively—removing a major source of downtime: a disk drive that has run out of space.

Figure 4–4 depicts these strategies, which can be generally categorized as host-based, in-band or symmetrical, and out-of-band or asymmetrical. The differences between the strategies are fairly straightforward. With a host-based virtualization scheme, the aggregation of physical disks and partitions is accomplished via software loaded onto every server individually. In-band approaches use a storage virtualization appliance, which is placed in the data path between the servers and the storage devices connected in a network or fabric. In an asymmetrical arrangement, the storage virtualization engine sits outside the data path of the storage network or fabric, creates virtual volume "device drivers" and delivers them to each server or host. The fourth strategy shown in the illustration is traditional virtualization—that is, the virtualization of disk drives in an array using the array controller to create "partitions."

The ramifications of virtualization for storage recovery are several. For one, the virtualization solution used in the production environment must be understood by the data backup and restore software deployed as part of storage management. There are already documented cases of one terabyte file restorals from tape requiring upwards of 100 hours to complete because of mismatched virtualization and backup software. The problem has to do with a "write penalty" that can accrue when reading data from one source and writing it to a virtualized volume. If certain compatibilities do not exist, the virtualization engine—which must read each bit of data and direct it to the appropriate physical disk device—can become a choke point in the data recovery procedure. Figure 4–5 depicts this situation.

Another issue related to virtualization that has great importance to disaster recovery planning is the potential hazard of losing data altogether during normal operations. The simple fact is that server operating systems want to "own" volumes, and they do not "understand" that a volume can scale. Many virtualization

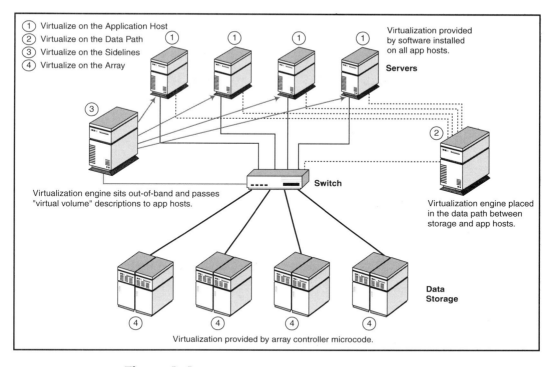

① Virtualize on the Application Host
② Virtualize on the Data Path
③ Virtualize on the Sidelines
④ Virtualize on the Array

Virtualization provided
by software installed
on all app hosts.

Servers

Virtualization engine sits out-of-band and passes
"virtual volume" descriptions to app hosts.

Switch

Virtualization engine placed
in the data path between
storage and app hosts.

**Data
Storage**

Virtualization provided by array controller microcode.

Figure 4–4   Four approaches to storage virtualization.

strategies—host-based strategies in particular—endeavor to surmount this limitation by "spoofing" the operating system. They are supplied with programs that "re-size" volumes by performing illegal operations on the operating system itself—causing the operating system to "forget" the previous size of the volume and to substitute a new volume size. When these spoofing approaches work, volume sizes can be changed dynamically in response to the storage demands of applications. But, when the spoofing program fails—and many do fail with greater frequency than vendors care to admit—all data on the existing volume can simply disappear.

Finally, virtualization needs to be carefully considered in terms of its impact on storage provisioning at the recovery site. Planners will need to ensure that storage volumes, whose capacities are changing more or less dynamically, are provided for at the systems recovery site. DR coordinators need to be aware that the sizes of virtual volumes can change rapidly and that the provisions made for data re-platforming at the recovery center can become obsolete just as rapidly. This is not a new challenge, of course, but it is one that is becoming more important as organizations embrace new, networked storage topologies.

Of course, the news on virtualization isn't all gloomy. Vendors of virtualization products are quick to point out that the technology can be useful in prevent-

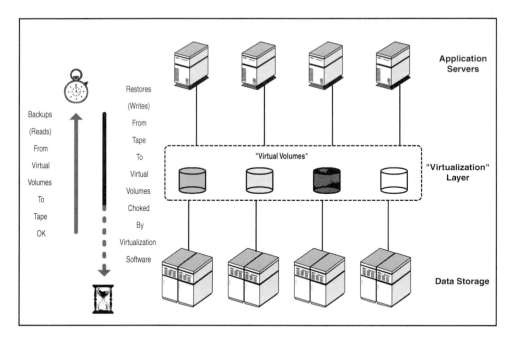

Figure 4–5   The virtualization choke point in tape-based data restore.

ing virtually all kinds of storage related downtime including disk full errors (by providing scalability on the fly), disk hardware failures (by enabling behind the scenes data replication and failover between physical drives), and routine disk maintenance (by enabling a replicated volume to carry the load while the primary components of a volume are taken off-line for maintenance). Moreover, virtualization of volumes may ultimately provide a solution for another knotty problem confronting DR coordinators: storage consolidation.

STORAGE CONSOLIDATION

In storage recovery planning, it is often incumbent on DR coordinators to develop a storage consolidation strategy—that is, to come up with a way to recover critical data on fewer, more capable platforms than those decentralized and heterogeneous platforms used to store data in the production environment. As shown in Figure 4–6, such a strategy may entail the aggregation of data stored on different arrays from different vendors into partitions of a single large array in the recovery setting. This is an important cost-savings strategy, since for most companies replacing every storage platform used in the production environment on a one-for-one basis would be prohibitively expensive.

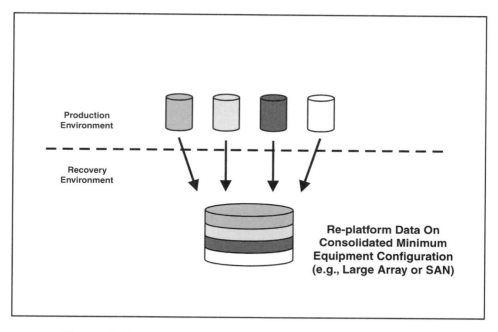

Figure 4–6   Storage recovery and platform consolidation: the ideal.

The problem is that disk-to-disk replication software provided by equipment vendors, including Symmetrix Remote Disaster Facility (SRDF) from EMC, only works to replicate data between two or more arrays from the same vendor (Symmetrix arrays in the case of SRDF). To restore data from different storage platforms in a consolidated platform has traditionally required the use of an intermediary: magnetic tape. In the not too distant future, according to vendors of virtual volume management software, the virtualization engine may be a key to cross-platform data recovery without the use of tape. As shown in Figures 4–7 and 4–8, describing solutions from StoreAge Networking Technologies and DataCore Software respectively, the virtualization engine may be able to be used to describe replicated volumes on two completely different storage platforms at different physical locations. This strategy is being pursued by vendors of backup and restore software, as well. Legato's RepliStor is an example, as shown in Figure 4–9.

Until such time as virtualization becomes more standards-based and the technologies for networked storage become more stable, however, the efficacy of these approaches as a comprehensive solution for data storage consolidation will continue to be limited. Most organizations will continue to restore data to consolidated platforms the old-fashioned way—via tape—as shown in Figure 4–10.

The bottom line is that storage management is a crucial technology for data protection and disaster recovery. According to several industry studies, storage

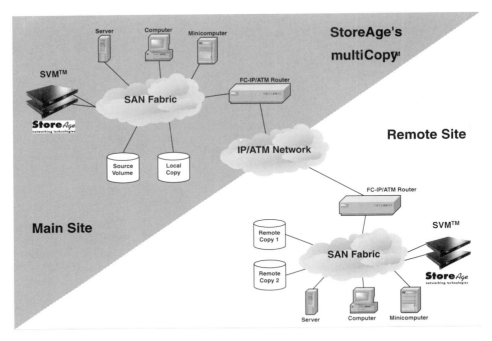

Figure 4–7   StoreAge's multiCopy™. (*Source:* StoreAge Networking Technologies, Irvine, CA and Nesher. Israel, www. storeage.com.)

component failure accounts for as much as 55% of server downtime. Thus, effective storage management is required to minimize downtime and avert disasters.

Of course, the risk reduction benefits of effective storage management are often de-emphasized by vendors in favor of compelling cost-savings arguments, but this is a result of marketing considerations rather than utility. From the standpoint of storage recovery, effective management is key and deploying a storage management capability should be considered a high priority by DR coordinators. That a well-managed storage environment is also considerably less costly to own is simply a side benefit.

TAPE BACKUP

The continued use of tape as the primary mechanism for data protection and storage recovery not only reflects the immaturity of alternatives, it also reflects robust development within the technology of tape itself. Tape capacity, performance, and resiliency is good and getting better.

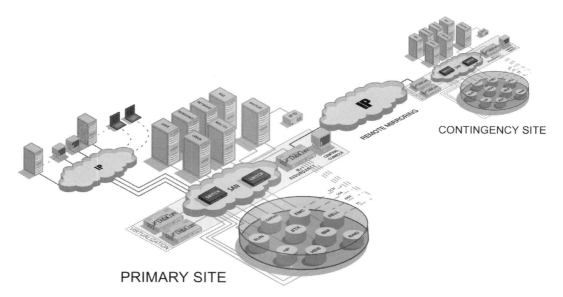

PRIMARY SITE

Figure 4–8 DataCore Software's SANsymphony for remote mirroring of virtual storage pools. (*Source:* DataCore Software,
Ft. Lauderdale, FL. www.datacore.com.)

Tape technology has a lengthy pedigree in the data storage marketplace.
Tape was among the original media used as "primary storage" for early computers. Over time, rotational media—magnetic disk—took over this role and tape
was relegated to the role of "secondary storage" (backup) and "tertiary storage"
(data archive).

The reasons for the rise of disk are well understood. Rotational media (disk)
offered faster access than streaming linear media (tape) to stored data. As CPU
speeds increased, and cost per MB for disk-based storage decreased, magnetic
disk became the preferred "primary storage" medium.

Of course, technically speaking, disk-based storage is not primary storage in
most computers. Rather, a nonrotational media provides the primary memory of
most computers: silicon chips. A small but growing market exists within the chip-
based storage industry for primary storage devices called "solid-state drives"
that may well eclipse the role currently played by magnetic disk in the not-too-
distant future. Many industry notables, including Microsoft CEO Bill Gates and
Sun Microsystems CEO Scott McNealy, have given credence to this view in numerous public statements.

However, just as the rising efficacy of solid-state disk does not diminish the
utility of magnetic disk, so magnetic disk has not diminished the utility of tape.
In fact, quite the opposite has occurred.

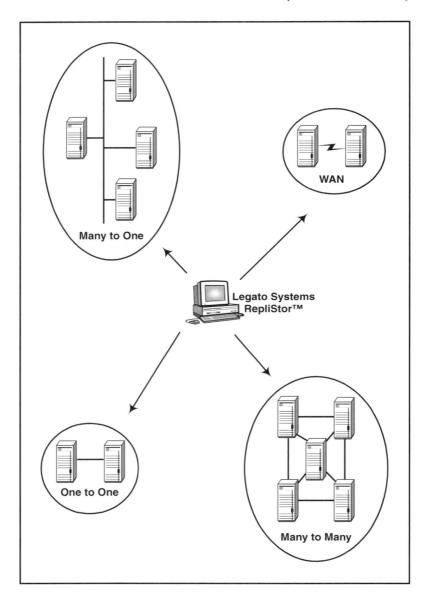

Figure 4–9　Legato Systems' RepliStor. (*Source:* Legato Systems, Inc., Mountain View, CA. www.legato.com.)

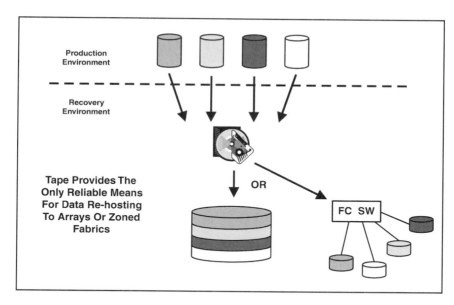

Figure 4–10   The continuing need for tape in storage consolidation.

Over time, tape technology has proven to be a robust technology that can adapt to the changing architecture of modern business computing. From its earliest days as a primary storage medium, tape evolved to become a secondary storage platform for production data within a hierarchically managed storage paradigm (HSM) advanced by IBM and other mainframe vendors throughout the 1960s and most of the 1970s.

In an HSM role, tape was used to store less frequently accessed production data that had been migrated from more expensive direct access storage devices (DASD). This role for tape may return into vogue as storage itself moves into a networked architecture (see Figure 4–11 for a classic HSM scheme).

With the rise of distributed "open" systems and networked client-sever applications in the 1980s, tape technology accompanied servers out of the glass house of the corporate data center and into the workgroup environment. It was in the open systems world that tape came into full flower as a flexible medium suited to the performance, capacity, and resiliency requirements of both server-based and PC-based computing.

Revenues for tape in the open systems market have soared, while revenues for older tape technologies aimed at mainframe data center markets have flattened substantially. Improvements in tape technologies aimed at this open systems segment have mapped closely to the improvements in server disk drive and storage interconnect technologies.

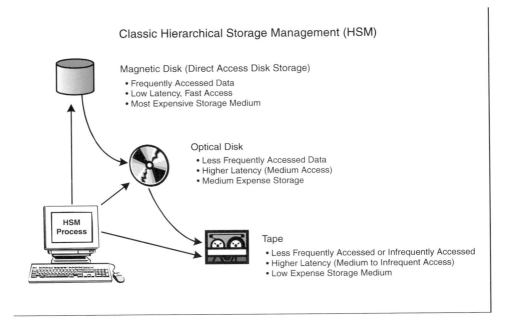

Figure 4–11   A classic HSM scheme.

As evidenced in Quantum Corporation's SuperDLTtape products (and others), tape has mirrored many of the same technologies implemented by disk drive manufacturers, including advances in read/write head technologies and media coatings that enable more data to be written and read more reliably to a fixed amount of recording surface.

- Super DLTape is the first to use PRML technology, first implemented on high-end server disk drives, to improve the read/write accuracy and efficiency of tape drives, while supporting ever-increasing data densities.
- Super DLTape's native capacity, which can be effectively doubled using compression algorithms depending on the data being stored, are moving from 160 GB per tape (320 GB compressed) in current generation drives to more than a terabyte per tape in Generation 4 drives anticipated by 2007. It is worth mentioning that Quantum is alone among tape manufacturers to provide such an aggressive capacity improvement roadmap. (See Figure 4–12.)
- Super DLTape technology also implements advanced storage interfaces such as Ultra2 SCSI, LVD, and HVD, first employed on disk drives, to improve transfer rates.

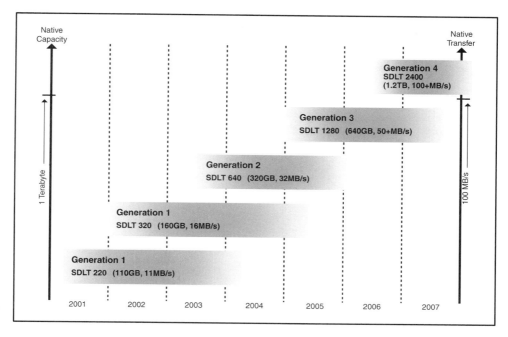

Figure 4–12   Quantum's SuperDLT roadmap. (*Source:* Quantum Corporation, Milpitas, CA. www.quantum.com.)

- The short-term roadmap for the technology goes further to implement Ultra160 and Ultra320 SCSI and Fibre Channel to facilitate the high speed transfer of data from tape to disk and vice versa. Current transfer rates of uncompressed data stand at 16 megabytes per second (MB/s), with Super DLTtape roadmaps projecting 32 MB/s in Generation 2 drives and 100+ MB/s in Generation 4 SuperDLT products.

In short, tape technology—led in the open systems space by Quantum's tape products, but with competitors such as Linear Tape Open (LTO), Sony Corporation, and Exabyte hot on Quantum's heels—has been keeping pace with advances in magnetic disk technology for nearly two decades. Whether as part of a hierarchical storage management scheme within the carefully controlled environment of a corporate data center, or as a highly available, highly flexible data backup medium in the distributed computing world, tape has proven to be a versatile and dependable medium for data storage.

Moreover, tape will continue to play a pivotal role at least until current generation networked storage topologies mature and stabilize—favoring disk-to-disk. Even then, tape will likely have significant traction as an inexpensive HSM medium and for archival storage. While some critics have adopted a "tape is dead" mantra, suggesting that disk-to-disk mirroring has already supplanted tape for disaster recovery given the shortened backup timeframes required by companies, such a perspective flies in the face of the transfer rates possible with tape automation.

The "tape is dead" view has surfaced from time to time in recent history. Not too long ago, organizations sought solutions for data backup that were consistent with available "backup windows." A backup window consisted of the time available within the normal operating schedules of systems and networks for performing large scale data movements from primary storage media (usually disk) to secondary storage media (usually tape). In the past, these windows were defined by application usage characteristics and network bandwidth availability.

Put another way, companies sought backup products that would enable them to copy mission-critical data to tape while production applications were not being used and networks were relatively quiet. These conditions usually existed after working hours, when everyone except janitorial staff and night operators had gone home for the night or weekend.

This scenario is increasingly anachronistic in many companies. With the growth of the Internet and the trend to extend corporate applications for access by customers or business partners via extranets and the World Wide Web, applications tend to be active on a 24×7 basis. That means that systems and networks are rarely quiesced for a sufficient period of time to enable a window for backup. Moreover, the amount of data to be backed up has increased to the point in many organizations where large-scale data movements could not be accomplished within any predefined window of opportunity.

Andrew Gup, a product marketing manager at Spectra Logic Corporation made a fascinating analysis of the problem in 1997.[13] He noted that terabyte-sized relational databases and 24×7 operating schedules had largely invalidated the traditional approach to off-line, or cold, database backup. In its place, database vendors enabled their products with application programming interfaces (APIs) that could be used to support "hot" backups (backups of active or in-use databases). Most leading backup/restore software vendors have since availed themselves of these APIs, which are also provided with many large ERP software suites.

In addition to hot backup API support, backup software vendors have added other capabilities to enable the performance of backups in a no window, multi-terabyte world. It is difficult to create a formal taxonomy of these approaches because vendors tend to give their technologies brand names in order to discriminate their products from one another. Table 4–3 provides a seminal effort in this area.

The new capabilities of backup software itself are addressing many of the "speeds and feeds" issues identified by critics with tape technology. These issues are also being addressed by improvements in the field of tape automation. Sim-

Table 4–3   Backup Strategy Taxonomy

Backup Strategy or Technology	Vendor	Functional Overview
IMAGE BACKUP Server Image Backup	Some vendors of backup software support variations of this method, which is probably the oldest method of electronic data backup on record.	Image backup creates a physical image of an entire disk. It operates at the physical disk level by transferring sectors or physical data storage blocks from hard disk to tape. Image backup delivers fast transfer rates by moving the hard disk head smoothly from one edge of the disk to the other as sectors are transferred. Complete server back-up is a relatively simple process since the entire contents of the hard disk are moved as a unit. The image contains the entire disk con-tents, but requires the system to be qui-esced prior to backup. Though a high-speed approach, the resulting backup tapes cannot be used to recover specific files, directories, or server specific ob-jects (Bindery and DNS for NetWare and the system registry under Win-dows NT).
Snapshot or Versioning Backups	Originated by CrosStor Software (formerly Pro-grammed Logic Corpo-ration), this capability has been added to many back-up software vendors' of-ferings.	Fast, block-level copies on a parti-tion basis, enabled for fast incre-mental (changed data only) backups to facilitate high-speed versioning.
FILE BACKUP Traditional Full Volume Backup on a File-by-File Basis	Most current vendors sup-port this approach, which varies from an image back-up in that data is recorded in accordance with the un-derlying file layout and structure of the host system controlling the disk volume.	Copy complete data sets via the pro-duction network to backup device(s) using a server-iniated, server-controlled process. The server maintains a database of file iden-tifiers and provides monitoring and reporting on process completion, errors and exceptions, and other factors.

(continued)

Table 4–3   Backup Strategy Taxonomy (continued)

Backup Strategy or Technology	Vendor	Functional Overview
Traditional Full Volume Backup with Hot Backup	Many vendors support Hot Backup APIs as either an integral function of their core product or as a modular add-on purchased on an as-needed basis by the customer.	Same as above, except that support is provided for database and application vendor application programming interfaces (APIs) that enable backup while active.
Traditional Full Volume Backup with Open File Support	Innovation attributed to St. Bernard Software but variations are now widely available from different vendors.	Open files are backed up to a "pre-write" cache, which is copied by the backup software instead of copying or skipping the open file entirely.
Incremental, Differential, or Delta File Backup	Most backup software supports the intelligent backup of data that has changed since the previous full or incremental backup. Methods for documenting changes and for facilitating file recovery vary from vendor to vendor.	Basically, file characteristics are compared to historical data (databases compiled in previous backup operations) to identify files that have changed since the last backup. Only changed files (and new files) are backed up. In some cases, differential differs from incremental backups in a subtle way. With differential backups, changed data files may be maintained as separate versions. With incremental backups, changed files replace their predecessors.
HYBRID IMAGE AND FILE BACKUP Full and Partial Backups Using Object Replication	Supported by products from Stac Software (Replica Tape) and others.	Object replication is a blend of file-by-file and image backup options. Logical objects are defined by the software, including disk partition tables, boot volume, security information, system volume, and user data volumes. All data on servers is treated as a single logical unit rather than as separate files, and all data can be copied at once. Object replication creates an exact copy of the entire server by saving it logically, block by block. Only data blocks that contain data are transferred.

(continued)

Table 4–3   Backup Strategy Taxonomy (continued)

Backup Strategy or Technology	Vendor	Functional Overview
ARCHITECTURE ADD-INS		
Host-free Backup	Supported by Legato Net-Worker following the company's acquisition of Intelliguard Software in 1999.	Using intelligent agents to initiate back-ups that then run independently of the host or server system, saving server resources and enabling direct storage device to storage device copies.
Full Backups with Parallelism Provisions	Essentially a hardware interconnect definition that enables multiple hard disks or a multiported disk array to be connected to multiple tape drivers or multiported tape arrays/libraries. Backup software must support interconnect device drivers.	Speeds the backup of large arrays by creating multiple, parallel paths for data movement. Some products, such as Ultera Systems', implement RAID striping and mirroring to facilitate multiple concurrent tape backups at high speed.

ply put, the speed with which tape technology can read and write data is no longer a function of the performance of a single tape drive. Automation is a multiplier of tape read-and-write speeds.

According to Quantum/ATL, just one of the company's high-end tape library subsystems using 16 SuperDLT or LTO tape drives is capable of backing up and restoring data from tape to disk at a rate of one Terabyte per hour. With more drives and more libraries, backup and restore rates can be increased almost exponentially.

Of course the use of multiple automated tape platforms to conduct backups requires some additional management according to Legato Systems' Symon.

> The challenge then becomes: how do we track the tapes? Tapes need to be tracked from the time they are used in the tape library, to their removal from the library, to their final move to an offsite vault for storage and protection. Products such as Legato's AlphaStor™ track the tapes/media so that customers not only know where their tapes are physically located but also it identifies which tapes they need to access immediately when a recovery is necessary.[14]

The strategies discussed in Table 4–3 are only the beginning of a broad array of solutions that will likely be developed to facilitate high-speed, reliable, and comprehensive backups of distributed corporate data. In many cases, the technologies for backup have begun to merge with the technologies for disk mirroring, reflecting less the problem of shrinking backup windows than the dilemma of fast restore.

DESIGNING A STORAGE RECOVERY PLAN

Many observers have pointed to restore as the critical part of the backup/restore equation. Rather than "windows for backup," they discuss backup/restore from the perspective of "windows of exposure" and emphasize both the impact of data loss and the time required to return data to a usable form following a disaster.[15]

While it is important to back up data accurately and with a minimal impact on normal operations, it is the speed of data restoral that is of key importance in a disaster recovery context. This premise is behind most of the recent technological advances in backup/recovery software and hardware platforms supporting its use.

Throughout 1998 and 1999, the press releases of major backup/restore software vendors cited new "world records" for terabyte database recovery on an almost monthly basis. This was more than a marketing effort to best the opposition. It was a response to the growing concern of business about the recoverability of such large and increasingly mission-critical data sets. Given the speed of popular tape devices of the day (DLTape, from Quantum, was the marketshare leader), transferring a terabyte of data to or from tape at a rate of 7 MB/s seemed a dangerously slow proposition. Moreover, with DLTape, it was necessary to scan an entire tape to find a particular file to restore, which could dramatically increase time to data in a recovery setting.

Advances in tape technology, especially in the areas of interface speed, parallel multiplexing capability, and tape RAIDing, provided a marked improvement in overall disk-to-tape data transfer rates. Backup/restore software vendors were quick to capitalize on these capabilities and added some tricks of their own to keep tape the dominant backup medium.

However, the key enablers of improved storage recovery timeframes have been less product-specific than systemic in nature. Beyond refinements and innovations in software and hardware, efforts to reduce time to data have also led to the reexamination of the traditional scenario for data recovery: tape backup with off-site storage.

In the traditional approach, the backup tapes and other documents needing backup are trucked off-site on a routine basis to a safe storage facility. In the event of a disaster, the tapes and other documents are collected from the off-site storage facility and transported via truck or airplane to a remote systems recovery facility, or hot site. There, the tapes are loaded into drives connected to the recovery platform, backup/restore software is loaded if necessary, and data is written from the tapes to the new storage devices on the backup platform.

The procedure had many steps—all of which required time—and was subject to many potential delays. Figure 4–13 depicts the factors affecting expeditious recovery from tape using the traditional approach.

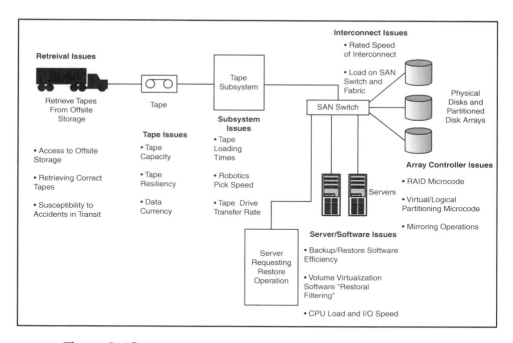

Figure 4–13   Potential delays in traditional tape-based storage recovery.

Despite these potential problems, the procedure continues to be used as the data restoral methodology for the majority of companies that plan for disaster recovery. Upon closer examination, however, several adjustments can be made to this procedure to save critical time to data.

Jim Grogan, Vice President of Alliances for disaster recovery facilities vendor SunGard Availability Services, says that the complexity of modern client/server platforms—including ERP applications, with their often huge and unwieldy distributed databases—have motivated many organizations to look for ways to shave precious hours off their data restoral processes.

> This basically comes down to some sort of data shadowing or mirroring technology that eliminates the need to retrieve data from off-site storage and places it directly on-site at the recovery data center. In the past, this was a prohibitively expensive proposition because it would have cost a company ten times more than [the traditional approach]. Today, with the deregulation in the telecommunications industry, the cost model has changed dramatically. We have been adding customers using high availability solutions for more than ten years now, with many advances in technology over that period of time. Our customers are embracing the technology advances, and they choose from several mature technology options for their HA configurations.[16]

ELECTRONIC VAULTING

Electronic tape vaulting replaces the manual procedures for handling tape in and out of off-site storage facilities and for transporting tape between locations. A Wide Area Network connection is established between the company facility and a remote tape library using channel extension technology or some similar high-bandwidth network interconnect. A classic implementation is one that partners off-site storage vendor, Iron Mountain, with long time channel extension and storage networking vendor, CNT. (See Figure 4–14.)

According to the vendors, the Electronic Vaulting Service, begun in March 2001, carves significant time off the traditional tape-based recovery timetable. Figure 4–15 shows the events involved in a 36-hour recovery process. But, by pre-staging the tape backup at the offsite storage provider (Iron Mountain), then providing incremental or journaled backups at routine intervals thereafter using CNT hardware to bridge internal systems with the remote electronic vault across a WAN, the total timeframe for recovery can be reduced to only 1 hour. Figure 4–16 illustrates how the time is saved—essentially by eliminating transportation and shipping, tape picking, and deployment of tape backups to automated tape

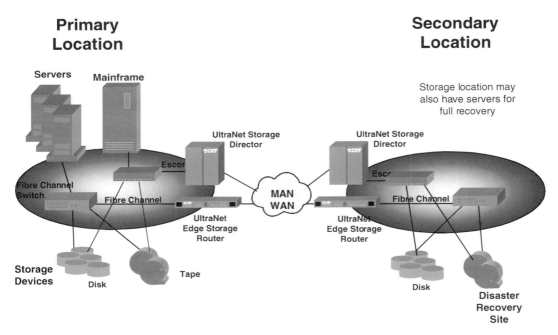

Figure 4–14   The CNT/Iron Mountain Electronic Vaulting Service
(*Source:* CNT, Minneapolis, MN, www.cnt.com.)

Traditional method of tape-by-truck
backup provides a standard recovery
point of 36 hours.

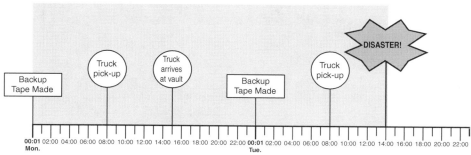

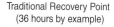

Figure 4–15   Before the electronic vaulting/journaling solution.
(*Source:* CNT, Minneapolis, MN, www.cnt.com.)

Adding electronic vaulting/
journalling drastically reduces
recovery point to 1 hour

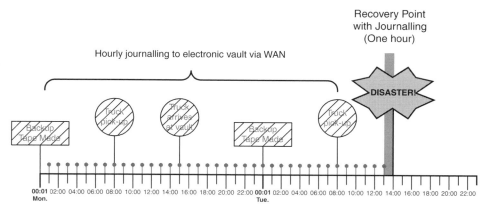

Figure 4–16   After the implementation of the CNT/Iron Mountain
electronic vaulting service. (*Source:* CNT, Minneapolis,
MN, www.cnt.com.)

libraries at the recovery site. With an electronic vaulting service, tape backups may be transferred electronically to the recovery site so that data is staged and ready to go when recovery teams arrive.

Of course, backups may also be required on site, at the corporate facility, to recover failed systems and to restore business processes before they have a chance to evolve into disastrous interruptions. To facilitate both local tape backup and remote electronic tape vaulting, intelligent tape controllers, like Ultera Systems Reflection, may be of service. (See Figure 4–17.)

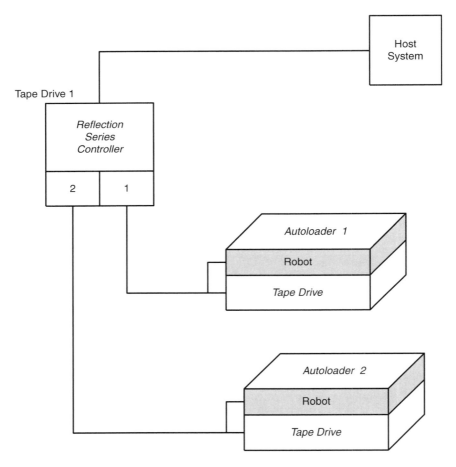

Figure 4–17   Mirrored tape backup operations. (*Source:* Ultera Systems, Laguna Hills, CA, www.ultera.com.)

Products like shadowing or multiplexing controllers provide the capability to duplicate backup data streams to two or more tape devices simultaneously. By directing a data stream across one link to a local tape autoloader and another data stream across a high-speed WAN link to a remote autoloader, both a local and a remote backup can be made expeditiously. This controller-based solution is compatible with most back-up/restore software products and with tape libraries and enables duplicate backup sets to be made in the amount of time typically required to make one backup.

Other approaches to mirroring or shadowing tape are beginning to appear in the market that leverage storage networks or fabrics. StorageTek's StorageNet 6000, for example, provides a means to enable local and remote tape writes while representing a single virtual tape subsystem to connected hosts. Figure 4–18 provides a simple diagram of the solution.

Another example is Quantum's DX30 product, based on its Adaptive Disk Array Management (ADAM) Technology. DX30, and future products in the family, will utilize a disk array platform wedded to tape in order to expedite tape reads and writes, and to facilitate the replication of data on any number of target storage devices.

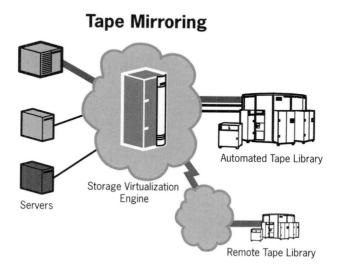

Figure 4–18   Leveraging virtual tape to support tape vaulting. (*Source:* StorageTek, Louisville, CO. www.storagetek. com.)

REMOTE MIRRORING

Another alternative to traditional tape-plus-off-site storage may be found in re-mote disk-to-disk mirroring. As suggested by its name, disk mirroring does not entail tape-based data copying at all. Instead, writes to one disk are duplicated in near real time on a duplicate disk volume.

Disk mirroring is not a new concept. In fact, it is a mainstay of Redundant Array of Inexpensive Disks (RAID) technology, affording RAID disk arrays an internal means of fault tolerance that is sometimes confused with disaster recovery backup.

With internal RAIDing, disks inside an array are mirrored as a safeguard against certain data loss scenarios. However, disasters can and do occur in which the building that houses the RAID disk array catches fire, loses power, or crumbles in any of a number of cataclysmic natural disasters, rendering the disk array—whether internally mirrored or not—inaccessible. In short, deploying mirrored storage within a data processing facility can contribute to the avoidance of certain types of disaster potentials, but it does not offer a comprehensive disaster recovery capability for the data asset.

Remote mirroring is essentially an extension of the concept of internal disk array mirroring. The idea is to perform duplicate writes to disks on identical (or at least similar) disk array platforms located some distance from the company facility—presumably far enough away so that the mirrored array is not consumed by the same disaster that affects the primary or production array.

In some cases, the mirrored array may be located at another site owned by the organization and remains a component of the organization's internal network. In other cases, the remote mirror may be located at a secure off-site storage facility. In still other cases, the mirror array may be located at a commercial system recovery facility that will be used to recover system platforms in the event of a disaster.

When the remote mirror is geographically distant from the production array, the two are typically connected to each other via a high-speed WAN link. As data writes are made to disk on the production array, they are replicated on the remote array.

In some mirroring arrangements, writes to production disks are placed in a holding queue while the system waits for the mirrored write to be completed and acknowledged. Known as synchronous mirroring, this technique introduces substantial latency into the production environment when mirrored arrays are located next to each other and share a high-speed interconnect. The problem worsens when arrays are separated by greater distances from each other and use slower WAN links for an interconnect.

For many years, extending the distance between mirrored arrays across hundreds of miles—say, between a corporate data center in California and a hot site facility in Pennsylvania—was the stuff of science fiction. The distance-related latency that would accrue to the production environment was enough to make remote mirroring a pipe dream. Over time, however, as the intelligence of disk array controllers improved, the speed and capacity of wide area networks increased, and the costs of high bandwidth WAN links declined, remote mirroring got a second look.

By the mid-1990s, vendors of large (sometimes called "mainframe class" or "enterprise class") storage array products were experimenting with new techniques for removing distance barriers to remote mirroring. One technique, quite simple in design, consisted of using three arrays instead of two. As illustrated in Figure 4–19, the idea was to use a surrogate mirroring array between the primary and remote array.

The surrogate array is "local" (within the reach of a high-speed serial link) to the primary array and affords protection against an equipment outage in the primary array. A second purpose of the surrogate array, however, is to initiate and manage a separate asynchronous mirroring process with a remote mirror array. The surrogate and remote arrays are linked via a WAN facility, and the latency of the mirroring operation between these arrays does not impact the primary array or the production environment at all.

Surrogate mirroring and other innovations in mirroring operation control and management began to move the technology out of the backwaters and into the mainstream of business continuity technology by the mid-1990s. Today, most hot-site vendors offer a remote mirroring solution for customers. Vendors recognize that remote mirroring entails substantial costs, which might include the purchase of surrogate platforms and the cost of WAN links. However, many vendors have found that customers with "zero downtime" tolerance can justify these costs.

A variety of remote mirroring solutions are available to meet a variety of applications and price points. Some are closely coupled with a particular ven-

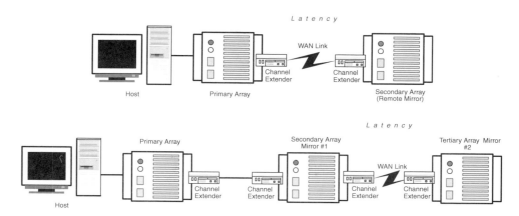

Figure 4–19   A surrogate mirroring configuration.

dor's array products. As depicted in Figure 4–20, EMC's SRDF may be used to provide synchronous or "adaptive copy" mirroring modes. Synchronous modes are preferred for short-distance mirroring, while adaptive copy—a technique for mirroring only changed disk tracks—produces smaller amounts of traffic and can save companies on bandwidth expense in wide area mirroring applications.

Most large hot-site facility vendors have adopted the EMC SRDF solution as part of their disaster recovery offerings. This is attributable in part to EMC's market share leadership in the enterprise disk array market through the second half of the 1990s. If customers are deploying EMC Symmetrix platforms in their production environments, they will likely seek comparable platforms in the hot site for use as remote mirrors.

According to SunGard's Grogan, another reason for the popularity of mirroring generally, and the EMC solution in particular, is product maturity.

> Mirroring products have matured over the past few years. They are proven. Cut and dried. They aren't rocket science anymore. SunGard was a beta customer of SRDF. From a usability perspective, the first generation product was not very friendly. You had no read access. If you wanted to see the data, you would basically have to stop the mirror operation. Today, with features such as [BMC Corporation's] Enterprise SnapShot and [EMC's] TimeFinder, you can see it, work with it and test with it. Again, with the costs of telcom links falling, the cost model is down. We have doubled the number of customers using remote mirroring in just the past couple of months.[17]

Sungard's first remote mirroring customer was the Philadelphia Stock Exchange. The organization set forth with an objective to recover its operations within two hours of a disaster that rendered its trade management applications unusable. In April 1996, the first tests of the configuration were conducted using mirrored EMC Symmetrix arrays, SRDF, and a SONET network ring interconnecting the Exchange and Sungard's disaster recovery hot site. Actual recovery in the test required only 58 minutes, which SunGard claims has since been decreased to 45 minutes.[18]

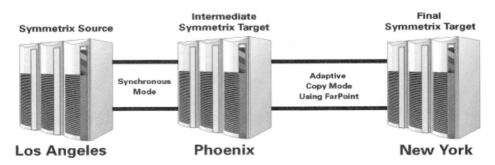

Figure 4–20   EMC SRDF multi-hop mirroring using synchronous and adaptive copy modes. (*Source:* EMC Corporation, Hopkinton, MA. www.emc.com.)

As suggested above, however, current mirroring schemes tend to be vendor hardware-specific. While vendor agnostic mirroring approaches continue to mature, establishing stable mirrored relationships between un-like storage platforms remains something of a holy grail.

MIRRORING NOT A PANACEA

Disk mirroring, especially the remote variety, has special appeal to disaster recovery planners because of its time to data characteristics and vendor promises of zero downtime. Zero downtime, however, is an unrealistic expectation even in a properly configured, perfectly operating, remote mirroring arrangement. Several factors mitigate the realization of this disaster recovery nirvana.

For one, remote mirroring is subject to data gaps. That is, because some sort of asynchronous mirror process is typically used in a WAN-based remote mirroring configuration, there is always a difference in the state of the data contained on the primary and mirrored arrays. This difference may be minor, or it might constitute a delayed shipment to a customer, a lost contract, or a missed investment. For remote mirroring to be effective, data gaps need to be identified and strategies for their resolution determined.

One approach is to use synchronous mirroring across the WAN, enhanced with a capability known as Mirrored Write Consistency mode.[19] This mode, available on some mirroring products, results in the creation of a detailed record of all write requests that have not been completed at both the local and the mirrored array. This record, in turn, can be used as a starting point for reentering older transactions and starting new transactions. A significant performance penalty must be paid for this type of security, however. Use of a synchronous operating mode combined with CPU-intensive transaction journaling can slow production system performance substantially. In general, the tradeoff between parity (synchronous mirroring with Write Consistency) and performance (asynchronous mirroring with data gaps) remains an issue for remote mirroring solutions.

In addition to the asynchronous mirror data gap, the zero downtime goal of many companies that choose remote mirroring is also mitigated by the fact that data restoration is only part of a recovery. In the wake of a disaster, many other activities need to occur before recovery can be accomplished. System hardware may need to be installed and operating system software loaded and configured. Networks may need to be rerouted. End-users need to obtain remote access to systems. These and many other tasks may need to be performed before the first transaction begins to be processed in the post disaster environment. From this perspective, remote mirroring is not a panacea for disaster recovery.

In addition to the above, more than one observer has pointed out that mirroring itself is not without risks. In some mirror configurations, improper array maintenance and disk swapping errors can cause the reference points for synchronized data to be lost, rendering the mirror array and the data it contains inaccessible and unusable. Moreover, any logic errors that affect the primary array and corrupt its stored data can also be transferred to the mirrored array, affecting its data efficacy and integrity as well. In short, mirroring can be a multiplier of disaster just as easily as it can be a mitigator.

In the event of a database corruption or human error, to get back to a good copy of the data, businesses had, until recently, no option but to use tape backup. Tape can have a place in a disaster recovery plan, according to Don Swatik, Vice President of Alliances and Information Sciences with EMC Corporation. But, the same content replication errors that can occur in a mirrored configuration are also the bane of tape. For critical data, he says, companies can use frequent point-in-time copies to get to a good copy of the data and to restart quickly in the event of one or more of the above data corruption issues.

> Here's a statistic: For every bit stored on a disk, there are ten bits stored on tape. Most companies that choose to have a mirrored copy of data that is in synch with its production data may well have an older generation of that data on tape. The difference is, if you have data on tape, it's data you hope you'll never have to use. If it's data you believe you will need to use, you ought to have it on disk.[20]

Swatik and others point to the declining price and increasing availability of high-speed telecommunications links as enablers of significant growth in both remote tape vaulting and disk mirroring implementations. Telecommunications providers, including AT&T and Sprint, are currently rolling out their "next generation networks"—albeit slowly—that promise to deliver redundant, high-speed, fiber-optic ring connectivity to corporate facilities. According to the vendors, the speed and performance characteristics of these networks will enable quality of service provisioning required to reduce the latency (and the costs) associated with electronic vaulting and remote mirroring. Ultimately, the intent of many telcos is to become vendors of high availability storage networking solutions themselves (see Chapter 7). This remains to be seen.

OPTIONS FOR RECORDS STORAGE

As of this writing, electronic data vaulting and remote mirroring are not part of the data protection strategies of most companies. This may be a function of the cost of these options or an acknowledgment of the greater tolerance to downtime inherent in their mission-critical applications. Whatever the reason, the preponderance of companies that do tape backups use manual methods for moving the tapes in and out of local and/or off-site storage.

It should also be noted that electronic tape vaulting and remote mirroring offer no solutions for the problems of paper and microform-based records storage. For these media, also, on-site or off-site storage may provide an answer.

Once documents and data files have been identified and classified, special attention must be paid to identifying any current methods that are being used to safeguard data from loss. Disaster recovery coordinators may find that the fear of potential data loss has motivated "owners" to develop their own strategies for safe storage. A host of capabilities may already be present within the company that provide varying degrees of records protection.

In certain areas of the company, auditors may have left their mark. Their comments about the security and recoverability of vital records may have led to the purchase of fireproof cabinets or to "informal" storage arrangements between company records administrators and vendors who prepare microform documents for remote storage of copies or source documents. Any number of "home-grown" strategies to safeguard data may have been devised by concerned departmental personnel.

Ferreting out existing strategies can be a challenging proposition. Migrating these individual strategies into a consolidated off-site storage plan can also be daunting. Not only are home-grown storage strategies often extremely informal and poorly documented, but they are also frequently a source of pride for those persons who formulated them.

The disaster recovery coordinator needs to be cognizant of the personal stake that people sometimes have in the most innocuous things. Applaud the ingenuity of the owner who has perceived the need for security and survivability and stored his or her backups in the safe deposit box at the local bank. Be diplomatic when telling the owner that a new strategy is being developed that will consolidate his or her off-site storage arrangements with those of less conscientious departments. Perhaps the owner can be recruited to assist in identifying and classifying other information assets in the company.

Once these steps have been completed, it is time for the disaster recovery coordinator to begin working toward a corporate solution to safe storage. Off-site storage is a common part of an overall strategy for data protection and survivability. However, off-site storage may be neither required nor appropriate for every data asset. The following options for data storage provide varying degrees of protection. A typical data protection strategy may integrate one or more of these approaches.

Local Storage Using Fire-Related Safes and Cabinets

A variety of fire-resistant cabinets and safes are available to safeguard data at the location where it is produced. Vendors typically reference performance ratings established by Underwriters Laboratories (UL) when describing their products. Table 4–4 summarizes the UL ratings of various fire-resistant safes and cabinets.

It should be noted that damage to magnetic tape and diskettes begins to occur at temperatures of 100 to 125°F and that newer, higher-capacity, hard disk media lose their integrity at temperatures of 145 to 149°F.[21] Paper and microform are considerably more resilient to heat (350°F for paper, 225 to 300°F for micro-

Table 4–4 Underwriters Laboratories Safe and Safety Cabinet Performance Ratings

Rating	Meaning
Construction Ratings	
B Rated	Steel construction, doors less than 1-inch thick, walls less than 1/2-inch thick.
C Rated	Steel construction, doors at least 1-inch thick, walls at least 1/2-inch thick.
E Rated	Steel construction, doors at least 1 1/2-inches thick, walls at least 1-inch thick.
ER Rated	Safe or chest labeled with "UL Inspected Tool Resisting Safe TL 15 Burglary."
F Rated	Safe or chest labeled with "UL Inspected Tool Resisting Safe TL 30 Burglary" or "UL Inspected Explosive Resistant Safe with Relocking Device X 60 Burglary."
G Rated	Safe or chest labeled with "UL Inspected Torch and Explosive Resisting Safe TR 60 Burglary" or "UL Inspected Torch and Tool Resisting Safe TRTL 30 Burglary."
PEFORMANCE RATINGS—BURGLARY CLASSIFICATIONS	
TL-15	Successfully resist entry for a net assault time of 15 minutes when attacked with common hand tools, picking tools, mechanical or portable electric tools, grinders, drills or pressure devices.
TL-30	Successfully resist entry for a net assault time of 30 minutes when attacked with common hand tools, picking tools, mechanical or portable electric tools, grinders, drills or pressure devices.
TRTL-30	Successfully resist entry for a net assault time of 30 minutes when attacked with common hand tools, picking tools, mechanical or portable electric tools, grinders, drills, pressure devices and oxy-fuel cutting or welding torches.
TRTL-60	Successfully resist entry for a net assault time of 60 minutes when attacked with common hand tools, picking tools, mechanical or portable electric tools, grinders, drills, pressure devices and oxy-fuel cutting or welding torches.
TXTL-30	Successfully resist entry for a net assault time of 60 minutes when attacked with common hand tools, picking tools, mechanical or portable electric tools, grinders, drills, pressure devices, explosives and oxy-fuel cutting or welding torches.
PERFORMANCE RATINGS—FIRE CLASSIFICATIONS	
4 Hour	Maintain an interior temperature of less than 150°F and an interior humidity less than 85% when exposed to fire up to 2000°F for 4 hours.
3 Hour	Maintain an interior temperature of less than 150°F and an interior humidity less than 85% when exposed to fire up to 2000°F for 3 hours.
2 Hour	Maintain an interior temperature of less than 150°F and an interior humidity less than 85% when exposed to fire up to 2000°F for 2 hours.
1 Hour	Maintain an interior temperature of less than 150°F and an interior humidity less than 85% when exposed to fire up to 2000°F for 1 hour.

form, depending on the presence of steam) and may derive greater benefit from fire-resistant safes and storage cabinets.

As a commonsense response to these facts, NFPA Standard 75[22] emphasizes the need to store duplicates of key, expensive-to-replace records in a location where they will not be affected by a disaster affecting the originals. The clear implication is that the practice of storing records in and around the data center or operations area of the business in which they are produced or used is ill-advised. Other options to strictly on-site storage, therefore, need to be considered.

Shell Game Strategy

One option, perhaps the least expensive, can be termed a "shell game." In this option, important data is moved around company offices but remains locally accessible.

If an organization's offices are dispersed around several buildings in an office park development, for example, copies of the records from one building may be stored in another building. This strategy has the advantage of providing ready access by those who would need to access records in an emergency. However, local storage may be vulnerable to the effects of the same disaster that damages the originating facility.

It may also be prohibitively expensive to outfit several sites within the company with the requisite safety and security capabilities to safeguard stored data. Storage rooms used for magnetic media, for example, should have features that approximate those in a data center environment, including temperature control, humidity control, static grounding, fire protection, water detection, environmental maintenance, and physical security. Table 4–5 summarizes NFPA recommendations regarding fire suppression systems and other elements of a protected computing environment and its storage facilities.

Cooperative Shared Storage Arrangements

A variation on the local storage option—one that might reduce some of the expense for redundant, specially equipped storage facilities within the corporate premise—is to share a storage room with another business. This, of course, is replete with issues of security and access control.

Subscribe to a Commercial Off-Site Storage Facility

Commercial records storage facilities remain one of the most often used options for secure, off-site storage. Commercial storage facilities are of two basic types: those offered by banks and moving-and-storage companies, and those offered by companies that specialize in off-site data and records storage.

Banks and moving-and-storage companies often make space available for records storage without knowing the types of records that are to be stored. Thus, their facilities do not generally meet the security and/or environmental require-

Table 4–5 Select NFPA Recommendations for Data Center/Records Area Protection

Building construction	Construction in accordance with NFPA 220, Standard on Types of Building Construction, preferably a single-story building, with protection provided where subject to damage from external exposure; separated from other occupancies within the building, including atria or other open-space construction, by minimum 1 hour fire-resistant-rated construction. All interior wall and ceiling finishes Class A rated per NFPA 101®, Life Safety Code® (if sprinklered, may be Class B); no exposed cellular plastics. Raised floors should include provisions for drainage from water leakage, sprinkler operation, coolant leakage, or fire-fighting operations. Structural supports and decking for raised floors should be of noncombustible materials. Access sections or panels shall be provided in raised floors and tools for providing access should be located in the room and their locations well marked. Cable openings or other penetrations through fire-related assemblies should be fire stopped. Openings, such as pass-through windows, should be equipped with automatic fire-related shutters. Air ducts should be provided with automatic fire and smoke dampers.
Materials and Equipment Restrictions	Only computer equipment and support equipment should be permitted in the computer room; office furniture in the room should be of metal construction. Records in the computer room should be kept to the absolute minimum. Tape libraries and record storage rooms within the computer area should be protected by a separate extinguishing system. Records storage rooms should be used only for storage, not for other activities, such as reproducing, erasing, etc. Paper stock, inks, and other combustibles should be restricted to the absolute minimum necessary for efficient operation. These materials should be kept in completely enclosed metal file cases or cabinets. Raised floor space should not be used for storage.
Fire Protection and Detection	Automatic detection equipment should be installed to provide early warning of a fire: at ceiling level throughout the computer area; below the raised floor over cable assemblies; and, above suspended ceilings/below raised floors where these spaces are used to recirculate air. Sprinkler systems should be provided if computer room enclosure is constructed of combustible materials, or the operation of the computer room involves a significant quantity of combustible materials, or the building is otherwise required to be sprinkled. Sprinklers for computer areas should be valved separately from other sprinkler systems. Gaseous Total Flooding Extinguishing Systems may be used when there is a critical need to protect data in process, reduce equipment damage, and facilitate return to service. Design, install, and maintain in accordance with NFPA 12A (for HALON), NFPA 12 (for CO2) or NFPA 2001 (for Clean Agents). Power to electronic equipment should be disconnected automatically upon activation of a gaseous agent total flooding system except where the risk considerations indicate a need for continuous power. Air handling systems that might exhaust the agent supply should be interlocked to shut down upon agent system actuation.

Source: Extracted from "NFPA Standard for the Protection of Electronic Computer/Data Processing Equipment 1999 Edition," National Fire Protection Association, Quincy, MA, 1999.

ments of data processing media or microform storage. Other drawbacks of using these facilities are that records are not available at all hours of the day, facilities are shared, access controls are insufficient, and physical storage sizes are limited.

Commercial off-site storage facilities specializing in electronic media storage cost about the same as bank or moving-and-storage company services. However, in these facilities, ideal conditions for environment, security, and accessibility are provided.

Commercial off-site storage centers are designed with magnetic and microform media storage requirements in mind. A well-designed facility is similar in all respects to one that a disaster recovery coordinator might wish to construct at his or her own facility, although costs are generally much lower because they are shared among several customers that make use of the same facility.

What makes the commercial facility preferable to a cooperative storage arrangement, however, is the use of trained, single-tasked personnel at the commercial facility to control access to stored data. Rarely are clients allowed to access their storage directly; they must rely instead on storage center staff to pull tapes and storage boxes.

For most medium to large companies, a combination of the preceding options is used to provide safe storage of critical and vital information. For example, companies may set up an in-house records center to facilitate day-to-day information requirements, may utilize a local but off-premise storage area for tape backup storage, and may contract with a commercial off-site storage vendor for longer-term media and records storage.

Some companies have gone even further to ensure backup survival by engaging redundant backup and redundant off-site storage. To wit, the case for redundant backup holds that if original data is lost and damage occurs to backed-up media while in transit to the backup site or during the effort to restore a system, a second backup would be needed to complete the system recovery process.

This may sound excessive, possibly even neurotic, until one considers the accidents that can and do occur in storage centers. In October 1996, for example, a fire at the Brambles Information Management Center in Chicago, IL, consumed 220,000 boxes of stored archival and vital records. The following year, three fires at supposedly impervious Iron Mountain Records Centers in South Brunswick, NJ, consumed over 1 million boxes of paper records and affected 200 companies. In May of the same year, the Diversified Records Services Center, a football stadium-sized building near Scranton, PA, burned to the ground with all of its paper and microfilm stores.[23] Whether the fires were accidental or deliberate, these events suggest that redundancy has value, even in backup strategies.

Other proponents of redundant backups point to the possibility of disasters that are regional in scope (i.e., hurricanes in coastline states, earthquakes in various parts of North America), which might affect both the subscriber company and its off-site storage facility.

Redundant backups would ideally be stored at separate locations: on-site, off-site locally, and off-site remotely. For many data processing centers, a three-cycle retention program is observed as a matter of standard operating procedure. "Grandparent" and "parent" backups are removed to remote and local off-site storage, respectively, while "child" backups are retained in-house for use in conjunction with day-to-day mishaps.

The point is that most businesses with a backup storage plan utilize a combination of redundant data backup procedures and complementary storage options to lessen their exposure to critical data loss. Most use, as part of their backup storage strategy, a commercial off-site storage vendor.

SELECTING AN OFF-SITE STORAGE VENDOR

One of the more controversial issues in disaster recovery planning revolves around criteria for selecting a vendor of off-site storage services. This, in part, reflects the nature of the data processing industry and the explosion of new companies that have formed to fill this niche over the past five to ten years.

The first commercial off-site storage facilities for magnetic media (and records generally) were designed for archival storage over decades or even centuries. Some were specifically constructed to withstand the anticipated force of an atomic explosion (see Figure 4–21 and 4–22).

Records were rotated in and out of these centers at the relaxed rate of once per month. Today, with an increased awareness of the need for off-site storage in

Figure 4–21 An underground commercial records storage facility. (*Source:* Iron Mountain/National Underground Storage, Inc., Boyers, PA. www.ironmountain.com.)

Figure 4–22   A tape vault at Iron Mountain. (*Source:* Iron Mountain/National Underground Storage, Inc., Boyers, PA. www.ironmountain. com.)

the face of other threats somewhat less devastating than nuclear war, numerous above-ground centers have been built for local and regional users.

In fact, one reason that commercial off-site storage facilities have become less expensive is that there are more and more facilities. In most metropolitan areas of the country, information managers now have a choice among several vendors. Added to this number are the dozens of vault-equipped banks, thrifts, and moving-and-storage companies who market their own facilities for media backup. This explosion of facilities has led to increased competition and relatively low prices; it has also had the positive effect of promoting a drive to establish "THE RULES" for identifying what makes one off-site storage facility superior to another.

In the search for distinction, vendors advertise that their facilities comply with any number of authoritative guidelines, including those articulated by the Association of Records Managers and Administrators (ARMA), the National Fire Protection Association (NFPA), American National Standards Institute (ANSI), the U.S. Government's National Bureau of Standards (NBS), the Underwriters Laboratories (UL), and various state and local agencies. Compliances often follow the facility logo in advertising literature like alphabet soup.

Despite all these guidelines, there is not a single set of rules that defines the "best" off-site backup facility. None of the above organizations, in fact, claim to have defined rules for selecting anything. Rather, each organization cites environmental or operational characteristics of a well-designed facility. Adherence by vendor facilities to these standards is a plus, but facility design alone is not a sound basis for selecting a vendor.

For example, the fact that a vendor complies with ANSI standard on temperature, humidity, and air purity requirements says little about the safety of the data of the business that uses the vendor. Similarly, vendor adherence to NFPA standards for vault construction or fire protection offers little consolation if the vendor has internal management problems, cannot effectively manage its stored inventory, or fails to answer emergency calls from clients over the holidays.

There is some truth in the arguments of some vendors who do not comply with certain standards in their facilities when they claim that technological advance has outpaced guideline revisions. Managers of storage facilities may decide that complying with outdated standards is less cost-effective than providing appropriate security, fire protection, and other quality services. For this reason, the selection of the right backup storage facility is less a function of counting compliances than evaluating vendor performance and capability.

At a minimum, the following evaluative criteria should be considered, and to the extent possible, validated by an independent third party:

- *Reputation.* How long a facility has been in existence, its association with a larger corporate entity, its financial statement, its record with the Better Business Bureau, and even its reputation within the community of information management professionals are all important factors in selecting an off-site storage vendor.
- *Site security.* Security at the storage site should be no less (and possibly a good deal more) stringent than at one's own facility. Some questions to consider:

    What are the access controls in the facility? Is visitor access restricted?
    Are client names concealed, even from one another?
    What security measures are observed during the transportation of media? (Unmarked vehicles, security in vehicles, employee monitoring, etc.)

How are employees screened?

Are cameras, videotape, or other devices used to monitor facility traffic?

How are emergency calls handled in terms of authorizations and so on?

- *Media management.* A very important factor, how the facility manages client records, may present the following questions:

  How is media of several clients segregated?

  Is magnetic media stored separately from microform and paper? Are there certain types of media that will not be stored in the facility?

  Is media transported in plastic containers or cardboard boxes?

  Are employees trained in proper media handling?

  Are media maintenance activities, including periodic tape rotation, performed as standard operating procedure?

  What kind of inventory management system is used? If an automated system, is it backed up?

  How often is a physical inventory of media performed?

  What controls exist to monitor the flow of media in and out of the facility?

- *Environmental factors.* Although much abused, a number of environmental standards are important in off-site vendor selection. Vendors should recognize the standards, and if they do not comply with them, have a good case for not doing so. Of course, to determine whether a vendor complies, one must first understand the standards involved. Table 4–6 lists several references with which the disaster recovery coordinator should become familiar prior to meeting with vendors.

  Having become familiar with the standards, the disaster recovery coordinator should seek answers and documentation from the vendor on the following points:

  What capabilities are installed to detect and signal smoke, heat, flame, water, and intrusion?

  What extinguishing capabilities are available?

  Is the alarm system tied directly to fire, police, and security services?

  How are temperature, heat, humidity, and contamination controlled?

  What are the facility's backup power requirements and how are they provided?

  How frequently are environmental protection and backup capabilities checked or tested?

  What is the company smoking policy?

- *Transportation.* There are statistics that purport to demonstrate that data is most vulnerable while in transit between the client facility and off-site storage house, and between the off-site storage facility and a data processing backup facility. In short, tapes and records are at higher risk of loss or damage while riding in the back of a van on a well-traveled street or highway or in the luggage compartment of an airplane than when they are sitting in a climate-controlled, fire-protected, contamination-reduced storage room.

Table 4–6   Selected References for Establishing Off-site Storage Vendor Selection Criteria

Source	Title	Abstract
ARMA International 4200 Somerset Dr., #215 Prairie Village, KS 66208 913/341–3808 • 800/422–2762	Records Center Operations —A Guideline ARMA International Standards Records Center Operations Task Force	This guideline will assist an organization or company in designing or selecting an appropriate records center site. It includes information on equipping, staffing, and overall management of the center with sample forms used in records center operations and discusses commercial records storage facilities. A section on computerizing a records center discusses design considerations and operating procedures. With appendices, annotated bibliography, and index, (51 p., 1986).
National Fire Protection Association, Batterymarch Park Quincy, MA 02269	NFPA 75: Standard for the Protection of Electronic Computer/Data Processing Equipment, 1999 Edition	NFPA 75 outlines requirements for computer installations needing fire protection and special building construction, building construction, rooms, areas, or operating environments. Application is based on risk considerations such as the business interruption as-pects of the function —as in computers used in the stock market —or the fire to the installation (18 pp., 1999).
	NFPA 232: Standard for the Protection of Records, 1995 Edition	NFPA 232 outlines requirements for records protection, equipment, including vaults, file rooms, safes, containers, and other devices, and for the management of records (17 pp., 1995).
	NFPA 232A: Guide for Fire Protection for Archives and Record Centers, 1995 Edition	NFPA 232A provides guidelines on fire protection for file rooms exceeding 50,000 cubic feet in volume, as well as all archives and records centers (20 pp. 1995).

(continued)

Table 4–6   Selected References for Establishing Off-site Storage Vendor Selection Criteria (continued)

Source	Title	Abstract
National Information Standards Organization (NISO) 4733 Bethesda Avenue Suite 300 Bethesda, MD 20814 Voice: 301/654–2512	NISO TR01–1995, Technical Report—Environmental Guidelines for the Storage of Paper Records, by William K. Wilson.	This technical report establishes appropriate environmental guidelines for the storage of records in libraries, archives, and other storage facilities. Recommended requirements for temperature, relative humidity, light, and air pollutants are given. Includes a detailed review of the technical and scientific literature. Suggests environmental parameters that influence the preservation of paper-based records in libraries and archives. Storage parameters addressed include temperature, relative humidity, exposure to light, gaseous contaminants, and particulate (30 pp. 1995).
National Technical Information Service Technology Administration U.S. Department of Commerce Springfield, VA 22161 Order Desk: (703) 605–6000 Fax: (703) 605–6900	Care and Handling of Computer Magnetic Storage Media PB 83 237 271 (Special Publication 500–101), 1989.	Covers tape management systems tape maintenance schedules, and environmental conditions for archivals storage computer media.
PRISM International (formerly Association of Commercial Records Centers) 16 E. Rowan Street Suite 400 Raleigh, NC 27609	Media Vault Guideline	Suggests operational guidelines for media storage.
	Demand the Best	Suggests evaluative criteria for selecting a storage facility vendor.

This underscores the fact that the transportation capabilities of the off-site storage vendor must be examined as part of the evaluation and selection task. The following questions can yield valuable insights:

Is media transported by vendor employees or by independent courier service?

Is media subjected to ambient climatic conditions during transport or are vehicles climate-controlled?

Under what conditions may drivers make stops, route changes, etc.?

Are vehicles equipped with antitheft devices, two-way radios, etc.?

How is media stored in the vehicle?

What is the longest estimated time to make a regular delivery? An emergency delivery?

Are different vehicles used to make emergency deliveries? Does the vendor provide an airport delivery service?

Does the vendor provide preparatory services (i.e., special services for readying media for long distance travel, including selection, crating, air or freight carrier contact, scheduling, delivery, destination transportation arrangements, etc.)?

The answers to all of the above questions should be verified, insofar as possible, with an on-site visit. Also, ask the vendor for the names of customers who would be willing to speak about the vendor's performance. Despite the security requirements of many companies, the vendor usually has the permission of several clients to disseminate their telephone numbers to prospective customers for validation and endorsement. Be aware, however, that the vendor will nearly always provide only the names of satisfied customers.

Once all evaluative criteria have been validated to the satisfaction of the disaster recovery coordinator, the next task is negotiating the contract and the schedule for regular pickups and deliveries.

Contracting for off-site storage is essentially a task of assigning a cost to each of the services that the vendor will provide. Contracts may be as straightforward as an initial invoice and a handshake, or they may be multipage documents loaded with fine print that need to be reviewed by a lawyer and/or auditor. Costs vary widely, and some storage facility managers have more latitude to negotiate than others.

Before examining the elements of an off-site storage contract, however, it is important to know what information the vendor will require about the prospective client prior to contract negotiation. Initially, the client will be expected to provide two items of information. The vendor will need to know approximately how much storage (and of what media type) the client will require. If the number of tapes or cartons can be estimated before the negotiation of a contract begins, this will help speed the process of setting a price for the service.

The second item of information concerns the frequency of pickups and deliveries. Are all records and media to be rotated to the facility daily? Are some to be rotated back to the client daily, some monthly, and some stored permanently by the vendor?

Until the disaster recovery plan is fully written, tested, and approved, the exact quantity of off-site storage and frequency of rotation may be difficult to determine. However, it may be possible to develop an interim off-site storage plan (for example, covering the storage of weekly system backups and daily transaction backups, plus the archival storage of critical and vital records) that will serve as the basis for negotiating the contract.

Some of the fees in a typical contract are the following:

- *Regular pickup and delivery fee.* This fee covers only the cost to the client of the courier's trip to the client facility on a regular or routine basis. It should state how often, and at approximately what time of day, the courier will arrive to drop off and/or pick up materials. The fee may be written as a per visit charge, or as a monthly aggregate.
- *Emergency delivery fee.* The contract should identify what "emergency delivery" means, whether all nonroutine visits are considered emergencies or only those visits in which an emergency time-frame for delivery is invoked. Some facilities will make unscheduled deliveries on a non-emergency basis by allowing the courier to deviate from his or her route during daily deliveries. If this is the case, it should be included in the contract and the fee stated. If an emergency delivery is defined as a visit made to the client site at a time other than normal vendor operating hours, be sure to have the vendor's working hours and holiday schedule spelled out in the contract.
- *Tape (or container) handling fee.* Delivery fees often cover only courier visits and media transportation. They do not necessarily cover the handling of media in and out of the storage facility. A per-tape or per-container fee for handling is often assessed, especially by vendors who must hire special staff to place, track, log, and maintain stored goods. For archival storage, particularly of tape, a fee in addition to a handling fee may pay for the rotation of archived tapes.
- *Storage fee.* In addition to delivery and handling fees, many facilities charge an additional fee for the actual amount of space occupied by client data. This rent is typically assessed on a monthly basis. If the amount of stored information changes during the month, the charge is usually assessed on the basis of the maximum amount of space occupied by client data at any time in the month.
- *Preparatory service fees.* Some vendors offer disaster recovery services in the form of preparing stored records and media for transportation to a recovery facility in the event of a disaster. These services may include boxing records and media for long distance travel by plane or freight, coordinating transport through freight routing services, moving media to an airport or train station, and arranging for the transportation (at the point of destination) of the records and media to the recovery facility. These services may be charged as a regular monthly fee or charged to the customer after the fact. If a regular fee is assessed, ensure that the vendor will provide one thoroughgoing test of the capability per year.
- *Other fees.* A host of other fees are becoming increasingly prevalent in the industry. These may include special insurance fees to cover media replacement (if the vendor is not insured or bonded for this eventuality, be sure to find out why), schedule revision fees (charged to customers who revise their regular pickup and delivery schedules), plan maintenance fees (for

customers who use the vendor to write the section of the plan pertaining to preparatory services), and special fees for upgrades to facilities (sometimes employed instead of price increases). Some facilities offer media maintenance and cleaning services that are also charged on a fee basis. All fees should be clearly spelled out in the contract.

In addition to fees, the disaster recovery coordinator should secure other items of information in writing from the off-site storage vendor. The vendor should indicate the exact steps that will be taken if records or media are misplaced in the vault or warehouse. The vendor should also identify the procedure for requesting and receiving a delivery, including emergency contact numbers, authentication of requests, and emergency delivery timeframes. The contract should also supply a complete definition of the vendor's liability for media in its charge, and identify the details of the vendor's insurance or bonding.

COST-JUSTIFY OFF-SITE STORAGE

Once the disaster recovery coordinator is satisfied that a vendor will provide competent, cost-effective service for the foreseeable future, the next step of the procedure may be to cost-justify the service to senior management. Pointing out a number of factors may help simplify this effort.

1. Off-site storage is not just a data processing-related expense. Every department, even administration, may have records and documents that need to be stored off-site. Most senior managers recognize the value of safe, secure storage when it comes to documents such as contracts, agreements, and accounting data.
2. As off-site storage is a solution to a business's overall vulnerability, it may be possible to divide the cost among all corporate departments. Better yet, off-site storage may be handled as a strictly administrative expense item, and may, in many cases, be tax deductible.
3. Off-site storage is rarely a politically charged issue. If the disaster recovery coordinator couches his or her rationale for storage in terms of protecting corporate assets, few detractors can persuasively argue against it.
4. Because of increased competition among vendors of off-site storage, the expense of the service is rarely prohibitive.

Of course, cost-justifications must reference benefits that accrue to the company from the acquisition of a subject product or service. In the case of off-site storage, cost-justifications devolve from the same risk analysis that was generated to identify corporate exposures. While it is difficult to assign a dollar value to the data that is being stored, it is a relatively common practice to demonstrate the cost to the company of prolonged downtime. Therefore, the coordinator can provide a scenario in which the cost of downtime to the company is attributable to the lack of backup data needed to restore the system.

The disaster recovery coordinator can further demonstrate the cost-effectiveness of the off-site option by developing a prospectus showing the costs and relative risks entailed in developing a comparable capability within company-owned facilities. In addition to the cost of environmental control, fire protection, water detection, furniture, shelving, and security, a "home-grown" shell for storage would also require the hiring of additional personnel.

IMPLEMENTING THE DATA RECOVERY PLAN

Once approval has been granted, the disaster recovery coordinator must finalize a schedule for removal of records to permanent off-site storage. The coordinator may need to coordinate with the IS executive to establish a routine for the preparation and rotation of computer media and other records requiring periodic update.

Special attention should be given to the requirement that users of PCs and user-administrated servers become participants in an off-site storage plan. For the first several weeks, their cooperation may need to be closely monitored. Given the increase in the average amount of disk storage shipped with PCs (10 GB drives are increasingly common in Windows/Intel personal computer configurations), as well as the proliferation of PCs in most organizations, this represents a truly staggering potential for data loss.

Obtaining the cooperation of users and administrators of decentralized systems may be a challenge, but it must be overcome if a company's disaster recovery capability is to be fully developed. There may be a need to involve senior management in forging corporate policy regarding data backup and participation in an off-site storage plan. Even then, it may be necessary to monitor the compliance of PC and LAN server users and administrators for a period of time until their participation becomes automatic.

The coordinator may also find it helpful to disseminate information about the backup program throughout the company so that new storage requirements or requirements that were not originally considered may come to light.

To establish controls, a formal log should be kept to record movement of media and records from the tape library and record center to the vendor site. This log documents when couriers were on site and what they took or delivered. The log may also be useful in billing issues or in assessing vendor compliance with established delivery schedules. The log further provides a backup that may be used to track down media or records that are misplaced at the off-site storage facility. The more detailed the log, the better its use in resolving problems.

Once schedules and controls are in place, the disaster recovery coordinator needs to arrange periodic reviews of the off-sight storage program. Depending on how rapidly company procedures and systems change, this review may have to be conducted quarterly or semiannually in order to identify changes in off-site storage requirements. This review should include an investigation of the following:

- *Vendor performance.* Periodically, the record of the vendor should be checked to ensure that billing is correct, media is being properly handled and stored, promised emergency delivery time-frames are being met, and media is being rotated on schedule and without apparent damage. This check should include an inspection of the vendor facility, a review of vendor financial statements and both financial and functional audit reports, and a sampling of opinions of the information management community regarding vendor performance generally.
- *Adherence to classification criteria.* Determine whether company information is being properly classified according to the scheme set forth in the development of the off-site storage plan. This may be done by sampling some of the records and documents as they are prepared for off-site storage. Trace the origins of the documents identified in the spot check, and ask the individual who classified the data to explain his or her rationale for the classification applied.
- *Changes in disaster recovery requirements.* An inventory of media and forms stored off-site should be discussed at a meeting of data "owners" to assess whether it is obsolete or otherwise irrelevant to company requirements. In some companies, this is done as part of departmental review of their sections of the company disaster recovery plan. If some materials stored off-site are no longer necessary or relevant to business recovery, have them removed. Be sure to have the vendor revise the storage fees if there is a substantial reduction in the volume of data being stored.
- *"Awareness" programs.* Verify that awareness programs established at the outset of the off-site storage program are continuing. This may include revising a handout on key characteristics of the storage program and disseminating it to department managers, application end users, and new employees within the company.

It is especially important that new PC-users be indoctrinated in procedures for backup and off-site storage of critical data. Having users read, initial, and return a memo covering their responsibility to participate in off-site storage may facilitate this requirement.

FINAL OBSERVATIONS ABOUT DATA RECOVERY PLANNING

Data recovery planning is not the most glamorous aspect of disaster recovery planning, but it is essential to successful recovery from a disaster. Without backups of critical data, and the capability to restore from those backups efficiently, most companies will never recover from a major disaster, regardless of other preparations they have made.

Some additional technologies that may facilitate effective data recovery capabilities include:

- *Electronic document management systems.* These systems enable more of an organizations nonelectronic information assets to be copied and shared efficiently and also provide an expedient means for creating backups for secure storage.
- *Enterprise storage management and backup/restore software.* These applications enable the policy-based management of data storage infrastructure (including backup and restore and mirroring functions) across a broad range of storage configurations. If an organization has not deployed a standardized enterprise storage management system, the task of managing the data recovery plan is magnified in proportion.
- *Standardized desktop configuration.* This is a part-policy/part-architecture solution that has been implemented by a number of large organizations to mitigate desktop management costs. Essentially, the applications that may be installed on an end user desktop are predefined by the organization, often on the basis of a user job classification, and application software itself is maintained on a central "library" server. The result is a common desktop with common directories that are much more readily backed up and restored in the event of an equipment outage.
- *Thin-client computing architecture.* The mention of standardized desktops provides a natural segue to another technology that has been gathering momentum in the modern IT world: server-centric or "thin-client" computing. Without delving into all of the permutations of this emerging technology, the fundamental premise is that data and application software are more cost-effectively maintained on a server than on a desktop device. The desktop device, a thin client, provides the user with an interface to the application, as well as local processing capabilities (in most, but not all, architectural definitions). By centralizing user data and applications onto a fewer number of devices, they can be more readily managed (and backed up) by a fewer number of personnel. This architecture, too, holds promise for increasing the efficacy of data recovery planning.
- *WORM media.* Certain types of data have special security, confidentiality or integrity requirements, even when stored as backups. The increasing availability of write once, read many (WORM) media provides a useful backup media for meeting such requirements. Once the exclusive domain of optical media types such as Compact Disk-Recordable (CD-R) and specialized magneto-optical products (MO-WORM), magnetic tape-based WORM was introduced to the market by Storage Technology Corporation in 1998. The VolSafe™ Redwood tape cartridge was the first to deliver the level of data security and integrity required under the Securities and Exchange Commis-

sion (SEC) amendment that allows brokers and dealers to store records electronically.[24] Recording to tape media can be accomplished at a significantly greater speed than recording to optical media, enhancing the value of this approach. Competitive products to the StorageTek offering are expected and tape vendors will likely leverage improvements in encryption technology to build out the features of these products over time.

Another point that should be made about data protection and storage recovery is that some of the ongoing management of processes, such as mirroring and backup, may be facilitated through the use of third party managed storage service providers. As shown in Figures 4–23 and 4–24, vendors like Storability or StorNet are offering services to corporate clients that off-load the heavy lifting of storage management and monitoring from IT staff so they can perform other useful work.

The Storability offering, which is being acquired by StorageTek as this edition goes to print, entails the provisioning of customer storage systems with agents to monitor backup operations. The agents are polled by AssuredStorage Communications and Operations Modules (ACOM) that, in turn, report to geographically dispersed AssuredStorage Operations Processing Systems (AOPS). AOPS also serve as knowledgebase repositories for status information on the en-

Figure 4–23   Storability's AssurENT Storage Management Architecture. (*Source:* Storability, Inc., Southboro, MA. www.storability.com.)

StorTrust Manager System

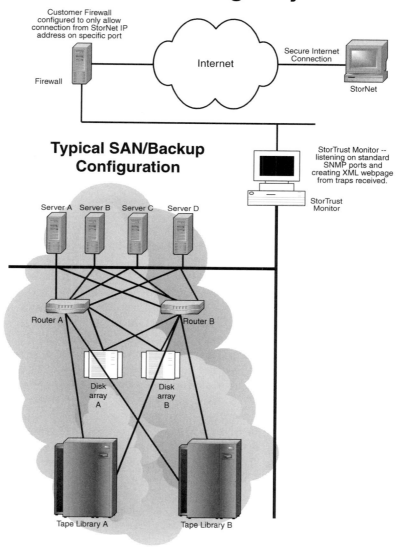

Figure 4–24   StorNet's StorTrust Monitor in action. (*Source:* StorNet, Englewood, CO. www.stornet.com.)

tire storage infrastructure (or subsets thereof), and as "automation engines" that control the operation of ACOMs and automate many storage management activities. Atop the architecture is Storability's own AssuredStorage Operations Center (ASOC), which can be used, much like a network operating center, to manage the entire management infrastructure.

Storability targets large enterprises for this service and has recently begun to sell the software developed to support the architecture as a service-based storage management product for larger customers.

StorNet, by contrast, takes an approach geared to companies with more modest budgets—reflecting the vendor's long experience as a value added reseller/integrator. For years, the firm provided telephone support on Veritas and Legato software that was sold in connection with its systems integration engagements, mostly for medium-sized customers. The vendor's storage management service solution is simple. It's StorTrust Monitor operates to collect status information on installed storage platforms at the customer facility. In one strategy, the information is maintained at the customer location and is referenced by StoreNet technical support engineers whenever the customer calls in to report a problem. Alternatively, the customer can opt to allow StoreNet's network operations center (NOC) on-going access to the managed infrastructure. Doing so offloads to StoreNet the responsibility for responding proactively to impending problems.

StoreTrust Monitor is powered by a customized version of Tek-Tools' Storage Profiler and capitalizes on that product's flexible deployment options. Using Storage Profiler's "agentless option," many types of storage platforms may be monitored and managed directly. Alternatively, a Simple Network Management Protocol (SNMP) agent option is also available and can be employed to gather status data on a broader range of equipment and processes, if desired.

The point is that, with selective outsourcing, some of the burden of disaster avoidance in storage—as well as the monitoring and management of distributed backup and mirroring operations—can be achieved. In addition to Storability and StorNet, doubtless other firms will come to market over time that will offer storage out tasking services. DR coordinators should keep the following in mind as they evaluate options.

- It is important to know the goals of the outsourcing strategy. It might help to set a dollar cost-savings objective or other measurable description of success that will help to measure the efficacy of the strategy once it has been in use for awhile.
- Avoid trying to codify in a contract every detail of the arrangement in advance. While certain service level minimums should be specified, together with legal remedies that will allow the arrangement to be terminated for cause, these are essentially imperfect working partnerships. As in a marriage, sound judgment and flexibility, rather than a codified litany of rules, regulations and remedies, are required if the partnership is to be sustained over time.

- Have an escape route. If things don't work out as planned, be sure that provisions are made for a transition of service either to an alternate provider or to internal staff as part of the service agreement.
- Pay close attention to security. With the StoreNet offering, all transactions between the vendor and customer essentially stop at the company firewall. Considering the many weaknesses and vulnerabilities that are being exposed daily in web servers, browsers and protocols, the DR coordinator should seek to avoid providing any additional inroads to hackers or other malcontents.
- Don't expect miracles. If it was troublesome managing the company's disjointed storage infrastructure before engaging an outsourcer, it isn't reasonable to expect the outsourcer to fix things overnight. Such expectations set the stage for failed relationships before they start.

ENDNOTES

1. Jon William Toigo, *The Holy Grail of Data Storage Management* (Prentice Hall: Saddle River, NJ), 1999.
2. Gregory Dalton, "Acceptable Risks," *Information Week,* 8/31/98.
3. Interview with George Symons, vice president of product management and development, Legato Systems, Palo Alto, CA, 3/02.
4. Ibid.
5. From the web page of Network One, Eugene, OR, http//:www.net1.com.
6. Laurie Hilsgen, "Document Management Still a Struggle," *InfoTech Weekly,* 2/8/99.
7. "DISASTER RECOVERY Information Assets—The Missing Link," a paper published on the web site of FIRELOCK, Kutztown, PA, http//:www.firelock.com/articles.htm.
8. Interview with Matt Fairbanks, backup exec product manager, Seagate Software, Lake Mary, FL, 3/99.
9. Interview with Jeff Wells, product manager, SAMS: Alexandria, Sterling Software, Boulder, CO, 6/99.
10. Interview with Ken Barth, CEO, Tek-Tools, Dallas, TX, 03/02.
11. Symons interview, op. cit.
12. Ibid.
13. Andrew Gup, "Survival in the Terabyte Age: Cost/Benefits of Safeguarding TB Databases," *Storage Management Solutions,* 7/97. While the dollars estimated in this article are somewhat out of date, the methodology for analyzing costs and benefits remains quite sound and may be particularly useful to DR coordinators.
14. Symons interview, op cit.
15. Jason L. Buffington, "Today's Window of Exposure for Data Loss," *Storage Management Solutions,* 1/98.
16. Interview with Jim Grogan, vice president of alliances, SunGard Recovery Services, Wayne, PA, 6/99.
17. Ibid.
18. SunGard Recovery Services case study, from the SunGard Recovery Services web site at http//:recovery.sungard.com/PHLX.htm.

19. Interview with Allan Mohess, Computer Associates, 6/99.
20. Interview with Dan Swatik, vice president of product management, EMC Corporation, Hopkinton, MA, 03/02.
21. Gary Herbst, "IBM's Drive Temperature Indicator Processor (Drive-TIP) Helps Ensure High Drive Reliability," IBM White Paper, IBM Storage Systems Division, San Jose, CA, 1997.
22. NFPA 75: Standard for the Protection of Electronic Computer/Data Processing Equipment, 1999 Edition, National Fire Protection Association, Quincy, MA, 1999.
23. Pat Moore, "Vital Records Protection Issues," Disaster Recovery Journal, Summer 1997.
24. Sets Industry Precedent; Delivers First Tape Technology To Meet Sec Requirements For Electronic Records Storage: StorageTek VolSafe is the Industry's First WORM (Write Once, Read Many) Tape-Based Storage Solution; Provides Cost-Effective, Scalable Alternative to Optical WORM," Press Release, Storage Technology Corporation, Boulder, CO, 07/08/98.

Perspective on Advanced Business Continuity Post–September 11

By

James Rothnie
Chief Technology Officer
EMC Corporation
Hopkinton, MA

*EMC's executive chairman, Mike Ruettgers said "in order to stay in business …
you have to have your people and you have to have their information." Barron's* January
9, 2002.

Crisis often shifts focus to what is truly important. In the wake of September
11, most if not all corporate boards and government agencies have shifted safeguarding their people, facilities, and information to the top of their agenda. In
large measure today, every organization is reducible to two things: people and
information. Now, regrettably both need new levels of protection and new ways
to think about such protection. This short article will focus on the changing customer view of how to protect their information.

Pulled from EMC's experience on the front lines, here are the bottom-line
information protection lessons from 9/11:

- DR plans need to be fully and repeatedly tested.
- E-mail is mission critical and so are HR, CRM, and SCM applications.
- Asynchronous remote replication is never acceptable for mission critical ap-
  plications.
- Think restore—not backup. Tape is unacceptable for fast restore. Disk repli-
  cas are the only way to go.
- Those working on the IT front lines of a disaster need to be as fully empow-
  ered as other kinds of emergency workers.
- Secondary sites must be a substantial distance from the primary data center.
- Automated information management is a prerequisite for advanced busi-
  ness continuity.

While business continuity awareness is at an all-time high, much work remains to be done and quickly. Organizations need to create a coordinated senior
level IT and business executive commitment to a business continuity plan that encompasses the entire value change, including customers, partners and vendors.
No longer is it sufficient to develop the DR plan and put in on the shelf. It needs
to be real, fully tested, and focused on enabling the business to continue operating even under the most awful circumstances. And disk storage replication is a
crucial component of DR planning.

Traditional discussions of disaster recovery planning gave scant attention to information continuity and the key role disk storage replication played in enabling it. This remained the case, even as EMC sold hundreds of millions of dollars of replication software each year. It continued to be the case even as other storage companies began offering their versions of replication software. But the events of September 11 changed that. *Barron's* on September 24, 2001, reported, "If any technology product emerged the hero from the recent disasters, it was an EMC product called SRDF (for Symmetrix Remote Data Facility)."

EMC has for a number of years suggested that disaster recovery planning is really a subset of business continuity planning: "How do I keep my business running in the event of a disaster, or in the event of other forms of planned and unplanned downtime?" Among other things the answer is to have replicated information on disk that is available immediately for business resumption. In the case of SRDF and September 11, every affected installation running SRDF had an up to the second mirror of business information at a second location. As a result, those businesses that invested in and tested synchronous remote mirroring technology had hundreds of TBs of usable critical and current data intact and ready for immediate access once the communications and server infrastructures were ready. It meant that these companies, even though their production data centers were destroyed, were back up and running quickly. Following September 11 these organizations did not want to have their information only in a single site, so instead of spending post-September 11 days recovering critical business data, they were able to concentrate their efforts on locating and creating a new second site. They were also establishing and testing communications and networks, and insuring that the complex infrastructures could support the business. They did not need to locate tapes and recover from them for those applications that failed over, but in many cases companies found that in hindsight they would have strongly preferred to have far more information remotely mirrored and immediately available.

One of the myths shattered on September 11 was that companies should only replicate mission critical data. Depending on the organization this mantra could be interpreted narrowly or broadly. After September 11, companies learned that e-mail was an application critical to running the business. It was often the glue that held the organization together. E-mail insured consistent and quick communications within the company, easily crossing organizations. E-mail also turned out to be an extremely important application for the company to communicate with its partners, suppliers, vendors, and customers, essentially everyone it touches. This was the case not just during the emergency, it turns out that companies used e-mail to do business. E-mail, along with applications such as ERP, CRM, and supply chain management, dramatically increased the externalization of information and the reliance on information for virtually every aspect of running the business.

September 11 also taught organizations that HR applications are mission critical. They have the phone numbers, addresses, and family contact information of our employees. It is the first place companies went to try and find their people. Without access to the HR files, this immediate and gut-wrenching task became many times more difficult.

Another myth that was shattered by September 11 was that asynchronous remote replication, even though it virtually guarantees data loss, was acceptable for mission critical applications. Unfortunately, the lesson from September 11 is that companies may never be able to fill in the missing data regarding thousands and perhaps hundreds of thousands of transactions. They will not be able to know if the transaction was a $100 ATM withdrawal or a $10,000 deposit; a $5M wire transfer to close a business deal or $1,000 transfer to the son or daughter in college.

Assumptions prior to September 11 that may have made asynchronous remote copy an acceptable risk were shattered. If a company or government needs the information to continue its business, data loss that may be permanent is not acceptable.

The criteria for determining when mirroring is a better strategy for data access restoration than tape

Tape is and will remain an important media for certain processes, including backup. But September 11 made one thing crystal clear, the issue for business is not backup, it is restore. Many companies restored from tape, but it took them days and weeks. Even 3 months after the disaster of September 11, some companies directly affected by the terrorist attacks were still restoring from tape. Even though these companies took a very long time to restore some applications and invested countless resources in this process, they were the lucky ones among those that relied on tape. Some companies had their most recent tapes at their data centers ready to be shipped off site. The tapes were destroyed. In other cases, the backup tapes were incomplete, the restoration time consuming, resource intensive and prone to errors.

There were instances of staff unable to get to the tapes or bring them to the remote site for days because the bridges and tunnels to and from Manhattan were closed. Planes didn't fly for days, so companies could not get their people to the tapes, and the tapes to the place and so on. Even if companies could live with days and weeks of delayed access to information, the traditional planning assumption that companies could get tapes and people to where they needed them doesn't work anymore.

Even the traditional assumption that you can get back into the building quickly is no longer operative. The presence of anthrax caused several buildings to close for days or weeks. We all hope these disasters never happen again, but we must plan to continue the business as if they might.

Even when no external disaster occurs, two other dynamics, scope and time, are driving organizations to implement restore strategies using disk replicas rather than tape. A database corruption may not be an external disaster, but unless appropriate steps are taken, it certainly will inhibit continuous business operations. To restore from tape to a point in time prior to the corruption, depending on how quickly you discover the problem, is likely to take 24, 36, or more hours to restore to that good point. Even if the database is remotely mirrored, the remote mirror will have the same corruption, so customers need to fix it locally and they need to fix it quickly.

This exact scenario that is prompting companies to move to disk replicas for very rapid recovery, and it is why EMC developed and is now selling software to schedule the entire disk replica process. For quick recovery of key applications and databases companies can create disk-based replicas as often as necessary, 4 to 6 times a day for example. In other cases, they will create replicas twice a day, once a day, or even less often. But these decisions are now no longer dictated by staffing or technical constraints. They are implemented based on business continuity plans that focus on the business processes that are directly impacted by the absence of access to data. Once the company identifies the database corruption, disk-based replicas can dramatically reduce the time it takes to determine when it occurred and to restore very quickly from the last known good replica. The difference is a few hours compared to days. As replicas become easier to schedule and manage, they will take on even greater importance in enabling continuous operations.

The need to provide for recoverability of data proactively

As companies plan for business continuity, two important staffing lessons come out of the response to September 11. First, this disaster required employees, both at the vendor and the customer sites, to be "enabled." For example, EMC enabled services staff at its headquarters to leverage all aspects of the company, logistics, manufacturing, professional services, customer services, and sales—everything to get the job done. No bureaucracy, no vice presidents. The attitude was, "Just do what needs to be done, do it well and worry about payment and permission later." It worked extremely well. Second, the empowered staff was at EMC's headquarters. They worked extremely closely with staff and customers in New York, but they had the luxury of a little distance and with it enough objectivity to make good decisions.

In New York, the first thing EMC and its customers did was to try and find their employees. Phone calls whether via cell or land lines within New York City were not getting through. Even though the telecommunications networks healed rapidly, the first day was extremely difficult. EMC discovered that calls from its Philadelphia office could get through, and it used this mechanism to find its staff and customers and to notify their families. EMC also had several satellite telephones that became extremely important when no conventional lines of communication could get through.

At corporate headquarters, within seconds of the first plane crashing into the World Trade Center, the EMC Symmetrix call home feature notified EMC of a significant increase in vibrations. Within 30 minutes of the second plane crashing into the World Trade Center, EMC set up a command center to assist affected customers. Within the next 24 hours, EMC and its partners and competitors, set up a coordinated command center to speed vendor communications in responding to critical customer issues.

EMC quickly identified its hundreds of customers in New York City, then those below Canal Street, then those in and around the World Trade Center. EMC then worked with its customers to identify the status of each customer and what, if anything, the customer needed.

SRDF worked. There was a good, available mirror of the data at the secondary site. But no customer wanted only a single site, and some customers only had mirrored some of the data they needed available at the secondary site. EMC, its customers, partners, and competitors all worked around the clock to get customers back up and running, implement a second site, ship in new hardware and software, configure and test SANs and do whatever else was needed. In one case, EMC found a used VAX server for a customer so they could get their application back up.

Throughout the following weeks, EMC leveraged its 24/7 global resources to have an expert in Australia or Ireland take a second look at the issues and solutions in real time, review options, give advice and whatever else needed to be done. This became extremely important as the dedicated local staffs both customer and vendor, became exhausted after working 2 and 3 days straight. This global resource helped avoid costly mistakes, but in another way, the availability of such fresh experts around the clock made it even harder for the local customer and vendor staff to take a break.

One lesson out of these events is that part of the business continuity plan needs to include time, no matter how precious, for staff to rest, to sleep, to see their families. Somehow, companies need to encourage, even demand it, because the staffs will just keep going. Two days after September 11, an EMC executive drove down to New York to help coordinate operations. He helped, by spending all day informally just talking to staff, listening, being there. He was profoundly moved by how important it was for people to talk about what happened, what they saw, what they felt, what happened to their families, friends, colleagues, and customers. There is no question that after an event counseling is important. What we learned is during the event listening and emotional supports are key.

In the case of one customer, EMC completed the remote data mirroring installation on September 7. This created a second copy of data at the company's second data center 35 miles away from the World Trade Center. But for this company, while what was traditionally considered mission critical application data was remotely mirrored successfully, the rest of the data was not. Indeed, this company needed up to 10 days to restore all of the other application data from tape. EMC delivered additional hardware (within 24 hours) to the secondary site to handle the tape restoration. Customer staff and vendors worked around the clock to insure that access to the key mirrored applications remained available and to migrate information from tape to disk, enabling other key applications to get back up and running. Fortunately, there was some staff at the remote site and other staff could travel to it without too much difficulty.

In another case, the company had most of its data remotely mirrored, and that worked fine. But some of its data was backed up only to tape. The primary site, while not destroyed, was running on backup generators. EMC worked with the customer to get the tape data onto local storage systems, immediately shipped additional capacity to a secondary site outside of New York and then used remote mirroring to move the data to the secondary data center. It worked. In this case, like many others, the teams of vendor and staff experts reviewed a number of options very quickly and decided on the most expeditious way to keep the company's information available.

The dust and debris on September 11 clogged and choked air conditioning and air handling systems in buildings that were not otherwise directly affected by the attacks on the World Trade Center. Indeed, had the wind been blowing toward New Jersey, the dust cloud could have caused considerable problems in the backup sites. Companies are reassessing the question of distance. Global companies are even looking at creating a third center on a different continent to avoid the enormous difficulties caused by travel, communication or other constraints.

As *Barron's* reported, successful synchronous remote mirroring was absolutely critical to the nations key financial institutions and markets being ready for business just a few days after these horrible events. We expect that even in these difficult economic times, organizations will commit the resources to plan and implement tangible business continuity infrastructures. Disk replicas will be part of those implementations.

But, after September 11, customers in New York and around the world are planning advanced business continuity with a new urgency and new ideas. These new plans will include, but not be limited to the following:

First, companies need to build information infrastructures that are coordinated by the senior business and IT executives to insure the plan includes the organization's entire value chain, including customers, partners, and suppliers.

Second, organizations treat nearly all its information, including e-mail, payroll, HR, and test data, as if it were mission critical.

Third, organizations build robust, highly automated information infrastructures that can withstand enormous shock and yet provide uninterrupted access to the organization's information.

Fourth, organizations duplicate and widely disperse sites for the organizations data and people. Some large customers are actively discussing having a third site and placing it on another continent. After September 11, it became clear that getting people to the secondary site can no longer be assumed. Air travel might be shut down for an entire country or region. Bridges and tunnels might be closed.

Fifth, "lights out data centers" which just a few months ago were usually deemed too expensive, will be revisited.

Perspective on Disaster Recovery

By

George Symons
Vice President Product Management and Development
Legato Systems, Inc.
Mountain View, CA

If your enterprise or regional data centers are vulnerable, then so is your business. In the event of a fire, flood, hurricane, or other natural disaster, protecting your data to tape is not enough. The time that it can take you to rebuild your server and storage configurations, find your tapes, recover information from them, and re-establish your data center operations could prove disastrous for your business.

Finding the tapes required to recover critical data can be particularly difficult for companies using paper documentation to track their locations. Paper-based tracking requires an operational staff to determine where the tapes are, what information is stored on them, and how they are rotated off- and on-site. In cases where the paper documentation is lost, it can require companies to take the time to scan the contents of thousands of tapes looking for the exact, for example, 1,500 tapes that they require to recover a typical enterprise database.

As enterprise businesses have broadened their operations and expanded from region to region, they are more vulnerable to disaster than ever before. At the same time, consolidated data in centralized locations is more critical to larger segments of the business than ever before; this means that an outage in that data center affects a larger segment of the business. Also, business-to-business connectivity means that when your data center is down, your doors are closed. Likewise, if a business partner has problems, then it can also slow down your business and even stop it.

Legato and other companies are changing the rules for how organizations can protect their business operations, by offering solutions that ensure the continuance of data center operations. These solutions automate and manage the movement of data from center to center, they constantly monitor and automate the process of recovering data center operations, and they help to manage the removable media such as tape that stores critical data. Legato simplifies these processes, to ensure rapid, efficient, and error-free recovery at the times that businesses need it the most.

Because Legato has simplified the process of switch-over and recovery, businesses are also using Legato's solutions proactively to optimize day-to-day operations to:

- Automatically switch selected operations from regional data center to regional data center, in a follow-the-sun strategy designed to lower connection costs and increase performance for business users

- Perform systems maintenance such as upgrading applications and servers during normal work hours, while ensuring the continuous operations that businesses require
- Manage complex replication configurations, combining bi-directional, synchronous, and asynchronous replication with automated throttling and other advanced options that are too difficult and time-consuming to manage without automation

To ensure the availability of your data center operations and to simplify it through automation, Legato combines solution components from three categories:

- Information protection, for backup, recovery and archive of data
- Application availability, for local and wide-area monitoring and restart of data center operations
- Management, for centralized monitoring and control of all capabilities

During Normal Operations

The foundation of data center recovery is ensuring that your data is protected, disk-to-disk and disk-to-tape.

For disk-to-disk replication of data across wide areas from data center to data center, businesses have several options to select from which are:

- Storage hardware-embedded replication tools, such as EMC Symmetrix Remote Data Facility (SRDF)

These capabilities require a dedicated network connection from a storage device to another like storage device, and support as many application servers as can be connected to the storage.

- Server-based replication tools, such as Legato RepliStor for Windows

These capabilities work over normal TCP/IP network connections between and among servers, and support data replication between and among mixed types of storage devices. You typically must install this type of solution on every application server from which you need to protect data.

There are also typically several modes of operation, whether the replication capabilities be hardware-embedded or server-based, as follows:

- Replication can be synchronous, which means that the data is written to a second disk with an acknowledgment received before the write is released back to the application. The advantage is that the secondary copy of data is guaranteed to be exactly the same as what is on disk at the primary location. The disadvantage is that network latency can slow down the application;

over very long distances, this proves to be impractical. In most real-world cases today, synchronous data replication is limited to about 60 kilometers. As wide-area networking capacities become cheaper over time, these distances will increase.

- Replication can be asynchronous, which means that the data is sent to the second location (disk or server) as fast as the network allows but that the application is not held up waiting for an acknowledgment. The advantage is that this type of replication can work over very wide virtually unlimited distances, and that there is no impact on the application's performance. The disadvantage is that the network latency causes the second copy of the data to be out of synch, or behind, the original copy of the data. How far behind depends on the rate of exchange of the data, and the amount of network bandwidth available to replicate that data, at any given moment.
- Replication can also be what is called semi-synchronous, which generally means that there is some type of threshold that a system administrator can set on an asynchronous deployment past which the system delays the application to allow the replication to catch up.

To protect their critical business operations, most companies consider combinations of synchronous and asynchronous replication strategies. They use synchronous replication to preserve their data to secondary disks located across campus, across town, or perhaps across a river. They then add asynchronous replication to move that same data across the continent, to also gain protection in the event of a regional disaster.

Most replication tools enable bi-directional replication of data, which allows each site in a two-site configuration to protect the data from the other site. Also, most replication tools enable what is called a "many-to-one" deployment, which out-sourcing service companies including Comdisco, IBM, and SunGuard have used to create what are called "data bunker" sites, each of which protect many production data centers. Finally, most replication tools also enable what is called "one-to-many" deployments, allowing businesses to actually divide the data from a single data center and send it to several secondary locations; this allows businesses to take advantage of extra disk capacity where they may have it across several regional data centers, instead of being forced to install extra capacity in a single location.

Replication tools can also be used in cascading configurations, sending data from a first location to a second, and then to a third, and so forth. Companies might use these capabilities to ensure that they have multiple copies of their data across many disks within a single location, such as to support web content publication within a large e-commerce deployment, for example. Companies might also use these capabilities to ensure that they continue to protect their production data after a wide-area failover of the original data center.

All of these options and the handling of application services along with the data, requires automation tools that can monitor, automate, and manage the replication of data along with the coordinated recovery of data center operations in the event of a disaster.

Transferring Data Center Operations

To make data center operations practical to transfer, Legato adds wide-area application availability.

Legato Automated Availability Manager (AAM) for WANs monitors key data replication states both locally and remotely to simplify its management and ensure data integrity at all times. When replication is disrupted or if a site fails, Legato AAM notifies you through a page or e-mail, so that you can take immediate action. When you decide to transfer data center operations from site to site, you push a button in the AAM Console and AAM automates the steps required to make the transfer.

In most cases, solutions including Legato AAM can be configured to automatically transfer data center operations when it first detects an outage at the production data center. However, it is recommended instead that AAM notify a system administrator who then makes the decision that a site-to-site transfer of data center operations is necessary. Typically, this also requires that the system administrator notify key company officers and take other actions required for comprehensive disaster recovery for the business.

Recovering a Data Center after Disaster

After you have transferred your data center to a second site, you need to recover the original site that failed. Legato also provides you with the tools that you need for this part of the job.

Legato NetWorker Recovery Manager (NRM) simplifies bare-metal, boot-level recovery of backup servers. NRM allows NetWorker to immediately begin file-data recovery from standard backups without having to first rebuild the operating system and the server configuration. And, you can perform NRM recovery over the network.

Legato AlphaStor eliminates the human decision-making process, allowing the administrator to set policies for when and what tapes get rotated offsite. AlphaStor helps to ensure that your tapes are safely off-site according to your rotation policies, and also records the inventory of where those tapes are located for easy look-up and recovery of the exact tapes required for each application that must be recovered.

Then, when you are ready, you can use Legato AAM to start the resynchronization of new production data from the secondary site back to the recovered data center. This allows you to transfer operations back smoothly and easily to the original site, all with continuous data center operations.

9/11: A Vendor's Perspective

By

Vickie Malis
Director of Marketing
Iron Mountain Off-Site Data Protection

For those of us at Iron Mountain, the most profound realization that we continue to associate with 9/11 is the horrific loss of life, and the emotional and physical trauma experienced by our customers and their business colleagues at the World Trade Center (WTC) and the Pentagon. For those of us who work at Iron Mountain Off-Site Data Protection, there is also a secondary realization, a reaffirmation, that our business isn't as much about off-site vaulting of computer backup tapes as it is about enabling our customers to recover from disaster—ensuring that they have their business data whenever and wherever they need it. Without the data, there is no recovery from a business disaster. The trust that our customers place in us, and the accountability that we assume for them, bore fruit many times over during the hours, the days, and the weeks following the 9/11 disasters.

Magnitude and Scope

The plane bombings of 9/11 and subsequent destruction of the WTC is the largest disaster event that Iron Mountain has ever dealt with, both in terms of the number of customer companies affected, as well as the degree of damage sustained by these customers. This is a sobering statement coming from the largest provider of backup data protection services in the world. We supported 111 customer disaster declarations from the WTC and another 3 from the Pentagon. For us, a disaster declaration is a customer call notifying us that, because of a disaster event, we need to retrieve and deliver their computer backup media— what is now likely to be much or all of their critical business data—to a designated recovery site as quickly as possible. Prior to 9/11 the Northridge California earthquake had been our largest disaster, with 29 customer disaster declarations. Prior to the Northridge quake, the 1993 WTC bombing, with 13 customer disaster declarations, had been our largest, a piece of irony not lost on any of us. The "lessons learned" that we took away from these previous disasters had been incorporated into our own disaster planning and the events of 9/11 proved that they served us well.

As a service provider, the first thing you do when a disaster strikes is to assess the breadth (involved geography), and scope (intensity) of the disaster and then activate your own disaster plan. For Iron Mountain, this starts with a "headcount" of our own employees and vehicles, to identify drivers and vehicles that might have been directly involved while servicing customers in the areas of the WTC and Pentagon at the time of the disasters. Fortunately, while we lost a truck, none of our employees were hurt. We are fortunate in this regard, since we had operated vault facilities underground in the WTC complex until earlier this same year.

Resources, Resources, Resources

Early establishment of "command and control" headquarters is essential for a vendor to provide quality disaster service. For Iron Mountain this meant that a command and control center was activated at our corporate headquarters and a regional command and control center was activated at one of our large facilities located a safe distance, yet close, to the WTC disaster site. From these headquarters, we maintained communication with outside news and information sources, continually assessed the breadth, scope and support requirements of the disaster, and organized and activated the resources needed to support our customers. This included anticipating customer needs so that our support is proactive, and not reactive.

For getting customers' critical data quickly to their recovery sites, the needed resources are people, communications, vehicles, and supplies—and big disasters require lot of every one of them. Disasters don't always unfold as planned or tested and the FAA airspace restrictions surrounding 9/11 forced the grounding of all airplanes, including the charter planes that we normally use to transport customers' backup media to their recovery sites. Iron Mountain's national network of facilities allowed us to mobilize people and vehicles from many locations to our regional command and control center to meet the need for rapid response. We were able to successfully respond to multiple, simultaneous disaster declarations in both New York and Washington, DC. This reaffirms the fact that one of our strengths is the ability to respond successfully to multiple, simultaneous customer emergencies.

The combination of our nation-wide network, with the caliber and character of employees, enabled us to respond to all 114 disaster declarations without negatively impacting the other 25,000 customers that we routinely service. We had employees who drove to our 9/11 regional command and control center from Chicago, Detroit, and Pennsylvania to help out. We moved customers' data from New York and New Jersey to hot sites and other recovery sites as far away as Chicago and Phoenix using truck convoy relays, not unlike the old "Pony Express." Loaded trucks from New York/New Jersey headed as far as, say, Pennsylvania, and were met by vehicles and personnel from the Iron Mountain vault in the adjacent region. Customer backup tapes were moved to the new vehicle and that new team drove them on to, say, Ohio, and so on.

Communication and Caring

In a crisis, people rise to the occasion, and we saw the power of adrenaline manifest itself throughout our employee population. We are incredibly proud of the huge numbers of our employees that put the needs of our customers before their own physical comfort. We were careful to watch for signs of "burn out," provided hotel facilities and food, and enforced scheduled shift work, so that our workers could get needed rest and replenishment. Having professional counseling available after the acute response period also has proved to be a benefit that employees appreciate.

Communication, both internal and external is essential to the effective functioning of a service provider during an emergency. It is essential that all employees, as well as their families, are kept informed. At Iron Mountain, we did this through regularly scheduled updates from Senior Management that we published on our company intranet and also circulated by e-mail.

Unaffected clients, suppliers and industry contacts must also be kept informed and it is important to do this using a single spokesperson or point of contact. The events of 9/11 demonstrated to us that some companies who believe that they are prepared for disaster, have overlooked planning related to their suppliers. Again, the breadth and depth of Iron Mountain resources enabled us to mobilize our own suppliers to meet customers' unplanned needs for items like containers and media that arose when they started up operations at their recovery site.

Like many disaster recovery service providers, Iron Mountain handled a heavy volume of press inquiries during the period surrounding 9/11. We have the utmost respect for the press, but cooperation with the press during disaster needs to be tempered with needs for the maintenance of proper security, protection of operations effectiveness and responsiveness, and total respect for the privacy of our customers. Use of a single point of contact was extremely valuable to us in maintaining this posture with the press. We were able to successfully control the flow of communication and yet be responsive to communication needs.

Our Clients

Our customers are companies of all sizes and from all industries. Regardless of size, industry, or type of information systems, they all are concerned with the following:

1. How current is their backup data? How much data, and what type of data will have been lost because it occurred or changed since the time of their most recent backup.
2. What is the availability of their backup data? Can it be taken to them wherever and whenever they need it?
3. Can we help them with access to additional resources that we have available, or that our suppliers have available? And
4. Can we arrange for direct and immediate access between our people who are involved with their data and their own people who are responsible for the recovery.

We found that our customers affected by the events of 9/11 needed us to anticipate and allow for some confusion on their part, to provide assurance in addition to assistance, and to be responsive in anticipating their needs before they were able to articulate them.

Our experiences during the disasters of 9/11 were consistent with other disaster recoveries that we have supported, in that the first customers to contact us are those that are indirectly affected. These customers are hungry for information about the magnitude of the event(s). They are trying to assess the likelihood that they will be affected at some later point in time and are looking for reassurance that we will be ready and able to help them should they need it. These customers often have multiple requests.

Customers that are directly impacted and have a tested disaster recovery plan in place were the next group to contact us. On 9/11, we received our first disaster declaration within 2 hours of the first attack on the WTC. These customers, those with active recovery programs were able to begin recovery hours, and in many cases, days, before customers who did not have tested recovery plans. For these customers, 9/11 certainly did not unfold as the "model" that they had planned and tested for, but their planning served them well in preparation for their recovery.

Customers that are directly impacted and don't have a plan are the last to call for help. They are the customers least able to identify what help they require. For some customers we (their off-site backup tape vaulting program) ARE their disaster recovery plan. We continue to work with customers such as these to help them understand the value of disaster recovery and business continuity planning.

Iron Mountain Off-Site Data Protection has 25,000 customers. In addition to providing support to customers indirectly and directly affected by the disaster, we need to make sure that all of our customers continue to receive the routine service of their off-site backup data protection services. We're very proud that we were able to continue this, without interruption, throughout the period of the 9/11 recoveries.

"Lessons Learned"

Much of what we know from supporting customers in recovering from previous disasters was reaffirmed with the events of 9/11. This includes things like the fact that customers with a tested plan recover quicker and more effectively than those who do not have one.

With the events of 9/11, we learned new things about how to rapidly assist customers across long distances without the ability to utilize air resources. That knowledge is now a valuable "arrow" in our quiver for the support of customers in the future. Unfortunately, we also learned the importance of having multiple people, in different locations, as contacts with authorization to declare a disaster and initiate our disaster recovery services. Nobody anticipated the massive loss of life associated with the disasters of 9/11 and, frankly, we will now keep that as a possible scenario in our own disaster planning.

Similarly, the massive loss of property and the fact that all affected customers needed to recover without the ability to get back into their original property meant that media needed to be available for all to start up "from scratch" including full backups of all systems. We have added this need to our own disaster planning as well. We also got a powerful reminder of the value of communication and strong relationships with our own business partners and suppliers so that we can assist recovering customers with whatever they urgently need.

From the events surrounding 9/11, we have learned to strategize new situations, such as "How do you get very large quantities of backup data to recovery sites outside of the United States when airspace is closed and the country's borders are on high security alert?" We are looking at new technologies that we are working with to help us find solutions to this question and others that will continue to present themselves over time.

In closing, once again we have been reminded of the tremendous strength, courage, ingenuity and resourcefulness of our customers and our employees. As our division President, Harry Ebbighausen, said "On September 17, when the opening bell on Wall Street rang and the Big Board lit up, and America got back on its feet, I can't tell you how much pride I [we] had for the outstanding job that we did and the contribution that we made."

Planning for Business Continuance and Disaster Recovery

By

Mark Santora
Senior Vice President, Marketing
Network Appliance, Inc.
Sunnyvale, CA

Organizations that depend on digital data to function—and today that includes virtually every organization of even modest size—owe it to their employees, shareholders, partners and customers to write, implement and regularly test a comprehensive plan for business continuance. Not to have one is to take unnecessary and unwise risks with prospects for the organization's ability to survive a disaster that damages or destroys its principal data storage locations.

Before September 11, 2001, some organizations questioned the need and expense of developing and implementing a comprehensive business continuance plan. Now, understandably, they see it as imperative, and are reexamining and strengthening their investments in the planning, facilities, and IT infrastructure necessary to ensure business continuance in a range of scenarios. Floods, fires, earthquakes, computer viruses, hardware failures, power losses, vandalism—regardless of the cause, the impacts of a catastrophic loss of mission-critical data have pushed business continuance and disaster recovery (DR) planning way up on the priority list of every management team.

In writing these plans, companies need to take into account key lessons from recent disasters, which include:

- Production sites and disaster recovery sites need to be separated by greater distances—or a third site needs to be built.
- Tape is useful for archiving, but using it as a primary restore strategy for mission-critical data can extend costly downtime.
- The definition of mission-critical data is much broader than was previously thought.
- The backup-and-recovery plan needs to be tested regularly to ensure it will work as intended when called upon.

Business continuance planning and implementation demand a complex, many-faceted effort for an organization. Network Appliance's (NetApp) role in that big picture is to provide hardware and software storage solutions, technologies, and strategies—these are our core competencies that can assist enterprises in addressing this critical requirement. From day one, NetApp has integrated disaster avoidance and data recovery features into our products; these capabilities were not built as an afterthought or added as a bolt-on to previous product releases but were designed into the product. In fact, many of our products, including our Snap family of software products, were developed expressly to provide data security and facilitate rapid data recovery and business continuance.

Digital data is the lifeblood of Network Appliance customers, and we're working with them to develop business continuance plans that take advantage of the unique capabilities of our products, partners, people, and services. To prepare for the unexpected, we're helping customers make realistic appraisals of the potential for unplanned downtime, devise comprehensive business continuance strategies, and understand the role the right IT infrastructure components can play in helping avoid and recover from business disruptions.

Major Disasters—A Real and Present Danger

In our increasingly global and interconnected business environment, major disasters are a real and present danger. There's no shortage of statistics making this point. For instance:

- One out of 500 data centers will have a severe disaster every year. ("Business Recovery Planning System Software: An Automated Technique for Developing, Maintaining, and Implementing a Comprehensive Disaster Recovery Plan," by RSM McGladrey, Inc., McGladrey & Pullen, LLP.)
- A company that experiences a computer outage lasting more than 10 days will never fully recover financially. Fifty percent will be out of business within five years. ("Disaster Recovery Planning: Managing Risk & Catastrophe in Information Systems," by Jon Toigo, Yourdon Press.)

Every hour—even every minute—that an organization's information resources are unavailable not only costs revenues and profits, it damages its reputation, employee productivity, and competitive advantage. The following figures bring home the magnitude of potential losses from unplanned downtime.

Business	*Average Hourly Loss*
Retail Brokerage	$6.5 million
Credit Card Sales Authorization	$2.6 million
Home Shopping Channels	$110,000
Airline Reservation Centers	$90,000
Package Shipping Service	$28,250
Manufacturing Industry	$26,761
Banking Industry	$17,093
Transportation Industry	$9,435

(*Source:* http:www.ontrack.com/datarecovery/cost.asp, Contingency Planning Research and Strategic Research Corporation)

It's simply not possible to anticipate and avoid every possible disaster scenario that could bring about these kinds of consequences. That's why having a disaster recovery plan in place to deal with them is so critical.

Assisting Customers after September 11, 2001

In addition to helping individuals directly affected by the tragic events of September 11, Network Appliance™ products and people helped companies cope with the loss of systems and data. Many NetApp® customers in New York City had disaster recovery locations in New Jersey or elsewhere in the city. The following examples present two different approaches to business continuance and two different outcomes.

Restoring Quickly from Mirrored Data

One of NetApp's New York-based customers is a worldwide financial services firm headquartered one block from the World Trade Center. At its headquarters site, the firm had Network Appliance filers—in a Clustered Failover configuration to protect against hardware failure—that stored and served data for an online trading application. High availability is critical for this firm because even 10 minutes of downtime could cost millions of dollars. It was using SnapMirror® software (see description below) to mirror the contents of the filers to another NetApp filer located at a disaster recovery (DR) site 10 miles away in Queens.

After helping evacuate the headquarters facility, the firm's systems administration staff went to the DR site. They ensured that the data on the remote filer was identical to that on the headquarters filers, then stopped the mirroring process. They proceeded to retrieve previous-week backup tapes containing non-mission-critical data from a remote vault so that this unmirrored data could be restored. Aided by the 3-day close of the NYSE, the firm increased capabilities at the DR site to enable it to handle as many as 200 traders and support staff. Within 48 hours, it also acquired another pair of filers from Network Appliance. The firm had them online the next day. Before the NYSE reopened the following Monday, the firm was back on-line and all data had been recovered. That day, September 17, was the busiest trading day in the firm's history, and it was able to handle the volume.

Simple setup and administration, centralized storage, on-the-fly scalability, automatic failover, streamlined remote data mirroring, and responsive technical support—those key benefits of a NetApp solution helped make possible the firm's rapid recovery from the disaster.

Restoring from Tape

Another major NetApp customer in financial services suffered serious and tragic losses in personnel and equipment on September 11, 2001. The firm's offices were destroyed, and along with them the 200-plus NT servers containing information for company traders. Data on the servers was backed up to tape at regular intervals and moved off-site to be stored in vaults. Because the data was not deemed mission-critical at that time, it was not backed up to on-line or near-line disk devices such as NetApp's NearStore™ R100.

Two days after the disaster, the company decided to consolidate its systems. It bought 50TB of storage in filers from Network Appliance and divided them between its production site and DR site. Rather than restore from the tapes to a new complement of 200 servers, the firm restored to the production filers and immediately instituted mirroring to replicate the data on filers at the DR site in New Jersey. Learning from September 11, 2001, the company now classified this restored data as mission-critical. Restoring from tape, which was unavoidable in this instance, was slow, but now the company has data mirrored on a filer—a rapid access storage device—and is much better prepared for future disruptions. Any future restores will be orders of magnitude faster. In addition, by consolidating storage and replacing the 200-plus lost servers with simple, easily administered NetApp filers, the company saved considerable expense and was able to get back online quickly.

Addressing the Spectrum of Business Continuance Strategies

NetApp offers a wide range of solutions that address the full spectrum of business continuance issues—from enabling an individual user to quickly recover an accidentally deleted file to making it possible for a company to recover from a tragedy like September 11, 2001. Our family of solutions, which companies combine to fit their needs, includes the following options. In addition to the software products highlighted (Snapshot™, SnapRestore®, SnapMirror, and SnapVault™), these solutions incorporate NetApp hardware in the form of filers, NetCache® and NearStore appliances, and tape drives.

Tape backup—For cost-efficient off-site storage and long-term retention of data, tape is an essential component of a business continuance strategy. Network Appliance and its partners give you the ability to choose the backup approach that best matches your environment. You can easily accomplish filer backups using traditional server-based tape solutions, or with a local tape device installed for each filer to minimize traffic over the network.

If you want to centralize tape devices and the associated administrative functions, you can protect NetApp filers using emerging approaches including Fibre Channel tape SANs and NDMP-enabled tape libraries. Both of these alternatives eliminate server overhead for backups.

Snapshots—Customers need a way to recover accidentally deleted files. This occurrence isn't as dramatic as a physical disaster, but is much more common and can be almost as disruptive. To handle this problem, the Data ONTAP operating system of NetApp filers includes Snapshot technology. Snapshots are easily accessible online backup copies of primary data. Snapshots store only data that has changed from the original file, so users can take Snapshots far more frequently compared to tape backup, minimizing data loss. In fact, users can capture data at any interval they choose—minutes, hours, or days. When a disaster occurs, the customer simply goes back to the most recent copy of the data and quickly resumes business.

SnapRestore—Where traditional data restoration techniques, such as restoring from tape, may take hours, SnapRestore recovers entire file systems or individual files in seconds. For example, in cases where a company loses a 1TB database from application corruption or an application upgrade fails, SnapRestore recovers it in seconds.

A perfect illustration of how Snapshot and SnapRestore software can help organizations avoid data disasters occurred when the Melissa virus struck in March 1999. One of the nation's largest telemarketing agencies uses a Network Appliance storage solution to support 70 call centers and handle more than 250 million phone calls annually. In this 24/7 operating environment, any type of downtime, planned or unplanned, is highly undesirable since it directly affects revenue.

The Melissa virus arrived over the Internet from one of the company's clients. A fix for the virus was not available at that time; as a result, it ended up infecting thousands of files on the filer. However, because the files in a Snapshot are read-only, the data in those Snapshots was protected from the virus. Using SnapRestore, the agency's IT administrators were able to avoid several hours of data loss and downtime by quickly reverting the data back to the most recent Snapshot copy. Snapshots and SnapRestore enabled the company to recover rapidly and avoid substantial losses in productivity and revenue.

SnapMirror—An integral part of NetApp business continuance solutions, SnapMirror software continually transfers copies of data from a primary site to one or more remote secondary sites using standard IP networks. SnapMirror provides a very high data availability and fast recovery solution for mission-critical applications.

In the event of a site-wide disaster, such as a flood at a primary data center, SnapMirror delivers fast access to the most current copy of the mission-critical data, minimizing business interruption. Unlike competing mirroring products, which require the user to mirror all the contents of a storage device, SnapMirror enables you to selectively mirror only the content you choose. This feature saves storage space on the backup device and requires less network bandwidth to transmit the smaller volume of mirrored data.

Because SnapMirror is based on Snapshots (which are consistent copies of the file system), the target system is also consistent and does not need recovery. Failing over to the DR site is very quick because it does not require a file system check. In addition, the complexity is hidden from administrators—they can set up a data replication system in less than 15 minutes with SnapMirror software.

One lesson many companies have learned is that essentially all data—even e-mail—is mission-critical information. However, restoring certain data as quickly as possible, such as transactional information, may be more urgent than restoring other data, such as home directories. Taking this into account, customers are now mirroring a greater volume of data, since they're classifying more of it as mission-critical, but are still selectively mirroring. Data that needs to be restored quickly is replicated on a filer at a DR site using SnapMirror; other data is backed up to tape and stored off-site. Such selective mirroring with SnapMirror does not require adding bandwidth; because it makes incremental backups and does not send entire data stores over connections, using SnapMirror can save on infrastructure expenses.

SnapVault—SnapVault and a NearStore R100 appliance protect important data that needs to be recovered quickly. The NearStore R100 is a low-cost, easy-to-use appliance for rapid data recovery and consolidated backup. By periodically backing up filer Snapshots to an economical NearStore R100 on the network, SnapVault provides extended and centralized disk-based data backup. Storing multiple Snapshots on the NearStore R100 lets enterprises keep weeks of backups on-line for faster on-line restoration. SnapVault also gives users the power to choose which Snapshots to back up and how frequently. The NearStore can be located nearby or off-site for site-wide disaster protection. NearStore devices add a crucial element of business continuance and data recovery for enterprises that need faster restore functionality and cost-effective online storage.

Supporting Customers and Enabling Business Continuance

At Network Appliance, we support our customers' business continuance plans with simple, powerful, highly dependable products that deliver data security, high availability, and, in the case of disruption, rapid and complete data recovery. The comprehensive approach that our hardware and software make possible is designed to mitigate the effects of all types of business interruptions, from a user accidentally deleting a critical file to the tragedy of September 11, 2001.

Although we design our products to minimize the effects of disruptions and disasters, avoiding them altogether is not possible. When disasters do occur, NetApp technology and people help organizations recover data more quickly and easily than is possible with other technologies or approaches. In the final analysis, disasters may be inevitable, but data loss and its associated business consequences are not.

The Evolving Role of Backup in Disaster Recovery

Dr. Kevin C. Daly
CTO
Storage Solutions Group
Quantum Corporation
Irvine, CA

The interaction between traditional data protection techniques such as backup and disaster recovery has begun to change significantly as the result of systemic change in information phenomenology, technological evolution and the increased awareness of the physical vulnerability of data systems as a result of the attacks of September 11th. While the initial reaction to the increased sense of vulnerability was a heightened interest in "hot sites" with synchronous data mirroring, the technical and economic realities of providing this level of disaster recovery has led to a much broader definition of the capabilities that can be brought to bear on this issue. In particular, as a result of the introduction of new technologies in both the backup and networking areas, a much more powerful set of options are becoming available to organizations that utilize backup to protect their data.

The most basic change in the role of disaster recovery is related to the fact that virtually all business information is "born digital" and, therefore, lacks the paper source documentation that was prevalent even 5 years ago. As a result, providing remote information archives for disaster recovery inherently means providing remote digital archives today. While the "what" of remote archives is, therefore, unambiguous, the "how" is a lot more problematic. While we have all become used to the facility with which we can move digital information (through the Internet, etc.) it is important to understand just how much this capability *does not scale* to the levels necessary for disaster recovery. That is why physically transporting removable media (typically tape cartridges) is de rigueur even in the age of the Internet and "free bandwidth." Shipping a 5-pound box of DLT tape cartridges by FedEx each day (at $400 per month) may not be elegant, but it is much more cost-effective than paying over $100,000 per month to obtain the equivalent bandwidth (78 MB/sec) to move the data electronically. While bandwidth costs are dropping rapidly, it will be a long time before a bandwidth equivalent to what we have become used to within local networks becomes economically available for transporting data far enough from the local environment to serve a disaster recovery function for all but the highest-end data centers.

The same bandwidth issues, to a somewhat lesser degree, dog the desires to run a synchronous "hot site" for disaster recovery. While this is done in those environments where operational continuity trumps the economic penalty, for most operations it is neither acceptable to constrain the primary site to the bandwidth that can be made available for synchronization nor affordable to maintain sufficient synchronization bandwidth to permit effective primary operation.

The growth of data in professional environments has been phenomenal. More than one-half of the organizations in the United States had at least 1 TB (1,000 GB) of data last year and the average organization had over 10 TB. Fortunately, these organizations almost never have to deal with all of this data at one time—except for disaster recovery. The closest that most organizations get to actually dealing with data on this scale is their periodic (typically, daily) backup. Even in this case, the data that is backed up is often limited for efficiency but, at least conceptually, backup provides organizations a complete and coherent image of the state of their enterprise at a point in time. Modern backup applications provide sophisticated tools and processes to make the backup process sure and effective and, as a practical matter, there is no other process that can provide a consistent image of the whole enterprise on the regular basis needed for effective disaster recovery.

So, why doesn't backup just solve the disaster recovery problem? Well, as always, it's just not that simple.

Conceptually, a backup system consists of two elements: a *backup target* and a *backup archive*. The backup target provides the repository for (typically incremental) backup activity while the backup archive maintains (often several) complete images of the system being protected. To be effective, the backup target must be local to the system being protected. It is, however, possible to structure a solution in which the backup archive is remote for the system being protected without facing bandwidth issues to the degree we discussed above. A remote backup archive can, therefore, constitute a key element of a disaster recovery solution. But there's a problem.

The problem arises because the backup target and the backup archive are today one physical system—a tape library that cannot be simultaneously local to and remote from the system being protected. While there are some ad hoc techniques that are in use today (e.g., mirroring of all tape cartridges created so that one can be transported off-site to a remote archive) to address this issue, there is an emerging technology called Enhanced backup which promises to provide a systematic solution to the separability of these backup functions.

In an Enhanced backup solution, the backup target is a disk-based system that is optimized for the large, high-speed data transfers characteristic of backup and the backup archive is the tape library. These two elements may either be co-resident local to the system being protected or may be separated—in which case the power and the flexibility of the disk-based element of the system can be used to transfer the necessary data across a distributed network which has very different characteristics than the network local to the system being protected.

An Enhanced backup system, then, can be used to create and maintain a remote image of the state of the system being protected. This state image, if properly constructed, can then be available for disaster recovery. Since the demands for disaster recovery are more severe than those for traditional backup, it is important to modify existing backup procedures and policies to meet these new requirements.

To be completely accurate, backup—even if implemented perfectly—does not preserve the complete state of a system. While it is, at least theoretically, possible to capture the complete *information state* of a system with backup, it is typically not possible to capture the complete *configuration state*. In today's topologically complex networked systems this configuration state is both complex and, often, highly dynamic. While there is not a single solution to this challenge today, there are a growing number of system and storage management tools that can aid in the process of maintaining a remote version of the system's configuration state that is usable for disaster recovery. While the challenge of maintaining current knowledge of the configuration state does increase with growing complexity of information networks, there is reason to hope that this problem will not grow without bound. Storage virtualization is beginning to emerge as an expected element in modern data system (why, some even consider it to be the "holy grail" of storage management). While it will be quite a while before truly virtualized storage systems become widely available, every step down the path of virtualization will reduce the dependency of disaster recovery on the details of the configuration state. While the need to maintain the configuration state for disaster recovery will not go away, there is good reason to believe that it will remain a manageable element of the solution.

The scope of disaster recovery is, of course, very wide. For environments requiring the highest levels of availability and uninterrupted operation continuity, solutions similar to today's high performance, high cost approaches remain the only choice. For disaster recovery needs that permit some degree of operational interruption, however, it is becoming possible to leverage emerging Enhanced backup technologies to provide practical disaster recovery capabilities at costs that are a small fraction of the costs of the high-availability solutions. The key technologies for this convergence of backup and disaster recovery are becoming available although the design of high-confidence disaster recovery solutions utilizing these technologies is just beginning.

The availability of these disaster recovery solutions will eliminate the Hobson's choice that most organizations face today. Unless it was possible to justify the level of investment necessary to support high availability disaster recovery solutions, most organizations had to function without a systematic, high confidence disaster recovery capability. A tightly integrated backup and disaster recovery design can substantially increase the ability of these organizations to meet their complete data protection obligations.

Why a Managed Storage Service? Outsourcing Can Protect Vital Data and Prevent Costly Downtime

By

Kirby Wadsworth
Co-Founder
Storability, Inc.
Southborough, MA

Once a mundane administrative task handled by the late shift, data backup has emerged from obscurity to become a strategic and resource-intensive function. As the value of information continues to rise, protecting and effectively recovering vital corporate data has become critical to the success of new economy companies and established firms alike.

On the surface backup appears to be a simple, straightforward task. And at one time, it was. But today, the sheer amount of data that must be managed is staggering. Data volume has doubled annually for the past several years, and is expected to continue to grow exponentially for the foreseeable future. I/O bandwidth strains to keep pace, and traditional architecture slows an already slow process.

When customers need to be served 24/365, applications can't afford downtime. Continual reduction of an already short backup window can force IT to risk data recovery to meet production needs. If the backup function fails, a crisis can easily erupt, making a "simple" restore far more labor intensive and difficult than necessary. New technologies offer real advantages, but effective deployment demands skills and experience that may not be available.

At the same time, the role of the IT organization itself has changed. Enterprises now look to IT to drive competitive advantage with faster time-to-market for new products, improved customer satisfaction and product quality, and new product and customer acquisitions.

With all this as a backdrop, outsourcing—or out-tasking—backup, recovery, and restore functions to a storage management service provider still makes a lot of sense. Here's why:

A storage management service provider uses best-in-breed technology, industry best practices, and proven processes to remotely manage backup and restore functions. Such a company can help customers:

- Successfully backup data enterprise-wide, despite disappearing backup windows
- Ensure that data is always protected and always available
- Implement critical Data Life Cycle Management Plans

- Maximize productivity of IT organizations
- Instantly access dynamic, up-to-the-minute reports on storage infrastructure status and performance

The goal of the storage management service provider is to develop a solution that meets each customer's unique business requirements. Architects work closely with each customer to understand requirements, current capabilities, and future plans. Once the analysis is complete, the customer gets a comprehensive set of recommendations to drive company achievement and increase the strategic value of IT.

Taking advantage of the latest advancements in hardware and applications, the storage management service provider can design the optimal IT infrastructure and carefully manage the transition to the new environment. They assume full responsibility for design, procurement, installation, configuration and on-going management. This frees the customer from the time-consuming tasks of vendor management and technology "clutter," enabling IT resources to focus on other strategic business issues.

Working closely with the customer's staff, a storage management service provider can create a Service Level Agreement (SLA) that specifically details the services to be delivered. The provider assumes full responsibility for all aspects involved in delivery of the SLA, including procurement, implementation, reliability, storage management automation/oversight, monitoring, and equipment service. SLA reports provide the customer with the detail necessary to ensure the provider is meeting its commitments.

Here's an example.

One of our customers is a leading provider of turnkey, private-label insurance agency solutions. The company successfully leveraged the Internet to create an innovative business model. The firm now provides technology and operations to enable its partners to sell insurance products from many insurance carriers on a single platform that integrates the Internet, call center and retails channels.

As a thriving e-commerce company, continuous availability is absolutely critical to the company's operations. Downtime of any length—whether planned or unplanned—has a significant impact on revenue. At the same time, information is the company's lifeblood, and the company urgently needed to implement a secure, reliable backup solution to protect its vital corporate data. With business rapidly expanding and new products and business applications constantly coming on-line, storage had become a critical issue.

Initially, the firm looked to the Internet Data Center (IDC), which was already responsible for the 24/7 operation of its 20 servers. However, the IDC's shared backup service did not meet the customer's stringent requirements for security and accessibility. In addition, the customer wanted a clear "exit strategy" in the event it decided to change its hosting provider or relocate its server and storage environment.

Storability conducted an objective assessment of the company's environment and developed a dedicated, secure solution based upon current and future backup requirements. The key component was AssuredRestore, Storability's automated remotely managed backup and restore service. The customized solution is based on the requirement to backup 2500 separate volumes per month. Storability designed the solution using VERITAS Netbackup Datacenter backup software, a SUN backup server, and an ADIC Scalar 100 library. Storability coordinated all aspects of equipment delivery, installation, testing and remote network connectivity. All of the firm's servers at the IDC are now successfully backed up by Storability, which is exceeding its service level commitment by completing over 99% of all backups within the defined backup window. Appropriate tape volumes are ejected for vaulting twice a week. The backup infrastructure is managed remotely 24/7 from Storability's operations center.

The customer has been able to implement best-in-class backup and restore procedures, along with 24/7 remote monitoring and management support at a fraction of the cost to do it themselves. When salaries, training, recruiting, and other expenses are factored in, the customer would be required to add more than $50,000 each month to its operating budget. With Storability, the company avoids those costs entirely while enjoying the advantages of around the clock monitoring to ensure continuous availability, access to storage experts, and a secure storage infrastructure.

It's clear that companies today can benefit from the assistance of a storage management service provider who can augment staff resources, assist in the development of a manageable storage infrastructure, and provide storage management services remotely using a customizable suite of storage management tools.

New Thinking on Business Continuity and Disaster Recovery

By

Robert F. Nieboer
Manager of Industry Relations
StorageTek
Louisville, CO

Introduction

Concerns about how to protect a business' information assets are not new. Backup is as old as computing. Disaster recovery planning as a recognized discipline is decades old. The shift to consider disaster recovery as more to do with the ability to keep the business running—business continuity—than it has to do with simply keeping IT "up" is at least 10 years old.

Today the world considers information to be the strategic corporate asset. The information assets of the business are considered its DNA; it says everything about who we are, what business we're in, who our customers are, who our suppliers are, and who our partners are. It documents every single aspect of our business in operation; market intelligence gathered, orders taken, inquiries made, shipments sent, invoices cut, payments received, goods manufactured, and services delivered.

The purpose of IT in this third millennium is to deliver information products and services into the hands of the people who run the business. Period. The ability of the business to survive today without the flow of timely information can be measured in hours and sometimes in minutes. The cost of downtime in some industries has been measured at millions of dollars per hour.

A Time of Reckoning

IT organizations everywhere have known these facts for many years. On September 11th, 2001, IT was put to the test. The good news is that the majority of those businesses affected in New York passed the test. Most were able to recover in a timeframe that minimized impact to the business. The key to this success was that most companies placed copies of their information in locations outside the radius impacted by the terrorist attacks.

Why were the businesses in New York around ground zero so well-prepared? Were they typical of the greater IT community or just lucky? The fact is that most of these businesses were among those who were most exposed to financial loss in the event of disruption to IT and so had taken the steps of securing offsite copies of their information, not in the basement, or in the building across the street, but in locations far enough away from ground zero to survive the attacks.

What is "far enough"? Since last September, more people consider that backup copies need to be at least 10 or 15 miles away from the primary site; others believe that backups need to be hundreds or even thousands of miles away.

What is more important for this discussion is that the boards of thousands of businesses around the world began asking their CIO's and IT management, "What if that had happened to us? How prepared would we have been?" The answers in many cases were not very encouraging. On a positive note, the visibility of business continuity and disaster recovery issues in the boardrooms of worldwide business was welcome to IT practitioners who have been trying to get budget for DR for years from boards that have just too many other initiatives to fund to pay much attention. The visibility is welcome; we have yet to see how quickly the increased visibility turns into dollars.

Options

Among the largest companies in the world, many of them have advanced techniques in place to protect the ability of the business to continue to function in the event of disruption to IT. These range from RAID schemes for disk to point-in-time copies (or snapshots) kept locally, to hot standby sites remotely located. The hot standby sites can minimize the outage to as little as a few minutes using mainframe techniques such as IBM's peer-to-peer remote copy (PPRC), which synchronizes remote disks with local disks.

This last methodology is a hugely expensive option for ensuring business continuity in the event of disruption to IT. It is the ultimate tool for disaster recovery and can protect the business from the loss of an entire enterprise data center. Those businesses that believe they need this level of protection have usually already done so. It is usually not an option for those businesses outside the Fortune 500 or 1000.

So what about those businesses for whom funding a duplicate data center is not a realistic option?

It was clear from the experiences of those in New York that the key to business continuity derived from their access to offsite copies of their information. Data recovery and application resumption involved installing new equipment in a new location and rebuilding files and data bases from backups, or simply restoring data from backups at an existing second site. Stories about data recovery in New York included accounts of boxes of cartridges being wheeled into buildings on hand trucks. Some businesses didn't know which cartridges were the latest versions of backups for which files.

For most businesses, the most cost-effective disaster recovery option will be built around tape backup. Even as conventional wisdom touts disk as the primary recovery vehicle because of its speed, no one is credibly suggesting that the fundamental need to save generations of files and databases on tape is no longer necessary. In fact, as long as the gap between the cost of disk and the cost of tape continues to be around 100:1, it will be impractical to eliminate the need to include tape backup in business continuity scenarios.

Next Steps

Among the lessons learned from New York in September 2001 were that while many businesses did protect business information via a combination of offsite disk and tape backup, it was not unusual to discover that knowledge of what generation of what backup data was stored on which cartridges was not also kept offsite. In addition, it was also not always known which volumes and files were successfully backed up and at which recent interval. This made the recovery process more tedious and time-consuming than it needed to be.

One of the next advances in cost-effective business continuity practices likely will be both the automation of offsite backup and its management—to ensure its consistency, and the continued exploitation of tape as a proven low-cost medium.

I suggest that automated and transparent tape mirroring will achieve both of the objectives of consistency in application and cost-effectiveness in execution.

Tape Mirroring

Today, we have already seen the beginnings of a strong adoption of storage networking. It is likely that by the year 2005, most, if not all, storage will be configured in storage networks. Whether Fibre Channel or iSCSI, whether Storage Area Network (SAN) or Network Attached Storage (NAS), it is likely that most, if not all, storage will be accessed by servers through some kind of storage network topology.

In fact, one of the strongest business cases for stimulating SAN adoption derives from tape consolidation. That is, reducing the number and variety of tape drive technologies that are typically dedicated to individual servers and applications, by using a SAN to share fewer—better—tape drives across many servers and applications.

The presence of tape-based storage networks now creates an interesting opportunity to achieve the goals of remote backup automation and cost-effective business continuity now that we are playing under the new rules of 9/11, where even the unthinkable can happen.

The following diagram shows the basic configuration for tape consolidation. This particular tape storage network includes heterogeneous servers, an in-band storage virtualization engine, and a robotic tape library that includes tape drives.

In this configuration, the servers are presented with a virtual or logical image of one or more tape drives. The storage virtualization engine is responsible for mapping data directed to these virtual tape drives, to real tape devices (which

Tape Mirroring

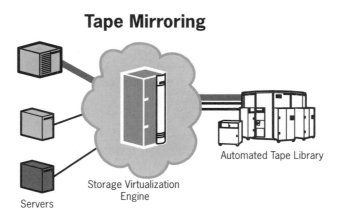

Servers

Storage Virtualization Engine

Automated Tape Library

may be a different device type) and real tape cartridges. We have, in effect, an environment in which the servers have no real knowledge of the physical tape devices.

This type of configuration is beginning to be installed by IT practitioners who are horrified by the weaknesses that were exposed by recent events. It is a desirable solution to the backup and recovery problem because it reduces the number and variety of tape drives being used, and, more importantly, because it reduces the human intervention in the tape and backup management processes that make those processes error-prone.

The virtualization engine essentially removes the need to extend tape storage management to each server platform. It allows changes to the physical environment to take place without the need to make those changes visible at the server and backup application level.

This type of virtualization engine already contains processor bandwidth and imbedded intelligence that allows data being written to one device type to be mapped to another. It includes intelligence that can handle error recovery without involving the server or the backup application. I propose that the configuration above can easily be adapted to a policy-based management capability that causes a second copy of the backup to be created. Further, the copy can be made locally or remotely. Within the context of business continuity and the desire to automate the backup process for consistency and to manage down the cost of off-site backups, I will discuss only a remote copy.

The diagram below is an adaptation of the earlier configuration diagram that now includes a remote copy of a backup tape.

In this scenario, the act of creating a tape backup of a file or volume can, using policy-based management constructs, trigger the synchronous or asynchronous creation of a second copy of the backup tape. Since the only knowledge of the second copy resides within the intelligence of the storage virtualization engine, the creation and management of the second copy takes place wholly within the sphere of influence of the storage virtualization engine.

Tape Mirroring

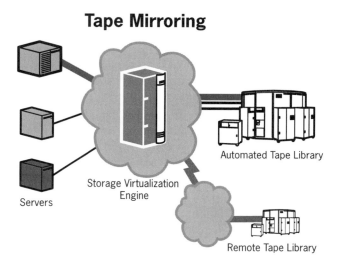

Servers

Storage Virtualization Engine

Automated Tape Library

Remote Tape Library

Also, since the backup application running on the application server has initiated the original backup process, and so therefore has the knowledge of the tape cartridge volume serial number assigned to the backup function, the virtualization engine should probably associate the remote second copy with the original tape cartridge volume serial number. That would certainly simplify the process of initiating a file restore. You either use the local original serial number, or if that is unavailable, for whatever reason, you use the same serial number from the remote site.

I like a few things about the proposed solution:

- The storage network drives efficiency in resource utilization
- The virtualization engine removes storage management from the server
- The success of the backup is guaranteed because it's driven by the virtualization engine which can perform automated error recovery

- The creation of the second copy is also guaranteed because it's also driven by the virtualization engine (with its own error recovery)

What has been achieved with this solution, relative to our original objective:

- "Supervision" of the backup process (automated error recovery)
- Automation of the offsite creation of a second copy of the backups
- Leveraging the low cost of tape for offsite backups

I see no end in sight to the exploitation of tape for protection against disruptive events. For those with deep pockets, mission critical applications will be protected via remote disk mirroring. For non-mission-critical applications, and for those without deep pockets, the ability to recover data must include tape and remote tape mirroring.

Disaster Avoidance through Effective Storage Management

By

Ken Barth
CEO
Tek-Tools, Inc.
Dallas, TX

The events of 9/11 underscored the potential that exists in every organization for an unplanned interruption of normal operations that could properly be described as a disaster. Such disasters can be the result of deliberate terrorism, as in the case of the World Trade Center and Pentagon attacks, or they can stem from a variety of other natural or man-made calamities.

Most unplanned downtime, however, is not the result of "smoke and rubble" disasters that command "center stage" on the nightly news broadcasts. According to numerous studies, most downtime events are the consequence of a much less dramatic cause: the improper or inefficient management and administration of data storage platforms.

Recipe for Disaster

Compelled by lack of resources and burgeoning data, many organizations have been deploying storage technology on an ad hoc basis, often in response to disk full error messages, with little or no concern for how these repositories of an organization's most critical asset—data—will ultimately be managed. In the process, entire organizations are being placed at risk.

Compounding the problem is the lack of standards-based storage management. Simple Network Management Protocol (SNMP), a protocol overseen by the Internet Engineering Task Force (IETF), provides one standards-based mechanism for managing network-connected equipment. The Storage Networking Industry Association (SNIA) is working on another standards based on the Common Information Model (CIM) that is garnering much attention.

The problem with SNMP, as recently revealed, is that it poses a potential security problem. According to the experts, SNMP could be exploited by hackers to attack the very "targets" that the protocol is intended to make more manageable. Even if this potential did not exist, implementation of SNMP controls on storage equipment is inconsistent across vendors and products.

CIM confronts other challenges. As an emerging standard, it is paid considerable "lip service" by the storage hardware vendor community, but few vendors have actually instrumented their platforms to facilitate management using the CIM approach.

As a result, IT managers are left to choose from among numerous proprietary approaches for storage management that may or may not support all of the gear that they have deployed. As more than one system administrator has observed, managing the current heterogeneous infrastructure of storage requires "a quiver of arrows approach" involving multiple products from different vendors. There is no "one-stop shop" solution offered today that can meet the needs of a truly heterogeneous infrastructure.

There are numerous storage management products called "frameworks" that endeavor to monitor storage components for error conditions so that corrective actions can be taken using storage resource management (SRM) software tools. The problems that vendors of management software confront are many, but they come down to a central challenge: how does one maintain the broadest possible configuration support (that is, the capability to support the broadest range of storage and server hardware components), while at the same time providing the best capabilities in terms of automated error condition response?

Most storage management software vendors (like network management software vendors before them) must maintain good relations with hardware vendors to maintain access to application programming interfaces, command line interfaces, or other proprietary mechanisms offered by the vendors to manage their gear. They devote nearly 80% of their resources just to keep up-to-date with the latest hardware device drivers. As a result, it is difficult for these vendors to dedicate resources that will add value and reduce costs for organizations that use their products in the form of time-saving or cost-saving automation.

Yet, a policy-based and highly automated solution for storage management is what consumers need to realize the promised business value of their storage acquisitions, which includes downtime risk reduction as well as cost savings and business enablement.

It is a conundrum for which there is no easy answer. And it is a problem that software developers alone cannot solve. Consumers of information technology need to demand that storage platform vendors enable their platforms for greater ease of management, whether by CIM, secure SNMP, or by some other means. The simple fact is that vendors will not enable their platforms to be managed by a common method until consumers demand it. And, until this common management approach emerges, the critical data stored by companies who use heterogeneous platforms and topologies will remain at high risk.

What Is Tek-Tools Doing?

Tek-Tools, while a relative newcomer to the storage management field, is no stranger to network management. The company comes to the problem of storage management with a distinctly network-oriented perspective and one that is well-suited to the evolution of storage technology away from server-attachment and toward new networking paradigms.

This is reflected in our Storage Profiler product, which features a web-based management console. Additionally, we are working to leverage the increasing number of storage products that articulate their own Web pages for monitoring and configuration control to aid in reducing our customers' dependency on hardware vendor "good will" and to deliver increased automation of storage management tasks.

Our technology is largely customer-driven. We have spent considerable time with customers to establish their requirements and to determine what is actually needed to model storage for improved management. Our customers agree with us that proactive measures are required to prevent avoidable downtime and we support them with the best monitoring, trend analysis, and reporting tools in the business.

We are further working to assist our customers by embracing the goals, and contributing directly to the development efforts, of organizations like SNIA in their work on CIM.

Managing Backups

As work proceeds in these important areas, Tek-Tools is already facilitating one very important requirement of its customers, which was underscored by the tragedy of 9/11: backup management. From our interaction with customers, we

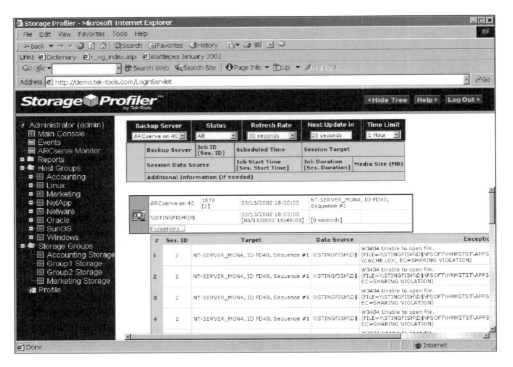

Figure 1

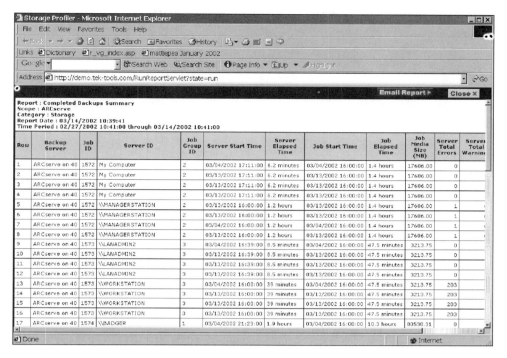

Figure 2

have identified three immediate needs that are not being adequately addressed by other products in the market:

1. The ability to simultaneously view and monitor the progress of backup systems,
2. The ability to report on the success and failure of backups to maintain integrity and to ensure that all data and applications are being backed up on a regularly scheduled basis, and
3. The ability to manage backup windows by reporting on the growth of data being backed up in order to adequately plan and budget for their storage needs well in advance of collapsing backup windows.

With the current and future releases of Storage Profiler, Tek-Tools, Inc. is implementing ways to coordinate the management of multiple backup software products deployed throughout an enterprise. See Figure 1.

With the ability to manage and monitor multiple copies of backup software distributed throughout an enterprise into one "near real-time" monitor, operators can view the jobs as they start and progress through the backup window. Any

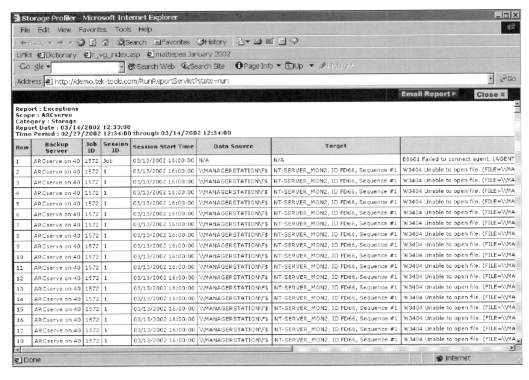

Figure 3

failures during the back up process are immediately displayed by creating an exception link so that operators can isolate and correct problems in real-time.

Extensive management reporting is also required to meet the needs of managers tasked with ensuring that company backup and disaster protection policies are observed. Backup reports are required that allow multiple managers to view and report the systems backed up on a routine basis and identify and correct procedures for new systems or failed backup jobs. See Figure 2.

With instant access to their nightly backup status reports of systems for which they are responsible, managers can be sure that there are no "holes" or gaps against company policy and backup schedules currently in place. This is increasingly important, given the tight backup windows most organizations confront. Figure 3 depicts Exceptions reports that notify systems administrators and users when there are failures. Such reporting capabilities can also be used to identify patterns of failure when critical systems haven't been backed up per schedule.

In addition to these capabilities, an effective storage management tool also needs to deliver historical trending reports that enable managers to understand

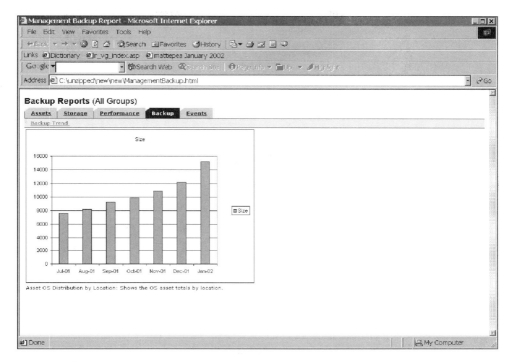

Figure 4

the growth of the data that is being backed up from month to month. This will allow managers to predict when they need to implement new policies and procedures and to understand how much data would need to be restored in the event of a catastrophic event. Figure 4 depicts a summary report.

Conclusion

Of course, managing and monitoring backup processes is only one part of the challenge of disaster prevention. Other processes, such as symmetrical and asymmetrical data replication from disk to disk, will also need to be managed and monitored as these techniques find greater use within the modern IT shop. Tek-Tools is evolving its products with appropriate capabilities to meet this need.

Storage recoverability is important to mitigate the consequences of disasters that can't be avoided. However, intelligent disaster recovery planning also requires proactive measures to stop downtime that can be prevented. At Tek-Tools, our primary objective will continue to be disaster prevention through effective management.

CHAPTER

5

Strategies for Centralized System Recovery

To many people, disaster recovery planning is synonymous with planning for the restoration of mainframe operations following a catastrophe. This should come as no surprise, considering that the traditional focus of disaster recovery planning was the recovery of the corporate computer, almost without exception a mainframe or large minicomputer.

Mainframe-centric disaster recovery plans dealt primarily with the procedures for replacing a damaged or inaccessible mainframe with compatible hardware. Tasks included loading system software and defining resources, starting the processes required for use by application software, loading data to direct access storage devices (DASD) from tape, establishing network connections—including a terminal network, and performing the many other preparatory tasks and tests to bring the corporate oracle back to life. Given the complexity of the task and the technical skills required, often disaster recovery planning was conceived as an activity confined entirely to the data processing department of the company.

Today, more and more, disaster recovery planning encompasses a wider set of objectives. It aims at the recovery of critical business processes, rather than the restoration of mainframe operations alone. This, in large part, is a response to changes in the business environment in which disaster recovery plans are developed.

Decentralization of data processing functions, the rise of personal computing, and the emergence of distributed computing architectures that leveraged local area networks are just some of the environmental changes that have forced contextual alterations in the field of disaster recovery planning. During the 1990s, a client/server "revolution" occurred in corporate computing that saw the migration of at least 20% of mission-critical applications off the corporate mainframe

220

and out onto the enterprise network. This trend was acknowledged by IBM with the release of its OS/390 operating system in 1995—the first OS from the mainframe vendor touted explicitly as a player in the "open systems" environment.

However, while decentralization has had the impact of broadening both the scope and the "targets" of disaster recovery planning, it has also created tremendous management burdens for corporate IT organizations. By the end of the 1990s, many companies had initiated projects designed to consolidate distributed servers into a fewer number of physical platforms and to recentralize distributed servers within the glass house of the data center. There, the thinking goes, they could be more effectively managed by a disciplined cadre of IT support personnel.

Even personal computers have not escaped the consolidation/recentralization trend. Many companies are considering new, server-centric, desktop computing paradigms that recentralize applications and data onto "application servers" and replace "fat client" PCs with "thin client" terminals as a means to improve management and reduce costs. To be sure, rumors of the death of the Microsoft Windows/Intel architecture-based ("WINTEL") desktop are greatly exaggerated, as were the rumors of the death of mainframe computing a decade before. However, the increasing availability of applications for thin client devices and the increasingly widespread use of the web browser and Java Virtual Machine, enabling technologies for many thin client desktops, have increased the appeal of this WINTEL desktop alternative.

According to one analyst, the application recentralization trend was inevitable, "When servers get more powerful, it just makes sense for them to get used more—for the server to get fatter."[1] Microsoft seems to have gotten this point when it released a Terminal Server Edition (TSE) of its popular Windows NT server operating system and more recently, as the vendor has begun to pursue an application-as-Web-Service model with its .NET initiative. Like other distributed servers, application servers too are being eyed for recentralization within the safe confines of the corporate data center.

One mitigator of this trend, however, has been the concern over the vulnerability of older, mainframe-based, COBOL applications to Year 2000 date issues. In a few documented cases (although the data here is suspect for a variety of reasons), businesses have actually migrated their mission-critical, mainframe-based applications onto distributed platforms—leveraging Y2K-ready software packages to provide an "end run" around the Year 2000 bug. It remains to be seen, however, whether this phenomenon will become less the exception and more the norm in the future.

To the extent that mission-critical business processes are supported by centralized platforms, older strategies for centralized systems recovery are still somewhat pertinent. These are discussed in this chapter. However, the introduction of three-tier and *n*-tier client/server application architectures pose entirely different challenges to the disaster recovery coordinator. They cannot be addressed effectively by simple hardware replacement strategies and are thus considered separately in the next chapter.

In the final analysis, the disaster recovery coordinator must think in terms of protecting and restoring business processes rather than CPUs. Specifically, the coordinator needs to look at the infrastructure supports for business processes, including hardware, operating systems, application software, and databases, as well as networks, interconnects and end users. Planning only for the replacement of a computer is no longer sufficient, if it ever was.

DEVELOPING CENTRALIZED SYSTEM BACKUP STRATEGIES

As indicated above, centralized system backup means more than hardware replacement and entails more than software or data backup. Centralized system backup strategies are interdependent with data protection strategies and with other disaster recovery plan elements.

For this reason, centralized system backup strategies are best developed concurrently with data recovery plans and with plans aimed at recovering business processes supported by distributed systems in which the mainframe plays a role. If mainframe recovery plans are created without careful consideration of the requirements and conditions imposed by these other plan elements, important interdependencies may be overlooked.

For example, even the most mainframe-centric application often has a role to play in other mission-critical applications residing on distributed platforms. The "legacy" transaction processing application that operates on the "back office" mainframe often has an important role to play with respect to the operation of Enterprise Resource Planning (ERP) applications residing on distributed platforms. A similar interdependency often exists between the legacy environment and the distributed e-commerce applications that companies are increasingly fielding to capitalize on the business potential market of the Internet.

Centralized system recovery procedures need to take into consideration important gateways and interfaces required by distributed applications, and process restoration must often be timed to meet distributed application requirements.

Figure 5–1 shows, in a simplified way, some of the relationships among these activities. While centralized system recovery is primarily a technical matter, it also requires the coordinator's complete understanding of the business processes that the system supports. Thus, data acquired during risk analysis is very important.

The risk analysis provides answers to the following questions that will impact directly on the strategies developed for centralized system recovery.

What Applications Are Critical or Vital?

One task of risk analysis was to rank the relative criticality of applications to business recovery following a disaster. Critical and vital applications are defined by the support they provide to critical business processes and also by the lack of

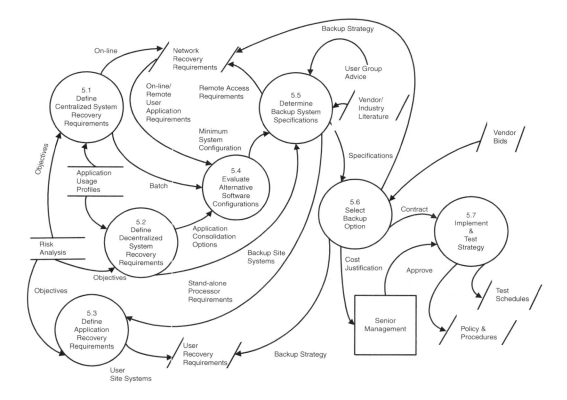

Figure 5–1   Systems recovery planning.

ready alternatives (e.g., manual methods) for providing their core functions. In short, these applications need to be restored within a short time following a disaster if business recovery is to be accomplished.

Having identified critical and vital applications, the disaster recovery coordinator can begin defining the infrastructure support requirements for the applications. Infrastructure support, in this context, may include users, input data and forms, output data and forms, processing hardware and necessary peripheral devices, and documentation.

It is important to note that, in addition to the personnel, equipment, networks, and data required to support an application, it may also be dependent upon the processes of another application for key inputs. Application interdependencies need to be clearly identified in order to determine accurately what applications are critical unto themselves and what applications may be critical based on inputs they provide to critical applications. Much of this analysis should have been completed during the initial analysis phase of the DR project.

What Is the Minimum Acceptable Hardware Configuration?

Once application criticality is defined, the risk analysis goes further to identify the hardware (both CPUs and storage devices) used by the application in performance of the critical or vital business function. From the perspective of disaster recovery planning, it may be possible to view hardware capabilities utilized by all noncritical and nonvital applications as "spare capacity."

Hence, during its emergency operations, the business may be able to settle for far less processor and storage capacity than it normally utilizes. The ramifications of this view are twofold.

If less capacity is needed to run critical and vital applications, the centralized platform required for recovery need not match the configuration of production system hardware on a one-to-one basis. A high-end model CPU may be adequately backed up with a lower-end processor of adequate capacity.

It also follows that, if critical and vital applications run on several homogeneous (or compatible) processors in normal business operations, it may be possible to replace several low-end servers with a single high-end server. Through the use of the right operating system software, even applications that reside on heterogeneous processors may be able to run successfully on a single processor. Again, the total capacity requirement of the backup server and related storage devices may be substantially less than that of the production environment.

The net result of this analysis is what may be called a minimum acceptable hardware configuration. This configuration, which must be implemented quickly in the event of a disaster, may require substantial technical assistance to design. Still more assistance may be required to deploy and test it. However, a workable minimum configuration can drastically reduce the costs of the disaster recovery capability.

How Many Users?

The risk analysis should also have identified the characteristics of application use, including the number of users who would need access to applications to continue business functions at emergency levels. The number of personnel required during emergency operations may be far fewer than the normal complement of personnel who use systems in day-to-day operations. Additional staff might be put to better use supporting business processes that are being continued by manual means, or aiding in other aspects of the recovery effort.

From the size of the "skeleton crew" using restored applications to provide critical and vital business functions, certain other facts may be discerned. For example, the number of users will help to define the recovery network for the application by identifying how many end stations (workstation/terminals) and what type of access and bandwidth will be required. This information, too, must be taken into account by the centralized system recovery strategy that is developed.

The strategy must account for peripheral devices as well as CPUs and mass storage devices. It must also provide for a location where recovery personnel will work, in addition to providing an environment where processors, tape drives, disk drives, and other equipment will be operated.

CAUTIONS AND CAVEATS

The above description may seem to oversimplify the task of defining the parameters for centralized system recovery. However, the task can be, and often is, just that straightforward. Having identified key business processes and their application supports, the balance of the centralized system recovery planning effort is made substantially easier because of the well-defined operating environment of the mainframe.[2]

According to Tim Humphreys, chief architect for Trident Services, assuming that a "floor system" is available for use and backups of data are available, OS/390 mainframe application recovery is typically a by-the-numbers (or by the acronyms!) proposition.

> First, you need to do a software-based Hardware Configuration Data (HCD) activation to dynamically change the configuration of the platform [to identify the network addresses of devices that will be used to interface with the system]. Then, load your initial program load (IPL) volume [which defines resources and parameters], followed by your master catalog pack, and you IPL the system. Next, you initialize the direct access storage devices (DASD) for use with Systems Managed Storage (IBM's DFSMS manages storage volumes), and you begin performing logical restores of your backups. This may be done using IBM's Data Set Services (DFDSS), or IBM's Hierarchical Storage Manager Application Backup and Recovery System (DFHSM ABARS), or third party data dump restore products like Innovation's Fast Dump Restore (FDR). With this done, you're basically ready for business.[3]

Humphreys's description makes centralized system recovery seem almost routine. He points out, however, that running an application on a platform having a different configuration, or in a system that is partitioned or shared with others, can introduce some problems. He notes that products such as Trident Services' Operating System/Environment Manager (OS/EM) may provide an easy to use mechanism for supporting ABARS data set recovery and for dynamically altering region sizes and memory resources available to applications.[4]

Even with environment management tools, however, problems can and do present themselves when defining a minimum system configuration that may require effort and creativity to surmount. First, not all applications have been written in such a way that they can be deployed in alternative configurations. Systems programmers are an important source for information about application resource requirements that might be missed by less technical analysts. Job Control Language (JCL), customized Job Entry System (JES) "exits," and a number of other factors may conspire with poorly written "spaghetti code" to mitigate the ability to move applications readily from one set of environment conditions to another.

In some cases, there is no minimum equipment configuration option for applications without a significant rewrite of application- and system-level code. Few organizations are inclined to modify or rewrite code merely to facilitate the recoverability of an application in a disaster situation. However, identifying such problems and alerting management to their existence might add another argument to an existing business case for rewriting or replacing the old application code.

In any case, minimum equipment configuration goes beyond the definition of the mainframe platform. The analysis of inputs and outputs to the business process, included in risk analysis, defines the equipment requirements to recover the business process overall, not just its application host. Based on the risk analysis, it is possible to formulate a fairly clear picture of how many users (or processes) will use the application, and what the network, end station, and peripheral requirements are for that use.

For example, if printed reports are a necessary output of a given business process, a printer may need to be added to the minimum configuration of the recovery system. Also, if input data needs to be received, via data communications from remote sites (for example, "lock box" transmissions used to update customer payment records), the minimum equipment configuration would need to provide for the network hardware and software for this function.

Business process analysis will also identify any special preprinted forms required for work, as well as voice communications, electronic mail, photocopying, facsimile transmission, and ground mail resources needed to do the job.

This brief overview should make evident that much of what is needed to develop an effective centralized system recovery strategy is available from the risk analysis. Given this information, it is up to the coordinator, in conjunction with technical staff, to select the best strategy for the restoration of critical and vital business functions.

MAINFRAME BACKUP STRATEGIES

As observed above, disaster recovery planning techniques were once limited to developing strategies for replacing mainframe computers. While this is not an adequate context for business recovery today, the focus on mainframe backup has yielded some time-tested techniques that can provide useful information for more sophisticated system recovery plans.

The following are typical strategies for backing up the corporate mainframe. The explanation of each strategy identifies the merits and demerits that have come to be associated with it.

"Next Box off the Line"

One strategy used by many companies in the past to backup their data processing mainframe was to absorb the impact of the disaster until a data center could be readied and a comparable or compatible mainframe and peripherals network could be installed to replace the lost facility and equipment. In the interim—until a new mainframe became available—the company would "make do" with manual procedures, locate and prepare a new facility or refurbish the existing facility, and retrieve a current backup of system and application software and data from storage. When the new mainframe was installed, IT personnel would load the software and data backup and users would frantically re-input interim data until files and records were up to date.

The drawbacks of this approach—which stands today as more a straw man than a strategy—are numerous. First, the plan could work only in an environment where there were no critical systems. By definition, if viable, manual alternatives existed to all mainframe-supported business processes, no application would be considered critical to business survival. Only in such an environment could the open-ended timeframes involved in replacing computer equipment with new hardware be tolerated. Certainly, very few companies today would find their automated systems so easily replaced with manual means.

Second, this option does not provide, in advance, for a facility in which the new mainframe can be installed. Locating a suitable facility may not be a very difficult task, but the preparation of such a facility, including the installation of a raised floor, air conditioning, UPS, electrical wiring, security systems, fire protection, etc., would be a major undertaking. In short, even if the "next box off the line" were available in a timely way, the facility might not be.

Cold Site

The cold-site (or shell site) strategy is similar to the "next box off the line" option in that the actual restoration of mainframe operations is on hold until replacement hardware can be obtained. By using the cold-site strategy, however, the business has already prepared a facility with the requisite physical capabilities to serve as an alternate data processing site.

Company-owned cold sites have the drawback of being expensive to outfit with all of the requisite disaster prevention systems provided in a production data center. However, the facility may be able to be used for other purposes, including off-site storage or new employee training, when not in use for disaster recovery.

Commercial Cold Site

This option is identical to the cold-site strategy above except that a commercial cold site is a contracted facility. The facility may be located in the subscriber's vicinity or distant from it. Or, a cold site may be able to be moved to the customer's location. Mobile cold sites have become widely available in the United States and are offered by leading disaster recovery services vendors, including Hewlett Packard Business Recovery Service, IBM Business Continuity and Recovery Service, and SunGard Availability Services. Figure 5–2 shows a typical mobile shell site offering from SunGard.

Commercial shell sites, whether mobile or not, provide a capability that is cost-effective because expenses for its construction and maintenance are shared by multiple subscribers. Like the preceding strategies, however, this approach to centralized system recovery assumes that the company can absorb the impact of being without a mainframe until one can be obtained from either a leasing company or system vendor. For many companies, this option is unacceptable.

As with the private cold-site option, commercial cold sites do not provide a means to test the effectiveness of this recovery strategy until a disaster actually happens. A company cannot verify its estimates for system restoration time-frames without testing restoration procedures on actual hardware.

Given their inherent systems recovery "lag time," the role of shell sites has been substantially recast in recent years. In some cases, the shell site is positioned as a transitional facility—a location to which company systems that have been supported on a "hot-site" platform (see below) in the hours or days following a disaster can be migrated for operation over a substantially longer period of time.

For example, if a data center has been demolished by a disaster, it is sometimes necessary to support mission-critical operations at an alternate site for an extended time-frame while a new facility is being located and equipped. A shell

Figure 5–2   Mobile MetroCenter®. (*Source:* SunGard Availability Services Inc., Wayne, PA.)

site can be equipped with company replacement hardware while the company's critical applications are being supported at a hot site. When the system is ready at the shell-site, the company can migrate applications to the shell-site host, freeing the hot-site platform for use by other subscribers. Hot-site contracts generally require this strategy and limit the period of hot site occupancy. In some cases, the shell site serves as a staging area for replacement systems from the mainframe vendor.

Mobile shell sites, too, have been largely retasked to support transitional operations, or to serve different functions in the recovery environment, such as small systems and/or user recovery. According to Jim Grogan, SunGard Recovery Services Vice President of Alliances, mobile shell sites can and do serve as mobile data centers:

> We can move one of our Mobile Data Centers within 48 hours anywhere in the country. We used them recently in several regional disasters, such as the Red River floods, after the California earthquakes, and so forth. Following a flood in Grand Forks, SD, one of our customers, a bank, operated from the Mobile Data Center and had to move the center two times to stay ahead of the water. . . . We have a total of 39 mobile support trailers of different sizes and configurations. With these, we have the capability to ship smaller processors with the mobile units, and to use them for end-user recovery, including workstations and [other office] equipment, and for distributed systems recovery as well.[5]

The 48-hour mean restoration time-frame has emerged as an industry standard for mobile shell sites. Both Hewlett Packard and IBM offer mobile shells, equipped with smaller server hosts, that can provide facilities for workgroup and distributed systems recovery. Cast in this role, vendors can make at least one test per year possible on actual equipment.

Reciprocal Backup Agreement

To address the problem of facilities and hardware outages in companies unable to manage for extended periods of time without their mainframes, one option, less frequently seen today than in the past is the reciprocal backup agreement. Essentially, two companies having spare processing time and compatible hardware capabilities agree formally or informally to back up each other's critical applications. In a simple arrangement, if Company A experienced a disaster, Company B would allow Company A to restore its critical applications on Company B's hardware. The reverse would be the case if Company B had a failure.

The problems with this strategy, even at the time that it was popular, were twofold. First, it was extremely difficult for a company to find a partner who had the right hardware, spare capacity, and the inclination to participate in such an agreement. Location was also a factor: The potential partner could not be co-located to the company seeking the arrangement, since the same disaster that affected Company A might at the same time affect Company B.

Second, if a suitable partner were found, it was difficult to find a mutually agreeable time to test the arrangement. Having an untested strategy is nearly as pointless as having no strategy at all.

Companies that experimented with these arrangements in the 1970s and 1980s found that it was also difficult to maintain the relationship on mutually acceptable terms. Managers chafed at having to notify their partners of changing configurations or new processing requirements. One could not cost-justify to one's own management the need to acquire a new item of hardware on the grounds that it would facilitate the disaster recovery capability of another company.

These arrangements also carried the risk of domino-effect disasters. The relocation of Company A's processing load to Company B's host might also disrupt Company B's operations. Company B would need to activate its emergency plan, requiring that its business operate in disaster recovery mode until Company A was recovered. Needless to say, this was unacceptable to Company B's management.

Today, reciprocal arrangements are rarely seen, except in large companies with numerous subsidiaries. Even in these cases, it is rare that enough spare processing time or equipment capability exists to support a mutual backup arrangement without deliberate planning to support such a scenario. Where there is substantial excess capacity, it has a tendency to be drawn into normal production use over time, making it unavailable for DR.

Service Bureaus

Some companies elect to back up systems against failure by contracting with a service bureau for emergency processing services. For example, the vendor of a loan administration application used by mortgage banking companies may offer a "service bureau" capability for the application.

Software vendors that provide service bureaus typically market the service to customers who prefer not to invest in their own computer systems and software. User terminals are installed in the client offices, and jobs are submitted to CPUs located at the vendor service bureau via data communications. In some cases, printers are also installed at the client office so that reports and other output can be printed locally.

For customers who purchase vendor software but operate independently of the vendor's service bureau, the service bureau offering may still be available in a disaster recovery situation. Service bureau backup may be part of a software sales contract, or may be a separately negotiated arrangement.

What are some of the potential drawbacks of this approach? Vendor service bureaus are typically application-specific. They process customer data all together, then distribute output to individual customers. This may create some difficulties for a company that has several critical applications, including some for which recourse to a software vendor's service bureau is not available. Also, the prospect of dividing numerous applications among several vendor-provided service bureaus is unsettling.

For a service bureau arrangement to be effective, several conditions must be met. First, the disaster-stricken company must have an existing facility where remote access to applications by users can be provided. Second, the customer's data backups must have been saved from the disaster that consumed the originals, and these data backups must be in the proper format for speedy integration with the service bureau storage and systems. If vendor-recommended maintenance procedures have not been observed, if applications have not been updated to the most current software release, or if file formats have been "customized" to better suit the business' needs, there may be incompatibilities with the service bureau application that will be difficult and time-consuming to correct.

It should be mentioned that, despite the caveats expressed above, there is a new spin on service bureau backup that is giving the concept a renaissance of sorts. As the 1990s drew to a close, the emergence of "virtual infrastructure outsourcing" descended. Companies have begun experimenting with remote application hosting via the Internet as a means to reduce internal system support costs.

One vendor that was quick to see the disaster recovery implications of this trend was Exodus Communications, now part of Cable and Wireless Internet Services. According to a spokesperson for the company in 1999, the e-commerce explosion was driving many top-tier companies to the Web and making small companies instant players in a bigger world.[6] Exodus' goal was to provide application hosting services to a significant percentage of the largest concerns on the World Wide Web, serving as a virtual data center for this clientele by providing service level guarantees exceeding those of non–Internet-based outsourcing service providers.

Exodus created its own network of redundant Internet Data Centers interconnected by OC3/OC12 backbone. Mission-critical e-business applications were mirrored across these data centers to provide enhanced performance and uptime guarantees. The vendor also worked with its customers to develop Internet disaster recovery (IDR) plans that enabled the application service provider to also play the role of disaster recovery provider.

Application service providers (ASPs) are quickly becoming the modern service bureau processors, not only for e-commerce applications, but also for databases, enterprise resource planning (ERP) applications, and other mission-critical applications.[7] While not technically a "mainframe backup strategy," the potential for the use of the Internet as a mechanism for application backup is intriguing. A new category of backup options, closely related to the service bureau strategy of two decades ago appears to be coalescing on the disaster recovery landscape, as evidenced in the offerings from long-time outsourcing companies-turned-managed web hosting providers such as Electronic Data Systems (EDS).

Hot Sites

Hot sites are rather like generic service bureaus. Typically, they are fully equipped IT operations facilities to which a number of companies having compatible hardware subscribe. Machine time is made available to subscribers for the purpose of testing their recovery procedures, and this testing schedule can be quickly interrupted so that facilities can be made available to any customer who declares a disaster.

Once a disaster is declared, the customer sends its backup media (or uses an on-site tape vault or remote mirror) and a team of operations personnel to the hot site. Critical applications are loaded and tested, users are provided with access from their work location, and IT services are restored.

Unlike a service bureau, a hot site is usually equipped to run any application that is compatible with its hardware and operating system. Hot sites are often equipped with technical support personnel to assist the company operations team in its efforts to get systems configured, data transferred, and applications up and running.

In addition to the fixed complement of hardware at the hot site, specialized equipment can be added to satisfy the customer's backup requirement. However, this is often done at the customer's expense, especially if other facility subscribers do not need the required equipment.

Some hot-site vendors also offer cold sites that a customer can lease if disaster conditions persist for an extended period of time. Hot-site vendors may also provide assistance in obtaining replacement hardware for use in the cold site or for delivery to the customer's own new or refurbished facility.

Hot sites have become the mainframe backup option preferred by medium to large companies. Their reliability and recent notable successes in recovering companies in the throes of a disaster have greatly offset initial concerns about their price. Some considerations and cautions in selecting a hot site are provided later in this chapter.

Recent public announcements of pricing for hot-site services by some vendors have contributed to the perception that this type of service offering is becoming a commodity. In January 1999, *Network Computing* magazine built a feature story around a hot-site services request for proposal (RFP) issued by hypothetical retailer, Dewey, Cheatham, and Howe.[8] The RFP specified requirements and invited hot site vendors to respond with solutions and pricing. Three vendors, Exodus Communications, IBM, and Comdisco, responded to the RFP, while several declined to participate. Of those who refused, only one vendor (SunGard) did so because, reportedly, it was unwilling to discuss price in an open forum.

In June 1999, Hewlett Packard BRS went public with "a portfolio of services" specifying estimated recovery timeframes, and, in conversations with the press, pricing (see Table 5–1). According to George Ferguson, marketing manager for HP BRS, "Our portfolio of services are designed to address the different criticality requirements of companies. Criticality is being determined today at the Chief Financial Officer and Chief Operating Officer level. It is no longer primarily an IT concern."[9]

Ferguson observed that the range of services provided by the vendor cater "to the differing recovery time objectives and differing recovery point objectives of various business processes. These are not linear to cost. For a high-availability uptime solution, companies can expect to pay upwards of $750,000 per year. For

Table 5–1   Hewlett Packard BRS Portfolio of Services

	BRS Continuous	**BRS Immediate**	**BRS Critical**
Typical end-user availability following disaster invocation (RTO)	Less than 1 hour	2 to 8 hours	8 to 24 hours
Service Level Objective	Less than 1 hour for end-user availability	2 to 8 hours for end-user availability (an exact number of hours will be specified based on the customer's environment)	7 hours for the system to be fully commissioned, operating system loaded, and volumes configured
Currency of data (RPO)	Nearly the same as the moment of the disaster	Nearly the same as the moment of the disaster	Same as the last backup
Customer access to recovery center following disaster invocation	Within 2 hours	Within 2 hours	Within 2 hours
Shared vs. dedicated components	Dedicated system Dedicated storage Dedicated networking	Shared system Dedicated storage Shared networking	Shared system Shared storage Shared networking
Location of recovery system	HP Recovery Center	HP Recovery Center	HP Recovery Center
Disaster rehearsals included	Yes	Yes	Yes

	BRS Core -HP Recovery Center	**BRS Core -Ship-to-Site**	**BRS Core -Mobile Data Center**	**BRS Basic**
Typical end-user availability following disaster invocation (RTO)	24 to 72 hours	24 to 72 hours	24 to 72 hours	Greater than 72 hours (based on no rehearsals)
Service level objective	24 hours for the system to be fully commissioned and operating system loaded	6 hours for the system to be fully commissioned and shipped; operating system will be loaded before or after shipping	6 hours for the system to be fully commissioned and shipped; operating system will be loaded before or after shipping	8 hours for the system to be fully commissioned and shipped

(*continued*)

Table 5–1   Hewlett Packard BRS Portfolio of Services (continued)

	BRS Core -HP Recovery Center	**BRS Core -Ship-to-Site**	**BRS Core -Mobile Data Center**	**BRS Basic**
Currency of data (RPO)	Same as the last backup	Same as the last backup	Same as the last backup	Same as the last backup
Customer access to recovery center following disaster invocation	Within 4 hours	Nonapplicable	Nonapplicable	Nonapplicable
Shared vs. dedicated components	Shared system Shared storage Shared networking	Shared system Shared storage Shared networking	Shared system Shared storage Shared networking	Shared system Shared storage Shared networking
Location of recovery system	HP Recovery Center	Customer-provided data center	HP Mobile Data Center at customer-specified location	Customer-provided data center
Disaster rehearsals included	Yes	Yes	Yes	Optional

Source: Hewlett Packard Company, Palo Alto, CA.

other business processes, in which recovery timeframes range from 8 hours to 3 days, there is a huge pricing drop—well below $100,000 per year."[10]

Menu-based pricing, unheard of in the industry a decade ago, reinforces the commodity view of hot-site services. SunGard's Jim Grogan, however, takes exception to the trend toward price disclosure on several grounds.

> There is little doubt that service pricing is a little more open now. Industry groups have challenged vendors on their pricing policies. But are disaster recovery services commodities now? I have heard it said over the past 2 years that they are. At SunGard, we have to disagree. There is no one-size-fits-all solution. The technology simply has not matured enough.[11]

Redundant Systems

Of course, the single, most reliable, system backup strategy is to have fully redundant systems. While most companies cannot afford to build and equip two identical data centers, those that can enjoy the comfort of full confidence in their ability to recover from almost any disaster.

In the event of a disaster, redundant systems at a separate facility—which must be far enough distant so as not to have been affected by the same disaster—are brought on-line. Users are either transported to an operations center that is co-located to the backup site or are provided remote access to the backup CPU via some sort of preestablished data communications network.

Besides being the most reliable method of centralized (or decentralized) systems recovery, redundancy also tends to be the most expensive. A commercial hot site, for this reason, is often a more acceptable alternative from a cost perspective, provided that the longer recovery window is acceptable.

This spectrum of alternative mainframe backup strategies are graphed in Figure 5–3 to show the relative measure of confidence afforded to the company whose survival depends upon each strategy. The highest measure of confidence is afforded by the redundant systems strategy in which hardware availability is immediate, facilities mirror those that were lost, and backup systems duplicate production systems so closely that only minimal adjustments to normal business processes are required. The least confidence is placed in the "next box off the line," or replacement strategy. Such a strategy provides no timetable for system replacement or restoration of business processes as hardware delivery dates, facility location, and preparation dates, and other factors are unknown. A caveat to this simple comparison goes without saying: No strategy affords any greater level of confidence than any other unless it is accompanied by a carefully thought-out, documented, and tested recovery process. Contracting for a hot site does not absolve the DR coordinator of the responsibility for planning for or testing its use.

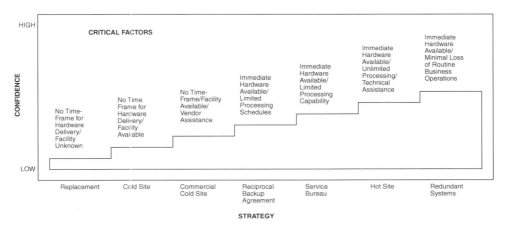

Figure 5–3   Centralized system recovery strategies and confidence levels.

WHICH STRATEGY IS PREFERRED?

Considering the large population of companies that have not prepared at all for the disastrous interruption of business processes, some crafty analyst might say that the most popular strategy for centralized system recovery is the "do nothing" strategy. The fact is that the preferred strategy for the recovery of centralized platforms is not known.

IBM Business Continuity and Recovery Service claims to have had 10,000 customers subscribe to its service since its inception in 1989.[12] IBM's original offering consisted of hot site facilities and consulting, but, like most hot site vendors, the company has rolled out additional services over the years, ranging from mobile shell sites to expedited delivery of replacement hardware (a sort of contractual next-box-off-the-line) for its smaller systems.

As of this writing, the company has added two offerings aimed at very specific and vertical markets to its portfolio of services: the recovery of call centers and the recovery of Enterprise Resource Planning (ERP) systems. These, according to IBM BCRS spokespersons, are part of the company's effort to provide "skills-based offerings" that meet specific market demands. In short, while IBM BCRS may have contracts with over 10,000 customers, the actual recovery method preferred by those customers is not public information.

So as not to single out IBM, SunGard Availability Services also boasts over 10,000 customers—a number substantially increased following its acquisition of Comdisco's disaster recovery services business in 2001 and Guardian iT in 2002. According to vice president of alliances, Jim Grogan, the average customer comes to the vendor today with at least three different types of system platforms to recover.[13] SunGard's service offerings range from consulting and disaster recovery planning software to hot site, workgroup recovery, call center recovery, and trade floor recovery. How many customers are purchasing hot-site contracts, versus mobile shell sites, versus other recovery or service offerings remains unclear.

This "information gap" regarding preferred centralized system recovery strategies is unlikely to be resolved in the near future. Industry surveys conducted by trade journals or analysts also do not provide a clear picture of strategy preference, in part because of the comparatively small number of companies surveyed. Disaster recovery–specific publications do offer periodic reader survey results, but they capture only the behavior of the small subset of planners who actually subscribe to the publications.

At least three studies are presently underway within academia, but these are hampered by numerous factors. Some use the World Wide Web to collect data, which inevitably skews results (falsified reports are common). Plus, academic surveys, like industry surveys, are subject to the "PBS factor." That is, just as surveyed television viewers overwhelmingly claimed to watch intelligent programming on Public Broadcasting System (rather than the intellectually mediocre fare on broadcast or cable television channels), companies almost inevitably point to DR plans that are "under development," rather than acknowledging that they have never undertaken any planning whatsoever. The latter would be politically incorrect.

For these reasons and many others, the best evidence regarding the preferred strategy for centralized system recovery is strictly anecdotal. It is derived from press accounts of recovery efforts, consultant tales, DR planner "war stories," and vendor-provided statistics. Added together, this less-than-scientific evidence favors the commercial hot site strategy as the preferred modus operandi for centralized system recovery in businesses with critical downtime sensitivities measured in the 1- to 48-hour range.

While some companies do build redundant data centers or have mutual assistance agreements with the data centers of their subsidiaries, most do not enjoy these luxuries. To them, the commercial hot site provides a less expensive and equally effective option for large system recovery.

Hot sites remove many of the unknowns inherent in strategies that involve the acquisition of replacement hardware in a disaster situation (i.e., replacement, cold site, and commercial cold site). Moreover, the increasing diversity of installed software products and a concurrent increase in the utilization of hardware capacities have rendered service bureaus and cross-firm mutual backup agreements increasingly anachronistic as competent mainframe backup strategies.

As of this writing, the Internet-based virtual data center strategy offered by managed Web hosting companies and some Application Service Providers is still very new. It is entirely conceivable that these services will come to rival traditional hot sites in the future, especially given the interest of telecommunications providers in delivering system hosting services within their Next Generation Networks.

For now, commercial hot sites, such as the facility pictured in Figure 5–4, are available to recover nearly all brands and sizes of large systems and mainframes. Most also offer recovery services for smaller server configurations, though the efficacy and price/performance of these solutions remains a debatable issue (see Chapter 6).

SELECTING A HOT SITE

Selecting a hot site is a straightforward process but one that requires the disaster recovery coordinator to have (1) a detailed understanding of the company's minimum acceptable system configuration and (2) some savvy about the hot site industry and its practices. Armed with this information, the coordinator will be better able to identify the vendor offering that best fulfills a company's mainframe backup requirements.

Since minimum acceptable configurations are company-specific, they cannot be treated here in any detail. Suffice it to say that considerable technical assistance may be required to define a system hardware configuration that is capable of restoring all critical and vital applications. These applications may include

Figure 5–4   A hot-site facility (*Source:* IBM Business Continuity and Recovery Service, Sterling Forest, NY.)

both those that are normally resident on a mainframe as well as portable applications that are normally deployed to distributed computers but may be recovered in a centralized system environment. It is obviously advantageous to have completed this analysis and to have a requirements list in hand before going hot-site "shopping."

In addition to system hardware specifications, DR coordinators need to understand the data communications requirements of their critical and vital applications. Most of the larger hot site vendors offer recovery networks for use by their customers in re-establishing links between the recovery system and peripherals located at user recovery facilities. While most organizations have moved from 3 to 4 Mb/s channel-to-peripheral-device interfaces to much faster interconnects, including 18 Mb/s ESCON, 40 Mb/s UltraSCSI, or 100 Mb/s Fibre Channel for connecting remote storage, printer, and other types of devices,[15] or have moved to an entirely ethernet-based peripheral attachment strategy,[16] there may continue to be the odd item sorter, controller, or other peripheral at a company branch office that requires special service. Be sure to know what requirements exist for reconnecting the recovered system to its peripheral network before approaching vendors.

Also, if critical or vital applications require the exchange of data between locations other than the user recovery site and the hot site (for example, electronic data interchange between the company's systems and the systems of suppliers, service bureaus, government agencies, etc.), these communications requirements must be specified in as much detail as possible. Information about the location and type of communicator, the communication methods, the access methods, protocols, encryption standards, and even the timing of scheduled communications should be at the DR coordinator's fingertips when he or she sits down to define backup requirements with a vendor marketing representative.

Technical suitability is a primary criterion for selecting a hot site vendor. However, there are several other factors that the coordinator would be well advised to consider. Many of these factors can be derived from the experience of other DR coordinators who have developed effective centralized system recovery strategies through the use of hot site facilities.

In the past, one consideration was the veracity of vendor claims that they could actually deliver promised services. In the 1970s and 1980s, disaster recovery planners confronted the reality of fly-by-night companies who misrepresented their facilities and capabilities. Legitimate vendors struggled to offset the damage caused by a few unethical charlatans who collected large monthly fees for nonexistent or phantom hot sites on the gamble that a customer will never have to declare a disaster.

In the 1990s, the DR industry underwent enormous change. The rise of organized associations of disaster recovery planners created a type of informal industry watch. Word spread quickly within these groups regarding any questionable practices by vendors, the adequacy of their offerings, pricing differences, and so forth.

In addition to tighter monitoring, the vendor community itself went through a winnowing-out period in the 1990s. Many smaller vendors either closed their doors or were acquired by larger companies. As a result, most hot-site solutions today are provided by established firms with extensive client references and demonstrable records of successful recoveries.

The last point is extremely important. Cases of disaster recovery plan implementation are now front page stories in the computer trade press. In the past, companies that experienced disasters—even those that recovered successfully from them—were very circumspect in disclosing information about the event. The fear was that stockholders, business partners, or customers would respond negatively to the perceived vulnerability of the company and its business processes to unplanned interruptions.

Corporate culture has changed in most (though not all) firms. No longer is the best information about disaster recovery locked away in confidential corporate records: Now, disaster recovery is grist for splash headlines in trade magazines and tabloids. Editors welcome the exciting visuals of wrecked buildings, flooded data centers, and shattered glass houses as a break from stock product photos, software screen shots, and mug shots of IT corporate luminaries.

With more information readily available to DR coordinators about the legitimacy of vendor offerings, attention can be focused on other important components of the system recovery service. These considerations become apparent upon review of the steps typically involved in contracting with a vendor for hot-site service.

Meet with the Marketing Representative

One of the first steps in selecting a hot site is to meet with a marketing representative of the vendor. During this meeting, the representative will seek information about company backup requirements, minimum configurations, communications requirements, and even the current status of the company disaster recovery plan.

Obviously, the representative will strive to inform the prospective customer about the merits of his or her facilities, identify some of its more prestigious subscribers, and even recount instances in which the facility rescued a subscriber in distress. Be sure to ask for the names of contacts in several subscriber companies for later use in vendor evaluation.

Do not accept the representative's word for the fact that his or her facility can meet recovery needs. Only in rare cases can a marketing rep make such a determination without input from the hot-site technical staff. Even if a technical support person has accompanied the marketing representative, verbal assurances are not sufficient.

Ask the marketing representative to develop, within a specified time, a written proposal responding to the specific recovery requirements that have been explained to him or her. The vendor should clearly define how the hot site facility being offered will fulfill each requirement. Hot-site vendors are highly competitive, so legitimate vendors will usually go out of their way to ensure that the prospective customer has all the information needed to make the right choice (presumably, a choice that favors their service).

The proposal should detail costs associated with both subscription to, and actual use of, the facility. It should also provide details of other vendor offerings. Many hot-site vendors also maintain cold sites that are available to customers in the event that the recovery period becomes protracted. Some will help the customer locate and install new hardware in the vendor cold site or at some other specified location. Some vendors are subsidiaries of larger concerns involved with disaster recovery consulting, equipment leasing, system manufacturing, or other data processing services. A list of the vendor's other services and interests may be a factor in a coordinator's decision.

Inspect the Facility

Once two or more potentially suitable hot-site vendors have been identified and their proposals and credentials have been evaluated, the coordinator should go no further until a physical inspection has been made of each candidate's facilities. It is often a good idea to have a systems expert and an auditor accompany the coordinator during the inspection, as their observations and criticisms may go beyond the scope of a purely disaster recovery-oriented focus to identify important vendor inadequacies.

Some hot-site vendors will purchase the plane tickets or underwrite lodging for serious prospects. The coordinator should strive to avoid being influenced by these or other perks that the vendor provides. Weighed against the monthly fee that the vendor will charge once the prospect signs a subscriber contract, these perks amount to very little indeed.

One of the purposes of the facility visit is to evaluate the vendor's non-emergency operations and staff. The coordinator should find out how processors are used during non-disaster periods: Are they idle, are they in constant use for customer tests, or are they used to provide other services?

If the vendor's own business applications reside on processors during non-emergency operations, or if the processors are utilized to provide service bureau functions, the coordinator should ask for an explanation of how these processing functions will be handled in the event of a customer emergency.

Be aware that, in many cases, the facility that a vendor shows to its prospective customers may not be the facility that will actually be used if recovery is required. Since the mid-1990s, some disaster recovery service providers have been selling MIPS (processing capability measured in millions of instructions per second) rather than sites. In other words, if a customer declared a disaster, the vendor might recover the customer not at the facility being toured, but on another system offering adequate MIPS located somewhere in the vendor's infrastructure.

While there is no obvious reason why the "MIPS, not sites" strategy will not work, there are several key issues that need to be addressed by the vendor to the satisfaction of the DR coordinator. For one, if the MIPS will be taken from system platforms that are used by the vendor for other purposes (time sharing with non-DR customers, for example), how will the user be displaced by the vendor and how soon will the MIPS become available for use?

Another important, though subjective, evaluation the DR coordinator needs to make of a "MIPS, not sites" offering is whether valuable "affinity" is being sacrificed in this strategy. Once a deal is made for a hot site, testing is usually undertaken one or more times per year. Through this process, the vendor's support staff becomes intimately familiar with the recovery requirements of the customer and affinity develops between hot-site staff and corporate recovery team personnel that can be of value in an actual disaster recovery situation. This is lost if different vendor personnel from those who tested with the customer implement an actual recovery at a different facility.

One IBM spokesperson minimizes the importance of such concerns, noting that recovery processes are "carefully documented and ISO 9001 certified" so "all of our 17 sites serving 62 countries throughout the world have the same look and feel." He credits this fact and the IBM BCRS Network, with the "31 simultaneous recoveries" accomplished by IBM BRS for its customers in the wake of Hurricane Georges (1998). "Some customers," he notes, "based on configuration requirements, require recovery at a specific site. But Georges provided evidence that we could do multiple recoveries at different locations."[17]

SunGard's Grogan agrees that "MIPS, not sites" is a technically feasible solution and acknowledges that SunGard's recovery agreement does not specify the site where a customer can expect to be recovered. He notes that regional disasters have often resulted in simultaneous disaster declarations that have required some shuffling by vendors to recover multiple customers.

> But just promising MIPS can be deceptive. There are cases in which a customer would need to engineer a recovery solution very differently based on the limitations of different environments. If this needs to be done during a recovery, it introduces some additional risk and usually lengthens the recovery timeframe. Some of our competitor's customers have come to us because they didn't like this strategy. Others are contracting with more than one hot site vendor at a time.[18]

It is also important for the coordinator to ascertain how many subscribers are assigned to the service. An excessive number of users assigned to a fixed set of processing capabilities can be a warning sign. The coordinator should tread cautiously with a vendor that promises that new capabilities are being added to take the overload within x months.

Regardless of whether the number seems high, the coordinator should follow up by asking how multiple, simultaneous disaster declarations would be accommodated. The coordinator should also ask for a list—or at least a count—of hot-site customers located in the same geographic region as his or her company. This is extremely important if the region is especially vulnerable to regional hurricanes or earthquakes.

Be sure to ask whether and how the vendor discriminates between customer disaster declarations and proactive alerts issued by customers in advance of a disaster event? Are these types of "declarations" treated equally or is preference given to the company that declares, rather than alerts?

For shared facility offerings, be sure also to obtain an explanation of how security will be provided to limit the access of unauthorized personnel (including recovery teams of other customers) to sensitive company materials and processes.

Contract for Service

Based upon information collected from the marketing representative, research, the vendor proposal, and the on-site visit, a final decision must be reached. In the best of circumstances, the ultimate decision will come down to price differences among two or three equally qualified candidates.

Hot-site agreements, like off-site storage agreements, typically contain a number of fees and provisions that the coordinator should understand and examine thoroughly.

- **Subscription fee.** This is the fee (typically expressed as a dollar amount payable to the vendor on a monthly basis) for the base equipment configuration that will be made available to the subscriber. Equipment covered will generally include all CPUs, storage devices, input devices (other than user terminals), output devices, and communications equipment that is held in common with other subscribers. A schedule of the exact equipment covered by the fee should appear in the contract. There is often a discount on the monthly fee for subscribers who contract for service over a period of many years.

- **Extra equipment fee.** This fee (also payable monthly for most facilities) covers special hardware that is not used by a preponderance of subscribers but is made available at the hot site for emergency use by companies that subscribe for it. The fee may also cover additional storage devices, tape drives, and other equipment not part of the base configuration. Extra equipment should be listed on a schedule that appears in the contract.
- **Annual test time allocation and additional test time fee.** The hot-site contract should spell out how many hours per year the subscriber will have to test its plan without charge and indicate the hourly fee for test time over and above this amount.
- **Disaster notification fee.** This fee is assessed by some (but not all) hot site vendors to "discourage frivolous use of hot site facilities." Fees may be nominal or quite expensive, depending on the vendor. In addition to stating the fee, the contract should indicate how the customer declares a disaster and when the fee will be collected.
- **Daily usage fee.** This fee is included in the contract to show daily (or hourly) rates for use of the hot site in a disaster situation. Other associated fees may be assessed for technical support, maintenance services, administrative office space rental, and cold site use. The hot site may also provide facilities for local and off-site storage of data and supplies. These charges should be spelled out in the contract.
- **Network services fee.** Some hot-site vendors will contract separately for the use of their network services, while others will specify the fees on the hot-site services agreement. Fees may be assessed on a monthly basis, or there may be a setup fee and a table for charges on a usage basis. If no fees for network services appear on a proposed agreement, ask for them so they can be added to the bid price. Only in this way can a fair comparison of multiple vendor pricing be accomplished.
- **Plan fees.** The hot site vendor may also contribute to the development of a disaster recovery plan and testing strategies and the documentation of tests. These services may be provided on a fee basis or at no charge to the customer. Be aware that even cost-free planning software tools provided by the hot site vendor may have far-reaching costs in terms of future software maintenance fees, user training, and so on. When in doubt, just say no, thank you.
- **Multiple simultaneous disasters.** The methodology that the hot site will observe in allocating resources among customers that experience concurrent disasters should be spelled out in the contract. In some cases, resources are allocated on a "first come, first served" basis, while vendors with multiple facilities may offer primary and secondary recovery sites. Declaration policy should also be formally stated.
- **Subscriber limitations.** The hot-site contract should also formalize its policy, assuming it has one, on the maximum number of subscriptions that will be taken for any extant facility.

- **Prior notice of price increases.** The contract should stipulate how much notice the subscriber will be given of fee increases. Ninety days' advance notice seems to be standard.
- **Equipment modifications and additions.** The contract should clearly describe how equipment changes and resultant changes in configuration fees will be handled. Contracts typically provide 60-day prior notice of hardware changes that significantly affect the configurations for which the subscriber has contracted. Longer-term (multiyear) contracts expose the customer to contract modification fees that would dramatically outstrip the cost of negotiating contracts on an annual basis.
- **Hot site liability.** The hot-site contract should indicate the extent to which the hot site assumes responsibility for providing services at contracted levels. Typical components include a "reasonable care" clause and a force majeure clause. The former is the vendor's guarantee that it will exercise reasonable care in the handling and processing of subscriber media and data. The vendor should also provide client confidentiality. Force majeure releases the vendor from liability for outages resulting from acts of God, nuclear wars, and so on. These caveats are fairly common to service contracts of any type. They take on particular importance when considering the location of the hot-site facility viz. the normal business IT data center. If a hot site is selected that is subject to the same regional disaster event that impacts its customer, force majeure may release the vendor from supporting the recovery of its customer. This is another reason to select a hot site that is sufficiently distant to prevent it from being included in a regional disaster such as an earthquake or hurricane.

Selecting a hot site vendor is an important step in building a disaster recovery capability for the company. It is a partnership with an outside vendor who is willing to share responsibility for corporate survival in the wake of an unplanned interruption. Some DR coordinators may seek to include intangible, yet important, factors in their selection of a vendor—especially when this will help to identify the best-suited vendor from among a group of more or less equally qualified vendors.

One method is to contact the sales rep for each company and explain that an impasse exists in selecting the winner, that the bids are too close to call, and that the offerings seem about equal to each other. The vendor representatives will probably react in one of three ways:

- **Criticize the competition.** Some sales reps will respond by criticizing their competitors. They may relay "off the record" information about competitor incompetence or competitor failures in supporting customers in actual disaster situations. While this practice is ethically questionable, it may provide a basis for further investigation. It may also say something about the vendor whose representative is doing the criticizing: If criticisms are found to be patently false, how much trust can one vest in the critic?

- **Negotiate the rate.** Like used-car salesmen, some vendor representatives enjoy a certain amount of latitude in pricing their services. If they perceive that they are losing a prospective customer because of price, they may seek to decrease the originally quoted price. Since the proposal solicited at the outset of the selection process was intended to show the vendor's best offer, some valid questions about negotiations and good faith may be raised by this practice of price cutting.

  This issue is also brought to the fore by vendors who will not provide pricing until competitive bids have been disclosed to them. Once the best offers of the competition are known, these vendors will proceed to undercut their price.

  Costs are as important in disaster recovery planning as in any other business activity. However, the coordinator must weigh pricing against the value of good faith negotiations, realizing that the latter, more than the former, may indicate how conscientiously the vendor will execute its responsibilities under the hot site agreement.

- **Offer pre-subscription testing.** Faced with the impasse of several qualified candidates, some vendor representatives will seek to reinforce their bid by inviting the prospective customer to conduct a live test at their facility. This "puppy dog sale" technique is intended both to demonstrate that the vendor can deliver what has been promised and also to ingratiate the customer to the vendor. The coordinator would be well advised to accept the vendor's offer. The test can provide important information not only about vendor capabilities but also about the solvency of the backup strategy itself.

  The willingness of the vendor to provide precontract testing time may demonstrate sincerity and a willingness to go beyond the stipulations of the contract to aid subscribers that are experiencing disasters. The value of this business ethic cannot be understated.

Any of the above factors can provide the intangible, yet compelling, basis for selecting one vendor from a field of several technically qualified candidates. When the selection has been made, the strategy for centralized system recovery needs to be documented and tested, then maintained in a state that reflects ongoing changes and modifications to business processes and their system supports.

THE BOTTOM LINE ON CENTRALIZED SYSTEM RECOVERY

On the preceding pages, some critical assumptions have been made that merit additional discussion. The first assumption is that the disaster recovery coordinator has selected a hot site vendor whose recovery facilities are not located near the company data center.

The rationale for selecting a "distant" hot site is fairly straightforward. Considering the company's exposure to regional disasters (hurricanes, earthquakes, local exchange carrier (LEC) central office (CO) failures, local long-distance carrier point of presence (POP) failures, power company failures, etc.), it makes little sense to select a backup facility that might be affected by the same adverse conditions as the company data center.

This issue is perhaps less critical for large hot-site vendors having multiple facilities and guaranteeing MIPS for recovery to their subscribers. Smaller vendors, on the other hand, generally have only one or two facilities. So, the issue of geographical proximity remains.

With hot sites available in numerous locations throughout North America, the one selected by the DR coordinator will probably be as near the company data center as possible (to save on travel expenses) while being sufficiently distant to insulate it from regional disasters.

This assumption leads to another. Since the hot site is located at a distance, chances are that relocating the entire management and staff of the company to the vicinity of the hot site would be cost-prohibitive for most businesses. Hence, the assumption is made that users will need to be restored independently of systems, then connected to remote systems via data communications networks.

The nature and scope of the disaster confronting the company will ultimately determine the requirements for restoring users. If the disaster affects only the data center, but leaves company offices and work areas intact, then user relocation will be unnecessary. Recovering user functions will consist mainly of reestablishing data communications links with operations at the remote processing site. Of course, if only critical and vital systems are restored, user function recovery may also entail the implementation of manual systems for nonvital applications, as well.

On the other hand, if both user work areas and the data center are rendered unusable by the same disaster, some sort of end-user recovery plan may be required to complement system and network recovery plans. Users will need to be directed to a work site outside the disaster perimeter, in new quarters equipped with all that is necessary to continue work at emergency levels—telephones, office supplies, desktop computers and peripherals, preprinted forms, typewriters, and a myriad of other essentials.

Each of these scenarios presumes planning. Without advanced planning, not only will employees not know where to go, but they will also have no means for performing work when they get there. Thus, planning for centralized system recovery is not a synonym for disaster recovery planning. It is only a component of a larger plan designed to provide a business continuity capability for the company.

It is worth noting that in the aftermath of the September 11, 2001 terrorist attack on the World Trade Center in New York City, roughly 220 of the 470 tenants of the Twin Towers activitated a hot-site contract with their preferred vendor. According to press accounts and statements by hot-site service vendors, the strategies of the companies executed flawlessly. Despite the large number of simultaneous declarations, the hot-site vendor community took the crisis as an opportunity to shine.

ENDNOTES

1. Greg Blatnik, vice president, Zona Research, Redwood City, CA, quoted in Jon William Toigo, "Thin Computing: Bustin' Out All Over," *Solutions Integrator,* 9/1/98.
2. For the purposes of this discussion, the term mainframe refers to IBM and IBM plug-compatible mainframe platforms. For non-IBM mainframes, readers should consult with their vendors for comparable recovery procedures.
3. Interview with Tim Humphreys, chief architect, Trident Services, Sausalito, CA, 8/99.
4. Ibid.
5. Interview with Jim Grogan, vice president of alliances, SunGard Recovery Services, Wayne, PA, 2/02.
6. Interview with Prabakar Sundarrajan, vice president of research and development, Exodus Communications, Inc., Santa Clara, CA, 6/99.
7. Jennifer Mateyaschuk, "App Alternatives," *Information Week,* 6/28/99.
8. Brian Walsh, "RFP: Heading for Disaster," *Network Computing,* 1/11/99.
9. Interview with George Ferguson, marketing manager, Hewlett Packard Business Recovey Service, Wayne, PA, 6/99.
10. Ibid.
11. Grogan interview, op. cit.
12. Interview with Tony Martinez, general manager, IBM Business Continuity and Recovery Service, Sterling Forest, NY, 6/99.
13. Grogan interview, op. cit.
14. Comdisco web site, Business Continuity, "History and Overview," 1999.
15. Interview with Dan Broadway, Director of ClearPath Storage, Unisys Corporation, Mission Viejo, CA, 7/99.
16. Humphreys interview, op. cit.
17. Martinez interview, op. cit.
18. Grogan interview, op. cit.

Perspective on Systems Recovery

By

George Ferguson
Marketing Manager
HP Business Continuity & Recovery Services

Businesses today depend heavily on access to electronic information so when disaster strikes the IT environment, it strikes the heart of the company. A disaster that cracks this foundation can generate huge losses. In some cases, it can compromise the survival of the company. It doesn't matter whether the crisis is a broken pipe or a fire, a computer virus or a power outage, a strike or a disgruntled employee; the impact on the business is the real disaster. Ensuring the continuity or recovery of IT-supported business processes, in the face of disaster, is essential.

The dependence of businesses on information technology continues to spur the need for disaster recovery support. For example, for companies providing mobile phone service to consumers, providing payroll services to other companies, or selling books and electronics on the Internet—IT is no longer a support function; IT is the business. For many other companies, such as manufacturing and financial service firms, the lines between IT and the "core business" continue to melt with the deployment of customer relationship management (CRM), enterprise resource planning (ERP), and supply chain management (SCM).

New Challenges with Distributed Computing

As recently as the late 1970s, companies could survive system interruptions of three to six days without significant revenue loss or disruption to operations. Today, in contrast, a two-day outage would undercut operations so seriously as to threaten the market position of many organizations. This point is supported by the U.S. Bureau of Labor, which reported 93% of companies that suffer a significant data loss are out of business within 5 years.

The concept and practice of business recovery began some 30 years ago, and the evolution of the discipline has paralleled the evolution of business computing generally. Historically, disaster recovery meant restoring mainframe operations after a catastrophe. As businesses have moved to client/server computing in the late 1980s and early 1990s and then to internet-based distributed computing in the late 1990s and the new millennium, the focus and complexity of disaster recovery planning has also evolved.

Traditional mainframe recovery focused on the recovery of the centralized computing environment housed in the mainframe. Even today much recovery of client-server computing environments is treated as recovery of a set of boxes tied together with a network. The real value of business recovery, however, is in the continuity or quick resumption of critical business processes. Even ignoring for the moment end-user recovery, successful recovery of the IT-foundation of business processes requires a new perspective.

- Application Recovery: As CRM, ERP, and SCM environments take the place of old, single-system, stand-alone applications, recovery must be planned for full, interrelated application environments. Recovery of these complex, multi-system environments requires significantly new and different skills from external vendors or internal staff than those skills associated with just assembling and cabling together hardware systems.
- Full Environment Testing: One of the many lessons from the 2001 World Trade Center disaster was that it is not sufficient to just test sub-environments in disaster rehearsals. Rehearsals that will build a foundation for company survival need to test full environments including extended system inter-relationships, alternate backbone network connections, and web connectivity.
- Application Management: Complex, distributed IT environments require first recovery and then operations management. As an example, a Los Angeles-based company approached HP and asked us to manage their SAP environment for up to five days following a disaster. Understandably, the company believes that following a major earthquake, their employees' attention would rightfully be focused on their family's needs—not the needs of the company's customers. Planning for operations management can make a huge difference following a disaster.

As organizations plan for the recovery of distributed IT-environments, they should be careful to remember that disaster recovery is much more than finding a spare box and recovering data. Organizations that want a successful, quick recovery must put a high premium on the expertise to test, deploy, and manage these complex environments.

Gradations of Service

The cost of unplanned downtime varies widely. According to Contingency Planning Research, the average financial impact of just one hour of data center downtime is $6.5 million for retail brokerage firms and $2.6 million for credit card sales authorization. Although these statistics represent the high end of the range, other kinds of operations also suffer financial damage when disasters disrupt normal processes. For example, Contingency Planning Research's figures peg average losses per hour at $90,000 for retail catalog sales centers and $69,900 for a telephone ticket sales operation. Even a $14,000 per hour loss for a small manufacturing system can total $1 million in less than 3 days. Besides the direct costs, of lost sales and opportunities, there can be significant indirect costs, such as negative publicity, loss of customer satisfaction, or loss in stock price.

Given these wide variations, it is to be expected that no one technical solution is right for all environments. Too often vendor sales representatives may implicitly answer the question of how much protection does a company need by determining the company's budget. To address the varying criticality requirements of businesses, HP and some other vendors have started to specify estimated recovery time-frames for the offerings in their disaster recovery service portfolio and assign prices accordingly. A company can thus address the differing recovery requirements of their business processes with a service that corresponds to the value of their business process. By tying the value of the business process to the appropriate recovery service, we can both satisfy the CFO's bottom line and allay the CEO's worst fears.

Assured Recovery

Another key lesson from the 2001 World Trade Center disaster was the importance of assured recovery. In addition to the technical expertise already mentioned as a key component for successful distributed IT recovery, assured recovery refers to mitigating risks resulting from shared recovery infrastructure and geographic proximity. These risks need to be considered regardless of whether disaster recovery is handled internally or sourced from an external continuity services vendor.

Except for very high-end implementations, nearly all disaster recovery environments rely on one or more elements of shared infrastructure. These may include shared servers, storage, networks, power grids, data centers, etc. Sharing may take place with shared cables from a telecommunications provider, shared servers and facilities from a business recovery services vendor, a shared power grid from the electric company, or a shared corporate campus provided by the recovering company itself. For example, a clustered (and, at first glance, redundant) computer environment located at separate ends of a corporate campus may rely on a shared power grid, a shared facility (the campus itself), and shared network connections. Sharing some portion of infrastructure is a reasonable choice that greatly reduces the cost of a recovery solution for all but the highest value business processes.

In spite of its high economic value, sharing does entail risks and conscious efforts should be made to determine which elements to share and how to mitigate the risks of those shared elements. During the World Trade Center disaster, all recovery vendors performed admirably in supporting the large number of IT-disaster declarations with shared servers and facilities. Market consolidation has many companies rightfully concerned, however, about recovery vendors having individual servers with 50 to 100 shared subscriptions. Likewise, the World Trade Center disaster showed the risk entailed by telecommunications networks with single points of failure. These risks may be reasonable depending on the value of the business process being protected. Companies should assuredly ask questions, however, of their continuity and telecommunications vendors regarding numbers of subscriptions and single points of failure, so that they can assess these risks.

Another key element of recovery assurance is geographic proximity (or its converse, separation). Tragically, some companies in the World Trade Center maintained a private recovery center across the street from the building. Of course, this really is not much different from the many companies who believe that they have disaster recovery because their local clusters are separated by only 1 or 2 kilometers. How much geographic separation is necessary depends on the propensity of an area to widespread disasters (particularly earthquakes, hurricanes, and floods—but also possibly including terrorist acts, civil unrest, and strikes). Thus geographic separation in San Francisco should probably be at least 100 miles (because of earthquake risk), while geographic separation in Atlanta could probably be adequate at 15 to 20 miles. When contracting with a business continuity vendor, special attention should be paid to how the vendor geographically separates shared subscribers.

Clearly, the continually increasing criticality of information technology generates new risks for businesses and organizations. At the same time, however, more and better disaster recovery resources are available to reduce the kinds of outages and to contain the damage they cause. By learning about the risks that disasters pose for IT systems and about strategies to avoid or limit interruptions, IT management can assure that one of their company's most valuable assets, its information technology, will survive.

**Disaster Recovery Isn't Enough:
Today's Enterprises Need Information Availability**

By

Jim Simmons
CEO
SunGard Availability Services
An operating group of SunGard
Wayne, PA

Since September 11 of last year, corporate executives, line-of-business managers, and, of course, IT managers have focused more than ever on disaster recovery and business continuity planning. Most of these individuals have long been aware of the importance of having plans in place to protect their information in the event of a systems disruption. But September 11 changed the very nature of the disaster recovery business.

The disaster recovery business is no longer just about protecting information—a data center here or a production facility there—in the wake of hurricanes, earthquakes, and fires. It's about more than anticipating and planning for the inevitable hardware and software failures and the even more inevitable human errors that occur. It's about information availability.

Information Availability: Connecting People and Information

Today, more people need more access to more information more quickly than ever before. As a result, anything that separates people from the information they need to transact business can be considered a disaster. The job at hand, then, is not disaster recovery; it's information availability—connecting people with the information they need. This is critical to the health of a business because information without people isn't very useful, and neither are people without information.

Ensuring information availability across an entire enterprise requires planning with three key components in mind: 1) people, 2) information, and 3) the infrastructure that connects people and information. September 11 provided a tragic and dramatic illustration of the need for this type of planning.

Although relatively little data was lost when the twin towers of the World Trade Center collapsed, that data was essentially useless. Most workers from the towers had nowhere to go to be reconnected with their data. There were a few exceptions, but most were stranded. Nothing in their disaster plans addressed the critical need for alternate work locations and points of access.

The Information Availability Continuum

While it's important to keep people connected to information, it's also important to recognize that all information is not equally critical. Organizations do not need the same level of access to all information. For example, it's more important to have constant access to a web-based ordering system than it is to have constant access to a personnel database. This fact—the difference between levels of importance—is what shapes the information availability continuum.

Envision the information availability continuum as a graph on which the horizontal axis represents the amount of time an organization can be without any given system or application and the vertical axis represents the technology and infrastructure required to meet each time requirement. On this graph, the lower-left side represents traditional disaster recovery: that is, shipping backup tapes to a remote location where they can be loaded onto hot site recovery systems.

The upper-right area of the graph represents those applications and systems that cannot be down more than a few minutes or seconds. The technology and infrastructure required to meet those time objectives includes a combination of managed services, such as data mirroring, automated fail over, and perhaps even complete IT outsourcing.

Along the curve between the two ends of the continuum are systems and applications whose various time requirements may dictate the use of other technologies such as hot storage or high availability solutions.

Although the technology employed to help ensure information availability across the continuum may vary, there is one constant: there must be provisions at all points along the continuum for people to access the information they need from alternate facilities. This "people" requirement cannot be stated strongly enough. And the alternate facilities need to be reasonably close to employees' regular offices and supported by the same robust infrastructure as their regular offices. Simply booking hotel ballrooms with ordinary telephone lines is not a solution that will allow an organization to resume its business with any sense of normalcy.

As you move rightward along the information availability continuum toward higher availability solutions, the cost of those solutions increases. Because resources are finite, companies must balance the need for constant access to information with the need to stay within budgets. Fortunately, as the need for information availability has risen, the cost of infrastructure to help ensure that availability—hardware, storage, and telco—has declined. Almost everything that enables information availability is more budget-friendly than it was just a few years ago. But again, while the cost of technology may be coming down, more applications are becoming mission critical and the cost of high availability solutions is still greater than traditional disaster recovery.

Most organizations already have a solution in place that can be refined or augmented to keep people and information connected. Some organizations will choose to engineer an internal solution. Others, wanting to maintain their focus on core businesses, will choose an external solution, perhaps outsourcing the entire undertaking. Others will choose a combination of the two. No approach is right or wrong. But while there is no single "correct" solution for helping to ensure information availability, there is one imperative: Make sure the solution works.

Information Availability Starts with Planning

Making sure a solution works brings us full circle because information availability starts with planning.

In preparing for the unexpected, organizations must assess the multiple points of failure in their enterprises, assess the impact of interruptions on business units, and develop strategies and detailed plans to help ensure people and information remain connected. In many cases, it makes sense to call in planning professionals. Planning professionals can assess the big picture from an objective perspective; help develop detailed plans that address information, infrastructure, and people requirements; and most important, help test the plans to make sure they work. Planning professionals can also help anticipate future needs and keep plans updated as technology and business requirements change.

Professional planners can also offer new planning products and new planning services. Planning has come a long way since the days when it merely drafted disaster recovery plans.

Today, top vendors in the planning industry can offer superior availability solutions. More than that, they can offer the resources—the people—with the skill sets necessary to help execute those availability solutions. Most businesses simply do not have these resources readily available. Even in those rare cases in which organizations do have the expertise on staff, they must ask themselves whether they want (and can afford) to devote those resources to information availability projects or to day-to-day production issues.

Begin by Answering a Few Questions

Successfully addressing most information availability challenges begins with questions. Addressing information availability needs and current levels of preparedness is no different. Begin by considering these broad questions:

- Do you have an information availability solution in place that addresses information, infrastructure, and people requirements?
- Does your solution meet current needs?
- Will your solution meet future needs?
- Does your solution have a track record of success?

The answers to these questions will establish a starting point and a pathway for developing an information availability plan that will keep people and information connected, and the business running, come what may.

No matter what your resources or your needs may be, the bottom line is this: Make it work. If an internal solution is right for you, make sure it works. If using an outside vendor is right for you, make sure it works. If a blend of the two is right for you, make sure it works. Call on planning professionals to help you make sure it works now and as technology changes our world.

CHAPTER

6

Strategies for Decentralized Systems Recovery

As described in the previous chapter, the centralized systems model identified with traditional mainframe computing lends itself readily to disaster recovery planning. Indeed, strategies for centralized systems recovery have evolved over the past twenty years to nearly the point of routine procedure. In the view of some observers, commercial mainframe recovery centers, or hot sites, have become veritable "commodity offerings" from disaster recovery vendors.

In addition to having a high degree of recoverability, centralized data centers avail themselves readily to the disaster avoidance and facility protection techniques discussed in Chapter 3. Data centers are typically raised-floor, environment-controlled, physically secured facilities operated and/or monitored by disciplined IT staff on a 24/7 basis. While the electrification requirements of such facilities can and do lead to facility fires, detection and suppression technologies work well in the positive pressure atmosphere of the "glass house," often enabling the cataclysmic outcomes from fire-related disaster potentials to be avoided completely.

Jim Grogan, vice president of alliances for SunGard Availability Services, has gone on record with an interesting observation about mainframe recovery:

> In recent years, there have been fewer mainframe disasters. Over the past three years or so, our customers have declared only six mainframe disasters, [considerably] fewer than there used to be.[1]

If SunGard's experience is mirrored by other hot-site vendors, and the frequency of "smoke and rubble" disasters affecting centralized systems has dropped dramatically, then DR coordinators should be able to rest easier each night. Perhaps they can begin concerning themselves less with the "dark side of corporate computing" and more with regrowing some of the hair they have nervously pulled from their scalps over the past two decades.

Or can they? With apologies to the advertising copywriter for the popular motion picture sequel, *Jaws II,* just when you thought it was safe to go back into the water, another shark has discovered the pleasures of dining alfresco at the beach. Like Chief Brody, the DR coordinator must return to work—vigilant bordering on paranoid—to develop new ways to keep corporate business processes from becoming box lunches.

DISTRIBUTED CLIENT/SERVER COMPUTING: THE ACHILLES' HEEL OF DISASTER RECOVERY PLANNING

From the perspective of disaster recovery planning, everything that centralized data centers are, distributed computing environments are not. In the realm of distributed computing, traditional disaster recovery planning methods and techniques confront a range of challenges that are distinctly different from those designed with the mainframe-based computing infrastructure in mind.

Today, most DR planning literature has a tendency to gloss over the special recovery requirements posed by client/server computing. Partly, this is attributable to a lack of understanding of client/server technology itself. However, part of the blame must be assigned to DR methodologists themselves, many of whom "came to maturity" during the bygone days of mainframe-only data processing.

Asked about the apparent oversight in their "core methodologies," they will emphasize that the majority of mission-critical information processing continues to be handled on mainframes in those organizations that have mainframes. This response begs several questions. For one, how is disaster recovery provided in shops that do not have mainframe platforms installed? For another, if it is true in those shops with mainframes that some mission-critical business processes are supported by distributed client/server computing architectures, why doesn't modern disaster recovery planning methodology account for these requirements?

Some who maintain a mainframe-centric view of disaster recovery planning disparage distributed servers and PCs as "children's toys," contrasting them to "Big Iron" mainframe processors. They continue to emphasize mainframe recovery techniques and ignore or oversimplify the requirements for distributed applications. Servers and PCs, they say, are commodity items that could be replaced at the local computer store, or in some cases, at discount retailers like WalMart.

DR coordinators who are dealing with modern corporate IT environments know better: Distributed servers are not "off-the-shelf products that can simply be replaced in the event of a disaster." To operate high-performance, mission-critical applications on a distributed computing platform typically requires considerable customization of that platform, including its server, client, and middleware components. It is foolish to believe that such applications and their system, network, and software infrastructure cannot be replaced "on the fly" or without substantial advanced planning following a disaster.

Moreover, the argument could be made that distributed computing tends to be more vulnerable to disaster than its mainframe counterpart. Some explanations include the following:

- The administrative tools and disciplined management, which are taken almost for granted in the IT data center, frequently do not exist in the realm of distributed computing.
- Operating systems are often heterogeneous, and in the absence of any willingness on the part of operating system vendors to "work and play well together," distributed computing often features a kludge of interfaces, gateways, and bridges to enable cross-platform cooperative computing. In short, there are more parts to break and more complexities involved in fixing or replacing them.
- Distributed computing environments tend to be less physically secure than centralized data centers. Servers may be located in closets, ceilings, or basements, or out on the cubicle farms and shop floors that constitute modern user work areas.
- As suggested in Chapter 4, coordinating data backups for distributed computing environments can be daunting; coordinating data restoration can be nightmarish.
- Disaster prevention systems are certainly more difficult and costly to deploy in a distributed environment.

It is only a small overstatement to compare the world of distributed computing to the Hobbesian "state of nature," where life is nasty, brutish, and short.

For all that is challenging about disaster recovery in distributed computing environments, there is one thing that distributed environments have that centralized computing lacks. In a geographically dispersed distributed computing environment—one designed with a bit of attention to disaster recovery requirements—it is unlikely that all resources will be consumed by the same disaster potential. Case in point is Tokio Marine and Fire Insurance Company, headquartered in Kobe, Japan, and its speedy recovery following the devastating Kobe earthquake in 1995.

Shortly before the earthquake, Tokio Marine had concluded work with Hewlett Packard Company to deploy a Distributed Computing Environment (DCE)-based client/server computing platform. By design, the DCE infrastructure provided for the replication of data and resources at different locations within the insurance company's offices. When disaster struck and demolished part of the company's network, including several key servers, replicated resources were quickly brought on line. Disaster recovery was accomplished in a matter of hours. By comparison, one of Tokio's competitors, a mainframe shop, was down for nearly 4 weeks.[2]

This example and others point to the potential resilience of distributed computing platforms to disaster. Of course, for such availability-enhancing characteristics to be present, companies have to have designed them into their distributed platforms.

Today, few organizations have gone to the extra expense and effort to deploy high availability architectures. Fewer still have any sort of plan for the recovery of distributed computing if and when an outage occurs.[3] This is the Achilles' heel of modern disaster recovery planning.

This chapter explores the requirements for disaster recovery planning in distributed environments. It does not include a separate data flow diagram because the broad tasks involved in developing a strategy to recover distributed environments are quite similar to those for recovering centralized systems.

- First, mission-critical business applications and their dependencies must be understood.
- Next, minimum equipment configurations need to be identified.
- Finally, an appropriate recovery option, from among a range of options, must be chosen and implemented.

The differences in planning for centralized and decentralized systems recovery reveal themselves at a finer level of analysis. This, quite possibly, accounts for the paucity of literature on recovery methods for distributed client/server systems. As stated previously, many DR coordinators do not understand enough about client/server to know what to do about recovering these systems. If it is any consolation, most client/server system developers, integrators, and product vendors know even less about disaster recovery.

To approach this subject intelligently, it is necessary to provide some historical background on the evolution of distributed computing and a brief review of client/server components and architecture before launching into a discussion of recovery options. For readers who are already familiar with these subjects, a bit of review won't hurt.

For DR coordinators who are totally unfamiliar with the rarefied world of client/server, numerous resources exist to facilitate a deeper understanding, including courses at local colleges, trade press publications, and informative web sites. DR coordinators are strongly encouraged to develop a deeper understanding of this technology, especially in light of the near total lack of concern for recoverability evidenced by the architecture of most client/server software products.

A BRIEF OVERVIEW OF DISTRIBUTED COMPUTING

As the name implies, distributed computing environments are defined by their lack of centralization. Processors and data are dispersed across the business enterprise—on end-user desktops and on minicomputer hosts (servers) located in workgroups, in department offices, and elsewhere. These resources are interconnected by physical networks and, at a higher level, by predefined processes or middleware functions that enable input, processing and output operations to occur as though within a single system.

Distributed computing emerged in the late 1970s and early 1980s in part as a redress for mainframe computing costs, delays, and accuracy problems. If the denizens of the glass house (the mainframe data center) could not meet the service levels that business managers required, the business managers were going to deploy local systems that would do the job.

Vendors contributed to the rebellion. They reassured non-technical business managers that inexpensive, easy-to-administer systems and software tools were becoming available that would enable them to do more than they were ever able to do with mainframes. PCs were secreted into offices without the Data Processing department's approval—sometimes recorded on invoices as typewriters or office machines.

Of course, there was more to the case for distributed computing than a simple rejection of mainframes. Advocates touted it as a means for moving information closer to decision makers who needed it to perform work. It was also a mechanism to enable and empower knowledgeable workers to do more productive work than ever before. (Though, in many companies, empowering and enabling knowledgeable workers was actually a code phrase that meant disbanding corporate typing pools and eliminating secretaries.)

The introduction of PCs and minicomputers was a tremendous success, automating departments and end user desktops. However, the phenomenon also introduced a problem of isolated, uncoordinated computing within the organization. In an effort to regain some control over these "islands of automation," networks were implemented to interconnect distributed servers and desktops. Predicated on the assumption that interconnected distributed computers would facilitate cooperative computing between workgroups, as well as improved manageability, local area networks were established and eventually linked to one another via backbone networks.

Thus, within the brief span of less than a decade, distributed computing evolved from a collection of independent processors, to a network with loose interconnections, and finally to a tightly integrated distributed computing platform.

CONTEMPORARY CLIENT/SERVER APPLICATIONS

Quick to capitalize on the increasing integration of networked computers, client/server architecture for distributed computing began to appear in the middle 1980s. Client/server remains a confusing concept for many—in part because of the variety of meanings applied to the term by vendor marketing departments. In essence, it is a software partitioning paradigm in which an application is split between one or more server tasks.

In a client/server application, server tasks accept requests for information or action from distributed client tasks. Client tasks communicate their requests to server tasks according to some predefined protocol. Server task components may be centralized or distributed across several computing platforms, enabling clients and servers to be placed independently on any nodes in a network.

Early client/server implementations featured a two-tier architecture (see Figure 6–1). Typically, client tasks were located on intelligent workstations, or PCs. Server tasks were located on a second tier of processors, called, appropriately, the server tier.

In a simple model, client tasks communicated requests to servers, and servers communicated with each other to process requests. In the end, the requested output (information or action) was returned to the client. This operation was transparent to the end user—that is, the end-user had no idea what was going on "under the covers." With a well-defined client/server application, it appeared to the end-user that all applications were being executed at his or her client workstation. The server components could be anywhere in the network.

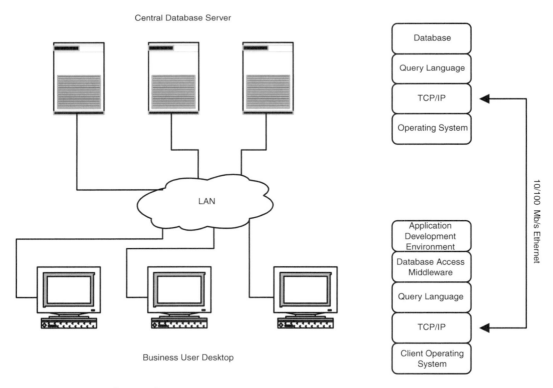

Figure 6–1   Simplified two-tier client/server implementation.

Subsequent implementations of client/server provided for three or more tiers (see Figure 6–2). In effect, client requests were received by a second tier of application server tasks that, in turn, relayed requests to another tier of server tasks (say, database servers), which responded to the request, allowing the second-tier server to complete request processing and to relay the results to the client tier. Specialized message handling software, called middleware, came into use as a mechanism for ensuring that requests and responses were conveyed to their intended destinations.

As the number of server tasks (and tiers) increased, the performance of client/server had a tendency to degrade. Requests would be lost or become corrupted. Server tasks would receive the wrong requests or would simply drop incoming requests when they were already busy processing other requests. Network or server interruptions (resulting from device failures, software failures,

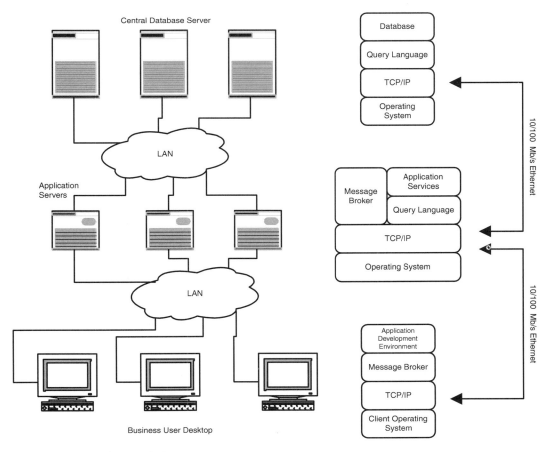

Figure 6–2   Simplified three-tier client/server implementation.

etc.) would cause synchronization problems in request processing. The bottom line was that the performance of client/server computing did not encourage companies to entrust the distributed architecture with mission-critical applications. Thus, disaster recovery planners did not need to concern themselves with these applications.

However, throughout the decade of the 1990s, vendors and integrators expended considerable effort to improve the performance and reliability of distributed, client/server applications. While initiatives to establish a common, vendor-agnostic, "open" framework for message exchange, security, fail-over, and other characteristics common in a single system environment (such as Distributed Computing Environment or DCE), met with limited acceptance, several proprietary middleware products emerged as market leaders.

By the middle of the decade, multi-tier applications were being deployed using a variety of proprietary message-oriented middleware (such as IBM MQSeries, Microsoft MSMQ, BEA Systems MessageQ, and PeerLogic Pipes), transaction-oriented middleware, and object-oriented middleware. The latter capitalized on Common Object Request Broker Architecture (CORBA) services, which were slowly added to popular server operating systems by the mid-1990s.

Regardless of the differences in approaches embodied in these middleware products, the objective was the same. Vendors and their customers were looking for ways to establish a distributed infrastructure that could deliver the levels of dependability and performance to client/server computing environments that were "givens" in centralized mainframe systems.

Middleware selection, however, was a confusing proposition. Somewhere along the way, vendors of mainframe-based enterprise planning applications decided to address the problem (and, in some cases, to prop up their own sagging mainframe product revenues) by porting their applications to the distributed platform in the form of "packaged" solutions. They introduced client/server application suites with integral middleware components or with pretested application programming interfaces (APIs) enabling quick deployment with third-party middleware product offerings.

Perhaps the ultimate expression of client/server computing today is to be found in the client/server application suites from vendors such as SAP, Baan, PeopleSoft, and Oracle. Companies have been deploying these packaged client/server products—known by acronyms such as Manufacturing Resource Planning (MRP), Enterprise Resource Planning (ERP), and Customer Relationship Management (CRM)—in record numbers throughout the 1990s. This trend portends to continue into the next millennium.

According to the 1999 Information Systems and eBusiness Spending Study, conducted by Computer Economics, 18.9% of organizations across all industry sectors had ERP software in place. Another 34.1% were researching, piloting, or implementing ERP software (see Table 6–1).[4]

Both "packaged" and "home-grown" client/server applications are now in evidence in most corporate environments and are depended upon to support a

Table 6–1   ERP Software Implementation Percentiles

Industry Sector	No Activity	Researching, Piloting, or Implementing	Already in Place
Composite for all sectors	47.0	34.1	18.9
Manufacturing	24.3	35.3	40.5
Distribution	50.0	31.7	18.4
Banking and Finance	38.7	48.4	12.9
Insurance	65.4	26.9	7.7
Healthcare	64.5	25.8	9.7
Trade Services	50.7	37.0	12.3
Professional Services	47.8	26.0	26.2
Utilities	50.0	34.6	15.4
Transportation	57.2	33.3	9.5
State and Local Government	62.5	25.0	12.5
Federal Government	76.0	20.0	4.0

Source: Computer Economics, Carlsbad, CA www.computereconomics.com.

broad range of mission-critical business processes. For this reason, DR coordinators must include provisions for their recovery in the corporate disaster recovery plan if the plan is to be comprehensive.

The requirement to consider client/server recovery becomes even more critical within the context of e-businesses—businesses that depend on the Internet and World Wide Web for their sales and marketing, supply chain management, or other mission-critical business processes. With the advent of e-commerce and the Internet, many companies added still more tiers to their client/server applications in order to enable data sharing, or actual application interaction, via the World Wide Web. Figure 6–3 depicts an *n*-tier client/server configuration designed to facilitate web access to internal corporate applications.

What is important to recognize is that most (if not all) of the *n*-tier client/server applications that are in use today within companies have been deployed through a cumulative process over a number of years. This basically means that a certain set of application functions were implemented at one time, then additional application functions (server and client tasks) were added later, and still others later, over the course of several years. (Client/server applications are rarely delivered as a single "turnkey" solution.)

The result of this application delivery process, in many cases, is that mission-critical business processes are supported by client/server application platform that includes a mixture of different technologies. As in most software markets, client/server and middleware software products have a tendency to be changed or upgraded by their manufacturers every few months. Thus,

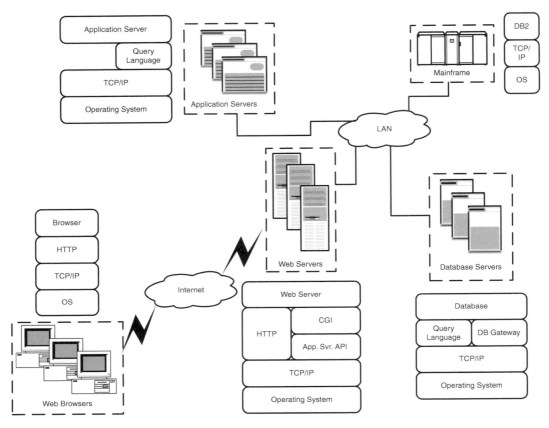

Figure 6–3   Simplified *n*-tier client/server configuration for web-enablement.

client/server applications that have grown their functionality over a period of years are typically a conglomeration of server task components that communicate with each other via a hodgepodge of different, proprietary, middleware products. The resulting application is a kludge of software and middleware that makes mainframe COBOL spaghetti code look like fine dining.

Among the first to identify the difficulties associated with this situation were integrators tasked with "web-enabling" internal business applications. Seeking to capitalize on the growing popularity of the Internet and the growing prevalence of the web browser as a "universal client," companies engaged integrators to add a web interface to their applications.

Delivering a robust solution (beyond that of simple "screen scraping") to the problem proved a significant challenge to integrators. They quickly realized that they were dealing with multiple client/server applications, each with its own mixture of software and middleware technologies. In a white paper from

Bluestone Software (now part of Hewlett Packard Company), the problem was summarized at a fairly high level,

> Information deployment is the most fundamental challenge facing the modern enterprise. To meet this challenge, corporations must overcome the difficulties of information sharing on a large scale. Over the years, various hardware and software technologies have been employed. The result? In most enterprise environments, you'll find a complicated patchwork of domain-specific solutions.[5]

Bluestone's web-enabling solution, Sapphire/Web™, was among the first to approach the problem of client/server Web-enablement by "nesting" the existing client/server environment inside its own "Enterprise Interaction Management" framework (see Figure 6–4). The approach capitalized on existing APIs in server task components and service interfaces offered by some middleware component vendors. To complement these, the vendor added custom-developed interface modules. In short, Bluestone endeavored to deliver a mechanism for adding a

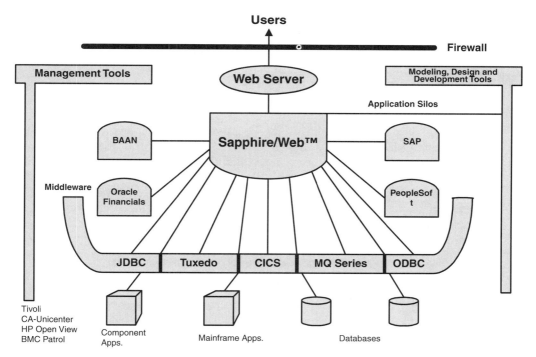

Figure 6–4   Nesting existing client/server applications in an Enterprise Interaction Management Framework. (*Source:* Alternative Technologies, Boulder Creek, CA. Sapphire/Web is a registered trademark of Bluestone Software, Mt. Laurel, NJ.)

web interface "non-obtrusively"—that is, without requiring client/server applications to be rewritten or existing architectures to be reengineered.

Subsequently, the Bluestone offering was followed by a broad range of "application server" software products from a number of vendors. Some, like Citrix Systems and Microsoft, followed the path of application interface extension or emulation, in which a single user application was simply operated in an application server environment with its graphical interface extended to a remote end user across a network. Other vendors, including Oracle Corporation, embedded an application server directly into their client/server software. A third category of application servers, which might be described as framework servers, came from IBM, BEA Web Logic, Allaire, Inprise, and many others. These products took advantage of the component structure of many modern client/server applications (a la Bluestone) and provided the minimum set of services required to deploy interoperable components as coherent applications. They also performed one or more of the functions associated with the "logical middle tier of a distributed multitiered environment": providing support for distributed, component-based solutions, providing security, handling transactions, delivering a single and well-defined developer interface, providing runtime load balancing, and ensuring data persistence.

The quest for the simplest path to application Web enablement persists today. New strategies, providing for application to application messaging via the extensible mark-up language (XML), are under development at Microsoft and elsewhere that seek to reinvent client/server applications as web services accessible via any network by any client anywhere in the world. This dream has both potential benefits and drawbacks from a disaster recovery perspective as discussed later.

For now, this brief discussion is offered as a reference point for thinking about the disaster recovery challenges posed by *n*-tier applications. From a disaster recovery planning perspective, the challenge is to recover the functionality of mission-critical client/server application quickly and cost-effectively—and also unobtrusively. Few companies would be willing, strictly on the basis of disaster recovery requirements, to rewrite their client/server applications or to reengineer them for recoverability. Other advantages that might accrue to Web enablement from a line-of-business perspective, however, may provide opportunities for DR planners to introduce disaster protection as well.

PREVENTIVE MEASURES

Existing client/server applications pose a challenge for disaster recovery planning because of the investment that companies have already made in developing and deploying these applications into production. For existing applications, coordinators may have little option but to plan for a one-for-one replacement of the entire hardware and software infrastructure in order to guarantee the business process continuation in the wake of a disaster. (This is discussed in greater detail below.)

With new or planned client/server applications, however, there may be an opportunity for DR coordinators to take a more proactive posture. If the DR coordinator can influence the design of new client/server applications, there is a chance that less expensive and more efficient strategies for recovery can be found.

To address the Achilles' heel of modern disaster recovery, DR coordinators need to become involved, in a consulting role at least, with the development of new client/server applications. Considerable diplomatic skills and a firm grasp of technical concepts are important prerequisites to earning the respect and attention of client/server application architects. It is critical that a relationship be established, however, since, in the words of Larry Finch, vice president of Prolifics, Inc., "application design elements favoring recovery will not be included in client/server applications unless they are put there deliberately."[6]

According to Finch, there are many design choices that can be made to enhance the recoverability of client/server systems. As evidenced by the experience of Tokio Marine, one strategy is resource replication.

> There are various methods for recovering databases [and other resources] within a client/server application. Providing for the replication of resources in real-time at different locations within the enterprise is one approach. It is expensive to do and you must explicitly plan for it in your design, but it can be done. Among other things, you need to provide the means for clients to know where servers are once a failure has occurred and resources failover to other servers. That will require configuration files in the server or other code-level approaches, but it can be designed to work. The nice thing is that replication can enhance performance in non-disaster operations, so it isn't like "you are just wasting money on disaster recovery."[7]

The selection of middleware components is also an important step to ensuring high availability and recoverability. According to Finch, some messaging middleware products can provide failover capabilities with less design effort than others can.

> Some messaging middleware products don't require addresses or identifiers for server components. If a block of servers fail that are replicated elsewhere in the network, the messaging [broker] broadcasts to all servers in the network and automatically updates itself with the locations of the available [failover] servers. In a disaster recovery situation, you may be able to use this feature to move the client/server configuration to a different platform. Just tell the [middleware broker] the location of a database resource, for example, and it will automatically update application servers and begin processing.[8]

Finch is quick to point out that this capability is only available if the right middleware components are selected and the design of the application facilitates this recovery mechanism. Some middleware, he notes, is highly address-dependent.

> Some of the componentware, the COM middleware, is not designed with recovery in mind at all. The design goal of the product vendor is to replicate an object model in the multitier environment, not to provide support for disaster recovery. In a COM

middleware environment, when a client needs a service, it initiates an object that addresses a server by name. [To recover a client/server application that uses this type of middleware], you would need to update all of the clients with new server addresses. In such a case, failover would not be transparent—mainly because reliability was not a design goal of the middleware or the designer who chose it.[9]

Finch's views are echoed by other client/server application developers and integrators, most of whom confess that they have never given disaster recovery a thought when designing and deploying client/server solutions. One, who works closely with one major ERP package vendor, communicated his concerns about the vulnerability of these applications. Asking not to be identified, he noted that the disaster recovery concerns manifested in custom-developed client/server applications are not mitigated through the use of packaged application suites.

> The fact is that the ERP application suite vendors are in a fiercely competitive business. They are constantly challenged to add features and functions to their integrated suites in order to compete with the functions and features that exist in competitor products. They often do this by acquiring another software house, adding its software components to their package. I know for a fact that, in the case of one major ERP product vendor, many functions in the current release are not fully tested or integrated and that a great number of problems exist that could bring the application down at any time. Disaster recovery isn't just a problem with homegrown client/server software that you can fix by buying a packaged product. The quality of the packaged products falls prey to the requirement to add functions in order to compete.

Beyond application design choices, another concern to some observers are the host platforms that are being used to operate client/server applications. Graham Thompson, Vice President of Marketing for InCert Software, notes that approximately 60% of client/server package products are being deployed on Windows NT platforms "without any benchmarking prior to deployment, or scalability testing."[10]

> The availability specification for the Windows NT server is about 99.5 percent. UNIX has something like 99.7 percent availability and OS/390 has 99.999. When you think about it, that means your unplanned downtime on an NT server will average about 50 hours per year. With UNIX, the number is around 26 hours per year. And, with OS/390, you are looking at 5 minutes of unplanned downtime per year. Considering the cost to companies for an hour of unplanned downtime—$100,000 for a retail operation, $6 million or more for a brokerage—you can see that the drive to client/server is a costly one.[11]

Thompson believes that if a company is committed to deploying mission-critical applications on distributed platforms, both design and deployment methodologies need to have a strong disaster recovery focus. This point of view derives from InCert Software's product focus. InCert is a vendor of mainframe-centered tools used in COBOL code execution tracing and debugging. The tool has proven useful in resolving Y2K code failures expeditiously and offers capabilities for software failure analysis that are now being ported into the client/server world to facilitate NT-based application fault detection and repair.

PROACTIVE MEASURES

What specific steps can disaster recovery coordinators take to ensure the speedy (and cost-effective) recoverability of mission-critical client/server applications following a disaster? These fall into two categories: proactive and reactive measures.

The goal of disaster recovery planning is to deliver capabilities for recovering business processes following unplanned interruptions within an appropriate timeframe and at an acceptable level of business risk. Since disaster recovery planning exists in the real-world environment of a functioning business, it is also important that planning take into account the cost of recovery strategies relative to the business revenue losses accrued to protracted outages.

That is a fancy way of saying that DR planners should never spend more money to recover from an outage than the outage itself would cost. In most companies, budgets for disaster recovery restrict spending to levels far below outage costs. DR coordinators can optimize their scarce resources by planning to avoid preventable disasters, while selecting the best strategy they can for coping with disasters that cannot be predicted or avoided.

Proactive and preventive measures are particularly important in client/server application recovery. While planners may need to "play the hand they are dealt" with regard to existing client/server apps, if they can become involved in new application development, they may be able to influence developers to construct applications in a manner that facilitates disaster recovery.

Emphasize Middleware Standards

Given the opportunity to influence client/server application design, DR coordinators should press for the adoption of middleware standards for present and future development. They should research middleware products to obtain an operational understanding of each product being considered for use by application designers and be prepared to advise designers and architects regarding the limitations of the product from a recoverability standpoint.

A middleware product that uses a "hard" resource naming scheme (specific names must be assigned to server and/or client tasks and each component must be "hard coded" or configured with these names) poses greater difficulties for recovery than does a product using a flexible or adaptive resource naming scheme (e.g., tasks are identified "on the fly" through broker broadcast messages). This is not to say that the DR coordinator can tell the designer which middleware product to use. There may be performance reasons for using a less flexible product. But, it is the DR coordinator's job, at least, to sensitize the designer to the importance of such considerations as recovery.

In addition, the DR coordinator should emphasize the importance of building applications around a single middleware product, rather than introducing new middleware products with each application upgrade. The use of multiple products has a tendency to reduce options for disaster recovery to a one-for-one replacement of client/server platform components.

Encourage Partitioned Design

DR coordinators should know from experience with non–client/server applications that the most expeditious recovery is accomplished when the data used by an application is clearly delineated and defined. In an ideal world, the data for a specific application can be backed up and maintained in a well-defined way and restored readily when needed. With deliberate effort, according to Prolifics' Finch, "the overall [client/server] work can be partitioned into discrete applications and data can be partitioned [to correspond with these applications]."[12] If this is done, it would be possible to enable processes and their related data sets to be restored and restarted individually.

Emphasize Resource Replication

Redundancy is expensive in large systems, but substantially less so in distributed computing environments where processor and storage hardware costs, as well as network bandwidth costs, are constantly dropping. DR coordinators can avoid some disaster potentials, such as hardware failures, by emphasizing redundancy and resource replication as an aspect of client/server application design. Where possible, the case for replication should be based on application performance improvements rather than disaster recovery advantages alone.

Unlike other redundancy strategies, where it is best to maintain redundant components as "hot standbys" that are unused except in the event of an outage, replicated client/server resources can play an active, ongoing role in day-to-day processing. They can be used to eliminate network congestion or to speed throughput or to provide extra capacity when primary resources are being utilized at near maximum capacity levels.

Lobby for High-availability Components

The failure rates of server operating systems are well known in the industry (as discussed above), even if they are debated by operating system vendors. Additional disaster avoidance capability can be obtained by acknowledging the reality that client/server host platforms can and do fail and recommending the acquisition of fault-tolerant hardware configurations.

Fault tolerance can be added at many levels of hardware. Servers can be clustered for failover. Disks can be mirrored through the application of various RAID configurations. Array controllers can be obtained that deliver failover and failback capabilities. Drives can be dual ported to facilitate hot swapping. Redundant power supplies, network interface cards, and even motherboards are available. DR coordinators need to research fault tolerance technologies and be prepared to recommend additional, and often low-cost, enhancements to client/server platforms that will enable them to withstand equipment failures that could become disasters for the company.

Lobby for Application Web-enablement

Many companies have come to the conclusion—without considering its potential disaster recovery benefits—that the web-enablement of legacy and client/server applications has definite business advantages. For the "dot.com" companies (businesses that execute primary business processes via the Internet and World Wide Web), providing a browser-based client interface to applications is a given. Other companies have seen advantages in web-enabling applications for use in internal intranets or in business-to-business extranets established with suppliers, business partners, and other external entities. Web-enablement provides opportunities for enhanced disaster recovery as well.

There are many approaches to web-enabling applications, but the net result is the delivery of secure access to necessary application functions via a browser software client. This capability can be harnessed to facilitate flexible end user application access in a post-disaster situation. From a disaster recovery perspective, flexibility has two meanings: If applications are web-enabled, end-users may be able to access applications via an intranet at a user recovery site using virtually any client device capable of supporting a browser. If web-enabled applications are accessible via the Internet, end users can access applications from virtually any location, including their homes. The bottom line is that, if an organization has web-enabled its applications, the range of user recovery options may be increased dramatically.

Of course, web enabling applications is not without its down side. DR coordinators also need to ensure that proper attention is paid to protecting web-enabled applications from security threats and that the applications themselves are accessible in the face of Internet disruptions and outages (see Chapter 7 on network recovery for more details).

PLANNING FOR RECOVERY

Fault-tolerance capabilities and resource replication designs do not substitute for disaster recovery planning, but they can help avoid some of the most commonly cited disaster potentials associated with client/server computing. According to SunGard's Grogan, while the number of mainframe disaster declarations has decreased substantially, the number of "component failure" disasters supported by his company has increased significantly.[13] He attributes this to the increasing importance of client/server applications and the vulnerabilities of their host platforms.

In addition to component failures, distributed computing platforms are as vulnerable as centralized computing platforms to regional power failures, weather events, seismic disturbances, cataclysmic fires, riots and civil unrest, telecommunications outages, and a number of other disaster potentials that deny access to corporate facilities generally. Unplanned interruptions can and do happen in the client/server environment, regardless of fault-tolerance capabilities. To prevent the interruption event from resulting in a full-blown disaster for the business, decentralized systems recovery strategies must be developed and tested.

Through the late 1990s, there were only two decentralized system recovery strategies available to DR coordinators.

- **Next Box off the Line.**   As in the case of mainframe recovery options, one alternative is to take copious data backups of client/server systems and to make arrangements with equipment vendors or distributors to provide replacement hardware on a priority basis following a disaster. This procedure was actually recommended in the past by some consultants and analysts because of the expense of the alternative: the redundancy option.[14]
- **Redundancy/Hot-Site Option.**   This option involves the establishment of a fully redundant distributed computing platform at an alternate facility, either business-owned or provided as a subscription service from a commercial hot site vendor. According to SunGard's Grogan, this expensive option is sometimes the only way to safeguard mission-critical client/server applications—especially when they have not been designed with disaster recovery in mind.

  > Client/server is a challenge, especially when the pieces of an application have been purchased à la carte. Even packaged applications such as SAP need to be integrated to back-end and front-end processors. It can be very convoluted. You literally have to restore each piece of equipment by itself. There is a high degree of risk involved in getting it correct. The time requirements for these restorals can be much greater than [mainframe application] recovery. SunGard has a new service called Silhouette OS that can assist in these situations. With Silhouette a system profile is periodically transmitted to a server at SunGard so that in the event of a disaster customers' servers can be rebuilt in a reliable, repeatable manner at any time.[15]

Spokespersons for other leading disaster recovery service providers agree with SunGard that the increasing mission-criticality of client/server applications is raising the bar for recovery timeframes and practically mandating that recoveries be performed on redundant hardware configurations. Hewlett Packard BRS marketing manager George Ferguson notes,

> As ERP applications move to full supply chain management, companies are dependent upon those applications as well. About 35% of the customer base is recovering [their client/server] applications with our service. We can bring their recovery times down to a modest 8 to 24 hours depending on the last backup. We also offer full replication via our network. Rather than copying database changes, the customer can just transmit Special Query Language (SQL) updates and the replicated server performs an identical change on a replicated database. That avoids the difficulties [associated with] pushing physical data across the wide area network. The trend is that higher-end services such as these require us to take on more responsibility for the recovery.[16]

More responsibility translates to increased expense, which vendors nearly universally agree is the price paid for fielding mission-critical applications on distributed platforms. However, two additional strategies for client/server recovery are becoming available that promise to deliver expeditious recovery at a lower cost.

- **ASP Service Bureau.**   In 1998, application service providers (ASPs) began to appear on the corporate computing scene. These modern Internet-based service bureaus provide remote hosting of applications, including client/server applications, on behalf of corporate customers. Some feature extensive Internet expertise and multiple data centers interconnected by high-speed OC3/OC12 networks, while others combine telecommunications network services with business automation management expertise. Even database giant, Oracle, has an ASP service that offers remote implementation and hosting of Oracle enterprise client/server applications. The value proposition of the ASP is cost-of-ownership reduction and many smaller and medium-sized companies are already leveraging these web-based outsourcing companies to obtain the benefits of client/server packages without the hassle. A growing number of ASPs, spearheaded originally by Exodus Communications, are placing disaster recovery capabilities high on their list of service benefits.

  Service bureau-based disaster recovery has been an alternative strategy for centralized systems recovery for some time. However, the diversity of applications in the typical corporate data center and the limitations of service bureaus to supporting only a set number of hosted software applications, has limited the strategy to a niche market.

  The current generation of ASPs presents similar limitations. Most ASPs offer support for only a short list of packaged client/server application suites. For some companies, this is sufficient. For others, especially those with "home-grown" client/server apps that support mission-critical business processes, ASPs, like their service bureau predecessors do not provide a complete solution.

  However, the ASP industry is growing. On the horizon, analysts expect a more diverse set of "infrastructure outsourcing" services to be provided. Of particular interest is the expressed intention of telecommunications giants, such as AT&T, SBC Communications, and others, to enter this market. Given their multiple data centers and core, inter-exchange carrier (IXC) network access capabilities, application outsourcing with disaster recovery provisions is a very real prospect early in the first decade of 2000.

- **Application Consolidation.** Another strategy for client/server application recovery will be possible only when applications themselves incorporate the design characteristics addressed above. If the middleware interconnecting application components is standardized, applications and their data are properly partitioned, and attention is paid to the selection of message brokers based on their adaptability to platform changes, it is possible to recover even the most distributed client/server application on a more centralized hardware platform. That is a much less expensive and configuration-intensive proposition to recovering platforms on a one-for-one basis.

It should be kept in mind that the rationale for distributing client/server application components in a production environment does not necessarily apply in a recovery environment where fewer end users and "emergency" (reduced) levels of performance are expected. If such a strategy is selected, the DR coordinator should work out the details of the alternative application configuration in advance and test the configuration on target hardware platforms and under actual conditions of load.

Server Recentralization versus Consolidation

Some observers point to the current trend toward server recentralization as a boon for client/server recoverability. Recentralization refers to the physical relocation of server hosts, once deployed throughout the work environment of the business organization, back into the data center environment. Enabling server recentralization are concurrent trends in local area networks toward increased bandwidth and decreased network equipment prices.

A snapshot of a business network in the late 1990s would likely find a high-speed network interconnect, such as switched Gigabit Ethernet (1 Gb/s), deployed as the "corporate backbone network"; medium speed networks, such as Fast Ethernet (100 Mb/s), deployed to connect departmental LANs and "power" workgroups to the backbone; and slower speed networks, such as 10 BaseT Ethernet (10 Mb/s), used as a general-purpose LAN interconnect for desktops (see Figure 6–5).

While the recentralization of servers in the controlled environment of the corporate data center may reduce certain disaster exposures and provide for better monitoring and management of equipment by trained IT personnel, the physical location of servers does nothing to enhance the recoverability of client/server applications themselves.

Server consolidation, too, does nothing to enhance the survivability of client/server applications, though the process of consolidating the applications re-

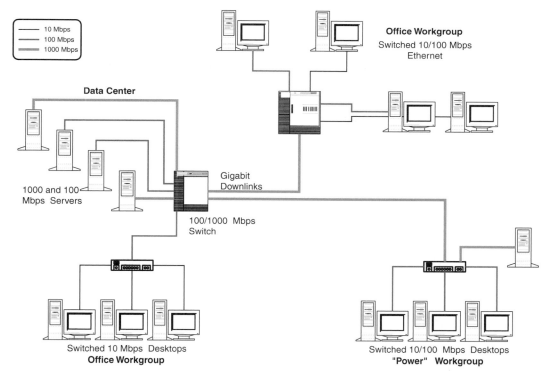

Figure 6–5   Typical Ethernet network, circa 2002.

siding on many smaller servers onto a fewer number of larger platforms can provide a fertile testing ground for client/server application consolidation strategies.

Of course, there are other types of applications in the decentralized computing environment besides client/server applications. The consolidation of these onto fewer platforms can benefit the organization directly from a disaster recovery standpoint, in part by providing a centralized location for backup and improved restoral speed.

One consolidation trend that received considerable press as the 1990s drew to a close was "thin client computing." Essentially, this is a desktop computing architecture aimed at the replacement of "fat client" personal computers (e.g., those running Microsoft's Windows operating system) with terminal-like devices running "thin" operating systems. One approach to server-centric architecture, promulgated by Citrix Systems, provides for client desktops to be connected to "application servers," which serve as central repositories for the software and data that previously resided on PCs. In operation, the client desktop receives only interface information from the application, which executes on the applications server (see Figure 6–6).

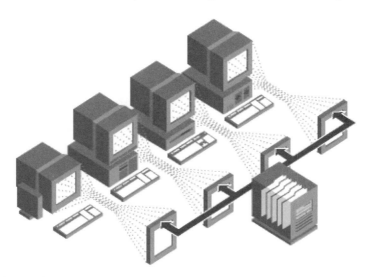

Figure 6–6   Server-centric computing. (*Source:* Citrix Systems, Inc., Ft. Lauderdale, FL.)

After an initial false start, the "fat server/thin client" architecture (not to be confused with client/server application architecture) shows signs of becoming an increasingly prevalent architecture for desktop computing in the new millennium.[17] From a disaster recovery perspective, consolidating desktop applications on fewer application servers provides numerous advantages. Such an architecture enables the umbrella of data protection and physical security that is closely associated with centralized data center operations to be extended around the most decentralized of corporate information assets: the hard disks of PCs.

Also, as shown in Figure 6–7, if the server-centric desktop computing architecture is deployed in a corporate environment, it can be used to restore desktop device configurations rapidly, regardless of the type of desktop device being used.

This server-centric desktop computing strategy, and others, will be discussed in greater detail in the following chapter on end user recovery. For now, it may be useful to close on a positive note.

Decentralized computing has multiplied the targets for consideration by modern disaster recovery planning and made the job of the disaster recovery coordinator more complex than ever before. However, it has also provided an opportunity for the disaster recovery coordinator to play a more active role in shaping the enterprise that he or she is assigned to protect.

Client/server applications, because of their underlying distributed paradigm, represent an unprecedented challenge to traditional disaster recovery methodology. However, by acquiring the necessary background knowledge, and

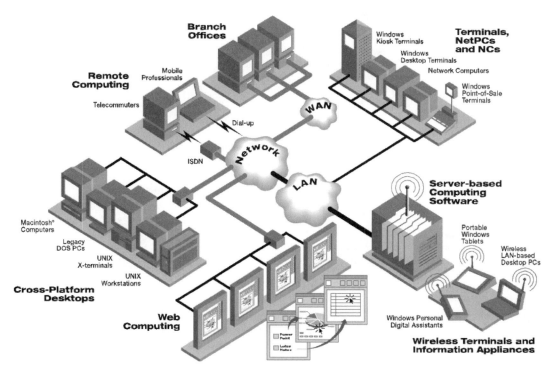

Figure 6–7   Delivering application interfaces to diverse client computing devices. (*Source:* Citrix Systems, Inc., Ft. Lauderdale, FL.)

by cultivating good working relations with application designers, developing frugal and effective recovery strategies for these mission critical applications is not beyond the capability of the DR coordinator.

For other decentralized applications, the disaster recovery coordinator needs to champion the implementation of consolidation strategies where they make business sense. Each success will simplify the requirements for putting the business back in business quickly following an unplanned interruption.

ENDNOTES

1. Interview with Jim Grogan, vice president of alliances, SunGard Availability Services, Wayne, PA, 2/02.
2. Jon William Toigo, "Mission: Impossible? Disaster Recovery and Distributed Environments," *HP Professional*, 6/98.

3. Thomas Hoffman, "Risk Mounts for Mission-Critical Data," *Computerworld*, 3/27/95, quotes Tari Schreider of Contingency Planning Research, who observes that fewer than 3% of the consultancy's 400 Fortune 1000 clients have contingency plans that incorporate client/server networks.
4. "Nearly 20 Percent of Businesses Have Implemented ERP," *Business Wire*, 6/11/99.
5. "The Heart of Sapphire/Web™: The Sapphire/Universal Business Server," white paper, Bluestone Software, Mount Laurel, NJ, 1999.
6. Interview with Larry Finch, vice president, Technology Division, Prolifics, Inc., New York, NY, 6/99.
7. Ibid.
8. Ibid.
9. Ibid.
10. Interview with Graham Thompson, vice president of marketing, InCert Software Corporation, Cambridge, MA, 6/99.
11. Ibid.
12. Interview with Larry Finch, op. cit.
13. Interview with Jim Grogan, op. cit.
14. Jaikumar Vijayan, "Client/Server Disaster Plans Fall Short," *Computerworld*, 11/3/97.
15. Grogan interview, op. cit.
16. Interview with George Ferguson, Hewlett Packard Business Recovery Service, Wayne, PA, 6/99.
17. International Data Corporation (Framingham, MA) is projecting a dramatic increase in the deployment of thin-client technology as the millennium begins, according to a press release dated 4/29/99, "Worldwide shipments of enterprise thin clients will jump 87% from 369,000 in 1998 to 1.2 million in 1999. By 2003, they will top 6 million." This projection is also supported by Zona Research, an IntelliQuest Company (Redwood City, CA), which issued its findings on 4/27/99 that predited the "growth of the worldwide commercial market to over 2,250,000 thin-client units by 2001, with factory revenues exceeding $1 billion."

CHAPTER

7

Strategies for End-User Recovery

Of all the outcomes of the September 11, 2001, attacks on the Pentagon and World Trade Centers, perhaps the most significant was an increased perception they helped create of the value of human life. In just a few minutes, the tragedy took away a parent, spouse, son or daughter from more than 3,000 families. For countless others, the attacks cost a friend, business associate, or co-worker.

From the standpoint of disaster recovery, the events brought into sharp focus to private companies and government organizations alike what happens when key personnel, both management and staff, and the years of knowledge and experience that they embody, are suddenly gone. In a few cases, the human resources that supported entire lines-of-business simply disappeared. As noted in the foreword to this book by Mike Shannon, at least one organization, the Port Authority of New York and New Jersey, lost much of its emergency management team at WTC, hamstringing the organization as it sought to execute its disaster recovery plan.

The events also reduced significantly the capabilities of organizations to continue productive work in the days and weeks following 9/11 as the psychological toll weighed in on those who survived their comrades in the workplace. Indeed, while we lack practical techniques by which to analyze and quantify it, the events had an impact on all American workers everywhere in the country: anger, shock, and depression resulted in significant degradation in work performance.

Surviving even the unthinkable means thinking about the unthinkable—to its fullest conclusion. It means confronting the possibility that a disaster will claim human assets and preparing for this contingency. And, above all, effective DR means doing anything and everything that can be done to protect personnel and prevent the loss of human life.

In the past, disaster recovery plans focused rather narrowly on the recovery of technology platforms: mission-critical applications, their data, and their server and network infrastructure components. The advent of "business continuity planning" in the mid-1990s refocused traditional disaster recovery planning on business processes rather than solely on IT platforms.

From the perspective of business continuity planning, company personnel (sometimes referred to as "end users" of information systems) and their work processes were elevated onto an equal plane with IT infrastructure as targets for recovery planning. Business continuity planners perceived that it was only the end user's interaction with systems and networks to provide critical business functions that made the recovery of IT infrastructure worthwhile. Without end user recovery in the wake of a disaster event, all other recovery strategies were rather pointless.

Why had traditional DR missed so obvious a point as the need for end user recovery planning? One explanation might be that the focus of early DR planning mirrored the interests of most corporations and the predominant information systems architecture of the day. Companies that undertook disaster recovery planning tended to focus their efforts on the mainframe data center, the primary source of processed information for roughly three decades. Since end users were typically restricted from entering mainframe data centers, and since end user access to mainframe applications was a fairly straightforward proposition (typically accomplished via a "dumb terminal" and communications controller), end-user recovery requirements were often taken for granted in the data processing recovery plan.

A frequent, though unstated, planning assumption held that end users would continue to work in their business offices even if the systems and networks they were using needed to be relocated to an alternate facility. Indeed, a goal of DR planning was to make the transition between primary and backup computer centers transparent to the user—an admirable objective, though not always practical.

Recent history (even before 9/11) is replete with examples of disasters that compromised entire corporate facilities—data centers and business offices. Regional disasters—whether the result of hurricanes or fires within telecommunication company central offices, tornadoes or terrorist bombings—can take out sprawling corporate campuses and high-rise headquarter buildings in a single blow. These disasters demonstrated the inadequacy of plans that focused on data center recovery while ignoring end-user recovery.

Moreover, unplanned business process interruptions can and do result from events that do not affect corporate computing infrastructures at all. The break of a sewer pipe in a ceiling or wall may require the evacuation of end-users from their offices, as may the overturning of a tanker truck transporting a noxious gas on a highway some miles away from the company site. While health hazards may require the evacuation of end users, systems and networks may continue operating undisturbed by such events.

Additionally, user work areas are often not as effectively protected as data centers and communications equipment rooms against fires and other avoidable disaster potentials. Lacking these prevention capabilities, which have contributed greatly to risk reduction in data centers, the statistical likelihood is actually greater that certain types of disasters will originate in user work areas, rather than corporate data centers.

With everything that we have learned about disasters over the past three decades, the failure to include a user recovery strategy in a modern-day disaster recovery plan must be regarded as a violation of one of the basic tenets of modern DR: Plan for the worst-case scenario. To be comprehensive, disaster recovery plans need to include documented and tested procedures that may include:

- The location and provisioning of backup end user work facilities
- The notification of employees who will staff the recovery site
- The transportation of employees to the recovery site
- The redirection of ground mails, telecommunications, and data networks to the recovery site
- The acquisition of supplies at the recovery site
- The application of remote access technologies for operating mission-critical applications from the user recovery site

In addition to the above, and as a matter of the highest priority, all disaster recovery plans should provide for emergency evacuation of personnel from the corporate premises in the event of a hazardous or life-threatening disaster event.

DEVELOPING AN END USER RECOVERY STRATEGY

Figure 7–1 provides an overview of the activities involved in end-user recovery planning. As depicted in the data-flow diagram, the definition of end-user recovery requirements draws upon the analysis and objectives-setting processes that were undertaken at the outset of the project and also the details of centralized and decentralized systems recovery strategies discussed in Chapters 5 and 6. Case studies providing the practical experience of other companies in the area of end user recovery can also provide valuable insights.

Based on this analysis, facility requirements, supply and logistics requirements, and application, system, and network requirements will emerge. These become inputs for activities aimed at delivering properly equipped facilities for use by end-users when and if they are required.

The term "user recovery facility" can be interpreted in a variety of ways. In many disaster recovery plans, the user recovery facility consists of a temporary working location, such as conference facilities rented from a local hotel in the hours following a disaster event. In other cases, end-user recovery may be accomplished using a permanent, company-owned facility put to a secondary use. In

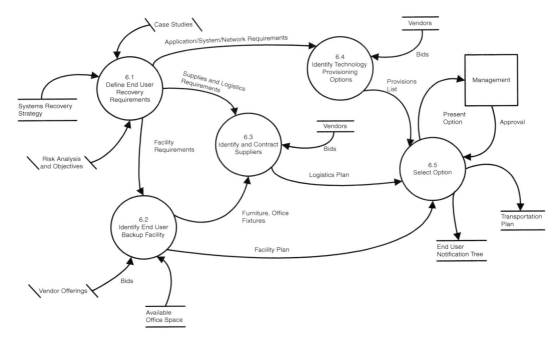

Figure 7–1   End-user recovery plan development.

still other cases, mobile shell facilities from commercial vendors may be deployed as temporary work areas, or employees may be able to work from home using dial-up connections to private networks or the Internet. These options are discussed in greater detail below.

The end-user recovery option that is selected by the DR coordinator needs to address all of the requirements users have for performing purposeful work. In addition to providing access to mission-critical applications, the fully developed option will consider everything from workspace ergonomics to preprinted forms; from telephones, fax machines, workstations, and email access to the personal hygiene, lodging, and transportation requirements of the users themselves.

Information security and disaster prevention provisions in the alternate worksite setting are also extremely important considerations in any user recovery plan. Among other things, planners need to become familiar with the ramifications of emergency work arrangements on corporate liability and insurance.

As with every other disaster recovery strategy, the time-frame for end-user recovery is an important consideration. Options must be evaluated in part on the basis of the amount of time they would take to implement. Evaluating the "time to implement" criteria presumes the ability to test the strategy in advance of its actual use. Thus, it follows that the best strategy will be one that avails itself of testing and validation.

OPTIONS FOR END-USER RECOVERY

With the recovery requirements defined by earlier processes in the planning project, and with the criteria cited above clearly in mind, options for end user recovery may be evaluated. The DR coordinator should note that the strengths and weaknesses of the fairly typical options discussed in the following pages are relative. Companies differ greatly in terms of their assessment of outage costs and their recovery priorities, as well as their existing infrastructure and technology preferences. Thus, the assessment of advantages and disadvantages of any given strategy will be a matter of perspective, which differs from one company to the next.

End-User Recovery "On the Fly"

This approach involves locating a user recovery facility only after a disaster oc-curs. Advocates argue that this approach is valid because of the large amount of unoccupied office space in most metropolitan areas that is generally available for lease on short notice. Even a conference facility at a hotel, advocates argue, could be turned into a temporary operations center within a short time. The option has the additional advantage of presenting little or no cost to the company until (and unless) a disaster actually occurs.

The potential drawbacks of this laissez-faire strategy are numerous however. Although it may be possible to locate a warehouse, hotel conference center, or office space within a short time following a localized disaster—such as a building fire, this approach offers little confidence in the case of a regional dis-aster. If a recovery team must look for new user quarters in "unfamiliar territory" (that is, areas outlying the disaster region), a significant amount of recovery time could be lost.

Time would also be lost while preparing the recovery facility for telephones and network interconnections and provisioning the facility with the necessary workstations, communications devices, disaster prevention systems, security sys-tems, and power distribution and protection capabilities once it has been located.

Considerable coordination would be required with vendors of technology products and services, with off-site storage vendors, and with others who need to direct products to the temporary facility. Additionally, because advanced arrangements could not be made for redirecting long distance and local telecom-munications traffic, data networks, and ground mails to the new facility, these ac-tivities would need to be accomplished at the time of recovery. So, too, would the notification of employees regarding where and when to report for work.

With so much planning left up to the post-disaster timeframe, a laissez-faire strategy introduces substantial risk and numerous opportunities for delay into the recovery process. However, its suitability to the requirements of a particular company is entirely contingent upon the sensitivity of the company to longer duration outages.

The Either/Or Approach

A second approach to user recovery planning—one that imparts only a slightly higher confidence level than the laissez-faire approach—is to implement a dual or "either/or" strategy. With such a strategy, if the disaster is localized, user recovery facilities are located "on the fly." If the disaster is regional in scope, employees are relocated to a predefined company-built user recovery facility at a remote location.

Advocates of this type of strategy observe that a "localized" disaster scenario does not manifest the same obstacles to a laissez-faire strategy that may be present in a regional disaster. For example, with a local disaster, such as a fire at a company's office building, company facilities may be lost, but local utilities and telecommunications infrastructure will probably be intact. Given the limited geographical scope of the disaster, finding and equipping replacement facilities on the fly might be accomplished more readily. Telecommunications providers may be able to respond to requests to reroute networks more promptly. Sources of supply for necessary provisions may be quite accessible. Notifications of employees regarding new work schedules and office locations could be made in an efficient manner.

By contrast, in a regional disaster, the expeditious completion of all of the activities outlined above may be compromised by the scope of the disaster itself. Following an earthquake, hurricane, or other disaster with geographically widespread impact, the integrity of the public infrastructure cannot be assumed. Vendors and providers may be fielding large numbers of emergency requests for services and products in the wake of such a disaster. Thus, to safeguard against the difficulties inherent in a regional disaster, a "hard" site is designated for user recovery.

This either/or approach has the merit of building flexible response into a disaster recovery plan. It embraces the worst-case scenario of a regional outage, but acknowledges that different circumstances might obtain that enable a scaled response.

Unfortunately, the laissez-faire strategy that is to be used in the event of a local disaster is still very amorphous. Any disaster recovery element must avail itself to testing and validation. Laissez-faire strategies do not.

Another potential problem with the either/or strategy is its designation of a company-owned "hard site" at a remote location that is to be used in the event of a regional disaster. Many companies would be hard pressed to cost-justify the construction and maintenance of duplicate user work areas at an alternate remote location to be used only in the event of a regional disaster.

An alternative to constructing a stand-by operations center may be to use a large remote branch office or other company-owned facility, such as a remote training or customer education center, as a backup site. The benefits of dual use of an existing facility are both compelling and deceptive. Dual-use facility strategies can present other problems that require close attention by the DR coordinator, including the following:

- Equipment and furnishings that will be used in a user recovery situation must be securely stored and routinely inventoried at or near the recovery site. If the designated recovery site is publicly accessible (for example, a customer education facility), providing the security of recovery supplies storage can be a difficult and costly proposition.
- Secondary network interconnects, WAN and telecommunications services, power and water utilities, and other infrastructure components, must be preinstalled. Whatever the primary purpose of the designated facility, its use as a user recovery center will likely place an enormous strain on available power, telecommunications, network infrastructure, and even plumbing. Secondary capabilities may need to be added, often at substantial expense, to augment those resources used during normal operations of the facility.
- Other logistical requirements such as proximity to highways, airports, lodging, and restaurants, must be considered to ensure that users who will be working from the remote site will be able to access the site and obtain suitable living quarters during the recovery period.
- Tests of the user recovery strategy must be conducted periodically and this may interfere with the primary operations of the dual-use facility. The requirements for testing the recovery option and for actually activating the strategy must not constrain, impair, or inhibit the normal operations of the dual-use facility. For example, DR coordinators should consider how testing will be coordinated with the scheduling of the training facility for normal use, or how normal branch operations will be impacted by the sudden influx of unfamiliar recovery personnel into the branch facility if a disaster occurs.

As the above suggests, while this either/or approach goes part of the way toward preplanning facilities for user recovery, it still leaves room for delays and problems. Other potential problems with the strategy may include the reluctance of employees, given a regionalized disaster scenario, to leave friends and families behind while they travel to a remote location for work.

Moreover, the costs of maintaining such a facility in a ready state may be high, including costs of leased communications facilities that terminate in the backup operations center, storage space rental, wiring and cabling, and so on. These factors, plus the costs for transporting a cadre of personnel to a remote site and sustaining them while there, must be carefully evaluated to determine the solvency of such a strategy for expeditious end-user recovery.

The benefits of having a "hard" relocation site are several. Such a strategy facilitates testing and logistical planning. Knowing a site location and capabilities in advance can ease the transition of critical and vital operations in an emergency as well as provide a location for storing emergency supplies of preprinted forms, office supplies, hardware, and others. An alternative to developing a company-owned facility is to contract for the services of a user recovery vendor.

The Commercial Work Area Recovery Center Option

A number of vendors, both of off-site storage and of hot-site facilities, are now providing a "user work area" recovery offering. For a monthly fee, companies can subscribe to the facility, much in the way they do for a systems recovery hot site, that will be used for end-user recovery. Presumably, this fee would be substantially lower than the cost to the company of renting, preparing, and maintaining a private user relocation site.

As a variation on this theme, some hot-site service vendors offer mobile shell facilities (see Figure 7–2) specially configured for rapid deployment as user work facilities at or near normal operating facilities. Assuming that public infrastructure (power and water) is available, the end user recovery facility can be positioned within 48 hours in the parking lot of the disaster-stricken facility. Some localities also require building permits and other formalities before a shell facility can be positioned on a site. Coordinators will need to check the requirements of local government when considering this option.

Subscription service-based user recovery plans, while expensive, can be tested and validated—increasing the DR coordinator's confidence in their success. Moreover, mobile end user recovery facilities provide tremendous flexibility in deployment in response to a wide range of disaster scenarios.

In addition to these benefits, coordinators also need to consider the potential drawbacks of mobile shells. In the event of a regional disruption, travel to a mobile facility site may be disrupted. Moreover, such sites may fall prey to post-disaster cataclysms such as aftershocks following earthquakes, post-hurricane floods or mudslides, or looting following building fires. One vendor reports that mobile sites enjoy a singular characteristic that may mitigate some of these drawbacks. Says Jim Grogan, vice president of alliances for SunGard Availability Services, his company's mobile offering was used frequently during regional

Figure 7–2   Mobile user facility (*Source:* Hewlett Packard Company
Business Recovery Services, Palo Alto, CA.)

disasters in the late 1990s. In one case, a Grand Forks, South Dakota–based bank set up operations in a SunGard mobile site, then moved the site a few miles from its original location in response to rising flood waters, then moved it once more when Red River flooding exceeded all anticipated levels.[1]

EMERGING TECHNOLOGY: HARNESSING REMOTE ACCESS CAPABILITIES

In a growing number of cases, end-user recovery may be possible without relocating users at all. In 1999, according to International Data Corporation, 35.7 million workers in the United States routinely worked from home—"telecommuted" to their company offices using direct dial-up or Internet-based remote access methods. The analysts expected this number to increase to 47.1 million by 2003,[2] however current trends seem to show a slowdown in growth. The reasons are several.

Despite the successful use of telecommuting by many companies following the 9/11-related telecommunications failures and building evacuations in several U.S. cities, economic reality, rather than DR value, seems to be squelching interest in the approach. As this book goes to press, the down economy appears to have shifted employer interests away from employee recruitment and retention measures (telecommuting is considered a perk by many companies), and also heightened employee concerns that telecommuting might reduce their visibility at the office and cost them their jobs in the next round of staff reductions. Moreover, attention and budget has shifted in many companies toward improving the security of existing networks, rather than fielding new telecommuting networks. The end result of these factors is a slowdown in the deployment of new telecommuting programs and, in some cases, elimination of funding for previously existing programs.

Still, many organizations have telecommuting programs today and continue to use them to provide employees with flexible work schedules for knowledge workers or to meet the needs of "road warriors"—staff that routinely travel and need to remain connected to corporate networks and applications. Within certain metropolitan areas, telecommuting programs have been developed as a means to offset long employee commute times or as an automobile pollution reduction measure encouraged by federal, state, and local government. Regardless of the company motives for enabling telecommuting, where remote access capabilities have already been deployed, these may be leveraged for the purposes of end user recovery planning.

TYPES OF REMOTE ACCESS

Numerous variations of remote access computing are available. Some companies utilize client-side remote access methods such as remote node or remote control.

Remote control typically utilizes a software package running on an office desktop and a remote desktop. The end-user working from home or some other remote

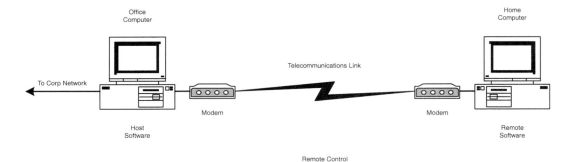

Figure 7–3   Remote control of a corporate desktop from a remote location.

site, uses a dial-up modem connection or other communications method to access and take control of a desktop system that is already attached to corporate networks. In effect, the end user operates the office desktop remotely, running applications on the remote desktop as though sitting in his or her office chair. Products in this category feature such capabilities as encryption and password protection to safeguard links from being misused or tapped. Figure 7–3 depicts a remote control scenario.

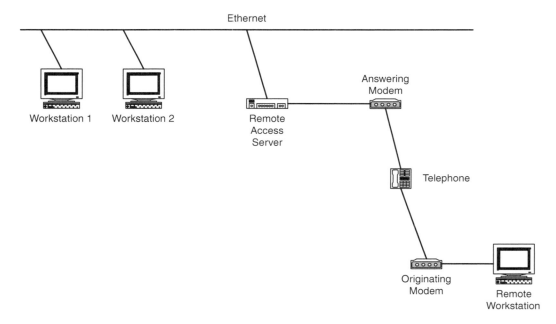

Figure 7–4   A simple remote node configuration.

With remote node methods, the end user dials into the company network and identifies itself as another member of the LAN. There are numerous techniques for accomplishing this feat, including direct dial-up to a remote access server (RAS), as depicted in Figure 7–4. Dial-up connections may utilize slower-speed 56K analog modems, integrated switched digital network (ISDN) services, cable modem services, or digital subscriber line (xDSL) technologies increasingly available from public telecommunications carriers.

As the number of external nodes increases, substantial investments in remote access configurations are made by companies in order to enhance performance and security. Remote access servers (RAS) are available in a wider range of configurations to meet varying connectivity requirements. At the high end, RAS devices enable the consolidation of hundreds of dial-up ports, handle communications from a mixture of link services (analog, ISDN, Frame Relay, etc.),

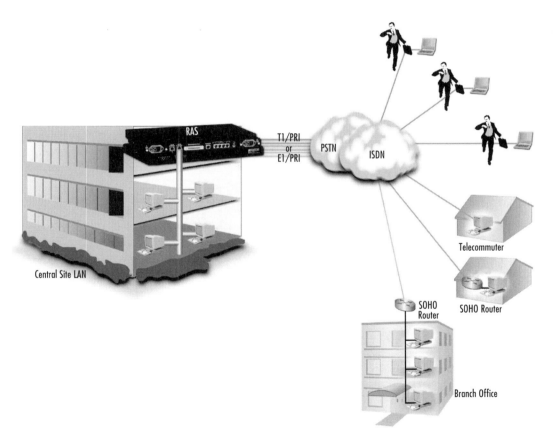

Figure 7–5   A consolidated remote access configuration (Patton Electronics Corporation, Gaithersburg, MD, www.patton.com).

and provide high-speed switching and routing functions to facilitate the smoothest possible operation and highest possible performance of applications. Figure 7–5 is an example of one vendor's product offering in this space.

Another method for achieving remote node access is via the Internet and virtual private networking (VPN). With a VPN, the end-user uses a desktop system and browser software, usually augmented with VPN client software, and connects to a corporate web address or Universal Resource Locator (URL). A secure session, or tunnel, is established between the VPN server and the end-user workstation, and the end-user gains access to internal corporate networks and systems (see Figure 7–6).

Establishing a VPN through the Internet is a comparatively new scheme with several competing standards for tunneling under review by the Internet Engineering Task Force. Some of the areas of difference between techniques involve the manner in which security will be handled and how quality of service will be guaranteed across the Internet backbone network. While universal standards have not been formalized, this has not prevented some companies from pursuing VPN technology to establish convenient remote access for end-users, smaller branch offices and suppliers, especially in situations where high-speed private network interconnects would be costly.

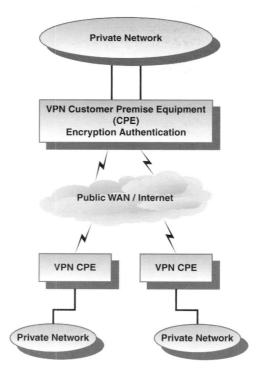

Figure 7–6   Simplified VPN tunneled through the Internet.

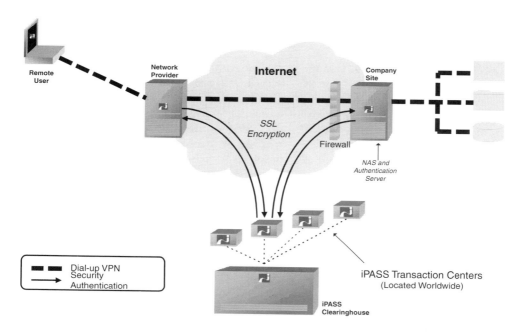

Figure 7–7   iPass VPN Service (*Source:* iPass Inc., Mountain View, CA. www.ipass.com.)

Especially keen to see an increase in VPN popularity are network service providers, including Internet Service Providers (ISPs) and telecommunications carriers, who are endeavoring to provide VPNs as a managed service to corporate subscribers. To build a market for managed VPN services, however, vendors must first enable them with security protocols that safeguard them from hackers but without constraining ease of deployment or use.

Currently, service providers are fielding security solutions to augment VPNs offered directly by carriers and others. They bundle their security and management services with subscription VPNs. An example is iPass. As depicted in Figure 7–7, iPass advertising literature describes several of the advantages of subscription VPN services generally:

- Remote access with a local call from all over the world
- Reliable, redundant connectivity through top-tier networks
- Comprehensive security and the VPN solution of your choice
- Simplified administration and complete administrative control
- 70 to 80% cost savings compared to modem bank solutions
- A simple point-and-click interface, easy for novice users
- Improved convenience with one consolidated account[3]

CONSIDERATIONS REGARDING THE USE
OF REMOTE ACCESS FOR END USER RECOVERY

The selection of which remote access method a company uses to facilitate the requirements of mobile workers, telecommuters, or small branch offices is not within the scope of this discussion. What is important about remote access technology is (1) that existing remote access capabilities may provide an alternative to user relocation in the event of a disaster that affects company facilities; and (2) that, generally speaking, some sort of remote access solution will need to be used in a recovery situation regardless of what strategy is selected to restore user operations following an unplanned interruption.

On the first point, it should be noted that existing remote access solutions, whether dial-up or Internet-based, need to be evaluated for their capacity to handle increased loads placed on them from end users who would normally conduct work at office locations. DR coordinators should obtain information from network management personnel about the feasibility of utilizing remote access services for critical personnel during a disaster. Moreover, coordinators should ascertain the viability of such a strategy from the standpoint of application requirements. Not all applications perform well across a low-speed dial-up connection or an Internet connection. As demonstrated in Table 7–1, transmission speeds of communications links have a great deal to do with application performance and response times. While newer high-speed line options are becoming increasingly available, they represent a substantial cost and may not be readily activated by telecommunications providers to meet the needs of a company confronting a disaster.

Simple file transfer speeds may not be the only indicator of the potential efficacy of a remote access solution for end user recovery, however. As touched

Table 7–1   File Transfer Speeds at Different Link Rates

File Type	File Size	33.6 Kb/s	56 Kb/s	64 Kb/s	128 Kb/s	512 Kb/s
Word Processing (20 pages)	40 KB	9.5 secs	5.7 secs	5 secs	2.5 secs	.625 secs
Spreadsheet	100 KB	23.8 secs	14.3 secs	12.5 secs	6.25 secs	1.6 secs
B&W Presentation	1 MB	4 min	2.4 min	2 min	1 min	15 secs
CAD/CAM	2 MB	8 min	4.8 min	4 min	2 min	30 secs
Digitized Photograph	4 MB	16 min	9.6 min	8 min	4 min	1 min
Color Presentation	10 MB	40 min	24 min	21 min	10 min	2.5 min
X-Ray File	100 MB	6.6 hrs	4 hrs	3.5 hrs	1.7 hrs	26 min

upon in the preceding chapter, thin computing technology is increasingly coming to the fore in many organizations. Thin computing solutions from companies such as Citrix Systems and Microsoft provide demonstrated high-performance characteristics even across "thin pipes" (low-bandwidth network connections).

Citrix Winframe technology, which is also used by Microsoft in its NT Terminal Server Edition and some flavors of its Windows 2000 operating systems, is a server-centric computing technology in which applications execute entirely on a server application host system. Rather than passing all data to the remote client device (a PC, terminal, or other device), only interface data is transmitted. In turn, the client passes only keyboard keystrokes and mouse clicks back to the server. The bandwidth required for such interaction is minimal, reflecting the heritage of the Citrix presentation services protocol in the days when slow modem technologies prevailed. Citrix's technology is optimized for Microsoft Windows and delivers specified performance for all native Windows applications.

Used in conjunction with remote access technology, server-based thin computing architectures have the potential to provide tremendous flexibility in application access. The same may be said of applications specifically enabled for use via the Internet and a web browser.

If end-users require access to additional capabilities besides applications themselves (for example, if they need to print copies of forms, send faxes, etc.) or must perform other manual tasks to sustain a business-critical process, the notion of at-home recovery may be moot. However, the presence of a preexisting telecommuting capability at a company implies that the end users who routinely use it can and do support critical corporate functions while at off-site locations.

Of course, basing a user recovery strategy on a telecommuting premise must also account for how remote access will be accomplished if local communications services are impaired. For companies using Internet-based VPNs, it may be possible for end users to connect to alternate ISP access numbers as a simple workaround if primary ISPs are unavailable. This is one of the advantages touted by the growing cadre of VPN service providers: Their services feature multiple access numbers, including an 800-number, so that access is assured wherever the end-user travels.

Assuming that a disaster is not so widespread as to have disabled the telecommunications infrastructure of a given region, access constraints may not be a factor. Once servers are recovered and applications are restored at a hot site or other systems recovery facility, connecting to the remote systems recovery center from home-based client systems will require only the restoration of the remote access system and any necessary private network or Internet access links. These activities are logically part of any systems recovery and network recovery strategy.

If a regional disaster does occur that renders all telecommunications services unavailable, user relocation to a remote recovery center (or provisions for an exotic replacement of local telecommunications service, such as satellite communications, see Chapter 8) may provide the only solution.

The second point made above, that remote access is almost always part of a disaster recovery plan, should also be discussed here. End-user recovery, whether accomplished via some home-based strategy, at a remote location, or even in normal offices following a disaster that affects only the corporate data center, will require the restoration of access to mission-critical systems, wherever they are being recovered. To this end, remote access technology of some type will be part of the network recovery strategy for a company.

OTHER ISSUES IN END-USER RECOVERY

The determination of which of these remote access approach will best meet the needs of a specific company must be made by the disaster recovery coordinator after reviewing all relevant options. Coordinators will need to have identified and prioritized in advance which business functions, resources, process, and employees need to have these capabilities. In addition to selecting a recovery option, other end-user recovery requirements also need to be considered and accounted for in the end-user recovery strategy.

Employee Notification Procedures

Depending on the selected approach to facility replacement, special procedures will need to be developed to ensure that employees who are vital to the recovery are notified in the event of a disaster. Recovery teams and operations staff will need to know when and where to report for work. (This topic is treated in greater detail in Chapter 9.)

Employee Transportation Arrangements

The disaster recovery coordinator also needs to make provisions for the relocation of users to the user recovery site. Preparations may be as extensive as establishing a provisional service contract for private air transportation or as limited as designating a recovery team to hire buses at the time a disaster occurs. Here, as in any dimension of disaster preparedness, the coordinator may face tradeoffs between the certainty of advance preparation and the cost savings of a more open-ended approach.

Redirection of Voice Telecommunications Traffic

For many businesses, the loss of voice telecommunications for any period of time is tantamount to the loss of business functions. For this reason, user recovery strategies must account for the recovery of voice telephony capabilities as well. Another factor making restoration of voice telephony at the user facility extremely important is that this often provides the means for coordinating the work of the various recovery teams involved with systems restoration, network restoration, and user recovery. Chapter 8 treats network recovery strategies (including both voice and data communication networks) in detail.

Supply Logistics

Once a facility is designated for user recovery and provisions have been made for notifying and transporting users to the location, the disaster recovery coordinator must determine what supplies users must have to perform productive work. Some supplies, identified in the risk analysis, may have been stored off-site as part of the off-site backup plan. Arrangements have to be made to ensure that they are retrieved and delivered to the user recovery site.

If some supplies (i.e., office supplies) are expected to be acquired from regular sources, the disaster recovery coordinator should so state in the recovery plan. Sources and alternates for needed supplies should be specified together with procedures for obtaining them (purchase orders, corporate accounts, etc.).

For items that may be somewhat more difficult to obtain because of size, cost, order processing intervals, and so forth—including computer terminals, PCs, peripheral devices, portable photocopiers, FAX machines, printer paper, diskettes, ribbons, and other computer-related supplies—advance planning may help minimize recovery time delays. The coordinator should compile a list of all necessary items and then identify possible sources for them in the general vicinity of the recovery site (if known in advance).

For electronic equipment, the coordinator may be able to make an arrangement with the vendor, a value-added reseller (VAR), or retailer to deliver replacement hardware within 24 hours. If this time-frame is unacceptable, either to the company or to the supplier, the coordinator should explore the possibility of purchasing needed hardware and storing it off-site with other critical supply items.

At least two suppliers should be identified for any critical item. Redundant supply arrangements can safeguard against the possibility that a critical item or a supplier will be unavailable when needed.

Where possible, emergency purchase orders should be completed so that only a signature is needed to activate them. Suppliers may require this and may wish to have copies of the purchase orders in their possession as a part of an emergency supply agreement.

Of course, all suppliers and the items they will provide must be listed, together with office and emergency contact telephone numbers. These contact lists will be included in the disaster recovery plan, kept up-to-date through regular plan maintenance, and included in the notification procedures set forth in Chapter 9.

Employee Accommodations

If a "hard" user recovery site is specified in the plan, it may be possible to make advance arrangements with a hotel or motel in the site's vicinity to accommodate recovery personnel in an emergency. At a minimum, an inventory of lodging facilities should be made prior to selecting a recovery site if the site is located too remotely for users to commute from their own homes.

FINAL THOUGHTS ON END-USER RECOVERY STRATEGIES

As with all aspects of disaster recovery planning, end-user recovery requires creativity and imagination. In addition to striving to minimize costs by leveraging existing capabilities and providing a flexible response to different disaster potentials, coordinators need to consider in this aspect of planning the very real human factors involved.

Depending on the nature of the disaster, end-users may be confused, terrified, or in a state of shock in the hours following the event. Their foremost concern may be with the safety and well being of their families and friends rather than with the survival of the business. Some may have experienced personal losses or even injuries. It is important to plan for the worst case and to discuss with management the possibility of including provisions in the plan for crisis counseling and family assistance.

Carol Dorris Andersen summarizes the situation succinctly:

> During disasters, employees sometime become dysfunctional. They are worried about families, have thoughts of inadequacy, or react to seeing an injured co-worker . . . . On a typical workday, under normal work conditions, a company will have approximately 10–20% of its labor force under enough work related stress to result in decreased performance, safety hazards, or poor work habits. After a crisis, performance is decreased from 30–75% for a period of time. Six to twelve weeks is considered average. However, individual needs may increase or decrease the time required.[4]

To address the problem of human factors in a disaster, Andersen recommends a two-phased approach. She suggests that certain activities conducted in advance of disasters by DR coordinators, such as disaster awareness programs and plan tests, that help to familiarize employees with disaster potentials and their roles in responding to emergencies provide important psychological benefits to the employees as well. Second, she recommends that "debriefings" be conducted with employees in the hours following the disaster event. Allowing personnel to talk about their experience typically provides a catharsis for pent-up stress, bringing "closure to the crisis."

> The memories of the event may last, but the impact is significantly reduced with an appropriate debriefing that includes large group meetings, small group support programs, and individual counseling for those who require it. These programs will get your workforce back to work quickly.[5]

This view is echoed by Dan Paulk, PhD, who serves as a senior consultant with Crisis Management International in Atlanta, GA. Plan provisions for post-disaster user recovery recommended by Paulk are summarized in Table 7–2.

Table 7–2   Structured Response Checklist for Post-Crisis Human Factors

Provide "psychological first aid"	Identify and assist those who are deeply affected by traumatic stress. These people need to be separated from the disaster scene, but not isolated. Move them to a safe place, under the care of counselors or caring friends. Get appropriate help.
Provide management-led deescalation meetings	It may seem kinder to simply let them go home, but people suffering from traumatic stress do not need isolation. They need structure, peer support, facts, and information. If these immediate concerns are well met, recovery will be greatly aided. The deescalation meetings should be provided before allowing employees to leave the worksite for their homes.
Contact family members of casualty victims	Death and serious injury notification (also known as next-of-kin notification) is a very difficult and stressful duty. It is best if two management representatives make the initial visit—quickly—before the message is delivered by the media or other less caring messengers.
Protect your employees from the media	Guard affected employees and family members from media contact. All employees are to be instructed not to comment if approached by the media. They are stressed, stunned, dazed, and confused following a traumatic incident—a poor time to make any public statements.
Plan your communications to the media	An Emergency Communications Team should handle all media interaction per a preestablished plan.
Telephone operators	Receptionists and others who must confront the public need careful instructions in what to say and do. These employees may be under particularly heavy stress. Consider short shifts, or relief from duty. Have them log all calls.
Assess the need for professional traumatic stress intervention	Having made prior arrangements with experienced professionals, determine the need for intervention. Traumatized individuals may need intervention services, such as group debriefings or private interviews. These sessions provide for emotional venting—to share and normalize reactions.
"At-risk" employees	Identify persons who may be at potential risk of continuing or escalating traumatic stress reactions. At-risk persons may be identified by the group debriefing leader, by local management and supervisors, by co-workers, or by self-referrals.
Provide management briefings for employees returning to work	Management briefings should be offered as the initial processing step for employees when they return to work.
Maintain communication with your employees	Employees have a great need for information and facts following a critical incident. They need this directly from management. It is important to give truthful, accurate, and complete information.

Source: Extracted from Daniel Paulk, "Human Factor in Disaster Recovery," *Disaster Resource Guide,* 1998.

While post-event counseling may be mandated in some situations, many DR coordinators who have activated plans in the wake of hurricanes and other cataclysmic events have discovered that, once the human needs of employees and their families were attended to, the employees became veritable zealots in corporate recovery activities. In some cases, companies have actually reported a surge in productivity during post-disaster periods. Disasters can create a common bond and mission among staff and management if provisions are made to attend to human needs first.

Like all other aspects of the disaster recovery capability, the user recovery plan will need to be tested and refined over time. Coordinators should make every effort as they assess the solvency of remote access strategies, the efficacy of recovery facilities, and the intricacies of logistics and supplies, not to lose sight of the human factor.

ENDNOTES

1. Interview with Jim Grogan, vice president of alliances, SunGard Recovery Services, Wayne, PA, 02/02.
2. "Working Outside the Office Spurs Demand for Remote and Mobile IT Products," *Recent News,* International Data Corporation, Framingham, MA, 08/99.
3. iPass Inc. marketing materials, from www.ipass.com, iPass Inc., Mountain View, CA, 1999.
4. Carol Dorris Andersen, "Critical Incident Stress Management," *Disaster Resource Guide,* 1998.
5. Ibid.

CHAPTER 8

Strategies for Network Backup

Planning for business recovery entails more than developing strategies for the backup of computer hardware, critical applications, and data. As discussed in the previous chapter, DR planning must also consider the recovery of those who produce and use information assets to provide critical and vital business functions.

This community of users may be quite vast. It typically includes employees and managers of the company (the classic definition of the end user community), but it may also include a host of others who trade with the company, invest in its growth, monitor or regulate its activities, or consume its products and services.

In the late 1990s, concern with the Year 2000 "bug"—a date-change error embedded in many applications and chips—forced many companies to redefine the concept of "user community" in disaster recovery planning. Given the dependencies that existed between internal business processes and the business processes of key suppliers, many firms "discovered" that defining disaster recovery and business continuity requirements solely in terms of company-owned facilities was inadequate. Key suppliers also needed to have adequate disaster recovery plans.

Of course, ensuring the preparedness of other companies is usually beyond the purview of corporate DR coordinators. As companies concerned about Y2K discovered, the only "stick" they possessed to encourage the preparedness of business partners was a threat. Assuming that other potential suppliers of some needed good or service were available, a company could threaten to change partner/suppliers if a current partner could not demonstrate requisite levels of disaster preparedness.

In the case of Y2K issues, however, these threats rarely translated into action.[1] One problem was the lack of any effective means to verify partner preparedness. Some companies did perform joint Y2K testing with their key suppliers, while others contented themselves with partner-supplied results of Y2K preparedness audits conducted by trusted third parties. All in all, these were the exception rather than the rule. The fact was that companies were often tied to their suppliers by business realities, including the expense of change, difficulties in acquiring customized goods or services from alternate suppliers within a short time, or contractual obligations that bound companies to their partners. Discontinuing a supplier relationship was often perceived as potentially more costly than a temporary Y2K-related supply interruption.

What this brief flirtation with "supply chain DR planning" did accomplish, however, was to demonstrate how interdependencies between external organizations and the company might also create exposure to corporate disasters. Moreover, for those who did not clearly understand up to this point the business criticality of communications networks—used to interconnect a company and its geographically dispersed user community—supply chain DR planning was a wake up call.

Awareness of the business interruption risks posed by networks has also grown with the expansion of the Internet. Business use of the public data network, which had long served the Department of Defense and the international university community as an information-sharing medium, exploded in the mid-1990s. Ubiquitous browser technology, email, and searchable directories established the public Internet and World Wide Web as a gateway to a vast user community. Sensing opportunity to access a global customer base, older businesses established a "presence" on the Web, while newer "dot coms"—businesses built literally out of Hypertext Markup Language (HTML) running on a web server (.com is a domain name extension signifying a business site address on the World Wide Web)—proliferated.

Today, business use of the Internet is varied, and applications run the gamut from simple presentations of corporate brochure information to electronic catalog displays and on-line order-taking and customer service systems. Many companies use Internet-centered electronic mail to extend corporate communications networks to remote offices and telecommuter sites. As security and performance improve, the Internet is becoming an increasingly viable alternative to expensive private line networks, an alternative vehicle for remote access to internal corporate applications, an alternative voice telephony service, and a platform for outsourcing applications and entire data center operations.

Even in the wake of the "dotcom debacle"—a general term used to describe the failure of many nascent Internet business ventures to realize profits following their warm welcome into world financial systems and stock markets—in the first years of the millennium, many companies continue to look to the Web as a medium for business-to-consumer and business-to-business commerce. In some industries, a phenomenon referred to as "business process deconstruction" is taking shape.

Deconstruction, simply stated, entails assigning of certain business process functions to supply chain partners. The expected result of companies engaging in deconstruction is that the costs associated with "out-tasked" functions will be pushed out of the business and into the supply chain itself.

For example, an automotive company that traditionally performed all of the tasks associated with vehicle manufacturing—from design and testing, to marketing and order processing, to assembly and delivery—may elect to deconstruct the process and assign to key suppliers responsibility for delivering their components directly to the assembly line and for providing workers to install the components on the vehicles on the line. The aim of this strategy may be to reduce costs associated with maintaining an inventory of parts and providing skilled labor for their installation.

In the new process model, the company retains the responsibility for design, marketing and order-taking, and oversees the work of supply chain partners with networked logistics and management applications. The networked applications are critical to the success of the process and may themselves be "web hosted"—made accessible to suppliers via the Web at a managed hosting services provider or application service provider. This removes any requirement for the automobile company to equip its suppliers directly with the technology required for them to participate in the strategy.

Business process deconstruction entails many risks, to be sure. It generally involves a staff dislocation as work is outsourced to third parties. Staff reductions invite labor unrest and potential sabotage.

Moreover, such a strategy creates dependency upon the smooth functioning of the Internet. Unplanned interruptions of Internet-based business processes can impact corporate revenues negatively and cause other significant damages to the company.

Of course, dependency on networks—both within company premises and between corporate offices—was perceived by many companies long before Y2K or the advent of business process deconstruction. The acquisitions and mergers of the late 1980s, particularly within the financial industry, saw the formation of large conglomerates whose operations often spanned vast geographical areas.

Following an acquisition, it was usually desirable to consolidate information processing assets under a single point of management and control. This often translated to closing the data centers of acquired companies and relocating applications and data to a central data center supervised by a corporate IT organization.

In the case of banks, this effort was often paralleled by a drive to substitute data communications networks for local data processing assets. High-speed data communications links enabled personnel in the branch offices of acquired banks to access remotely hosted applications and data and to continue to deliver the same levels of customer service and support despite the consolidation of the IT architecture. The reliability of these wide area networks (WANs) was understood to be as critical to business success as the operation of automated teller machine (ATM) networks.

Within company offices themselves, local area networks (LANs) took hold throughout the 1980s as well. LANs were initially introduced as a technology for interconnecting "islands of automation" created by the PC revolution and later provided the "plumbing" for client/server computing. The evolution of LANs from a simple conduit for data transport and file exchange into a strategic framework for distributed business-critical applications is a subject of computing lore. Business dependency on LANs, interconnected by enterprise backbone networks, grew over time. Based upon experience with network interruptions and outages, companies quickly discovered that network availability was as much a determinant of business success as application integrity and system uptime. Fault tolerance and high availability have become the buzzwords of LAN architecture today.

One network that has always been recognized as critical by modern business is the public telephone network. In recognition of this fact, most disaster recovery plans, whether developed in the 1970s or the 2000s, provide procedures for the restoration of voice telephony services following a disaster. The dependency of business processes upon voice telecommunications during normal operations is a given. During a disaster, telecommunications becomes even more vital as a vehicle for coordinating recovery activities and communicating with shareholders, customers, suppliers, and corporate end users.

The public telephone network has undergone (and is undergoing) significant changes over the years. From its roots in analog switchboards and relays and copper transmission lines, the telephone system has evolved into a complex, fully meshed network of high-speed digital switches transporting data through fiber optic and copper cabling. Note the use of the term data: whether voice, computer signal transmission, or video, everything is data.

As of this writing, modern interexchange carriers (IXCs) provide "long distance network core switching services"—that is, long distance calls—using redundant, high-speed (mostly) fiber-optic networks interconnected via digital switch equipment. Access to the IXC network is made at points of presence (POPs) located throughout the network. IXC POPs may be co-located with the central offices (COs) of local exchange carriers (LECs), which, in turn, maintain their own switched fiber optic or copper line networks to meet the local calling requirements of business and private consumers. Local exchange carriers generally provide "last mile services"—that is, switching and cabling from the LEC central office to the "demarc" or physical termination point at the customer premises—as well as "gateway service" interconnections to the IXC POP and into the long distance network (see Figure 8–1).

Also as of this writing, the telephone network provides the bulk of resources used for corporate WANs and for the Internet. Some companies utilize private network facilities that include a mixture of lines leased from the public telephone network, satellite communications links, and even digital radio. However, the preponderance of medium and smaller companies use the Plain Old Telephone System (POTS), enhanced with some specialty networking services and facilities, to meet their business WAN and voice telephony requirements.

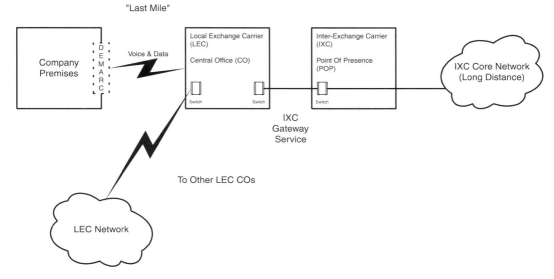

Figure 8–1   Simplified diagram of the public telephone network.

By 1999, there were 13.3 million fiber circuits in North America and some 123 million copper lines that had been in service for approximately twenty years. The system was showing significant indications of strain as demands for performance, access, and availability increased. By the millennium, most analysts agreed that an entirely new public network infrastructure was required. Vendors are steadily working toward a next generation network, the New Public Network (NPN), "overhauling most of the equipment hanging off [the old Public Switched Telephone Network]—upgrading everything from the POPs and COs to the core infrastructure."[2]

As a result of both the current strain and upgrade activities (as well as the occasional line cut, CO fire, CO power outage, or switch equipment failure), many significant interruptions of POTS services occurred in the final years of the 1990s. These outages have impacted virtually every company in North America at one time or another within a given year, alerting everyone to the need for recovery plans that address public network outages.

WHAT IS INVOLVED IN FORMULATING A NETWORK RECOVERY STRATEGY?

Network recovery planning often eludes DR planners because, on the surface at least, it seems far removed from the central issue of business continuity: the recovery of mission-critical business processes. The plethora of terms and acronyms used by network specialists obfuscates matters further, as does the fact that a strategy must encompass three very different networks: LANs, WANs, and telephony.

The watchword of modern networking is convergence. Just as the public telephone network now carries voice, computer data, and video—all digitized and packaged into data packets or cells—so, too, eventually, will a single network infrastructure within a company premises serve as a common carrier for different data types. That is the holy grail of enterprise network convergence. Opinions vary widely as to when the transition will occur. Until it does, network recovery strategies will need to contain several subordinate strategies.

As depicted in Figure 8–2, network recovery plan formulation involves the development of at least three discrete recovery strategies to cover:

- Internal enterprise networks (loosely defined as departmental or work-group LANs interconnected via a switched or routed backbone network, as well as separate or converged telephony networks used to provide dial tone at the desktop for company employees)

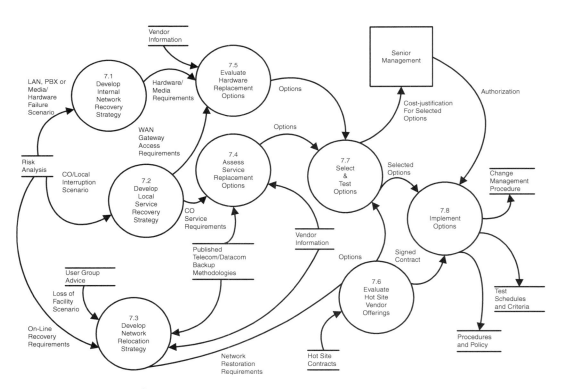

Figure 8–2 Building a network recovery capability.

- "Local loop" (Local exchange carrier services connecting the company facility to the LEC central office) and wide area networks (connecting the company to IXC network-based services), including voice and data networks
- Network relocation—providing a means to rebuild mission-critical internal network services and to reroute WANs and telephony services to alternate end user and/or systems recovery sites in the wake of a disaster.

Of course, the three-strategy approach is only one method that may be used to tackle the problem of network recovery strategy building. Depending on company configurations and requirements, there may be a need for other subordinate strategies to cover the restoration of cellular, satellite, or digital radio networks.

Some coordinators may elect to develop a separate network recovery plan for telephony-intensive call centers or for Internet operations or for video broadcast systems. The above approach is adequate for the preponderance of companies that have based internal networks on Ethernet, Token Ring, or other standard networks using common protocols such as Netbios, Novell Netware, ATM, SNA, or TCP/IP, as well as those that utilize public telephone network services for WANs and telephony.

The strategy formulation effort does not occur in a vacuum. Networks, in and of themselves, are not appropriate objects for disaster recovery unless they enable mission-critical business functions. Thus, network recovery objectives should be determined, preliminarily at least, by risk analysis and business process analysis activities conducted earlier in the planning process.

As with system platforms and applications, it may not be necessary to recover production networks in their entirety in the wake of a disaster. Network recovery requirements are determined in part by the requirements of mission-critical applications and by the details of system and end user recovery strategies formulated in prior processes.

To assist in formulating effective strategies, it may be useful to define a loss scenario that will guide planning. To assist in the development of internal network recovery strategy, for example, DR coordinators may wish to use a scenario of equipment or media failure. To facilitate the development of a local loop/WAN recovery strategy, a scenario envisioning the disruption of normal access to CO services may be used. The third strategy, for network relocation, is based on a scenario of user and data center facility loss, though it may be implemented in response to a wide range of actual disaster scenarios that force the relocation of end users, systems, or both.

This scenario-based approach has the benefit of enabling flexible response to network interruptions of different kinds. It also provides a basis for analyzing and implementing preventive measures to protect against certain types of outages.

As shown in Figure 8–2, the requirements generated by strategy-building activities serve as inputs to other activities aimed at evaluating options for hardware and service replacement. Once options have been evaluated, selections can be made, senior management approvals can be solicited, and capabilities can be implemented and tested.

ANALYZING NETWORKS: A LAYERED APPROACH

As Figure 8–3 suggests, network recovery planning can be thought of as an effort to address the disaster avoidance and recovery issues associated with three distinct layers or domains of networks. In the diagram, these domains are represented as a series of concentric circles. Each layer contains a functionally related set of technologies, transmission facilities, and components that enable data to be propagated over greater and greater distances. At the hub of these circles are the mission-critical business applications themselves.

The innermost layer surrounding the application hub consists of internal networks—networks that exist within the physical boundaries of the business itself. Included in this layer are:

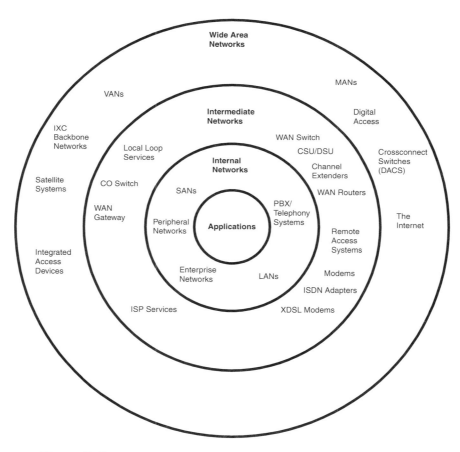

Figure 8–3   A conceptual model of networks grouped by functionality.

- Peripheral device networks, connecting terminals, printers, etc., to large processors
- I/O device networks, such as storage area networks, connecting disk arrays and storage pools by means of a high-speed serial network fabric directly to a server or set of servers
- Enterprise and local area networks (LANs) that may be used to provide shared access to network attached storage (NAS) devices, server-based applications, and databases and intranet web sites, and to facilitate network mail and file exchange
- A voice communications network, often consisting of a separate cable infrastructure interconnecting a private branch exchange (PBX) switch and numerous communications devices, including telephones, modems, facsimile machines, and various network management and troubleshooting devices

Taken together, the internal network layer (generically depicted in Figure 8–4) provides telephony services and business-critical application access to end-users situated within the company premises. In most businesses, dual networks—one for telephony and another for data—persist. The two are frequently managed by separate organizations within the company. Thus, DR coordinators may need to develop separate recovery strategies for coping with voice and data network outages resulting from internal causes, such as equipment failures or cable cuts. In the future, the development of convergence technologies (including as IP telephony—a technology for combining voice traffic on IP data networks) may see the consolidation of voice and data within the corporate premise, thereby consolidating recovery plans.

The second, or intermediate, layer of corporate networking encompasses technologies for extending internal networks from the company "demarc" across the local loop to the Central Offices of Local Exchange Carrier. (By the way, coordinators are likely to find LECs referred to as "ILECs" and "CLECs." This contribution to the alphabet soup of telephony acronyms was introduced in the wake of local phone service deregulation. ILECs are incumbent local exchange carriers—service providers who used to own all telephone services within a specific local exchange. CLECs are competitive local exchange carriers, new service providers who compete with the incumbents to provide services to a local exchange area.)

From the ILEC/CLEC central office, voice and data traffic can be passed to the IXC-controlled network, or it can be switched to local Internet Service Providers that provide Internet access (sometimes called "on-ramp services") and/or to telecommuters located in the local region covered by the ILEC/CLEC.

Simply put, functional components of this layer include customer premise equipment and demarc facilities (switch and router WAN ports, MODEMs, etc.) that provide interfaces to local area transmission facilities (groups of lines or "trunks" provided by the local carrier), the physical trunks themselves, and CO-

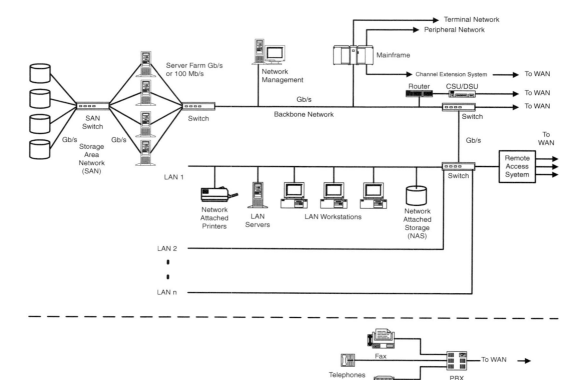

Figure 8–4 A generic enterprise network.

based switches that receive and route voice and data communications traffic. (Figure 8–5 provides a high-level diagram of how connections are typically made between a company premise and a CO currently.) Typical components of this layer include:

- Enterprise network equipment such as WAN switch "ports" (hardware connections that bridge internal network switch to telco transmission facilities), WAN router ports, and similar data networking interface devices such as Channel Service Unit/Digital Service Units (CSU/DSUs), mainframe channel extenders, modems, etc.
- Remote access systems facilitating dial-up access to internal networks for off-site users equipped with analog modems or ISDN and DSL connection devices
- Connections, often made via CO-provisioned or CO-switched facilities, to Internet Service Providers that provide on-ramps to the Public Internet

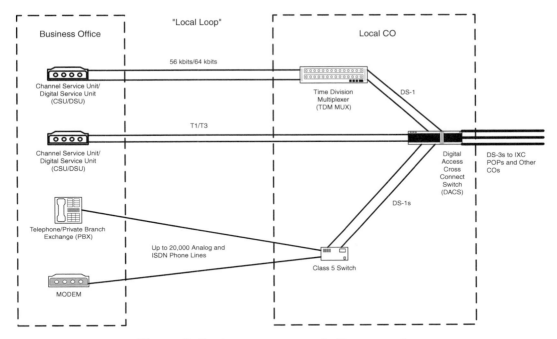

Figure 8–5   Company-to-central office connections.

- Trunk connection points on PBX systems interfacing the internal telephony network to the local telco provider (CLEC/ILEC)
- Transmission facilities themselves—the physical media for connecting the company voice and data networks to CO switches
- CO switches and multiplexers that provide the gateway to the third layer of wide area or long distance networks (although there are now a number of options for circumventing the local CO in accessing the third network layer)

The third network layer consists of wide area network services that handle the movement of voice and data traffic between COs in different local exchanges whether via the IXC network, value-added networks (VANs), or satellite networks. At present, most connections to the IXC occur via digital access cross-connect switches (DACS) located in CLEC/ILEC COs. The DACS aggregate data and voice traffic from customers onto high capacity links and forward it to larger switches located in IXC POPs on the boundaries of the IXC network.

In some cases, it is possible to direct traffic from the company premises directly to switches located in an IXC point of presence, though the cabling involved usually remains the property of the ILEC/CLEC that controls the "last mile"—as fiber and copper cabling to the CO or POP is sometimes called.

It is worth noting that in many metropolitan areas of the United States, IXCs and CLECs have been rolling out broadband metropolitan area networks (BMANs) that connect corporate sites directly to the high-speed IXC backbone networks. The current economic slowdown in the telecommunications industry, and the subsequent cutbacks of certain programs, such as Sprint's Integrated On-Demand Network (ION™), have limited the availability of telco-operated BMAN services to certain key cities. However, CLECs such as Yipes Communications, which provides broadband LAN-to-LAN connections, have continued to roll out high-speed services to a corporate clientele.

The Yipes network is based upon a three-tiered ring architecture. A high-level diagram of the architecture is presented in Figure 8–6.

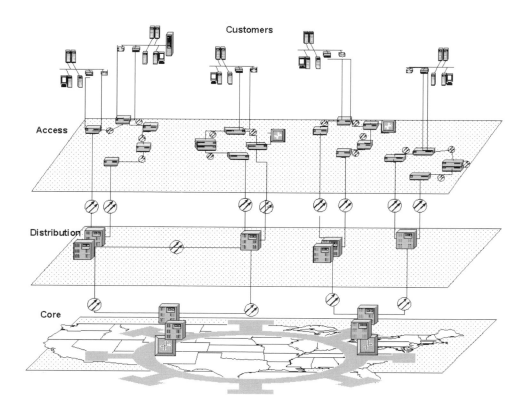

Figure 8–6   Yipes network architecture (*Source:* Yipes Communications Inc., San Francisco, CA. www.yipes.com.)

At the top tier of the Yipes network is the customer access level. Local fiber-optic rings, which span city streets, are used to connect customer premise equipment at customer distribution points. The distribution points consist of gigabit ethernet switches located in multitenant buildings to which customers can connect their internal, copper cable-based, or multimode fiber-based, LANs.

The access level is connected with fiber-optic rings operating at 1 gigabit per second full duplex (using layer-2 switching) or at "wire-speed" (using routing protocols). This topology provides redundancy in the event of ring failure. Figure 8–7 depicts the architecture in greater detail.

At the middle level of the Yipes network architecture is the Metropolitan Distribution tier. At this level, multiple fiber rings connect to a common Yipes point of presence (POP), where an aggregating gigabit router—the "Giga-PoP"—is located. Also at this level, multiple Giga-PoPs are linked around adjacent metropolitan regions forming a regional optical internetworking infrastructure.

For example, all Giga-PoPs in the San Francisco Bay Area are linked by a ring of fiber constituting a Yipes regional backbone (Figure 8–8). Since switches at a customer's location and the Giga-PoPs are all "non-blocking" gigabit devices, all network connections on a regional level will see latency times on the order of a few milliseconds or less.

The Metropolitan Distribution network is used by Yipes to deliver managed IP-over-fiber network services. This network consists of one or more gigabit links, as determined by traffic demands, and again features a ring topology to ensure redundancy. This topology extends the effective area of MAN services throughout an expanded metropolitan geographic region, creating a regional managed network services infrastructure.

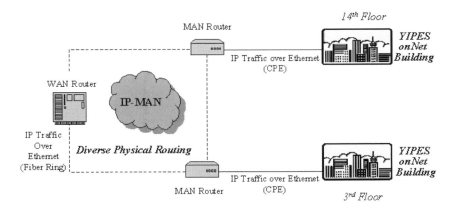

Figure 8–7   Yipes customer access level (*Source:* Yipes Communications Inc., San Francisco, CA. www.yipes.com.)

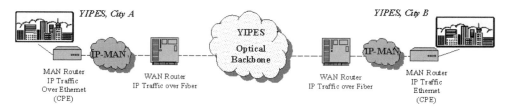

Figure 8–8   Yipes metropolitan distribution tier (*Source:* Yipes Communications Inc., San Francisco, CA. www.yipes.com.)

Multiple buildings in a city, or dispersed throughout a region, can be interconnected on a customer-specific basis to create virtual private links between customer locations, or to link business partners in extranets. This is achieved by entering switching or routing configurations that link specific ports on the customer premise ethernet switches. Since interconnection latencies across regional areas are on the order of a few milliseconds, excellent quality of service can be provided for delay-sensitive traffic.

The third tier of Yipes' architecture connects regional areas across the nation, and potentially around the world. This is referred to as the "core network." This level is implemented through multiple IP backbone carriers to transport traffic between Yipes regions. Connections are made from the Yipes metropolitan gigabit backbones to Tier-One backbone carriers using gigabit wire-speed WAN routers (see Figure 8–9).

These routers are connected via gigabit ethernet, OC-12, or OC-48 links at multiple peering points. At this level, routers are running special protocols to route traffic over the most efficient path. Traffic traveling between Yipes private regions is carried via Tier One IP backbones operated by Yipes' partners. These

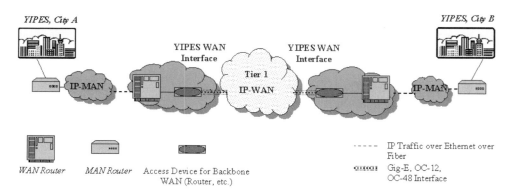

Figure 8–9   Yipes core network architecture (*Source:* Yipes Communications Inc., San Francisco, CA. www.yipes.com.)

partner network providers have specific service level agreements (SLAs) with Yipes that the vendor says ensure that the Yipes SLAs provided to customers can also be met.

In order to ensure multiple paths and complete redundancy throughout a metropolitan region, multiple co-location and peering arrangements are established. For example, in the San Francisco Bay Area region, Yipes has co-location facilities in San Francisco, Palo Alto, and Santa Clara. Both public and private peering and transit agreements provide Yipes with capabilities to pass traffic directly to Tier One IP backbones such as Level 3, Qwest, or UUNet via Gigabit Ethernet, OC-3 and OC-12 links. The company is replicating this model throughout the United States in all major cities. The result is a scalable, redundant, multi-path architecture that offers the maximum flexibility in traffic management, QoS, and provisioning-on-demand.

Advocates of broadband MAN and WAN services, including Yipes, argue that the redundancies in their network topologies provide a guarantee against interruption. Touting the self-healing characteristics of meshed networks or dual fiber rings, vendors argue that using their services negates much of the planning and provisioning that companies must undertake to recover from interruptions in last mile facilities and CO problems. Potentially, services from providers such as Yipes will eliminate the expenditure of company resources on technologies for ensuring WAN-access survivability, while delivering a several-orders-of-magnitude improvement in production WAN operations. (This claim is addressed in greater detail below.)

Convergent voice and data traffic delivered directly to the IXC network is one of many innovations expected to characterize the New Public Network (NPN) over the next decade. Additional use of wireless networking and cable modem-based technologies is also anticipated throughout the early 2000s. These last-mile technologies, combined with new fiber optic signaling and switching technologies, promise to increase the performance and capacity of the IXC infrastructure for the foreseeable future.

Viewed from the perspective of multiple network layers, DR coordinators may be able to see more readily the threats to mission-critical networks and the disaster avoidance and disaster recovery capabilities that are required to address them. The primary objective of network recovery planning is to prevent avoidable interruptions of network services that might impact critical business processes and to minimize the consequences of interruptions that cannot be prevented. A second, though equally important, goal is to develop a capability to transition vital networks to meet the needs of system and end user recovery strategies.

PRELIMINARY ACTIVITIES IN NETWORK RECOVERY PLANNING

It is the disaster recovery coordinator's job to identify the dependency of business functions on the proper operation and the availability of each layer of network services as summarized above and to evaluate the impact of a loss of a service. Some activities that may be part of this undertaking include the following.

Review Risk Analysis and Business Process Analysis Documents

These documents, created at the outset of the disaster recovery planning project, contain information about critical business functions and the automated systems and networks that support them. Analyses should be reviewed to identify dependencies on networks, the criticality of network services, and the minimum network service levels that will be required for business continuation.

Obtain Network Configuration Documentation

In addition to the insights obtained through analysis, the coordinator may need to solicit the assistance of a company telecommunications manager, network administrator, and/or network security manager to develop an understanding of network configurations used to support business processes under normal operating conditions. For companies that have implemented network management systems (NMS), configuration information may be readily available, together with network traffic data, and even hypothetical outage impact projections. A number of NMS vendors are following the lead of Micromuse, Inc. to deliver impact analysis tools "designed to help corporations and service providers rapidly assess the business impact of IT service outages and accelerate service restoral by following procedures that are closely aligned with business objectives."[3] (See Figure 8–10.)

Subordinate diagrams may also have to be compiled showing specific characteristics of specific LANs or subnetworks, including topologies and protocols, characteristics of transmission media between network nodes, and traffic patterns, loads, and transmission rates.

Good network documentation is prerequisite to the task of relating critical business functions and applications to specific communications services. It provides a framework that the disaster recovery coordinator can use to analyze what effect the loss of a particular network service will have on the company. This, in turn, can guide the disaster recovery coordinator in planning measures to safeguard against network failures that threaten critical functions.

Build Disaster Scenarios

Once network configuration documentation has been prepared, the disaster recovery coordinator may find it useful to develop scenarios to account for failures within networks that could lead to unacceptable network service levels for critical business functions.

Often scenario building begins with an examination of internal networks for single points of failure. The disaster recovery coordinator looks at the topology of

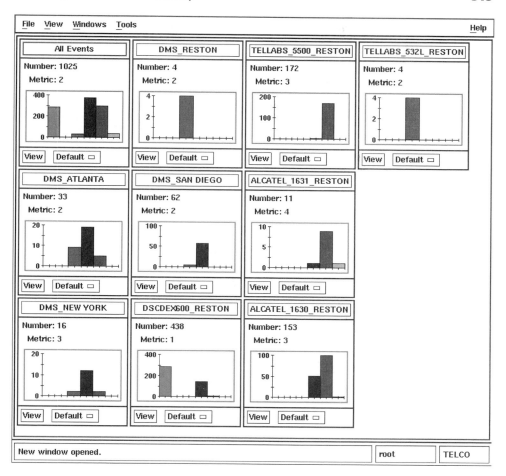

Figure 8–10   Micromuse Netcool/Impact depicts what-if outage impact scenarios (*Source:* Micromuse, Inc., San Francisco, CA.)

voice and data networks and subnetworks with an eye toward identifying the impact of device or network media failure. The coordinator then develops recommendations for network enhancements that will eliminate single points of failure where possible and strategies for recovering network operations in the event of failures that cannot be prevented.

A similar approach is then taken to develop a scenario for intermediate network interruptions. Device or media failures within company premise equipment, within the local loop, or at CLEC/ILEC COs can compromise such key corporate networking requirements as access to WANs, local and long distance telephone services, remote access services for telecommuters, virtual private network access, frame relay network access, and the Internet, just to name a few.

According to a first quarter 1999 Macro-Analysis Report of the Alliance for Telecommunications Industry Solutions (ATIS) Network Reliability Steering Committee, which correlates network outage information accumulated by the US Federal Communications Commission, there were 41 outages in the opening months of 1999 that fit FCC reporting criteria (at least 30 minutes in duration and affecting a minimum of 30,000 lines).[4] Significant increases were seen in certain root causes for the outages, such as procedural errors, while the frequency of outages attributed to other root causes—including CO power failures, facilities (mainly cable cuts), and non-procedural error-based CO switch failures—remained in-line with previous reporting periods or declined slightly (see Figure 8–11).

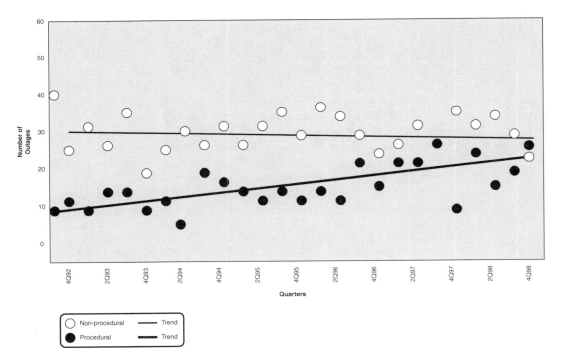

Figure 8–11   Procedure error and nonprocedure error outage frequency by quarter (*Source:* Procedural Outage Reduction: Addressing the Human Part, Alliance for Telecommunications Industry Solutions [ATIS] sponsored Network Reliability Steering Committee [NRSC], Washington, DC, May 1999. Reproduced with permission of ATIS.)

While NRSC numbers cover only a subset of intermediate network outages (those that meet FCC reporting requirements), DR coordinators may be able to leverage the organization's causal hierarchy to identify threats and build a scenario to guide recovery planning. (See Table 8–1.)

In addition to central office and local loop interruption potentials, outage scenarios in the IXC network should also be considered as a prelude to planning. In the first edition of this book, as well as in other writings by the author on the subject of disaster recovery, remarks regarding the potential vulnerability of Frame Relay services provided by IXCs elicited a barrage of criticisms from carriers themselves. Critics responded that Frame Relay service failures were highly improbable given the safeguards and redundancies inherent in IXC network itself.

Short of a complete failure of the network, the loss of a specific service such as the Public Frame Relay Network was inconceivable. AT&T's April 1998 Frame Relay Network outage, followed by MCI WorldCom's August 1999 Frame Relay Service failure, demonstrated that the inconceivable was entirely possible.

In the case of AT&T, the 20-hour outage affecting 6,600 customers started on a Monday at 3:00 P.M. EST and ended at approximately 1:00 P.M. the next day. During that period, only customers with backup networking provisions were able to conduct business using their WANs. Wells Fargo Bank in San Francisco lost one-half of its automated teller machine network during the period, while Unisys, the American Red Cross, TRW, and a host of other organizations were unable to provide normal customer services and other operations.

MCI WorldCom's outage (in fact, a succession of several outages of varying duration over a week-long period) resulted from a software upgrade being conducted by the IXC to its legacy network switches. Instead of backing out the destabilizing software, which had already been deployed across 30% of the network switches, when outages first began to occur, the company made a controversial decision to forge ahead after temporarily stabilizing the network during the first affected weekend. By the following weekend, several short-term outages and various system measurements confirmed that it was time to take action and the new software was backed out. In the process, the vendor earned the public wrath of thousands of its customers, including the Chicago Board of Trade, which was unable to use the network to conduct trades for nearly 5 days.[5]

As these events demonstrate, the paths through the IXC network created by special switch services (Frame Relay, ISDN, etc.) can and do fail, requiring DR coordinators to consider alternatives for providing mission-critical network functions.

The same logic applies to the Internet, which is increasingly used by companies to provide virtual private networks (VPNs) and other business-critical services. Like Frame Relay Network services, Internet services, which use the IXC network as a transport, can also be interrupted without the complete failure of the public network. DR coordinators whose companies use these special services may wish to develop specific interruption scenarios that can then be used to create recovery strategies.

Table 8-1   Causal Classification of Telco Outages Used by ATIS NSRC

Cause	Subcategory	Explanation
Procedural— Service Provider	Failure to follow standard procedures/ documentation.	Work error by telco personnel; correct procedures exist and were generally available, but correct procedures/documentation were not used or were used incorrectly.
	Followed procedures/ documentation that were incorrect.	Flawed documentation or procedures used by telco personnel.
Procedural— System Vendor	Failure to follow standard procedures/ documentation.	Work error by system vendor personnel; correct procedures exist and were generally available, but correct procedures/documentation were not used or were used incorrectly.
	Followed procedures/ documentation that were incorrect.	Flawed documentation or procedures used by system vendor personnel.
Procedural—Other Vendor	Failure to follow standard procedures/ documentation.	Work error by other vendor personnel; correct procedures exist and were generally available, but correct procedures/documentation were not used or were used incorrectly.
	Followed procedures/ documentation that were incorrect.	Flawed documentation or procedures used by other vendor personnel.
Design—Software	Faulty or defective software design.	Includes inadequate fault recovery strategies or failures; ineffective software fault isolation performance that triggers system reinitializations, or requires manual system recovery action for resolution; and insufficient software/memory capacity allocation problems.
Design—Firmware	Faulty or defective firmware design.	Includes inadequate fault recovery strategies or failures and ineffective fault isolation performance that require manual recovery action for resolution. Includes problems associated with incomplete firmware restoral (with or without accurate state indicators) following re-initialization.
Design—Hardware	Faulty or defective system hardware design.	Includes problems with component independence and single-point-of-failure problems between otherwise duplex components, as well as physical hardware design problems (i.e., bad connectors, inadequate grounding techniques).
Hardware Failure	Random hardware failure not related to design but due to the inherent unreliability of the system compo-nents.	If (single) hardware failure causes loss of dupli-cated critical systems, consider procedural or de-sign fault. If system outage resulted from hard-ware failure occurring during simpler operation, consider root cause procedural fault if simplex mode resulted from inappropriate deferral of normal maintenance.

Cause	Subcategory	Explanation
External Environment	Natural (storms, lightning).	External environmental conditions that exceed limitations documented in the vendor's technical specifications; includes direct effects of flooding, freezing, excessive temperature changes; includes outages resulting from lightning or external high voltage transients introduced into the system. If bonding and grounding violations caused the entry of lightning into the system, consider root cause procedural or design fault. If water damage was the result of cable pressurization failure, consider root cause procedural fault.
	Man-made (vandalism, accidents).	External man-made conditions that exceed documented (or reasonable) technical specifications; includes direct effects of water system ruptures, fires, vehicular accidents, vandalism, and explosions. If incident was the result of inadequate security precautions, consider root cause procedural fault.
	Cable damage.	Cable damage caused by dig-ups, (fiber) micro-bending, rodent damage, falling trees, etc.; includes underground and aerial cable failures associated with natural and man-made external environments. If incident was the result of faulty cable installation, or of cable locating activities, consider root cause procedural fault.
Internal Environment	Water.	Entry of water into the system, including roof leaks, air conditioning leaks, excessive humidity, fire suppression activities, flooding, etc., If failure was the result of environmental systems failure (e.g., AC leaks, pressurization failures), or inadequate property management (e.g., unreasonable delay in repair or roof leak, predictable flooding), consider root cause procedural fault.
	Temperature.	Excessive ambient temperatures, excessive rate of temperature changes. If failure was the result of environmental systems failure and a more effective response to the failure would have prevented/minimized impact of incident, consider root cause procedural fault.
	Corrosion/contamination.	Corrosive contamination that enters the system from surrounding environment; includes dust, airborne dirt, and smoke and/or fire suppression chemicals. If failure was the result of inadequate air filtration strategies or maintenance, consider root cause procedural or design fault.

(continued)

Table 8–1   Causal Classification of Telco Outages Used by ATIS NSRC (continued)

Cause	Subcategory	Explanation
	Fire.	Fires within the telecommunications facility environment; includes fires in test sets, peripheral equipment, power equipment, and building systems. If incident was the result of telco/others' activities, consider root cause procedural fault.
Traffic /System Overload	Reduced capacity due to system trouble.	System overload or congestion associated with decreased system throughput or trouble-caused resource limitation; does not include system congestion associated with simple high-volume traffic conditions. If failure was the result of excessive out-of-service conditions, consider root cause procedural fault. If failure was a result of overload triggered by moderate increase in traffic/attempts, or recovery-associated activities, consider root cause design fault.
	High call volume.	System overload or congestion associated with high traffic traffic or load conditions that exceed the engineered capacity of the system; includes unexpected traffic that was the result of media-stimulated calling, natural disasters, political or social activities, or other external conditions. If failure was the result of poor event notification and planning, or network management response to media-stimulated call-in, or a result of inadequate capacity engineering, consider root cause procedural fault.
Commercial and/or Back-up Power Failure	Instances of outage directly related to failure of the external power system, or failures of telco back-up power systems.	Includes failures associated with commercial power, standby generators, building electrical systems, Direct Current (DC) power plants, DC distribution systems, and alarms/monitoring systems. Does not include failures of DC/DC converters or fuses embedded in switches and transmission equipment, unless the problem was caused by the power plant. If the failure was the result of inadequate/no response to (alarmed/unalarmed) failures, consider root power alarm fault. If the failure was the result of over loaded or undersized power sized power equipment, consider root cause procedural or design fault.
Other/ Unknown	The cause of the outage cannot be determined, or the cause does not match any of the classifications above.	Does not include cases where outage data was insufficient or missing or where direct cause is still under investigation investigation. When direct cause cannot be proven, it is usually still possible to determine probable cause, which is preferred to the use of "unknown." When classifications provided do not match direct cause, approximate match is preferred to the use of "other."

Source: Procedural Outage Reduction: Addressing the Human Part, Alliance for Telecommunications Industry Solutions (ATIS) sponsored Network Reliability Steering Committee (NRSC), Washington, DC, May 1999, Reproduced with permission of ATIS.

Depending on the company, additional scenarios may need to be developed to address specific network vulnerabilities. For example, companies that have adopted integrated access strategies (i.e., Yipes or AT&T INC) or are early adopters of voice/data network convergence may need to make special plans to recover these types of network technologies. Also, companies that use value-added networks (VANs) from third-party providers may need to make special provisions for the replacement of these services in the event of a failure. In many cases, VANs are simply companies that lease lines from the IXCs and pay to colo-cate their own switch equipment in IXC POPs. They operate their own applications across these "private network services"—such as enhanced financial market ticker-tape feeds, for example—and sell subscriptions to the service to customers. If these services are important to business-critical processes, plans must be made for their replacement in the event of a service failure.

Finally, DR coordinators need to leverage the scenarios that have guided the development of system and end user recovery strategies to define a set of network recovery capabilities to "reconnect the dots" if a disaster forces the relocation of either data centers or user work facilities or both.

FORMULATING STRATEGIES
FOR INTERNAL NETWORK RECOVERY

Once the preliminary steps outlined above are completed, the disaster recovery coordinator will be able to address specific network recovery issues. At first glance, the multiplicity of scenarios might seem overwhelming. Fortunately, the principles of redundancy and replacement can be successfully applied to creating strategies to cope with most network failures. By making plans for less-than-worst-case scenarios, the coordinator may also find that a pattern of problem escalation emerges that will support emergency management decision making.

Several generic options for recovering failed networks are presented in the following sections.

Internal Voice Communications Systems

Planning for the recovery of internal communications networks must consider two aspects of the network: station failures and PBX failures. In most modern PBX-based voice communications networks, the failure of a station or group of stations will not cause the PBX to fail (though a facility power failure will affect a switch that does not have a backup power supply such as a UPS). Indeed, station failures, because of media faults or hardware malfunctions, are often treated as maintenance issues rather than disaster recovery issues. Conceivably, however, the loss of network wiring integrity could create an emergency for the affected operational area of the company. Thus, line redundancy may be a valid measure to ensure network integrity for critical business functions. It is also important to acquire appropriate network diagnostic and troubleshooting software and to train technicians in its use so that sources of trouble within the network can be rapidly localized, identified, and repaired.

In the event of a PBX failure, two alternatives may speed recovery. First, sufficient dedicated lines (i.e., analog or digital lines that do not have to operate through the switch itself) may be installed for critical, telecommunications-dependent business functions. These lines can be used to handle critical traffic until the PBX malfunction can be resolved or the unit replaced.

For some companies, however, leasing sufficient private lines to sustain critical functions may be more costly than purchasing and installing second switch as a backup to the primary unit. In such cases, purchasing or leasing a backup PBX may provide a cost-effective recovery option. If a second PBX is obtained, common sense dictates that it be installed in a different location than the primary unit. In this way, the second unit may be insulated from disaster conditions that may affect the primary switch. Both the primary and secondary PBX installations should also be backed up for power (via UPS), have appropriate environmental controls, and be equipped with a suitable fire detection/suppression capability.

Most modern PBXs are programmable. Station services and capabilities (i.e., call pickup, call forwarding) may be defined in a series of program statements or "translations." It is important to ensure that these programmed instructions are backed up regularly to portable media, and that a copy of the backup is stored off-site, together with documentation, for recovery purposes.

Computer Peripheral and Terminal Networks

Computer input and output devices, together with the servers to which they are attached, comprise a straightforward (though often complex) data communications network. Once the mainstay of the centralized mainframe computing environment, device networks have recently returned into vogue with the increasing interest in server-centric and thin client computing architectures.

Provided that systems management software—either delivered with the server operating system or purchased from a third-party provider—is used, peripheral device failures and access interruptions can usually be detected promptly. Redundant hardware should be stocked for use in the immediate replacement of failed critical devices.

Cabling can be another vulnerable aspect of these networks, but exposures to severe loss due to cable cuts or other problems can often be predicted and limited. Proper upfront planning for long cable runs will help ensure that obvious hazards are avoided. Careful attention to proper grounding and surge protection can prevent lightning and other power variations from being conducted back to the server or attached device—resulting in damage. If cable cuts occur, it may be possible to utilize alternative media to handle data traffic while repairs are made. Balun™ adapters, for example, may be employed with some systems to convert coaxial cables for use with PBX station wiring.

Storage Area Networks

Another peripheral network, the storage area network (SAN), is rapidly gaining presence in modern IT architectures. SANs derive their heritage from the ESCON-managed Direct Access Storage Device (DASD) "farms" of a decade ago, and while still evolving, comprise a network of storage devices shared among servers and accessed by means of a SAN switch or hub. Because of the sensitivity of applications and server operating systems to storage latency, the interconnect technology for a SAN is typically a high-speed serial interface such as Fibre Channel.

As of this writing, SANs lack any sort of "in-band management" mechanism (in-band management refers to a mechanism for managing and monitoring the operation of connected devices via some technology that operates over the link connecting the devices themselves). Instead, the monitoring SANs for proper operation is a function of Simple Network Management Protocol (SNMP) agents operating over a separate Ethernet network that interconnects SAN networking and storage devices via management ports.

This is not to say that early SANs are disasters waiting to happen. First-generation SANs feature homogeneous storage components combined with data networking products that have been selected by vendors based on demonstrated interoperability. These proprietary SANs, while not the "open storage nirvana" ultimately sought from the architecture, do capitalize on proprietary storage management and resiliency capabilities provided by their vendors and deliver high-availability performance in some configurations. Switch fabrics can and are constructed with link redundancy and failover in mind, and fault tolerance is considered a key design criteria considering the critical nature of the SAN: It is the repository for a significant percentage of corporate data.

DR coordinators within companies that have adopted SAN technology should understand how SAN availability is being provided. They may also wish to find out how SANs can be leveraged to support the timely mirroring or tape backup of mission-critical datasets.

LANs

Local area networks (LANs) pose a challenge for disaster recovery planning because of the diversity of types, functions, transmission media, equipment, and topologies currently in use. In many cases, LANs enable mission-critical client/server applications by providing a medium though which distributed servers and workstations can participate in the processing of data.

Some types of LANs can be readily protected against catastrophic loss due to the failure of a node (an individual workstation), loss of media integrity, or software-related factors. The solution resides in the software used to create and control the LAN as well as the topology of the LAN itself.

At a generic level, LAN communication may be viewed as a multifaceted programming problem. It is depicted as such by the International Standards Organization (ISO) in its open systems interconnection (OSI) model of data communications. Figure 8–12 illustrates the OSI model as it applies to peer communications within a LAN.

As the model suggests, there are seven levels, or layers, of data communications between nodes attached in a LAN. These layers correspond to software components imbedded in the node device operating system (or the network operating system). The following summary describes the layer functions within the OSI model.

- **Layer 7: Application.** The application layer provides the commands or functions, such as file transfer, document printing, or electronic mail, by which the node communicates with other available or open nodes on the network. The command will not result in the actual performance of the function, however, until it has been interpreted by other protocol layers. Common application service elements defined in the application layer allow application programs to find each other and exchange information without requiring special user intervention and guidance.

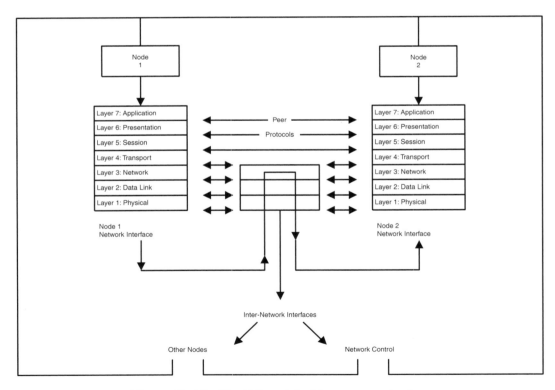

Figure 8–12   The OSI model of data communication.

- **Layer 6: Presentation.**   This layer provides translation, and sometimes encryption and compression, functions in intranetwork communications. The presentation layer thus provides communication between nodes with disparate internal codes as well as security in network communications.
- **Layer 5: Session.**   The session layer is responsible for handling conversations between network nodes. In addition to managing node interaction, the session layer oversees network operating conditions and can reestablish communications after temporary disruption of network connections. The session layer also provides a means for mapping network node addresses to names, thus minimizing the impact to application programs of hardware changes within the network.
- **Layer 4: Transport.**   The transport layer provides error checking between nodes during communication. In the event of an erred transmission, layer 4 may generate error messages and requests for retransmission of data.
- **Layer 3: Network.**   This layer provides internetwork communications as well as the translation of logical addresses (node names) into physical addresses. It also serves as a traffic controller, selecting the best route on the network for communications between two nodes.
- **Layer 2: Data Link.**   The data link layer handles the packaging of data to be communicated and its successful entry onto the network. Data may be packaged as frames or packets and, depending on the network software, may conform to certain packaging standards such as those articulated by the Institute of Electrical and Electronic Engineers (IEEE). If packets arrive at their destination in a corrupt or improper form, layer 2 may notify layer 4 to signal an error and request retransmission.
- **Layer 1: Physical.**   This layer consists of the hardwired instructions of the network—cabling and physical circuitry. Depending on the media, this layer defines the signaling method that is to be used to represent on and off bits.

It is important to understand clearly that the OSI layer functions are provided by the network software and hardware used in a company LAN that is to be safeguarded against disaster. DR coordinators also need to familiarize themselves with the specific network products deployed by the company, as vendors differ widely in their adherence to the OSI model, with some software packages and hardware products providing the functions of several layers in a single layer. Generally, the functions of layers 1 and 2 are provided by network interface cards (NICs) and cabling. The functions of layers 3 through 5 are usually provided through a combination of network software and switch, router, and hub firmware. The functions of layers 6 and 7 may be provided by nodal operating systems, application software, or both.

The OSI network model can provide a useful analytical tool for approaching the subject of LAN disaster recovery. However, the flexibility of LAN technology facilitates highly customized deployments that mitigate efforts to develop a "boilerplate" methodology for protecting and recovering LANs.

For example, knowing how the OSI model functions are provided with respect to company LANs may help the disaster recovery coordinator to set important parameters on recovery procedures. The coordinator can use the information collected about the LAN to determine how network nodes are identified (i.e., by name or physical address). If nodes are identified by name, node hardware may be able to be changed readily in the event that a node fails or if new workstations need to be used to restore the LAN at a recovery site. If hard-coded addresses are used to identify nodes (i.e., firmware associated with specific network interface cards), replacement of node hardware and restoration of network operations may be more complicated and time consuming.

Depending on the OSI layer 1 through 4 characteristics of a LAN, which describe the physical, data link, network, and transport parameters for normal LAN operation, it may be possible to specify a wireless LAN interconnect as a temporary substitute for a cabled interconnect in the event of a cable infrastructure problem. Wireless LAN products (see Figure 8–13) have been growing in capability and corporate presence since the adoption of a wireless Ethernet standard (IEEE 802.11) in 1997. While companies have largely deployed these slower-speed network interconnects in locations where conventional cabling is difficult,

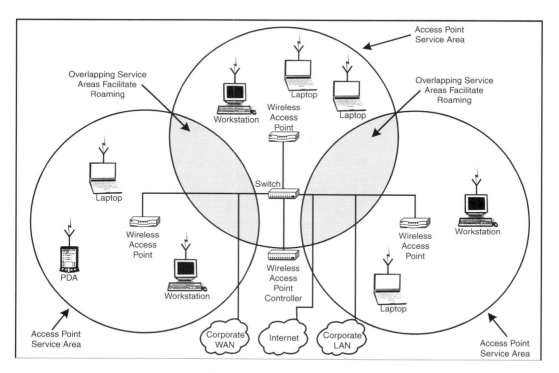

Figure 8–13   A wireless LAN topology.

the technology has merit both as a short-term workaround for network cabling breaks and as a quick deployment solution for emergency LAN restoral with certain applications.[6]

Wireless LANs, it is worth mentioning, came into common use in the wake of the terrorist attack on the World Trade Center in September, 2001. Many companies that were forced to relocate personnel to alternative working sites were able to use wireless LANs effectively to extend existing network connectivity at those sites and to handle the additional user load.

Security-related factors are also of importance in network software. Generally, layers 6, 4, 3, and 2 in the OSI model are utilized to provide security for data and applications on the LAN. The disaster recovery coordinator needs to understand the security measures being employed to determine the extent to which they might interfere with node or network recovery.

Depending on how OSI layer functions are provided, the recovery of LAN-based applications may not need to be accomplished on a LAN at all. In certain cases, the applications and data that are being shared across the LAN are portable to alternative processing platforms. If LAN applications are critical, it may be possible to plan to move them onto a centralized host system for emergency operation. There, the programs and data can be accessed, in a dial-up mode, by users from a recovery site.

As the above examples suggest, understanding how a LAN is physically interconnected is only one part of the equation for defining recovery strategies. An understanding of topology enables the identification of single points of failure, either in cabling or hardware, that can be addressed through configuration enhancements or additional, redundant hardware. However, LANs also need to be understood at the level of internodal communications to identify both impediments to recovery and opportunities for disaster prevention. In these efforts, DR coordinators may be well served by an understanding of the OSI model and the development of a good working relationship with corporate network administrators.

The importance of establishing an effective dialog with corporate network management cannot be understated. The fact is that network administrators work to leverage the capabilities of network equipment and infrastructure to provide quality of service guarantees for mission-critical applications on a day-to-day basis. In most modern networks, this activity involves a combination of application review and policy setting on the one hand and ongoing network monitoring on the other. Network managers understand the service level requirements of applications and endeavor to meet them through a combination of network design and policy-based traffic switching. This knowledge extends to disaster recovery planning in several important ways.

First, network managers can usually identify what service levels will be required for restored LAN-based applications in an emergency operations mode. They can identify the bandwidth requirements and traffic patterns of applications from which hardware and cabling infrastructure requirements can be gleaned. They are also familiar with the security requirements that must be upheld in a recovery setting and can work with DR coordinators to ensure that appropriate security is applied even in alternative recovery network configurations.

Network managers may also have access to Network Management Systems (NMS) that can provide "views" of the IT infrastructure that pertain to specific applications. Network managers often use an NMS to provide less technical business managers with simplified information about the complex networks and systems that support their specific application or business function. This type of utility can aid DR coordinators in focusing recovery planning efforts on specific business processes rather than becoming overwhelmed by the complexities of the entire enterprise network.

The resources and insights of the network manager extend beyond the internal LANs of the company. DR coordinators can leverage the relationships they cultivate with corporate network professionals to obtain a clearer understanding of the service-level requirements for applications distributed beyond the corporate boundaries as well, as discussed in the following section.

BACKUP STRATEGIES FOR THE LOCAL LOOP AND WIDE AREA NETWORK SERVICES

In addition to internal network failure scenarios, the disaster recovery coordinator also needs to consider how the company will replace mission-critical local loop and wide area network services in the event of interruptions. Despite the assurances of IXCs with respect to the resiliency of their new SONET ring services (one, who shall not be named, went so far as to claim in an interview that DR planners for businesses using her company's service no longer need to plan for the recovery of local loop facilities), the fact remains that these offerings are (1) not available on a widespread basis, (2) meeting challenges from ILECs and CLECs who will not surrender last mile services without a fight, or (3) still require some kind of local loop interconnect technology such as xDSL to connect the company Integrated Access Device with the IXC-provided metropolitan area network.

Thus, ensuring the solvency of connections between the corporate premises and the outside world remains within the scope of DR planning. Coordinators need to address the issues involved with an eye toward avoiding interruptions.

Local Loop Protection Through Link Duplication

The last mile—shorthand for the cable connections between the LEC Central Office (CO) or IXC point of presence (POP) and the company premise—is vulnerable to a broad range of disaster potentials. Conduits containing thousands of voice and data lines can be cut, deliberately or accidentally, or can fall prey to natural hazards (gophers that chew on casings, for example, or natural cataclysms such as earthquakes, lightning strikes, hurricanes, etc.). It is beyond the purview of the DR coordinator to protect telco-owned facilities, but it is within the coordinator's power to develop backup schemes for critical links.

One strategy for coping with line cuts is to secure lines from two different COs or POPs. With full-line redundancy, supplied through different conduits from different sources, line dig-up resiliency may be guaranteed. Typically, an automatic switch or PBX cutover is made from one set of trunks to a redundant set if a failure is detected, though additional details for switching trunk identities may need to be worked out with the telecommunications service provider.

Coordinators opting for a replacement strategy need to work together with service providers to ensure that redundant lines are not provided through the same physical conduits or the presumed resiliency of the solution is defeated before it is implemented. It is also important to note that different carriers often lease circuits from each other and share the same fiber, conduits, and/or rights-of-way. Thus, obtaining backup services from different carriers does not of necessity ensure that primary and backup services are physically separate from one another. Coordinators need to get the facts before settling on a solution.

In some cases, it is possible to replace land-based links with satellite or wireless transmission options available from third-party providers such as value-added network (VAN) companies. These options are worth investigation, especially if geographic distances or right-of-way issues prohibit link duplication through land-based COs or POPs.

Properly implemented, a strategy of link redundancy has the additional merit of safeguarding mission-critical communications against a number of disaster potentials linked to CO or POP operations, including switch port failures, power outages, fires, and other internal problems.

Local Loop Protection with Unlike Link Substitution

Of course, duplicating all communications services, from voice-grade lines to T-3 links, with fully redundant backup facilities that are to be used only in an emergency may be beyond the DR budget of a company. Jeff Davis, director of service level management products with Paradyne Corporation observes that

> [Like kind or one-for-one] link backup is not always economical for "always-on" services [like T-1 or xDSL]. Analog lines and Integrated Switched Digital Network (ISDN) lines may be better suited for transient use. With these you have a minimal fee, then a toll charge assessed on a per use basis. [Suggesting that you replace high-speed facilities with slower links may seem questionable,] but not when you consider that most T-1 connections to business offices are actually running at a fraction of the available link rate. They are often configured at 56k or below.[7]

According to Davis and others, consolidation and creativity are usually required to come up with the most effective link replacement solution at the right price. Network managers can be of enormous assistance, given their knowledge of application bandwidth demands and typical traffic patterns, to identify link substitution strategies that might be adequate to handle application traffic loads during an emergency operations period.

Service Failure Circumvention with Unlike Link Substitution

In addition to replacing last mile links, DR coordinators also need to consider how companies will circumvent IXC or VAN-provided networking services in the event that these services become unavailable. One obvious example is Frame Relay. Most IXCs offer some sort of Frame Relay Network services as a replacement for expensive private point-to-point networks. With these services, company offices establish connections to the IXC's Frame Relay Network "cloud," which handles all necessary switching functions to establish secure, private network sessions between communicators. These services are vulnerable to interruptions caused by any number of problems and alternatives need to be found for reestablishing point-to-point connectivity in the event of an outage—in effect, to circumvent the service when needed.

For the last 5 years, many companies have replaced high-speed connections to Public Frame Relay Network services with a fewer number of less capable ISDN facilities. This ISDN "safety net" was credited with seeing many firms through the infamous AT&T Frame Relay network outage in April 1998 as well as the MCI Frame Relay network failures of August 1999.[8]

The ISDN safety net strategy offers a number of valuable considerations that can be applied in other service circumvention scenarios. For one, it is important to test and evaluate any non-like replacement strategy for its impact on applications. If normal link bandwidth is 256 kbit/s (fairly standard for Frame Relay links), replacing the normal link with an ISDN basic-rate interface (BRI) backup link, which offers 64 kbit/s, will have a noticeable impact on application performance.

A company may be able to get by despite the diminished bandwidth if fewer end-users utilize applications during the period of interruption in primary link services. Another fix may be to quiesce less essential applications for the duration of the primary link outage, saving all available BRI bandwidth for the mission critical application(s).

Another consideration that can be derived from the ISDN backup strategy and applied in other circumvention strategies involves the implementation of such an alternative service. DR coordinators need to look closely at how the replacement strategy is provisioned. In the case of ISDN backup, many companies have discovered that some service providers take circuits out of service when they are not being used regularly—even when the customer keeps subscription payments up to date.[9] This can create havoc if primary link services fail and recovery teams must spend hours with backup service providers trying to get backup link services restored.

This is one reason, according to Paradyne Corporation's Davis, why some vendors of ISDN backup devices (including Paradyne) are building in "background test features that check to ensure that the ISDN link is up and running."[10]

In addition to capacity and provisioning, another important consideration when defining a service backup strategy is configuration. As the diversity of ISDN backup products demonstrate, there are often several competing hardware and/or software solutions to address any given link replacement/service circumvention requirement. For example, one method, encouraged by router vendors, for responding to a Frame Relay service outage is to reprogram routers to utilize an ISDN backup link if a primary link or service fails (see Figure 8–14).

On the surface, this strategy has the advantage of requiring a minimum of additional equipment to be provided at the customer premise. Assuming that ISDN interfaces are provided in the router WAN ports directly, no additional hardware is necessary to make a connection to the replacement network. If interface support is not provided, an ISDN interface device will need to be connected to a router port at each communicating site.

Paradyne Corporation, as well as ISDN backup equipment providers such as Controlware Communications Systems, argue that the router-based ISDN backup solutions are inherently inefficient and flawed. Consolidating both normal operations and backup capabilities in the same router introduces a potential single point of failure, critics contend. Moreover, programming a router to use an ISDN link as a substitute for a Frame Relay link is a complex and time-consuming undertaking—so much so, observes Davis, that router vendors teach it as part of their advanced router programming course.[11] The performance of consolidated router-based offerings also suffers, he contends:

> The speed of the [implementation of the backup] is slower using Layer 3 routers. It may take more time for the router to sense that the Frame Relay net is down. When alternative ISDN backup lines are implemented, the routers can take several minutes to exchange protocols and routing tables across the network [before the network

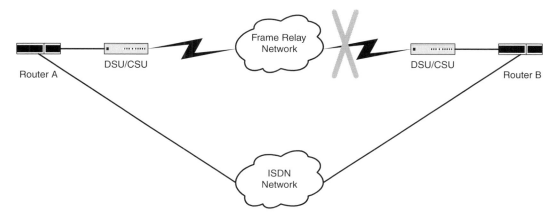

Figure 8–14   Router-based backup (*Source:* © Paradyne Corporation, Largo, FL.)

connection is reestablished]. With an [ISDN backup device placed between the router and the WAN], the device quickly senses that the Frame Relay network is down and cuts over [immediately and transparently] to ISDN backup links [see Figure 8–15].[12]

Router-based implementations of ISDN backup are also short on specialty features, according to vendors of the devices. One vendor touts the advantage of its product in being able to combine multiple ISDN B-channels into one large virtual channel, or to package data for transport via satellite.[13] These operating modes, not available with generic ISDN dial backup capabilities in general purpose routers, may be more or less important within the context of corporate network backup strategy.

Another vendor offers "Time-of-Day backup" settings that enable network managers to indicate certain times of the normal workday when, if a network outage occurs, the backup network (ISDN links) will *not* be activated. The vendor says there may be certain times during the day when Frame Relay networks are not being used and outages do not represent a cost to the company. Time-of-Day settings avoid the costs associated with turning on backup links unnecessarily.[14]

Yet another special feature of some ISDN backup devices is a toll charge savings algorithm. According to Jeff Davis, Paradyne's "Dial Nearest Neighbor" capability enables the ISDN backup device to identify and connect to the closest node, avoiding long distance fees (see Figure 8–16). Davis also adds that vendors of ISDN backup units typically add capabilities for collecting statistics on latency, availability, and throughput that can be used to evaluate the adequacy of the link.

In addition to discriminating their products from router-based solutions, ISDN backup device vendors also strive to discriminate their products from one

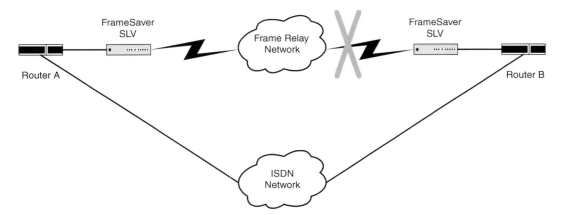

Figure 8–15   ISDN backup device implementation (*Source:* © Paradyne Corporation, Largo, FL.)

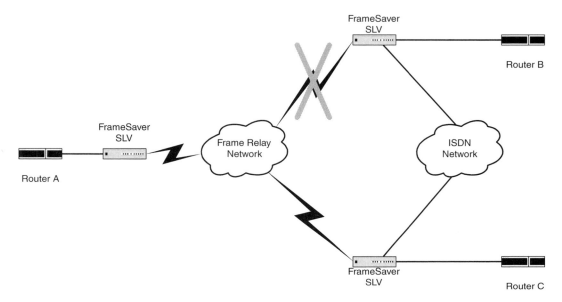

Figure 8–16 Dial nearest neighbor implementation (*Source:* © Paradyne
Corporation, Largo, FL.)

another. DR coordinators need to work with knowledgeable network specialists
to wade through the features and functions of each product offering to determine
the best fit, given recovery requirements.

Frame Relay services are not the only services that may require circumvention in the event of an outage. Similar strategies may be required to circumvent
carrier or VAN-provided Virtual Private Networks (VPNs) in the event of a service outage. It should be noted that leading disaster recovery systems backup
vendors such as Hewlett Packard Company, IBM, and SunGard Availability Services offer value-added networks as a feature of their total recovery solutions.
In some cases, these services may be available to subscribers who are confronting
IXC service failures. However, they may come into greater use when companies
experience disasters in their data centers and/or user work areas, and relocation
to hot sites or other vendor-supplied facilities is required.

PLANNING FOR THE RESTORAL OF WIDE AREA VOICE AND DATA
NETWORK LINKS FOLLOWING A USER OR SYSTEMS RELOCATION

The previous discussion of network recovery strategies has focused on the recovery of critical network operations in the face of a LAN- or WAN-specific outage.
A mixture of proactive (preventive) and reactive (recovery) techniques were dis-

cussed. A third strategy that must be developed by the DR coordinator considers the network recovery dimension of a systems and/or end user relocation. Following a fire, earthquake, or other disaster event that forces the relocation of the data center and/or end user work areas to an offsite location, it is necessary to reestablish a LAN/WAN infrastructure that will accommodate the resumption of business-critical operations.

A good place to begin this analysis is with a simple assertion: If a disaster leaves company offices intact but without necessary local loop or WAN connectivity, activation of system and end user recovery plans will likely be mandatory. Just as a company without power to its offices cannot continue productive business, so too communications are part of the vital business support infrastructure. If telecommunications outages occur that promise to exceed in duration the maximum acceptable thresholds established in DR risk analysis, it stands to reason that the relocation and recovery strategies developed for IT and end user operations will need to be invoked.

To the above assertion must be added a corollary. Even if network infrastructure is intact, the relocation of end users or data center operations in response to a disaster will necessitate the activation of network recovery strategies that support the relocation. Note that network recovery will be necessary whether data center relocation, end user operations relocation, or both are necessitated in response to a disaster.

Recovering critical networks expeditiously following a relocation requires advanced planning. From the perspective of local area networks, a suitable LAN infrastructure will be needed to ensure that applications and other resources are available to end-users at prescribed service levels. From the perspective of WAN links and services, adequate capabilities must be provided to meet the voice and data communications networking requirements of business critical processes. WAN links must connect the end-user community—including suppliers, partners, and other external entities with which the company must interact—to recovered systems and the applications they support.

The general objective of this type of network recovery strategy is to enable the restoration of network services at acceptable service levels in the shortest possible timeframe. This can only be achieved through upfront planning.

Acceptable service levels are determined in a number of ways. Depending on the type of application, the speed of a transaction may be an determinant of an acceptable service level. In other cases, service levels may be dictated by the number of end-user sessions that can be supported concurrently over a link. In still other cases, service levels may be evaluated in terms of queue lengths (how many operations await processing at a given time, or how many customers are placed on hold awaiting an operator or service response). Appropriate service levels are generally determined at the time that a business impact analysis is conducted. Information gathered from end users identifies the numbers of personnel who must have access to applications and the response times required of those applications. DR coordinators must consider these requirements as performance baselines for recovery strategies when selecting between options.

Achieving network restoration to acceptable service levels within the shortest possible time implies that plans must be formulated and tested to ensure that recovered networks are deployed in as automatic a fashion as possible. This assertion has several components:

1. Expeditious network recovery is dependent, in part, on the extent to which system and end user recovery strategies have been "concretized." This essentially means that the greater the number of unknowns in the end user and systems recovery strategies, the more difficulty DR coordinators will face in endeavoring to field an efficient network recovery capability. Ideally, end user recovery facilities and systems recovery facilities are known in advance of a disaster. If this is the case, DR coordinators can leverage IXC and CLEC/ILEC services for on-demand rerouting of communications links to the alternate work locations and WAN links can be reestablished rapidly from new operating locations.

2. Expeditious recovery is possible only when underlying assumptions are carefully considered. Network recovery strategies should not depend upon conditions that may or may not exist in the wake of a disaster (i.e., that local CO services will continue to be available following a hurricane that demolishes corporate data centers or user work areas). Network recovery plans have frequently run afoul of "unpredictable post-disaster conditions"—translated simply to mean the failure of the DR coordinator to plan for the worst-case scenario. Even simple assumptions about the availability of cell phone and pager services must be questioned to prevent erroneous expectations from creeping into plans.

3. Expeditious recovery is enabled by cautious generalization. Network recovery strategies are arguably the most difficult components of DR planning to keep current. Ask any network administrator in any company: Most changes, no matter how small, to applications or end-user responsibilities have consequences for network resources and consume most of the administrator's time. Security settings, disk and resource allocations, telecommunications station identifiers, and a host of other details are adjusted on a daily basis. Network recovery, therefore, should be based where possible on general, rather than specific, environmental parameters. That is, individual user accounts should not be recovered unless absolutely necessary. Instead, plan for recovery by role, or by function—according resources, access, and security on a group, rather than an individual, basis where practical.

4. Consolidation is key to efficient recovery. Where possible, network recovery planning should seek to capitalize on consolidation opportunities. Not all applications require immediate restoration in the hours following a disaster, nor will networks necessarily be required to support the full traffic loads that characterize normal operations. The same may be said of support for end-users: The number of staff who must work with applications in a post-disaster environment to maintain minimally acceptable service levels may be

dramatically fewer than the number of staff using network resources during normal operations. These two facts provide the basis for estimating network resource requirements and providing them in a consolidated fashion.

5. Network recovery can be efficient only when recovery technologies are thoroughly tested and proven. Innovate but don't recreate. Network recovery can be innovative in support of new computing paradigms, such as rehosted applications and server-centric computing. With proper planning, entirely new network technologies can be introduced to augment existing methods (e.g., wireless networking or virtual private networks tunnelled through the Internet). However, any and all strategies implemented to facilitate recovery should have a specific justifying rationale and must be thoroughly tested. The purpose of network recovery planning is not to test out technology, but to identify appropriate techniques for meeting service level requirements quickly.

The above considerations go to the efficiency of a network relocation strategy and its capability to deliver acceptable service levels throughout the period of a corporate emergency. In addition to the general considerations enumerated above, it may be useful to discuss a few specific points before concluding this discussion.

Restoring End-User Access to Networks

As stated in a previous chapter, end-user restoral may no longer require a remote facility equipped in advance with office furnishings, desktop workstations, and telecommunications switch hardware. The rise of the Internet and advancements in dial-up remote access technology provide alternatives for enabling productive end-user operation of remote applications. Such an end-user recovery strategy is typically only realistic for companies that have already instituted a program of telecommuting within day-to-day operations. From a network recovery standpoint, technologies for web-based or dial-up telecommuting should already be in place; they should not be tried for the first time in a disaster situation.

If telecommuting is a component of normal operations, it may still be inappropriate for end-user recovery from a network recovery perspective. A scenario of total loss requires planners to think in regional terms. If a CO serving the company is lost in a cataclysm that also forces the company to relocate its operations to another venue (a total loss scenario would embrace this view), then end users who must also access the same CO for Internet or dial-up access services would also be without the ability to connect. The work-at-home strategy for end-user recovery is practical only if a sufficient number of key end users are located outside of the area served by the business office's primary LEC CO so that their communications access is handled by a different CO or POP.

Assuming that at-home end user recovery is practicable, network recovery planning requires that access methods be examined for potential cost and efficacy.

If planning assumes that 50 end-users will need to dial-up to a distant data center remote access system, a certain cost is associated with this approach. Coordinators may wish to check with hot site providers to determine whether toll-free access can be provided, and at what cost. To determine the efficacy of such an approach, prospective end users need to be polled to determine how many have (1) telephone service provided by a CO located outside of the anticipated disaster zone and (2) two or more incoming lines to the CO. Doubtless one line would be required for network access, while the other would be needed for voice communications.

Connections Through Value Added Services

These connections, including IXC broadband metropolitan area networks and hot site provided WANs, need to be carefully assessed. Despite vendor claims regarding the internal resilience of these services, value added networks are usually still at the mercy of CLEC/ILEC-provided last mile services, which are already at risk in a regional disaster. If a local CO or POP is devastated, the "on-ramp" provided to the company by the local exchange carrier for access these services may also be lost. Once again, network recovery planning must consider alternative methods for restoring access to critical voice and data WAN services. This may include an examination of alternative CO or remote POP access utilizing either special ground lines or more exotic methods such as satellite and/or digital radio services. Be aware that these alternatives can introduce new issues to networks, including new security requirements and even operational issues related to propagation delay in signaling.

Security and Integrity in the New Network

Special consideration should be given to the security and integrity of data communications in the new network. Data that is deemed sensitive in normal operations remains sensitive in a recovery operations mode. All levels of program and database security should be rigorously tested both at the systems recovery site and at the user recovery site to ensure that one disaster does not lead to another. Integrity in data communications refers to the susceptibility of the data being transmitted to corruption due to a hostile communications environment. If data is being transmitted over new routes, there may be new environmental factors that can corrupt it. It is therefore important to obtain the "cleanest" media possible to handle communications between the user recovery facility and systems backup facility. Coordinators may also wish to consider installing new error-checking software to facilitate detection and correction of data communications errors due to link noise and other environmental factors.

While the parameters of the network relocation strategy may be largely determined by end user and systems recovery strategies, DR coordinators will still have much to do to formulate, test and select component options. For the network relocation strategy to deliver timely communications restoral at acceptable service levels, careful attention will need to be paid not only to technology, but also to the realities of the recovery environment. Simply put, it is not enough to recover applications, provide end user work arrangements, and restore network connections. The successful implementation of a disaster recovery capability also depends on the quality of decision making that governs its execution. The meaning of this assertion is the subject of the next chapter.

ENDNOTES

1. Tim Wilson, "Severed Chains," *Information Week,* 07/19/99, reported that only 15% of 250 surveyed companies had suspended contracts or replaced non-Y2K suppliers. Some had requested written information about Y2K compliance, a lesser number had conducted joint tests or requested third-party certification, and most had taken no action or had determined that non-Y2K compliant suppliers could not be replaced in any case.
2. Andrew Cray, Peter Heywood, with additional reporting by Joanna Makris, "New Public Network: Building the Brave New World," *Data Communications,* 10/98.
3. "Micromuse Unveils Netcool/Impact™," Micomuse Press Release, 08/16/99, *Micromuse Inc.,* New York, NY.
4. Raymond F. Albers, "Macro-Analysis: 1st Quarter 1999," Alliance For Telecommunications Industry Solutions (ATIS), Network Reliability Steering Committee, Arlington, Virginia. ATIS is responsible for analyzing telecommunications outage reports submitted by telco providers to the Federal Communications Commission. Mr. Albers chairs the NRSC and oversees the production of quarterly analyses of outage data. Visit www.atis.org to view documents of NRSC on line.
5. Carol Sliwa, David Orenstein and Kathleen Ohlson, "MCI Network Outage Hits Chicago Trading Board Hard," *Computerworld,* 08/13/99.
6. Jon Toigo, "Wireless Wends Its Way," *Solutions Integrator,* 05/01/99.
7. Interview with Jeff Davis, director of service level management products, Paradyne Corporation, Largo, FL, 08/99.
8. Many accounts of the impact of AT&T's Frame Relay outage are available in the trade press. Some good reportage included: Ben Heskett, "Nationwide Breaks in AT&T Service," CNET News.com, 04/14/98. Robin Gareiss, "Frame Relay," *Data Communications,* 06/98. Kate Gerwig, "AT&T Network Outage: Disaster for Customers without Backup Systems," *Internet Week,* 04/15/98. Kate Gerwig, "Companies Tap Contingency Plans as AT&T's Frame Network Crashes," *Internet Week,* 04/20/98. John Rendleman, "AT&T Users Regroup," *PC Week,* 04/17/98. Rebecca Sykes, "AT&T Outage Points Up Network Weaknesses," *Computerworld,* 04/15/98.
9. Andrew Cray, "Leased Line Backup: The ISDN Safety Net," *Data Communications,* 10/96.
10. Interview with Jeff Davis, Paradyne Corporation, op. cit.
11. Ibid. See also, Vince Ciletti, Theresa McGuire, and Jeff Davis, "Improved Frame Relay Quality of Service Using ISDN Dial Backup Solutions," Paradyne Corporation White Paper, 01/14/99, Paradyne Corporation, Largo, FL.
12. Ibid.
13. "A Guide to the TAXI-System," Controlware Communications Systems, Neptune, NJ, 01/98.
14. Davis interview, op. cit.

Perspective on Broadband Storage Networking

By

Jim Morin
VP Strategic Planning
CNT Corporation
Minneapolis, MN

Businesses today increasingly rely on computer operations and information access as the lifeblood of their organizations. Disruptions in these operations, or rejected access to information will have an immediate negative effect on the business, and potentially the economy at large.

It is therefore extremely important to design redundant systems for non-stop operation of critical functions, and to have a reliable and timely business continuity strategy. Much has been written about the need for disaster recovery and business continuity plans justified by the potential cost of downtime. These plans are now under revision to improve recovery period objectives from 72 hours to less than 1 hour, and recovery point objectives from 24-hour loss of data to almost no loss of data. In fact, continuous availability designs are becoming mandatory for core operations.

Relatively little is known about the evolving networking infrastructure that enables the business resumption process. Broadband storage networking is a new term that gets at the heart of what it takes to achieve continuous access to critical information: the bandwidth, the connections, and the infrastructure. This article addresses the advancements being made in each of these areas and how they interconnect to help businesses achieve higher confidence in the safety and accessibility of their information.

Broadband Options for Storage Networking

Broadband is a telecommunications term that means a data communications service faster than a regular phone connection, which is typically limited to dial-up speeds of 56 Kbps. Broadband is an advanced telecommunications capability that enables applications requiring faster connections for high-quality voice, data, graphics, and video. For example, digital subscriber line (DSL) is a broadband consumer service to push a faster speed over the copper wire used for phone connections. Cable modems enable a similar high-speed service over cable TV coaxial cable.

In the context of storage networking, broadband means a connection that typically runs over a fiber infrastructure and enables faster speeds than traditional leased line services of T1 (1.54 Mbps) or DS-3 (45 Mbps). For example, broadband services like SONET come in speeds several times faster than DS-3, called OC-3 at 155 Mbps, OC-12 at 622 Mbps and SONET services past 10 Gbps. Wavelength services at 2.5 Gbps per wavelength can also run over fiber. Internet Protocol (IP) or Asynchronous Transfer Mode (ATM)-based services provide a packet level utilization of these lower level connections to route and deliver the information across the network.

Table 1 Bandwidth options for storage networking

Service	Speed	Typical US Price per Circuit per Month	Storage Networking Application
Dial-up phone line	56 Kbps	$20	Low-speed synchronization e.g. Microsoft Outlook
Cable Modem	200–300 Kbps	$45	High speed internet access; VPN service for remote file access
T1	1.54 Mbps	$500–2,000	Grouping several T1's and using data compression can enable lower capacity data replication
DS-3	45 Mbps	$5–7,000	Typically the minimum bandwidth for data replication or remote tape; universally available over any distance
SONET OC-3	155 Mbps	$8–18,000	Use when bandwidth requirement exceeds 2 DS-3 circuits and for ATM/SONET services
SONET OC-12	622 Mpbs	$25–40,000	Mostly shorter distance MAN applications due to pricing per circuit mile
Ethernet IP	3 Mbps to 1 Gbps	100 Mbps = $6–7,000 1 Gbps = $20–25,000	Very scalable for multiple requirements; some vendors offer bandwidth on demand pricing; available in the MAN and WAN
Wavelength	1 Gbps to 2.5 Gbps per wavelength 8–32 wavelengths per DWDM	N/A	Available in some locations as a wavelength service or can install DWDMs when fiber is available; typically limited to MAN distances of 80 km (48 miles)

Note: International bandwidth designations and speeds vary slightly and typically are priced 2 times or 3 times US prices.
Source: CNT.

Latency and packet loss are two additional considerations for broadband in the context of storage networking. To understand the latency concept, consider the time it takes to travel from point A to B and back. If we add an infinite number of lanes to a highway, thereby removing any potential bottleneck due to congestion, we still have some time required to travel the distance between the points. This delay concept is the latency of the network, bound by the speed of light, and is typically 1 millisecond per 100 miles. We'll see how a millisecond becomes important later in this paper.

Packet loss is an important consideration in storage networking because high packet losses mean more frequent retransmissions that will significantly slow down the application performance. CNT's experience has shown that corporate IP networks are often undersized for storage networking applications. CNT offers an IP Assurance and Analysis Service to test an IP network for its suitability for data compression, throughput and latency at various packet sizes, bandwidth utilization over time, packet loss and data errors and protocol distribution. The results from this testing are used to make recommendations for adjusting the routing or bandwidth to accommodate broadband storage networking.

Storage Networking Connections

Storage is connected to computers in several different ways. Embedded storage means systems like the disk in laptops or servers, directly cabled within the computer. Direct-attached storage means the storage unit is externally connected to the computer via a cable, typically a small computer systems interface (SCSI) cable.

Network attached storage is a collection of disks and automated tape systems locally connected to the computer through a network or fabric. Network attached storage connections typically use Ethernet, Fibre Channel or Escon, and are limited to a campus or within a building distance. Analysts predict that in five years over 70% of all storage shipments will be networked attached.

Although network attached storage enables a limited extension from the computer, a big benefit is that it is also ideally suited to connect to remote storage over metropolitan area networks (MAN) or wide area networks (WAN) of hundreds or thousands of miles via storage networking technologies.

Adding Extended Distances to the Equation

Broadband interfaces and networking technologies enable network-attached storage to be located far beyond the direct cable distance limitations between the storage and the computer. Specialized hardware and software systems called storage routers or channel extenders are used as the networking device to interconnect the storage over the network.

The state-of-the-art devices today typically have Fibre Channel ports to connect to the Fibre Channel switch fabric, and Ethernet ports to flow the data over an IP network. Leading software implementations perform data compression, efficient payload conversion from Fibre Channel to Ethernet, load balancing, buffer credit management, end-to-end data integrity checking and guaranteed data delivery features. These software features ensure maximum throughput over long distance networks (high latencies), even with random errors.

Storage router performance needs to be certified by testing the operation of data flows over various broadband network connections. Additional testing is required to ensure specific application performance is not affected by the broadband storage networking implementation.

Broadband Storage Networking in Use Today

To maintain business continuity, broadband storage networks need to provide all the data a business needs to continue operations on a 7/24/365 basis. This means information must be accessible during both planned and unplanned outages. There are several factors that need to be considered in building networks for business continuity.

The network needs to move data transparently in real time or close to real time between different locations and different environments. The locations for storing original and backup copies of data should be far enough apart so they are not subject to the same disaster. Recent events have caused rethinking of acceptable distances from under one hundred miles to several hundred miles.

In addition, multinational or multi-site organizations need up-to-date data in multiple locations due to the real-time, transaction-oriented nature of their business. It is not unusual for corporations to dynamically manage six different copies of their active data. This requires that the system be able to roll over automatically to secondary servers when primary production servers become unavailable. Those secondary servers must contain the same up-to-date data as the primary servers. When the primary servers are again available, the system must roll over back to them. And everything has to be done without missing a beat.

Time has a key business value in this application. The network specialist sizes the broadband network to address throughput performance, so that congestion does not slow performance during peak loads. This enables data intensive operations like backup to be accomplished with a minimum of time.

The delay time or latency also has a key impact. For example, a CNT customer needed to perform synchronous mirroring of data between two locations one hundred miles apart. The initial testing showed a total latency close to 20 milliseconds. Unfortunately this short delay to synchronize the local data with the remote location was enough to seriously disrupt the normal read/write performance of the application to the storage. Improvements to the customer's application, the telecommunication provider's cable topology, the storage vendor's software, and CNT's software gained a savings of 11 milliseconds. This brief time improvement proved enormously significant because the customer was now able to synchronously mirror data during 85% of his critical time period.

Evolving Storage Networking Technologies Drive Quicker ROI

CNT's technology has evolved to make IP a powerful option for serving as the backbone for business continuance applications. For example, IP-based data replication made it possible for one securities firm to replace their labor-intensive tape backup system and add distance into the equation without having to set up new, dedicated links between the primary and secondary sites. Now they mirror their Microsoft Exchange data over their excess IP bandwidth.

By merging storage and IP in the IT department, companies leverage existing staff skills and management tools. At the network level, IP storage leverages the existing IP switch/router infrastructure, minimizing capital investments. And companies lower the total cost of ownership by sharing bandwidth costs between storage and client/server applications.

While the cost of bandwidth has been declining, it is by no means an insignificant factor. Efficient bandwidth utilization is key. CNT technology is available that compresses the data, reducing bandwidth use and maximizing throughput. Some companies have found that the reduced bandwidth requirements can represent savings that outweigh the cost of implementing their new storage solution. Typical compression ratios range from a minimum of 2:1 to 6:1 or even over 10:1 depending on the data type.

Those companies that have access to fiber-optic cable have the ability to take advantage of one of the most cost-effective and scalable network connection options available to support business continuance applications in metro area networks. CNT's dense wavelength division multiplexing and time division multiplexing (DWDM/TDM) product provides economical multi-Gb/sec bandwidth across a single fiber-optic cable. And it supports the consolidation of multiple intersite links and networks.

The advantage is scalable capacity without leasing or installing multiple fibers. Companies can achieve single-fiber capacity of up to 64 ESCON channels or dual-fiber capacity of up to 128 ESCON channels over distances of up to 80 kilometers. CNT has achieved certification with all the major storage vendors for their data replication and remote tape operations over the DWDM broadband storage network.

Summary

CNT is the global leader in end-to-end storage networking solutions. In close partnership with vendors such as Compaq, EMC, Hitachi, HP, IBM, STK, and many others, we've helped businesses of all sizes in virtually all industries implement storage and networking solutions.

CNT's UltraNet technology, field-proven in over 10 years of demanding service, enables storage networking applications such as disk mirroring, backup/restore, and data migration over fiber optic, dedicated T1/E1 or T3/E3, ATM, and IP networks of any distance. UltraNet performance and advanced network management features, such as data integrity checking, data compression, alternate pathing, and dynamic load balancing, optimize bandwidth utilization, maintain application response over unlimited distances, and reduce the incidence of service disruption—ideal for business continuity plans.

CNT's solutions, technology, and services combine to meet today's needs for cost-effectiveness, scalability, and above all, reliable and seamless business continuation, no matter what man or nature dishes out.

Perspective on The Role of Wireless Systems in Disaster Recovery

By

Klaus Bader
Director of Spectrum Services and RF Engineering
SiteSafe
Arlington, VA

Summary

When a disaster occurs, the important issue is to "re-connect" the systems and the people. Wireless technology is a viable solution to fill this gap in a disaster recovery plan.

In this uncertain world, where critical resources are subjected to natural and man-made threats, one role of wireless communications systems is to provide a lifeline for both infrastructure and personnel. Enterprise networks are growing in complexity and capacity, serving not only as a "back office" resource, but also as a major factor in generating corporate revenue. As these networks grow and resources are pushed to their limits, disaster recovery planning is left as an afterthought. The loss of a fiber backbone that supports the enterprise system can, in one quick moment, ruin months and years of planning and development. Use of wireless technologies as redundancy can allow for planned infrastructure recovery.

The availability of communication between key personnel can help minimize the impact of a catastrophe. Most disaster planning tends to focus on hardware and software, ignoring the "people" aspect of an emergency situation. Planning redundancy in infrastructure—servers, routers and T-01 links—seems trivial in comparison to the task of planning for loss of personnel. Direct communication between team members can save infrastructure and lives. Private wireless systems can provide this connectivity when commercial carrier systems are either overloaded with call traffic or facing devastating infrastructure loss. It is this aspect of wireless communications in disaster recovery that is the focus of this discussion.

Network disaster planning looks at critical components and communication paths, determining a procedure for the loss of connectivity, whether this loss is due to a server failure or the loss of a network switch. Voice communication, PBX's, and voice mail systems are often included in this planning, as these functions become more integrated in the IT network. Many firms stop their planning here, assuming that key personnel can coordinate their activities via the land line network or cell phone. In the event of a major disaster, both the corporate network communications systems and the public switched network communications system can be wiped out. This leaves critical personnel with no communications paths.

9/11/01 Disaster Recovery

During the tragedies in New York and Washington at the end of 2001, the scenario mentioned above became all too real. The crumbling of the World Trade Center towers wiped out both wireline and wireless communications systems throughout Manhattan. The wireline carriers were able to route traffic around faults in the systems, but the wireless carriers that lost cell sites were not as quick to recover. Cell sites remaining in service immediately following the disaster were unable to meet the needs of the customers in the area, leaving safety workers and people fleeing the area with no means of communication.

Through the admittedly heroic efforts of wireless carriers, such as Verizon and Nextel, and equipment manufacturers like Motorola, mobile cell sites, or cell-on-wheels (COWs) were brought into the area in an attempt to restore cellular and PCS coverage. But this effort took hours, if not days. In the critical time immediately following the disaster, the only mobile communications available to public safety workers in the area were the traditional private wireless police, fire, and EMS dispatch systems.

A similar situation occurred in the nation's capitol. The workers fleeing the Pentagon, as well as the District of Columbia and surrounding environs, clogged the roadways and the cell sites in the area. The Virginia, Maryland, and D.C. rescue workers were able to coordinate their efforts because each agency used privately licensed radio frequencies to communicate. Each local jurisdiction had an interoperability plan that ensured each organization could efficiently communicate with other rescue workers.

Private wireless systems do not rely on commercial cell sites and land lines to function. For the most part, they are owned and operated by the companies that they serve. Also called "push-to-talk" (PTT) systems, this technology has developed slowly since the 1950's and now incorporates digital modulation and the ability to transmit slow speed data in addition to voice communications. Police, fire, and emergency medical service workers are no longer tied to their vehicles for voice communications. Handsets are now available that incorporate the tools needed for these critical workers into a device no larger than a cell phone. This technology need not be limited to public safety agencies.

Frequencies Available for PTT Systems

These systems operate in several different frequency bands. Available spectrum is lower in frequency than cellular or PCS systems, and such frequencies are licensed by the FCC for a reasonable fee, with the licenses being valid for ten years. Channels in most bands are shared among users, though there are provisions for licensees to attain exclusive use of the frequencies they license. When companies share the use of a channel, a user must listen to the traffic on a channel and transmit only when no one else is talking. Newer technology radios "listen" to the channel for the user and transmit only when the channel is clear. Firms seeking to implement this technology can purchase radios from dealers and use the frequencies licensed by the dealers, further simplifying the implementation of a disaster plan.

When approaching potential vendors, the first question the vendor will ask is, "What frequency band would you like to use?" Each frequency band has its own unique characteristics. One popular band is the VHF band (150-180 MHz). The VHF band has good propagation characteristics, meaning the signals travel further than those at higher frequencies; therefore, fewer signal repeaters, if any, are required to cover a given area.

However, VHF antennas tend to be larger than those used at higher bands. Also, VHF is one of the first bands used for this type of service and tends to be crowded in metropolitan areas. Such crowding means more users are sharing the frequency.

The UHF band is divided into two parts. The frequencies 450-470 MHz are shared, as in the VHF band. However, the higher frequency allows for the use of smaller antennas. The UHF signals do not travel as far as VHF. Alternatively, UHF frequencies are available in some markets of the US at 470-512 MHz. These channels have the same characteristics as the 450-470 MHz channels, but the frequencies can be assigned on an exclusive basis, meaning no sharing with other users.

Finally, frequencies in the 800 MHz and 900 MHz bands are assigned on an exclusive basis, use smaller antennas, but have less range than lower frequencies. The reduction in range for this spectrum necessitates the use of a repeater station in most applications. Because these channels are assigned on an exclusive basis, finding a channel in a major market is next to impossible. There are commercial firms that offer service in this band; the most notable of these vendors is Nextel Communications. However, smaller firms also provide services in these bands and firms who do not wish to own their own systems are natural clients for such companies. More information is available from vendors, the FCC, and consulting firms who specialize in PTT system engineering.

Blueprint for Communications Recovery

So how does one integrate this technology into a disaster plan? Knowledge of available resources and a logical plan is the key to any disaster plan. What follows is one blueprint for the addition of private wireless communications into the plan.

First, disaster planning must consider the loss of wireline and wireless communications between critical employees. Planners must decide which positions within the company are critical in the event of a disaster. Generally, these positions are representatives of senior management, the IT group and other operations employees. The number of employees in this group will determine the number of radios required and, ultimately, the number of radios will determine the number of frequencies required.

The geographic location of the critical staff will determine the configuration of the system. A small company with one office can normally stock radios for critical staff, and the radios will need no other infrastructure to communicate with one another. Firms with multiple locations in a given market should map the locations and determine the distance separating these facilities. In some instances, multiple locations can establish communications through a repeater site, located centrally to the distribution of company locations. The repeater accepts communications from one location and retransmits these signals to other company offices. A repeater system can be owned by the company, or leased from a radio dealer. In either case, the company must total the number of radios required for each location.

At this point, planners must decide if they wish the company to own the system outright, or lease the services from a communications provider. Providers operate small systems within a market and lease the capacity to customers. The firms differ from cellular and PCS providers in several ways. They generally are not tied to the public switched network and therefore are not impacted by a disruption in the public network. These systems allow direct connect, or push-to-talk communications, so radios can communicate directly with each other without the need to go through a cell site. While firms with multiple locations may need a repeater to communicate between locations, the employees at each location need not rely on a repeater to communicate. Firms seeking to lease services from a provider need only negotiate a contract with the provider, purchase or lease the radios, and they are ready to implement their disaster plan.

Some firms desire more control over the system they operate and so chose to license the system directly from the FCC. The FCC has designated several organizations to recommend the frequencies the licensees use and applications must first be submitted to a coordination firm, which in turn files the application with the FCC. The licensee must purchase and install its own equipment, ensuring that the system is operated within FCC rules. Many firms find designing such a system and application for its use attractive, as evidenced by the thousands of FCC licensees operating their own systems.

Regardless of whether the choice is to purchase services from a third party, or build and license an internal system, installation and training services are also available commercially. While the operation of a private wireless handset would appear simple, users should be briefed on etiquette and other criteria for using the system. In effect, disaster planners can outsource the entire process of adding private wireless communications into their disaster plan.

Consider PPT During the Planning

PTT systems are only a small part of wireless communication solutions available today. Point-to-point microwave systems are used as backup for backbone communications, GPS systems track the location of service fleet vehicles, and radios are used to control devices like utility substations. PTT systems can provide a link between personnel when commercial services are rendered inoperable. Incorporating PTT into a disaster plan requires firms to analyze how critical staff interacts with one another in times of crisis. This should be the intent of any disaster plan and, with a knowledge of PTT technology, wireless communications integration can be straightforward, with a little effort. As the events of September 11th have taught us, anything can happen.

SiteSafe is located in Arlington, VA. We provide a variety of engineering, systems design, and FCC consulting services related to private wireless systems, including frequency recommendation services to utilities *(http://spectrum.utc.org)* unications providers *(http://www.amtasite.com)*. Sitesafe also provides RF safety screening and training services. *(http://www.sitesafe.com)*.

Perspective on High Availability and Fault Tolerant Networking

By

Michael Linett
President and CEO
Zerowait Corporation
Newark, DE
Prevention and Planning. The Inseparable Twins of High Availability

Every one wants to build a high availability network. Has anyone met an IT director who specifically sets out to build a low availability network? Of course not. Yet low availability networks exist. Included among them are networks with enough fault tolerance and redundancy to choke a T-1. How is this possible? Isn't fault tolerance synonymous with high availability? The short answer is no. In fact, high availability is actually a combination of fault tolerance (prevention) and disaster prevention (planning), rather than one or the other.

Pilots are taught to handle system emergencies in the air. It's a big help that all major instruments have a primary and secondary purpose. For instance, if the vacuum pump goes, affecting the gyros that tell the pilot his heading, he can still navigate using electric instruments and magnetic compass. That's fault tolerance, and most aircraft have a lot of it built in. On the other hand, as every single engine pilot knows, there are always going to be a few single points of failure in an airplane that can't be addressed. The engine is one of them! So what happens if the engine sputters to a halt and the plane is still three thousand feet up? Well, if the pilot has remembered his or her training, then he or she will have a couple of emergency landing areas already in mind and will, within seconds, be going through a well-practiced checklist for making that emergency landing. That's disaster prevention, or planning. Therefore, if the pilot has prepared himself or herself well, the odds are that that pilot will live to fly another day—and that equals high availability!

Coming back to the world of networking, fault tolerance and high availability, while often used interchangeably, are really two very different things. Fault tolerance is best thought of in terms of hardware resiliency and redundancy: Examples of this would be removing those single points of failure by doubling up routers, switches, and bandwidth providers; and using server farms and load balancers to provide intelligent fail over between them. That would be fault tolerance. High availability, on the other hand, is best defined as the ability to always get the data from its source to its destination. Consider the web server farm, for example. It is entirely possible for the physical unit to be up and running, returning pings or a variety of other health-checks, and yet still be unable to respond correctly to user requests. Is that data available? What does it take to make that data available? Rebooting might be necessary, or perhaps something even simpler. Fault tolerance is all very well, but providing high availability has to go beyond that into the realm of action. Being prepared to perform the action or series of actions to bring a system back on line, servicing customer data, is what high availability is all about.

High availability, then, is more closely aligned to a service level agreement with your end users. After all, they don't care if only one of your two routers is working. What they care about is getting their data. The prudent and careful IT manager will require a process of identifying the detail and requirements of his client base to provide the service level they require. The end result of this process will be a high-availability network that meets the needs of the organization and provides a disaster prevention plan instead of a disaster recovery scenario.

Similar to a flight plan, the high-availability networking plan needs to clearly identify the beginning and ending point of the project before the journey begins. In a flight you must always know your two end points to make sure that you have the range, weather, altitude and course to make the flight. In a networking situation, you also have the beginning network diagram and the current service level, including speeds and capacities of all of your equipment. If you have bottlenecks it is best to identify them early so you can build your HA plan around the obstacles. For example, in flying, the flight plan includes reserve fuel to make an alternate airport in case the destination is weathered in. In HA networking, you include a fail over site that will take over in case of an unplanned outage. Planning early will allow you to increase the reliability of your network without penalty to your clients.

So how do you go about creating a high-availability network? First you begin at the beginning, with a network diagram and a list of hot spots and bottlenecks. Then you devise networking strategies that target these issues, trying to anticipate as many areas of trouble you can imagine. One problem area may require duplicate routers for fault tolerance, another might require documenting the steps to take in case x occurs. The high-availability plan will develop over time; there are very few cookie cutter answers in this business. Flexibility is a requirement; so is vigilance. You really, really need to know what is going on in your network. Tools are available that will help you track metrics such as data traffic patterns, firmware revisions, and storage capacities.

During the design and implementation phases, and even later during normal day-to-day administration of the high availability network, monitoring of metrics such as the above will help you ensure continued levels of service. It's also a good idea to identify milestones and document whether you are on course as you pass each milestone—and take corrective action when you are not. Occasionally, you will have to readjust your plan to meet unexpected obstacles. But as long as you have a plan you can correct and improve as you go along. A constant scan of all of the variables will keep you on course. Avoid focusing on one area of your network as you may pass over a significant change in another area. At each stage in the process you must make certain that you have a period in which your systems are unchanged so that you can create a baseline from which to judge. We have all made the mistake of making several small changes and then not being able to go back and isolate a problem.

Once in place, your HA network would be like the portion of a flight plan where the pilot is in cruise mode and occasionally receiving new vectors for small course corrections. However, in flying as in networking, just when things are going well up pops a big storm cloud—someone wants to add a whole new functionality to your network—what do you do?

Actually, as you will discover, adaptation to new requirements is really quite simple when you have a high availability plan in place. For example, if management wants to increase capacity in storage or throughput, since you know the throughput and possible bottlenecks already all you have to do is highlight your possible routes of expansion.

Creating a high-availability network is a process that involves many calculations for performance, speed, capacity and growth. Success is dependent on having a clearly defined starting point and a clearly defined ending point. Each step along the route must take into account the performance envelope of your current system. There will be bad patches and problems along the way. But with the proper planning you will have a back up prepared for almost every contingency to provide the level of service your user groups require. Working with the twin aspects of high availability—fault tolerance and disaster prevention—you will able to provision you network to provide your organization with a smooth ride from where you are to where you are going.

CHAPTER 9

Emergency Decision Making

One aspect of disaster recovery that is particularly elusive and difficult for many disaster recovery coordinators to treat adequately in their plans is emergency management. Emergency management planning aims at the management of three projects that are intrinsic to disaster recovery: evacuation, recovery, and relocation or reentry.

An emergency management plan provides the skeleton of a disaster recovery capability implementation. It is the organizational and policy structure that will be referenced to determine whether and by whom the disaster recovery plan will be invoked and who will do what when. Development of the emergency management plan (see Figure 9–1) requires the disaster recovery coordinator to:

1. Define recovery teams and their missions.
2. Work with business and technology managers to staff the teams and to develop mechanisms for their notification and activation in an emergency.
3. Develop timelines and flowcharts identifying the sequence of and interrelationships between various disaster recovery tasks—in short, draft the disaster recovery plan document itself.

The third activity, developing procedural flowcharts, often poses the greatest problem to novice DR coordinators for a number of reasons. First, most coordinators have never directly experienced a company disaster. Many endeavor to compensate for this lack of direct experience through detailed description. They try to predict and chart every conceivable decision point and write procedures that spell out too rigidly what each recovery team member will do.

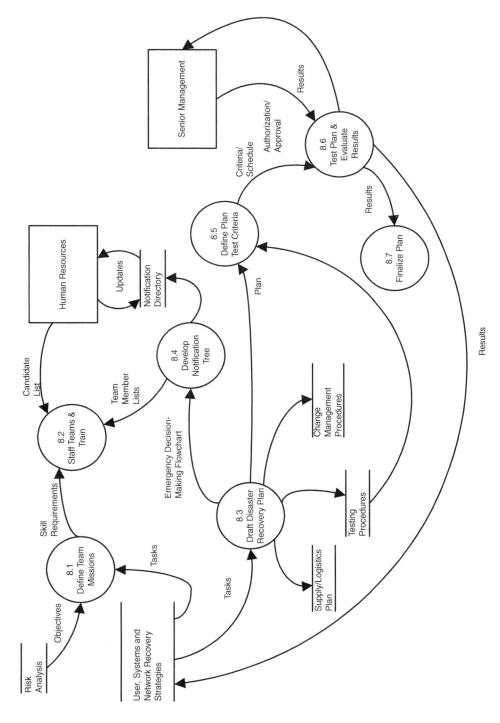

Figure 9–1 Developing an emergency management plan.

An overly detailed approach ignores the realities of plan implementation. In an actual crisis, flowcharts purporting to map crisis decision making on a step-by-step, thought-by-thought basis are often set to one side. This fact underscores the point that there is no script for the frantic, urgent, and imperfect world of disaster recovery.

In other cases, novice planners may seek to compensate for a lack of direct experience by understating emergency management requirements. The flowcharts they develop embrace a view of crisis management as a mere extension of normal management practices. Little thought is given to how the extraordinary impact of a disaster will affect managers as they perform their recovery duties.

Between these extremes of excess and defect, there is a workable medium: a plan that is sufficiently detailed to guide decision making without dictating it—a plan that provides, at a glance, a holistic appreciation of what is to be done and where efforts stand at any given point in the recovery process. Experience dictates that, in the absence of such a plan, the coordination of strategies for systems, network, and end user recovery can be an even more difficult task.

Without an emergency management plan that provides for top-down direction and coordination of recovery tasks, inefficiencies can result that will extend the length of downtime following a disruption of normal business processes. If the business is out of operation for too long, regardless of the integrity of plan components, the plan itself may be ineffective in supporting business recovery.

Thus, coordinators need to develop an emergency management plan that will formalize certain aspects of the management process and provide guidance for managing situations that cannot be anticipated prior to a disaster. Such a plan is less than a script for emergency management from which actors dare not stray, but it is also more than a collection of platitudes.

The following discussion aims to clarify emergency management planning by detailing its several dimensions and providing simplified examples of some of its typical components. Note that the flowcharts offered here are for illustration only. The decision-making processes developed by a DR coordinator will need to fit the specific strategies that have been developed for corporate business processes and their IT infrastructure supports.

As depicted in Figure 9–1, the activities comprising this effort include the development of test criteria and the performance of plan testing. A more detailed discussion of testing is reserved for a later chapter.

One final point deserves mention before proceeding with this discussion. Both practical and philosophical, it is simply this: Too much of the writing surrounding DR planning concerns itself with the plan document. DR planning projects often, and incorrectly, take as their primary objective the creation of a paper or electronic document. Among business people and IT professionals alike, the DR planning effort is often reduced to a simple objective of creating a paper volume that will pass muster with auditors and examiners.

While documentation is important and good organization is always a plus when addressing any complex subject, DR planning is less about building a paper document than creating a demonstrable capability for ensuring business continuity in the face of unplanned interruptions. Clearly, strategies need to be documented together with the options that were evaluated and the rationale for their selection, in order to satisfy auditors and others who are interested in the planning process. The emergency management plan is a particularly important component of the plan document because it provides a high-level roadmap for the implementation of the DR capability. However, the primary purpose of DR planning is ultimately the preparation of corporate personnel to respond rationally to the great irrationality of a disaster.

DESIGNATING TEAMS

One of the first steps in emergency management planning is to identify where personnel resources will be needed in order to implement the strategies that have been developed for business recovery. At this stage, the task is not to assign specific individuals to specific teams. Team assignments will be discussed in greater detail later this chapter. For now, the objective is to identify the roles and missions of teams themselves.

Teams should be created to support a critical recovery process—defined as a set of tasks for achieving a plan objective. With well-organized plans, an overview of recovery processes, organized as a time line or consolidated flowchart, should be the first item of information presented to the reader. The rationale for this is simple: Such a diagram provides a snapshot of the recovery process as a whole, which then provides links to the compilations of procedures associated with specific system, user, and network recovery strategies.

In a typical user-friendly plan document there is usually a section devoted to each of the following processes.

SECTION 1.   Emergency Action Processes—procedures for reacting to crises, ranging from fire suppression activation procedures to emergency evacuation procedures.

SECTION 2.   Notification Processes—procedures for notifying relevant managers in the event of a disaster. A contact list of home and emergency telephone numbers is typically provided. This section may also include processes for setting up an emergency operations center (EOC) that will subsequently be used to coordinate additional recovery activities.

SECTION 3.   Disaster Declaration Processes—instructions pertaining to the assessment of damage following a disaster, criteria for determining whether the situation is a disaster, and procedures for declaring a disaster and invoking the plan.

SECTION 4.   Systems Recovery Processes—procedures to be followed to restore critical and vital applications at emergency service levels within a specified timeframe in accordance with the systems recovery strategy defined in the plan. Separate procedures may be established for centralized and distributed systems-based application recovery.

SECTION 5. Network Recovery Processes—procedures to reinstate voice and data communications at emergency service levels within a specified timeframe in accordance with the network recovery strategy defined in the plan.

SECTION 6. User Recovery Processes—procedures for recovering critical and vital user functions within a specified timeframe in accordance with planned strategy.

SECTION 7. Salvage Operations Processes—procedures for salvaging facilities, records and hardware, often including the filing of insurance claims and the determination of the feasibility of reoccupying the disaster site.

SECTION 8. Relocation Processes—procedures for relocating emergency operations (system, network, and user) to the original or a new facility, and the restoration of normal service levels.

The above is a generic example. Plan sectioning may vary substantially from one company to the next. For example, a company may have a set of processes designed to bring Internet-based e-business operations back on line, or it may have a separate set of processes for activating an emergency operations center. In some cases, companies assign different names to the processes shown here or adopt recovery strategies other than those described here (for example, end-user recovery via work-at-home telecommuting rather than a new end-user hard site). The point of this illustration is to provide a stepping-off point for readers of this book who will be developing their own plans.

When viewed from the perspective above, one begins to see that the disaster recovery project actually consists of three distinct projects. The procedures in sections 1 to 3 pertain to an evacuation project; sections 4 to 7, to a business recovery or business resumption project; and section 8 to a relocation or reentry project. Teams are designated to fulfill the functional requirements of each project.

COMMON EVACUATION PROJECT FUNCTIONS AND TEAMS

What are the functional requirements of the evacuation project? Basically, there are three. First, the emergency must be met with an appropriate response. Responses range from use of an extinguisher to suppress a small fire, to performing last-minute backups and evacuating hardware in the hours before a hurricane, to evacuating personnel in a bomb threat.

Another function of the evacuation project involves the preliminary assessment of damage caused by the interruption event and the determination of whether disaster declaration criteria have been met. If DR planning has determined that 24 hours is the maximum length of time that the company can be without critical or vital business operations, this may serve as the primary criterion for declaring a disaster. If the critical business functions will likely be unavailable for more than 24 hours, it may be necessary to declare a disaster and activate the plan. However, to make this determination, event impact will need to be accurately assessed and realistic recovery timeframes estimated.

A third function in the evacuation project is to declare a disaster and invoke the plan. The plan may need to be activated in whole or in part, since a data center disaster may not affect user facilities, or a telecommunications switchroom fire may leave both key servers and user work areas intact.

Activating the disaster recovery plan also entails certain risks from a public relations standpoint. Al Czarnecki, APR, who helms a Canadian PR firm specializing in crisis communications, recommends that the items identified in Table 9–1 be part of any organization's crisis communications readiness checklist.

Table 9–1   Crisis Communications Checklist

These ten items should be in place PRIOR to a crisis situation. This is of great help in maintaining poise and being able to concentrate on your top priority, the crisis response plan.

Public relations policy and procedures	A statement of mandate, values, program, leadership.
Crisis communications action plan	Key people, roles, action sequences, scenarios.
"Big Picture" information piece on your organization	This could be your annual report.
"Window" information piece on every major program	Content and being up-to-date is most important. Can be kept as text files and printed on special masthead.
Reference files on potential crisis situations	Minutes, reports, clippings—indexed and portable.
Key person list	Work and home phone numbers, one-page job summary and one-page bio—board, senior management, senior person at every physical location—indexed and portable.
Designated spokesperson(s)	Establish default assignments prior to a crisis. Arrange for everyone to have some public speaking experience. These people and your public relations counsel should know each other.
Designated media coordination	This function should be established as credible and helpful with BOTH your staff and the media prior to a crisis. Trust is an outstanding asset in the midst of mayhem.
Media directory or detailed list	[Commercial Media Contact Database] or your own contact database. You should have a concise list of the major media and your public relations counsel at home with your key spokespeople.
Media contact log	You can have a dozen or more newspapers and radio and television stations on the go at one time. Keep a separate tracking sheet for every journalist/story. Know who contacted you, when, about what, how to contact them, what their deadline is, what you promised, who you've delegated to, when they're due to get back to you, whether you need to follow up.

Source: Al Czarnecki Communications, Toronto, Ontario, Canada. http://www.alczarnecki.com.

Some companies designate "crisis communications center activation"—establishing a central point for handling communications with the media and other interested parties—as a separate function of the evacuation project. Experience has shown that implementing an effective vehicle for crisis communications as early as possible in a disaster can make the difference between a hostile or a supportive response from corporate shareholders, business partners, and customers.

As a rule, however, a crisis communications center should be established away from a company's emergency operations center (EOC), which is often used to control actual recovery activities, and from other recovery sites. EOCs, hot sites, end-user recovery centers, and the like are not appropriate venues for the media—particularly in the early stages of recovery. Their operations are sensitive to disruption. Plus, observation of recovery efforts by untrained media personnel may result in a misapprehension of the progress of the recovery effort. The object is to avoid the communication of erroneous information to those who might have an interest in the company.

This above list of functions associated with evacuation is not exhaustive and there may be others that are specific to a given company. However, to fulfill the three basic requirements for evacuation, the following teams may be developed.

Emergency Action Teams

Sudden emergencies rarely lend themselves to team efforts. However, in some companies, there are designated "fire wardens" and "bucket crews" whose function is to deal with fires. Emergency action teams are trained in their functions and drill regularly. They may handle the evacuation of personnel or provide informational support to local fire fighting officials, explaining security systems or structural features of the facility.

In most cases, the emergency response function is provided by individuals rather than teams. A night operator may report a fire, then evacuate himself or herself from the danger area. A late-working employee, confronting a water leakage alarm, might perform emergency program shutdowns, power down electrical equipment, and notify management. Detection of a computer virus might originate in an end user work area, with the desktop operator reporting the situation per a standard operating procedure to a department head or help desk.

These individual responses can be expected only if reaction procedures are developed and employees are trained to perform them.

The point is that response may be a function that does not require a team (except in the sense that every employee is a member of the team). Effective response may be provided by an individual, or it may be automatic, as with a fire suppression system. Indeed, in some cases, there may be no immediate action or response available for a sudden emergency.

Besides sudden emergencies, companies are also subject to phased disasters. Phased disasters are disaster potentials that are known well enough in advance to allow for the implementation of planned response procedures.

One example of a phased disaster scenario, familiar to businesses near the coastlines of North America, is the hurricane or typhoon. Early warnings of a potential storm landfall (or associated tidal surges, tornadoes, etc.) may be issued well in advance of an actual disaster. Procedures can be developed as part of the disaster recovery plan to make the best use of this advance warning.

Reaction to a phased-disaster scenario may include such tasks as the evacuation of backup hardware and supplies, last-minute data backup, notification of hot site and off-site storage vendors, and advance notification of personnel about recovery site relocation. Emergency action teams can be formed to provide these functions, or the functions can be performed at the direction of company managers without the formal designation of teams.

Damage Assessment Team

The second function of the evacuation project is to estimate the extent of damage following the disaster. The team providing this function should be comprised of individuals who are qualified to assess damage and estimate the time required to recover operations at the affected site. Their reports will likely trigger the decision to activate the recovery plan.

This team should include persons who are skilled in the use of testing equipment, knowledgeable about systems and networks, and trained in applicable safety regulations and procedures. The team's product is a report identifying possible causes of the disaster and, more importantly, its impact in damage and predictable downtime.

Emergency Management Team

One team common to nearly all disaster recovery plans is an emergency management team. This is the group that will coordinate the activities of all other recovery teams and that will provide a key decision-making role. In the context of the evacuation project, the emergency management team receives the report of the damage assessment team and makes the decision to activate the plan, in part or in toto.

Other functions of the emergency management team in the evacuation project may include arranging the finance of the recovery, documenting losses and damages for insurance purposes, handling health and legal matters evolving from the disaster, and activating a crisis communications mechanism tasked with handling public relations and media inquiries.

If system recovery or end-user recovery facilities have not been defined in the plan, the emergency management team may also need to undertake the mission of finding facilities on the fly from which to operate. An additional set of teams would then need to work in a coordinated way to ensure that the sites are equipped and ready for work within the shortest possible amount of time.

In short, the roles of the emergency management team need to be defined in the plan. In some cases, the plan must go so far as to assign specific functions to specific members of the team.

COMMON RECOVERY PROJECT FUNCTIONS AND TEAMS

The functions of the evacuation project define the missions, skill requirements, authority requirements, and activities of the teams that will be active in performing project tasks. The same is true of the recovery project whose basic functions may include the following:

- Retrieving critical and vital data from off-site storage. Off-site backups may have to be obtained from off-site storage, if the company has contracted for this service, and shipped to the systems, network, and user recovery facilities.
- Installing and testing host operating systems software and environmental configurations at the systems recovery site (hot site, cold site, service bureau, etc.). Depending on the recovery strategy that has been developed, a number of tasks will have to be performed in order to recover critical system operations. Restoration of host environments—including their security and management components—is usually a component of any strategy. This must be done before applications can be recovered.
- Application restoration and testing. This must be undertaken to ensure that applications required by mission-critical business processes are available to end users once network connections are reestablished. Performance service levels should be baselined and monitored on an ongoing basis once applications begin to be used in emergency mode.
- Identifying, purchasing, and installing hardware at the system recovery site. If a system recovery option has been selected that does not provide access to installed hardware, another recovery function may be to locate a supply of equipment, lease or purchase that supply, arrange its delivery to the systems recovery site, and install it.
- Operating from the system recovery site. System operations tasks, including host administration, job management and accounting, data transfers, storage management, help desk operations, and other system tasks need to be provided on an ongoing basis once systems, networks, and end users are reconnected. The objective of system recovery, after all, is not simply to restore systems, but to operate them over the duration of the disaster to support critical business processes.
- Rerouting network communications traffic. Network recovery is another typical function of a disaster recovery plan. Rerouting voice and data communications links to the user recovery site and system recovery site may be more or less complicated depending on the strategies selected. As with sys-

tems recovery, additional functions may include the acquisition and installation of new hardware as well as communications device programming and software installation. Security and quality of service (QOS) must also be implemented and baselined, then monitored throughout the recovery period.

- Reestablishing network links to external entities. Related to the rerouting function above is the reestablishment of data communications between the user recovery site and system recovery site and external entities such as branch offices, suppliers, and others. This function should be provided as a strategy within the recovery plan and may include the lease or purchase of communications devices and public or private network services.

- Transporting users to recovery facility. Depending on the user recovery strategy that has been developed, it may be necessary to provide transportation and housing for employees at the user recovery facility. If prior arrangements have not been made for a user facility, a preliminary function may be to locate a suitable workplace and equip it with the basic furniture, communications capabilities, workstations, and so on required. Another preliminary step may be to notify all employees of the new work location, transportation schedules, and emergency accommodations that will be provided.

- Reconstructing databases. If data is lost in the disaster, it may be necessary to restore or reconstruct production databases prior to application use. Typically, this is done by an end user team using available documents. In addition to company personnel, outside contractors may be brought in to aid in the data entry effort. The training and oversight of these personnel may also be viewed as a recovery function.

- Sourcing supplies. Yet another function of the recovery project involves the requisition, delivery, and distribution of office supplies and other items, such as computer paper and printed forms, needed to perform useful work. Vendors must be contacted, logistics coordinated, costs and inventory monitored, reorder points established, and so on.

- Coordinating systems use and employee work schedules. To utilize minimum system configurations efficiently, it may be necessary to schedule system use rather tightly. The scheduling of user input, processing, and output periods may be necessary, and implementing a regimen of shift work is not uncommon.

It is self-evident that sustaining operations under emergency operating conditions requires considerable supervisory skill. Moreover, preventing and resolving technical and operational problems before they reach disastrous proportions are vital for business recovery.

The above list, which is partial at best, suggests the multiplicity of functions that may be undertaken during the recovery project. In addition, the emergency management team has a continuing role to play—coordinating team efforts, financing the recovery project, and maintaining a focal point for business planning and public information. However, to provide the functions required for the recovery of critical operations the following teams may also be created.

Off-site Storage Team

This team obtains, packages, and ships media and records required for recovery to the end-user and system recovery facilities. It may also have an ongoing role of establishing and overseeing an off-site storage schedule for information created during operations at the recovery sites. The off-site storage team may also assist in records salvage and storage efforts as described below.

Software Team

Some companies designate a special team whose mission is to restore host systems, load and test operating system software, and monitor and resolve system-level problems when they arise.

Applications Team

The applications team, together with the software team and emergency operations team (see following section), travels to the system (and end-user) recovery site and restores applications programs on backup host systems. The complexities in restoring n-tier client/server and consolidated mainframe applications should be reduced by advanced testing of new configurations. As the recovery progresses, this team may have the responsibility for monitoring application performance, security, and integrity.

Emergency Operations Team

The emergency operations team may consist of shift operators and a shift supervisor who will reside at the systems recovery site and manage system operations during the entirety of the disaster and recovery projects. It may also be called upon to coordinate hardware installation if a hot site or other equipment-ready facility has not been designated as the recovery center.

Network Recovery Team

This team is responsible for rerouting wide area voice and data communications traffic and reestablishing host network control and access at the system and end-user recovery sites. This team provides ongoing support for data communications and oversees security and communications integrity as well as network performance and quality of service.

Communications Team

This team travels to the user-recovery site where it works in conjunction with the remote network recovery team to establish a user/system internetwork. The communications team may also be responsible for soliciting and installing communications hardware at the user recovery site and working with LEC COs, internet service providers (ISPs), and carriers or value-added network providers to ensure last-mile services and remote access. The team may also have responsibility for reestablishing local area network (LAN) services within the user recovery facility itself.

Transportation Team

This team, which may also serve as a facilities team to locate a user recovery site if one has not been predetermined, is responsible for coordinating the transport of company employees to a distant user recovery site. Transportation may also assist in contacting employees to inform them of new work locations and schedules and arranging employee lodgings.

User Hardware Team

In addition to locating and coordinating the delivery and installation of user workstations, printers, photocopiers, and other necessary equipment, this team may also support the communications team, and ultimately the hardware salvage team in their functions.

Data Preparation and Records Team

This team updates the applications database, using workstations installed at the user recovery site or at some vendor facility. The team may oversee contract operators and support records salvage teams in acquiring primary documents and other input information sources.

Administrative Support

This team may provide clerical support to the other teams and serve as a message center for the user recovery site. Administrative support personnel may also be tasked with rerouting ground mail and overnight delivery services to new work locations. Accounting and payroll functions as well as ongoing facility management issues may also be controlled by this team.

Supplies Team

The supplies team supports the efforts of the user hardware team and coordinates logistics for an ongoing supply of necessary office and computer supplies.

Some of the teams identified above may, in actuality, perform functions that can be handled by one person. Again, the complexity of the disaster recovery plan for a specific business will determine whether functions require a team, or a single properly trained individual. Conversely, coordinators may find that additional teams are needed or that some of the listed teams need to be combined into a larger conglomerate. Business recovery needs will dictate these adjustments.

Teams are not static entities and they may dissolve after performing their function. Teams may also change and their members may be shifted to other responsibilities as the recovery project gives way to the relocation or reentry project.

RELOCATION AND REENTRY PROJECT FUNCTIONS

Relocation or reentry refers to the two options that may confront a business following a disaster. If the original facility is salvageable, it may be possible to reenter it once cleanup and refit activities are completed. If the facilities are uninhabitable, or prohibitively expensive to reconstruct, the business may choose to relocate to new quarters. In either case, there is usually an interest in salvaging whatever corporate assets can be salvaged, especially when expensive hardware, critical documents not off-site, and other company assets are involved.

Functions commonly associated with the relocation or reentry project include:

- *Facility and hardware salvage.* This function of the relocation and reentry project is to make a more detailed assessment of the damage to facilities and equipment than was performed immediately after the interruption event. The purpose of this assessment is twofold. First, it will provide the emergency management team with the information it requires to determine whether planning should be directed toward reconstruction or relocation; second, it will provide a basis for certain insurance claims that may provide an important funding component for recovery activities.

    If salvage is determined to be economically desirable, salvage operations may be undertaken concurrently with recovery project activities. As teams complete recovery tasks, they may be reassigned to aid in salvage operations.

    If facilities are not salvageable, teams may be directed to the task of identifying comparable facilities and preparing them for company occupancy.
- *Records salvage.* Important paper records and documents, damaged by smoke and water, require immediate attention if they are to be salvaged. They need to be cleaned of visible debris, logged and packed, and then moved to a cold storage environment to forestall loss to fungi and mold. Following pack-out and cold storage, they may be recovered through a vacuum freeze-drying process available through records reclamation vendors. Excellent publications are available from federal and private sources describing all facets of this process that can produce amazing results. More discussion follows in this topic later in this chapter.
- *Relocation.* Many of the same activities that were involved in the recovery of systems, networks, and users immediately following a disaster may be repeated for the purposes of relocating systems, communications traffic, and user operations to the new or restored business facility.

- *Transition to normal service levels.* The final function of disaster recovery is to provide a smooth transition from emergency service levels to normal service levels. Although important to full recovery, this function is not generally documented in detail within a disaster recovery plan. It is typically a function of planning undertaken following successful recovery and while salvage or site preparation activities are underway.

To provide these functions, many of the teams previously defined are reassigned to relocation or reentry project duties. However, there are a few specially trained teams, such as a facilities salvage team, hardware salvage team, and records salvage team, that may perform critical tasks depending on the nature and impact of the disaster and the consequent decisions reached by the emergency management team.

STAFFING TEAMS

Once teams are defined by the disaster recovery coordinator, it is important that their tasks be clearly documented in written procedures. If teams are organized by recovery functions, they need to understand in detail only those procedures that pertain to their functions. Thus, they will be trained to perform only the procedures in one section of the well-written plan.

However, someone in the team, such as a team leader, must know how the team's work affects and is affected by other teams. A team leader may also be given the responsibility of reporting on the progress of tasks that his or her team has been assigned and maintaining records of costs associated with team activities.

Staffing teams, then, requires the identification of personnel who have the prerequisite skills and knowledge to perform the technical tasks that are assigned them. Moreover, it is vital to select one person—a team leader (and an alternate)—who has the supervisory and communications skills required to manage team activities effectively.

Staffing efficient teams is a challenge for the disaster recovery coordinator. The coordinator can develop a fairly comprehensive list of skills and knowledge needed for each team. However, the fact that team members possess the listed requirements may offer little indication of how the team will perform in an emergency. The skills and knowledge possessed by a team member cannot guarantee that the person will remain calm in an emergency, think creatively, or handle stress. In the end, team selection may come down to judgment calls rendered with the support of business unit/departmental managers and human resources personnel.

The experience of several companies that have recovered from disasters offers little guidance about the best method of selecting team members and team leaders. For this reason, the following points should be considered in establishing evaluative criteria rather than blueprints for selecting individuals.

Worker Performance

An employee's performance record may not be the best criterion on which to judge suitability for team membership or leadership. That the employee is not punctual, or, conversely, that he or she always comes to work early and stays late may be meaningless in the context of recovery. The same is true of a worker's motivation and attitude. Disasters can reveal surprises about personal mettle.

However, some important dimensions to work performance should not be ignored. A worker who requires a considerable amount of structure and supervision is probably not the best candidate for a leadership position where some creativity and self-direction are desirable. Also, a worker who is technically astute, but who cannot communicate ideas, is probably a poor choice for leadership in a functional area requiring these characteristics. Similarly, the optimal team leader is seldom an employee who has great difficulty in reaching decisions or reasoning to conclusion in normal operational environments.

The difference between the ideal team leader and the marginal candidate is the difference between a troubleshooter and a technician. The troubleshooter has added analytical thinking to technical skills. Teams need both technicians and troubleshooters, but the troubleshooter is the person who should lead the team.

Worker Tenure

Tenure is another factor that may be considered in staffing teams. Tenured workers may understand the business better than novices. They may have a greater stake in business survival (higher salary, well-developed pension, etc.). They may also command greater respect from fellow, less-senior employees.

On the other hand, tenured workers may lack the exposure to alternatives that would be the forte of a worker who may be new to the company, but not the workplace generally.

Since some team leaders will necessarily be privy to security information (passwords, filenames, etc.), tenure may also be a consideration in this regard. While there is no correlation between tenure and trustworthiness, a more senior employee is often perceived as a better security risk than a new hire.

Worker Marital Status

Despite studies performed by the Defense Department, there is little data to establish that a married worker will handle responsibilities in an emergency any better or worse than an unmarried one. However, many coordinators still assert that married persons are less reliable because of a distraction factor. In the event of a regional disaster, so the argument goes, the married employee is going to be more worried about the well-being of his/her family than about the company. This distraction could affect performance.

This argument has little merit as even unmarried persons can have parents, siblings, or significant others to distract them. In acknowledgment of this fact, some companies have gone so far as to have their facilities approved for use as evacuation shelters. In the event of a regional cataclysm such as a hurricane or earthquake, employees and their families and friends are urged to utilize the shelter. Thus, recovery team personnel will know that their relatives and friends (though not necessarily their property) are safe as they proceed in their recovery tasks.

Residence of Recovery Personnel

One factor that may be important in the consideration of candidates for recovery teams is the location of their homes in relation to the company offices. Employees who must travel 2 hours (in good traffic) to reach the workplace may be less suitable for critical disaster recovery roles than those who reside in nearer proximity to the company.

Even when travel time is not an issue, there may be compelling reasons to select employees who are located in the general vicinity of the facility. In some disaster scenarios, including natural disasters and civil disturbances, there may be restrictions imposed on movement into and out of the affected region or area. The author's personal experience provides one example, which has been repeated many times in many locations since.

Following the passage of Hurricane Elena in September 1985, along the shores of southwestern Florida, the police cordoned off Pinellas County. Until damage could be assessed, no one from neighboring Hillsborough County was allowed in or out of Pinellas County. Following cessation of disaster conditions, many hours passed during which only those who could prove residence in the county to which they wished to travel were allowed into that county. Thus, employees who resided in one county were not permitted to travel to their workplace in the neighboring country for a protracted period of time. Had significant storm damage been sustained by companies in the Tampa Bay area, it is doubtful that many could have activated their disaster recovery plans very effectively.[1]

The above considerations illustrate that there is a lack of hard, experiential data available to disaster recovery coordinators to guide them in team staffing. Coordinators may find themselves completely dependent upon the judgment of the business unit/departmental managers whose aegis extends over the teams and functions in question. Since there are no objective grounds for challenging department management decisions, the only hedge that the coordinator may have against seemingly poor choices is a procedural one.

Coordinators should strive to portray the role of team leader or member as nonglamorous, even clerical. This may be accomplished by requiring team leaders to be responsible for maintaining the integrity of "their" section of the disaster recovery plan according to a plan maintenance schedule. It should also be made clear that plan testing may interfere with off-work activities of those who are designated to play recovery roles. For some, the added responsibility and interference in their personal lives will dissuade them from lobbying for the position of team leader.

If a seemingly inappropriate selection of team leader is made, regardless of the above procedural checks, another hedge against incompetence is to train an alternate person to lead the team if the primary candidate is unavailable. The selection of an alternate may be up to the coordinator if the department manager is appeased by his or her selection of the primary team leader. Where this is not the case, and the coordinator's confidence in both primary and alternate team leaders is low, all team members may need to be cross-trained in recovery team operation and management.

This is not intended to imply that business managers will always make bad choices about team leaders and members. In most cases, not only will the managers identify appropriate candidates, but their insights will be of considerable value to the coordinator, who is not in a position to evaluate the personal qualifications of each and every company employee. As a control against team incompetence, teams can be trained and tested in detailed procedures until the procedures become routine.

DEVELOPING A NOTIFICATION DIRECTORY

Once recovery teams have been staffed, the coordinator will have most of the information needed to develop a notification directory of persons to be notified in the event of a disaster. Besides team members and company employees, phone lists may include the numbers for representatives of equipment and software vendors, contacts within companies that have been designated to provide supplies and equipment, contact persons at recovery facilities (including hot-site representatives, representatives of predefined network communications rerouting services, etc.), and insurance company agents.

Primary and emergency telephone numbers for each critical contact person should be compiled and kept in the back matter of the disaster recovery plan. In the case of company employees who will be called on to staff the user recovery facility (other than teams), the human resources or personnel department is often a good resource for compiling a telephone directory and keeping it up-to-date and off-site.

In conjunction with the directory, many disaster recovery planners develop a notification schema or "tree" to indicate who will be responsible for contacting whom. Sometimes the responsibility for contacting team members is vested in the team leader (and alternate). The team leader or his or her designee may also have responsibility for notifying vendor representatives whose roles relate directly to the team's area of recovery responsibility.

Other branches of the notification tree may provide for the notification of company personnel by a team designated to provide this function. Employees will need to know where and when to report for work once a user recovery facility has been prepared and systems and networks have been restored.

Notification trees may also indicate triggers, or chronological points, at which a branch of the notification tree is to be activated and contacts on the branch notified of some impending activity or event. A trigger in a notification tree may be the declaration of a "voluntary evacuation order" in a hurricane scenario. Such orders are usually issued one to three hours in advance of a mandatory evacuation order and may be used as a trigger not only for notification trees, but also for activation of other plan components (emergency system and data backups, safe power down of hardware, evacuation of redundant hardware, etc.).

The notification tree, with its carefully defined branches and triggers, is one of several tools that may help emergency managers make order out of chaos following a disaster. Communication is essential for command and control in a disaster situation. Communication of impending disaster conditions can help reduce the impact of the disaster when it occurs, and communication about the extent of damage can be used to determine whether the disaster recovery plan must be invoked and whether to activate it in whole or in part. Finally, communication between recovery teams and emergency managers—regarding the progress of recovery activity, new strategies and directions, decisions and plans, and so on—will determine how effectively business resumption may be realized. Table 9–2 summarizes command, control, and communications factors as they relate to the management of the three projects within disaster recovery: evacuation, recovery, and relocation or reentry.

Table 9–2 Command, Control, and Communications in Emergency Management

Phase I Evacuation	Phase II Recovery	Phase III Relocation/Reentry
Command	*Command*	*Command*
Emergency Response: On-site personnel react to situation in accorance with emergency action procedures. Emergency Management Team assesses impact, invokes plan. Phased Emergency Response Emergency Management Team decides when to take action. Emergency Management Team assesses disaster impact; invokes plan.	Command of Recovery Phase activities vested in Emergency Management Team supported by subordinate recovery team leaders.	Relocation to the evacuated or new permanent operating site will require management oversight and coordination; lines of reporting established by the disaster recovery plan will continue until systems and networks are stabilized and normal service levels are reestablished.

(*continued*)

Table 9–2 Command, Control, and Communications in Emergency Management (continued)

Phase I Evacuation	Phase II Recovery	Phase III Relocation/Reentry
Control **Emergency Response:** Minimal control over employee reaction to crisis; routine drills in emergency action procedures will help to ensure adherence to procedures. **Phased Emergency Response:** Emergency Management Team exercises direct control over last-minute preparations and evacuation of personnel, equipment, and supplies. Management controls disaster declaration. *Communication* **Emergency Response:** Initial communications conditions uncertain; possible difficulties in locating authorized Emergency Management Team member; possible difficulties in accessing site to perform evaluation; potential for miscommunication of damage assessment if Emergency Management Team available for site inspection. Disaster definition and inspection criteria may aid in prevention of unwarranted disaster declarations. **Phased Emergency Response:** Generally favorable communications conditions may exist at outset of disaster. However, damage assessment may be delayed. Evaluation of damage and communication of situation reports enhanced if Emergency Management Team is present. Communications with media regarding details of disaster controlled through Crisis Communications function.	*Control* Control of Recovery achieved through management of teams performing tested procedures. Service level monitoring will be used to aid the Emergency Management Team in managing emergency operations. *Communication* Voice and data network restoration is a priority; until networks are restored communication between Emergency Management Team and other operational teams may be impaired. Recovery activities are thus conducted according to tested procedures and accomplished within agreed-upon timeframes. Following network recovery, communications will be normalized, beginning channels for Emergency Management Team reporting. Communication with external entities and the media controlled by Crisis Communications functionaries.	*Control* Control of relocation/reentry activities accomplished through management channels established by the disaster recovery plan; the Emergency Management Team will control the acquisition and preparation of the salvaged/new facility, direct facility preparation teams, and oversee the relocation of systems and networks; the transition from emergency to normal service levels will be controlled in accordance with a management plan. *Communication* Communication of management plans for preparation and relocation to the salvaged or new operating site are likely to occur within a stabilized communica-. ---tions environment Communictions with external entities and the media controlled by Crisis Communications functionaries.

CREATING THE EMERGENCY MANAGEMENT FLOWCHART

As stated at the outset, most disaster recovery plans contain an emergency management flowchart that graphically depicts the sequence in which recovery tasks will be undertaken. This flowchart can be of substantial value in helping disaster recovery teams and emergency managers understand the disaster recovery plan as a whole.

The following sample flowcharts are segments of the detailed master flowchart, which can be downloaded from the companion website for this book at http://www.drplanning.org. To enhance their usefulness to teams, flowchart segments, such as these, may be placed at the front of the sections of the plan to which they pertain.

The diagrams provided here may be less detailed than those that would be developed for an actual recovery plan, but the coordinator should strive in every case to keep the charts he or she develops clear and straightforward. If possible, the coordinator should relate chart symbols to specific plan procedures using a numbering scheme common to both.

EMERGENCY RESPONSE

Figures 9–2 and 9–3 are simplified examples of decision-making flowcharts that may be placed at the front of a plan section treating emergency response.

Figure 9–2 deals with a sudden crisis in which on-site employees may be called upon to take immediate action procedures as outlined in the plan. Since personnel may not have the luxury of time (or presence of mind) to refer to the manual and perform a written procedure, they should be thoroughly trained and drilled in procedures such as interpreting alarms, powering down equipment, initiating security or safety systems, and, of course, evacuating the facility quickly and safely. While these procedures will probably be conducted without reference to a plan document, it is a good idea to document them in a section of the plan both for use as a training aid and as evidence to the auditors that response procedures have been developed and tested.

Following emergency actions, the flowchart indicates that the emergency management team is to be notified. Again, the plan document may not be accessible to the evacuated worker, but all personnel should be provided with contact numbers, possibly on a wallet-sized card, that can be referenced in an emergency. The existence of the card and the telephone numbers listed on it should be documented in the written plan as well.

The next activity denoted on the chart calls for an assessment of the damage caused by the disaster and an estimate of anticipated downtime or inaccessibility to business-critical applications or their system/network infrastructure. If the facility has to be evacuated, it may not be possible to reenter immediately to assess damage. However, even the "best guess" of fire officials or other emergency officials may be sufficient to determine whether a prolonged business interruption is probable.

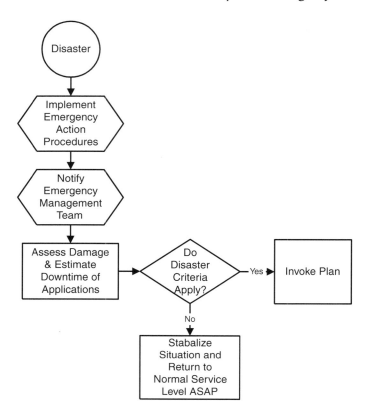

Figure 9–2   Decision-making flowchart (emergency response).

Thus, the next symbol indicates that a decision needs to be made whether to activate the disaster recovery plan. If disaster recovery criteria, which should be spelled out in the plan document but are usually common sense considerations (i.e., will downtime exceed 24 hours?), are met, a decision is made to invoke the plan.

If the event does not meet disaster criteria, the situation will be stabilized as soon as possible and operations returned to normal service levels. For example, if the crisis is a power blackout, but power company representatives assure the company emergency management team that power will be restored within eight hours, and this timeframe is acceptable, the emergency management team may decide to ride out the situation and work to restore operations to normal as soon as power is restored.

Figure 9–3 portrays a different type of emergency response: response to a phased emergency. In a phased disaster scenario, the company has advance notification of an imminent crisis. The plan document may contain procedures for bracing for such an event—a hurricane, a labor strike, or even a possible civil dis-

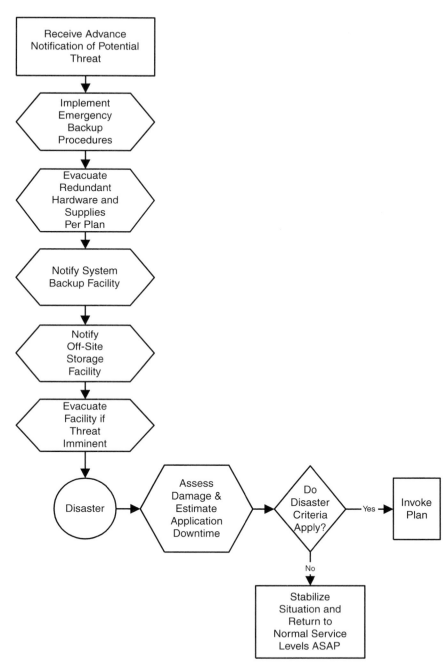

Figure 9–3   Decision-making flowchart (phased disaster scenario).

turbance. These emergency procedures may be activated by a "trigger" event such as a warning issued by the National Hurricane Center in Miami, FL, or the Storm Prediction Center in Norman, OK, or on the basis of reports from local TV or radio, police bulletins, or civil voluntary evacuation orders.

Once triggered, planned procedures may include performing last-minute system backups to reduce the amount of "catch up" work that will be required later to restore databases to a current form. Redundant hardware may also be deactivated and evacuated to a designated safe location. The system recovery facility may be placed on alert. Off-site storage facilities may be contacted and teams sent to retrieve stored backups and prepare them for transportation to recovery destinations. Finally, personnel will be evacuated if the threat exceeds safe levels.

If the disaster then occurs, these prophylactic measures should speed the recovery of the company. However, before a disaster is declared, damage will need to be assessed, disaster criteria will need to be applied, and a decision will need to be reached as to whether the plan should be invoked.

Given the variety of possible disasters that can confront a company, the assumption that one or two simplified decision-making flowcharts can cover every contingency is foolish. Whether the disaster is phased or sudden, the decision to invoke the plan rests on human judgment and is subject to all of its foibles. For example, in recent history, a major metals distributor in the Chicago area sustained more than $10 million in hardware and facility damage (and an incalculable amount in lost revenue) due to flooding. The MIS director reported that he held off on declaring a disaster in the early hours of a torrential downpour, expecting the rain to stop and the water level to fall. Twelve hours (and 10 inches of rain) later the plan was finally invoked. Systems went off-line on Friday and were not restored at a hot site until the following Monday. The company's extensive data communications network was out until Tuesday. Despite his fully tested disaster recovery plan, the director conceded, critical on-line order processing and inventory systems were out of commission for a protracted period—because the plan had not been invoked at the first sign of trouble. On the other hand, added the director proudly, without the plan—although implemented late—the company would never have survived.[2]

The story, one of many with a common theme that have taken place in the last decade, illustrates one of the major flaws with the expectation that emergency management flowcharts will be implemented without delay or modification in an actual disaster. It doesn't fit the facts. However, these charts do provide the means—for testing purposes at least—to "black box" the disaster and superimpose rationality upon a complex, multifaceted, and irrational phenomenon.

SITUATION ASSESSMENT

Once the initial response to a disaster has been made, Figure 9–4 begins the project of recovery from the disaster.

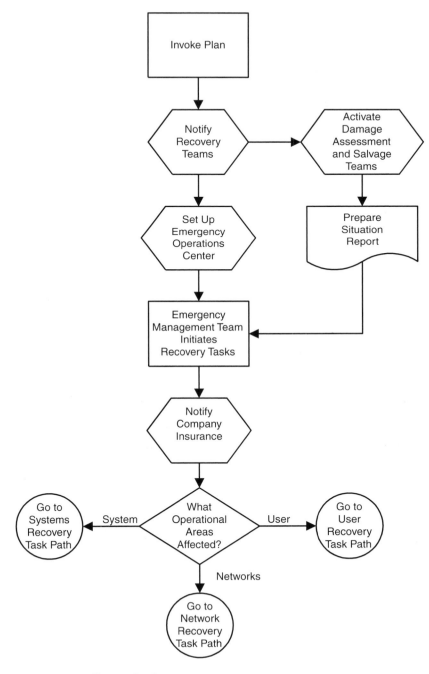

Figure 9–4 Situation assessment and response.

Once the plan is invoked, a number of plan components come into play automatically. As seen in Figure 9–4, recovery teams are notified by the emergency management team. Two teams—responsible for damage assessment and salvage—go directly to the disaster site, if this is possible, to make a more comprehensive evaluation of the situation. Meanwhile, an Emergency operations center (EOC) is set up (see below for more information) for use by the emergency management team throughout the duration of the recovery project. The emergency management team—often headed by a senior corporate officer—reviews reports of the damage assessment and salvage teams, determines which parts of the disaster recovery plan must be implemented. If the data center has been rendered unusable, but user work areas and the communications are intact, the decision may be made to implement only the systems recovery section of the plan. If user work areas are untenable, but data centers and networks are intact, user recovery plans are activated. Plan and team activation are contingent upon the nature and scope of the emergency.

It should be noted that damage assessment and salvage teams may have some critical tasks to perform. They may tour the facility with electrical contractors and construction vendors to obtain cost and time estimates for repair work. If damage has been done to user areas, there may still be working hardware that can be salvaged, tested, and relocated to the user recovery site. They may also obtain eyewitness accounts from persons who were in or near the facility when the disaster occurred. Finally, an insurance claims adjuster may also need to be part of the damage assessment team in order to facilitate the claims adjustment process.

The disaster recovery plan should indicate, generally, what tasks are to be performed by the recovery teams at the disaster site. Videotape or photographic records may need to be made. If eyewitness accounts are to be gathered, the plan may provide a standard form, possibly developed with the assistance of an attorney, for gathering this information. In addition, hardware testing routines may be summarized in the plan, although it would be wise to have someone on the salvage team who is thoroughly conversant with the procedures for testing hardware. The plan should also contain safety guidelines to instruct teams in avoiding personal risks.

EMERGENCY OPERATIONS CENTER ACTIVATION

Based on the best information available, the emergency management team decides to activate the disaster recovery plan may be activated in whole or in part. As suggested above, many plans call for the gathering of management personnel at an emergency operations center (EOC), a facility from which they will operate to receive updates and status reports and provide ongoing command, control, and communications functions throughout the emergency operations period.

EOCs are sometimes construed as the equivalent of a NASA command center, the stuff of motion pictures, consisting of a hardened site or bunker equipped with the latest communications and computer technologies used to monitor every aspect of an event from mass media descriptions to stock market ticker tapes to the display screens of network and system monitoring applications. While certain organizations, such as government emergency management organizations, may construct such facilities to provide management capabilities in a disaster, most do not. A number of alternatives exist, including:

- *Facilities Retasked as EOCs.* Some companies select a facility used for other purposes during an normal operations to serve as an EOC in an emergency. They place communications and computer devices in storage at the site that are accessed when needed for an actual recovery or for plan testing. This strategy has the obvious advantages of reduced facilities cost, but may present other problems, including the disruption of normal operations and/or the displacement of end users whenever plan tests need to be conducted. Security issues may also arise if publicly accessible facilities are designated for use as EOCs. Such sites are also of questionable utility in the event that they cannot be accessed by team members in an emergency because of regional disaster impact (roads destroyed, etc.) or to police cordons.
- *Hot-site-based EOCs.* Some vendors of commercial systems recovery facilities are more than happy to provide workspace for corporate executives and emergency management teams for the purpose of managing disaster recovery plan implementations. These sites may be part of the hot site contract and provide an appropriate location for work if management is comfortable with managing the disaster from a remote location (hot sites that are in close geographical proximity to normal work locations are usually regarded as poor choices in systems recovery planning). Should such an EOC option be selected, coordinators need to provide for the relocation of management and emergency operations team members to the remote facility.
- *Mobile EOCs.* An alternative to the facility retasking and hot site-based options is the Mobile EOC—an EOC facility staged on a trailer or other mobile vehicle that can be positioned wherever it is needed. Lynch Diversified Vehicles, self-styled as "the nation's premiere supplier of mobile command/communications vehicles," is one of several vendors offering "special service vehicles" that can be customized to meet the budget and features requirements of a customer (see Figure 9–5). These vehicles have come into common use by civil emergency management organizations including police, fire, and hazard materials management as a means to place command, control, and communications functions at or near the location where they are necessary. A vehicle-based approach has the merits of flexible deployment and nondisruptive testing. It may also serve the needs of an organization whose management prefers to remain around the disaster site during recovery. However, this option can also be expensive and may have limited utility in the event that transportation is constrained by disaster impact or local civil emergency management activity.

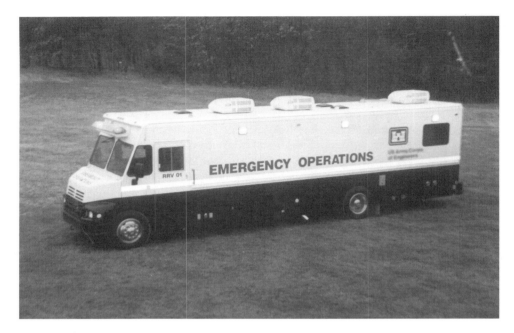

Figure 9–5   Special service vehicle used as EOC. (*Source:* LDV/Lynch
Diversified Vehicles, Burlington, WI.)

- *Commercial Mobile Facility.* As with end-user recovery, many hot-site vendors offer mobile trailers that can be tasked for use as emergency operations
  centers. These offerings have many of the same advantages and constraints
  of company-owned mobile EOCs but without the acquisition costs. The
  drawback of this strategy is the timeframe for deployment. Most mobile
  shell facility vendors promise delivery within 48 hours of notification. DR
  coordinators need to ascertain whether this timeframe is acceptable or if a
  more immediate response capability is required.

All of the above options share a common assumption: that emergency management team members will wish to gather in a single location to oversee the response, recovery, and relocation/reentry phases of the disaster recovery project.
This assumption must be questioned rigorously by DR coordinators because it is
highly dependent upon corporate culture. In some cases, business managers will
defer all recovery tasks to an IT manager or CIO, preferring to focus on their own
higher-level tasks at some remote location. In other cases, senior management will
wish to have the ability to be on-site as a show of support to workers or to communicate an impression of stability and normalcy to business partners, investors, and
others. These factors need to be taken into account when planning the EOC.

An alternative to deploying an EOC hard site is to use a virtual EOC (VEOC). Leveraging the ubiquitous web browser and the public Internet, a secure, Web-based mechanism can be fielded to facilitate command, control, and communications during a recovery effort. The author has deployed similar solutions in the past on behalf of clients and is currently developing a generic version of a virtual EOC for adoption by web-based service providers and vendors of web server appliance products. The value proposition of such a solution is summarized in the paragraphs below, which are abstracted from the author's prospectus for a VEOC:

> The VEOC is essentially a private web site that is activated when a disaster occurs. The domain for the site is preestablished with Internet domain name registration services such as the INTERNIC and is "parked" until its activation is required.
>
> The VEOC can be hosted on a web-server appliance, retrieved from secure off-site storage as a function of plan activation, or it can be an Application Service Provider service customized in advance of use, then stored on a fee-paid basis, until its activation is required.
>
> When activated, the VEOC provides a central point of information about the disaster for company personnel and DR teams. The site is used to disseminate reliable information about the recovery effort, to communicate recovery process status and issues requiring resolution, and to maintain contact with and between recovery teams. The web browser interface provides ubiquitous access for company employees, and features such as chat and email enable near-real-time interaction between management, recovery teams, and corporate personnel as necessary. This approach eliminates the need for predesignated and preequipped EOC facilities, since it can provide a virtual conference facility for all involved in the disaster recovery effort.
>
> As a module of [a larger package of web-based DR planning tools], the VEOC can convert the electronic DR plan into a recovery flowchart and procedural checklist that can be referenced at any time to understand the status of the recovery effort. The VEOC can also be used to capture data on plan tests and to prepare test reports (or reports on actual disaster recovery plan implementations) that capture information about plan efficiency and guide the refinement of the plan. Reports can be appended to the plan document to meet the needs of auditors.
>
> Potential enhancements for this product over time include support for IP telephony and video conferencing.[3]

The decision to deploy an EOC in a building, vehicle, or via the web must be based on an assessment of how management will actually be provided in a disaster situation. Those who will play a role in emergency management need to be personally involved in plan testing so they are familiar with the scope of the recovery effort, the strategies involved, and the decisions they will be required to make.

THE RECOVERY PHASE

Systems

Figures 9–6 and 9–7 depict events in the recovery of systems. In these flowcharts, systems recovery will involve the use of a remotely located commercial hot site. Be aware that the systems recovery strategy will probably already have been initiated if a decision has been made to activate the plan. If, after further examination the original center is found to be inhabitable, the systems recovery plan may advance quickly to the reentry phase.

System Recovery Task Path

In Figure 9–6, the need to activate the systems recovery plan has been acknowledged by the emergency management team, which issues a formal disaster declaration to the hot site. The systems recovery team leader assembles/notifies the teams whose activities must be coordinated to restore both centralized and distributed server hosts that provide mission-critical applications required by key business processes.

An off-site storage team retrieves backups from the storage facility, crates or otherwise prepares them for transportation, and transports them to the hot site. (This may already have been done in the event of a phased disaster, or it may be unnecessary if the company has chosen a remote tape vaulting or remote mirroring that places the data at the remote recovery facility on an ongoing basis.) The team may also arrange for the pickup of backup media at the remote recovery facility destination and their transportation to the hot site. Once these tasks are completed, the off-site storage team so reports to the systems recovery team leader.

The off-site storage team then inventories remaining storage and, if necessary, prepares stored documents, preprinted forms, and other user supplies for transport to the user recovery site. The team will then coordinate new storage arrangements for vital and critical records generated during recovery operations. An off-page connector indicates that the reader should go to the user recovery task path in Figure 9–9 to see additional off-site storage team tasks.

Meanwhile, the emergency operations, software, and applications teams travel to the hot site. Once there, the emergency operations team prepares system hardware and the Software team restores system core datasets (or "packs") from tape, loads host operating system software, and reports task completion to the systems recovery team leader. The applications team restores user data, installs and tests application software, reports task completion to the team leader. Off-page connectors direct the reader to go to the remote systems operations task path in Figure 9–7. With systems prepared for operation, the systems recovery team leader so reports to the emergency management team.

The above is a simplification intended to show the manner in which an emergency management flowchart depicts the interrelationships between tasks

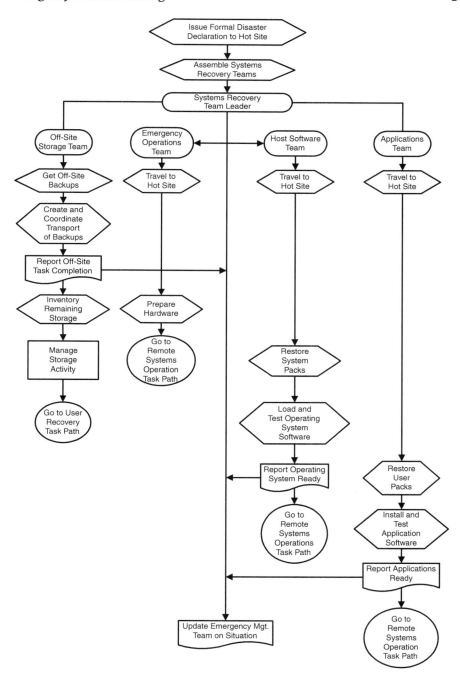

Figure 9–6   Systems recovery task path.

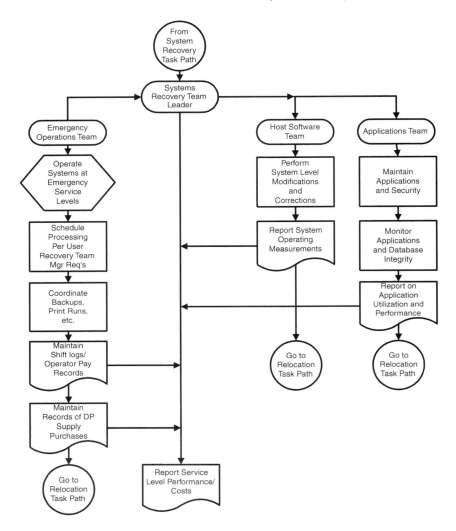

Figure 9–7   Remote systems operations management (remote systems operations task path).

and provides reporting procedures. In actuality, a number of additional steps may be required.

For example, the complexity of a client/server platform restoral may be much greater than what is depicted here. Client/server platforms that must be recovered on a one-to-one basis (with respect to platforms used in the production environment) often entail more than host operating system and application software installation from backups. Middleware must also be installed in many cases. Dynamic directories that identify and link messaging nodes in the multi-tier platform may need to be updated with new nodal identifiers. Security, performance measurement, and system/application monitoring resources need to be deployed and configured. It is also a good idea to perform workload simulations and to measure outputs to ensure that client/server configurations produce predictable results and acceptable service levels.

In general, a combination of the restoral requirements for an application and the advanced provisions made in DR planning will dictate the number and complexity of tasks involved in any restoral. Indeed, as noted previously, team designations are generally linked to such considerations as task complexity and recovery time-frame requirements.

Regardless of the complexity and number of tasks involved, each task should be thoroughly documented in the disaster recovery plan, linked by some sort of numbering scheme to the emergency management flowchart, and regularly tested at the hot site. Also, in point of fact, systems are not restored until databases are current, communications have been reestablished with users and data communicators, and users are on the system performing work. Network and user recovery tasks occur concurrently with systems recovery, as shown in the master flowchart available on the companion website to this book. (See http://www.drplanning.org.)

Remote Systems Operation Task Path

In some disaster recovery plans, procedures for operating applications from a remote hot site are documented only in broad sweeping strokes. However, a better approach is to detail the tasks and responsibilities for application and host performance management and to implement a program of service level accounting that will keep the emergency management team apprised of how well business process needs are being met. Specific attention should also be paid to cost accounting and reporting. In Figure 9–7, the ongoing responsibilities of systems recovery teams during operations at the hot site are set forth.

As depicted in Figure 9–7, the emergency operations team is responsible for operating systems and applications at emergency service levels. This may include scheduling jobs, performing backups, and maintaining system recovery team time and expense records, as well as records of other accrued expenses. Expenses are reported on a regular basis to the systems recovery team leader, who includes them in his or her regular reports to the emergency management team.

The host software and applications teams monitor system performance, work to resolve problems, maintain applications security and data integrity, and report performance and utilization measurements to the systems recovery team leader. Presumably, the team leader will advise the teams of changing requirements and the decisions of the emergency management team that pertain to their activities.

These tasks are ongoing until the recovery phase gives way to the relocation of systems to the original or newly constructed facility. Relocation may need to happen more than once in a recovery. As mentioned in a previous chapter, with some commercial systems recovery vendors, facility use in excess of a set number of days is prohibited. The hot site may be used only until a cold site at or near the vendor location can be fitted with necessary hardware. Then, the customer is moved to the cold site. This allows the hot site to be used by other subscribers wishing to test their plans or needing a recovery facility in a disaster.

Networks

Network recovery consists of a set of tasks, such as those depicted in Figure 9–8, which may be undertaken concurrently with system recovery and remote system operation tasks. In this flowchart, it is assumed that the company has contracted with a wide-area network service vendor for rerouting WAN services and voice communications along a preplanned alternate path. Such services can be used effectively if systems and end user recovery facilities are designated in advance of any disaster. In situations where this is not the case, additional procedures may be needed to accommodate the on-the-fly rerouting strategies (for example, the solicitation of services from IXCs or value-added network service providers, the acquisition of requisite hardware, testing of new facilities, etc.)

In addition, the flowchart shown in Figure 9–8 describes a response to a total loss of both user work areas and systems facilities. Hence, a network recovery team located at the systems recovery site and a Communications Team located at the user recovery site work cooperatively to facilitate full recovery of corporate voice and data communications networks. Other flowcharts may need to be developed to reflect a partial disaster scenario in which only a part of the corporate voice and data networking capability needs to be restored or rerouted.

Network Recovery Task Path

As depicted in the flowchart, once the network recovery section of the disaster recovery plan is invoked, the network rerouting service vendor is contacted and communications are rerouted along predefined paths. The network recovery team leader activates teams responsible for restoring voice and data interconnects at the systems recovery and end user recovery site respectively. Each team travels to its intended destination. The network recovery team leader proceeds to one location or the other per plan specifications.

The network recovery team is responsible for implementing the WAN rerouting strategy and for deploying remote access technology that will be used by end users to access and operate hot-site-based applications. Other tasks may include the installation and preparation of communications hardware at the hot site for use in the network, the deployment of network management software, the implementation of network security hardware and software and the notification of remote communicators about changes to network configuration and anticipated service levels. Thorough testing of the new systems recovery site-user re-

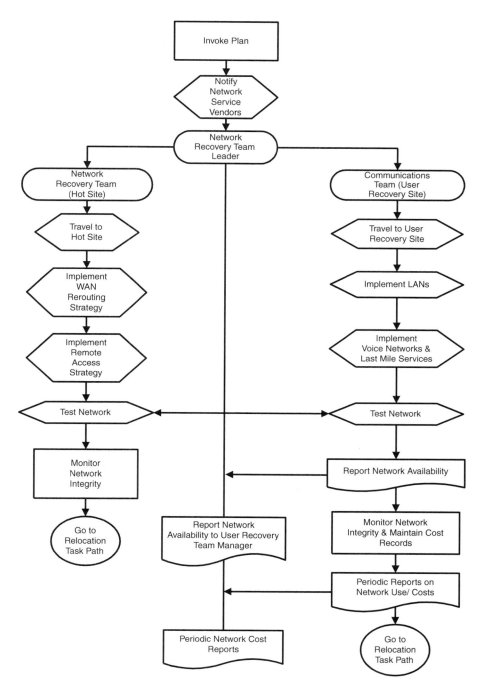

Figure 9-8 Network recovery task path.

covery site network can only be accomplished after tasks have been completed at the end user recovery site by the communications team.

Following successful completion of the above tasks, the network recovery team will monitor network traffic for performance, utilization, and integrity throughout the recovery period and will report on network costs and service levels to the network recovery team leader. The team leader will provide these reports to the emergency management team. This will persist until systems and end users are relocated to their original or to new company facilities.

At the user recovery site, the communications team works with user recovery teams to install and make operational local area networks used to support local end user business processes. The communications team installs telecommunications hardware received from backup inventory or from prearranged vendor sources. This team also works with ILECs/CLECs and other last-mile service providers to implement both local communications circuits and any WAN or Internet gateway services designated in the disaster recovery plan.

Tests of wide area network and remote access services between the systems recovery site and end user recovery site are conducted and performance levels baselined according to a planned testing strategy. When network tests are completed, the availability of the network for use is reported to the team leader who in turn reports this to the emergency management team.

Until systems and networks are relocated to original or new company facilities, the communications team monitors network performance at the end user recovery facility and maintains cost records that are periodically summarized and reported to the network recovery team leader for inclusion in management reports.

End-Users

Figures 9–9 and 9–10 refer to user recovery tasks, which are undertaken concurrently with system and network recovery tasks. These flowcharts assume that a user recovery site has been preplanned and designated in the recovery plan. Were this not the case, advanced planning for the automatic rerouting of communications networks would be impossible and recovery would be delayed by the need to locate and outfit a recovery site, then to notify end-users of the new address.

As telecommuting-based end-user recovery becomes more viable, the recovery tasks involved will be very different from those depicted here. As of this writing, however, the preferred strategy for end-user recovery is to relocate end-users to an alternate facility that is either company-owned or leased from a vendor.

User Recovery Task Path

As depicted in Figure 9–9, once the decision has been made to activate the user recovery section of the plan, the emergency management team notifies the company insurer so that extra expense coverages for user relocation and extraordinary operating costs can be activated. The user recovery team leader activates an

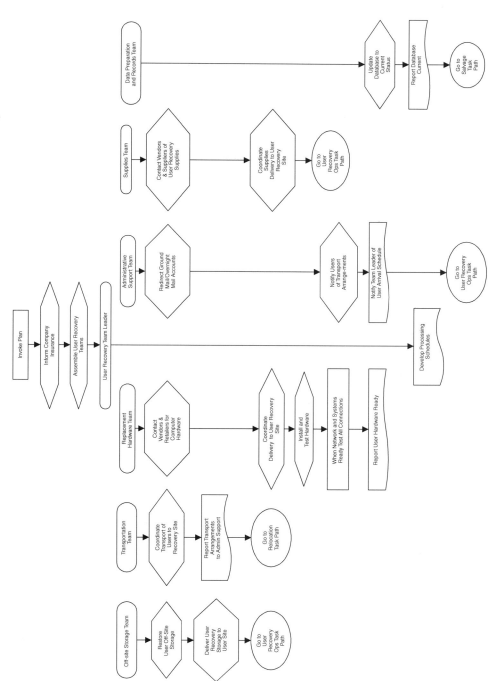

Figure 9–9 User recovery task path.

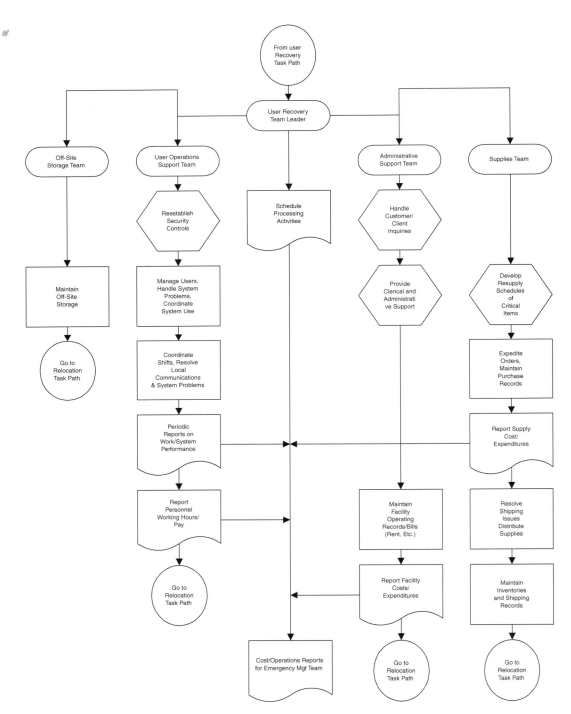

Figure 9–10 User recovery operations task path.

off-site storage team, transportation team, replacement hardware team, administrative support team, supplies team, and data preparation and records team to begin the work detailed in the DR plan.

The off-site storage team is responsible for retrieving stored materials required by the user recovery site and delivering them to the site. They also assist in preparing off-site stores, particularly magnetic media backups and restoral software, for use.

The transportation team coordinates the transportation of end users to the recovery site, although this is not done until other aspects of site preparation are completed. Transportation arrangements are reported to the administrative support team.

A replacement hardware team contacts vendors and retailers, identified in the plan, to coordinate shipments of workstations and peripherals, photocopying equipment, fax, and other office equipment to the user recovery site. This team is then responsible for installing and testing hardware in cooperation with the communications team, which will be working on the restoral of office LANs and voice communications capabilities at the user recovery site. Following LAN and communications tests, the replacement hardware team reports readiness to the user recovery team leader.

While systems and LANs are being readied, the administrative support team contacts ground mail and overnight delivery services and arranges for the redirection of services to the new end user recovery facility. Upon receipt of the details of transportation arrangements from the transportation team, and at the direction of the user recovery team leader, administrative support advises end users to report to work. Administrative Support staffs work shifts and coordinates end user arrivals, meals and lodging.

Meanwhile, a supplies team coordinates the acquisition and delivery of office supplies from vendors identified in the plan. Supplies are delivered to the recovery site, shipments are verified, and records are maintained of costs and deliveries.

Once systems and networks are ready, a data preparation and records team uses salvaged records as well as documents stored off-site to bring databases to as current a state as possible. Once databases are current, this is reported to the user recovery team leader and the user recovery site is ready for operation.

The user recovery task path depicted above assumes that certain capabilities already exist and will not need to be hastily developed. This may not be the case for every business. Additional teams, such as a Facility Location Team, may need to be commissioned and staffed to handle additional functional requirements of user recovery.

Note also that the data preparation and records team, unlike the other teams in this task path, may have responsibilities in the salvage task path, as they will assist in records reclamation and other salvage activities. With application access restored, operations in the end user recovery site may commence. The ongoing activities of the user recovery teams during this period are depicted in Figure 9–10.

User Recovery Operations Task Path

As illustrated in Figure 9–10, this task path comprises the ongoing procedures for managing day-to-day operations at the user recovery site. The off-site storage team maintains a storage schedule for records and data generated at the site. The user operations support team oversees premise security, manages users, handles system problems, provides help desk functions, coordinates shifts, and supervises work, making routine reports of work and system performance, personnel time, and payroll to the user recovery team leader. Administrative Support handles customer and client inquiries, provides clerical and administrative support for the other teams, and maintains operations cost records. Reports of facility costs and expenditures are made by the team to the user recovery team leader on a regular basis. Finally, the supplies team coordinates the resupply of critical office and computer supplies. This team escalates orders, maintains purchase and inventory records, resolves shipping issues, and distributes supplies upon arrival.

The activities described above may or may not have corresponding procedures in the disaster recovery plan document. However, special forms and report formats may be developed and included in the plan with instructions for their use.

Salvage

The user recovery team continues its operations until a plan is developed to relocate the users to the original or a new facility. Decisions regarding where and when to relocate are made by the emergency management team, based in part upon the findings and progress of the salvage effort.

Salvage Task Path

Salvage activities may begin the moment that entry is permitted to the disaster-stricken facility. These efforts continue concurrently with response and recovery activities undertaken by other disaster recovery teams. Figure 9–11 provides an overview of some of the activities that may be a part of a salvage effort.

As indicated above, once the plan is invoked, a damage assessment team— possibly comprised of the salvage team leader, a qualified member of the emergency management team, and others familiar with source records and computer hardware—enter the facility. A photographic record is made of facility damage by a team member (or a professional photographer on retainer to the company for this purpose). Witness accounts may also be collected at this point.

Some plans provide for a claims adjuster from the company's business interruption insurer to accompany the damage assessment and salvage teams to the disaster site. Since payment on insurance claims may provide part of the financing for the recovery, the quicker that claims can be filed and adjudicated, the better.

Following this initial visit, formal salvage operations commence under the auspices of a salvage team leader. A facility salvage team determines whether the data center and user operations area environments can be restored, and at what cost.

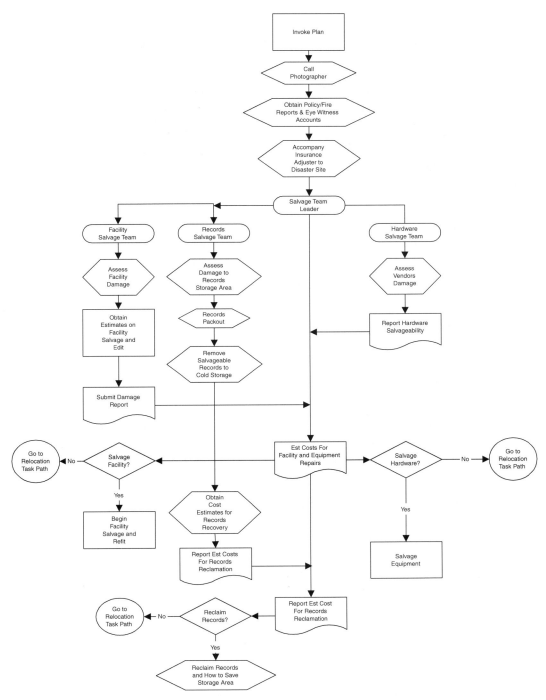

Figure 9–11 Salvage task path.

An itemized report of team findings is provided to the salvage team leader. Similar reports are filed by the hardware salvage team, whose task it is to determine how much computer and networking hardware can be restored reliably to service.

Concurrently, the records salvage team sets to work. The job of the team is to determine what magnetic media, paper-based, and microform records can be rescued at the disaster site; to clean, pack, and inventory these records; and to remove them to cold storage. Generally, this must be done within 24 to 48 hours, before mold and fungi begin to corrupt salvageable documents, though some documents may be vital to database restoration activity and may require faster action.

The procedure for packout should be set forth in the disaster recovery plan, as should a list of cold storage facilities in the vicinity of the company.[4] Alternatively, DR coordinators may wish to place a data recovery vendor and a records reclamation vendor on retainer and utilize their services to recover magnetic media and records, respectively. Table 9–3 summarizes some of the media-specific procedures that may be performed by the records salvage team.

Following packout, and once the extent and quantity of damaged records are known, the records salvage team should obtain a salvage work cost estimate from a records reclamation vendor (also noted in the disaster plan) detailing the expenses for restoring the volume of records salvaged from company facilities. This cost estimate should be reported to the salvage team leader.

In the case of magnetic media, firms such as ontrack data recovery services offer cleanrooms and laboratories distributed around the world, as well as on-site engineering support, to facilitate data reclamation from damaged disk media. Typical recovery of data takes about three days on average, though special services are available in a post-disaster context that can cut restoral time by half.[5] Recovering data from client workstations may be necessary to facilitate database restoration or to access special workstation-based information that has been added since the last backup. However, the records salvage team should work with other recovery teams to ensure that only the most important data is submitted for fast-turnaround recovery services to minimize expense.

The salvage team leader is responsible for reporting cost estimates for facility, equipment, and records salvage to the emergency management team. The emergency management team will decide whether to undertake salvage or to write off the loss and look for new hardware and new quarters for the company.

If the decision is made to salvage and reenter the original facility, the facility salvage team initiates contract work and provides a completion schedule to the salvage team leader. The other salvage teams move forward with salvage activities, identifying task progress and anticipated completion schedules as work proceeds.

THE RELOCATION/REENTRY PHASE

Whatever decision is reached by the emergency management team, it is followed up by the development of a relocation or reentry plan. The components of the

Table 9–3 Salvage Priority by Media Type

TYPE OF MEDIA	Color films and photographs	Silver or emulsion films and photographs	Diazo or vesicular (duplicate) films	Bond, rag, or duplication paper	Magnetic media (including tape, disk, floppy disk, audio and video-tape)
PRIORITY	Immediate.	Immediate.	Last.	Within 48 hours (depending on temperature and humidity levels at the disaster site, and upon the extent of damage).	Immediate.
IMMEDIATE ACTION	Once wet, keep wet.	Immerse totally in water.	If time and staff available, rinse off and lay out flat on clean surface to dry; otherwise, leave until last.	Air dry in well-ventilated area. If volume of wet records is large, consider freeze or vacuum drying.	Contact vendor.
PURPOSE OF ACTION	To avoid further damage and loss of image.	To avoid further damage.	To prevent water spotting and curling of films or fiche.	To prevent further deterioration of paper materials and eruption of mold and fungus.	To obtain professional advice and service.
FOLLOWUP ACTION	Within 48 hours, obtain professional advice and assistance and cleaning, drying and restoring. Freeze if professional help is delayed longer than 48 hours.	Seek professional assistance with cleaning and drying. Freezing may cause image damage. If freezing will be delayed more than 48 hours, immerse films in 1 percent solution of formaldehyde in cool water.	Wash with liquid detergent and rinse. Dry on flat, absorbent paper towels.	May include freeze- or vacuum-drying. If mold erupts, treat with an approved fungicide.	May include special cleaning techniques and professional assistance in retrieving data.

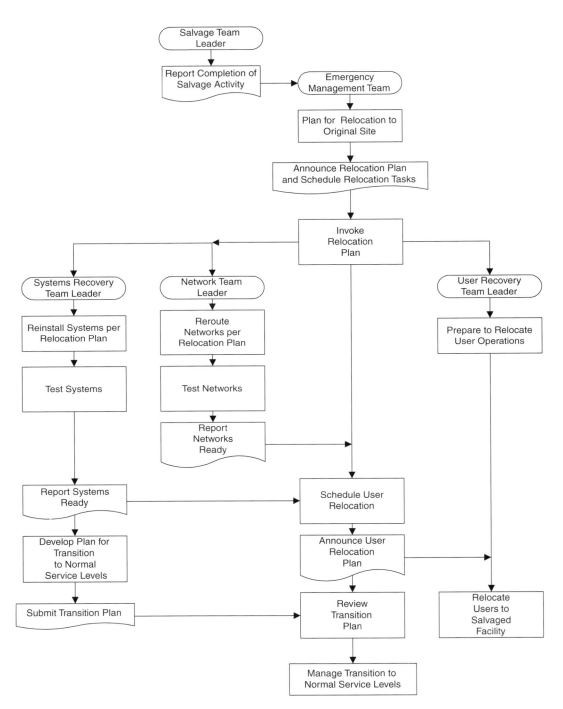

Figure 9–12 Relocation task path.

relocation plan cannot be determined in advance by the disaster recovery coordi-nator. However, if the relocation plan capitalizes on the same team structures that were defined in the disaster recovery plan, this may facilitate efficient relocation of systems, networks, and users to the original or new company facility.

In addition, the relocation or reentry plan should provide a scheme for the gradual transition back to normal service levels from the emergency service lev-els in effect during recovery operations. Presumably, this transition will be sched-uled following the successful relocation of critical and vital systems to the company site.

Figure 9–12 summarizes the tasks that may be involved in the relocation of emergency operations to the original (salvaged) facility. The task path mirrors re-covery task paths in many respects, except that emergency service levels are gradually replaced by normal service levels per a plan developed by the emer-gency management team during recovery operations.

FINAL THOUGHTS ON EMERGENCY MANAGEMENT DECISION MAKING

The above is only one example of an emergency management flowchart. The team descriptions and roles depicted, the specific tasks described, and the recov-ery procedures enacted will, by necessity, differ from one company to the next. The purpose of designing an emergency decision-making flowchart is to help readers (including those who must implement the plan and those who merely want to understand plan provisions) to see the interrelationships between the strategies developed for systems, network, and end-user recovery.

Emergency management remains as much art as science. In an actual emer-gency, senior managers and technical managers together need to use the emer-gency management flowchart as a jumping-off point for the innovation and creativity that is always required to surmount the hurdles of critical business process restoration.

In extreme cases, such as the terrorist attack on the World Trade Center in 2001, those tasked with executing the disaster recovery plan may themselves fall prey to the disaster. In such cases, an easy-to-understand emergency manage-ment flowchart that can be executed by personnel other than the experienced cadre of disaster recovery team members may become the most important com-ponent of the disaster recovery plan. The wise old axiom applies: Keep it simple.

ENDNOTES

1. Jon William Toigo, "Storm Warnings Sound," *The Databus,* 07/86.
2. Richard Sandhofer, "Chicago Not Prepared for a New River," *Disaster Recovery Jour-nal,* 01/88.

3. Jon William Toigo, "The Disaster Recovery Planning Assistant and Virtual Emergency Operations Center: A Brief Prospectus," 01/99. The VEOC and Disaster Recovery Planning Assistant described in the document are copyright to the author. However, beta test versions of the solution are expected to be provided on the companion website to this book, www.drplanning.org.

4. Some excellent background reading on records salvage include Richard Harms et al., *A Program for Disaster Response in Michigan*, Michigan Archival Association, East Lansing, MI, 1981. See also *A Primer on Disaster Preparedness, Management and Response: Paper-Based Materials Selected Reprints*, issued by Smithsonian Institution, National Archives and Records Administration, Library of Congress, and National Park Service. A Collaborative Publication Sponsored by the Conservation Analytical Laboratory and the Office of Risk Management, SI; the Preservation Policy and Services Division, NARA; the Preservation Directorate, LC; and the Curatorial Services Division, NPS, October 1993, available on the World Wide Web at the National Archives and Records Administrators site: www.nara.gov/nara.

5. See "Data Recovery Services," on Ontrack Data Recovery's (Eden Prairie, MN) website at www.ontrack.com. This site provides a wealth of information on the causes of magnetic media failures and restoration techniques.

CHAPTER 10

The Recovery Management Environment

As discussed in Chapter 9, the emergency decision-making plan provides the framework of the disaster recovery plan. Its flowcharts and notification directory depict the interrelationships between all of the strategies, tasks, and procedures that have been developed to recover critical business processes in the event of a disaster.

However, flowcharts—and the scenarios on which they are built—are only theoretical constructs. Disaster recovery teams and emergency managers may have to deviate from preplanned paths in order to respond effectively to the demands of an actual event and its recovery requirements.

In some cases, a disaster can overwhelm the emergency management team itself, as occurred in the case of some companies impacted by the attack on the WTC in New York. As reported in Michael Shannon's Foreword to this edition, the Port Authority's Emergency Operations Center was activated following the collision. Emergency teams set up shop in their designated location, the Marriott Vista Hotel, only to have Tower Two collapse on them. Those who survived managed to set up a backup EOC at another location hours later. Had the entire team been lost in the 9/11 tragedy, it would have been up to others to manage the recovery effort—possibly with no understanding of the carefully constructed strategies and plans previously developed.

The point is that there is no way to predict or to develop suitable responses to every recovery scenario in advance. However, there are ways to identify potential obstacles to plan implementation, educate team leaders about them, and, in some cases, develop the means for surmounting them.

To better understand the recovery management environment, disaster recovery coordinators need to research the experience of other companies that have implemented plans. Research entails more than reading this book or disaster-related articles in back issues of popular business computing journals. An important part of the research involves conducting interviews with those who have led or served on recovery teams in a business disaster. Research also entails interviewing local and state civil emergency management authorities and representatives of local utility companies, telephone companies, and others who will help define the milieu in which corporate disaster recovery will take place. Disaster recovery coordinators can perform this research themselves, or they may be assisted by team leaders who will profit from direct participation in the endeavor.

The purpose of this research is twofold: to learn about external factors that may impact the implementation of a plan and also to obtain a greater understanding of the impact of disaster on the behavior and psyche of company personnel, recovery teams, and the community at large. Some of what is discovered may not be useful in writing the disaster recovery plan. However, it may help those who will implement the plan to see their roles more clearly and perceive the parameters within which improvisation (in the face of obstacles to recovery) may be successful.

RESEARCHING LITERATURE

There is an old saying that best information about disaster recovery is locked away in company filing cabinets—often in the exit interviews of business and IT managers who have been fired in the wake of a disaster! While this may be a bit of an exaggeration, it is true that businesses often wish to suppress any information that might indicate instability or vulnerability to investors, customers, stockholders, and auditors.

Despite this desire, accounts of successful (and, to a lesser extent, unsuccessful) recovery projects are increasingly finding their way into the press. Part of the reason, of course, is that some disasters are highly visible events, spectacles for the media or significant in terms of human tragedy. However, even a software malfunction can achieve prominent media attention when it causes a federal reserve bank to borrow billions at the discount window, destabilizing the securities market, or when it prompts the customers of an online brokerage to complain en masse to the Securities and Exchange Commission (SEC) and makes front-page news in the *Wall Street Journal.*

The point is that more and more information about the problems and pitfalls of disaster recovery is available in the public media. This information can be helpful in identifying potential obstacles to the implementation of disaster plans.

In some cases, lessons are preeminently practical. For example, companies located in Canada with hot sites in the United States learned significant lessons from published accounts of the 1986 Steinberg disaster in Montreal. As reported in the trade press, the evening after a fire demolished company headquarters, 25 employees gathered together 10,000 reels of tape containing payroll systems data and other necessities, such as blank check stock, and formed a caravan headed for a hot site in New Jersey. They were prevented from crossing the border into the

United States, however, by customs agents concerned that the software and checks could be used for illegal purposes.[1] It took the company CEO, working in conjunction with the U.S. Consulate, to straighten out the matter.

More recently, the press has offered a broad range of practical lessons concerning the efficacy of plans. A small sampling:

- After Hurricane Hugo in 1989, an automotive parts manufacturer impacted by the storm discovered that its plans to coordinate the activities of recovery teams using cellular phones ran afoul of local civil emergency management mandates.[2] Cellular communications were reserved for use by emergency services, and the IT manager was told to cease using the phones.
- Following Hurricane Fran in 1996, a Bank in North Carolina learned the vicissitudes of counting on the availability of certain key personnel to facilitate recovery. The MIS director had to dodge power lines to drive to the home of a key systems programmer whose car had been demolished by a tree felled by the storm.[3]
- During Hurricane Floyd in 1999, many planners discovered their error in counting on both ground and air transportation to move personnel and supplies to recovery sites at the same time that massive civilian evacuations were taking place. The flood of requests stimulated by the event overwhelmed the reservation systems for airlines and travel agencies and the millions of people seeking shelter inland in advance of the storm turned interstate highways into parking lots.[4]

In addition to print media accounts of disaster recovery efforts, coordinators may profit by spending time reviewing tapes of "on-the-scene" coverage of disaster events made by television media. The advent of all-news television networks (CNN, MSNBC, and others) has made the "dynamic" media (i.e., television, as opposed to "static" or print media) a factor in disaster recovery—in ways that are both positive and negative. On the plus side, television and radio provide a means for disseminating information about the recovery milieu quickly and efficiently. Weather-related warnings, information about earthquake damage areas, locations of civilian disturbances or emergency shelters, and so on, can be communicated quickly via electronic reporting. Accurate reports enable business managers to identify alternative transportation routes, obtain appropriate infrastructure assistance, determine appropriate plan implementation strategies, and even disseminate information to employees regarding alternate schedules or work locations.

On the downside, however, dynamic media accounts can protract emergency timeframes by exaggerating the extent of damage accrued to an event (see below). They can also portray recovery efforts in a less-than-flattering light. For example, following the 1993 bombing of the World Trade Center in New York, CNN covered the efforts of some businesses to recover key operations. Video broadcasts showed the emergency operations center of a "Big Five" accounting and consulting firm impacted by the event, capturing images of frantic employees and recovery personnel engaged in heated arguments and, worse yet, a clearly visible white board on which was scrawled numerous instructions to recovery team members, including what appeared to be IDs and passwords and emergency phone numbers. If nothing else, the coverage communicated a potentially damaging impression of the firm's disaster preparedness (ironically, the firm also provides disaster recovery planning services!) to clients and shareholders watching the broadcast. It further demonstrated the importance of maintaining EOC operations at a different location from crisis communications.

Of course, it would be impractical for coordinators to gather all of the publications covering all of the subjects that might offer insights into disaster recovery planning. However, vendors of products and services used by the DR coordinator often survey this literature and forward relevant articles to the coordinator's attention. Many vendor sales representatives cite their practice of forwarding news clips to customers as part of an ongoing effort to inform and educate clientele.

In addition to subscription publications and vendor clips, many hardware and software companies generate their own disaster recovery guidelines. Coordinators can obtain these through marketing representatives for the various companies. While this literature rarely provides a comprehensive treatment of disaster recovery, it may provide useful information about a specific application or platform used by the company.

INTERVIEWS AND TOURS

Other DR Coordinators

Another way to learn about the milieu in which a company disaster recovery plan will be implemented is to conduct interviews with DR coordinators in other companies, as well as providers of public infrastructure services and government officials concerned with public safety and emergency management. From these discussions, coordinators can identify what measures similar or neighboring companies are taking to facilitate disaster recovery, and how the coordinator's plan will be affected by the plans of those whose plans shape the recovery environment.

In some instances, vendors of disaster recovery products and services can provide the names of contacts in neighboring companies or arrange introductions between coordinators. By discussing everything from how the coordinator for another company cost-justified his or her plan to management, to the technical details of how a certain type of local area network can be backed up, to the other coordinator's evaluation of the performance of various vendors, a great deal of useful information can be gathered.

Public Services and Utilities

Coordinators would also be well-advised to interview representatives of public services and utilities and local government officials tasked with emergency management. It would be useful to gather information on the following:

- *The Power Company's Policy on Repairs and Service Restoration.* Most power companies are willing to allow disaster recovery coordinators to tour their facilities. The coordinator should ask questions and develop a thorough understanding of how the provider goes about localizing and repairing the causes of outages. In addition, the coordinator should identify how a "trouble report" is handled: What is the emergency telephone number for reporting an outage? Is more than a single report required to initiate corrective action? What is the typical length of a power outage? What has been the maximum length of an outage in the past 2 years? Is there a policy regarding priority of service restoration (who is turned on first, second, third, etc.)?

  The answers to these questions can lead into a detailed discussion of the coordinator's company power requirements. Ask the representative to show how the company is supplied and what redundancies exist in the system to supply power should system outages occur.

  Power company representatives can also provide information that may guide further research. For example, an office park or high-rise building may be supplied power by the public utility at a central service entry point. Power is then distributed from this service entry to offices within the complex or building using secondary lines, transformers, and other hardware that is owned and maintained by the building management company. The power company can point out where its responsibility (and ability to correct problems) ends, and where the building manager's responsibilities begin. This may lead to a subsequent interview of the building manager to understand problem reporting procedures, job order methods, and power restoration timeframes from the management company's perspective.

  The coordinator may also wish to identify what hardware the management company is using and whether redundant hardware is available to replace malfunctioning equipment. If the management company is using obsolete or hard-to-find hardware, some tenant pressure may persuade the management company to upgrade to newer, more readily obtained equipment.

- *How Local Telephone COs Are Configured and How They Will Handle Service Restoration in an Outage.* Coordinators will find that many of the same questions asked of the power company also need to be discussed with a local telephone company representative: where to report trouble, how to escalate response, what are the restoration priorities in the event of a regional outage, and how long an outage may persist. It would be useful to coordinators to tour the facility containing local exchange and IXC gateway switches. Find out what redundancies exist and where other COs are located in proximity to the company. This information may be used to determine whether it is necessary, or possible, to obtain local area and gateway services from a second CO.

  Find out also what services the CO offers in the areas of line grading and automatic rerouting of local traffic. If the coordinator is able to speak with a CO engineer who has helped other companies with their network planning or disaster recovery projects, he or she may be able to obtain useful information about the techniques and strategies others have applied with success.

Similar visits may need to be made to IXC POP sites used by the company, to local Internet Service Provider facilities, and to cellular carrier offices. In every case, efforts should be made to identify outage scenarios, understand disaster recovery procedures of vendors themselves, and to learn about the recovery practices of other customers of vendor-provided services.

- *Local Civil Emergency Management Plans.* Because of the threats posed to entire communities by natural and manmade disasters, many state and local governments (as well as the federal government) have developed emergency management plans. These plans provide for the evacuation and relocation of the public in the event of hurricanes, typhoons, floods, earthquakes, or nuclear, biological, or chemical disasters.

  While not every disaster experienced by a company will entail government intervention, businesses located in "high-risk" areas (i.e., those located on the coastlines of North America, or near chemical or nuclear plants) need to be aware of the impact that civil plans will have on the implementation of their own plan.

  A local administrator is usually responsible for the maintenance of a civil emergency management plan. In some localities, the administrative function is given to a local law enforcement or fire protection agency. It may take some time to sift through the bureaucracy to locate the individual or group responsible for emergency planning, but the coordinator should make the effort and meet with the responsible party.

Some coordinators may view this recommendation as superfluous. The concept of civil defense conjures up images of 1950's planning for bomb shelters, air raid sirens, and emergency broadcasts. This perception aside, residents of disaster-prone regions of the United States are aware of the ongoing need and true benefit of emergency management agencies in local and state governments. In the event of a natural or man-made threat such as a hurricane, city, county, and state governments have developed strategies for notifying the people and safely evacuating them.

Following cessation of disaster conditions, governmental emergency management plans often provide for controlled reentry into the evacuated areas. These plans have proven their worth time after time and have probably accounted for saving more lives than the polio vaccine. However, such plans are not without their cost to a business if disaster recovery coordinators have not anticipated how they will impact on their company disaster recovery plans. The following brief story from the author's own experience illustrates the point.

In 1985, Hurricane Elena forced the evacuation of metropolitan areas up and down the Florida Gulf Coast. (Later that same season, Gloria forced civil governments to relocate populations away from coastal areas all along the Atlantic seaboard.) The Tampa Bay Metropolitan Area was evacuated while the hurricane was still more than 21 hours distant and had less than a 30% chance of making landfall anywhere near the area. Officials called for the early evacuation because they added a 15-hour period of "prelandfall hazard" to the 9 to 15 hours they calculated it would take to evacuate the residential populations of all flood-prone areas, including the Gulf Beaches and low-lying areas. Local and state emergency managers had to take into account the period of sustained gale force winds (40+ miles per hour) preceding the storm's landfall during which travel would be extremely hazardous. (The length of this period is determined by the size of the hurricane and its rate of movement.) Because of these factors, civil planners anticipated that up to 15 additional hours should be added to the time requirement for safe evacuation. This, in turn, affected the timing of the evacuation order.

While many business planners expected evacuation orders to be inconvenient whenever they were issued, most did not anticipate being ordered out so long before the storm even appeared on local TV radar. Local law enforcement officials ordered the disaster recovery teams of many Bay Area businesses out with last-minute backups only partially completed and other planned procedures implemented haphazardly or not at all.

Responding to post-Elena criticisms of their evacuation policy from area businesses, local officials noted that at the time that the mandatory evacuation for Elena was ordered, the storm had been sustaining a 10-mile-per-hour speed toward Tampa Bay for several minutes. Applying the government formulas for calculating the prelandfall hazard, there were actually only about 6 hours in which to safely evacuate flood-prone areas. To provide for the safety of all of the people, there could be no deviation in the evacuation schedule.

As the story suggests, in order to plan effectively for a disaster such as a hurricane, coordinators must develop a firm understanding of governmental emergency management plans. The government will place the safety and well-being of the citizenry before the interests of the business and, in so doing, may create a recovery environment in which business recovery plans will flourish or flounder. When there is a threat, governments will evacuate too often and too early. They will also be unsympathetic to the objectives of business planners if they are perceived as coming into conflict with civil plans aimed at preserving the lives of the population.

Evacuation is the first phase of the two-phase plan employed by most civil emergency management officials. The second phase is reentry. As noted previously, the Elena experience demonstrated that coordinators must consider where their recovery personnel reside when planning for facility reentry and damage assessment. If arrangements cannot be made to utilize only personnel who reside in the same area where business offices are located, coordinators may wish to pursue one of the following alternatives with civil defense professionals.

1. Determine whether an evacuation shelter exists or can be set up near the company facility for use by employees and their families. Not only will this reduce the distraction factor, but it will also reduce the likelihood that recovery will be delayed by prohibitions on travel in and out of the disaster area.

2. Discuss with emergency management officials the possibility of approving company ID cards as valid passes into disaster areas. In efforts to avoid looting, reentry into evacuated areas is often controlled by law enforcement officials who seek proof of residence (rather than employment) as the criterion for admission. As in the case of Hurricane Elena, company recovery personnel who cannot prove residence in the area of the business they want to access may be turned away, stalling damage assessment and disaster recovery. Preapproval of company ID with civil defense officials may expedite reentry into evacuated businesses once safety hazards have been cleared.

Coordinators from all types of businesses might find it useful to explore some of the generic issues, raised by the experience of Elena (and more recent storms such as Floyd in 1999), with local government authorities. Depending on the business and its geographical location, there may be other issues that a coordinator may wish to explore in detail to bring business disaster recovery plans into agreement with civil emergency management plans.

For example, local law enforcement and fire department officials may be consulted to determine the manner in which bomb threats or arson investigations will be handled, or to explore the roles that public safety officials will play in approving the reoccupation of salvaged facilities following a fire, flood, earthquake, storm, or other event. The results of these and other investigations will aid in finalizing a plan that can coexist with other emergency management plans that comprise the recovery environment.

PROFESSIONAL DR ORGANIZATIONS

Information about the recovery management environment is available from a variety of sources besides publications and one-on-one interviews with infrastructure providers and civil emergency management officials. Many professional organizations, such as those organized for risk managers, internal auditors, IT and records management professionals, and other industry specific fields, occasionally offer special programs related to various dimensions of disaster recovery planning that the disaster recovery coordinator may wish to attend.

In addition to these educational forums, an increasing number of disaster recovery planning specific associations are available to coordinators. These organizations focus on the disaster recovery issues facing the business communities they serve rather than treating the subject as a peripheral issue. Members can compress a great deal of time-consuming research into several hours of concentrated discussion at a group meeting.

Through participation in a group, members can quickly develop an extensive network of contacts, including other users (and vendors) of disaster recovery plans, products, and services. In addition, members are kept up to date with the latest advancements in disaster recovery techniques and technology and can profit collectively from shared information on vendor or product performance, or from member discounts on expensive services.

Table 10–1 contains contact information for disaster recovery groups and emergency management organizations in the United States that existed at the time of this book's publication. Contact names, telephone numbers, Web URLs, and, in some cases, addresses are provided for further information. With the assistance of the organizations involved, it is hoped that this list will be maintained in an up-to-date form on the website that serves as the companion to this book at http://www.drplanning.org.

It is worth noting that the number of disaster recovery information groups has proliferated since the first edition of this book. In 1990, there were approximately 10 such grassroots groups located mainly in the Eastern United States and in Canada—the oldest of these being the Delaware Valley Disaster Recovery Information Exchange Group. Each group comprised a mixture of IT and records professionals who perceived the need for DR and acknowledged the dearth of reliable information on the subject. Vendors were pleased to sponsor these organizations and to provide "expert" speakers for their meetings and conventions. Where else could vendors gain such direct access to such a cadre of potential customers?

Over time, these groups wittingly or unwittingly distinguished themselves as reliable DR information brokers and as a "quasi-police force" for an otherwise largely unregulated industry as IT and records managers swapped stories about the performance and cost of vendor products and services. As members exchanged their experiences with plan strategies and testing techniques, a consciousness about DR best practices began to coalesce. Organizations have since sought to replicate this experience on a national and international basis. Today, in the United States, the Association of Contingency Planners (ACP) boasts numerous regional chapters, while in Canada, the Disaster Recovery Information Exchange (DRIE) has grown to more than 450 members in six chapters across the country.[5] While some have complained of the bureaucratic infighting that has characterized some of the newer national and international organizations, DR information groups remain the best venue for learning about disaster recovery technologies and techniques and for gleaning an understanding of the actual disaster recovery milieu.

Table 10–1   U.S. Disaster Recovery Groups and Emergency Management Organizations by State

State	Group or Agency
ALABAMA	State of Alabama Emergency Management Tel: (205) 280–2200
ALASKA	State of Alaska Emergency Services Tel: (907) 428–7000
ARIZONA	Central Arizona Chapter of the Association of Contingency Planners Barbara Martinez Tel: (602) 587–3810 Fax: (502) 587–3999 E-mail: jim_groark@apsc.com
	State of Arizona Emergency Services Tel: (806) 411–2336, or (800) 411–2336
ARKANSAS	State of Arkansas, Office of Emergency Services W.R. "Bud" Harper Tel: (501) 730–9750 Fax: (501)730–9754 E-mail: wharper@state.ar.us
CALIFORNIA	Association of Contingency Planners (ACP) Los Angeles Chapter Deborah Serina Tel: (310) 456–1040 Fax: (310) 456–1040 E-mail: disasterhelp@email.msn.com
	Association of Contingency Planners (ACP) Orange County Chapter Patti Scanlan Tel: (310) 335–4501 Fax: (310) 322–0130 E-mail: pati_scanlan@infonet.com
	Association of Contingency Planners (ACP) San Diego Chapter Marti Lee Tel: (618) 651–1478 E-mail: mlee@qualcomm.com
	Association of Sacramento Area Planners (ASAP) Darrell Baxter Tel: (916) 845–6911 Fax: (916) 845–0525 www.zetsite.com/asap.htm E-mail: darell_baxter@ftb.ca.gov
	Business and Industry Council for Emergency Planning and Preparedness (BICEPP) Los Angeles Chris Wright Tel: (213) 386–4524 Fax: (805) 499–8804 www.kfwb.com/bicepp/bicepp.html

(*continued*)

State	Group or Agency
	Business Recovery Managers Assoc (BRMA) Northern California Tel: (925) 355–8660 www.brma.com
	California Emergency Services Assoc (CESA) Southern Chapter Laura Hernandez Tel: (805) 644–0899
	California Emergency Services Assoc (CESA) Coastal Chapter Ray Riordan Tel: (510) 287–1327
	California Emergency Services Assoc (CESA) Inland Chapter Nellie Lee Barber Tel: (530) 224–4113
	City of Los Angeles Emergency Preparedness Division Ellis Stanley Tel: (213) 485–5231 Fax: (213) 847–7143 E-mail: eooweb@cao.ci.la.ca.us
	Southern CA Emergency Services Association Wendy Milligan Tel: (805) 644–0899 Fax: (805) 642–2883 http://scesa.com
	State of California Office of Emergency Services Tel: (916) 262–1800
COLORADO	Association of Contingency Planners Rocky Mountain Chapter Bob Niehoff Tel: (303) 768–2857 Fax: (303) 768–3019 www.acp-crmc-colorado.com E-mail: rniehoff@oppenheimerfunds.com or 103473.1215@compuserve.com
	State of Colorado Emergency Management Tel: (303) 273–1622
CONNECTICUT	Connecticut Disaster Recovery Information Exchange Robert Urion Tel: (203) 925–3900 Fax: (203) 944–9008
	State of Connecticut Emergency Management Tel: (860) 566–8517

(continued)

Table 10–1 U.S. Disaster Recovery Groups and Emergency Management Organizations by State (continued)

State	Group or Agency
DELAWARE	Delaware Emergency Management Agency John P. (Sean) Mulhern, Director P.O. Box 527 Delaware City, DE 19706 Phone: (302) 659–3362 Contact: Jane Gooding, jgooding@state.de.us Delaware Valley Business Resumption Information Exchange Group (DVBRIEG) Patricia Bennett Tel: (609) 635–9770 Fax: (609) 635–9766
DISTRICT OF COLUMBIA	Association of Contingency Planners Capital Area Chapter Greg Brown Tel: (301) 803–6168 Fax: (301) 803–6168 E-mail: gsbrown@us.ibm.com DC Emergency Preparedness Tel: (202) 727–6161
FLORIDA	Association of Contingency Planners North-East Florida Chapter Brian Vigue Tel: (904) 464–5671 Fax: (904) 464–4264 E-mail: brian.vigue@nationsbank.com or bvigue@aol.com Association of Contingency Planners Mid-Florida Chapter Marsha Bacsko Tel: (407) 805–5441 or Fax: (407) 858–8876 E-mail: marshalb@sms.att.com Disaster Prevention & Recovery Alliance Lee Keller Tel: (813) 969–3614 State of Florida Emergency Management Tel: (850) 413–9886
GEORGIA	Association of Contingency Planners Atlanta Chapter Tel: (800) 445–4227 State of Georgia Emergency Management Tel: (404) 635–7000

(continued)

Table 10–1 U.S. Disaster Recovery Groups and Emergency Management Organizations by State (continued)

State	Group or Agency
HAWAII	Hawaii Association of Contingency Planners Ray Trombley Tel: (808) 526–7125
	State of Hawaii Civil Defense Tel: (808) 733–4300
IDAHO	State of Idaho Disaster Services Tel: (208) 334–3460
ILLINOIS	Business Resumption Planners Assoc (BRPA) William Lundquist Tel: (312) 540–3717 E-mail: William.Lundquist@US.PwCGlobal.com
	Illinois Emergency Services Management Assocation (IESMA) Bill Keller Tel: (217) 384–3826 www.iesma.org
	State of Illinois Emergency Management Association Tel: (217) 782–7860 www.state.il.us/iema/
INDIANA	Midwest Contingency Planners Gary Wyne Tel: (317) 276–6632
	State of Indiana Emergency Management Tel: (317) 232–3984
IOWA	Iowa Contingency Planners Roberta Holmes Tel: (515) 225–5489
	State of Iowa Disaster Services Tel: (515) 281–3231
KANSAS	Association of Contingency Planners Kansas Chapter Don Martens Tel: (316) 523–6820 Fax: (316) 523–6815 E-mail: don.martens@boeing.com or dmart10299@aol.com
	Business Contingency Planning Forum of Northeast Kansas Dan Swearingen Tel: (785) 296–7422 Fax: (785) 296–8932 E-mail: dansw@dadisc1.wpo.state.ks.us

(*continued*)

State	Group or Agency
	Kansas Emergency Management Association Gary Rogers, President Tel: (785) 332–2560
	State of Kansas Emergency Management Tel: (785)274–1409
KENTUCKY	State of Kentucky Disaster & Emergency Services Tel: (502) 564–8630
LOUISIANA	State of Louisiana Emergency Preparedness Tel: (504) 342–1588
MAINE	Maine Business Continuity Information Exchange Linda Norden Tel: (781) 398–8062
	State of Maine Emergency Management Tel: (207) 287–4080
MARYLAND	Mid Atlantic Disaster Recovery Assoc (MADRA) Mike Slingluff Tel: (703) 450–3232
	State of Maryland Emergency Mgt. Agency David McMillion Tel: (410) 486–4422 Fax: (410) 486–1867 www.mema.state.md.us
MASSACHUSETTS	Northeast States Emergency Consortium Tel: (781) 224–9876
	Northern New England Disaster Recovery Information Exchange Bill Bruce Tel: (603) 437–2179
	State of Massachusetts Emergency Management Tel: (508) 820–2000
MICHIGAN	Great Lakes Business and Recovery Group Gwen Pfaff Tel: (248) 265–5724
	Michigan Emergency Management Association Charles Seehase Tel: (810) 469–5270
	State of Michigan, Police: Emergency Management Division Capt. Edward G. Buikema Tel: (517) 333–5042 Fax: (517) 333–4987 E-mail: buikemae@state.mi.us

(*continued*)

Table 10–1 U.S. Disaster Recovery Groups and Emergency Management Organizations by State (continued)

State	Group or Agency
MINNESOTA	Business Continuity Planners Association Tel: (612) 223–9801 State of Minnesota Emergency Management Tel: (651) 296–2233
MISSISSIPPI	State of Mississippi Emergency Management Tel: (601) 352–9100
MISSOURI	Mid America Contingency Planning Forum St. Louis Tom Roseler Tel: (314) 466–6662 Fax: (314) 466–4731 Partnership for Emergency Planning (PEP) Kansas City Barb Ortmeier Tel: (913) 928–6862 State of Missouri Emergency Management Agency Cathy Zumwalt Tel: (573) 526–9146 Fax: (573) 634–7966 E-mail: czumwalt@mail.state.mo.us
MONTANA	Association of Disaster & Emergency Services Jim King Tel: (406) 873–2084 State of Montana Disaster & Emergency Services Tel: (406) 841–3911
NEBRASKA	Great Plains Contingency Planners Jerry Tritz, President Tel: (402) 351–3178 State of Nebraska Emergency Management Tel: (402) 471–7410
NEVADA	County of Clark, Local Emergency Planning Committee Robert Andrews Tel: (702) 455–5710 Fax: (702) 455–5718 State of Nevada Emergency Management Agency Tel: (702) 687–4240
NEW HAMPSHIRE	State of New Hampshire Emergency Management Tel: (603) 271–2231
NEW JERSEY	Society for Computer and Information Protection (SCIP) Richard Critchley Tel: (973) 430–6725

(continued)

State	Group or Agency
	State of New Jersey Emergency Management Lt. Eric Sorchik Tel: (609) 882–2000 Fax: (609) 538–0345
NEW MEXICO	New Mexico Office of Emergency Management Emergency Management Center Tel: (505) 476–9600 Preparedness/Mitigation/Training Bureau Chief Tel: (505) 476–9640 Response & Recovery Bureau Chief Tel: (505) 476–9611 Hazardous Materials Bureau Chief Tel: (505) 476–9620 Information Systems Bureau Chief Tel: (505) 476–9692 http://www.dps.nm.org
NEW YORK	Contingency Planning Exchange James Certoma Tel: (212) 983–8644 www.cpeworld.org State of New York Emergency Management Tel: (518) 457–2222
NORTH CAROLINA	Contingency Planning Association of the Carolinas (CPAC) Al Wallis Tel: (704) 271–4650 www.cpaccarolinas.org E-mail: awallis@ncdc.noaa.gov State of North Carolina Emergency Management Tel: (919) 733–3825
NORTH DAKOTA	North Dakota Emergency Management Association Tim Heisler Tel: (701) 662–7001 State of North Dakota Emergency Management Tel: (701) 328–3300
OHIO	Contingency Planners of Ohio Dr. Calvin L. Taylor, President Tel: (614) 799–3688 Fax: (614) 799–3678 E-mail: ctaylor@dps.state.oh.us State of Ohio Emergency Management Agency James Williams, Acting Deputy Director Tel: (889) 880–7150 Fax: (614) 889–7183 www.state.oh.us/odps/division/ema

(*continued*)

Table 10–1   U.S. Disaster Recovery Groups and Emergency Management Organizations by State (continued)

State	Group or Agency
OKLAHOMA	Association of Contingency Planners Oklahoma Chapter Mick Myscofski Tel: (918) 595–4389 Fax: (918) 595–4374 E-mail: rmyscofski@tulsa-health.org
	State of Oklahoma Emergency Management Tel: (405) 521–2481
OREGON	Oregon Emergency Management Association Kelly Jo Jensen Tel: (503) 378–1329 Fax: (503) 391–9152 www.navicom.com/~oema
	State of Oregon Emergency Management Tel: (503) 378–4124
PENNSYLVANIA	Delaware Valley Business Resumption Information Exchange Group (DVBRIEG) Patricia Bennett Tel: (609) 635–9770 Fax: (609) 635–9766
	Northwestern Pennsylvania's Disaster Preparedness Committee Rick Robie, Committee Chairman Tel: (814) 835–1199 Fax: (814) 835–9203
	State of Pennsylvania Emergency Management Agency Tel: (717) 651–2001
	Three Rivers Contingency Planning Association Kathleen Criss Tel: (412) 641–4860
RHODE ISLAND	State of Rhode Island Emergency Management Agency Tel: (401) 946–9996
SOUTH CAROLINA	Contingency Planning Assoc of the Carolinas (CPAC) Al Wallis Tel: (704) 271–4650 E-mail: awallis@ncdc.noaa.gov
	State of South Carolina Emergency Preparedness Tel: (803) 734–8020
SOUTH DAKOTA	State of South Dakota Office of Emergency Management Tel: (605) 773–3231

(continued)

Table 10–1 U.S. Disaster Recovery Groups and Emergency Management Organizations by State (continued)

State	Group or Agency
TENNESSEE	Association of Contingency Planners Middle Tennessee Chapter Mark Brewer Tel: (615) 781–7257 Fax: (615) 365–5550 E-mail: mark.brewer@fanb.com
	Business Emergency Preparedness Council (BEPC) Rex Holloway Tel: (901) 756–5103 Fax: (901) 756–5190 www.bepc.net
	Emergency Management Association of Tennessee Libbi Rucker-Reed, CEMP EMAT Secretary/Treasurer 1220 W. College St. Murfreesboro, TN 37129–1720 Tel: (615) 898–7764 Fax: (615) 898–7840 www.emat.org E-mail: ematweb@aol.com
	State of Tennessee, Emergency Management Tel: (615) 741–0001
TEXAS	Association of Contingency Planners North Texas Chapter John Small Tel: (214) 515–1226 Fax: (214) 515–1201 E-mail: jsmail@swst.com
	Association of Contingency Planners South Texas Chapter John Link Tel: (713) 216–2524 Fax: (713) 216–2524 E-mail: john.link@chase.com
	Association of Contingency Planners Capital of Texas Chapter Joan Light Tel: (512) 463–4218 Fax: (512) 305–9785 E-mail: joan.light@cpa.state.tx.us
	County of Jasper, Emergency Management Billy Ted Smith Tel: (409) 423–4200 Fax: (409) 994–2543 www.ih2000.net/jasperem E-mail: btsmith@ih2000.net
	State of Texas, Emergency Management Michelle Johnson Tel: (512) 424–2430 Fax: (512) 424–2444

(continued)

Table 10–1 U.S. Disaster Recovery Groups and Emergency Management Organizations by State (continued)

State	Group or Agency
UTAH	Association of Contingency Planners Utah Chapter Michael Stever Tel: (801) 535–6030 Fax: (801) 535–6190 E-mail: mike.stever@ci.slc.ut.us State of Utah Emergency Management Tel: (801) 538–3400 Utah Emergency Management Association Steve Layton Tel: (801) 774–7217
VERMONT	State of Vermont Emergency Management Tel: (800) 347–0488
VIRGINIA	Business Recovery Association of Virginia (BRAV) Clarence Elliott Tel: (804) 272–1549 Mid Atlantic Disaster Recovery Association (MADRA) Mike Slingluff Tel: (703) 450–3232 State of Virginia Emergency Services Tel: (804) 897–6500
WASHINGTON	Association of Contingency Planners Washington State Chapter Rick Roller Tel: (425) 865–3639 Fax: (425) 865–3327 E-mail: richard.l.roller@boeing.com Western Washington Emergency Network (WWEN) Shad Burcham King County Office of Emergency Management 7300 Perimeter Rd. South, Room 128 Seattle, WA 98108–3848 Tel: (206) 205–8106 Fax: (206) 296–3938 http://hrs.crgnet.com/wwen E-mail: Shad.Burcham@METROKC.GOV
WEST VIRGINIA	State of West Virginia Office of Emergency Services John W. Pack, Jr. Tel: (304)558–5380 Fax: (304) 344–4538 E-mail: dirwvoes@mail.wvnet.edu

(continued)

Table 10–1   U.S. Disaster Recovery Groups and Emergency Management Organizations by State (continued)

State	Group or Agency
WISCONSIN	Business Recovery Planners Association of Wisconsin Paul Bergee Tel: (608) 231–7502
	State of Wisconsin Emergency Management Tel: (608) 242–3232
	Wisconsin Emergency Management Association Wayne Baetsen Tel: (715) 478–3430
WYOMING	State of Wyoming Emergency Management Agency Bob Bezek, Coordinator Tel: (307) 777–4900 Fax: (307) 635–6017 http://132.133.10.9 E-mail: wema@wy-iso.army.mil
	Wyoming Emergency Management Association Chuck Young Tel: (307) 877–9835

PROFESSIONAL ASSOCIATIONS

Over the course of this discussion, a number of professional associations in fields not specifically related to disaster recovery planning have been cited for the insights they offer to business preparedness and recovery. Table 10–2 provides a list of some of these associations for further reference by planners.

THE "FRICTION" OF DISASTER

In addition to DR planner/emergency management groups and non-DR-specific professional associations, a number of resources exist for coordinators seeking information that will aid them in planning efforts. From severe weather tracking to virus alerts to emergency assistance (both financial and personal), the World Wide Web provides a wealth of resources. Table 10–3 summarizes information resources that may be useful in understanding the milieu in which disaster recovery may take place, and in seeking assistance and information, before, during and immediately following a disaster event.

Participating in DR organizations, reading the case studies, and talking to infrastructure service vendors and emergency managers are all part of an ongoing "sanity check" in DR planning. They are as important as any other plan

Table 10–2 Partial Listing of Non-DRP Professional Associations with DR-Related Focus

Association of Records Managers and Administrators	ARMA International 4200 Somerset Dr., #215 Prairie Village, KS 66208 Phone: 913–341–3808 800–422–2762 (U.S. and Canada) FAX: 913–341–3742 (fax) hq@arma.org URL: www.arma.org	ARMA International is a not-for-profit association serving more than 10,000 information management professionals in the United States, Canada, and over 30 other nations. ARMA International members include records and information managers, MIS and ADP professionals, imaging specialists, archivists, hospital administrators, legal administrators, librarians, and educators. The mission of ARMA International is to provide education, research, and net-working opportunities to information professionals, to enable them to use their skills and experience to leverage the value of records, information, and knowledge as corporate assets and as contributors to organizational success.
National Fire Protection Association	NFPA 1 Batterymarch Park PO Box 9101 Quincy, MA 02269–9101 Phone: 617–770–3000 URL: www.nfpa.org	The National Fire Protection Association (NFPA), headquartered in Quincy, Massachusetts, is an international, nonprofit, membership organization founded in 1896 to protect people, their property, and the environment from destructive fire. In more than 100 years of advocacy, NFPA has established its role as the leading worldwide advisor on the topics of fire safety and protection. More than 65,000 strong, NFPA's membership represents nearly 100 nations and is open to all individuals interested in promoting a safer world.
Association of Information Technology Professionals	AITP 315 South Northwest Highway Suite 200 Park Ridge, IL 60068–4278 Phone: 847–825–8124 800–224–9371 FAX: 847–825–1693 URL: www.aitp.org	AITP is the professional association comprised of career-minded individuals who seek to expand their potential—employers, employees, managers, programmers, and many others. The organization seeks to provide avenues for all their members to be teachers as well as students and to make contact with other members in the IS field, all in an effort to become more marketable in rapidly changing, technological careers.

(continued)

Table 10–2 Partial Listing of Non-DRP Professional Associations with DR-Related Focus (continued)

Information Systems Security Association	ISSA 7044 South 13th Street Oak Creek, WI 53154 Phone: 414–768–8000 FAX: 414–768–8001 URL: www.issa-intl.org	The primary goal of the Information Systems Security Association, Inc. (ISSA) is to promote management practices that will ensure the confidentiality, integrity, and availability of organizational information resources. To achieve this goal, members of the Association must reflect the highest standards of ethical conduct and technical competence. Therefore, ISSA has established Code of Ethics and requires its observance as a prerequisite and continuation of membership and affiliation with the Assocation.
Information Systems Audit and Control Association	Information Systems Audit and Control Association/Foundation 3701 Algonquin Road, Suite 1010 Rolling Meadows, IL 60008 Telephone: 847–253–1545 FAX: 847–253–1443 URL: www.isaca.org	With more than 20,000 members in more than 100 countries, the Information Systems Audit and Control Association (ISACA) is well on its way to achieving its vision of being the recognized global leader in IT governance, control, and assurance. Founded in 1969, ISACA sponsors international conferences, administers the globally respected CISA® (Certified Information Systems Auditor) designation held by more than 12,000 professionals worldwide, and develops globally applicable Information Systems (IS) Auditing and Control Standards. An affiliated Foundation under takes leading-edge research in support of the profession.
International Association of Emergency Managers	IAEM 111 Park Place Falls Church, VA 22046–4513 Telephone: 703–538–1795 FAX: 703–241–5603 URL: www.iaem.com	The International Association of Emergency Managers (IAEM) is a nonprofit educational organization dedicated to promoting the goals of saving lives and protecting property during emergencies and disasters.
National Emergency Management Association	National Emergency Management Association C/O Council of State Governments P.O. Box 11910 Lexington, KY 40578 Telephone: 606–244–8000 606–244–8239 URL: www.nemaweb.org	NEMA is the professional association of State and Pacific Caribbean insular state emergency management directors committed to providing national leadership and expertise in comprehensive emergency management; serving as a vital information and assistance resource for state and territorial directors and their governors; and forging strategic partnerships to advance continuous improvements in emergency management.

(continued)

Table 10–2   Partial Listing of Non-DRP Professional Associations
                 with DR-Related Focus (continued)

Network Professionals Association	NPA 710 East Ogden Avenue, Suite 600 Naperville, IL 60563 Telephone: 630–579–3282 FAX: 630–369–2488 npa@npa.org URL: www.npa.org	NPA endeavors to unite network computing professionals in a worldwide association; determine member needs and interests; deliver programs and services to meet those needs and interests.
Risk and Insurance Management Society	RIMS 655 Third Avenue New York, NY 10017–5367 Phone: 212–286–9292 FAX: 212–986–9716	The Risk and Insurance Management Society, Inc. (RIMS) serves its member entities by proactively providing the highest-quality products, services and information to manage all forms of business risk.

development activity because they help to "condition" the coordinator and his or her DR teams to the world in which their plans will execute.

In some respects, disaster recovery planning can be likened to the preparations for a battle during war. The classic military thinker, von Clausewitz, expresses the difference between planning and execution as the "friction" of battle.

> Everything is very simple in war, but the simplest thing is difficult. These difficulties accumulate and produce a friction that no man can imagine exactly who has not seen war. . . .Friction is the only conception, which in a general way corresponds to that which distinguishes real war from war on paper. The military machine, the army and all belonging to it, is in fact simple, and appears on this account easy to manage. But let us reflect that no part of it is in one piece, that it is composed entirely of individuals, each of which keeps up its own friction in all directions.[6]

Without bending the metaphor too far, von Clausewitz's description of friction in battle can also be applied to the implementation of disaster recovery plans. Many factors—from human to milieu—can and do impact the execution of most plans. Regardless of the theoretical soundness of the paper plan, it is at best a jumping off point for disaster response.

The DR coordinator and his or her lieutenants need to understand and rehearse the strategies and procedures detailed in the plan until they have honed their ability to perform their assigned roles within acceptable timeframes. Plan testing, discussed in the next chapter, helps to build this type of ability.

However, in the absence of actual experience with disaster, coordinators and teams need to exploit every possible avenue for understanding the "friction of recovery," albeit, secondhand. They need to listen to the accounts of those who have actually experienced disasters (the only true "gurus" in this field) and

Table 10–3   Milieu Information Resources on the Web

Books and Magazines	The Rothstein Catalog on Disaster Recovery URL: www.rothstein.com	Since 1989, one of the most comprehensive resources for books, DR software tools, videos and research reports related to disaster recovery.
	The Disaster Resource Guide URL: www.disaster-resource.com	An excellent guide to the latest articles on DR-related topics, and up-to-date lists of product/service vendors, disaster recovery related web resources, and forth-coming conferences and tradeshows.
	Summit Online URL: www.summitonline.com/white.html	The latest industry white papers on systems and network management issues including DR
	Prove-IT Initiative URL: www2.dlttape.com/proveit/index.htm	Quantum's DLT tape contextualized as a disaster recovery solution. However, good generic information and whitepapers on DR planning.
Alerts and Emergency Information	Federal Emergency Management Administration Tropical Storm Watch URL: www.fema.gov/fema/trop.htm	Latest FEMA information on tropical storms and disaster relief activities.
	U.S. Geological Survey Water Data URL: h20.usgs.gov/public/realtime.html	Latest data from USGS on drought, floods, and other water-related issues.
	National Oceanic and Atmospheric Administration URL: www.noaa.gov/	Portal provides links to the National Hurricane Center, National Weather Service, and Weather Satellite Imaging Information.
	National Earthquake Information Center URL: www.neic.cr.usgs.gov/	Another USGS site with up-to-date earthquake information.
	Symantec Antivirus Research Center URL: www.symantec.com/avcenter/	Two websites from anti-virus software makers providing alerts about computer viruses and tools for removing them from systems.
	Trend Micro AntiVirus Alerts URL: www.antivirus.com/vinfo/	

(continued)

Table 10–3   Milieu Information Resources on the Web (continued)

Emergency Response	CERT Coordination Center URL: www.cert.org/	The CERT Coordination Center is part of the Survivable Systems Initiative at the Software Engineering Institute, a federally funded research and development center at Carnegie Mellon University. CERT was started by DARPA (the Defense Applied Research Projects Agency, part of the U.S. Department of Defense) in December 1988 after the Morris Worm incident crippled approximately 10% of all computers connected to the Internet. Originally, the work of CERT was almost exclusively incident response. Since then, the organization has worked to help start other incident response teams, coordinate the efforts of teams when responding to large-scale incidents, provide training to incident response professionals, and research the causes of security vulnerabilities, prevention of vulnerabilities, system security improvement, and survivability of large-scale networks.
	Forum of Incident Response and Security Teams (FIRST) URL: www.first.org	Since November 1988, an almost continuous stream of security-related incidents has affected thousands of computer systems and networks throughout the world. To address this threat, a growing number of government and private sector organizations around the globe have established a coalition to exchange information and coordinate response activities.
		This coalition, the Forum of Incident Response and Security Teams (FIRST), brings together a variety of computer security incident response teams from government, commercial, and academic organizations. FIRST aims to foster cooperation and coordination in incident prevention, to prompt rapid reaction to incidents, and to promote information sharing among members and the community at large. Currently FIRST has nearly 70 members.

(continued)

Table 10–3   Milieu Information Resources on the Web (continued)

American National Red Cross URL: www.redcross.org	The American Red Cross, a humanitarian organization led by volunteers and guided by its Congressional Charter and the Fundamental Principles of the International Red Cross Movement, will provide relief to victims of disasters and help people prevent, prepare for, and respond to emergencies.
National Infrastructure Protection Center URL: www.nipc.gov	The mission of the NIPC is both a national security and law enforcement effort to detect, deter, assess, warn of, respond to, and investigate computer intrusions and unlawful acts, both physical and "cyber," that threaten or target critical infrastructures, including telecommunications, energy, banking and finance, water systems, government operations, and emergency services. The NIPC's job is not simply to investigate and respond to attacks after they occur, but to learn about preventing them. The site lists current advisories and warnings

attempt to define better the milieu in which their plans will be executed. This milieu focus is critical to the translation of capability into recovery.

ENDNOTES

1. Wendy Goldman Rohm, "That's All That's Left!" *InfoSystems,* 02/87.
2. Jon William Toigo, "Bosch Overcomes Hurricane Hugo," *Contingency Journal,* 03/90.
3. Carol Silwa and Julia King, "Storm Tests IT Plans," *Computerworld,* 09/20/99.
4. Carol Silwa, "Plans Being Laid for Next Time," *Computerworld,* 09/20/99.
5. The DISASTER RECOVERY INFORMATION EXCHANGE (DRIE) can be contacted via telephone at (416) 491–2420 or on the web at www.drie.org. According to the DRIE website, the six chapter organizations include:

    DRIE Toronto
    Graeme Jannaway
    2175 Sheppard Avenue East, Suite 310
    Willowdale, Ontario, Canada M2J 1W8
    (416) 359–6218 Fax: (416) 491–1670
    E-mail: Graeme.Jannaway@NesbittBurns.com

DRIE Ottawa
Brian Miller
(613) 238–2909 Fax: (613) 238–2902
E-mail: bp.miller@sympatico.ca

DRIE Montreal
Andre Gagnon
(450) 466–4911
E-mail: agagnon@zercom.net

DRIE West (serving Calgary, Edmonton & Vancouver)
Cheryl Bieson
(403) 543–4699
E-mail: cbieson@telusplanet.net

DRIE SW Ontario
Rod Mabley
(519) 895–1213 x 795 Fax: (519) 895–1215
E-mail: mableyr@recall.com

DRIE Central (serving Manitoba, Saskatchewan, & NW Ontario)
(204) 985–4854

Another organization endeavoring to establish an international presence for disaster recovery planning is SURVIVE! INTERNATIONAL, Tel: 011–800 SURVIVE 5, Fax: +44 181 874 6446, with a web presence at www.survive.com.

6. Carl von Clausewitz, On War, translated and edited by Michael Howard and Peter Paret (Princeton, NJ: Princeton University Press, 1976 and 1984).

CHAPTER 11

Plan Maintenance
and Testing

The plan is finished at last! Strategies for system, network, and user recovery have been meticulously honed into straightforward, step-by-step procedures, tied together by a solid-but-flexible emergency decision-making flowchart. To the extent possible, a documented capability has been put into place that will safeguard the company against the vicissitudes of nature and man.

Coordinators who reach this point in the disaster recovery planning project often sense a special moment of exhilaration. Too many, however, end their efforts here.

The disaster recovery document for a large company with numerous critical functions can be voluminous and impressive in appearance. Perched atop a shelf in the office of the coordinator or information manager, it may be a source of pride, evoking praise from senior management and auditors alike. However, there on the shelf, gathering dust, the document is also useless.

Disaster recovery plans are living documents that must grow and change as the businesses they are to safeguard grow and change. In short, plans must be tested frequently and maintained in a state that is consistent with the requirements of changing business processes.

As previously cited, plans must exist not only on paper or electronic media, but in the minds of those who will enact them. This presumes training and education.

These points are more than philosophical. Given the increasing pressure of federal regulation and state legislation, the increasing scrutiny of the media and of shareholders, and the decreasing tolerance of companies to even short-term interruptions of critical applications, auditors are less inclined to pass untested plans without comment. They want to see proof that the plan will work and that the company's money has not been invested in anything less than the best capability their money can buy.

Unlike science fiction television dramas, in which desperate last-minute repairs made to critical systems are tested in mortal combat, disaster recovery plan testing should occur in advance of disaster itself. Clearly, it is the wrong time to discover erroneous conclusions and errant strategies when the company is in the throes of an unplanned interruption of mission critical business processes. At that point, the plan's disaster is the company's as well. Plan components need to be tested in a context of rationality, not crisis, so that lessons learned are not learned at the expense of business survival.

Some of the elements of plan maintenance and some approaches to testing planned strategies and procedures are discussed in the following sections. Many coordinators, including those who owe their expertise to having recovered from smoke-and-rubble-type disasters, argue that testing is the most important element of disaster recovery planning. For all of the reasons cited above, they are probably correct.

TEAM EDUCATION

Before a disaster recovery plan can be implemented, whether in a test situation or in an actual crisis, those who will be called upon to implement the plan must understand their roles. Educating recovery teams may require a mixture of classroom, distance learning, and hands-on instructional methods. Getting all team members to become committed to and conversant in the plan is sometimes as great a challenge as developing the plan itself.

The coordinator needs to keep in mind that those who attend DR training may not be terribly enthusiastic participants. Some may have been compelled to attend and may view the training as an unwelcome interference with their important work. Conversely, to others, training may be viewed as a vacation, an escape from day-to-day work schedules. Generally, the majority of trainees do not share the coordinator's zeal for disaster recovery planning. Being cognizant of this will help prevent misunderstandings on the part of the coordinator and dissuade him or her from seeking or expecting the appreciation of the planning effort undertaken up to this point.

The coordinator should focus team training as narrowly as possible on the specific components of the plan that pertain to the team being trained. (Teams, by the way, should be trained separately, then team leaders and alternates should be given special education in the "bigger picture"—the ways in which the activities for which they are responsible interact with other activities documented in the plan.) Teach trainees what they need to know, not how well the plan is organized.

There are a number of guidelines that coordinators need to keep in mind when presenting the plan in a training environment. Knowing what they are can aid in training even the most reluctant student.

1. Be brief and to the point. Especially when training technical teams, it is important to package the information in short, digestible amounts, appropriate to the skill level of the trainees. Unless asked, avoid lengthy digressions into the rationale behind the selection of a particular strategy.

2. Target the audience for level of presentation. Coordinators need not explain the differences between multi-drop and point-to-point circuits to a network team. Where possible (i.e., where the coordinator clearly understands the concepts and jargon), use terms and language familiar to the trainee.

3. Use multimedia teaching methods. Coordinators should try to mix their methods for communicating information. Provide text handouts. Use overhead projectors, video, slides, flip charts—whatever is available and appropriate. Nothing is duller than an hour of lecture.

4. Make the presentation formal. Prepare an agenda. Rehearse. Designate start and stop times. Set objectives for the group and meet them. This demonstrates respect for trainees and earns their respect.

5. Address all questions to the extent possible. If the coordinator cannot answer a question competently, he or she should make a note and follow up at a later time. Encourage constructive participation and make notes of serious questions or concerns the trainees offer. They may be valuable considerations that will improve the plan.

6. Finish on time. If there is more material to cover, plan another session.

7. Advise the trainees that there is no test at the conclusion of the training, but that their performance in a forthcoming plan test may be evaluated by their managers.

8. Give the team members copies of the plan sections that pertain to them. Ask them to review the procedures, submit any comments or corrections that they feel may be needed, and designate a date. If the next test date is known, announce it so they are prepared.

Team leaders and their alternates require extra training to familiarize them with the "big picture"—the interdependencies of the activities of their teams and how they combine to provide the business recovery capability. Here, some informality is recommended in order to create a sense of self-confidence and team unity. Team leaders are generally assigned several time-consuming tasks, such as maintaining their sections of the plan and ensuring that staff turnover does not leave a team position vacant. To facilitate their cooperation, coordinators should strive to develop a good personal rapport with team leaders.

Often the most difficult training problem exists at the senior management level. The Emergency Management Team is typically comprised of senior managers. If possible, the coordinator may be able to offload the task of "training" senior management to his or her manager (usually an IT director or CIO). If this is not the case, the coordinator needs to be prepared to provide senior managers with a high-level overview of the plan, emphasizing the emergency decision-making flowchart.

Most decision-making flowcharts are rather vague when it comes to the emergency management task path. The idea is that the team will coordinate the activities of other teams and make key decisions along the way, as well as arranging the financing of the recovery effort. Thus, "procedures" for the Emergency Management Team plan section often consist of lists of issues that the team will need to address as recovery proceeds. Criteria or guidelines for addressing the issues within the context of planned recovery strategies may also be offered.

Because of these characteristics, the emergency management section of the plan requires little maintenance. Thus, training senior managers in their recovery role may take the form of a presentation rather than a formal training session, often combining a tour of emergency operations center facilities.

PLAN MAINTENANCE

One of the more challenging aspects of the disaster recovery coordinator's job is maintenance of the plan over time. Changes to the business processes that the plan seeks to protect (or changes in the technology infrastructure that supports these processes) come to the coordinator's attention in one of three ways. The first (and preferred way) is through the change management procedure. This procedure should be outlined in the plan to provide a means for regularly auditing plan procedures for their continued adequacy.

The second way in which changes reach the coordinator's attention is through tests. Tests are conducted for a variety of reasons, such as acclimatizing teams to their roles, verifying new strategies, establishing or validating restoration timeframes or other plan assumptions, appeasing auditors, and so on. However, a test can also identify where deficits exist within the plan in the recovery of a given business process.

The third way in which changes affecting the plan are discovered is through audit reports, which may call into question the adequacy or effectiveness of the overall plan or the competence of the plan coordinator. With adequate testing, however, problems can be detected before an audit notes their existence. This is one reason why auditors should be involved in testing: They tend not to criticize test results, even if deficits are discovered, inasmuch as testing is a sign of intent to correct. There is no such thing as a failure in testing. Tests are used to gain knowledge, not to disparage plans.

Of course, there is one other way that problems in the plan can reveal themselves: in actual implementation. However, this is the least desirable way to discover plan inadequacies.

CHANGE MANAGEMENT

Suffice it to say that change management procedures, combined with periodic testing, comprise the preferred approach to plan maintenance. The question remains: Is there an approach to change management that can streamline and make the plan maintenance function less burdensome?

The answer to this question is yes. An important first step is to examine the business processes and their IT infrastructure supports in order to identify elements that are likely to change over time. These elements probably include data, programs, documentation, supplies and forms, hardware, and personnel. Of these items, changes in the size and shape of company databases are probably the most expected and self-evident.

Changes in data have two ramifications for disaster recovery planning. First, the disaster recovery coordinator needs to be familiar with the procedures for purging old data and archiving data that needs to be preserved. The coordinator needs to ensure that backup and off-site storage procedures remain adequate to safeguard data against loss.

Also in the realm of data change management issues is the creation of specialized databases on servers and workstations within the company. As new PCs and servers are acquired, their purpose and use need to be documented and provisions need to be made to securing and backing up their data. This task requires vigilance on the part of the coordinator and may be greatly facilitated through a combination of corporate policy and data discovery and classification tools discussed in Chapter 4. In the absence of these mechanisms, tracking data recovery requirements alone may pose as great a challenge as the entire disaster recovery planning process.

If IT acquisitions (including PCs) are controlled through a company IT department, the coordinator only needs to develop an interface to the acquisition process to remain informed about new installations. Controlled server and workstation acquisition can yield other benefits as well. For example, users requesting workstations may be required to schedule time for disaster recovery and security awareness training in conjunction with their acquisitions.

However, it is still the case in many companies that workstations are not acquired through conventional IT channels. As prices decline and user knowledge increases, the disaster recovery coordinator may find that PCs are acquired in the same manner as office supplies and that the number of company "data centers" increases from week to week. In this case, the coordinator may need to solicit a senior management policy to be kept apprised of acquisitions. Even if management cannot be convinced to place control over the purchase of computer technology in the hands of corporate IT professionals, few would disagree with efforts to track distributed computing assets and most would agree to implement policies aimed at safeguarding assets from loss. With management support, the coordinator may be able to arrange with departmental managers to be informed of technology purchases.

The second ramification of data change is its impact on hardware. As data grows, it may be necessary to acquire additional mass storage devices, including hard disks, arrays, network attached storage (NAS) devices, or storage area network (SAN) peripherals. These acquisitions need to be documented in the equipment inventory included to the plan and will need to become part of a hot site agreement if their replacement is expected as part of the vendor's services.

In addition to changes in data and its storage, coordinators also need to remain vigilant to the introduction of new applications as well as changes, enhancements, and modifications to existing applications that may impact the plan. Such additions and changes may also be an indicator of changing business processes that must be accounted for in the plan.

While some application changes do not affect the procedures for restoring critical systems in the event of a disaster, each change should be documented—usually as a function of IT development operations. At a minimum, the DR coordinator should ensure that copies of the documentation are removed to off-site storage for use in recovery efforts.

By contrast, major modifications or additions to the software inventory of the company must be investigated for their impact on recovery requirements and strategies. New applications may introduce significant new demands on processors, memory, and storage, altering the recovery systems configuration envisioned in the plan and provided for in a systems recovery service agreement. New applications may also impact network requirements and end user recovery.

Of even greater significance, enhancements or additions to the software inventory may also reflect changing business processes and associated criticalities. Company business plans may offer insights into these changes, but more often the managers of end user departments can provide information about new directions for their operational areas. Thus, periodic questionnaires, accompanied by a copy of the original responses, should be circulated to end user managers with the request that managers update their information.

In the case of software changes and enhancements prompted by technical rationales (that is, changes required by operating system or applications software upgrades, etc.), recovery team leaders, who are generally members of IT department staff, should be directed to update their sections of the plan at periodic intervals. It is worth noting that the term "software changes" may include changes to telecommunications switch or data networking device programming as well as computer software.

Documentation changes associated with software additions, modifications, and changes nearly always entail a review of the disaster recovery plan's provisions for off-site storage. Coordinators, or their off-site storage team leaders, should regularly inventory documentation that is off-site to ensure that only the most current documentation is stored and outdated or obsolete documentation is destroyed. This includes the disaster recovery plan itself.

As business processes change, support requirements such as preprinted forms and other supplies are also likely to change. If stores of these materials are kept off-site or at a user recovery facility, they need to be inventoried periodically and outdated materials culled from useful supplies. The emergency supplier list (persons to be contacted to obtain replacement supplies and materials in the event of a disaster) also needs to be reviewed to ensure that changing supply requirements can be met by listed suppliers. This review should reveal whether a designated supplier has gone out of business. Where this is the case, any open purchase orders with the former supplier should be closed out and new suppliers should be identified.

It is worth noting that, despite the earnest efforts of many vendors to support their customers in the wake of the 9/11 tragedy, there were also cases in which the vendors completely dropped the ball. The following is a report of one instance in which a company impacted by the World Trade Center attacks almost failed to recover because of bureaucratic infighting between an equipment vendor and reseller:

Even from my remote vantage point—in Atlanta attending that ghost town called Networld + Interop—it was clear that everyone shared in the shock, disbelief, and emotional malaise following the attack on 9/11. It was difficult to think about business, let alone to do much of it. Suddenly, the technical and political minutiae of the data storage industry seemed terribly unimportant.

That is, until a friend, who was also attending the show, joined me in the CNN Center on Wednesday evening for dinner. At first glance, it was clear that he was agitated. Red-faced and shaking when he slid into the booth, he explained his dilemma.

As a reseller/integrator of high-availability storage solutions, he had provided a storage platform to a customer located in the NYC metro area several months before. In the intervening months, hard times had hit the storage product supplier whose equipment he had used in the customer's system. As a result, the vendor had changed sales strategies, as many have, to favor "direct sales" (sales by the vendor's own sales force) over "channel sales" (those made by third-party integrators and resellers). Doing business through direct sales looks better on the corporate earnings reports and delivers more revenue directly to the vendor's bottom line. A year or two ago, channel partners were being courted to help vendors keep up with customer demand. But the recent reversal of fortune in most areas of the storage market has led to decisions by vendors that have left many channel partners blowing in the wind.

And, in this case, a customer, as well.

As a consequence of the vendor's sales strategy shift, the customer was no longer located in my friend's "territory." Instead, the customer was located in the sales territory of someone from the direct sales organization based in California.

To make a long story short, the customer had contacted his solution provider, my friend's firm, to seek another storage platform that could be used to mirror data at an alternate site. The customer was fearful that the frequent power and telecommunications outages affecting Southern Manhattan and much of the surrounding area would eventually cause his primary site to become untenable. He was playing "beat the clock" to develop a fallback strategy.

The customer complained that he was getting no support from the storage array vendor. He had been told that the vendor could not supply him with new equipment promptly because of constraints in shipping and airline transportation.

My friend, on the other hand, had exactly the equipment required by the customer: it was just sitting on a shelf at his shop. He was prepared to have his people load the equipment into a truck and drive it to the customer's location. However, the vendor stood in his way. The vendor threatened the reseller with the rescission of his reseller license if he took any such action.

The N+I conference provided my friend an opportunity to speak with the CEO of the storage company involved. After hearing the story, the CEO assured him that an accommodation could be made. A few hours later, that assurance had resulted in a quagmire of politics. Several heated phone calls and a faxed letter from a bureaucrat at the vendor's headquarters stated that my friend had done wrong by going directly to the CEO rather than "working through channels." Epithets were slung and everyone's blood pressure hit the boiling point.

In the end, the decision of whether to allow my friend deliver support to the customer became moot. Either the customer secured a solution elsewhere, or his business had simply failed: no further voicemails or emails were received despite the fact that neither my friend, nor the vendor, had come to his rescue in a timely way.

As you have probably noticed, I have elected not included any names in this brief account. Mainly, this is because I have not been able to confirm all of the details and do not wish to stir up more problems in an already difficult situation. The bottom line, however, is that for the customer, the vendor and the integrator, this was not their finest hour.

- The customer should have had done due diligence well in advance of the September 11 disaster to anticipate and provide for business continuity requirements. While no one could have anticipated the specific scenario that unfolded, solid disaster recovery planning assumes the interruption of infrastructure and business processes from any number of causes and provides a capability for ensuring that the time-to-data requirements of critical applications can be met.

- The vendor in this case was guilty of inflexibility in the face of an exceptional situation. Good management requires the articulation of policies and rules for doing business and their consistent application across the organization. However, there are exceptions to any rule. In this case, the vendor would have better served the customer by creating a new rule. Without sounding flip, what would have been the harm of deciding that resellers can support customers of the direct sales organization whenever a force majeur or Act of God interruption occurs. The exception would have benefited both the customer and the vendor.

- The reseller is guilty of nothing except for, perhaps, a lack of initiative. The support for the former customer could have been delivered swiftly, without attention to the bureaucrats. Vendors are a dime a dozen and I doubt that the current vendor would have made good on threats given the exceptional nature of the event once the crisis subsided and cooler heads prevailed.

Perhaps the lesson that can be learned from this situation is that IT managers need to expect unexceptional performance from vendors even during exceptional situations. This assumption, while somewhat pessimistic, has the advantage of assuring business survival. The simple fact is that many vendors and solution providers will not deliver best-of-breed support during a crisis for any number of reasons. If some do—and fortunately many, including EMC and Yipes!, have in the current situation—this will only aid a positive outcome of recovery plan implementation. Plan for the worst is a good strategy going forward.[1]

In addition to monitoring sources of hardware, coordinators also need to look for changes in hardware configurations that in turn require that plan inventories be updated and that hot sites be notified of these changes. Major system conversions may invalidate the existing hot site capability by creating backup requirements that the hot site vendor cannot meet. Thus, a major hardware change may necessitate evaluating new hot site vendors and negotiating a new contract.

Hardware change is a broad category that includes changes to communications as well as computer configurations. It is also important to review network configurations for line changes and additions, communications hardware changes and upgrades, and other network modifications that threaten to invalidate traffic rerouting plans or network backup strategies.

Personnel turnover poses a major challenge to disaster recovery change management. New personnel must be trained in the roles they will play in disaster recovery. Emergency contact directories also need to be updated to reflect new personnel and changed home and emergency telephone numbers. For the company as a whole, the maintenance of a general employee contact directory might best be delegated to the human resources or personnel department; while for teams, team leaders should be responsible for keeping contact lists up to date.

Tools for Change Management—No Easy Fix

As of this writing, no commercially available DR planning tool exists that can reasonably claim to improve the efficiency of disaster recovery plan maintenance. Some vendors claim to provide ease of maintenance features as a function of their "canned plan" product. In other words, if the coordinator uses the template provided by the vendor to develop the plan, data elements inserted by the coordinator into the planning tool boilerplate will be neatly organized in a table or database for ease of editing.

While there is value to collecting changing data elements in a discrete table, the proposition that this simplifies change management assumes several things. First, the vendor is implying that the boilerplate plan tool is compatible with the specific requirements of each and every company that uses it. As previously suggested, the disaster recovery requirements of any two companies are often highly dissimilar, mitigating the efficacy of such boilerplate planning tools generally. This limitation extends to the "ease of maintenance" features as well.

Second, simple changes to data elements, as noted above, are rarely all that is needed to maintain a plan in its current state. For example, it is rarely an adequate response to a change in application software to simply note the new application filename in a table. The impact of an application change may be, and often is, much more far reaching.

In some cases, an application change may require the reengineering of the recovery hardware platform, the creation of a new team, changes to supplies lists, new data storage requirements, and so forth. The "change management features" of boilerplate plan tools offer little to streamline the review that must accompany each and every data element change; they simply make the easiest task—editing an element list—a bit easier.

To facilitate the change management task requires several things. First is good communications traversing over well-defined processes.

The coordinator needs to define routine intervals for gathering change data and standard reporting mechanisms for collecting change data. Intervals may be based on calendar periods (that is, team leaders will make a quarterly report of business process and IT infrastructure changes and their impact on the disaster recovery capability) or events (that is, changes will be undertaken following plan tests or significant corporate events such as the implementation/reorganization of new/existing business units, deployment, upgrade or migration to new host systems, and so forth). However reporting intervals are defined, they need to be articulated as a matter of policy, and team leaders and business unit managers need to be made responsible for adherence to established change management policy and procedures.

Modern e-mail and collaborative computing software provide powerful resources for coordinating the collection of change management information. Based on the input from reporting sources, the DR coordinator needs to review existing tasks and provisions, solicit additional input as needed, and make the necessary modifications to the existing plan. Teams need to be trained in new requirements and tasks and testing and validation activities need to be scheduled.

By organizing the plan document on some rational basis—sectioning recovery plan procedures by business process, for example—change management may be somewhat simplified. However, no amount of upfront organization can substitute for the application of careful analytical reasoning to the evaluation of change and its impact on plan elements. Were it otherwise, the DR coordinator could hand off the maintenance of the plan to a tech writer once it was first implemented and tested.

Testing to Maintain the Plan

Plan testing is an important component of plan maintenance activity as tests are the crucibles in which the plan's validity is demonstrated. The central purpose of testing is to ensure that plans can be successfully applied to recover the business processes that they have been developed to safeguard. However, there are other purposes for testing the plan.

- *Testing as an audit tool.* Plan tests are often used to evaluate the efficiency of the plan and to reveal its shortcomings. If the criteria for evaluating test results are properly defined, tests can provide useful information about deficiencies in the plan so that they can be corrected.
- *Testing as benchmarking.* Plan tests may also reveal useful information about performance of the recovery capability. Certain tests can benchmark how quickly, under optimal conditions, recovery can be reasonably expected to occur following plan activation. Live tests (involving the actual implementation of plan provisions) can also provide information on the service levels that are likely to be provided from remote system and network configurations during a period of emergency operations. This data can be used to fine tune plan provisions and to evaluate the adequacy of business interruption insurance coverage.
- *Testing as rehearsal.* Tests are a valuable training experience for team members. They provide an opportunity for teams to become familiar with their roles in disaster recovery as well as how their activities relate to the activities of the other teams. Moreover, post-test debriefings of test participants can provide insights into implementation factors that the disaster recovery coordinator may not have considered.

Testing also provides a psychological benefit to participants. They become better prepared to function in a crisis due to the familiarity they acquire with procedures and tasks in a test situation. Furthermore, testing can help to build team unity by demonstrating the interdependence of team members upon each other.

Testing methods are numerous and the ones employed should be customized to the needs of a given business. Disaster recovery coordinators differ in their approaches to testing. Some prefer to test without prior notification of test participants in order to simulate the shock and crisis of an actual disaster. Others believe this approach has little merit, claiming that tests should be routine exercises that provide a basis for calm, rational implementation of plan procedures in an actual emergency. Some companies test sections of the plan separately (i.e., they perform a hot site test on one occasion and test various other plan components, one at a time, on other occasions). Other coordinators prefer a dry run of the total recovery process.

The approach taken by a specific company will generally be determined by the tolerance of the company to interruption of normal work for testing. Few companies are willing to allow a coordinator to "pull the plug" on their computer systems in order to see how efficiently teams will react to a mock disaster. Not many more are willing to shut down normal operations for an evacuation drill. However, it may be argued that effective testing does not require these approaches. The following procedures are some of the basic requirements for effective testing of the disaster recovery plan.

- *Establish a scenario in advance.* Before undertaking a test, a test strategy needs to be developed. The strategy, often set forth in a document, should identify the scope of the disaster scenario (total loss of facility, loss of CO services, fire in the user working area, flooding of the data center, etc.). The document should also indicate any assumptions that are being made, such as the anticipated duration of the outage, the availability (or unavailability) of key recovery personnel, or the opportunity to perform a last minute backup of critical data.

    In addition to these stage-setting directions, the coordinator may wish to provide details on specific production files that will be recovered, special security requirements, or other factors that will define the elements that are to be tested. In other words, although the disaster may encompass all systems, the coordinator may wish to test only the part of the system recovery plan that pertains to distributed systems application recovery or accounting system recovery. This will limit the actual procedures that are executed in the test.

- *Set test objectives.* Tests should be performed only after formal objectives have been set. Objectives should state clearly what the exercise is to test. For example, the test may seek to determine, under certain conditions, how quickly system and applications software can be brought up on hot site hardware. Or, the test may seek to determine how long data reconstruction will take if a disaster occurs at 3:00 PM on a working day and transactions entered since 9:00 AM have been lost. The test may also seek to measure the performance of a concentrator used in conjunction with a set of user workstations thought to have low activity profiles.

    Whatever the objectives, they should be clearly stated prior to the test exercise to aid in the interpretation of test results at the conclusion of the exercise. Generally, the narrower the objectives, the more useful the information derived from the test will be.

- *Define the rules.* The rules in a test may be to perform the required recovery operation in strict adherence to planned procedures. Where deviation from the plan is required to accomplish the task, this reveals something about the adequacy of plan procedures, and participants may be required to make careful notes of what undocumented steps they must take to accomplish the objective.

In rare cases, the rules for the test may be open-ended. Traditionally, this type of test rule is used to evaluate how well a team participant can improvise or develop procedures where none previously existed.

- *Identify participants and observers.* A list should be made of the team members and observers (often internal audit, IT management, and others) who will participate in the test. Each should be made fully aware of his or her role before the test occurs (unless the test is a surprise). Observers should be told what to look for and what to do (i.e., take notes, ask questions). Team members should be told the rules and given any other directions that will help them to collect valuable information during the test.
- *Document the test results.* Depending on the objectives of the test, output may be printed in the form of system performance measurements, transaction logs, or other reports containing data sought from the test. This data will be analyzed, and both the original documents and the conclusions drawn from them retained with the plan. Test conclusions and source documentation are an important part of the documentation an auditor will require when auditing the disaster recovery plan.

  In addition to machine-generated data, test objectives may require written reports from test participants. Specific performance measurements, such as elapsed time to perform a given task or delays in recovering systems, may be included in post-test documentation. In addition, subjective assessments of plan performance may be sought from participants. These subjective assessments may be balanced by obtaining more than a single viewpoint on a given subject. Conflicting views or interpretations necessitate a group discussion with the results summarized in a final test report. Written reports, like the machine output, should be kept with the plan document for review by auditors.

There is no guideline for how often plans should be tested, but tests should be conducted as often as necessary. In stable, evolutionary data processing environments, system recovery plans should be tested quarterly or semiannually. However, in shops where system configurations and applications change often, more frequent testing may be required.

In addition to what is presented here, much more detailed information on testing methods is available from a number of sources:

- *Consultants and vendors.* Many DR planning and business continuity planning consultants specialize in developing and overseeing tests. They offer experience and a "fresh perspective" that may be of use to DR coordinators in ensuring that tests are performed efficiently and yield productive results. Vendors of disaster recovery services, such as hot sites, can also provide assistance on test definition and management. Coordinators should consider using the resources, especially if they have never tested a DR plan before.

- *Books and other educational resources.* The number of books on disaster recovery and business continuity have increased almost exponentially since the publication of the first edition of *Disaster Recovery Planning* in 1990. One book in particular, *Disaster Recovery Testing* (1995), edited by consultant Philip Jan Rothstein, provides the views and techniques of numerous practitioners. This book and a host of others on related subjects can be acquired via the web-based *Rothstein Catalog on Disaster Recovery* (http://www.rothstein.com), arguably the most complete repository of information about books, software tools, videos, and research reports in the disaster recovery field.

- *Consult fellow planners.* The disaster recovery groups listed in the previous chapter provide yet another opportunity to learn about the testing methods used by disaster recovery planners. The meetings, conventions, and other forums offered by DR groups typically include educational presentations geared to a practical business environment. Additionally, some junior colleges, colleges, and universities offer short courses (and a few degree programs) on disaster recovery and emergency management. Program administrators may be able to recommend a particular class that treats testing methods and issues in detail.

MANAGING THE RESULTS

Given the massive amounts of information that will often be generated by maintenance and testing, it is possible for the disaster recovery coordinator to lose sight of the purpose of plan testing itself. Testing provides more than back matter to the paper plan. While good test documentation will satisfy auditors and others that the plan is not simply gathering dust on a bookshelf, this is not the central objective of testing any more than producing a paper plan is the primary objective of DR planning.

Testing provides the means to cultivate understanding and preparedness among those who will need to behave rationally in the face of the great irrationality of disaster. For this reason, the old saw—that there are no failed tests—continues to have merit. Testing provides a period of time during which participants focus on the difficult "what ifs." Through testing, participants may find that strategies and procedures have missed important requirements and these insights will yield important improvements to the corporate recovery capability. A test cannot fail. Regardless of the outcome, testing always achieves its two primary objectives: (1) rehearsing teams who will be responsible for coping with a disaster and (2) identifying ways to improve the coping capability that has been established in advance of a disaster.

A final thought on plan maintenance and testing is this: It is important to have a copy of the plan stored on magnetic media to facilitate edits and changes. If this approach is adopted, however, it is essential that both hard copy and magnetic media backups be made of the plan. Every effort needs to be made to ensure the accessibility of the plan to decision makers and implementers if and when an unplanned interruption occurs.

Beyond this, to quote Shakespeare, "All things are ready if our minds be so."

ENDNOTES

1. Jon William Toigo, "Special: Customer due diligence in DR planning," Toigo's Take on Storage, www.searchstorage.com, 09/20/01. Reprinted by permission.

CHAPTER

12

Conclusion

When originally released in 1990, this book was conceived as a practical guide for information managers. In fact, it was a compilation of all of the information that I wished I had known when, as a technical staff member within the MIS Division at a medium-sized financial services company, I was first handed the task of disaster recovery planning. At that time, when asked how long I thought the project would take to complete, I estimated confidently, "About two weeks." Little did I know!

Two months and one hurricane later, I found myself still wrestling with the myriad details of a thousand what-if scenarios. Not one procedure had been written. Not one strategy had been developed. No testing had occurred. Yet, somehow, the document had grown to exceed the page count of the *New York Times* Sunday Edition.

Assistance came in the form of two persons: a marketing representative for an off-site storage vendor, who possessed a wry sense of humor and a disdain for unmerited self-aggrandizement, and a contingency planner-turned-consultant, who gave away more valuable advice than he should have—a practice that ultimately required his return to the secure embrace of corporate employment. Through these persons, I was introduced to a network of fellow DR coordinators struggling to improve their skills in the disaster recovery craft—now, as then, as much an art as a science.

One thing led to another, and my associates and I co-founded one of the first DRP user groups in the United States—a not-for-profit, Florida-based, professional association called the Disaster Avoidance and Recovery Information Group (DARING). During the next two years, both as a planner and as the president of DARING, I became conversant in the practices and jargon of the disaster recovery trade—and developed and tested several DR plans in the process.

Of particular importance, I learned to discriminate the charlatans of the unpoliced DR industry from the earnest souls who continue to populate this shadowy world of corporate continuity planning. Through ongoing interactions with industry peers and continuing efforts to develop disaster recovery capabilities both for employers and clients, I developed most of what I now know about DR planning.

Disaster recovery planning is, in essence, a pragmatic undertaking. Despite the Byzantine mystique that is perpetuated around the endeavor by some consultants and vendors, DR planning is an undertaking that is well within the grasp of common sense individuals possessing good analytical and communications skills. It also helps to have some political sense and a willingness to keep apprised of new business information technologies.

In 1990, I took it as a personal mission to dispel the myths and mysticism surrounding this activity—hence, the first book. Its publication coincided, purely by accident, with the decision by IBM to enter the disaster recovery field. The vendor was closing several regional facilities in the late 1980s when some bright soul came up with the idea of converting them into a new systems protection service offering. Leveraging its tremendous position within the IT industry in those days, IBM transformed disaster recovery planning almost overnight from back-burner concern to a systems management priority for many companies.

The significance of this transformation can be expressed this way: As late as 1988, IBM systems engineers assigned to our corporate account were still assuring us that mainframes were invulnerable to all but the most cataclysmic disaster potentials (building fires, building explosions, etc.) Data backup was important, to be sure, and IBM had a number of tape products and software to meet this need, but the resilience of "Big Iron" was a given.

The announcement of IBM's Business Recovery Service was a profound departure from this line and a wake-up call for those who had been lulled into complacency about DR. For the first time, the vendor was sending a message to its customers that even Big Blue systems were vulnerable and that some sort of contingency response capability was intrinsic to what IBM defined as "good systems management." While this piece of information may strike many as intuitively obvious ("a duh moment," as my teenage daughter might say), it sent hundreds of IT professionals in hundreds of companies on a quest for current information about DR planning. My book, one of the few in print at that moment, was the beneficiary of this newfound concern. Thanks, IBM.

In the years that followed, *Disaster Recovery Planning* was both celebrated as "an industry standard" by those who used it to guide their own planning endeavors and assailed by others, mainly a few high-priced consultants, as a terrible encroachment upon their daily bread. Imagine, portraying the "black art known only to a privileged few" as a straightforward application of common sense accessible to virtually anyone! I delighted in both characterizations, however undeserved.

Of course, the world of business information technology did not stand still over the next decade. By 1995, distributed client/server computing models had taken hold, data storage was exploding, and the Internet Revolution was revving up. Against this increasingly complicated IT backdrop, many novice planners began to perceive disaster recovery planning as an activity beyond their grasp. Driven by repeated requests from readers of the first book to publish a new work that provided an illustration of how one might apply the methods and techniques discussed in the first edition of *Disaster Recovery Planning,* I did so—albeit, through gritted teeth. The number of books in print on the subject of DR had exploded since 1990 (a good thing), but so had the number of "canned plans"—boilerplate DR planning tools that sought to fit the disaster recovery requirements of all companies into a neat, one-size-fits-all template (a not-so-good thing).

I did not want the second the book to fall into the latter category—and it didn't. Released by another publisher, book number two offered a sample implementation of the common-sense methodology described in the original book and added generic forms and checklists as a starting point for readers.

The decision to do the book was a response to two new "products" that had taken hold in the industry: "canned plans," as described above, and DRP certification programs, which were addressed in an earlier chapter. The approach favored by vendors in marketing these "products" struck me as profoundly cynical: play on the lack of self-confidence that many novice planners have in their abilities to develop a testable plan. Prey on their fear, uncertainty, and doubt. It seemed a resurgence of the same technique used by some DR consultants to cultivate contracts with corporate clients in the late 1980s. All of my experience militated against what I considered to be a return to old DR mythology. The mission was rekindled and book two was published.

In the years that have followed, the advent of *n*-tier client/server application suites (ERP, MRP, and the like), the development of new storage architectures (storage area networks), and the growth of the Internet and intranet technologies (including server-centric computing, web-based infrastructure outsourcing, thin client computing) have changed the landscape of disaster recovery planning. In response to these changes and, in part, as a result of the "business process reengineering" craze of the late 1990s, DR has shifted its focus from system recovery to business process recovery and has acquired a more fashionable moniker in some quarters: "business continuity planning."

Jargon aside, the "new focus" of DR is the same as the old focus: recover critical business operations as expeditiously as possible following an unplanned interruption. The difference, however, is that the complexity of business computing technology has increased, while corporate tolerance to downtime has decreased.

These facts are driving the first real changes in the scope and mission of disaster recovery planning since the discipline first appeared. As a new millennium dawns, it is no longer sufficient for DR coordinators to follow behind business and IT decision makers, discovering ways to ensure the continuity of the processes and infrastructures that they leave in their wake. Given the increasing dependence of business on technology and its near-zero tolerance for outages, DR considerations need to become part of the business and IT decision-making process. Coordinators need to develop a new presence: helping to guide the risk calculus of business managers and influencing the application designs of corporate IT architects. In short, coordinators need to find ways to become more proactive.

As indicated in the forewords to the second edition, which have been retained in this third edition, the DR industry takes many views on this topic. Understanding that modern DR coordinators have a broader mission than in the past, systems recovery service vendors such as IBM and Hewlett Packard Company are developing menu-based service portfolios to simplify certain aspects of recovery planning. With the right service selections, most vendors claim that they can recover systems without any on-site presence by company personnel whatsoever. Automatic recovery is possible, they claim, with the right combination of data mirroring or vaulting, automatic network rerouting, and top-notch operations support from your friendly service provider.

Meanwhile, web-based infrastructure outsourcing providers are insisting that companies concerned with potential interruptions are best served by the site replication services offered by the new breed of web-based outsourcing companies. The best disaster recovery plan, they argue, is an instantaneous, transparent failover from an interrupted system to a fully replicated, "hot" standby. Leave it to web guys, they argue, who have elevated site mirroring to an art form.

Even Paradyne Corporation's approach to Frame Relay network replacement by ISDN safety net facilities embodies a notion of hassle-free, machine-intelligent guarantees of process continuity. Disaster recovery has begun to blend with high availability, which concerns itself not with speedy restoral from outages, but with the preservation of "five nines" (99.999 percent uptime).

When and if this transition is ever complete, disaster recovery planning may fade away in its current form and become a component of corporate stewardship. However, for the foreseeable future, a mixed scenario will persist.

That, in a nutshell, is what prompted the second, and this third, edition of Disaster Recovery Planning. In this period of rapid technological innovation, there are new challenges and new risks that call into question older, mainframe-centric methodologies and recovery techniques. At the same time, however, DR coordinators cannot afford to be distracted by the promises of a forthcoming disaster recovery "nirvana," described by both new and old vendors of DR products and services.

DR coordinators need to turn their attention to new challenges and meet them with a combination of time-tested techniques as well as innovative approaches that are appropriate to the modern business. In this endeavor, there are no experts, only fellow novices. What was true in 1990 persists today.

Conclusions serve two purposes. One is structural, as the book must have an ending.

The ending of this book is hopefully a beginning. Newcomers to the field of disaster recovery planning are now, I hope, a little better oriented to the task that is before them. Maybe this book will confirm that they do not labor alone and, just maybe, it will give them some added confidence that their self-made efforts are at least as valid as those of any self-styled expert.

Pragmatism dictates that this book must also end with a sobering thought. It is this: No amount of planning can cover every contingency. When a disaster strikes, even the best plans may prove unequal to the challenge. In an actual disaster, creativity, improvisation, and hard work will determine whether the business will recover.

What then is the value of disaster recovery planning? Just this: A company's chances of survival are better if it has a plan than if it doesn't. The enterprise of disaster recovery planning, involving as it does numerous company employees, forces the company as a whole to face a reality that most would prefer to ignore. This has the effect of sensitizing persons to the causes of disaster, and perhaps helping to avoid one.

Of course, this new edition does come on the heels of perhaps the most widely witnessed disaster event of our time: the terrorist attacks of 9/11. From a human perspective, that tragedy was a significant event. We will exchange stories in the years that follow about where we were when the World Trade Center was destroyed. Those of us who were on the ground aiding in the recovery efforts in the weeks that followed will remember forever the almost surreal milieu of Lower Manhattan in those days.

From a disaster recovery perspective, however, there were few lessons to learn that we should not already have learned from the many natural and man-made calamities that organizations have sustained over the past twenty to thirty years. Writing for *Enterprise Systems* magazine in the aftermath of the Trade Center attacks, I struggled to re-contextualize familiar themes and to illustrate the dictums of disaster recovery with events I witnessed or learned about second-hand from individuals in and around Ground Zero. The editors kindly agreed to permit me to reprint the story here.

PREPARING FOR THE UNTHINKABLE: CONTROL THE DAMAGE

By

Jon William Toigo

(Originally published in *Enterprise Systems*, December 2001. Reprinted by Permission.)

The disasters at the World Trade Center and Pentagon in mid-September, while appalling in terms of their origin and horrific in terms of their human cost, could've been far worse, according to most emergency management experts. If the hijacked aircraft had struck the WTC an hour later, as many as 50,000 occupants and an incalculable number of tourists may have been counted among the missing. Similarly, had the Pentagon not been undergoing significant remodeling around the time that the building was attacked, the number of civilian and military personnel packed into those office spaces might have been much greater.

While these facts in no way mitigate the human tragedy that occurred, they did have a significant impact on the overall death toll from the events. As smoke-and-rubble disasters go, the direct impact of the Sept. 11 terrorist attacks was actually more limited than many. Within the past decade, for example, earthquakes in Japan and Turkey claimed a larger number of lives in a much shorter amount of time.

Aside from the social and political consequences of Sept. 11, perhaps the most extraordinary thing about the disaster was that so few of the impacted companies appear to have had any sort of disaster recovery plan. Of the 440-odd businesses occupying the WTC, and the numerous governmental entities in the Pentagon, only a small subset—perhaps as few as 200—evidenced pre-planned continuity strategies. My estimate is based on press accounts of the number of firms that formally declared a disaster and activated their contracts with any of the several leading "hot site" vendors, such as Comdisco, IBM Business Continuity and Recovery Services, Sungard Recovery Services, and HP Business Continuity and Recovery Services. A hot site contract provides for a facility, computer equipment and networks that can be put rapidly into service to replace a subscriber's "production" IT infrastructure if normal operations are interrupted by a disaster.

To be generous, a few companies may not have needed the services of a hot site vendor in the wake of the disaster. In some cases, only "branch office operations" were hosted within the WTC or the Pentagon, rather than a primary headquarters or important data center. In a few other cases, companies may have instead used homegrown recovery strategies and capabilities that didn't require the participation of a commercial service provider.

Even with these exceptions factored in, however, the number of companies that had prepared for the possibility of a disaster were well in the minority. The sad truth is that, as in the case of the 143 companies that simply disappeared in the months and years following the 1993 bombing of the WTC, many of the companies that endured the Sept. 11 tragedy without a continuity plan will not be around this time next year. These companies will learn their lessons about the importance of disaster recovery planning the hard way, adding further pain and anguish to the already sad memory of that awful event.

Based on published reports, along with interviews I conducted in early October with several WTC survivors, some lessons can be gleaned that may help planners to safeguard mission-critical business processes from future disasters. Most have to do with the settings and circumstances in which the disaster recovery capability may need to be activated and used.

1. Plan for Total Disaster

    Assume the worst, that critical infrastructure components over which businesses have no control (including telecommunications, power and transportation) are unavailable. This was certainly the case for hundreds of businesses located near the WTC. Most lost power, communications, and, in many cases, physical access to their facilities due to police and emergency management cordons. According to one person with offices near the disaster area, "Our facility wasn't directly impacted by the attack, but we lost all telephone communications with our [financial] clients and all of our overseas lines for almost a week following the event. We had to activate our disaster plan, despite the fact that we had no visible damage." The company, and many of its neighbors, were part of the secondary disaster that almost inevitably follows any regional disaster: Their business operations were stopped cold, despite the fact that they were not directly in the path of the terrorist-controlled aircraft. A well-designed disaster recovery plan takes the worst-case scenario as its premise and is designed for modular implementation in response to any "lesser" disaster events that confront the business.

2. Focus on Key Assets

    The most important assets of an organization cannot be replaced. Disaster recovery strategies come in two basic flavors: replacement or redundancy. Since it's impossible to replace skilled personnel or data, a redundancy strategy should be implemented. In terms of data, this means implementing a data mirroring or tape backup strategy and ensuring that it's scrupulously observed and periodically tested.

    Many spokespersons for companies in the World Trade Center reported that they had plans in place to account for everything—except for the loss of key personnel that resulted from the attack. According to a spokesperson for the Port Authority of New York and New Jersey, "We didn't anticipate an instantaneous loss of so many senior managers. In the blink of an eye, the fire department lost most of its upper echelon. I remember being asked by a fireman whether I had seen his battalion commander, captain, lieutenant or any other officer. I hadn't and I didn't realize until long afterward that we had lost so many of the hierarchy when the towers collapsed."

As awful as it is to contemplate such human loss, a redundancy strategy may mean cross-training numerous personnel to perform mission-critical tasks, then dispersing them around the corporate campus or into field offices. Companies most profoundly impacted by the Sept. 11 attacks will be those who lost not just electronic- and paper-based information assets, but irreplaceable personnel.

3. Size Doesn't Matter

A lesson that many organizations are learning the hard way from this incident is that they've seriously underestimated the importance of data stored on PC hard disks. When DR planners and IT managers in most organizations think about mission-critical data, they tend to focus on "big iron." That means large arrays, large network-attached storage volumes, storage area networks or mainframe DASD.

However, the lowly PC, with its 30 to 100GB hard disk drive and innocuous Excel spreadsheet used to track key corporate financial hedges, may have significantly greater importance from a business recovery standpoint than all the data in the corporate ERP system. The company that survives a disaster will be one that has ferreted out all of these small-but-critical apps so that they can be replicated off-site.

One planner whose company is recovering from the attack reports that, "We are discovering that the really important data was on hard disks of PCs and laptops that were never backed up and didn't survive the disaster."

4. Work with Law Enforcement

For the first full week following the disaster, police and emergency managers were not allowing personnel into the cordoned area, which extended several blocks from the actual WTC disaster site. When authorities began opening the area to some traffic, only those who were able to show that they resided in the restricted areas were allowed to pass.

Survivor companies recognize that their continuity plans will need to execute under the aegis of law enforcement and public safety professionals who are less interested in how they're going to access offices to power down equipment or take last-minute backups than they are in preventing looting and ensuring public health and safety. It's a good idea to meet with local civil emergency management and police agencies and to obtain "clearances" for your corporate ID badges in advance of any disaster. But, don't rely on the "clearances" counting for much in the event of a major calamity.

5. Expect People's Best—and Worst

The spirit is willing, but the flesh is weak. The stories of courage coming out of the WTC and Pentagon disasters are more than "hero building." It's an almost signature characteristic of disasters that they tend to bring out the best—and the worst—in people. Consider the story of the man who lost his briefcase under a car where he sought shelter from the dust and debris of the second tower collapse. Several days later, the briefcase was returned by a rescue worker who had discovered it while removing the automobile from the rubble. The man was delighted to see that the briefcase still contained his wallet, which was filled with cash and other personal effects. However, a day or two later, the man also discovered that his credit-card number was being used to purchase goods and services all over the city, apparently by the same man who had returned the case, and that this had been going on almost from the day of the disaster. The point is that you cannot assume unilateral heroism in a disaster. The purpose of rehearsing and testing a disaster recovery plan is not to teach recovery team members how to perform procedures by rote, but to get them acclimated to thinking rationally in the face of a great irrationality. Human nature also requires that security safeguards be provided in the recovery environment.

6. Watch Out for Third Parties Affected

Be careful about planning assumptions that involve third parties. Some companies continue to use a "next-box-off-the-line" approach in their strategies for replacing hardware in the wake of a disaster. That is, their plan is to replace damaged components by requesting a priority shipment of new gear from suppliers as soon as possible following the disaster. The shutdown of air transportation following the Sept. 11 calamity compromised quick hardware replacement for many firms.

One survivor reported that his company was running on batteries in the days following the attack. "Power was sketchy and we wanted to mirror our NAS [network-attached storage] across the Hudson River. Our vendor told us that because of a change in their sales territories, we couldn't get more product from the local reseller who had originally sold us the gear. It had to be delivered to us by our new direct sales account representative, located on the West Coast. Our reseller was livid—he was close by with gear on his shelf that he could get to us in an hour, but he was being told he would violate his reseller agreement if he supported us. Ultimately, he told them to go to hell and brought us what we needed."

For reasons like this, it's a good idea to maintain critical spare components at a secure off-site facility.

7. Plan Employee Work Space

Many disaster recovery plans stop at provisioning for systems and network replacement. They don't provide for new user work locations. This not only compromises the recovery timetable, it can lead to employee confusion. Going forward, companies may want to consider using application service providers or managed Web-hosting providers to make mission-critical applications accessible via dial-up connections or the World Wide Web. Such an approach would enable work-at-home strategies for workers who are equipped to do so—a useful hedge until suitable replacement work areas can be located.

8. Try to Avoid the Media

You'll want to establish a command center away from the media. After the bombing of the WTC in 1993, one "Big Five" accounting firm established an ad hoc command center in a nearby office complex. The location proved to be a preferred backdrop for television journalists covering the event. Inadvertently, TV cameras captured images of a whiteboard containing two credit-card account numbers intended for use by the company's recovery teams as they secured supplies and equipment. The numbers were broadcast around the country and were repeatedly misused by nefarious viewers of the program. After Sept. 11, no such mistakes were made. The need to establish a command center away from the disaster site, and to deal with media through the vehicle of corporate communications or experienced PR firms, seemed to be recognized by most disaster-stricken firms.

9. Consider Your Workers

The impact of any disaster, whether the result of terrorism or some natural calamity, exacts a toll on the psyches of workers. Shorter workdays, half shifts, on-site counseling and other compassionate considerations may aid more in a successful recovery than all the logistics and plans combined. The good news is that most companies, including many impacted by the WTC incident, find that concerns about employee availability in the aftermath of a disaster are often unfounded. In most cases, disasters have a galvanizing impact on company teams: More than one planner reported that he needed to turn away personnel offering to assist recovery efforts. It's important to keep employees apprised of the situation, rather than having them draw conclusions from TV reports. When you need employees' help, most planners report, it's available.

10. Reward Innovation

Disaster recovery plans are not scripts for recovery efforts; they're guidelines at best. Given the "shifting battlefield" of recovery efforts, preplanned approaches sometimes need to give way to expediency.

According to one company spokesperson, "We had planned to keep in touch with our recovery teams by cell phone. But there were times after the incident when the cells in Manhattan were completely saturated. We started using runners to carry verbal messages from one site to another. [Sticking to the cell phone plan] would have slowed down our recovery a lot, but some teams simply abandoned the planned procedures and moved forward on their own initiative. As a result, we were able to keep the recovery effort on track."

Reports like this emphasize the importance of encouraging innovation and creativity on the part of recovery teams. When team leaders feel empowered to take the initiative, planners should reward this, either immediately or in debriefing meetings well after the fact. If mistakes are made, forgive them, at least in the short term, since customers, shareholders and others who are waiting for a return to normalcy will do the same. Most will understand that disaster recovery is difficult work.

TOUGH JOBS ALL AROUND

Disaster recovery planning is difficult work, but it pales in comparison to actually executing the plan. This is true whether the disaster situation confronting a company is a minor software glitch that threatens to place the company on the front page of the *Wall Street Journal* in a less than flattering light, or a terrorist attack that kills thousands of people and reduces statuesque buildings to mountains of dust and rubble in the space of a few hours.

In the final analysis, the events of Sept. 11 have clearly illustrated to complacent companies that disasters do happen. The result has been a surge of interest in disaster recovery planning that may or may not last beyond the current crisis. While the iron is hot, take the opportunity to get senior management signatures on purchase orders for high availability and recovery provisions.

But as the WTC and Pentagon incidents demonstrate, there are no silver-bullet technologies or best-of-breed solutions that guarantee the successful outcome of a disaster recovery strategy. Disaster recovery is less about a product or document than a process: It's a way of thinking about the unthinkable.[1]

In the final analysis, the events of 9/11 confirmed what we already knew about disaster recovery — the principles and practices that have been advanced by practitioners who have labored in obscurity in the field for the past thirty years. The poignant reality is that most of the organizations that will rise like the mythological Phoenix from the ashes of 9/11 owe their good fortune to the real heroes of their organizations: to those who did the work of DR planning over the years and often without much support from senior management or fellow workers. Readers of this book, whether experienced hands or novice planners, should take note of their critical role in guaranteeing the survival of their charges and always remember that theirs is among the most noble tasks in any organization—even if it is among the least celebrated.

The second purpose of a conclusion is to serve as a repository for all the justifications of those quiet judgments that were rendered in the earlier chapters. It is where the author tries to comment on observations that he is sure will come in response to the book (although sometimes he only rationalizes his own complaints).

These are some of the issues that require closure.

1. "Short shrift was given to quantitative risk analysis techniques." This is true. I have dealt with the subject of quantitative risk analysis methods at some length elsewhere.[2] Those who know me know that I am not an adherent of any quantitative methods, and since there are already so many books dedicated to the subject, readers are directed to bookstores or The Rothstein Catalog on Disaster Recovery (www.rothstein.com/catalog.html) for further research.

2. "Some disaster scenarios were brushed over in the book—for example, what if senior managers or other key corporate decision makers are lost in a disaster?" This comment was actually received from a reader of the first edi-

tion in the UK. He was, no doubt, disappointed by the absence of a treatment of the issue in the second edition as well. While the loss of a key decision maker is a potential hazard faced by all companies, both of the earlier editions of this book assumed that, in the majority of cases, some management element would be intact to facilitate the recovery process. The sharp decline, in the United States at least, in human casualties associated with business interruption events suggested the validity of this assumption. In the last edition of the book, the author even glibly noted that selling management on disaster recovery planning with arguments premised on its own demise would not be politically expedient! Perhaps the reader, who hailed from a country with significantly greater experience in coping with deliberate terrorist attacks, was issuing a veiled warning that this author failed to heed. In the wake of 9/11, few of us will be so cavalier in dismissing such critiques.

3. "You have not fully explored systems/network/user recovery options that are most appropriate to my company." Again, this statement may be true. However, this book has sought to devote the greatest attention to those options that the apparent majority of companies with backup capabilities are using and also to introduce evolving strategies that are likely to become favored approaches over the next five years or so. Of course, companies with tested disaster recovery capabilities, as stated in the Introduction and elsewhere, comprise only a small percentage of all companies in North America. If coordinators who read this book determine that a different recovery more closely meets their backup requirements than those strategies explored here, then, by all means, pursue the strategy. Different companies clearly have differing needs. The recovery options presented here are just that: options to consider when formulating a suitable approach. If cautions associated with specific options are viewed as inapplicable in a given case, coordinators should go with their best judgment.

4. "If I have only twenty employees, how can I have ten to twenty recovery teams?" or "I run my entire company on a single server and a handful of local and long distance lines, so why do I need to use teams to perform tasks that a single individual could do blindfolded?" The size of a disaster recovery team should be guided by the following considerations.

- Complexity of the task. If a task can be performed by a single person within an acceptable timeframe, no team may be needed. If the task is somewhat complex, at least one other individual should be available to assist in the event of a problem. Very complex tasks may require several persons.

- Extent of preplanning. If a task has been clearly defined, and no improvisation is required or expected, and one person can perform the task, designate a one-person team. If the strategy is not formalized, and/or the task is to be performed by "the seat of the pants," it may be necessary to allocate more than one person to the team assigned to perform the task.

- Availability of trained backup personnel. If the person responsible for performing the task cannot be reached in a recovery situation, is there another qualified individual to whom the task can be assigned? If the answer is no, then a team approach—with cross training of team members—may be required.

5. "You did not describe in any detail the way in which the financing of a recovery will be accomplished." True. In this edition, based on experience, I made a conscious decision to relegate recovery finance to the amorphous category of tasks belonging to the Emergency Management Team. In my experience, companies vary greatly in terms of their approach to handling the ongoing accounts payable/accounts receivable processes during an emergency. After Hurricane Andrew, one national company actually paid employees out of a "war chest" without so much as recording the monies taken by employees during the emergency. They found that employees worked very cheaply and that payroll costs were actually lower during the post-disaster period. In other cases, formal arrangements have been made with third-party providers or through branch operations to handle finances following a disaster. It will be necessary to document how management will prefer to handle the financing of emergency operations. However, little guidance of a generic nature can be offered on this point, so it was omitted for the discussion.

6. "You said that there is no such thing as a failed test. Considering the money, time, and effort spent in developing a plan, wouldn't the plan be a failure if the test proved the plan inadequate?" Personal embarrassment aside, coordinators need to view as beneficial any information that a test provides. If the plan fails in testing, the test is not a failure. It has succeeded in identifying areas of the plan that need to be reviewed and revised to make the plan better.

With those issues addressed, all that remains is to preview the companion web site for this book. The first edition of Disaster Recovery Planning featured multiple appendices including resource lists that were rendered obsolete over the course of time. What is needed to keep a resource list up-to-date is a "living appendix." That is what readers of this book will find on the World Wide Web at http://www.drplanning.org. This site offers a vendor-neutral clearinghouse for the latest thinking on disaster recovery planning as well as listings of products, services, and informational site links that may be of use to DR coordinators. If you are a vendor, feel free to contribute information about your products or services to the site. If you are a coordinator or someone interested in disaster recovery, feel free to join in the discussion groups that will be established on the site.

One final issue needs to be addressed: "When should I start to develop a disaster recovery plan?" The question is typically followed by a lengthy list of all of the reasons why now is not a good time. Here is a brief summary of the rationalizations and how I respond to them.

- "We're just in the planning stages for bringing IT in-house. We have no computers yet, except a few workstations. Most of our processing is done by a service bureau or outsourcing agent and they have a plan."

  In this instance, the disaster recovery coordinator is afforded a rare opportunity. Not only can current business processes be documented fairly quickly, but the coordinator is in on the ground floor of a IT migration project and may be able to influence how that project develops in order to favor disaster recovery considerations.

  Second, the coordinator should participate in the service bureau's or outsourcing agent's disaster recovery tests. This can provide some useful information about recovery requirements for applications as presently configured.

  Third, if facilities are being developed to house the company's new IT capability, the coordinator should attempt to become involved in planning disaster avoidance capabilities for the new facility.

  Finally, disaster recovery planning is not planning for the recovery of IT infrastructure alone; it is planning for business recovery. Thus, all other components of the plan can be developed, leaving the systems recovery strategy for last.

- "We've been changing over to a new software package (or to new hardware) and I wonder if we shouldn't wait until the conversion is successful and complete before we take on disaster recovery planning."

  Again, the coordinator has much more to protect than one system or application. Development of user and network recovery strategies should proceed, even if the systems recovery strategy cannot be finalized at this point.

  Additionally, conversions are not only destabilizing, they can also create disasters if not properly managed and controlled. Thus, a disaster recovery plan should be written before a conversion begins to handle the possibility of a disaster involving the conversion project.

- "We've had a shaky quarter, lots of expenses. I don't think that management will underwrite the costs of disaster recovery planning until maybe next quarter or next year."

  Disaster recovery planning need not be a cost born solely by corporate IT. It is the protection of corporate assets from loss that may result in savings in the cost of business interruption insurance. Even in difficult financial periods, the coordinator may be surprised to find management receptive to the notion of disaster recovery planning, especially if such planning seeks to leverage existing capabilities as dual-use disaster recovery capabilities. Financial hard times provide an excellent time for DR planning, since the pace of business change often slows somewhat during these periods affording the opportunity to complete "housekeeping" tasks—an unfortunate categorization that is often applied to DRP.

- "We're putting out daily fires. There's not much time for disaster recovery planning and no personnel are available for the job."

This comment suggests two things. One, the coordinator is saying, "What we have right now is such a headache, I'm not sure that it's worth saving." If systems and networks provide critical functions for the company, they are worth something. Discerning that value and creating a plan that is commensurate with it is prerequisite to good management. If the DR coordinator or IT manager doesn't agree, he or she is in the wrong job.

The second comment, regarding the availability of personnel, is a valid one. Unless a full-time employee is available or can be hired for the purpose of coordinating the disaster recovery planning project, the project will probably not yield a workable plan. Assigning or hiring such a person should be a higher priority than hiring a new programmer or analyst, since an investment in disaster recovery protects an investment in new software.

The bottom line is that the time to begin developing a disaster recovery capability is now. Stop reading about it. The way to develop a DR plan is to get out into the trenches and do it.

ENDNOTES

1. Jon William Toigo, "Preparing for the Unthinkable: Control the Damage," *Enterprise Systems,* 12/01. Reprinted by Permssion.
2. Jon William Toigo, *Disaster Recovery Planning for Computers and Communications Resources* (John Wiley and Sons: New York, 1995).

Glossary

ACCESS CONTROL: The process of limiting access to the resources of a system only to authorized programs, processes, or other systems (in a network). Synonymous with controlled access and limited access.

ACCESS CONTROL MECHANISM: 1. Security safeguards designed to detect and prevent unauthorized access, and to permit authorized access in an IT (information technology) product. 2. Hardware or software features, operating procedures, management procedures, and various combinations of these designed to detect and prevent unauthorized access and to permit authorized access in an automated system.

ADVANCED PROGRAM-TO-PROGRAM COMMUNICATIONS (APPC): A set of IBM protocols also known as LU 6.2 and Type 2.1 architectures. It functions within SNA's APPN to support peer-to-peer communications between workstations attached to SNA LANs and the applications running on those workstations. It was added to SNA as part of the "new" SNA to support peer-to-peer networking, unlike the traditional hierarchical SNA approach in which the mainframe acts as host or master and treats the other computer as a terminal or slave.

AGENT: A software-driven process running on a communications or networking device that allows that device to participate in a management system. For example, an SNMP agent running on a router provides the ability for the router to exchange information with an SNMP network management system through the use of the SNMP protocol.

ALTERNATE ROUTING: Safety technique enabling communication to continue in the event of node failure or congestion. The network design allows for alternate paths through the network to arrive at the same destination.

ALTERNATING CURRENT (AC): An electric current that reverses its direction at regular intervals. See DIRECT CURRENT.

AMERICAN NATIONAL STANDARDS INSTITUTE (ANSI): A group that defines U.S. standards for the information processing industry. ANSI participates in defining network protocol standards and represents the United States on other international standards-setting bodies like ISO.

APPLICATION PROGRAMMING INTERFACE (API): An interface between the operating system and application programs, which includes the way the application programs communicate with the operating system, and the services the operating system makes available to the programs.

APPLICATION SERVICE PROVIDER (ASP): An Internet-based application service bureau.

APPLICATION SOFTWARE: A set of programs that provides a specific function or set of functions.

ARCHITECTURE: The design of a system, network, or application.

ARCHIVAL BACKUP: A data backup that will be stored for a long time.

ARCHIVE: 1. To transfer files off the computer into long-term storage. 2. A file that has been archived. 3. A group of files which must be extracted and decompressed in order to use them; software to be installed sometimes comes in this format. 4. A file stored on a computer network, which can be retrieved by FTP or other means.

ARMA: Association of Records Managers and Administrators.

ARRAY: A group of disk drives that have been combined into a common array and appear as a single LSU (Logical Storage Unit). (See also DISK ARRAY.)

ASYNCHRONOUS TRANSFER MODE (ATM): A type of fast-packet switching that uses a fixed-size packet called a cell. This technique makes it possible to transmit data at great speed, and can make voice, multimedia, full-motion video, and video conferencing available to all users. It also makes dynamic allocation of bandwidth possible; telephone and cable TV companies can charge individual customers based on the amount of bandwidth they use.

AUTOMATIC REROUTING: A method of re-terminating wide area or local telecommunications traffic at alternate facilities in the event of a disaster. Automatic suggests that the rerouting of traffic may be accomplished rapidly by pre-planning the alternate traffic routes with a carrier service vendor.

BACK END: A computer that does the main processing but has a smaller, more-friendly computer that the user interacts with (called the "front end"). Or, a program that takes care of details behind the scenes, performing tasks not directly controlled by the user.

BACK UP: To make copies of important files in case the originals are damaged. Data can be backed up on secondary hard drives, floppy disks, optical media, tape, etc.

BACK-UP SERVER: Software or hardware which copies files so that there are always two current copies of each file. Also known as a shadow server.

BANDWIDTH: A characteristic of a communication channel that is the amount of information that can be passed through it in a given amount of time, usually expressed in bits per second.

BAUD: A baud is a unit that measures the speed of data transmission. The baud rate of a data communications system is the number of symbols per second transferred. A symbol may have more than two states, so it may represent more than one binary bit (a binary bit always represents exactly two states). Therefore the baud rate may not equal the bit rate, especially in the case of recent modems, which can have (for example) up to nine bits per symbol.

BIOMETRICS: Technologies for authenticating the identity of an individual by using fingerprints, palm prints, retinal scans, or other biological signatures.

BIT: Short for binary digit.

BITS PER SECOND (bps): Bits per second, a measure of data transmission.

BRIDGE: A device that connects two local-area networks (LANs), or two segments of the same LAN. The two LANs being connected can be alike or dissimilar. For example, a bridge can connect an Ethernet with a Token-Ring network. Unlike routers, bridges are protocol-independent. They simply forward packets without analyzing and re-routing messages. Consequently, they're faster than routers, but also less versatile. Brouters, or Bridge-Routers, are devices that functions as both a router and a bridge. A brouter understands how to route specific types of packets, such as TCP/IP packets. Any other packets it receives are simply forwarded to other network(s) connected to the device (this is the bridge function).

BUSINESS CONTINUITY PLANNING (BCP): A re-casting of traditional Disaster Recovery Planning that focuses on business process (rather than IT infrastructure) as the central objective of recovery planning.

BUSINESS PROCESS: A routine or standard process or procedure for accomplishing a business-related task.

BUSINESS PROCESS REENGINEERING: To change business processes with the objective of improving performance and/or making more efficient use of resources. The concept of BPR generally includes the use of computers and information technology to organize data, project trends, etc.

BUSINESS RECOVERY SERVICES: Vendor-provided services intended to aid businesses in recovering critical business processes following an unplanned interruption. IBM and HP both provide a BRS offering.

BYTE: The amount of memory space used to store one character, which is usually 8 bits. A computer that has 8-bit bytes (most large and small computers today) can distinguish 28 to 256 different characters.

CANNED PLANS: Somewhat disparaging term applied to fill-in-the-blanks DR planning software tools.

CENTRAL OFFICE (CO): A telephone company facility that joins subscriber telephone lines to switching equipment. This allows subscribers to connect to one another, through local and long distance connections.

CHANNEL EXTENSION: A set of technologies used to extend a mainframe (typically) channel across a Wide Area Network connection.

CHANNEL LATENCY: The waiting time for a communications channel to be available to transmit data.

CHECKLIST TESTING: The team reviews the plan and identifies key components that should be current and available.

CIRCUIT: A single communications facility or combination of facilities including satellite, microwave, fiber optics, or copper wire.

CLEAN AGENT: One of several replacements for halogenated fire suppression agents thought to be less detrimental to the environment and the ozone layer.

CLIENT/SERVER: An application architecture client/server in which applications are divided into discrete client and server components that may coexist on the same host platform or be divided among several hosts. A client machine sends a request to a server machine, which provides files, database searches, and other services.

COLD SITE: Cold site is a synonym for a shell site. It is a facility that is prepared to receive computer hardware and that may be used on an on-going basis for emergency system operations if a primary computer facility is destroyed or rendered uninhabitable.

COMMUNICATIONS CHANNEL: The physical media and devices which provide the means for transmitting information from one component of a network to (one or more) other components.

COMMUNICATIONS LINK: The physical means of connecting one location to another for the purpose of transmitting and/or receiving data.

COMMUNICATIONS PROTOCOL: A standard way of regulating data exchange between computers, including the rules for data transmission and the formatting of messages. Some communications protocols are TCP/IP, DECnet, AppleTalk, SNA, and IPX/SPX.

COMPUTER EMERGENCY RESPONSE TEAM (CERT): An organization formed by DARPA in 1988 after the Internet worm incident. CERT watches for threats to Internet security, educates the public about computer security issues, and conducts research to improve the security of existing systems. CERT issues advisories and provides 24-hour technical assistance in response to computer security emergencies.

CONCENTRATOR: A programmable device that combines the functions of a multiplexer with a data storage buffer, message error checking capability, and device polling capability.

COMMON OBJECT REQUEST BROKER ARCHITECTURE (CORBA): An architecture that enables pieces of programs, called objects, to communicate with one another regardless of what programming language they were written in or what operating system they're running on.

CUSTOMER RELATIONSHIP MANAGEMENT (CRM): Software that allows companies to manage every aspect of their relationship with a customer. The aim of these systems is to assist in building lasting customer relationships—to turn customer satisfaction into customer loyalty. Customer information acquired from sales, marketing, customer service, and support is captured and stored in a centralized database. The system may provide data-mining facilities that support an opportunity management system. It may also be integrated with other systems such as accounting and manufacturing for a truly enterprise-wide system with thousands of users.

DATABASE: (1.) A large collection of data organized for rapid search and retrieval. (2.) A program that manages data, and can be used to store, retrieve, and sort information.

DATA COMMUNICATION: The transfer of data from one computer to another.

DATA COMPRESSION: The encoding of data so that it consumes less storage space or transmission bandwidth.

DATA ENTRY: The process of entering data into a computer.

DATA PACKET: A format in which data is transmitted over a network. A packet contains the data itself as well as addresses, error checking, and other information necessary to ensure the packet arrives intact at its intended destination.

DATA PORTABILITY: The possibility for a set of data to be transferred from one operating system to another.

DATA RECOVERY: Salvaging data stored on damaged media, such as magnetic disks and tapes. There are a number of software products that can help recover data damaged by a disk crash or virus. In addition, there are companies that specialize in data recovery. Of course, not all data is recoverable, but data recovery specialists can often restore a surprisingly high percentage of the data on damaged media.

DATA WAREHOUSE: A large centralized database designed to hold and manage a company's information over a long period of time. Data warehouses are often used to mine key data for reference, for example, to detect trends, spot new market opportunities, and monitor business results.

DE FACTO STANDARD: A standard that is widely used and accepted even though it is not official.

DEFENSE ADVANCED RESEARCH PROJECTS AGENCY (DARPA): The Federal agency that began as ARPA, and created the Internet. It became ARPA again in 1990.

DEBUG: To fix problems in hardware or software.

DEDICATED LINE: A telecommunications line that lets your computer have a direct, permanent connection to the Internet or some other network. Different from a dialup connection which is only opened for temporary use. A dedicated line is assigned to only one purpose, and is always connected to the same equipment.

DIAL BACKUP: A technique for backing up a dedicated line or connection using a dial-up connection.

DIALUP CONNECTION: A temporary network connection usually established through Dual Tone Modulation Frequency (DTMF) "touch tone" telephone signaling.

DIGITAL SERVICE UNIT/CHANNEL SERVICE UNIT (DSU/CSU): A way of connecting a communications line to an external digital circuit.

DIRECT CURRENT (DC): An electric current flowing in one direction only. See ALTERNATING CURRENT.

DISASTER: An unplanned interruption of mission-critical business processes for an unacceptable period of time.

DISASTER RECOVERY PLANNING: Advanced planning intended to provide an organization with capabilities for preventing avoidable disasters and for mitigating the impact of disaster potentials that cannot be avoided.

DISK ARRAY (or ARRAY): A linked group of small, independent hard disk drives used to replace larger, single disk drive systems. The most common disk arrays implement RAID (redundant array of independent disks) technology. (See also RAID.)

DISTRIBUTED ARCHITECTURE: A set of interacting computer systems, databases, and workstations situated in different locations, typically dispersed across a department or enterprise-wide network.

DISTRIBUTED COMPONENT OBJECT MODEL (DCOM): A Microsoft developed system for exchanging objects over a client/server network.

DISTRIBUTED COMPUTING ENVIRONMENT (DCE): A set of middleware standards that defines the method of communication between clients and servers in a cross-platform computing environment; enables a client program to initiate a request that can be processed by a program written in a different computer language and housed on a different computer platform.

DLT TAPE: Quantum Corporation's widely installed Digital Linear Tape format. A type of 1/2" wide magnetic tape used for backup.

DOCKING STATION: A piece of hardware that a portable computer can be plugged into when it is at a fixed location. The docking station makes available devices that the portable computer is not able to support, such as a battery charger, a larger screen, additional drives, or a network.

DOWNLINK: (1.) In satellite communications, a link from a satellite to one of its earth stations. (2.) To receive data through a downlink.

DOWNLOAD: To transfer files or data from one computer to another. To download means to receive; to upload means to transmit.

DOWNSIZE: (1.) To reduce the size of staff at an organization. (2.) To move to a smaller host platform. (3.) To reduce an operating budget.

DOWNTIME: The time during which a computer is nonfunctional because of problems with hardware or system software, etc.

DOWNWARD COMPATIBILITY: The characteristic of hardware, software, or standards to coexist or be compatible with older versions of the hardware, software, or standard. Also called backward compatible.

E-BUSINESS: Business use of the Internet and World Wide Web.

E-COMMERCE: The use of computers and electronic communications in business transactions. E-commerce may include the use of electronic data interchange (EDI), electronic money exchange, Internet advertising, websites, online databases, computer networks, and point-of-sale (POS) computer systems.

ELECTROSTATIC: Relating to static electricity, or nonmoving electric charge.

EMERGENCY OPERATIONS CENTER (EOC): A location from which an emergency management team controls the execution of a disaster recovery plan.

ENCAPSULATION: The process of sending data encoded in one protocol format across a network operating a different protocol, where it is not possible or desirable to convert between the two protocols. For example, where Ethernet LANs attach to an FDDI backbone, it is not possible to convert between the different packet formats, so the Ethernet packet is encapsulated in its entirety inside an FDDI packet as it crosses the bridge on to the FDDI network. When the encapsulated Ethernet packet reaches the bridge connecting the destination Ethernet LAN to the FDDI network, the Ethernet packet is stripped out of the FDDI packet and put, unchanged, on to the destination Ethernet LAN. Also known as protocol tunneling.

ENCRYPTION: A method of defeating attempts to eavesdrop on data communications by encoding the data according to a scheme known only to the originator and recipient of the transmission.

ENTERPRISE: An enterprise consists of all functional departments, people, and systems within an organization. In some cases, the enterprise can include partners—even vendors and customers.

ENTERPRISE RESOURCE PLANNING (ERP): Typically, software designed to tie together all of an enterprise's various functions including human resources, finance, manufacturing, sales, etc. This software also provides for the analysis of this data in order to plan production, forecast sales, analyze quality, and so on.

EPCOT CODE: A set of building codes, including a fire code, developed in conjunction with the construction of the EPCOT Center at Walt Disney World in Orlando, FL. Considered one of the most advanced codes in existence.

ETHERNET: The most popular type of local area network, which sends its communications through radio frequency signals carried by a coaxial cable. Each computer checks to see if another computer is transmitting and waits its turn to transmit. If two computers accidentally transmit at the same time and their messages collide, they wait and send again in turn. Software protocols used by Ethernet systems vary, but include Novell Netware and TCP/IP. Named after the "ether" which was thought to be the medium through which electromagnetic waves propagated. The medium was initially a thick (about 1 cm in diameter) coaxial cable, usually yellow, and specially designed for the purpose. Today, there are several varieties of the Ethernet standard including 10 Base-T, 100 Base-T or Fast Ethernet, and 1000 Base-T or Gigabit Ethernet.

EXTRANET: The part of a company or organization's internal computer network which is available to outside users, for example, information services for customers.

FAILURE: The malfunction of a system or component; the inability of a system or component to perform its intended function. A failure may be caused by a fault.

FAST ETHERNET: A local area network that transmits data at 100 Mbits/s. Officially, IEEE 802.3u, Fast Ethernet is an implementation of 802.3 "Ethernet" that uses 100 Mbits/s transmission and different bit encoding but otherwise is identical to 10BASE-T (same frame and message lengths, same collision detect scheme, same Ethernet drivers). Fast Ethernet is promoted by the Fast Ethernet Alliance, whose main members are 3Com, Intel, Standard Microsystems (SMC), Sun Microsystems, Lucent Communications, and Cabletron Systems. Also supported by Cisco Systems.

FAT CLIENT: Somewhat derogatory reference to the Windows/INTEL desktop PC architecture. PCs are called fat clients because of their large memories and hard drives. They store information and run programs locally from software loaded on hard drives. Fat clients are typically deployed in client/server environments, where they enable local execution of client applications. As a rule, fat clients are much more customizable than thin clients.

FAT SERVER: In a client/server environment, a server that does most or all of the processing leaving little or none that must be done by the client.

FIBER DISTRIBUTED DATA INTERFACE (FDDI): a high-speed (and usually local) networking technology. A 100 Mbits/s user data rate, dual ring (for redundancy), connectionless LAN. With configurable distances of up to 2 kilometers, some would say that this is also a Metropolitan Area Network (MAN) technology.

FIREWALL: A system designed to prevent unauthorized access to or from a private network. Firewalls can be implemented in both hardware and software, or a combination of both. Firewalls are frequently used to prevent unauthorized Internet users from accessing private networks connected to the Internet, especially intranets. All messages entering or leaving the intranet pass through the firewall, which examines each message and blocks those that do not meet the specified security criteria. There are several types of firewall techniques: (1) Packet filter: Looks at each packet entering or leaving the network and accepts or rejects it based on user-defined rules. Packet filtering is fairly effective and transparent to users, but it is difficult to configure. In addition, it is susceptible to IP spoofing. (2) Application gateway: Applies security mechanisms to specific applications, such as FTP and Telnet servers. This is very effective, but can impose a performance degradation. (3) Circuit-level gateway: Applies security mechanisms when a TCP or UDP connection is established. Once the connection has been made, packets can flow between the hosts without further checking. (4) Proxy server: Intercepts all messages entering and leaving the network. The proxy server effectively hides the true network addresses. In practice, many firewalls use two or more of these techniques in concert. A firewall is considered a first line defense in network security and is typically used in conjunction with encryption.

FIRMWARE: Vendor-written software usually stored in read only memory (ROM) on a vended product.

FRAME RELAY: A protocol for sending small packets of data over a network. Frame relay uses packets of variable length, unlike cell relay, and requires less stringent error detection than other forms of packet switching because it is designed to take advantage of the more reliable circuits that have become available in recent years. Frame relay is often used for wide area networks, where it can transmit data at high speed more efficiently than point-to-point services. Frame relay is used with digital lines.

FRAME RELAY ACCESS DEVICE (FRAD): A combination of hardware and software that is used to convert communications packets from formats like TCP, SNA, IPX, and others into frames that can then be sent over a frame relay network.

FRONT END COMMUNICATIONS CONTROLLER: A programmable device that interfaces a communications network with a host computer. Some controller functions may include polling, speed control, code conversion, error detection, data buffering, and security authorization checking.

FULL-INTERRUPTION TESTING: Testing the DR plan by interrupting normal operations. This test is costly, could disrupt normal operations and should be used and scheduled with extreme caution.

GATEWAY: Gateways are points of entrance to and exit from a communications network. Viewed as a physical entity, a gateway is that node that translates between two otherwise incompatible networks or network segments. Gateways perform code and protocol conversion to facilitate traffic between data highways of differing architecture. In OSI terms, a gateway is a device that provides mapping at all seven layers of the OSI model. A gateway can be thought of as a function within a system that enables communications with the outside world.

GIGABIT ETHERNET: (1000 Base-T) A standard for a high-speed Ethernet, approved by the IEEE (Institute of Electrical and Electronics Engineers) 802.3z standards committee in 1996. It supports the extension of existing Ethernet and Fast Ethernet standards, providing increased network bandwidth and interoperability among Ethernets at operating speeds from 10 Mbps to 1000 Mbps. Gigabit Ethernet can be used in backbone environments to interconnect multiple lower speed (10 and 100 Mbps) Ethernets.

GIGABITS PER SECOND (Mbps): 1000 bits per second, a measure of data transmission.

GIGABYTES PER SECOND (MBps): 8000 bits per second, a measure of data transmission.

HEAD CRASH: A serious disk drive malfunction. A head crash usually means that the head has scratched or burned the disk platter. In a hard disk drive, the head normally hovers a few microinches from the disk. If the head becomes misaligned, if platters warp as a result of heat, or if dust particles come between it and the disk, read/write heads can contact or crash the disk platter. Data loss is often the result. For this reason, it is important to operate disk drives, particularly hard disk drives, in as clean an environment as possible. Even smoke particles can cause a head crash. Head crashes are less common for floppy disks because the head touches the disk under normal operation.

HOST: Any computer-based system connected to the network and containing the necessary protocol interpreter software to initiate network access and carry out information exchange across the communications network. This definition encompasses typical "mainframe" and "midrange" hosts and workstations connected directly to the communications subnetwork and executing the intercomputer networking protocols. A terminal is not a host because it does not contain the protocol software needed to perform information exchange; a workstation (by definition) is a host because it does have such capability.

HOT SITE: A commercial systems backup facility. A vendor-provided facility equipped with computer host hardware, telecommunications hardware and personnel to aid subscribing companies in restoring critical business application processing following an unplanned interruption of normal IT operations.

HYBRID PRIVATE/PUBLIC NETWORKING: The creation of a network using both private leased lines and public switched facilities (digital dial-up bandwidth). The goals of combining both networking technologies are increased performance and flexibility at reduced cost.

INCREMENTAL BACKUP: A routine that makes it possible to back up only the files that have changed since the last backup, instead of backing up every file.

INSTITUTE OF ELECTRICAL AND ELECTRONICS ENGINEERS (IEEE): An organization that maintains the standards for 10BaseT and other communications standards.

INTEGRATED SERVICES DIGITAL NETWORK (ISDN): An international communications standard for sending voice, video, and data over digital telephone lines or normal telephone wires. ISDN supports data transfer rates of 64 Kbps (64,000 bits per second). Most ISDN lines offered by telephone companies provides two lines, called B channels. One line for voice and the other for data, or both lines, when used for data, provide data rates of 128 Kbps, three times the data rate provided by today's fastest modems. The original version of ISDN employs base band transmission. Another version, called B-ISDN, uses broadband transmission and is able to support transmission rates of 1.5 Mbps. B-ISDN requires fiber optic cables and is not widely available.

INTER EXCHANGE CARRIER (IXC or IEC): Common carrier providing communications channels between local telephone companies (LECs, or Local

Exchange Carriers). Also known as long distance carriers, such as AT&T, World-Com (Sprint and MCI WorldCom), WilTel, etc.

INTERNET: A global network connecting millions of computers. As of 1998, the Internet has more than 100 million users worldwide, and that number is growing rapidly. More than 100 countries are linked into exchanges of data, news, and opinions. Unlike online services, which are centrally controlled, the Internet is decentralized by design. Each Internet computer, called a host, is independent. Its operators can choose which Internet services to use and which local services to make available to the global Internet community. Remarkably, this anarchy by design works exceedingly well. There are a variety of ways to access the Internet, including the use of a commercial Internet Service Provider (ISP).

INTERNET SERVICE PROVIDER (ISP): A company that provides access to the Internet. For a monthly fee, the service provider provides the user a software package, username, password, and access phone number. Equipped with a modem, the user can then log on to the Internet and browse the World Wide Web and USENET, and send and receive e-mail. In addition to serving individuals, ISPs also serve large companies, providing a direct connection from the company's networks to the Internet. ISPs themselves are connected to one another through Network Access Points (NAPs). ISPs are also called IAPs (Internet Access Providers).

INTRANET: A network based on TCP/IP protocols (an internet) belonging to an organization, usually a corporation, accessible only by the organization's members, employees, or others with authorization. An intranet's Web sites look and act just like any other Web sites, but the firewall surrounding an intranet fends off unauthorized access.

LAST MILE SERVICES: A circuit, facility, or service used to connect an intercity cable, microwave system, and so forth to a customer of a point of presence (POP).

LAYER TWO FORWARDING: Often abbreviated as L2F, a tunneling protocol developed by Cisco Systems. L2F is similar to the PPTP protocol developed by Microsoft, enabling organizations to set up virtual private networks (VPNs) that use the Internet backbone to move packets. Recently, Microsoft and Cisco agreed to merge their respective protocols into a single, standard protocol called Layer Two Tunneling Protocol (L2TP).

LAYER THREE SWITCH: See ROUTING SWITCH.

LOAD BALANCING: The practice of splitting communications on one route into two or more routes to balance traffic on each route. Load balancing makes communications faster and more reliable. In remote internetworking, bridges and routers perform load balancing by splitting local area network (LAN)-to-LAN traffic among two or more wide area network (WAN) links. This permits a combination of several lower speed lines to transmit LAN data simultaneously.

LOCAL AREA NETWORK (LAN): A communications system that links computers into a network, usually via a wiring-based cabling scheme. LANs connect PCs, workstations and servers together to allow users to communicate and share resources like hard disk storage and printers. Devices linked by a LAN may be on the same floor or within a building or campus. It is user-owned and does not run over leased lines, though a LAN may have gateways to the PSTN or other, private, networks.

LOCAL EXCHANGE CARRIER (LEC): Local telephone company, providing connections between local points or to long distance carriers for extended connections. Examples are Pacific Bell in California, Illinois Bell in Illinois, GTE in Hawaii, etc.

LOCAL LOOP: A channel between a customer's terminal and a central office (CO). The most common form of loop, a pair of wires, is also called a line.

MATERIAL RESOURCE PLANNING (MRP): software for effectively managing material requirements in a manufacturing process. MRP II is better known as Manufacturer Resource Planning, a system based on MRP which allows manufacturers to optimize materials, procurement, manufacturing processes, etc., and provide financial and planning reports.

MESSAGING MIDDLEWARE: A middleware architecture where clients can send and receive higher-level messages—accomplishing an entire transaction or even a complete set of transactions with multiple servers.

METADATA: (1) Data referring to other data; data (such as data structures, indices, and pointers) that are used to instantiate an abstraction (such as "process," "task," "segment," "file," or "pipe"). (2) A special database, also referred to as a data dictionary, containing descriptions of the elements (e.g., relations, domains, entities, or relationships) of a database.

METROPOLITAN AREA NETWORK (MAN): A network established to serve a specific metropolitan area. AT&T INC and Sprint ION are two examples.

MICRON: A unit of length equal to one millionth of a meter or 39.3 microinches.

MIDDLEWARE: Software that connects two otherwise separate applications.

MIRRORING: A method of storage in which data from one disk is duplicated on another disk so that both drives contain the same information, thus providing data redundancy. A popular term for RAID-1.

MISSION CRITICAL: Any computer process that cannot fail during normal business hours; some computer processes (e.g., telephone systems) must run all day long and require 100 percent uptime.

MISSION CRITICAL DATA: Data or information considered to be so important that its loss would cause grave difficulty to all or part of a business. For example: customer account information at a bank, or patient information at a hospital.

MODEM: A peripheral device that connects computers to each other for sending communications via the telephone lines. The modem modulates the digital data of computers into analog signals to send over the telephone lines, then demodulates back into digital signals to be read by the computer on the other end; thus the name "modem" for modulator/demodulator. Modems are used for sending and receiving electronic mail, connecting to bulletin board systems, and surfing the Internet.

MULTIDROP CIRCUIT: A configuation for connecting communications devices that allows the sharing of a communications facility. Like a party line, several devices share a single line. Generally, only one device can be active at a time.

MULTIPLEXER: A device that combines different data streams into a single stream for transmission at high speed. Multiplexed transmissions are commonly received by a multiplexer at the destination site, where they are separated back (demultiplexed) into their component data streams.

MULTI-TIER TRANSACTION PROCESSING: The use of a two-, three-, or *n*-tier application architecture to perform transaction processing functions.

n-**TIER CLIENT/SERVER:** A client/server application architecture using more than three tiers.

NATIONAL FIRE PROTECTION ASSOCIATION (NFPA): An organization that develops standards related to fire protection.

NETWORK ARCHITECTURE: The communication equipment, protocols, and transmission links that constitute a network, and the methods by which they are arranged.

NETWORK ATTACHED STORAGE (NAS): This is the provision of storage in a form that is readily accessible on a network. A disk array storage system that is attached directly to a network rather than to the server. NAS devices typically present a networked file system in accordance with a protocol such as NFS or CIFS/SMB. These devices are often referred to as thin servers as they have the functions as a server in a client/server relationship. A typical NAS thin storage server has a processor, an operating system or micro-kernel, and processes file I/O protocols.

OBJECT REQUEST BROKER (ORB): A component in the CORBA programming model that acts as the middleware between clients and servers, receiving, redirecting, and routing real-time inter-object messages.

100 BASE-T: See FAST ETHERNET.

OPTICAL CARRIER LEVELS (OC): Used to specify the speed of fiber optic networks conforming to the SONET standard. The following table shows the speeds for common OC levels.

OSI ARCHITECTURE: The Open Systems Interconnect Architecture advanced by the International Organization for Standardization (ISO) provides a framework for defining the communications process between systems. This framework includes a network architecture, consisting of seven layers. The architecture is referred to as the Open Systems Interconnection (OSI) model or Reference Model. Services and the protocols to implement them for the different layers of the model are defined by international standards. From a systems viewpoint, the bottom three layers support the components of the network necessary to transmit a message, the next three layers generally pertain to the characteristics of the communicating end systems, and the top layer supports the end users. The seven layers are: (1) Physical Layer: Includes the functions to activate, maintain, and deactivate the physical connection. It defines the functional and procedural characteristics of the interface to the physical circuit: the electrical and mechanical specifications are considered to be part of the medium itself. (2) Data Link Layer: Formats the messages. Covers synchronization and error control for the information transmitted over the physical link, regardless of the content. "Point-to point error checking" is one way to describe this layer. (3) Network Layer: Selects the appropriate facilities. Includes routing communications through network resources to the system where the communicating application is: segmentation and reassembly of data units (packets); and some error correction. (4) Transport Layer: Includes such functions as multiplexing several independent message streams over a single connection, and segmenting data into appropriately sized packets for processing by the Network Layer. Provides end-to-end control of data reliability. (5) Session Layer: Selects the type of service. Manages and synchronizes conversations between two application processes. Two main types of dialogue are provided: two-way simultaneous (full duplex), or two-way alternating (half-duplex). Provides control functions similar to the control language in computer system (6) Presentation Layer: Ensures that information is delivered in a form that the receiving system can understand and use. Communicating parties determine the format and language (syntax) of messages: translates if required, preserving the meaning (semantics). (7) Application Layer: Supports distributed applications by manipulating information. Provides resource management for file transfer, virtual file, and virtual terminal emulation, distributed processes and other applications.

OUTSOURCING: Outsourcing is the third-party performance of functions once administered in-house. Outsourcing is really two types of service: ITO—IT Outsourcing, involves a third party who is contracted to manage a particular application, including all related servers, networks, and software upgrades; and BPO—Business Process Outsourcing, features a third party who manages the entire business process, such as accounting, procurement, or human resources.

PACKET SWITCHING: A data communications technique that allows messages to be divided or segmented into packets and routed dynamically through a network to a final destination point.

PACKOUT: A stage of records salvage in which specific cleaning, packaging, labeling, and storage procedures are performed.

PARTICULATE: A small particle of organic or mineral material that can collect in sensitive electronic equipment resulting in damage or destruction.

PASSWORD: A character string, often a word, that must be entered by the user and validated by the system or network before the system or network may be accessed.

PERMISSIONS: Read and write privileges assigned to users by the system administrator for programs and data sets. Permissions are often linked, via software, to device identifiers or user passwords.

POINT OF PRESENCE (POP): A location (and telephone number) that provides users dial-up access to the Inter Exchange Carrier network, to value added network services, or to the Internet.

POINT-TO-POINT CIRCUIT: A method for connecting communications devices in which a dial-up or dedicated circuit provides the connection between two communicating devices.

POTS: Plain Old Telephone Service.

PRIVATE BRANCH EXCHANGE (PBX): A leased or owned programmable device that facilitates communications between numerous voice and data communications devices at the customer premise and the public switched telephone network (PSTN).

PROTOCOL: Software-controlled rules that govern data transmission between communicating devices.

PUBLIC SWITCHED TELEPHONE NETWORK (PSTN): The name for a generic telephone network. One of the few acronyms consistently spelled out when spoken.

RAID (Redundant Array of Inexpensive Disks): A method of combining hard disks into one logical storage unit which offers disk-fault tolerance and can operate at higher throughput levels than a single hard disk.

REDUNDANCY (of a network): There are no perfect methods of transmitting signals—each one has inherent error rates, and all physical media is subject to damage. To safeguard against line and equipment failure during a transmission, a second, redundant line or unit can be active in the background to take over at any time. Network administrators always have a redundant (backup) module for multiplexers and other critical equipment.

REGIONAL BELL OPERATING COMPANY (RBOC): Any of the child companies created by the 1984 break-up of AT&T.

REMOTE ACCESS: The ability to log onto a network from a distant location. Generally, this implies a computer, a modem, and some remote access software to connect to the network. Whereas remote control refers to taking control of another computer, remote access means that the remote computer actually becomes a full-fledged host on the network. The remote access software dials in directly to the network server. The only difference between a remote host and workstations connected directly to the network is slower data transfer speeds.

REMOTE ACCESS SERVER (RAS): A server providing connectivity in the form of modems or other devices and software, to facilitate remote access to internal networks. RAS is also short for Remote Access Services, a feature built into Windows NT that enables users to log into an NT-based LAN using a modem, X.25 connection or WAN link. RAS works with several major network protocols, including TCP/IP, IPX, and Netbeui. To use RAS from a remote node, you need a RAS client program, which is built into most versions of Windows, or any PPP client software. For example, most remote control programs work with RAS.

REMOTE MIRRORING: Mirroring disk writes to a duplicate disk array located at an off-site facility using an WAN or Internet link.

REMOTE PROCEDURE CALL (RPC): A type of protocol that allows a program on one computer to execute a program on a server computer.

REMOTE TAPE VAULTING: Writing data backups to a tape library or loader located at an off-site facility via a WAN or Internet connection.

ROUTER: A device that connects any number of LANs. Routers use headers and a forwarding table to determine where packets go, and they use Internet Control Message Protocol (ICMP) to communicate with each other and configure the best route between any two hosts. Very little filtering of data is done through routers.

ROUTING SWITCH: A switch that also performs routing operations. Usually a switch operates at layer 2 (the Data Link layer) of the OSI Reference Model while routers operate at layer 3 (the Network layer). Routing switches, however, perform many of the layer 3 functions usually reserved for routers. Because the routing is implemented in hardware rather than software, it is faster. The downside of routing switches is that they are not as powerful or as flexible as full-fledged routers. Because they perform some layer 3 functions, routing switches are sometimes called layer-3 switches.

SERVICE BUREAU: A computer facility that provides processing services to subscribers on an on-going basis. In the context of disaster recovery planning, the vendor of a software package may be willing to make software available on its own hardware platform for emergency use by the customer.

SHELL SITE: See COLD SITE.

SIMULATION TESTING: A disaster is simulated so normal operations will not be interrupted. Hardware, software, personnel, communications, procedures, supplies and forms, documentation, transportation, utilities, and alternate site processing are thoroughly tested in a simulation test. Extensive travel, moving equipment, and eliminating voice or data communications may not be practical or economically feasible during a simulated test.

SOFTWARE: See APPLICATION SOFTWARE.

STORAGE AREA NETWORK (SAN): A network comprising multiple hosts and storage peripherals, currently conceived as Fibre Channel/SCSI Command Set-based. However, any interconnect and any network protocol could be used, theoretically, to establish a SAN, provided that the strict latency and throughput requirements of storage are met.

STRUCTURED WALKTHROUGH TESTING: Team members verbally "walk through" the specific steps as documented in the plan to confirm effectiveness of the plan and identify gaps, bottlenecks or other weaknesses in the plan.

SWITCH: In networks, a device that filters and forwards packets between LAN segments. Most switches operate at the data link layer (layer 2) of the OSI Reference Model and therefore support any packet protocol. However, increasing use is being made of ROUTING SWITCHES, which combine layer two and layer three operations. LANs that use switches to join segments are called switched LANs or, in the case of Ethernet networks, switched Ethernet LANs.

SYNCHRONOUS OPTICAL NETWORK (SONET): A standard for connecting fiber-optic transmission systems. SONET was proposed by Bellcore in the mid-1980s and is now an ANSI standard. SONET defines interface standards at the physical layer of the OSI seven-layer model. The standard defines a hierarchy of interface rates that allow data streams at different rates to be multiplexed. SONET establishes Optical Carrier (OC) levels from 51.8 Mbps (about the same as a T-3 line) to 2.48 Gbps. Prior rate standards used by different countries specified rates that were not compatible for multiplexing. With the implementation of SONET, communication carriers throughout the world can interconnect their existing digital carrier and fiber optic systems. The international equivalent of SONET, standardized by the International Telecommunication Union (ITU), is called Synchronous Digital Hierarchy (SDH).

SYSTEMS NETWORK ARCHITECTURE (SNA): IBM's layered communications protocol for sending data between IBM hardware and software. Shortly to celebrate its Pearl anniversary (it was first announced way back in September 1974), it is defined today in terms of a stack of seven layers. While there is some commonalty between the layers of OSI and SNA, it is difficult to make a direct mapping. SNA has traditionally been a hierarchical network architecture for homogeneous networking between IBM systems, but in the "new" SNA IBM has added increasing support for peer to peer networking through the development of Advanced Peer to Peer Communications. SNA is managed through the NetView network management system.

T-1 CARRIER: A dedicated phone connection supporting data rates of 1.544 Mbits per second. A T-1 line actually consists of 24 individual channels, each of which supports 64 Kbits per second. Each 64 Kbit/second channel can be configured to carry voice or data traffic. Most telephone companies allow customers to buy just some of these individual channels, known as fractional T-1 access. T-1 lines are a popular leased line option for businesses connecting to the Internet and for Internet Service Providers (ISPs) connecting to the Internet backbone. The Internet backbone itself currently consists of faster T-3 connections. T-1 lines are sometimes referred to as DS1 lines.

T-3 CARRIER: A dedicated phone connection supporting data rates of about 43 Mbps. A T-3 line actually consists of 672 individual channels, each of which supports 64 Kbps. T-3 lines are used mainly by Internet Service Providers (ISPs) connecting to the Internet backbone and for the backbone itself. T-3 lines are sometimes referred to as DS3 lines.

TELECOMMUTER: A work-at-home computer user who connects to the corporate LAN backbone using remote access technologies (for example, using a modem over analog lines, ISDN Terminal Adapter (TA) or ISDN router over ISDN lines, or CSU/DSU over Switched 56 lines).

10BASE-T: A local area network that transmits data at 10 Mbits/s over copper cabling. An IEEE 802.3 media option that supports 10 Mbits/s Ethernet over UTP.

A non-standardized full-duplex version (sometimes called full duplex switched Ethernet, FDSE) is available from Compaq and a few other vendors.

TERMINAL EMULATION: Software that allows a PC to mimic the attributes of a dumb terminal normally attached to a mainframe or mini-computer, giving the user with access to function keys and control sequences which the host applications normally use when communicating with one of their own dumb terminals. The most commonly emulated terminals are Digital Equipment Corporation's VT100 terminal and IBM's 3270.

THIN CLIENT: In client/server applications, a client designed to be especially small so that the bulk of the processing occurs on the server. The term has also become symbolic of a dividing line within the computer industry between Sun Microsystems advocating Java-based thin clients running on network computers, and Microsoft and Intel advocating large applications running locally on desktop computers. Although the term thin client refers to software, it is increasingly used to describe computers, such as network computers and Net PCs, that are designed to serve as the clients for client/server architectures. A thin client is a network computer without a hard disk drive, whereas a fat client includes a disk drive.

TRUNK GROUP: A group of circuits in a telecommunications network.

TUNNELING: A technology that enables one network to send its data via another network's connections. Tunneling works by encapsulating a network protocol within packets carried by the second network. For example, Microsoft's PPTP technology enables organizations to use the Internet to transmit data across a virtual private network (VPN). It does this by embedding its own network protocol within the TCP/IP packets carried by the Internet. Tunneling is also called encapsulation.

UNINTERRUPTIBLE POWER SUPPLY (UPS): A battery power backup for utility-provided electrical power.

VALUE ADDED NETWORK (VAN): A data transmission network that guarantees data security and integrity through added computer control and communications from the sender to the recipient, often in the manner of a door-to-door courier or freight forwarder.

VIRTUAL CIRCUIT: A link that seems and behaves like a dedicated point-to-point line or a system that delivers packets in sequence, as happens on an actual point to point network. In reality, the data is delivered across a network via the most appropriate route. The sending and receiving devices do not have to be aware of the options and the route is chosen only when a message is sent. There is no prearrangement, so each virtual connection exists only for the duration of that one transmission.

VIRTUAL PRIVATE NETWORK (VPN): A network that is constructed by using public lines to connect nodes. Many VPNs use the Internet as the medium for transporting data. These systems use encryption and other security mechanisms to ensure that only authorized users can access the network and that the data cannot be intercepted.

VIRUS: (1) Malicious software, a form of Trojan horse, which reproduces itself in other executable code. (2) A self-propagating Trojan horse, composed of a mission component, a trigger component, and a self-propagating component. (3) Self-replicating malicious program segment that attaches itself to an application or other executable system component and leaves no external signs of its presence.

WEB-ENABLED APPLICATION: An application provided with an HTML interface to facilitate web access.

WIDE AREA NETWORK (WAN): A network which covers a larger geographical area than a LAN and where telecommunications links are implemented, normally leased from the appropriate IXCs. Examples of WANs include packet switched networks, public data networks and Value Added Networks.

WIRELESS LOCAL LOOP: Wireless service systems that compete with or substitute for local fixed-line phone service.

WORKSTATION: Term used freely to mean a PC, node, terminal or high-end desktop processor (for CAD/CAM and similar intensive applications)—in short, a device that has data input and output and operated by a user.

WORLD WIDE WEB: A system of Internet servers that support specially formatted documents. The documents are formatted in a language called HTML (HyperText Markup Language) that supports links to other documents, as well as graphics, audio, and video files. This means users can move from one document to another simply by clicking on hot spots. Not all Internet servers are part of the World Wide Web.

WRITE ONCE READ MANY (WORM): An optical storage technology that burns pits into the recording layer of an optical disk, allowing the disks to be written just once but read without limit. WORM drives write directly to an optical disk from a host computer. Both the drives and disks include built-in safeguards to assure that data, once written, cannot be erased, overwritten or altered. Tape-based WORMs have just begun to enter the market.

YEAR 2000 (Y2K) PROBLEM: The Year 2000 problem refers to the inability of software to handle dates beyond 1999.

Index